INTERNATIONAL BOXING YEAR 1989

Mike Tyson prepares for his next challenge

Tom Casino

Edited by Barry J. Hugman

Macdonald
Queen Anne Press

A Queen Anne Press BOOK

First published in Great Britain in 1988 by
Queen Anne Press, a division of
Macdonald & Co (Publishers) Ltd
3rd Floor
Greater London House
Hampstead Road
London NW1 7QX

A BPCC plc Company

British Library Cataloguing in Publication Data
Hugman, Barry J.
International Boxing Year 1989
1. Boxing — Records
I. Title
796.8'3'09 GV1137

ISBN

Typeset by Techniset, Newton-le-Willows, Lancashire
Printed in Great Britain by
Butler & Tanner Ltd, Frome and London

Contents

Acknowledgements

Once again many people made this book possible and I have made every effort not to forget anyone.

Ron Olver — Assistant Editor of the British Boxing Yearbook; British correspondent of the Ring, America; former Assistant Editor of both Boxing News and Boxing World; author of The Professionals, Boxing (Foyles) and the boxing section of Encyclopaedia Brittanica; a member of the British Boxing Writers' Club, the Commonwealth Championships Committee and the BBBC Benevolent Fund; Vice-President of several ex-boxers' associations — who, with his great experience of boxing and of boxing people, was the ideal man to put together The Hall of Fame section within this book.

Fred Snelling, the author of White Hope and A Bedside Book of Boxing among many others, has once again produced the month-by-month narrative in his own inimitable fashion. He began writing prior to the war and follows a long tradition of outstanding penmanship that has entertained the boxing public since the days of bare fist fighting. O. F. Snelling, or Fred as he prefers to be called, spends most of his spare time these days, producing boxing magazines for several ex-boxers' associations, a task he delights in.

Eric Armit, who is undoubtedly one of the leaders in compiling international records, has yet again assembled over 400 for The World's Leading Fighters section. He is the man to whom boxing authorities and promoters turn to for an accurate record of any fighter that they are proposing to use. It was about 1958 that Eric began to compile boxing records and by 1962 he was involved with Boxing News, through his good friend, Ron Olver. Since then he has written countless articles for various world wide boxing magazines as a recognised authority and is a member of the World Boxing Council Ratings Committee.

Derek O'Dell, who always makes himself available however great the problem, was again to the forefront when it came to last minute jobs. General help was also given by Joe Koizumi, Tony Woodward, Neil Blackburn, Stan Pratt and David Roake and as in every book that I compile, my wife Jennifer does her fair share of typing, for which I am always indebted.

Last year I relied heavily on Peter Goldfield for all of the USA based boxers' photographs. Peter has again supplied many great pictures for the latest book and can be reached at 3161 Alabama Road, Camden, New Jersey 08104.

Other magical action shots from the States were captured on film for the International Boxing Year by the photographer for the Boxing Beat Magazine, Tom Casino. Tom, another top man, can be reached at 9 Everett Street, Jersey City, New Jersey 07304.

Chris Farina looked after our action requirements in Las Vegas with style. He does work for the Ring Magazine and lives in Las Vegas at 4000 Vaquero Avenue.

My very good friend, Thierry Chambefort, who writes about boxing in France, managed the European photograph requirement and Shigeru Yamamoto of the Japan Boxing Magazine very kindly gave us access to his library.

In London, Sporting Pictures (UK) Ltd., 7a Lambs Conduit Passage, London WC1R 4RG, through Steve Smith, another true friend, looked after our varying needs.

Other special mentions regarding photographs should be made of Peter Shaw and John McDonald of the World Boxing Fan Association, a new group who are going great guns under the auspices of Paul Thorpe; Action Images Ltd.; Derek Rowe (Photos) Ltd.; Harry Goodwin; All-Sport (UK) Ltd and last but certainly not least, Bobby Lee and Sy Roseman of the International Boxing Federation.

As in last year's book a special mention must be made of Edwin Cook and Ray Hedley for their expert handling in the area of design.

Preface

Welcome to the second edition of the International Boxing Year. The stage is almost certainly set for the book to go truly "international", following in the tradition of The Ring Record Book.

The International Boxing Year summarizes all of the major fights for the period, January to April 1987, within the introduction, which is a foretaste to the World Boxing Season, running from May 1987 to April 1988. It is in this part of the book, which is a 64 page colour section and carries 60 great colour shots covering the past twelve months, that the reader can recapture some of the more recent action, yet again.

When we began to compile The World's Leading Fighters section, it soon became apparent that the biggest problem was who to leave out. In the day and age of three major boxing commissions, fighters can virtually come from "out of the blue" to win the title. However, Eric Armit basically selected over 400 fighters from within the "Top 30", allowing for any aspiring young prospects, if credible.

The Hall of Fame will eventually aim to portray potted histories of all of the world champions since gloves and follows no specific sequence.

Once again, an essential item in the International Boxing Year, is the inclusion of all world title bouts since 1890. The results are in weight order and alongside each entry is recorded the name of the body or bodies involved in giving the contest world title status.

During 1987, the World Boxing Association decided to reduce the extent of championship contests held under their auspices, from twelve to fifteen rounds. This brought them into line with the World Boxing Council, who had already set the standard back in 1983. Many of the boxing public felt, however, that the WBA and the WBC, both South American based, were merely trying to squeeze the International Boxing Federation out. But at their recent convention, the IBF decided that very shortly they too would reduce to twelve rounds.

I personally feel that the IBF have been good for boxing in many ways and one of their strengths, repeating what I said last year, is in allowing a larger selection of quality fighters to aspire to title bout status. In a changing world, boxing included, it enables more champions to earn the kind of purses that television backed promotions, linked to sponsorship, can afford.

Regarding the fighters that the editor wished to see matched last season, it is interesting to note that of the names mentioned only Mike Tyson versus Michael Spinks became a reality. I say a reality with tongue in cheek, as the two men are not due to come together until the end of June, and by the time you read this book you will know the result. Tyson has been good for boxing and has created much renewed interest in the sport.

In an era where great fighters do not grow on trees, one of the most impressive must surely be Julio Cesar Chavez. The unbeaten Mexican WBA lightweight champion, would if given the opportunity, undoubtedly unify the division.

On the British front, Lloyd Honeyghan became the first man since Ted "Kid" Lewis, to regain a world championship when he flattened Jorge Vaca in the third round of their WBC welterweight title rematch and Barry McGuigan, the idol of Ireland, came back with a win. Elsewhere, especially among the middleweights, things livened up considerably with Michael Watson and Nigel Benn coming through to join Herol Graham in the world ratings.

I close by wishing the sport of boxing and all of the people involved, much prosperity in 1988–89.

Barry J. Hugman

Editorial Office: 6 River Court,
Ickleford, Herts. SG5 3UD.

In Defence of Boxing

by Teddy Atlas, the well known American boxing trainer

High noon in Catskill, New York, and the noise shot through the town, Echoes of Dodge City? Just compressed air coughing from the village horn. When E. F. Hutton speaks . . ., and when the old horn screams nobody talks, except this day. Eleven-year-old Gary jumped on this chance like Larry Bird on a loose ball.

His timing proved his Catskill heritage as he synchronized his words with each blast of air. He sounded like any other kid trying to out-talk a horn, until it stopped. Then Gary stopped. He had a silent look of disappointment. Enemies to my ears, the horns' bellows were Gary's allies.

With all the noise I hadn't noticed his hand never moved from the side of his mouth. Now it did, slowly, and I saw the lip. It was disformed; a harelip. Already obvious was the severity of the mental scar. Now, with the air still, he steadied himself.

"Damn horn," I complained, as I stuck my head closer as unassumingly as possible. Some words I understood, all of them I acknowledged. Instinct took over like it had for him when he went partners with the horn. My head seemed to nod on its own.

What had to be done seemed simple enough. My trade was training fighters. We had a gym full of youths. Get Gary into the gym and teach him to box. After all, I wasn't a speech therapist.

His desire for normalcy and acceptance overcame his shyness. In two years he beat a group of other thirteen-year-olds, while winning the Adirondack Junior Olympic Championships in the 75-pound division.

In just as impressive and determined fashion, he demolished a speech impairment like a Tyson left hook erasing an opponent. Gary attained a normal reading level and participated in class for the first time. On his next report card his teacher commented on the success of the speech classes he was obviously attending and suggested they be kept up.

Mane Moore was different. Noon didn't cause this twelve-year-old to talk, just cringe. The air blasts meant lunch time and that meant a tough kid named Goo would be collecting his lunch money.

After Mane stumbled upon the gym, heads were put together to do some real brainstorming. We figured that, since he wasn't too comfortable around horses, becoming a jockey was out, so his 85-pound frame began the chore of mastering the heavy bag. After a couple of rounds at under 100 pounds, hitting the heavy sack with no lunch was like swimming with your legs tied.

After a couple of consultations with his new management team, it was decided that a new routine was in order. Let Goo buy his own lunch. With the confidence of the gym and the growls of his stomach, Mane confronted Goo, and any dreams of ever riding in the Kentucky Derby ended.

Of course, boxing isn't always that romantic. There are also the echoes of Howard Cosell's impassioned, if not self-committed, documentation of Tex Cobb's imitation of a light bag against Larry Holmes' fists. Howie dramatically removed himself from the sport of professional boxing like any other true humanitarian would do to protest such a brutal contest.

In the previous years, when Howie was developing on the airwaves and in his pocketbook, he had a tougher skin; he could take more. But, as time passed, scar tissue formed; therefore, the sudden bleeding heart.

There are other blows in today's society that strike harder and cut deeper than even the great Sugar Ray's combinations ever did, haymakers like drugs, unparented and unwanted children, or political crimes that leave more than one body on the canvas.

Today, congressmen and the educators and the whole of this world will say we need to direct our youth into schools and teach them productive trades. I agree! That's what Gary is doing now in his second term in Columbia Greene College and Mane as he strives toward a basketball scholarship on a frame that was built on refunded lunches from an old nemesis.

Yes, we need education and we need stronger family principles and guidance but we also need to learn defense from the hooks and jabs of life and we need confidence and we need direction and boxing can sometimes teach those things. Just ask Gary; he'll tell you.

Introduction

Few followers of boxing would deny that the game is at present passing through a magnificent era. Although there are far fewer promotions than in tougher and less affluent times, and relatively fewer lads feel attracted to scrapping, the sport continues to flourish.

Thanks to television, both multi-million dollar extravaganzas and modest small-hall offerings are regularly brought into the home. Many a fan is now a knowledgeable armchair critic, and is far, far more familiar with the style and capabilities of a champion than was his counterpart of yore. The latter, for the most part, had to rely upon newspaper reports and the occasional cinema news-reel, which was confined only to leading contests.

While there is no refuting the fact that a fledgling fighter has little opportunity to test his wings and hone his talents with considerable experienced opposition in the company of a wide variety of stylists, and is often rushed into high ranking contendership after a mere handful of contests, it is also irrefutable that many of our present top men bear comparison with the best battlers of the past.

A man like Mike Tyson — and, indeed, even several of those he has humbled — would have given many heavyweight champions of the past a lot to think about. At the time of writing, there are those who would rank Tyson as the best of all time! And few would insist that men like Marvin Hagler, Thomas Hearns, and Ray Leonard could not have held their own with legends like Harry Greb, Mickey Walker, Barney Ross, and those of the earlier part of this century.

* * *

To recapitulate, glancing back at events of the recent past, the earlier months of 1987 were rich in attractive contests. Outstanding, by far, in capturing the imagination of the whole world, was the meeting of that fabled pair, "Marvelous" Marvin Hagler and "Sugar" Ray Leonard.

Ruthless two-fisted fighter versus immaculate and implacable super-boxer? The immovable object facing the irresistible force? Describe it any way you will. So many so-called "naturals" of former days — brilliant pairings on paper which turned into dull fiascoes on the night — had tended to make the public more than a trifle cynical. But here was one heroic contest which will go down in the annals of the ring as a classic of the art and science of pugilism.

Absolutely spell-binding from first bell to last, the battle presented a contrast in styles which was evident to any watcher with even the

Larger than life promoter, Don King, comes between Mike Tyson (left) and his rival, "Bonecrusher" James Smith, prior to their heavyweight battle in Las Vegas.

Tom Casino

In one of the greatest comebacks of all-time, "Sugar" Ray Leonard scored a stunning victory when he upset Marvin Hagler. Leonard (right) always fought back when under pressure.

Christopher M. Farina

minimum knowledge of the sport. Never for a minute was one man overwhelmingly the better of the two; never at any time did a dramatic knockout ending seem likely.

And while both men ladled out plenty of punishment with their gloves, the bout was entirely free of those accidental gashes, which often mar a good contest and bring it to a premature end. In fact, there was little blood evident to disturb the more squeamish, but the whole twelve rounds were so action-packed and full of interest that at the final bell no man on earth — including the contestants — could have been certain of the official outcome.

Ray Leonard was awarded the verdict on a majority tally, and yet for every person who agreed that he was the victor there was another who insisted that Marvin Hagler was the winner. This fight was truly an epic encounter: one of the best of all time.

The youthful "Iron" Mike Tyson, fierce, strong, and utterly ruthless in his thrilling rise to the World Boxing Association heavyweight championship of the world, faced James "Bonecrusher" Smith, the hard-punching veteran who had snatched the World Boxing Council version of the same title in a single round from the hitherto redoubtable "Terrible" Tim Witherspoon. Quite a firework display was anticipated with the clashing of two such phenomenal hitters, but Smith turned out to be little more than a damp squib.

For all his pre-fight talk of coming out fighting, the so-called "Bonecrusher" decided that discretion was the better part of valour. He crushed nothing more than the spectators' hopes for a thrilling battle. He took the money and ran — literally. Smith back-pedalled as the aggressive Tyson moved forward, and claimed his opponent in tight clinches whenever he got too close for comfort.

Mike was a unanimous winner, but a very frustrated one. Still, he now had the satisfaction of wearing both the WBA and WBC championship belts, and he looked impatiently towards any presumptuous adversary who might question his right to annexing the International Boxing Federation belt as well, and thus unifying the whole heavyweight championship business.

Among the cruiserweights — those fighters of still considerable poundage who would, in the days before the heavyweight division commonly produced men of well over 200 lbs, have been obliged to face up to such stalwarts as Dempsey, Louis, and Marciano — Evander Holyfield (WBA) came through with flying colours by stopping the highly-touted Henry Tillman in seven rounds. His victory made him a strong favourite to wipe the slate clean at his weight and to nullify the claims of Carlos de Leon (WBC), and Rickey Parkey (IBF). The same month, however, de Leon forced the Italian Rottoli to retire in the fourth round, and a few weeks later Parkey also successfully defended his laurels when stopping Chisanda Mutti in the twelfth.

Unfortunately the light-heavyweight division was, alas, another of the weight-classes marred by three separate title-claimants. While the WBA named Marvin Johnson as the rightful champion, the WBC backed Britain's Dennis Andries, and the IBF nominee was the exciting hitter, Bobby Czyz.

The latter was an active battler. Having won and defended the title in 1986, he again placed his honours in jeopardy early in 1987, and knocked out Willie Edwards rather easily in the second round. Marvin Johnson remained inactive during this period, but Dennis Andries was only too ready to travel to Detroit and face the somewhat surprising challenge of Thomas Hearns!

Tommy was an ambitious man. Having already held world titles at welter and light-middleweight, he sought to join the select few who have annexed major championships in three divisions. While certainly tall enough to compare with many a heavyweight, the consensus of opinion was that he was far too slight to stand an even chance with a natural 175-pounder.

He entered the ring appearing surprisingly bulky about the chest and shoulders, and more than held his own against the bustling Andries. Hearns then proceeded to do a real destruction job on a game but outclassed adversary. The fight was stopped in the tenth round.

Super-middleweight, a division at 168 lbs by no means universally accepted, had been dominated since 1984 — the year of its inception — by the South Korean, Chong-Pal Park, who must appear a veritable giant among his tinier countrymen. With no fewer than five successful defences of this IBF title under his belt, he encountered quite a surprise when opposing the Brisbane aborigine, Doug Sam. The fight went into the fifteenth and final round before Park established a supremacy so evident that the referee stepped in to halt proceedings.

Among the true middleweights, the hard-punching southpaw, Marvin Hagler, had long remained supreme. As already described, it took the incredible Ray Leonard to enter the lists once again and to outpoint the champion in one of the most absorbing contests in the whole history of the game.

At light-middleweight, Thomas Hearns had relinquished his hold on the WBC version of the title to mix it with heavier men, and Duane Thomas had beaten John Mugabi to take the belt in 1986. Buster Drayton, the IBF champion, forced the plucky but inadequate Said Skouma to retire from their fray early the following year, while the WBA claimant, Jamaican Mike McCallum, demolished the favoured Milton McCrory in a grim and hard-punching struggle.

Because most youngsters taking to the fight game scale something in the region of 147 lbs, a fairly average weight, the welters have always had an absorbing interest. But although Lloyd Honeyghan defeated Don Curry in 1986, thereby fortifying unity with all three ruling bodies, this happy state did not last for long. Honeyghan somewhat prematurely discarded his WBA belt because that body's foremost contender happened to be a South African! Harold Volbrecht, the gentleman in question, had not, at that time, seriously sought a match with the apartheid-conscious champion.

In February, under the auspices of the WBA, Mark Breland knocked out Volbrecht in seven rounds, while Honeyghan set about establishing his right to the other two belts. He utterly demolished Johnny Bumphus in a couple of rounds, but had a far tougher time when sneaking home following a close twelve-rounder against Maurice Blocker.

At light-welter, the WBA champion, Patrizio Oliva, outpointed Rodolfo Gonzalez over fifteen rounds before an Italian crowd, while the IBF nominee, Joe Manley, journeyed to England to defend his title against Basildon's Terry Marsh. The challenger created a great impression when stopping his man in ten rounds.

"Marvelous" Marvin Hagler (right) sets up another blistering attack, but again Leonard fights back.

Christopher M. Farina

No lightweight claimants risked their laurels early in 1987, but among the super-featherweights, Brian Mitchell (WBA) boxed a draw with Jose Rivera, and Julio Cesar Chavez (WBC) gave an impressive display when stopping Francisco Tomas da Cruz in three rounds. Barry Michael (IBF), after a busy 1986, was in no great hurry during the new year.

Steve Cruz, the Texan featherweight, who had looked so good when beating Barry McGuigan the previous summer, lost his WBA title in his first defence, against Antonio Esparragoza, but his WBC counterpart, the powerful Azumah Nelson, had little trouble with Mauro Gutierrez, who succumbed on a knockout in six rounds.

The super-bantamweight division, first instigated as long ago as 1922, but only popularised in 1976, and necessarily largely confined to Orientals and the smaller-statured men of the Latin-American countries — as, indeed, are all of the lighter weight-classes these days — found Seung-Hoon Lee and Prayoonsak Muangsurin meeting at Pohang for the vacant IBF title. Lee scored a nine-round knockout, and soon afterwards tackled Jorge Urbina Diaz, putting the quietus on his challenger in ten rounds. Louie Espinosa halted Tommy Valoy in four, for the WBA title, after Victor Callejas had forfeited the crown by failing to defend.

Thomas Hearns collected his third world title when he relieved Britain's Dennis Andries of the WBC light-heavyweight crown in March 1987

Peter Goldfield/USA

Once again the traditional bantams, at 118 lbs, were well-represented by Bernardo Pinango, who outpointed Frankie Duarte over fifteen rounds for the WBA championship, only to announce his retirement from the game. Takuya Muguruma and Azael Moran crossed gloves to decide a new title-holder, and the little Japanese scored a clean knockout in five rounds.

Gilberto Roman, the very busy Mexican, successfully defended his WBC super-flyweight honours, first by stopping Antoine Montero in nine, and then outpointing Frank Cedeno over twelve. The WBA was represented by Kaosai Galaxy, who knocked out Elly Pical in the fourteenth round, but the first four months of 1987 saw no IBF champion in action, Pical having forfeited that title to challenge for the WBA crown.

Two of the three claimants to the traditional flyweight class jeopardised their honours as the year began. Hi-Sup Shin took the full count in five rounds against Dodie Penalosa, to surrender his IBF title, while Hilario Zapata was outpointed by Fidel Bassa, who forthwith travelled to Belfast and beat Dave McAuley in the thirteenth after a terrific battle for the WBA crown. Sot Chitalada, the WBC champion, was not active.

South Korea would appear to hold a monopoly among the tiny 108-pounders of the light-flyweight group. All three rival bodies had a local fighter in possession of their championship belts, and with each of them emerging triumphant in title defences. Myung-Woo Yuh (WBA) stopped Eduardo Tunon in the opening round, Jung-Koo Chang (WBC) served Efren Pinto similarly in six, and Jum-Hwan Choi (IBF) outpointed Tacy Macalos over fifteen. What an opportunity for unification this exciting division now presented!

Thus a summarily-described account of events as the year got under way. Little more remains to be said, except to stress that the three-cornered rivalry of the governing bodies continued unabated.

There now follows a month by month resumé of all championship contests during the twelve months following, together with mention of the outstanding occasions among contenders which had some bearing on the pugilistic scene.

The victor thus added the IBF belt to that of the WBA; Holyfield looked towards Carlos de Leon and his WBC honours in anticipation.

Port of Spain was the scene of great enthusiasm when Trinidad's light-heavyweight, Leslie Stewart, faced Marvin Johnson in a second attempt to win the championship. The pair had faced each other before in a battle for the vacant WBA title, and Stewart had been unfortunate to lose with cuts over both eyes.

On this occasion Stewart lost no time at all in taking the initiative, and he met Johnson's opening attack with a fierce barrage of his own. Twice in the opening round he dropped his man for long counts, and at the bell Johnson was in a distressed state.

The veteran title-holder thereafter had little to offer but courage, and he took a sound beating for the next seven rounds. At the close of the eighth he was unable to continue and his corner signalled his retirement from the fray. Stewart thus became the first Trinidadian to win a major boxing title, an event which spells nothing but good for the game in the Caribbean.

Bobby Czyz, the rumbustious and active holder of the IBF title at the same weight, had very little trouble with "Diamond" Jim MacDonald. The challenger, once having tasted the power behind the champion's blows in the first exchanges, showed an obvious reluctance to mix matters, and spent practically the whole of a disappointing bout posing and clowning. After five uninspiring rounds a ringside official demanded that the referee stop the contest if MacDonald refused to make a fight of it. The challenger did offer a token effort during the sixth, but he was so far outclassed that matters were brought to a quick conclusion.

Chong-Pal Park, the South Korean holder of the IBF super-middleweight crown, faced the challenge of the American Lindell Holmes in a rugged fifteen-round battle at Inchon. Holmes had much the better of the exchanges in the early stanzas, and even scored a surprise knockdown in the fifth, but Park forged ahead during the latter half of the bout and did well to dominate matters.

The result was by no means a foregone conclusion, but the champion managed to scrape home by a majority decision. It was one

"Pinky" Thomas (left) boxed well during the early rounds, but succumbed to a vicious Tyson attack and was blasted to the canvas in the sixth, thereupon being rescued by the referee.
Sporting Pictures (UK) LTD

of his hardest tests, but he was a popular victor.

Australia was justly proud of Jeff Fenech, who had ruled the IBF bantamweight roost since 1985, but recently had found great difficulty in reducing to the required 118 lbs limit. When Jeff announced his intention of challenging for the WBC super-bantamweight honours the Aussie fans were right behind him as he faced the champion, Samart Payakarun, at Sydney.

Although the hard-hitting champion dropped his man in the opening round, Fenech soon settled into his stride and went in with both fists flailing. Payakarun did his best to match the little Aussie's fierce attack, but by the close of round three the challenger was well in front.

The following session saw the finish. The referee quickly brought matters to an end when a sustained bombardment stretched Payakarun unconscious, and seldom has one fighter shown such complete superiority over another.

The bantamweights proper were also quite active during May. Kelvin Seabrooks, the US Boxing Association champion, faced the Colombian, Miguel Maturana, for the vacant IBF world title before an expectant crowd at Cartagena. The local lad had much the better of things in the early rounds, but his American opponent floored him heavily in the third. From that moment, the Colombian did his best to stay on top by boxing off his aggressive adversary, but in the fifth round Seabrooks caught him with a beauty which stretched him for the full count.

Tony Tucker (right) sets himself up for a unification bout with Mike Tyson when he beat James "Buster" Douglas in the tenth round of their IBF heavyweight title bout

All-Sport/Duomo

This WBA bantamweight crown was also at stake in May, on this occasion at Osaka. The Japanese champion, Takuya Muguruma, got a shock when he faced the Korean, Chan-Yung Park. The aggressive challenger dominated the fight and stopped his man in the eleventh round. Gilberto Roman, the WBC super-flyweight kingpin, met the former WBA flyweight title-holder, Santos Laciar, who had relinquished his championship belt a couple of years earlier in order to mix it with the slightly heavier fellows. The bout, which was staged at Reims, was closely-contested, and Roman was rather unlucky to sustain a bad cut from a collision of heads. The wound was so aggravated by the eleventh round that the reference had no alternative but to halt proceedings.

Battling for the vacant IBF title at the same poundage, the two South Koreans, Tae-Il Chang and Soon-Chun Kwon, faced each other at Pusan in a hard-fought but very even fight. The split decision in favour of Chang was not entirely popular.

* * *

Perhaps the outstanding event among the world title contenders was Herol "Bomber" Graham's ill-fated defence of his European championship against the Italian-based African, Sumbu Kalambay. Graham had the better of things by just a slight margin until the twelfth and final round, when a right-hander caught him beautifully and sent him staggering. He was fortunate to last out the remaining minutes, but he heard a unanimous decision go against him — the first loss of his career.

Hector Camacho, in his first outing as a light-welter, did well to outpoint the former brilliant amateur, Howard Davis, although the verdict was not a popular one, and Don "Golden Boy" Lalonde, the Canadian light-heavyweight, endured much facial damage as he won a hard twelve-rounder over Mustafa Hamsho, of Brooklyn.

At cruiserweight, Ossie Ocasio and Dwight Muhammad Qawi, both former world title-holders, fought a grim battle at Las Vegas in a supporting bout to the Holyfield-Parkey championship meeting. Two judges had Ocasio slightly in front, while the third scored the fight a draw, reflecting how close the two men were.

JUNE

It was a great boost to find this month offering several title defences and a non-championship thriller so attractive that it grossed astronomical figures at Atlantic City, and was watched with great interest in every corner of the world.

At Montreal, the hard-hitting and ever-dangerous Buster Drayton was well beaten by the Canadian hero, Matthew Hilton, in a fight with the IBF light-middleweight championship at stake.

Such an encounter, between two established powerful punchers, was expected to finish relatively soon. Although a crashing right to the jaw in the first round felled Drayton early, his experience enabled him to weather the onslaught which followed. He fought back gamely against an obviously better man, and at the finish there seemed little need for the ceremony of an official decision. Hilton was an overwhelming winner by the scores of all three officials, and he became the first Canadian to win a world title for over 40 years.

Another IBF title bout upset, this time in Providence, Rhode Island, found the local hero, Vinny Pazienza, staging the fight of his life when opposing Greg Haugen, the tough holder of the lightweight crown.

It was a fierce and bruising battle from start to finish: fifteen rounds of closely-contested skill, science, and hard punching. The scoring of the judges, who awarded a three-point lead in Pazienza's favour on each card, accurately reflected the way in which the bout was waged. Haugen had no argument with the decision, and the spirit in which this little thriller was boxed guaranteed a certain sell-out in the event of the proposed re-match.

Further afield, South Korea was the scene of much rejoicing among Oriental fans. Eastern boxers more than established their supremacy in the lightest weight divisions, and no fewer than three of the tinier men starred in title matches during the month. All came through with flying colours in exciting battles.

For starters, Myung-Woo Yuh, popular holder of the WBA light-flyweight crown, defended his belt successfully for the fifth time when he staged a magnificant scrap against the Panamanian, Benedicto Murillo, at Pusan. The South Korean stopped his man in the last round of a contest scheduled for fifteen.

A week later, at Bujok, Kyung-Yung Lee, also of South Korea, faced Masaharu Kawakami, of Japan. This fight, under the auspices of the IBF, was staged to decide the holder of the recently-inaugurated mini-flyweight championship. The Korean had little difficulty in scoring a devastating two-round knockout victory.

And before the month was out, to the delight of an enthusiastic crowd at Seoul, Jung-Koo Chang, the local favourite, stopped the thirteenth challenger for his WBC light-flyweight title, the Colombian Agustin Garcia, in the tenth round of a hard-punching encounter.

* * *

Overshadowing all other pugilistic events of the month was the long-awaited clash between Michael Spinks and Gerry Cooney. Spinks had twice taken close decisions over the ageing but formidable Larry Holmes, and was also the erstwhile IBF heavyweight champion. But it was the gigantic left hook specialist, Cooney, who had himself come very close to winning boxing's greatest prize at the expense of the same Holmes, who was the major money-spinner.

The ambitious plan devised by Home Box Office to stage a series of eliminating matches in

Vinny Pazienza, "The Pazmanian Devil", came good in June when he wrested the IBF lightweight crown from Greg Haugen over fifteen tough rounds

Peter Goldfield/USA

The unfortunate Gerry Cooney seen in a bemused state shortly before the referee stopped the proceedings, leaving Michael Spinks the winner

Japan Boxing Magazine

order to determine the one true champion of the world had originally included Michael Spinks, at that time recognised as the IBF title-holder. But his volatile manager, "Butch" Lewis, had upset things just a trifle in pulling his man out of the tournament and promoting what he considered to be a much more lucrative contest against Gerry Cooney.

Lewis took a calculated risk in opting for what he viewed as the ultimate big money match, and felt that the survivor of the HBO tournament could wait. He would still be available when his will-o'-the-wisp protégé, Michael Spinks, had subdued Cooney!

Earlier in the year, the IBF authorities had summarily deposed Spinks from his championship throne for backing out of the elimination series, but neither he nor Lewis was worried. The fight versus Cooney was, as a matter of fact, actually billed as being for the world's heavyweight title! But nobody took that very seriously. Those onlookers who paid small fortunes to be present at the ringside of the Convention Centre, Atlantic City, and the millions who watched the contest at home on television did so in anticipation of a real thriller, with Cooney favoured to score a knockout if one were forthcoming.

Spinks came in at just a pound or two under fifteen stone — the most he had ever scaled — but his opponent outweighed him by a full two stone, and at six feet seven inches he dwarfed his adversary.

The first four rounds, packed with action, were fairly evenly-waged. Cooney became the aggressor from the opening bell and bulled his way forward, smashing over vicious hooks and uppercuts in an effort to end the fight quickly. Spinks, always the superlative boxer, rode or avoided most of the punches and jabbed effectively with a stinging left as he boxed on the retreat.

The end came quickly and unexpectedly in the fifth session. Spinks opened the round by meeting Cooney in the centre of the ring and whipping over blows to the head with both fists. The bigger man, who had showed no great distress on receipt of his opponent's earlier puches, was momentarily halted in his tracks. Spinks now smashed home blow after blow and dropped the New Yorker to the canvas.

Gerry was obviously hurt, and he took his time in arising, as Spinks piled in once more with his relentless attack. Again he went down heavily, and this time he had difficulty in climbing erect. His opponent forced him to the ropes and he was landing almost as he pleased when the referee jumped between the two men and led a bemused Cooney to his stool.

A week later came another surprise among the heftier men. "Smokin'" Bert Cooper, the protégé of former champion Joe Frazier, was tipped to continue his impressive rise when he faced Carl "The Truth" Williams, whose career had taken a turn for the worse after he had been battered to defeat by the veteran Mike Weaver a year and a half earlier. In a bout described as being for the vacant United States Boxing Association championship — a somewhat hollow and dubious honour — Williams showed scant respect for Cooper's impressive record.

He walked in and dumped Bert to the boards almost right away, and although Cooper was more surprised than hurt his morale was undoubtedly damaged. Williams thereafter had little difficulty in avoiding the powerful but ponderous hooks Cooper hurled over, and treated his rival to a taste of his own heavy artillery. It came as no surprise to anyone when Joe Frazier, at the close of the seventh round, signalled that Cooper could no longer continue.

Two veteran bantamweight contenders, Frankie Duarte and Albert Davila, staged an exciting and gory contest at Los Angeles in a battle described as being for the North American Boxing Federation title.

Although Davila suffered an injured eye early in the fight, which bled continuously, he had the better of things for most of the rounds. He outscored Duarte all the way, and even felled his adversary. But by the tenth round his eye was in a terrible state, and the referee was obliged to halt proceedings in Duarte's favour.

The British scene saw a dourly-contested struggle between Lloyd Christie, light-welterweight champion of Great Britain, and the Commonwealth lightweight king, Mo Hussein.

While the consensus of opinion was that Mo would be giving away too much poundage in this challenge for a heavier title, he weighed in at only a little less than Christie. It was a close and magnificent battle all the way, with neither man gaining a really marked advantage in the earlier rounds. But Christie was beginning to look the stronger of the pair, although Hussein fought back fiercely all through the sixth and did so well in the seventh that it looked as if he might come through successfully.

But by the twelfth Hussein was very tired, and was boxing on instinct alone. A powerful right sent him staggering, and at this point the referee had probably already seen enough. But before he could intervene another smashing right sent Hussein pitching into the ropes and almost out of the ring. It came as no surprise when the battle was stopped immediately.

George Navarro, the undefeated featherweight contender from New Jersey, advanced up the ladder towards a championship contest when he met the former WBC super-bantamweight title-holder, Jaime Garza.

Although it was the latter who had the reputation of a hard puncher, having stopped almost all of his opponents inside the distance, it was Navarro who surprisingly scored the one knockdown of the fight. Garza went to the boards, on one knee, very briefly, just before the end of the second round, but he was not greatly affected.

The former champion forced the fight for the whole ten rounds in the only manner he knew how, but his younger opponent's superior boxing skills were a thing apart, and Navarro showed a complete superiority in every round. The decision in his favour was unanimous.

Michael Spinks, all smiles, at a press conference the day after the Cooney fight. Following his demolition of the Irishman, a big money match against Mike Tyson was a distinct possibility

Christopher M. Farina

JULY

Rather remarkably, there were no fewer than fifteen world title contests decided during the month. While this averages out at just about one such match every couple of days, and from one point of view might suggest that such a state of things is demeaning and lowers the standard of championship honours, it also certainly reflects the healthy state of boxing throughout the world. The three administrative bodies, the WBA, the WBC, and the IBF are undoubtedly on the ball, despite their disinclination to play ball with each other!

South Korea's "giant" world champion, the IBF super-middleweight title-holder, Chong-Pal Park, who dwarfs most of his countrymen and all other prominent boxers from that part of the globe, had little difficulty in opposition to Emmanuel Otti, the Ugandan challenger. Park was putting his belt on the line, for the eighth time, on this occasion at Kwangju, and he stopped his man in the fourth round after a powerful, two-fisted attack to the body.

In what was to be his last contest, Terry Marsh (facing the camera) successfully defended his IBF light-welterweight title in London against Akio Kameda of Japan.

Sporting Pictures (UK) LTD

Park, whose activities had largely been confined to Seoul and district, and who was therefore something of an unknown quantity to the cognoscenti, was now viewed as a worthy champion, and probably able to hold his own with any super-middleweight in the ranks.

There were two unanticipated results among the light-middleweights. At Bordeaux, defending his WBC title for the first time since winning it in his controversial contest against John Mugabi, Duane Thomas was completely out-boxed and outfought by the Californian Mexican, Lupe Aquino.

The challenger established his superiority as early as round two, when he floored Thomas with a strong left hook for a count of eight. Thereafter, the champion could do little to overcome Aquino's harder punching, although he fought back gamely despite two badly-cut brows and several other injuries to the face.

Thomas was struggling hard at the finish, and another powerful blow sent him flat on his back shortly before the bell. He managed to beat the count, but there was no chance of his saving the contest. All three judges scored Aquino the victor by good margins.

In Las Vegas, with the WBA light-middleweight title at stake, Mike McCallum, the capable but hitherto under-rated Jamaican, defended his honours for the sixth time, on this occasion with the formidable former welter-weight champion, Don Curry, coming from the opposite corner.

Curry, whose early career had been so successful and dominating that many observers had been inclined to view his surprise defeat at the hands of Lloyd Honeyghan as being largely due to weight reduction, was strongly fancied to defeat McCallum in fine style. In fact, he had the better of the exchanges during most of the time the contest lasted, and up until the sudden finish it looked as if he might well breeze home by a comfortable points margin.

The knockout punch came right out of the blue. In the fifth round, McCallum launched a perfect left hook to counter a lead from Curry. It caught the Texan beautifully and sent him crashing to the canvas. It was instinct, rather than anything else, which led the fallen man to sit up at the count of eight and dazedly make an attempt to rise. But he was quite unable to beat the referee's toll, and would have been in no condition to continue the fray had he arisen.

Things kicked off in London, when Terry Marsh placed his IBF light-welterweight belt at stake in opposition to the Japanese challenger,

Akio Kameda. Although Marsh employed the first couple of rounds in testing and feeling out his southpaw adversary, he must have very soon come to the conclusion that this was one occasion when he must get a fight over as soon as possible. A couple of head clashes left Marsh cut over the brows and in imminent danger of having the bout stopped if the blood continued to flow.

Once he had summed up the Oriental's capabilities, and felt that he had little cause for concern in that direction, the champion stepped up the pace in the ensuing rounds. Kameda was very soon all at sea and floundering. By the sixth round Marsh had his opponent in bad trouble and obliged to take a mandatory eight count.

The challenger was hopelessly lost as Marsh piled in with both fists, and at the bell, when the Japanese tottered groggily to the wrong corner, it came as no surprise to anyone that he was no longer in a state to continue.

Also at light-welterweight, in this instance under the auspices of the WBA, Juan M. Coggi, the Argentinian challenger, travelled to Riberia to do battle with the Italian-born champion, Patrizio Oliva.

The title-holder was a strong favourite to retain his honours without too much trouble, and in the opening round he was able to outbox his man fairly comfortably. But at the start of the second, Coggi settled down to his task and began to force matters with a strong attack.

Even so, it was a considerable surprise when the challenger came out for the third and knocked the champion through the ropes with a powerful left hook to the jaw. Oliva had some difficulty in getting back on his feet and continuing the fight. When Coggi caught him again with a left flush on the jaw he went down heavily and had no chance at all of beating the count.

A third light-welterweight title battle took place at Tokyo, this time to decide the WBC championship. Almost a year after winning the title from Mexico's Rene Arredondo with an amazing and thrilling knockout in the opening round, the Japanese Tsuyoshi Hamada faced the same man again in a return fight.

But this time the Oriental did not have things all his own way. Arredondo outboxed him comfortably and had Hamada's eyes puffed and closing with punishing jabs. Only in the third round did the champion show anything of his earlier form, but he was unable to retain the initiative. By the sixth round he was so badly cut, and his right eye had closed so rapidly that the contest was stopped in the Mexican's favour.

Altogether, this was not a particularly good month for Japanese light-welterweights.

When Hector "Macho" Camacho relinquished his WBC lightweight title in order to box as a light-welter, the two contenders nominated to box for the vacant throne were Jose Luis Ramirez, of Mexico, from whom Camacho had won the crown two years previously, and the Guyanan, Terrence Alli, a man who had looked extremely impressive in his more recent outings.

Their contest, which was staged at St Tropez, went the full distance of twelve rounds, with Alli doing all of the clever boxing and Ramirez scoring points with strong but less scientific attacks. Things were fairly even until the final session, when both men stood toe to toe in an effort to clinch matters. Ramirez was the more powerful of the two, and he caught Alli with a left hook which had him staggering. The Guyanan was barely able to weather the ensuing onslaught, but he did manage to stay on his feet until the bell. The decision in the Mexican's favour, although unanimous, was very close, and was reflected in the tallies of all three officials.

Terry Marsh (left) piles on the pressure after a clash of heads left him badly cut. Kameda was eventually rescued by the referee at the end of the sixth round when he was deemed to be in no fit state to continue

Sporting Pictures (UK) LTD

A crashing right hand from Mike McCallum (right) stuns his opponent, Don Curry, and was a taste of things to come. McCallum, defending his WBA light-middleweight crown, kaoyed the former welterweight champion in the fifth round with a tremendous left hook

Japan Boxing Magazine

Among the junior-lightweights, the WBA kingpin, Brian Mitchell, of South Africa, entered the enemy's camp when he journeyed to Panama City to defend his crown against the local Francisco "Rocky" Fernandez.

Although the challenger was a game adversary, he had little more to offer than courage. Mitchell was superior in almost every phase of the game, and although the Panamanian struggled hard to finish the full distance, the referee wisely stopped the bout early in the fourteenth round, when the South African had completely dominated his opponent.

Antonio Esparragoza, the Venezuelan featherweight, who had so unexpectedly relieved Steve Cruz of his WBA championship in the Texan's first defence, took on Pascual Aranda, also of Texas, in Houston. It was the South American's own initial defence of the title.

The fight was one of those ding-dong battles which have the onlookers on the edge of their seats, and Aranda certainly did his best to give his home-town followers a thrilling outing. He went forward continually, taking the fight to his opponent all the way, but Esparragoza was too heavy and sharp a puncher for the challenger.

It appeared ominous when the Venezuelan opened up a cut on Aranda's right brow as early as the second round, and damaged the left eye in the eighth. But the game Texan was determined to give of his best, and although it was evident almost from the start that he stood little chance of winning the contest he put up a brave show.

Not surprisingly the end came in the tenth round, when Esparragoza caught the challenger with a solid right to the jaw. Aranda was on his knees and listening to the referee's count, but was utterly exhausted and in no condition to continue the fight.

All three versions of the super-bantamweight title were placed on the line during the month of July, finding each of the champions defending with success.

The brilliant Louie Espinosa, of Phoenix, Arizona, the WBA title-holder, met a very tough nut indeed in the brave and dogged Venezuelan challenger, Manuael Vilchez, but finally cracked him in the fifteenth and final round.

Although there was hardly a moment during the fight when Espinosa was really worried, Vilchez never stopped trying, with fierce, two-fisted attacks. Going into the last session the champion was well ahead on points, and at first it looked as though he would sail through to a comfortable decision via the officials' cards, but after a minute or so he scored with a hard left to the head which dropped Vilchez heavily. The South American staggered erect to beat the count, but Espinosa was now able to land effectively with both fists, and the referee quickly intervened to save the challenger from unnecessary punishment.

Jeff Fenech, the popular little Aussie WBC super-bantamweight title-holder, delighted his home-town Sydney crowd when he faced the challenge of American Greg Richardson. But the latter did not earn any plaudits from the onlookers by boxing in a purely defensive and negative fashion.

He seemed in no mood to force exchanges with the champion, and Fenech was obliged to take the initiative from the opening bell, chasing his man about the ring in a frustrating effort to catch him with an effective blow. He eventually managed to slow Richardson up a trifle in the fifth round, when he cut the American's brow and also floored him for a long count.

Although he was able to arise in time to continue, the challenger had no further taste for fighting that evening and withdrew from the unequal contest to the derisive jeers of the assembly.

At Seoul, the super-bantamweight champion in the eyes of the IBF, Seung-Hoon Lee, faced the challenge of Lion Collins. The latter did his best, but he was no match for the South Korean title-holder and Lee had little trouble in retaining his belt, with the Filipino being counted out in the fifth round.

Two of the three traditional bantamweight champions, coming in at 118 lbs or under, were also in action during the month, and one of the fights for the title ended in confusion and considerable uproar.

This happened at Calais, when Kelvin Seabrooks, the American holder of the IBF belt, was at the centre of a total mix-up when his bout against the native French challenger, Thierry Jacob, was declared "no contest" following a

The winner and still champion, Mike McCallum, is obviously elated following his great victory over Don Curry

Christopher M. Farina

different earlier ruling. After an exciting battle, with knockdowns coming from both men, and the outcome by no means certain, Jacob's corner pulled their charge out at the end of the ninth round, owing to a badly-damaged eye, whch had been caused by an unintentional clashing of heads.

The reasoning, apparently, was that the man ahead on points would be given the verdict. But the official IBF ruling was that this applied only when an incapacitating wound was caused by a deliberate butt, so Seabrooks was officially declared the winner. However, after an hour's wrangling among the officials it was eventually announced from the ring that the fight had become a "no contest".

Miguel Lora, the WBC champion at bantamweight, stopped Antonio Avelar, of Mexico, in a contest held at Miami. After an uncertain start, the title-holder's superior class began to tell, and by the fourth round he was hitting his challenger so easily that the fight was halted.

Seoul was the scene of a light-flyweight meeting under the auspices of the IBF, when Jum-Hwan Choi faced the Japanese challenger, Toshihiko Matsuta. It was an uninspiring bout with the talents of the two adversaries being poles apart. The champion had very little difficulty in sizing up his man early on and then stopping him in the fourth round.

* * *

Veteran Joe Bugner, an unexpected crowd-puller in his adopted Australia, pleased his fans there by outpointing erstwhile heavyweight champion, Greg Page, over ten rounds. In his middle 30s, Bugner was big enough, strong enough, and experienced enough to stay out of trouble and jab his way to victory in his usual dull fashion.

Considerably more action was shown at Atlantic City when Frank Tate, the former Olympic gold medal winner, faced up to Troy Darrell, of Bermuda, in a contest described as being for the United States Boxing Association middleweight championship.

The tall, slim Tate made full use of his long left jab and dominated the whole twelve rounds. He was content to take no chances, and boxed his way to a comfortable victory.

Another bout which was billed as being for the USBA title — this time among the light-heavyweights — took place at Philadelphia when "Prince" Charles Williams had little trouble versus Joe Dolphin. Williams knocked all the stuffing out of his opponent after dropping his man in the second round and action was stopped almost immediately.

Also contesting USBA honours — this time at lightweight — Pernell Whitaker, unbeaten since he turned professional after winning gold at the 1984 Olympics, won another vacant championship when he easily defeated the New York-based Puerto Rican, Miguel Santana, inside six rounds.

In Sardinia, Mark Breland, the world welterweight titleholder according to the WBA, undertook a non-title bout when meeting the tough Venezuelan, Juan Rondon. It was Breland's first outing since defeating Harold Volbrecht for the championship, and despite his adversary's persistent aggression, he won the fight easily on points.

Kelvin Seabrooks (right), the IBF bantamweight champion, seen defending his title in France against the local hero Thierry Jacob. The bout was declared a "no contest" amid confusion and controversy after both men had visited the canvas. P. H. Duval

him to the ropes. Ocasio was quite unable to defend himself when the referee quickly stepped in and halted matters.

Two matches with rival versions of the welterweight title at stake took place during the month. First, the highly-touted Mark Breland, former gold medal winner at the Olympics and undefeated as a professional, placed his recently-acquired WBA belt in opposition to the Connecticut war-horse, Marlon Starling. It was considered to be a routine defence and something of a warm-up before tackling Lloyd Honeyghan in a unification contest. Second, Honeyghan himself placed his own WBC and IBF championships on the line when facing the veteran Gene Hatcher, erstwhile WBA light-welterweight champion.

The lean and extremely tall Breland found it an easy task to jab off the persistent Starling and to accumulate a considerable points lead during the earlier rounds of their contest at Columbia, South Carolina. But as the fight progressed, so the young champion began to show increasing signs of tiredness. But he was still managing to fob off his tormentor almost until the sudden end.

This occurred in round eleven, when Starling launched a spirited attack and caught his man with a hard right to the jaw. He was quick to see that this was his moment, and he forced Breland across the ring and dropped him with a combination of heavy blows. Mark tried desperately to regain his feet before the referee completed the count, but he was unable to do so. Had the contest continued he would have been completely at Starling's mercy.

Marbella was the scene of Lloyd Honeyghan's defence of the other two versions of the championship. This was one of the quickest and most dramatic title fights ever witnessed. Both men came from their corners aggressively, and after a brief flurry in mid-ring the Bermondsey man connected solidly with a devastating right to the head. Hatcher went down in a heap, face forwards, but he struggled up at four and seemed in control of his wits.

But at the completion of the mandatory count of eight Honeyghan rushed in with a fierce two-fisted attack. Hatcher was trapped on the ropes and had no reply at all to the hurricane of blows which descended upon him. As he began to slump to the canvas, arms hanging limply, the champion turned away and the referee jumped in and signalled that the brief affair was over.

Puerto Rico-born Edwin Rosario, lightweight champion of the world in the eyes of the WBA, faced his fellow-countryman, Juan Nazario, at Chicago in a hard and bitter struggle in which the "needle" element between the two men had been stressed by the press.

The southpaw challenger was the aggressor throughout, but Rosario had that little bit extra, known as "class", and he was the superior point-scorer in the majority of the exchanges. Nazario was cut over both eyes by the title-holder's sharp and deadly punching, but

Evander Holyfield (left) moves in on Ossie "Jaws" Ocasio while defending his WBA and IBF cruiserweight titles. Held in Saint Tropez, the challenger was overwhelmed in the eleventh round and rescued by the referee. P. H. Duval

although he showed signs of wilting as the fight progressed, he never faltered in his efforts to take the coveted championship.

Nazario's dream ended in the eighth round. Rosario connected solidly with a fine left hook to the jaw which sent his game adversary face down to the canvas. Nazario tried hard to pull himself erect, but the shattering effect of the blow had done its job, and he stood no chance of being able to continue as the referee completed the count and spread his arms wide.

Barry Michael, the Australian-based holder of the IBF super-featherweight belt, fought a courageous battle when defending that emblem versus the tough Rocky Lockridge from Tacoma, at Windsor, but all his skills and experience were not enough to hold off the harder punching and extra determination of the challenger.

Rocky had obviously come to Britain with the full intention of winning the championship, and he never let up his fierce attack for a second. It was a hard and bruising battle, with Michael being subjected to most of the damage. His left ear swelled up alarmingly, his nose was broken as early as the second round, and it was later announced that the drum of his right ear had also been broken. In addition, the champion suffered several abrasions about the face, and it was surprising that he held on for as long as he did.

While Barry was perhaps the better stylist of the two, he was not strong enough to keep his challenger at bay, and as the rounds passed it grew increasingly evident that the bout would not last the scheduled fifteen rounds.

The end came at the close of the eighth, when Michael, totally exhausted and looking very much the worse for wear, agreed with his corner-men that it was time for surrender. He announced his retirement from the ring immediately afterwards.

Julio Cesar Chavez, the holder of the WBC super-featherweight championship, did not have nearly so hard a time when he opposed Danilo Cabrera, the hard little warrior from the Dominican Republic. Before a largely Mexican crowd of onlookers at the border town of Tijuana, Chavez proved that, pound for pound, he is one of the finest pugilists active in the ring today.

Defending his laurels for the ninth time, the Mexican sent his challenger to the boards in the opening round. Thereafter, although he was unable to fell his man again, his amazing combinations of clever long-range boxing and deadly body-punching at close quarters, had Cabrera all at sea. The three officials adjudged Chavez to have won every one of the twelve rounds.

A few pounds lighter, at the featherweight limit, Azumah Nelson, Ghana's hard-hitting WBC title-holder, faced the challenge of Mexican Marcos Villasana for the second time, over twelve rounds at Los Angeles.

The busy champion was now placing his crown on the line for the sixth time, facing the rugged Villasana in an effort to erase the slight blot on his record of a disputed decision on the last occasion they met. This time Nelson was far and away superior in every respect. Only the challenger's sheer toughness saved him from a knockout defeat or the ignominy of being dropped.

At the closure the judges' unanimous verdict in favour of Nelson was not at all well-received by a predictably partisan crowd, but there was no doubt at all to the independent observer that it was easily the champion's fight.

Among the junior-featherweights, or super-bantams, Louie Espinosa, of Phoenix, Arizona, strengthened the already acknowledged belief that he is a good champion when he beat the Texan, Mike Ayala, at San Antonio, for the WBA version of this title.

Although the challenger went forward all the time and did his best to make a fight of it, he was outscored in almost all of the exchanges, and as the rounds advanced so Espinosa's superiority began to show. It was early in the ninth session when the champion backed his man to the ropes and hooked a vicious left to the body. It felled the Texan, and the referee counted him out.

Santos Laciar, of Argentina, made his first defence of the WBC super-flyweight title when he crossed gloves with Colombian Jesus Rojas over twelve rounds at Miami.

Laciar, who had formerly held the WBA flyweight championship before moving up to the intermediate division, was expected to win this engagement without too much trouble, but the contest proved to be that of the challenger in almost every round. He opened proceedings by dominating the battle with a bewildering diversity of punches. Once on top he stayed there, and although the champion gave him a hard fight and forced him to work throughout, there was seldom any doubt that a new champion was about to be crowned. All three judges named the Colombian as the victor by a wide margin of points.

Another Colombian, this time at flyweight, was in action when champion Fidel Bassa met Panama's Hilario Zapata in their long-awaited return fight. Bassa had won a disputed victory before his own crowd in February, and on this occasion the pair met at Panama City, with the great majority of onlookers naturally supporting Zapata's efforts to regain his belt.

He gave early promise, when he dropped

Bassa heavily with a well-executed left in the opening round, and the champion had great difficulty in regaining his feet. But he came back superbly. He rallied in a manner which recalled his amazing recovery earlier in April, when he rose groggily from a similar knockdown at the hands of Ireland's Dave McAuley.

Thereafter, these two closely-matched fighters waged a very even bout. The official decision of a draw caused an immediate riot among part of the Panamanian element in the crowd, who threw missiles into the ring, injuring many ringsiders. Although Bassa retained his title, both contests between this pair have been so close that a third and hopefully decisive meeting is almost a certainty and a box-office winner. The only problem will be the venue.

Jum-Hwan Choi, South Korea's wearer of the IBF light-flyweight crown, defended his diadem before his Indonesian challenger's home-town crowd at Jakarta. His opponent, in the form of Azadin Anhar, stood very little chance from the opening bell.

A very confident Choi took the opening round easily, and then, in the second, sent his adversary to the canvas and gave definite indication that the contest would not last very much longer. A fast and bewildering attack right at the start of the third indicated that Choi was out to finish things and few onlookers were surprised when Anhar crumpled before the devastating onslaught.

*   *   *

Among the contenders, two former holders of the cruiserweight title were matched in the chief supporting contest on the Holyfield–Ocasio bill at St Tropez. Dwight Muhammad Qawi, who had held the WBA version before losing to Holyfield in 1986, faced Lee Roy Murphy, who had surrendered his IBF championship the same year to Rickey Parkey. Both men were out to win convincingly, with a shot at the reigning kingpin as an almost certain reward.

In the event, the durable and thick-set Qawi proved far too strong for Murphy. After pounding his man throughout the early rounds, and felling him in the fifth, he came out for round six intent upon finishing the job. Murphy was sent to the boards again, and being in no condition to defend himself the bout was rightly stopped and Qawi was named as the victor.

Also as a chief supporting contest — on this occasion on the Honeyghan–Hatcher bill at Marbella — Frank Bruno sought to re-establish himself in the eyes of British fans after the disastrous mis-match versus Chuck Gardner, when Terry Lawless, Bruno's manager, had been accused of "picking lemons".

This time a former WBA champion, Greg Page, had been chosen, but a week before the fight Page cried off, and a hasty substitute had to be found. The best available was Reggie Gross, a one-round victim of Mike Tyson's, who had not boxed seriously for well over a year.

Bruno established authority in the very first round, and from that point onwards Gross was only interested in surviving. It was a wearisome spectacle, with only one man doing any fighting, and it was a relief to all concerned when the referee — severely criticised in many quarters for his inability to handle matters properly — eventually stopped the farce in Bruno's favour in the eighth round.

The WBA lightweight champion, Edwin Rosario (right), is seen setting up an attack against his deadly rival Juan Nazario. Nazario was counted out in the eighth round after a fierce struggle which was described in some quarters as a "blood feud"

Japan Boxing Magazine

SEPTEMBER

Compared with the summer months of July and August, September was a fairly inactive one for champions. Of the four who did place their titles at stake, two were soundly beaten.

After fighting so hard at becoming the first Trinidadian to annex a world title, Leslie Stewart, the WBA light-heavyweight champion, did not wear his laurels for very long. Although he was favoured strongly to retain the title in his initial defence, his opponent, Virgil Hill, from Williston, unceremoniously upset all the odds and hopes when he opened up with his big guns in their battle at Atlantic City.

The American had come from a brilliant career as an amateur, gaining a middleweight silver medal at the Los Angeles Olympics. Turning professional late in 1984, and now with a bit more flesh on his bones, he had won all his contests to date, having picked up the Continental American light-heavyweight title almost exactly two years after entering the paid ranks.

But for all his impressive record, he was not considered sufficiently experienced to combat the wiles of Stewart, and it is possible that the champion erred in rating him too lightly. This was evident from the opening bell, when the challenger surprised his opponent and most of the onlookers by taking command almost immediately.

Hill was far more aggressive than Stewart and appeared to be a much heavier puncher. He took the first three rounds by a clear margin, although the champion did not show signs of being in trouble.

However, Hill stepped up the action in the fourth even more. He threw a masterly combination of lefts and rights to the jaw which dumped Stewart in a heap on the canvas. He was obviously hurt badly, but he had no intention of surrendering his belt too easily. He managed to beat the count, but was immediately subjected to a fast two-fisted attack

Brilliant action from the Leslie Stewart-Virgil Hill battle in Atlantic City. Stewart, the WBA light-heavyweight champion, is seen on his way to the canvas after being caught by a tremendous right cross. He managed to get up, but was counted out shortly afterwards, thus losing his title

Tom Casino

which again sent him to the boards. He was still struggling to rise when the third man in the ring waved the contest over.

Manila was the scene of considerable excitement when the Filipino world flyweight champion with the blessing of the IBF, Dodie Penalosa, defended against his South Korean challenger, Chang-Ho Choi.

It was a hard-fought battle between two game little warriors. Penalosa, who had hitherto lost only one contest in his career, and that to the extremely capable Hilario Zapata in a challenge for the latter's WBA title the year before, was now making his first defence since winning the IBF belt in February against Hi-Sup Shin. But although he had the plaudits of a partisan crowd to spur him on, they availed him little on this occasion.

Chang-Ho Choi became the second South Korean of that ilk, emulating light-flyweight IBF ruler, Jum-Hwan Choi, to win a world championship. The better and cleaner puncher of the two, he knocked out Penalosa in the eleventh round of a tough contest.

In Bangkok, little Sot Chitalada, one of Thailand's national heroes, made the fifth defence of his WBC flyweight laurels. Far too experienced for the South Korean challenger, Rae-Ki Ahn, he had little difficulty in reaching his man with damaging punches, and he knocked out his challenger in the fourth round.

At the light-flyweight poundage Myung-Woo Yuh, also from South Korea, successfully defended his WBA title for the sixth time when he knocked out the Colombian, Rodolfo Blanco, in the eighth round in Inchon.

Leslie Stewart shown in confident mood, before he was shorn of his title by Virgil Hill

Peter Goldfield/USA

* * *

High-ranking contenders for world titles were far more active than the champions. In the middleweight division, the hard-punching Juan Carlos Giminez, of Paraguay, sought to bludgeon his way nearer to a title battle by electing to face the ageing but ever worthy Roberto Duran, from Panama.

The former holder of the lightweight, welterweight, and light-middleweight championships, and now in his middle 30s, was reckoned by most observers to be a game old war-horse just carrying on at the only job he knew, in order to retain the life-style he had come to expect.

It is quite possible that Giminez viewed him in this manner, too, when they faced each other in Miami. But the Paraguayan received a shock when the bearded veteran displayed much of his former skill.

Duran had taken a little time to get into his stride during the initial session, admittedly, and Giminez seemed too strong and fast for him. But thereafter the old warrior both outboxed and outfought his much younger opponent, and at times it looked as if Giminez might not last the full distance.

A storming attack throughout the later rounds gave glimpses of the great Roberto Duran of the past. Spurred on by the cheers of a wildly-excited crowd, he took the fight on points by a good margin, with each of the three officials voting for him clearly. This victory put Duran back among the leading contenders for the crown, giving much cause for speculation as to whether he might, at nearing 40 years of age, win a fourth world title!

Also in the middleweight division, Leicester's Tony Sibson was another on the comeback trail. He had first won the British title as long ago as 1979, and had since failed in brave world championship challenges in opposition to both Marvin Hagler and Dennis Andries. Undefeated for British and European honours at the middleweight poundage, he had voluntarily

PALACE
WORLD
CHAMPION

Despite being floored by this big right in the second round, the challenger for the IBF light-heavyweight title, "Prince" Charles Williams, recovered strongly to force the defending champion Bobby Czyz, to retire at the end of the ninth minus his belt

Tom Casino

The latter was a dejected and well-beaten man at the final bell, with all three officials scoring the bout in favour of Frank Tate by overwhelming margins.

Also at middleweight, the incredible Thomas Hearns became the first fighter in history to hold four world titles at different weights when he knocked out Juan Domingo Roldan to annex the WBC belt relinquished by "Sugar" Ray Leonard.

Although it might be argued that this is no amazing feat — with three different "champions" in almost every division — it must nevertheless be viewed as something of an exceptional achievement to box in top company, over the years, at welterweight, light-middleweight, middleweight, and light-heavyweight!

The fight looked to be all over in the opening round, when "Hit Man" Hearns twice floored the tough and aggressive Argentinian. Roldan was decked again in the second round, but came back strongly. He swarmed all over Hearns in the third, and during the fourth he had the man from Detroit shaken and wobbling. At this point it seemed to be even money as to which man would win, but as Roldan moved in, intent upon a finisher, Hearns shot over a solid right to the jaw which dropped the South American flat on to his face and thoroughly beaten.

A third middleweight title-holder was crowned at Livorno when Sumbu Kalambay, the Italian-based African and conqueror of Herol Graham, battled it out with the New Yorker, Iran Barkley, to decide a new WBA champion.

Although Barkley was favoured to win the twelve-rounder, the little-known Kalambay caused a great surprise by scoring the cleaner and more effective blows throughout. The judges' decision was unanimous, with a clear-cut points advantage to the man from Zaire.

The light-middleweights were on view at Atlantic City in a supporting bout to the Tyson–Biggs contest, when Canadian Matthew Hilton defended his IBF championship against Indiana's Jack Callahan. Although the challenger had won 24 contests in a row and seemed, on paper, to be a worthy opponent for the champion, the contest proved to be a mismatch almost from the opening bell.

Displaying plenty of aggression, Hilton had no trouble at all in reaching Callahan, and gave

Frank Tate made it 21 wins in a row when he won the vacant IBF middleweight title, beating Michael Olajide over fifteen rounds. Olajide (left) looks pensive as Tate comes swarming in, both hands firing

Christopher M. Farina

him a good going over in the first round. Early in the second session a cut was opened over the luckless challenger's right eye, and not too long after that he was sent to the canvas by an accurately-placed left hook. He managed to rise, but Hilton pounded him round the ring and felled him a second time towards the end of the round. The bell rang before the count could be completed, but the groggy Callahan was obviously in no state to come out for the third round as he staggered erect and then fell back.

At the same poundage, in Perugia, a new WBC king was crowned when Gianfranco Rosi, the awkward Italian holder of the European title, pounded out a very close twelve-round points victory over Lupe Aquino, the California-based Mexican.

Although Aquino was favoured to win this battle, he was obviously surprised at his opponent's ability. Despite a bad cut over the eye, which the Italian suffered in the fourth round, most of the exchanges were dominated by the hard-pressed Rosi. He boxed well to stay slightly in front, and while the battle was admittedly a hard one for him, the verdict in his favour was anything but a home-town decision. All three judges voted for Rosi, gaining him a unanimous victory.

The welterweight division witnessed an unusual happening when Lloyd Honeyghan, holder of both the WBC and IBF championships, clashed with the Mexican challenger Jorge Vaca, at Wembley.

Confusion reigned for some minutes when, after a closely-waged bout, a clash of heads in the eighth round caused a bad cut over the challenger's eye and brought the contest to an end. Since the fight, scheduled for twelve rounds, involved only the WBC title, that body's ruling was to the effect that the major scorer of points over the preceding seven rounds should be declared the victor.

Vaca proved to be ahead on the officials' cards by a single point, and was announced the winner amid scenes of dissent. And while the IBF championship had not been involved, owing to the affair having been limited to twelve rounds, the Federation declared its title now vacant!

The long and honourable career of that tough old war-horse, Cornelius Boza-Edwards, finally came to an end in Paris, when Jose Luis

Ramirez put him down for the full count in a bout for the WBC lightweight championship of the world.

In a dour battle between two southpaws, the veteran Boza showed little form except in the opening round. But soon afterwards it could plainly be seen that he had gone to the well once too often, and that it was only a matter of time before the crunch. This eventually came in the fifth, after Ramirez had dealt out a considerable pounding throughout the earlier rounds. A barrage of head blows, culminating in a right to the jaw, sent Boza flat on his face to take the full count.

Among the super-feathers, two championship defences were decided. The first, fought in the French town of Gravelines, found South African Brian Mitchell, the WBA's nominee, clearly outpointing the French national title-holder, Daniel Londas over twelve rounds, in an uninspired exhibition by both contestants.

Considerably more action was shown at Tucson, Arizona, when Rocky Lockridge put up his IBF crown against Johnny de la Rosa. The challenger caused quite a surprise when he dropped the champion for a count in the third round and punished him badly, but Lockridge came back strongly to wear his man down with powerful attacks. By the tenth round there was very little in it between the two men, one of the judges seeing the challenger ahead on his card while the other two officials had the champion in front. But de la Rosa went to pieces very suddenly, and he fell to the boards from a terrific onslaught. He staggered erect somehow, but the referee had seen enough and stopped the bout.

The end looks in sight for the brave Michael Olajide, but he hauled himself up for the second time in the twelfth to bravely go the distance. Frank Tate won the fight, billed as "Glitter versus Gold", going away

Christopher M. Farina

Thomas Hearns (left) makes ring history when capturing the vacant WBC middleweight crown by becoming the first man to win four world titles. His opponent Juan Domingo Roldan is seen slipping the left lead

Tom Casino

"Hit Man" Hearns (left) moves in for the kill as an exposed Roldan comes rumbling forward. Three times Rolden hit the deck, before he was counted out at two minutes and one second of the fourth round

Tom Casino

Lloyd Honeyghan (left) on his way to losing the WBC welterweight title against Jorge Vaca at Wembley. The Londoner boxed in a low key fashion and following an "accidental butt", the challenger, unable to continue because of bad cuts, was awarded the title on a technical decision

Sporting Pictures (UK) LTD

The end of the road comes for Cornelius Boza-Edwards (right) as he attempts to wrest the WBC lightweight title held by Jose Luis Ramirez, in Paris. Ramirez took the challenger's best shots before unloading his own to Kayo Boza in the fifth round

Denis Vilma

Frank "Bomber" Bruno (left) stabs out the left jab into Joe Bugner's face, a punch that the former "Golden Boy" had no answer for during their heavyweight battle
Sporting Pictures (UK) LTD

Super-bantamweight WBC champion Jeff Fenech retained his belt in a disappointing contest at Sydney versus Carlos Zarate, of Mexico. The Australian was well ahead on points after four rounds, and might have gone on to win by a knockout, but the referee stopped the fight when an accidental clash of heads opened a nasty gash under the champion's eye. The rule being that the boxer who was ahead on the judges' cards should be deemed the winner, Fenech's arm was raised in this technical decision.

The WBA bantamweight championship changed hands at Seoul when Chan-Yung Park, of South Korea, was stopped by Puerto Rico's Wilfredo Vasquez. By the fifth the challenger was dominating matters, and Park was felled on a couple of occasions before he finally turned his back on his opponent in the tenth round, apparently acknowledging defeat, and the fight was stopped.

Junior-bantams, or super-flyweights, were represented first of all at Bangkok, when Thailand's WBA title-holder, Kaosai Galaxy, made his sixth successful defence when stopping South Korea's Byong-Kwan Chung rather easily in the third round. The champion had things much his own way throughout the brief contest, flooring his opponent on three occasions before the referee had seen enough.

A few days later, at Jakarta, the IBF title at this weight was on the line when Tae-Il Chang, another South Korean, came in against the Indonesian Elly Pical, who had earlier given up this championship belt when making an unsuccessful bid for Galaxy's WBA belt. After a hard battle, Pical regained his old title when he outpointed Chang by a split decision over the fifteen round route.

The third championship at this poundage, that of the WBC, was also at stake during the month, this time at Miami. Unbeaten Jesus "Sugar Baby" Rojas, of Colombia, pounded out an impressive victory over Argentina's Gustavo Ballas. The challenger tried hard to make a fight of it, but the title-holder was far too powerful for him, and obliged the referee to stop the bout in the fourth round.

Osaka had the distinction of witnessing the first world championship contest for the WBC's new division, mini-flyweight. The contestants were Hiroki Ioka, of Japan, and Mai Thornburifarm, of Thailand. The bout went the full scheduled distance of twelve rounds, with the 18-year-old Ioka being returned the victor on points. He had the added distinction of becoming Japan's youngest ever world champion as well as its tiniest.

* * *

A much-boosted promotion which would not have "drawn flies" outside of England or Australia, but which packed 'em in at Tottenham in the open air, proved to be something of a disappointment when Frank Bruno and Joe Bugner met in a big-money bout with a reputed "needle" element to it.

While Bruno soon took the initiative and boxed well to keep on top with a commanding left jab, his older and heavier opponent proved to be the same old Bugner.

Joe just took the money and ran, almost literally. He backed off after a taste of Bruno's heavy artillery. Frank caught up with him at the end of the eighth round. Against the ropes and with nowhere to go, the badly-trained and cumbersome Bugner took a brief beating as he squatted on the hemp, before stumbling and pitching almost from the ring. The bell to end the round sounded just as the referee decided that he had seen enough and waved the affair over.

Francesco Damiani, a native son of Italy, made quite a name for himself at Aosta when he won the European heavyweight crown by stopping the holder, Anders Eklund, in six rounds. The challenger, a former Olympic medallist as an amateur, did well to floor his bigger adversary and eventually to oblige the referee to halt proceedings owing to a cut. But negotiations to match the new continental kingpin with "Iron" Mike Tyson for world honours in the foreseeable future seem premature, to say the least.

At the age of 37, Joe Bugner concedes to "Father Time", as he folds under the bombardment of punches thrown by Bruno. The referee rescued Bugner at the close of the eighth round to end what had been the most over-hyped fight in British boxing history

Sporting Pictures (UK) LTD

NOVEMBER

This was the month when the light-heavyweights shone. There were two world championship fights decided during November: first of all a WBA defence, and then a week later a battle to determine a new holder of the vacant WBC title.

In addition, two strong contenders, one of whom was a former champion, emerged as potential challengers for world honours. The month certainly highlighted the achievements of the top twelve-stone-seven men.

Virgil Hill, who had won his title at the expense of Leslie Stewart, the Trinidadian, a couple of months earlier, felt confident enough to take on his first challenger in an "away match", so to speak. He travelled to Paris and boxed the French champion, Rufino Angulo, in a twelve-rounder.

The Frenchman was a willing enough adversary, but that was about all. He survived a knockdown in the opening round, and for the rest of a one-sided encounter he went forward all the time but did very little damage. Hill's vastly superior boxing ability enabled him to jab off the persistent challenger and work his way through to a fairly easy points victory. All three judges voted for the champion overwhelmingly, with one of them awarding Hill every round.

Port of Spain was the scene of the second light-heavyweight title battle, staged to find a new WBC king when Thomas Hearns dropped back to the middleweight division, after demolishing Britain's Dennis Andries and later becoming the first man in boxing history to win four world championships at different weights when flattening Juan Domingo Roldan. The contestants on this occasion were veteran Eddie Davis, of New York and the sensational Canadian "golden boy", Don Lalonde.

This was Davis's third shot at the top honours, having previously been beaten by Michael Spinks and Dwight Muhammad Qawi, but he was still considered to be far too experienced and dangerous for the young, if sensational, Lalonde. But the underdog proved to all doubters that he is a long way from being merely a pretty face with a glamorous aura. He came out punching, and after measuring his man he shot across a right-hander which felled Davis like a pole-axed steer.

The New Yorker had a hard job making it to his feet, but he just managed to pull himself erect before the final count. Thereafter he was hard put to avoid a one-round knockout. After ducking and dodging as best he could he was finally caught again right at the end of the round and slumped to the boards once more.

On arising, he was given the compulsory eight count, but looked in no condition to survive. The bell came to his rescue, but it was only delaying the inevitable. A further heavy barrage of rights dropped Davis in a heap early in the second round, and the referee stopped the uneven contest immediately.

It is, perhaps, worthy of mention that when Matthew Hilton defeated Buster Drayton back in June he became the first Canadian to win a world title for 40 years, and less than six months later along comes another Canuck to annex boxing's greatest prize at his weight! The Dominion certainly has good cause for celebrating, in pugilistic circles.

Among the light-middleweights, Virgin Islander Julian Jackson became the new WBA champion when he outclassed South Korean In-Chul Baek in a bout staged at Las Vegas for the vacant title.

Jackson went into this fight having lost only one previous contest, and that to the formidable Jamaican, Mike McCallum, who was now forsaking this championship among the eleven-stoners to mix with the bulkier full-grown middleweights. Baek was a little-known quantity before he and Jackson shaped up, but it very soon transpired that while South Korea produces some magnificent scrappers among the smaller men, it is not nearly so fortunate with its bigger fellows. Baek revealed that he was certainly no Chong-Pal Park.

Julian Jackson was the better man from the opening bell. He had no difficulty at all in scoring, and he punched his game but inadequate adversary all round the ring. Baek was floored twice, and was being hit almost without return when the referee wisely called a halt in the third round.

The Mexican faction turned out in full force at Los Angeles when Rene Arredondo, light-welterweight champion according to the WBC, defended his belt against the former holder of the WBA super-featherweight crown, Roger Mayweather.

Both men were understandably cautious in the early rounds, but once they had settled down it developed into a keen battle, with neither showing an outstanding supremacy. The challenger boxed well and chalked up a slight lead on points, but as the contest developed so the champion came right back, and after five rounds it was anybody's fight on the score-cards.

But early in the sixth Arredondo went in slugging, a tactic which Mayweather seemed to find ideal. He matched the Mexican in this respect, and from that moment onwards the end was only a matter of time.

Three times the challenger pounded the Mexican to the boards, and the third time

Arrendondo dropped he was so obviously beaten that the referee waved the fight over without even bothering to count him out.

If Arredondo's defeat was a disappointment to his Mexican followers, the fans of fellow-countryman, Julio Cesar Chavez, were highly delighted in Las Vegas. This little battler is Mexico's greatest present-day boxing hero, and he proved himself to be a ring warrior worthy of comparison with contemporaries like Marvin Hagler, Ray Leonard, and Thomas Hearns. Having reigned supreme among the super-featherweights in a magnificent and unbesmirched career, defending his championship against all comers no fewer than nine times, he now faced Edwin Rosario for the WBC lightweight title.

The Puerto Rican, himself highly regarded by the boxing cognoscenti, did everything he could. But his efforts only brought out the best in a dazzling combination of brilliant boxer and fierce fighter who, at just under the lightweight limit, proved to be by far the harder puncher of the two.

There was no time at all during this brilliant battle when Rosario looked as though he might win it. Chavez matched him move for move and punch for punch, and piled up an impressive points lead. Rosario was badly-marked about the face, and was looking a sorry sight when the doctor made a close inspection of his condition in the corner after the tenth round.

He came out for the eleventh in what was obviously a do-or-die effort to swing things his way with one pay-off punch, but Chavez took everything he could deliver and really turned on the pressure. Rosario was rapidly developing into a mere punching bag when the towel of surrender fluttered in from his corner and the referee called a halt to the proceedings.

Louie Espinosa, the Arizonan WBA super-bantam king, got a rude shock when he faced the Dominican, Juan Gervacio, in San Juan.

The undefeated challenger, who is Puerto Rico-based, had most of the onlookers well behind him as he pounded out a well-deserved and unanimous points victory. Espinosa was defending his title for the third time, and was favoured to win, but the battle had not lasted very long before it became apparent that he had tackled the biggest job of his life.

At no time in the fight until the final session was the issue absolutely clear, but in that twelfth and last round Gervacio punched his man to the canvas. Espinosa managed to beat the count, but it was this knockdown which made the local favourite an undoubted winner and new champion.

Two bantamweight title-holders were on view this month when they put their versions of the championship at stake.

In Miami, Miguel "Happy" Lora, the Colombian holder of the WBC version, took on Ray Minus, the Commonwealth king from the Bahamas, and although he eked out a unanimous points decision over his dogged challenger it was anything but a one-sided battle. The deciding factor was the world champion's superior strength of punch, although throughout the contest only one knockdown was scored, when Minus went to the boards for a count in the sixth round.

Even so, it was a close thing until the final stages, when Lora managed to catch the eye of all three officials with a strong finish.

Kelvin Seabrooks, the tough little holder of

Julio Cesar Chavez (left) crosses a battered Edwin Rosario, who defended his WBA lightweight title at Las Vegas with great dignity. Whatever Rosario did, Chavez did better

Japan Boxing Magazine

The end is near as Chavez (left) sinks in body punches and Rosario wilts on the ropes

Japan Boxing Magazine

Chavez proudly displays the WBA belt after he had overpowered the defending champion, Edwin Rosario, in the eleventh round of a bout scheduled for twelve

Christopher M. Farina

the IBF bantamweight belt, was treated to a rude shock in the opening round when he faced Ernie Cataluna in a routine title defence at San Cataldo. The man from the Philippines unexpectedly dumped the champion on the canvas and had him in a very bad way for a short time. Only Kelvin's experience enabled him to last out that hectic first session.

But, once he had settled down, Seabrooks came back steadily to dominate matters, and in the fourth round he landed his own big punches which brought matters to a halt.

* * *

The outstanding contender of the month was Trinidad's Leslie Stewart, who had briefly held the WBA version of the light-heavyweight title. Although he was billed in what was nominally the chief supporting bout to the Don Lalonde-Eddie Davis WBC championship contest, it was undoubtedly Stewart's presence, as much as anything, which made this Port of Spain outdoor promotion such a big success.

Leslie's opponent was the Philadelphian, Dawud Shaw, and the Trinidadian favourite turned in a workmanlike performance by outclassing his opponent and forcing Shaw's corner to withdraw their principal from the unequal combat.

No doubt members of Lalonde's retinue were on hand at ringside to watch points. After his popular victory, Stewart — who had been ranked above the Canadian in the world ratings — could well be the new champion's next opponent in a WBC title defence.

Chicago's light-heavyweight, Tony Willis, continued his unbeaten march towards a world title chance when he stopped the locally-based Jordanian, Ramzi Hassan, to annex the vacant USBA championship, at Los Angeles.

But it was by no means a walkover. After dropping his opponent in the eighth round, Willis found that Hassan was coming back strongly and scoring most of the points. A ding-dong battle ensued, and although Hassan was cut badly and was beginning to wobble slightly during the eleventh, he came out for the twelfth round with a clear lead on all three cards.

But Willis piled on the pressure strongly, and in a grandstand finish he floored his opponent again and then proceeded to execute the finish. Hassan was now in a state of grogginess, and the battle was rightly stopped in the Chicagoan's favour.

In Johannesburg, veteran Mike Weaver, the erstwhile heavyweight champion according to the WBA, disappointed American Civil Rights spokesmen by electing to face the unbeaten white-skinned South African, Johnny du Plooy, on his home ground.

Weaver proved to be far too strong and experienced for the youngster, and he scored heavily with no serious returns. It came as no surprise when, after six rounds, du Plooy's seconds signified surrender.

Atlantic City was the scene of a super-featherweight punch-up when the undefeated Harold Knight, of New Jersey, boxed Erskine Wade, of Detroit, in a bout with the former's USBA title at stake.

Wade was the cleverer boxer of the two, but Knight proved to be the tougher, and the harder puncher. He floored his man in the third with a fine left hook, and thereafter Wade did his best to stay out of trouble. He managed this pretty well until the penultimate session of the scheduled twelve-rounder, when Knight finally caught up with him and dropped him to the boards again. The challenger was in so distressed a condition that the referee had no hesitation in stopping the fight.

DECEMBER

Some interesting activity took place during the last month of the year, which is often a slack one for boxing. Although the half dozen title bouts contested were in the main among the lighter men, the bout which gained the lion's share of publicity and attracted the attention of fight followers involved two hard-punching cruiserweights.

Evander Holyfield, holder of both the WBA and IBF titles, faced the ever-dangerous Dwight Muhammad Qawi at Atlantic City, the pair having boxed a close contest the previous summer. On that occasion Holyfield had notched up a majority verdict, and was far from being outstanding, but this time he was definitely the superior of the two.

This was probably due to the fact that Qawi was now something of a veteran, finding the going harder at each outing, while the champion was still young, improving with each successive match, and was punching with more power as he grew in confidence.

Only the IBF championship was placed at stake in this meeting, since the WBA's decision to limit title bouts to twelve rounds clashed with the other authority's adherence to fifteen. In the event, only four rounds were needed for the stronger and younger Holyfield to establish his supremacy, and the ringside odds of 5–1 in his favour were amply justified from the opening bell.

Qawi seemed well aware that with his advancing years his only real chance was to catch his man with telling blows early on in the contest, and he became the aggressor from the start. But Holyfield was by far the faster and more powerful of the pair and had no great difficulty in scoring heavily during the first couple of rounds.

The challenger did better in the third, and he actually took this round on points with heavy blows to both the head and body. But his rally was something of a last desperate effort, even so early in the bout, for in the next round the champion caught him with a good left hook and sent him to the boards for the first time in his career.

Although Qawi was up at three, the knockdown had done great damage, and Holyfield now stalked his prey calmly and methodically. As his opponent threw a desperate right to the head, the champion countered swiftly with a right-hander of his own which dropped Qawi heavily for a second time. On this occasion he was slower in trying to arise, and although he was fully conscious of the referee's toll he made no effort to beat it.

The loser announced his retirement after this fight, while the victor's manager talked enthusiastically of a challenge to Mike Tyson in the near future! There is little doubt that Evander Holyfield might develop into a realistic opponent for the devastating heavyweight champion, but a year or two's more experience and considerably more weight might make all the difference between triumph and defeat.

In Seoul, the former holder of the IBF Super-middleweight belt, South Korean Chong-Pal Park, boxed Mexican Jesus Gallardo for the vacant WBA title.

Hopes for a step towards unification in this weight division were dashed when Park relinquished his claim to the IBF belt. The WBA nominated him number one in their ratings, but Gallardo was hardly in the same class.

Evander Holyfield, the WBA and IBF cruiserweight champion, in pose, prior to his defence against Dwight Muhammad Qawi

Peter Goldfield/USA

The Mexican, however, very nearly caused an upset early on in the fight, which, although a brief one, did not lack for thrills and incidents during the time it lasted. Park, who came out punching from the very onset, soon ran into a hard blow himself, and was unexpectedly dropped to the canvas. He was not greatly hurt, but he took the mandatory count of eight and then piled back into the battle with both fists weaving, while Gallardo lacked the experience to follow up the advantage he had scored.

He tried hard to make a battle of it, but it soon became evident that he was not really in the same league as Park, who was by far the stronger man, and who excelled in all directions. In fact, before the bell to end the first round came to Gallardo's rescue he had twice been floored by stunning blows to the head.

A desperate attempt was made by his seconds, during the minute's interval, to freshen him sufficiently, but the effort proved fruitless. Park was now feeling good, and had the measure of his man. It took only a few seconds of the round before the South Korean was able to land with a right to the jaw which floored Gallardo and the referee stopped the contest without picking up the count.

Among the super-featherweights, Brian Mitchell, the South African holder of the WBA championship, faced Salvatore Curcetti, the European title-holder, over twelve rounds at Capo d'Orlando, in what proved to be a somewhat one-sided event.

Mitchell was the better boxer of the two, and had little difficulty in piling up a good lead on points. The challenger fought almost throughout with the disadvantage of a cut brow, which he claimed had been caused by a clash of heads as early as the second round. But it seemed doubtful that he could have turned the tide had the injury never occurred.

The champion was apparently boxing his way to a comfortable victory on the judges' scorecards when, in the seventh round, Curcetti was sent to the boards from what appeared to be more of push than a clean punch. Although the challenger claimed that he had not been dropped by a blow, he was obliged to take a count.

Again, in the following round, he went to the canvas, but this time there was no doubt at all that a powerful punch to the body had been responsible. Curcetti was in a sorry state by this time, with the cut eye still bleeding profusely. It therefore came as no surprise at all when he retired from the fray during the interval after the eighth round.

Dwight Muhammad Qawi is down and out for the first time in a long career as the victor, Evander Holyfield, successfully defends his IBF cruiserweight title

Tom Casino

Jose Luis Ramirez, the WBC lightweight champion, seen here showing off the belt he defended against Cornelius Boza-Edwards in Paris last October, went back to the French capital in December to depose of John Rafuse in a non-title bout

Denis Vilma

Pohang was the scene of an interesting bout scheduled for the fifteen-round route when South Korea's IBF super-bantamweight champion, Seung-Hoon Lee, placed his title on the line against Jose Sanabria, of Venezuela.

Surprisingly, the battle went the full distance, with the title-holder having the better of the exchanges throughout. The South American challenger was a worthy enough adversary, but he lacked the spark to defeat the Oriental champion on his home ground. Lee was naturally enough a popular victor and fully deserved the plaudits of the crowd.

Also in South Korea, on this occasion at the light-flyweight poundage, another popular native son, Jung-Koo Chang, the WBC title-holder, had no great difficulty in boxing his way to a unanimous points victory at the expense of his Mexican challenger, Isidro Perez.

Fidel Bassa, the busy little Colombian, the holder of the flyweight championship with the blessing of the WBA, was seldom extended when he defended his title at Cartagena against Felix Marty, of the Dominican Republic. The challenger made a brave show, but he was not in the same class as his opponent, who won almost every one of the twelve rounds and earned the vote of each of the three officials.

* * *

There were also several very important non-title contests during the month which had considerable bearing on the championship situation. Perhaps the most important of these was the one which saw the return to activity of the lanky welterweight, Mark Breland, who had looked so good until losing his WBA belt so unexpectedly and dramatically to the old war-horse, Marlon Starling, during the summer.

Breland appeared in the chief supporting

contest to the Holyfield-Qawi title bout at Atlantic City. He faced the Mexican, Javier Suazo, but neither boxer was particularly imressive. Although the former champion was staging something of a come-back, and the uppermost thought in the minds of his advisers must have been to re-establish him in the eyes of those responsible for compiling the rankings, Mark erred on the side of caution.

Very soon after the start of the contest it became quite obvious that the Arizona-based Suazo had come only in order to survive the scheduled ten rounds, while Breland, whose deficiences had been exposed by the hard-hitting and rumbustious Starling, was in no mood for recklessness. He seemed quite content to box his way to a comfortable points victory without taking any chances at all.

Inevitably, the result was a dull fight, which proved to be hardly more than a workout for the former world champion. The onlookers were not backward in making their feelings known and both boxers were being roundly booed long before the end of the bout, when Breland's arm was raised in token of a unanimous victory.

Another former champion whose fortunes had not been particularly bright in the preceding months was Don Curry, who was now returning to the ring for the first time after his shock knockout defeat at the hand of the Jamaican light-middleweight title-holder, Mike McCallum.

Understandably a trifle gun-shy after so devastating a defeat, Curry was at first apparently reluctant to open up with the full force of his own considerable artillery when facing the Californian, Rigoberto Lopez, at Reseda. Although he was by far the superior boxer of the two, he performed very warily for the first three rounds. It was only in the fourth that he felt sufficiently confident to walk in and throw a few of the hard and accurate punches which had led him to be held in such high esteem a year or two previously.

It was noticeable that Lopez had little defence against a good body shot, and few of the onlookers were surprised when Curry sank a wicked left hook to the Californian's stomach which dropped him to the canvas. The fallen man had great difficulty in arising, and when he did Don followed up with another vicious hook to the body. Once again Lopez was felled, and the referee wisely stopped the contest to save him from further unnecessary punishment.

Over in Sydney, the fans got a very brief but satisfactory glimpse of their super-bantamweight hero, Jeff Fenech. The WBC titleholder came in as a featherweight and announced his intentions, with deeds, towards the top nine-stoners, when he opposed the ranked Argentinian, Osmar Avila.

Fenech lost very little time in getting to work. He went in with both fists, and had his man on the retreat immediately. It was a matter of mere seconds before he sent over a left hook to the jaw which connected perfectly and prostrated Avila on the canvas. The fallen man made no movement at all as the referee counted him out, and it took some time for his handlers to bring him to a condition fit for a return to his stool.

Michael Dokes, erstwhile WBA heavyweight champion and almost three years out of competitive action — long since believed to have retired — made a return to the ring at New York's Felt Forum when he opposed K. P. Porter, of Michigan, in a contest billed as being over ten rounds.

Dokes, who had a three stone advantage over his adversary, was obviously far from being in peak condition and was carrying much superfluous weight. Even so, he was too good for Porter, who tried to make a fight of it but was unable to make much impression on the bigger man.

A right-hander, just before the end of the fourth round, sent Porter to the canvas, but the bell intervened to prevent a possible finisher as the fallen man arose. Dokes so established his supremacy as they crossed gloves in the fifth round that the referee very quickly intervened and waved the unequal contest over.

Paris was the scene of two very one-sided matches, which were obviously staged merely as "appetisers" for a feast to come.

Mexico's Jose Luis Ramirez, holder of the WBC lightweight crown, had been signed to defend his title against the exciting former Olympic star, Pernell Whitaker. If the powers that be promoted the two warm-up contests in order to get some indication of the eventual outcome between champion and challenger then the exercise was hardly worth it. Both men barely raised a sweat in outclassing the sacrificial lambs chosen to oppose them.

Ramirez, coming in at well over the lightweight poundage, had no trouble at all with John Rafuse, of Massachusetts. After outclassing his adversary for the first three rounds he set out to end matters in the fourth, and after Rafuse had been sent to the boards on a couple of occasions his seconds threw in the towel as a token of surrender.

Whitaker, a flashy performer on most occasions, had ample time to play to the crowd as he outboxed a game but inadequate Davey Montana. Once again the first three rounds were extremely one-sided, while the fourth saw the end. Montana was given a standing count by the referee, who then took a hard look at the unfortunate fighter and signalled the contest over.

JANUARY

By far the outstanding event of the month was the one which many informed observers of the ring had labelled a mis-match, but one whose outcome was awaited eagerly, nevertheless. Nobody at all believed that the fight between Mike Tyson and Larry Holmes for the WBA and WBC titles would travel the full distance or be devoid of incident and excitement; few saw Holmes lasting, comparatively unruffled at first, for as long as he did.

The present challenger had been heavyweight champion of the world for some seven years, and had defended his laurels a full score of times, thus inviting comparison with great former title-holders like Joe Louis and Muhammad Ali, but he had never enjoyed popularity and the esteem of the crowd. To return to the ring just a year or two short of 40, offering defiance to a man not much over half his age and one who had the reputation of being the hardest-hitting heavyweight of them all was viewed as a somewhat rash endeavour — albeit a most lucrative one. There were no empty seats at Atlantic City, and the fight was beamed to all corners of the earth.

Larry had usually been the aggressor in most of his earlier contests, even when facing established hitters like Gerry Cooney and Ernie Shavers — but like almost all opponents who had faced Tyson since his complete annihilation of an oncoming Trevor Berbick, the veteran challenger was content to box at arm's length at the start of this fight, picking off the champion's hooks on his elbows and shoulders and clinching desperately whenever the powerful champion got too close.

It was admitted later that Holmes had planned to stave off his energetic opponent until he began to tire from his vicious assaults, and then to begin to step in with a few hard deliveries of his own. During the first three rounds this plan seemed to work well enough. Tyson took each round on points simply through sheer aggression, but he was never able to connect solidly enough to do much damage.

Holmes caused a mild surprise by coming out for the fourth round high on his toes, dancing in and out with the famous "stick and run" tactics popularised in his prime by the legendary Ali. But "Iron" Mike showed almost contempt for this attitude. He simply stepped in with what time-honoured pugilistic ploy, "the old one-two". Tyson shot a fast left jab towards the oncoming dancing Holmes then followed it rapidly with a devastating right to the head.

The blow was fantastic! It was clearly audible as it caught Holmes high on the temple and deposited him flat on his back. With that punch the fight was virtually won and lost, although the game challenger, his mind in a whirl, staggered erect at the count of four. But the referee continued the toll until eight before waving Tyson in, and Mike charged forward with one of the most ferrocious attacks ever seen.

Mike Tyson (right) moves in on the comebacking former heavyweight champion Larry Holmes, just prior to the finish

Sporting Pictures (UK) LTD

A bombardment of fierce left and right hooks now assailed the bemused Larry Holmes as he vainly sought to staunch the barrage. Again he was caught with a glancing blow to the head, but one which was sufficiently hard to send him tumbling again. He was now palpably beaten, but pride would not allow him even to rest on the boards until the count of eight or nine, and once again he struggled upright as soon as he could with senses reeling.

Tyson bulled him to the ropes near a corner, and once caught with no retreat the unfortunate Larry tried to slug it out in one final and desperate rally. But for the third time that lethal right fist of Mike Tyson's thudded to his head and down went the veteran for the last time, arms spread-eagled and utterly defeated. This time the referee did not count. He waved the fight over and bent to minister over the beaten gladiator.

To be billed on the very same programme with such a fistic star as Mike Tyson is disconcerting enough — something akin to a capable but not-yet-fashionable entertainer being obliged to perform his act before a star such as Bob Hope taking the stage — but to be faced with a middling opponent capable of making one look ordinary must be really demoralising.

Thus, on an unusually strong bill featuring such names as John Mugabi and Michael Dokes, the WBC cruiserweight kingpin, Carlos de Leon, boxed his way to a desultory twelve-round victory at the expense of his foremost challenger, Jose Mario Flores, of Uruguay, and failed to cover himself with glory.

De Leon took almost every round in an unexciting contest, with the judges' unanimous decision in his favour showing a marked advantage on their score-cards. But the Puerto Rican title-holder was unimpressive, and his performance did nothing to cause anxiety to the WBA and IBF champion, Evander Holyfield.

At light-middleweight, the awkward-looking and normally unspectacular Gianfranco Rosi brought about a late-night gala in Genoa when he sensationally stopped his opponent, the former title-holder Duane Thomas, in the seventh round of a defence of his WBC championship.

The American had been looked upon as the harder puncher and more aggressive of the two, with the Italian being expected to attempt to box his way to a points victory. But Rosi surprised the onlookers by taking the initiative and soundly trouncing his adversary by slugging it out with him and reducing him to fistic impotence before the referee stepped in to halt a thoroughly one-sided contest.

There was an exciting upset in the featherweight ranks when Antonio Rivera, Puerto Rican holder of the IBF title, faced the little-known Pennsylvanian, Calvin Grove, over fifteen scheduled rounds at Gamaches.

Grove, although coming into the battle with an unbeaten record, was not expected to give the title-holder too much trouble. Indeed, during the first couple of rounds Rivera looked all set for a good win, although the challenger managed to hold his own in the third. The thrills were mainly confined to an explosive fourth round, when Rivera had the onlookers on their feet with a perfectly-timed left hook which dropped Grove in his tracks. It looked all over bar the shouting, but Calvin somehow pulled himself upright and fell into a desperate clinch. Then, aware that he now had little to lose, he threw all caution to the winds and tore into the champion with a fierce two-fisted attack.

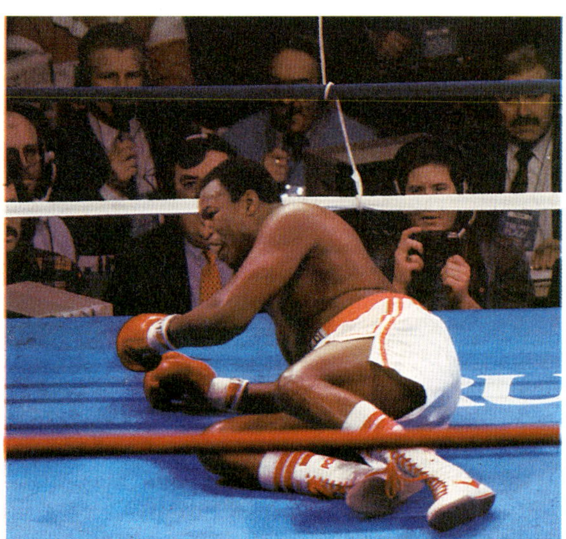

The finish of the Tyson-Holmes fight, with Larry on the canvas, but saved the ignominy of being counted out when rescued by the referee

Sporting Pictures (UK) LTD

To everyone's surprise, he sent the Puerto Rican heavily to the canvas. Rivera, upon arising, was now subjected to another devastating rally, and again he collapsed to the canvas. But although he managed to regain his feet for the second time he was now at the mercy of his opponent, and the referee wisely stepped in and signalled Grove as the victor.

Yet another Puerto Rican got something of a shock, this time in Osaka, and in the bantamweight division, when the WBA king, Wilfredo Vasquez, entered the enemy's camp to do battle against Japan's Takuya Muguruma.

It was a close and desperately-contested confrontation, travelling the full scheduled twelve rounds, and with the officials in disagreement at the close. One gave the champion the majority of points, another saw the challenger as the victor, while the third judge reckoned the bout an even one. A draw was declared, and Vasquez was lucky to retain his title.

All indications are that this eight-stone-six division will very shortly be graced by a formidable title challenger in the form of Kaosai Galaxy, the holder of the WBA super-flyweight belt. He had the greatest of difficulty in making the weight when defending his title against fellow-Thailander, Kongtoranee Payakarun, at Bangkok.

Although he suffered a surprise knockdown, Galaxy had little difficulty in winning the contest, but this was the first of his seven defences to be decided by a points decision at the close of twelve rounds.

In Manila, the local favourite, Rolando Bohol, exacted true revenge on behalf of his compatriot Dodie Penalosa, when he outpointed the IBF flyweight titleholder Chang-Ho Choi to gain the 112 lb crown. Back in September Penalosa had lost the title to Choi and this was the South Korean's first defence.

At the end of the month, Osaka, which had earlier witnessed the Vasquez-Muguruma contest, was also the scene of two further world championship fights, both of them on the same bill and involving Japanese boxers.

Hideoki Kamishiro, the local southpaw, was given a tough task when challenging the brilliant and popular little WBC flyweight kingpin, Sot Chitalada. It was an extremely one-sided encounter, with the champion having things pretty well much as he liked. He opened bad cuts over both of Kamishiro's eyes, and after the end of round seven the ringside doctors advised that the bout be stopped.

The WBC mini-flyweight title holder, Japan's Horoki Ioka, had a hard fight in opposition to his South Korean challenger, Kyung-Yung Lee, in the chief supporting contest on this attractive bill. Although the plucky Lee made a terrific battle of it, and came out for the twelfth with an aggressive burst, the champion felled him halfway through the round. The visitor regained his feet but was in a dazed condition and unable to defend himself properly, with the result that the referee called a halt.

Earlier in the month, the WBA held their inaugural championship bout at the 105lb limit when Luis Gamez from Venezuela boxed his way to a disputed twelve-round points win in Pusan, South Korea, over the local, Bung-Jung Kim. Following the announcement of the decision there was almost a riot as Kim had looked to be way ahead in the scoring stakes. And in an effort to pacify matters the officials ordered a rematch to take place within 120 days.

* * *

Among the contenders, the lanky and stylish Carl "The Truth" Williams continued his impressive return to big-time heavyweight boxing when he faced Rodney Frazier in a bout at San Diego which was styled as being for the United States Boxing Association championship.

With Mike Tyson the undisputed pugilistic king of the world, and far too active in other directions to lay claim to such a purely domestic title, few or no onlookers at all viewed Carl Williams as being truly the top dog among all heavyweights in his own country, although this quick and successful defence of the national crown did bring him one step nearer a lucrative battle in opposition to "Iron" Mike.

"Smokin'" Joe Frazier, former heavyweight champion of the world, had not been altogether successful in coaching both his son, Marvis, and his protége, Bert Cooper, to the top of the heap, and he had no more luck on this occasion with his nephew, Rodney Frazier, of Philadelphia.

The youngster lacked nothing at all in gameness, and he answered the bell in an aggressive, two-fisted fashion: the general rule with fighters from this stable. He managed to land one or two heavy blows in the opening exchanges, but the taller and more stylish Williams was able to keep his opponent at bay and on the end of accurate jabs.

It certainly looked like settling down into an interesting and evenly-waged struggle until Williams threw over a hard right which had the Philadelphian tottering. This was followed up by a barrage with both fists, and Frazier was backed to the ropes almost defenceless. The first round was almost over when the referee jumped between the pair to stop the fight, but had the bell saved Rodney it would only have postponed the inevitable.

The former undisputed welterweight champion of the world, "Texan Cobra" Don Curry, gave the light-middleweight title-holder, Gianfranco Rosi, considerable food for thought when he boxed the Californian Mexican, Lupe Aquino, over twelve rounds in the chief support to the Italian's contest against Duane Thomas at Genoa.

Aquino was a stubborn and very durable adversary, but at no time, except briefly in the third round, when he made a spirited rally, did he look like winning the battle. Curry was at his supreme best, and he boxed beautifully to take the judges' unanimous decision.

Right on the full middleweight poundage, and defending his North American Boxing Federation title, the up-and-coming Michael Nunn gave clear warning that he is on the title trail when he faced the rugged Kevin Watts at Reseda, California.

At no time did the young man look like being beaten, and he won every round in a rather one-sided contest. Watts was willing enough to mix matters, and did his utmost, but Nunn's dazzling speed and altogether superior boxing proved to many discerning onlookers that he

Carlos de Leon (right), the Puerto Rican WBC cruiserweight champion, tries to unlock the defences of his Uruguayan challenger, Jose Mario Flores

Sporting Pictures (UK) LTD

Calvin Grove, the new IBF featherweight champion, in pose, following his great win over Antonio Rivera

Peter Goldfield/USA

has the stuff of which world champions are made.

In an overweight contest, and with his championship not at stake, the holder of the WBC light-welterweight crown, Roger Mayweather, did not have too much trouble in overcoming the Philadephian, Marvin Garris, when they boxed a scheduled ten-rounder at Las Vegas.

Indeed, Mayweather was streets ahead of his rival in all departments of the game. He piled up an early points lead, and his supremacy grew more evident with each succeeding round. By the sixth he was so full of confidence that he was able to walk in and drop his opponent for a count. In the next session, after a cut had opened over Garris's left eye, the referee stopped the one-sided bout on the advice of the ringside doctors, with only a few seconds of the round to go.

Also at light-welterweight, Atlantic City was the scene of a real thriller when New York's John Meekins completely overwhelmed the hard-punching Othal "Choo-Choo" Dixon, from Texas. Brief as the meeting turned out to be, there was no lack of action during the time it lasted.

Dixon came out blasting, determined to halt his man inside the distance, and for a time he had Meekins on the defensive. But the New Yorker quickly settled down and soon began to match his opponent punch for punch. He felled Dixon right at the end of the opening round, and the Texan was in such distress that he might not have been able to continue had not the bell come to his rescue.

Meekins began the second with the obvious intention of finishing matters, and he soon had Dixon wavering. A powerful right to the head sent "Choo-Choo" to the canvas, but he was up almost immediately, although the referee gave him the mandatory eight count. Dixon tore in with a desperate final attack, but Meekins was now picking his punches. He was landing so easily that the fight was stopped to save Dixon from further unnecessary punishment.

In a contest at Calais to determine a new man to ascend the vacant throne among European bantamweights, the local favourite, Thierry Jacob, was strongly supported when he crossed gloves with the French-naturalised but Spanish-born Fabrice Benichou.

Jacob had little difficulty in outpointing his man during the early rounds, but after the sixth he began to tire, and the stronger Benichou started to take control. He sensed that the end could be near during the ninth round, and a powerful attack sent the local man to the boards. He struggled erect, but was now too tired and befuddled to offer much resistance. Benichou calmly measured him and then stepped in with a two-fisted barrage which dropped Jacob face down for the full count.

George Foreman, the former world heavyweight champion, who eventually hopes to gain a crack at Mike Tyson, scored his sixth successive win on the comeback trail when he flattened a substitute, Tom Trimm, in 47 seconds of the first round. Fighting just a day after his 40th birthday, the veteran backed his rival to the ropes and took him out with a single shot to the head.

FEBRUARY

Ten championship contests were decided during the month, with half of them being held under the auspices of the IBF and the majority involving title-holders and contenders from the lighter divisions.

The heaviest champion seen in action during February was the lean and rangy Texan, Frank Tate, who journeyed to Stafford to make the first defence of his IBF honours, with his opponent being that Leicester war-horse, Tony Sibson. "Sibbo" had recently appeared to have taken out a new lease of life with a dramatic victory to win back his British championship, and he felt that he had what it takes to win the elusive world title.

It was something of a gala occasion for that area of Britain, but it was marred somewhat by hooliganism and crowd disturbance, culminating in the throwing of gas canisters. One of these exploded at ringside and caused considerable distress among some onlookers.

The fight itself proved to be the swan-song of the ageing Sibson, who was here making his third attempt to win a world title; he had failed gallantly in opposition to the phenomenal Marvin Hagler at middleweight, and equally gallantly against Dennis Andries, when he gave too much weight away in a battle for the light-heavyweight crown. After a long and honourable career he simply found that the stamina and the will to win were no longer part and parcel of his pugilistic make-up, and he was beaten in ten exciting rounds.

For all that, Sibson put up a magnificent showing for most of the time the contest lasted. He met the younger Tate on even terms and managed to hand out as good as he got. Always an aggressive and willing fighter, he matched the champion's superior long-range boxing with excellent jabs of his own, coupled with vicious and powerful hooks from either glove, and up until the end of the eighth round there was very little in it as far as points were concerned.

But Tate came out for round nine in a more determined mood, and with the obvious intention of stepping up the pace. He really shifted into top gear, and it was at this juncture that Sibson began to falter. He did his best to match the younger man's attack, but suddenly appeared to become an old man, and for the first time in the bout started to show distress signals.

He came out for the tenth round apparently still fairly strong, and he waved Tate to come in and mix it. But it was an act of sheer bravado, a last gesture from a man who knew that he had now shot his bolt. It came as no great surprise when the champion landed with a heavy right and dropped the weary challenger to the boards. Sibson was still very much aware of all that was going on, but no longer had that fighting urge to climb erect and continue.

The gallant loser announced his retirement immediately after the fight was over. It was a sad but perhaps inevitable end to the career of one of Britain's most popular warriors. Still only 29, he had been boxing against top class opposition for so long that it was hard to believe that "Sibbo" was an old man as far as boxers go.

There were two main contests in the welterweight division. The first was at the traditional poundage, when Marlon Starling, the rugged

Tony Sibson (left) tries a sweeping left hook in an effort to prise open Frank Tate's defence during their IBF middleweight battle in Stafford, England

Action Images

holder of the WBA ten stone seven championship, defended his laurels against Fujio Osaki, of Japan, at Atlantic City. The second took place at Corpus Christi, Texas, where local boy James "Buddy" McGirt boxed Frankie Warren for the vacant light-welterweight title at ten stone.

Topping an all-star programme, which included Mark Breland, the man he had beaten to win the title, and also the veteran Roberto Duran, Starling won a somewhat dull contest against a man who tried hard enough but who quite simply lacked championship class. The fighters boxing "underneath" Starling drew far more appreciation from the onlookers than did the lack-lustre champion.

To the credit of the outclassed Japanese challenger, he tried to make a battle of it throughout, but Starling had no trouble at all in blocking or avoiding almost all of his leads and counters. He saw, very early, that he had little to beat in Ozaki, and he was quite content to coast along for much of the bout. His tactics did not win appreciation from the onlookers, who voiced their disapproval, but Marlon was not to be lured into any dangerous activity. All three judges scored the twelve rounds overwhelmingly in favour of the champion, but when the decision was announced it drew few plaudits from a discontented crowd.

The second championship contest — that for the vacant IBF title at ten stone — found Frankie Warren, the squat, powerful-punching little Texan, facing James McGirt, a man he had beaten convincingly before a home-town Corpus Christi crowd almost two years earlier. It was no wonder that Warren should enter the ring a firm favourite to annex the championship, with many of the onlookers having seen him soundly defeat McGirt earlier, but both Frankie and his followers were in for something of a shock.

McGirt came out for the opening round fully intent upon wiping the one blot from his escutcheon, and he so overwhelmed his hitherto unbeaten opponent that many shrewd judges of the game could see very early on the way this contest was going to go. He not only completely outboxed the rugged Texan but landed heavily to the jaw in that opening session and had Warren almost on the verge of defeat.

Warren seemed unable to get into his stride, and was taking quite a battering when he was felled heavily in the eighth round. He managed to rise and avoid the ignominy of a knockout defeat, but McGirt continued to pile on the pressure as the contest proceeded.

By round twelve Warren was in a sorry state, with one eye closed and the other one rapidly swelling to the same condition. Although he desperately sought to last out the full distance he was literally helpless when the referee stopped the bout to save him from unnecessary punishment.

Atlantic City, the pleasure resort which had been the scene of the Starling-Ozaki match, was also the venue for an IBF lightweight title bout the following day, when Vinny Pazienza defended his championship belt against the former holder, Greg Haugen.

This time there was no cause for discontent among the onlookers, as the pair waged an exciting, all-action scrap over the full fifteen rounds. Pazienza had won a clear and unanimous decision at Haugen's expense the previous summer before Vinny's own home crowd at Providence, Rhode Island, but on this occasion he was facing a much more determined

Frank Tate moves in on a pensive looking Tony Sibson in the tenth. The American retained his title by a Kayo with just seven seconds remaining of that round

Action Images

adversary who was convinced that he was the better man and who dearly wanted to win back his title.

In fact, once again the judges were in complete agreement over their view of the fight, but this time it was in Greg Haugen's favour. Despite a bruising and almost non-stop attack from Pazienza, Greg was in control of matters virtually from start to finish. Although neither boxer was able to score a knockdown, there was no lack of fire-power, with the Las Vegas-based Haugen getting the better of most exchanges. It was a gory set-to, with the reigning champion cut badly from the opening rounds, but he had no quarrel at all with the verdict, and expressed his desire for a third and final battle to decide the issue.

The hard-punching former featherweight champion, Azumah Nelson, of Ghana, had a very tough time of it when he crossed gloves with Mario Martinez, of Mexico, to decide a new holder of the WBC super-featherweight belt in Los Angeles.

Before a partisan and largely Mexican crowd, Martinez made the running, while Nelson seemed content to box easily on the retreat without getting into too much trouble. But the African got a nasty shock in the tenth round when Martinez stepped in with a fine right to the jaw and then followed it up with a left hook which dropped Nelson to the boards.

He was on his feet after a short count, grinning in embarrassment, and was easily able to foil his opponent's efforts to drop him again. He boxed his way out of trouble and took no more chances during the remainder of the bout. The majority verdict in Nelson's favour did not meet with a good reception from the onlookers, most of them believing that the Mexican had done enough to win. There was a very disturbing ringside demonstration before peace was restored.

At super-bantamweight, and as the second half of the Los Angeles double-header, Daniel Zaragoza and Carlos Zarate, each a former holder of the WBC title at eight stone six, came together to decide a new WBC champion at eight stone ten. This followed the announcement that Australian Jeff Fenech had vacated this throne through difficulty in making the weight.

The 36-year-old Zarate, although game and willing enough, did not have sufficient speed or artillery left to match his much younger opponent. Zaragoza dominated the battle from the outset and subjected his man to a gruelling battering before the referee intervened just before the end of the tenth round.

Also at super-bantamweight the WBA title-holder, Juan Gervacio, of the Dominican Republic, had a very tough time when defending his title at San Juan against the Venezuelan, Bernardo Pinango.

The challenger was no stranger to championship-class fighting, having held the WBA bantamweight belt the previous year, but had been obliged to relinquish his hold on the crown owing to increasing poundage. He proved beyond any doubt that he was stronger and more able in the heavier class, and managed to sneak a close verdict over the younger but very capable Gervacio.

The San Juan-based Dominican started off well in the earlier rounds, and at first looked as if he might control the contest, but Pinango stormed in with both fists and began to have the better of things as the contest proceeded. Midway during the twelve-round bout, Gervacio rallied again, and despite a bruised and badly-cut eye he evened up matters for a time.

In a thrilling contest, "Buddy" McGirt (left) hammered the favoured Frankie Warren to win the IBF light-welterweight title. This action shows Warren coming inside the left lead

Tom Casino

The bout was a see-saw slog right until the final round, when the challenger put everything he had into the last three minutes. Storming in, he sent the champion to the boards, and although Gervacio managed to rise, that knockdown tipped the scales in Pinango's favour. While one judge scored the fight a draw, the other two gave the Dominican challenger a one-point advantage.

At the traditional bantam poundage of eight stone six pounds, Kelvin Seabrooks, the holder of the IBF title, had very little trouble with his Mexican challenger, Fernando Beltran, in a contest scheduled over fifteen rounds before a Paris crowd.

Beltran lacked nothing at all in courage, but was quite outclassed. Seabrooks got his measure during the opening round and sent him to the canvas halfway through the session. Although the Mexican beat the count and managed to last

Over fifteen bloody, tremendously exciting rounds, the former IBF lightweight champion Greg Haugen (right), regained his title from Vinny Pazienza

Tom Casino

until the bell, it was apparent that the fight would not last very much longer. A powerful right-hander in the second round again sent Beltran to the floor, but although he struggled up and was game to continue, the fight was immediately stopped.

Both the super-featherweight and light-flyweight titles were on the line during this month. At Pontianak, in Indonesia, Elly Pical was very fortunate to retain his IBF honours. Three times he was sent to the canvas by his challenger, the Colombian Raul Diaz. Only the fact that he came back strongly towards the end of the battle and floored Diaz a couple of times himself enabled him to sneak a narrow points decision.

But the popular South Korean, Myung-Woo Yuh, had a much easier time with Wilibaldo Salazar, of Mexico, when defending the WBA light-flyweight crown at Seoul. He boxed in an extremely clever fashion to take a unanimous twelve round points decision and notch up the seventh successful defence of his title on his belt.

* * *

Greg Haugen (right) leads with the the jab, but the tough Pazienza who never stopped trying still tries to come through with his own slugging punches

Tom Casino

Foremost among the contenders hoping for a title chance was that evergreen man of iron, the Panamanian Roberto Duran, who overshadowed top-liner Marlon Starling when he pounded out a popular victory over the younger Ricky Stackhouse on the Atlantic City bill.

At the age of 36 Duran was still capable of defeating the majority of the world's middleweights, but whether or not he would be able to add a fourth world title to the three he has already held is a far different matter . . .

Although he managed to score two knockdowns, and won the fight fairly comfortably, Duran was unable to stop the South Carolinan. He was blowing considerably at the close of this hard ten-rounder, and he might find it harder still to go twelve or fifteen rounds with one of the eleven-stone-six champions.

Yet another veteran, the former heavyweight champion, George Foreman, pounded out an additional victory in his comeback when he stopped Guido Trane, the Italian title-holder, in the fifth round at Las Vegas. The ultimate goal for the 40-year-old Foreman was, of course, a big-money title match with Mike Tyson. While the hard-punching ex-champion has numerous followers who feel that he is still good enough to defeat "Iron" Mike, he did not impress against the mediocre Trane. Although he was able to outbox his man he was unable to knock him out or even drop him for a count. And it has yet to be seen how Foreman might fare when caught by a blow as hard as some of those that Tyson can deliver.

A third veteran on the comeback trail was Michael Dokes, erstwhile holder of the WBA heavyweight belt, who took on the lanky Eddie Richardson in a ten-rounder in New York.

Dokes made very heavy weather of it throughout, and although he managed to floor his opponent in the final round and the ringside doctors insisted upon the contest being stopped, the former champion was not particularly impressive. He claimed to have been thumbed in the opening round, with his sight being affected throughout the fight. He pointed to this as a reason for his mediocre showing.

Robert Shannon, former US representative at the Olympic Games, met Azael Moran, the one-time challenger for the WBA bantamweight title, in an eliminator for super-bantam honours.

Although the Panamanian was favoured to win the bout, the little southpaw from Washington State caused an exciting upset when he came out for the second round, threw a terrific left to the jaw and flattened Moran for the full count.

MARCH

Any month in which the heavyweight champion of the world, Mike Tyson, is scheduled to box now automatically becomes one to look forward to. March was no exception, when former holder of the WBA version of the title, Tony Tubbs, made his challenge for both the WBC and WBA championships before a hushed crowd of some 50,000 spectators in the vast domed stadium in Tokyo.

As was expected, Tubbs was the underdog in what betting there was, with practically nobody at all — including himself — really believing that he stood much of a chance against "Iron" Mike's devastating punching. His own attitude, quite apart from the statement he made before the contest to the press to the effect that he was "merely a stepping-stone", was reflected in his obvious lack of proper physical fitness. Weighing in at just over 17 stone, he carried far too much superfluous flesh to go twelve hard rounds with any man — Tyson least of all.

But although Tubbs probably knew that he was a sacrificial lamb, and took the fight for the half million dollars he was guaranteed, he neither spoiled nor stalled. He came out to try to make a fight of it, and in the opening round he matched his adversary in most exchanges, and did well enough to share the session on points.

Nevertheless, Tyson answered the bell for round two with a determined look, and very soon he was sinking home vicious and painful punches which palpably caused the heavier man distress. To his credit, Tubbs did his best to get back on to equal terms, when, towards the end of the round, Mike suddenly stepped in with a paralysing blow to the temple. It was almost an exact replica of the "delayed action" punch which had suddenly demolished Trevor Berbick in 1986.

It caught Tony Tubbs just above the right eyebrow and laid it open to the bone. Literally like a pole-axed ox, he wobbled uncertainly and then staggered back a pace or two, reaching instinctively for the ropes. And as Tyson charged in and threw another sweeping left hook, the challenger crashed heavily to the canvas, as Mike's intended finisher mercifully missed by only an inch or two.

As Tubbs hit the boards it was evident that the fight was over. Even as the referee commenced the count, Tony's chief second was up through the ropes and into the ring, ministering to his beaten principal.

This fight, perhaps not nearly so exciting nor so dramatic as most of Tyson's contests, particularly those versus Biggs and Thomas, and with the quiet and cathedral-like atmosphere of the surroundings doing nothing at all to help, nevertheless did much to boost the champion's already healthy stock. It promised well for the proposed Tyson-Spinks match during the coming summer, which gave indication of being an epic encounter and looked certain to be the richest boxing match of all time.

Top-class super-middleweights were well to the fore in March. Chong-Pal Park, the busy South Korean, made his first defence of the WBA championship when he faced up to the challenge of Polly Pasieron, of Indonesia, at Chungju. Park gave every indication that he might well be the best man at his weight in the world when he came out with both fists pumping and overwhelmed his opponent.

That Pasieron lasted into the fifth round says much for his grit and ability to take a hard punch, but when the title-holder opened up with a powerful attack to the body the challenger had no answer at all. He slumped to the boards, with no chance of beating the referee's count, and it took some minutes before he had sufficiently recovered to leave the ring.

The victor had been expected to make a bid for unification before he rather surprisingly relinquished his IBF belt prior to the above contest. Dusseldorf was chosen as the venue and Graciano Rocchigiani, the popular German twelve-stoner, had no great trouble in vanquishing Vincent Boulware to become the new IBF champion.

With an explosive third round count-out, Lloyd Honeyghan (right), regained his WBC welterweight title in the third round. Jorge Vaca, the defending champion, is seen here missing with the jab

Sporting Pictures (UK) LTD

"Honey" reigns again. Lloyd Honeyghan receives the acclaim of the crowd following his great win over Vaca

Sporting Pictures (UK) LTD

Rocchigiani dominated the battle throughout, and although Boulware rallied occasionally, the young German hit far too hard for his opponent, several times having him on the verge of a knockout. By the eighth round the bout had developed into a somewhat one-sided affair, and it caused no surprise when the referee stepped in to save the gallant Boulware from further punishment.

Among the men at eleven stone six, the incredible African-born Sumbu Kalambay continued his run of unexpected victories when he faced the challenge of Jamaican Mike McCallum before an enthusiastic crowd at Pesaro, Italy. With the WBA middleweight title at stake, McCallum, who had outgrown the light-middleweight division and had given up that championship to mix with the heavier men, was strongly favoured to win this contest and to continue his amazing string of victories.

But the Italian-based African was a clear winner on points, over the scheduled distance of twelve rounds. He had an answer for each one of McCallum's ploys, and although neither man ever looked like scoring a knockout, the West Indian was staggered on more than one occasion. Kalambay was a popular victor in his adopted country, while Mike McCallum suffered the first defeat of his 33 professional contests.

Wembley was the scene of action when Jorge Vaca, of Mexico, fought the Jamaican-born Londoner, Lloyd Honeyghan, in a welterweight contest with the WBC championship of the world on the line. It was their second meeting, Vaca having been declared the winner on the earlier occasion with a "technical" victory after an unintentional clash of heads.

While the Mexican had been ruled just ahead on points at the time of the disaster, Honeyghan had since claimed that he was far from his best on that occasion, and was now determined to regain the championship in this return engagement. He did, in fact, look an entirely different fighter from the one who had made such heavy going of things previously, and Vaca was very soon in trouble.

Honeyghan took the first two rounds fairly easily, beating his man to the punch time and again, and whipping home powerful blows which clearly distressed the champion. Lloyd was much the more dominant of the two, and he dictated matters so obviously that at first it appeared that the Mexican must surely be biding his time and waiting for his opponent to run out of steam.

But the Londoner showed no signs of tiring in the third round. He forced Vaca to the ropes and smashed home both fists to the head and body in a spirited rally. The Mexican wilted, and then a perfect blow to the solar plexus dropped him heavily to his knees. Although he was badly hurt, it seemed to most onlookers that he would beat the count. However, as the referee tolled off the seconds, Vaca remained hunched on the boards, unable to rise. With this victory, Lloyd Honeyghan became the first British boxer to regain a world championship for over 70 years.

At the light-welter poundage, Roger Mayweather, the Nevada-based WBC title-holder, made a storming and successful first defence of the championship he won from Rene Arredondo at Los Angeles. Boxing in the same city, he had little trouble with his Mexican challenger, Mauricio Aceves.

Mayweather gave an indication of the way things would go when he decked Aceves for a long count in the opening round. Although the challenger managed to avoid the ignominy of a first-round knockout defeat, he took quite a battering, and while he showed to better advantage in the second session, he was still looked at very closely by the ringside doctor before leaving his stool for the third.

The end came rapidly. Mayweather measured his man and shot across a devastating right-hander to the head. It dumped the luckless Mexican on to the canvas and into the ropes, where he lay bemused and beaten as he was counted out.

Pernell Whitaker, the Virginian-born gold medallist at the 1984 Olympics, hitherto undefeated as a professional, was favoured by the cognoscenti to defeat the French-based Mexican WBC lightweight champion, Jose Luis Ramirez, when they faced each other at Paris in a battle of southpaws.

It was a contest between two good boxers, with neither man gaining a marked advantage at any time during the fight. No knockdowns were in evidence and, indeed, no particularly hard and dangerous punching, but it was interesting all the way, and when the bell clanged for the close of round twelve, each felt he had done enough to win.

The three ringside judges were not unanimous in their reckoning: the British and Brazilian officials differed as to which man had won, while the French judge saw Ramirez as the victor by a single point. The decision in his favour was not received particularly well, and the Whitaker corner was vehement in their accusations. A return engagement between these two protagonists, either in the United States or Europe, was looked forward to eagerly.

Some 12,000 enthusiastic spectators turned out in Sydney when the little Australian hero, Jeff Fenech, faced Puerto Rico's Victor Callejas in a battle to determine a new WBC featherweight kingpin.

Although damaging his right hand as early as the second round, Fenech completely outclassed the experienced Callejas, and won every round, flooring his antagonist in both the third and eighth sessions.

An all-southpaw battle in Paris, saw Jose Luis Ramirez (right) hold on to his WBC lightweight title with a controversial twelve-round split decision over Pernell Whitaker

Thierry Chambefort

As the bout progressed, so Jeff's dominance became more apparent, despite the Puerto Rican's game efforts to stave off the inevitable. But by the tenth round Fenech was scoring almost without return, and halfway through the referee stopped the now one-sided contest to save Callejas from further unnecessary punishment.

After the exciting set-to the previous year between WBA flyweight champion Fidel Bassa and Northern Ireland's Dave "Boy" McAuley, which had been nominated as the Fight of the Year, there were no empty seats when the pair came together for a second time, once again at Belfast's famous King's Hall.

The previous engagement had been a ding-dong battle from start to finish, embellished by clever boxing, hard fighting, and several thrilling knockdowns, with the eventual issue at all times in doubt. Had that bout been a twelve-rounder the verdict would almost certainly have gone to the little Irishman, but at that time all WBA title contests were still scheduled for fifteen, and it was in the unlucky thirteenth that McAuley finally ran out of steam and had been punched to defeat by the more experienced Bassa.

It has often been said that sequels never match up to the originals, and this old maxim is particularly true with boxing. Thrillers which pave the way for a return fight between the principals rarely excite with the same brand of calculated recklessness and determination. The respective opponents have invariably learned much from the first outing and are wary about exposing themselves to too much punishment. This second Bassa-McAuley contest certainly rammed home the point.

But while many of the thrills were lacking this time, it was still a hard and dogged battle of twelve well-fought rounds, with Bassa's speed and superior boxing gaining him the edge in almost all of the rounds.

The challenger was sent to the canvas and on to his back with a well-delivered right-hander in the ninth round, and things looked very ominous for him at the time. But he rallied well in the tenth and eleventh, and had the spectators on their feet as it briefly appeared as if he might dramatically pull the fight out of the bag.

But Bassa was just too good and too wily. He boxed his way out of trouble and sailed home to a unanimous decision, although the points adjudged to have been scored by either man were very close. McAuley was a definite second-best, and looked none too strong at eight stone.

Back in January, when Kyung-Yung Lee had voluntarily relinquished his IBF straw- or mini-flyweight title, in order to make a bid for the WBC championship — a contest which, incidentally, he lost — the Thailander Samuth Sithnaruepol was matched with "Pretty Boy" Lucas of the Philippines at Bangkok. The outcome was a stirring battle between two diminutive gamecocks which ended in the eleventh round when the bout was stopped in the local man Sithnaruepol's favour.

* * *

The veteran erstwhile heavyweight champion of the world, George Foreman, who had been such a formidable antagonist before meeting his match in the form of the legendary Muhammad Ali, continued his comeback with a bout in Las Vegas where he failed to cover himself with glory at any stage of the proceedings.

Standing six feet four and looking very much overweight at almost 17 stone, he lumbered to a desultory victory over the squat and much lighter Dwight Muhammad Qawi, the former cruiserweight title-holder. Foreman had no trouble at all in reaching his opponent with cuffing, half-hearted blows, but rather surprisingly the smaller Qawi found no difficulty either in scoring with cleanly-placed punches, although he could not make much impression on the bigger man.

It was in the seventh round that Qawi, more in frustration than anything else, it seemed, abruptly turned his back on Foreman and walked to his corner, signifying surrender.

The contest was an unedifying spectacle, and

Pernell Whitaker (right), the challenger, comes onto the attack, but Ramirez's defences are once again in order

Thierry Chambefort

Iran "The Blade" Barkley (left) looks menacing as he comes in search of a shot at the world middleweight title. Michael Olajide, on the defensive, was crushed in the fifth round

Tom Casino

the ease with which the much smaller man landed his punches on Foreman's head and jaw boded ill for the veteran should his campaign ever earn him a match with the lethal and all-conquering Mike Tyson.

On the same bill at Las Vegas, "Smoking" Bert Cooper, of Philadelphia, defended his North American Boxing Federation cruiserweight title against the Tonga-born Arizonan, Tony Fuliangi.

Cooper came out in the two-fisted, all-action style of his former manager and trainer, Joe Frazier, and showed that as a cruiser he is a match for perhaps any man in the world. Bert forced the battle with sharp and accurate jabs, following up with short, powerful hooks which landed accurately.

Fuliangi, who had the reputation of being a big puncher, seemed overawed by the reputation of his shorter adversary, and seemed disinclined to do anything at all but try to take his man's best blows on arms or shoulders. On the few occasions he tried to mix matters he came off second best and soon retreated into his shell.

Cooper finally caught him properly in the fourth round. A right to the head followed a shattering left hook and Fuliangi dropped heavily on to his back. Although he beat the count and made ready to continue, his eyes were glazed and the referee had no hesitation in waving the contest over.

An eagerly-awaited confrontation was the New York matching of the two slightly tarnished middleweight contenders, Iran Barkley and Michael Olajide. The outcome was a thrilling and well-received fight full of skill and heavy punching.

At first there looked to be little in it between the two men, but in the second round Barkley floored his opponent with a well-timed left hook. Olajide came back strongly from the upset and caught the other with a terrific left of his own in the fourth and dumped Barkley to the boards.

But the fallen man recovered well. In the fifth round Barkley's superior strength began to tell, and again he floored the English-born Canadian with his favourite hook. Although Olajide insisted to the referee that he was all right as he climbed to his feet, he backed to the ropes and was being subjected to a severe battering when the contest was stopped.

Atlantic City witnessed a blistering set-to between lightweight contenders Terrence Alli and Darryl Tyson — no relation — in a ten-rounder. The Guyanan Alli forced the pace early on and soon began to pile up a lead on points, but in the second half of the contest he appeared to be tiring, and the Detroit-based Tyson came on strongly to even up matters.

Going into the final round it was anybody's fight, but Alli clinched the session using a powerful uppercut to the jaw which had Darryl in trouble. The judges disagreed on the decision, with one of them awarding the verdict to Tyson, but with the other two scoring Alli a close but definite victor.

APRIL

Hooray for Holyfield! — to paraphrase a popular American show-biz tag. In these days of rival authoritative bodies, with some champions seemingly content to hold a third share in a world title — more often than not preferring to defend in opposition to a contender rather than a claimant to the same weight-division honours — it is always refreshing to see a boxer so confident in his ability that he achieves unification. Names like Marvin Hagler, Don Curry, and Mike Tyson spring to mind immediately as outstanding fighters who mopped up thoroughly in their own divisions. We can now add the name of Evander Holyfield to the select list.

Already the proud owner of the WBA and IBF championship belts, the undefeated Holyfield came through with a convincing victory in Las Vegas when he pounded the WBC title-holder, Puerto Rican Carlos de Leon, to defeat in eight rounds to become undisputed cruiserweight champion of the world.

However, in the experienced de Leon, the all-conquering Holyfield found an adversary who was a hard nut to crack. Although two of the ringside judges had Evander on top in each of the first seven rounds — with the third judge awarding the opening session to the Puerto Rican — Holyfield by no means found this contest a mere walkover.

De Leon came out with the intention of making a real fight of it, and the former Olympic medallist was obliged to pull out all the stops in retaliation. It was a hard and bruising battle, but with Holyfield's superior strength tipping the balance.

Although there were no knockdowns in evidence throughout the bout, the WBC champion suffered a bad cut over the left eye in the sixth round. This worsened as the contest proceeded, but it was Holyfield's power and continued aggression which were responsible for the eventual stoppage. De Leon was backed to the ropes and barely in a condition to defend himself when the referee hastily stepped in and stopped the now unequal match.

Bismarck, North Dakota, was the unlikely scene of a light-heavyweight championship contest, and the town witnessed the first such occasion in its history when the WBA title-holder, "local boy" Virgil Hill, thrilled a partisan crowd as he defended in opposition to the Paris-based African, leading contender Jean-Marie Emebe.

The challenger was not exactly a stranger to title fights, having made a bid for this same championship two years earlier, losing on a stoppage to Marvin Johnson. But he proved to be no match for the younger North Dakotan, who had little difficulty in outboxing his man and piling up a generous lead in the early rounds. Still, Emebe did his best to make a fight of it, and several times he had the champion looking more than merely thoughtful with one or two powerful blows which landed solidly.

The game African made a supreme effort in the eighth round, and he managed to open a cut over Virgil's eye, but the title-holder now felt that he had the measure of his antagonist and he rallied well to take the majority of points for the round.

Although Hill looked to be well on the way to victory at this stage, he took a breather throughout the ninth and did little but box on the retreat and avoid the challenger's blows, while in the following session he accidentally landed a punch which was well below the belt. Emebe showed distress, and the referee halted matters until the African had recovered.

At this point it looked as if the contest might well go the full distance, and with the chance that the outclassed challenger might well finish the stronger man. But in the eleventh the champion attacked viciously and sent his man to the boards with heavy right-handers to the head. The fallen Emebe took the compulsory count of eight, but he was only delaying the inevitable as he resumed the bout. Hill was punching him at will and without return when the third man in the ring stepped in and halted matters.

WBA welterweight champion Marlon Starling had a tough time of it when he placed his title at stake, over twelve rounds, in opposition to lanky Mark Breland, the man from whom he had unexpectedly won the title.

This return engagement, at the Las Vegas Hilton Hotel, was watched by several million viewers on pay-TV, with the prospect of it being an exciting battle, but the fact is that Starling boxed an uninspired and disappointing contest — one not particularly enlivened by the efforts of his adversary, either. Although Starling began in fine enough style, and his rough and bustling attack was palpably superior to Breland's cleverer work at long distance, the champion was unable to retain his early lead.

Breland came on pretty well during the latter half of the fight, but he seemed overawed by the champion's undoubted power of punch, which he had experienced to his cost in their previous engagement, and he lacked the inspiration to launch anything like a spirited attack. By this time Starling was doing very little and the challenger even less. The bout developed into an unexciting scramble.

The decision of a draw was not at all well received, with most onlookers and critics feeling that Starling had done enough to earn the verdict.

At the same welterweight poundage an IBF championship contest between Washington's Jamaican-born Simon Brown and Tyrone Trice, of Detroit, took place at Berck-sur-Mer, in France, to establish a new holder of the title, which had been in abeyance ever since it had been declared vacant after the unsatisfactory head-clash ending of the first Lloyd Honeyghan-Jorge Vaca contest.

However, the fight between two relatively little-known contenders proved to be quite a thriller, if nothing else. Trice, a six-footer with a similar build to that of Thomas Hearns when he was a welter, also showed something of the power of punch wielded by his illustrious predecessor when he floored Brown in the second round after a spirited barrage. His opponent managed to arise before the full count and pitched in with some heavy banging of his own to stave off early defeat.

The West Indian showed true courage and championship status as he battled back in the ensuing rounds to even matters. Midway through the scheduled fifteen-rounder the shorter man was matching his antagonist's eye-catching aggression, and Trice soon began to show signs of weariness.

Brown gradually took charge of the battle as the rounds progressed, but Trice had no intention of giving up this world title chance too easily, and he fought back as best he could. But he experienced a very rough time in the twelfth round. A mighty left hook dropped him to the canvas and when he staggered up at nine, he was beaten to the boards a second time soon afterwards. Although he appeared unhurt, the referee insisted upon the mandatory eight before beckoning the men together. Brown now threw everything into an attack to finish his man, and Trice tumbled yet again.

The bell to end this amazing round found the man from Detroit tottering to his stool, with every appearance that he would not be strong enough to leave it for another session.

But Trice somehow weathered the thirteenth round as Brown still piled on the pressure, and he even came out aggressively for the fourteenth, pluckily attempting to score a knockout punch to save the day. Unfortunately for Trice, the stronger Jamaican caught him with a smashing right-hander to the jaw which dropped him face-downwards. He struggled erect yet again, but it was his last effort and he was utterly defenceless as the referee stepped in to end proceedings.

April also witnessed two contests for different versions of the lightweight championship. WBA title-holder Julio Cesar Chavez defended against Panama's Rodolfo Aguilar at Las Vegas, and Greg Haugen put his IBF belt at stake versus the Puerto Rican, Miguel Santana, at Tacoma, Washington.

Simon Brown became the new IBF welterweight champion when he stopped fellow-American, Tyrone Trice, over fourteen tough rounds in France

Peter Goldfield/USA

Local favourite Haugen boxed a disappointing bout before a large crowd of well-wishers, and he was having something of a hard time when both fighters clashed heads during the eleventh round. The champion was seen to have a very bad gash above the right eye, and the contest was immediately halted at the request of the ringside doctor.

There now occurred yet another of these confused and unsatisfactory verdicts. Although two of the three judges had Haugen ahead by three points after the eleven completed rounds, and the other judge saw Santana as being in front by three points, the challenger was actually announced as the winner from the ring. It was

Rocky Lockridge (right) is stunned by a big left hook thrown by Harold "The Shadow" Knight during their IBF super-featherweight title battle

Peter Goldfield/USA

only after many disappointed spectators had left the arena and the fighters were back in their dressing rooms that the "result" was reversed and Haugen was told that he had retained his title on a technical decision!

The fight had been a grim struggle all the way, with the champion doing effective work in the earlier rounds but with the Puerto Rican coming on strongly until the accidental head-clash.

The meeting between Mexico's Julio Cesar Chavez and Rodolfo Aguilar, held at Las Vegas on the same bill as the disappointing Starling-Breland meeting, was a different matter entirely. The WBA champion proved once again that, pound for pound, he is probably the finest fighting machine in the world today when he stopped his foremost challenger in the sixth round.

In fact, the contest was almost decided in the very first session. Chavez turned on the pressure early against his taller opponent, and late in the round he dropped his man with a powerful right-hander. The bell saved the Panamanian challenger from the ignominy of a first-round knockout, but he had come to make a fight of it. Yet try as he might he was no match for the chunkier Mexican champion.

By the fifth, Chavez had established complete authority, and when he floored his opponent in the sixth the unequal contest was rightly stopped.

Two versions of the super-featherweight championship were also contested during the month. The first was in Atlantic City, when IBF title-holder, Rocky Lockridge, outpointed Harold Knight over fifteen rounds to retain his belt by a wide margin. The hitherto undefeated challenger made a brave effort, but this was the first occasion on which he had faced a man of the champion's class, and Lockridge had little difficulty in out-boxing and out-punching a game but inadequate antagonist.

It was not quite so easy for the WBA champion, Brian Mitchell, of South Africa. Facing Puerto Rico's Jose Rivera over twelve rounds before a Spanish crowd at Madrid, he defended his crown successfully for the fifth time, but he had to work hard all the way. Although Rivera had earlier boxed a draw with the champion he found that Mitchell knew just a little too much for him on this occasion. Rivera did score a surprise knockdown in the second round, but thereafter Mitchell dominated the action. Although the verdict was decided by a majority decision, the fact that one of the judges saw the challenger as the victor flattered Rivera.

At bantamweight, the Colombian WBC champion, Miguel "Happy" Lora, pounded out a very popular twelve-round victory before his delighted followers in Cartagena when he faced Argentina's Lucio Lopez.

But both Lora and the onlookers received an early shock when he was floored in the second

The boot is on the other foot as Lockridge (left) crashes his own left hook through Knight's guard. Rocky retained his title over fifteen hard rounds in Atlantic City

Tom Casino

round by his bustling and eager opponent. However, the champion survived, and he got up to fight back strongly and once he had hit his stride he dominated the action, earning a clear-cut and unanimous victory over his challenger.

A super-flyweight championship bout took place during the month in Miami Beach, when Jesus "Sugar Baby" Rojas, from Colombia, put his WBC title up against the former champion, Gilberto Roman, of Mexico.

Roman had been unfortunate to lose this self-same championship a year earlier, when Santos Laciar stopped him with a badly-gashed brow, and he was now intent upon regaining the belt from the man who had taken it from the Argentinian.

Although Rojas set out to dominate the battle from the start, and even looked as if he might win the contest early when the Mexican was again cut over the right eye, the challenger proved his true worth by doggedly boxing a brilliant campaign. At the conclusion of the full twelve rounds all three officials voted him a clear winner.

Meanwhile, in defence of the WBA mini-fly or "straw-weight" title, Luis Gamez of Venezuela took on the local Kenji Yokozawa, in Tokyo.

The bout started in fine style, and at first it seemed that the Japanese challenger was going to give Gamez a hard time of it. But the Venezuelan floored his rival for a long count in the second round and then opened up a bad gash over Yokozawa's eye in the third. It was so deep that the referee had no hesitation in calling a halt.

* * *

A big crowd turned out at the newly-furbished Alexandra Palace arena to see the return to the ring of Irishman Barry McGuigan, after almost two years of inactivity. Arguably the most popular British fighter for many, many years, and most definitely the best money-spinner among our lighter men of all time, he was still considered to have been unlucky in having lost his WBA featherweight crown to Texan Steve Cruz in the dehydrating heat of Las Vegas.

On this occasion, coming in as a super-featherweight, at which poundage he claimed he felt much stronger than at nine stone, Barry and his manager certainly did not pick a mug for starters. Coming out of the opposite corner was Nicky Perez, NABF title-holder at super-featherweight, but he was no match for the fast and heavy-hooking McGuigan.

Turning on the heat in the all-action style which had made him such a pleasure to watch in the past, he was far too good for the Arizonan in every respect. After settling down and getting the measure of his opponent, Barry shifted into top gear in the fourth round and dropped Perez on to all fours with a scythe-like left hook.

Milton McCrory (left) reached the end of the road when he was convincingly beaten by Lupe Aquino. The former world welterweight champion is shown being caught by a heavy right

Peter Goldfield

Although up at eight and eager to get back into the fray, Perez was again floored, this time by a right to the head. Although he very quickly regained his feet, the referee had seen quite enough to know that the plucky visitor had been completely outclassed, and he stopped the action immediately.

At light-middleweight, the former welterweight star, Milton McCrory, faced Lupe Aquino, who had reigned briefly as the WBC light-middleweight kingpin.

McCrory put up a game struggle, but he was just not strong enough for his hard-hitting opponent. Aquino felled him on two occasions, while in the eighth round McCrory was given a standing count. Although he lasted out the full ten rounds there was no doubt as to which man had scored the majority of points, and McCrory announced that he would now be retiring.

Donovan "Razor" Ruddock, Jamaica's hope for a world champion in the heavyweight class, had little to beat when he faced his "jumbo" opponent, Larry Alexander, at Camden, New Jersey.

The Canadian-based Ruddock, a powerful puncher, completely outclassed his man in the opening round, and after a strong combination he dropped Alexander heavily to the boards in the second. The referee took one look at the prostrate fighter and did not bother to complete the count, waving the one-sided contest over as the stricken man's handlers hastily entered the ring. "Razor" now steps one rung up the ladder towards a big-money battle with "Iron" Mike Tyson.

Another young hopeful with his eye on a lucrative clash with the champion was South African Johnny du Plooy, who faced the former WBA heavyweight title-holder, Mike Weaver, at Sun City.

The 35-year-old Weaver, on the comeback trail, and the only man to have defeated du Plooy, whom he had stopped in seven rounds a few months previously, found the young South African to be an entirely different proposition on this occasion. Although the American opened a cut over du Plooy's eye in the opening round, Johnny came out for the second session cool and determined. He floored Weaver for a long count with a heavy right to the head, and after that he went in for the finisher with confidence. The former title-holder was literally flattened, face-foremost, and scarcely moved as the referee counted him out.

The World's Leading Fighters

Shows the complete career records of 408 leading fighters from the current international boxing scene compiled by Eric Armit. The records set out to cover all the top-rated active men in their respective divisions as at the end of April, 1988.

Results Code:

PTS	– Points
CO	– Count Out
RSC	– Referee Stopped Contest
RTD	– Retired
DIS	– Disqualified
NC	– No Contest
ND	– No Decision
TD	– Technical Decision
T DRAW	– Technical Draw

Title Bout Code:

ABU	– African Boxing Union
CON AM	– Continental American
EBU	– European Boxing Union
FECARBOX	– Central American & Carribean
IBF	– International Boxing Federation
NABF	– North American Boxing Federation
OPBF	– Orient & Pacific Boxing Federation
USBA	– United States Boxing Association
WBA	– World Boxing Association
WBC	– World Boxing Council

Mauricio Aceves
Mexico City, Mexico. *Born* 18.12.60
Lightweight

14.07.79 Mario Castelan W PTS 4 Mexico City
18.08.79 Juan Soto W RSC 3 Mexico City
10.10.79 Lupe Martinez W PTS 6 Mexico City
01.12.79 Juan Soto W RSC 2 Mexico City
16.02.80 Pedro Molina W CO 8 Mexico City
24.03.80 Pedro Molina L DIS 3 Mexico City
24.05.80 Maximo Guevara W CO 4 Guadalajara
07.06.80 Angel Mata L CO 2 Mexico City
09.10.80 Cayetano Correa W RSC 8 Mexico City
25.11.80 Armando Villalobos W CO 7 Guadalajara
16.12.81 Cayetano Correa DREW 10 Mexico City
.81 Chuchu Ramirez W CO 2 Mexico City
10.03.82 Rene Arredondo L PTS 10 Mexico City
03.11.82 Raul Guerrero W PTS 10 Mexico City
.83 Alejandro Garcia W CO 4 Acapulco
23.04.84 Jorge Mercado W RSC 5 Mexico City
14.07.84 Agustin Vincenteno W CO 2 Mexico City
08.09.84 Miguel Dominguez W PTS 10 Mexico City
27.10.84 Ricardo Peralta L CO 5 Merida
23.03.85 Herminio Delgado W RSC 9 Mexico City
21.12.85 Arturo Hernandez W RSC 5 Minatitlan
28.04.86 Eduardo Dominguez W RSC 8 Tijuana
07.08.86 Martin Morado W TD 8 Los Angeles
09.10.86 Ernie Landeros W RSC 8 Los Angeles
26.03.87 Mark Fernandez W RSC 5 Los Angeles
28.05.87 Julio Ruiz W CO 6 Los Angeles
29.08.87 Alfredo Layne W RSC 5 Los Angeles
14.12.87 Tony Contreras W PTS 10 Tijuana
24.03.88 Roger Mayweather L CO 3 Los Angeles
(*WBC L. Welterweight Title Challenge*)
Summary: 29 contests, won 23, drew 1, lost 5.

Rodolfo Aguilar
Panama
Lightweight

21.05.83 Alfredo Ashley W PTS 4 Colon
17.09.83 Carlos Rodriguez W PTS 4 Panama City
15.10.83 Tomas Palacios W PTS 4 Colon
19.11.83 Daniel Melo W PTS 4 Panama City
17.12.83 Juan Perez W RSC 5 Panama City
16.04.84 Ray Best W RSC 4 Colon
28.04.84 Leroy Durant W RSC 3 Panama City
03.06.84 Jose Williams W PTS 10 Colon
25.08.84 Esquiel Mosquera W PTS 10 Colon
27.10.84 Geronimo Luquez W PTS 10 Panama City
28.12.84 Felipe Julio W CO 3 Panama City
15.02.85 Aurelio Benitez W RSC 3 Panama City
27.04.85 Enrique Ramirez W CO 4 Panama City
15.06.85 Ray Williams W RSC 7 Panama City
16.11.85 Julio Ruiz W PTS 10 Panama City
21.03.86 Ildemar Paisan L PTS 10 Caracas
20.12.86 Aquilino Asprilla W RSC 4 Panama City
14.02.87 Rafael Williams W PTS 10 Colon
31.07.87 Ismaldi Pineda W PTS 10 Panama City
15.08.87 Luis Portocarrero W RSC 5 Panama City
20.02.88 Pedro Padilla W RSC 9 Panama City
16.04.88 Julio Cesar Chavez L RSC 6 Las Vegas
(*WBA Lightweight Title Challenge*)
Summary: 22 contests, won 20, lost 2.

Kyung-Duk Ahn
South Korea. *Born* 21.09.62
Former Undefeated South Korean L. Welterweight Champion. Former OPBF L. Welterweight Champion

12.06.81 Wang-Soo Kim W PTS 4 Kwangju
24.07.82 Suk-Nam Woo W PTS 4 Seoul
05.02.83 Yung-Wan Kim W PTS 4 Pusan
20.02.83 Chong-Lim Suh W RSC 2 Chinju
27.03.83 Heung-Sik Shin W RSC 3 Chinju
01.05.83 In-Sun Kim W RSC 3 Chinju
05.06.83 Byung-Sun Yuh W RSC 3 Chonju
21.08.83 Kuk-Jim Lim W PTS 8 Daejon
24.09.83 Hong-Kyu Lim W CO 7 Chinju
(*Korean L. Welterweight Title Challenge*)
04.11.83 Suh-Aeng Lee W CO 9 Chinju
(*Korean L. Welterweight Title Defence*)
27.11.83 Hwa-Yung Song W PTS 10 Masan
(*Korean L. Welterweight Title Defence*)
29.11.83 Daeh-Yun Oh W CO 9 Pusan
11.03.84 Joe Lim W CO 4 Chinju
08.05.84 Chong-Hak Lee W PTS 10 Chinju
(*Korean L. Welterweight Title Defence*)
09.09.84 Tae-Wang Kang W PTS 10 Inchon
(*Korean L. Welterweight Title Defence*)
19.01.85 Wha-Yung Song W PTS 10 Daejon
(*Korean L. Welterweight Title Defence*)
27.04.85 Ki-Young Park W RSC 9 Ulsan
(*Korean L. Welterweight Title Defence*)
13.07.85 Rang-Ku Park W PTS 10 Chungju
(*Korean L. Welterweight Title Defence*)
01.10.85 Eung-Shik Kim W PTS 12 Seoul
(*OPBF L. Welterweight Title Challenge*)
03.01.86 Yodkan Donjadee W RSC 3 Chinju
(*OPBF L. Welterweight Title Defence*)
05.04.86 Allan Alegria W PTS 10 Masan
01.11.86 Sang-Ho Lee L PTS 12 Pohang
(*OPBF L. Welterweight Title Defence*)
26.04.87 Tae-Wang Kang W PTS 10 Chinju
29.08.87 Pyung-Sup Kim W PTS 10 Chinju
27.12.87 Ruben Rabago W PTS 10 Pohang
05.04.88 Boy Romero W CO 3 Jinju
Summary: 26 contests, won 25, lost 1.

Rae-Ki Ahn
South Korea. *Born* 02.02.65
Former Undefeated South Korean Flyweight Champion

06.05.81 Manam Pyun W PTS 4 Seoul
09.05.81 Jung-Hwan Kim W PTS 4 Seoul
31.07.81 Jung-Oh Kim DREW 4 Pusan
08.11.81 Tae-Il Chang L PTS 4 Seoul
20.12.81 Ken-Sik Yuh W PTS 6 Daejon
07.03.82 Yong-Chae Kim DREW 6 Seoul
24.07.82 Choong-Woo Lee W RSC 3 Seoul
29.08.82 Ki-Yung Kim W RSC 4 Seoul
09.10.82 Keum-Jing Yun W PTS 6 Seoul
27.11.82 Ik-Won Kim W PTS 6 Seoul
19.12.82 Kwang-Chul Ahn W RSC 3 Seoul
02.01.83 Woo-Yong Kim W RSC 3 Daejon
05.03.83 Myung-Woo Yuh L PTS 8 Seoul
28.01.84 Woo-Hyun Cho W RSC 2 Seoul
04.03.84 Yong-Chae Kim DREW 8 Seoul
14.07.84 Chun-Woo Koom W PTS 8 Seoul
16.09.84 Dol Suk W PTS 8 Seoul
06.11.84 Sung-Kyu Kim W RSC 5 Seoul
23.02.85 Ha-Sik Lim W CO 7 Seoul
27.04.85 Hae-Yul Kang W RSC 6 Seoul
(*South Korean Flyweight Title Challenge*)
09.06.85 Jae-Youn Lee W RSC 9 Seoul
(*South Korean Flyweight Title Defence*)
07.09.85 Suk-Bong Kim W PTS 10 Seoul
(*South Korean Flyweight Title Defence*)
05.12.85 Miguel Mercedes W PTS 10 Seoul
15.03.86 Shunichi Nakajima W PTS 10 Seoul
01.08.86 Petchaint Donjadee W CO 4 Seoul
23.01.87 Thamin Sithseemork W CO 2 Seoul
13.06.87 Tim Balantay W CO 4 Seoul
05.09.87 Sot Chitalada L CO 4 Bangkok
(*WBC Flyweight Title Challenge*)
13.03.88 Davrung Technicutradit DREW 10 Seoul
Summary: 29 contests, won 22, drew 4, lost 3.

Larry Alexander
Peter Goldfield/USA

Larry Alexander
New York, USA. *Born* Mississippi 17.10.55
Former NABF Heavyweight Champion

25.07.77 Don Martin W CO 3 Memphis
20.09.77 Clifton Haynes W RSC 1 Memphis
08.11.77 Robert Echols L PTS 5 Memphis
04.12.77 Raul Rodriguez W CO 2 Memphis
30.11.77 Nick Wells L CO 6 Topeka
10.01.78 James Dixon DREW 4 Memphis
29.01.78 Louis Tillman W RSC 3 Knoxville
08.02.78 Lynn Ball L PTS 4 Memphis
21.03.78 Robert Reynosa W CO 1 Greenville
04.04.78 Edward Baines W RSC 1 Greenville
25.04.78 Lee Holloman W CO 3 Greenville
09.05.78 Walter Santemore L PTS 6 Memphis
23.05.78 Carlton Morris W CO 3 Greenville
22.07.78 Willie Brown W CO 1 Knoxville
03.08.78 Joe Gorilla Griffen W CO 1 Birmingham
21.09.78 Walter Santemore L PTS 10 Birmingham
01.11.78 Rochelle Norris W RSC 7 White Plains
09.02.79 Tom Nickson L PTS 6 Mobile
16.02.79 A. J. Staples W RSC 2 Louisville
24.05.79 John Hudson W RSC 6 Detroit

26.09.79 George Chaplin L PTS 12 Baltimore
04.12.79 Marvin Stinson L PTS 8 Upper Derby
24.02.80 Jerry Thompkins W RSC 2 Atlantic City
15.04.80 Jeff Simms W CO 6 Miami
24.04.80 Bob Stallings W RSC 8 Totowa
16.05.80 Greg Page L CO 6 Lexington
17.09.80 Renaldo Snipes L RSC 2 White Plains
03.09.81 Leroy Boone W PTS 8 Atlantic City
24.10.81 Ralph Cuomo W CO 1 Brooklyn
04.02.82 Barry Funches W PTS 8 Bronx
24.02.82 Leroy Boone W PTS 8 Washington
16.04.82 Art Robinson W PTS 8 New York
07.01.83 Harold Rice W CO 1 Hartford
21.01.83 Mel Daniels ND 6 New York
22.07.83 Woody Clark W PTS 6 New York
17.11.83 James Broad L PTS 12 Atlantic City
03.03.84 Jesse Clark W CO 1 Hamilton
06.04.84 Larry Givens W CO 2 New York
10.05.85 Mike White W RSC 9 New York
11.07.85 Larry Frazier W PTS 10 New York
11.04.86 Tom Trimm W CO 1 Hamilton
21.04.86 Stan Ward W CO 2 Los Angeles
10.07.86 Eric Curry W PTS 10 Los Angeles
25.09.86 Mark Wills W PTS 12 Los Angeles
10.04.87 Dorcey Gaymon W RSC 7 Jacksonville (*Vacant NABF Heavyweight Title*)
25.11.87 Orlin Norris L PTS 12 Las Vegas (*NABF Heavyweight Title Defence*)
26.04.88 Donovon Ruddock L RSC 2 Camden
Summary: 47 contests, won 32, drew 1, lost 13, nd 1.

Olian Alexander

Olian (Baby O) Alexander

Huntington, USA. *Born* 17.02.60
Cruiserweight

12.10.84 Paul Madison L RSC 6 Wichita
15.12.84 James Wilder W RSC 3 Waukegan
02.04.85 Londale Freison W CO 1 Colorado Springs
14.09.85 Jim Berry W CO 3 Oklahoma City
16.11.85 Bob Wiggins W RSC 1 Oklahoma City
14.12.85 Charles Jamison W CO 2 Oklahoma City
02.08.86 Orlin Norris W PTS 4 San Jose
14.08.86 Mike Bardwell W RSC 1 Vallejo
26.09.86 David Kliewer W CO 2 Wichita
02.10.86 Mike Bardwell W PTS 4 San Jose
30.10.86 David Smith W PTS 6 San Jose
13.11.86 Mike Bardwell W RSC 2 San Jose
04.12.86 Rafael Fimbres W RSC 1 San Carlos
04.03.87 Lorenzo Boyd W CO 6 San Rafael
16.04.87 Calvin Sherman W RSC 2 San Rafael
05.06.87 Dwain Bonds W RSC 6 Pleasanton
09.07.87 Mike Gans L PTS 8 Oakland
02.10.87 Henry Hearns W RSC 8 Pleasanton
19.03.88 Eric Williams W CO 6 Pleasanton
Summary: 19 contests, won 17, lost 2.

Bashiru Ali

Oakland, USA. *Born* Lagos, Nigeria 27.02.56
WBC International Cruiserweight Champion. Former NABF & USBA Cruiserweight Champion

01.06.78 Junior Albers L PTS 6 Sacramento
21.06.78 Charles Terrell W PTS 6 Concord
12.07.78 Jim Ingram L PTS 6 Oakland
22.07.78 William Tavake W PTS 6 Truckee
28.07.78 Reggie Phillips L PTS 5 San Diego
06.12.78 Tony Stone W PTS 6 Stockton
27.02.79 Greg McPherson L PTS 10 San Carlos
27.03.79 Basheer Wadud W PTS 6 San Carlos
24.04.79 Greg McPherson W PTS 10 San Carlos
27.06.79 Pete McIntyre L PTS 10 Los Angeles
05.10.79 Yaqui Lopez L PTS 10 San Carlos
31.01.80 Len Provo W RSC 8 San Carlos
29.02.80 David Smith W PTS 10 San Carlos
11.04.80 Yaqui Meneses W DIS 8 San Jose
25.07.80 Jim Ingram W CO 7 San Carlos
28.08.80 Byron Campbell W RSC 5 San Carlos
16.10.80 Young Alvaro Lopez W RSC 10 San Carlos
03.12.80 Jesse Burnett W PTS 12 Anaheim (*USBA Cruiserweight Title Challenge*)
15.02.81 Reggie Patrick W PTS 8 Atlantic City
28.02.81 Marcus Jackson W PTS 8 Atlantic City
02.10.81 Marvin Camel L PTS 12 San Francisco (*USBA Cruiserweight Title Defence*)
12.11.81 Wilbert Albers W RSC 4 Oakland
25.02.82 Jesse Avila W RSC 4 San Jose
12.03.82 King David Smith W PTS 10 San Francisco
17.04.82 Fernando Montes W RSC 9 Mexico City
27.05.82 Greg McPherson W RSC 5 San Jose
25.08.82 Roger Braxton W PTS 10 Concord
02.10.82 Henry Hearns L RSC 2 Las Vegas
07.11.82 Mario Rosa W PTS 8 McAfee
20.11.82 Don Addison W RSC 2 Atlantic City
18.03.83 Leon Taylor L PTS 6 Atlantic City
09.06.83 Ruben Williams W PTS 10 San Jose
02.06.84 Carlos de Leon L PTS 12 Oakland (*WBC Cruiserweight Title Challenge*)
12.09.84 Yaqui Lopez W PTS 12 Stockton
29.09.84 Michael Arms W CO 6 Anchorage
07.05.85 Young Joe Louis W CO 2 Reno
19.06.85 Anthony Davis W RSC 9 Reno (*NABF Cruiserweight Title Challenge*)
14.08.85 Dee Dee Collier W CO 2 Reno
14.01.86 Michael Arms W PTS 10 Reno
22.04.86 Henry Tillman L RSC 1 Las Vegas (*NABF Cruiserweight Title Defence*)
10.04.87 Tommy Richardson W PTS 12 Jacksonville (*Vacant WBC International Cruiserweight Title*)
05.12.87 Kevin Wagstaff W CO 1 Ibadan (*WBC International Cruiserweight Title Defence*)
Summary: 42 contests, won 31, lost 11.

Terrence (Halley) Alli

Atlantic City, USA. *Born* Georgetown, Guyana 29.06.60
Former Undefeated USBA Lightweight Champion

02.12.79 Winston Goodridge W PTS 4 Georgetown
26.12.79 Walter Smith L PTS 6 Georgetown
14.01.80 Lloyd John W CO 3 Port of Spain
26.02.80 Clyde Wilson W PTS 6 Georgetown
05.03.80 Ricardo Croquer W PTS 6 Port of Spain
30.04.80 Cleophas James W PTS 6 Port of Spain
29.03.81 Cleophas James W PTS 8 Port of Spain
27.05.81 Walter Smith W PTS 6 Port of Spain
15.08.81 Michael Drayton W RSC 8 Port of Spain
28.11.81 Ismael Santana L RSC 3 Port of Spain
22.01.82 Nedric Simmons W RSC 4 Toronto
20.03.82 Rick Pappa W PTS 6 Toronto
16.04.82 Johnny Summerhays L PTS 10 Toronto
11.09.82 Norberto Velez W PTS 6 Atlantic City
07.10.82 Thomas Baker DREW 6 Atlantic City
16.12.82 Primo Ramos W RSC 2 Atlantic City
27.02.83 Edwin Luis Rivera W RSC 8 Atlantic City
02.06.83 Danny Avery W PTS 8 Atlantic City
18.06.83 Gonzalo Montellano W PTS 10 Atlantic City
05.11.83 Jerome Artis W RSC 2 Atlantic City
12.11.83 Ivan Montalvo W RSC 5 Las Vegas
05.04.84 Ezzard Charles Adams W RSC 7 Atlantic City
17.05.84 Melvin Paul W PTS 12 Atlantic City
21.06.84 John Senegal W RSC 2 Atlantic City
02.08.84 Efrain Nieves W PTS 12 Atlantic City
05.09.84 Frank Newton W RSC 3 Atlantic City
24.10.84 Victor Babilonia W PTS 10 Atlantic City
12.01.85 Harry Arroyo L RSC 11 Atlantic City (*IBF Lightweight Title Challenge*)
04.09.85 Eduardo Valdez W PTS 10 Atlantic City
23.10.85 Erskine Wade W RSC 10 Atlantic City
27.11.85 Denny Vargas W PTS 10 Atlantic City
10.01.86 Anthony Williams W PTS 10 Atlantic City
30.03.86 Cornelius Boza-Edwards DREW 10 Las Vegas
15.08.86 Pedro Montero W DIS 2 Atlantic City
27.09.86 Miguel Santana W PTS 12 Atlantic City (*Vacant USBA Lightweight Title*)
02.01.87 Roberto Medina W PTS 10 Atlantic City
11.03.87 Jeff Bumphus W RSC 8 Atlantic City
19.05.87 Rodney Moore W RSC 9 Atlantic City
19.07.87 Jose Luis Ramirez L PTS 12 St Tropez (*Vacant WBC Lightweight Title*)
04.09.87 Joey Olivera W PTS 10 Las Vegas
23.12.87 Miguel Santana W PTS 10 Atlantic City
21.03.88 Darryl Tyson W PTS 10 Atlantic City
Summary: 42 contests, won 35, drew 2, lost 5.

Dennis Andries

Hackney, England. *Born* Guyana 05.11.53
Former WBC L. Heavyweight Champion. Former Undefeated British L. Heavyweight Champion

16.05.78 Ray Pearce W CO 2 Newport
01.06.78 Mark Seabrook W RSC 1 Heathrow
20.06.78 Bonny McKenzie L PTS 8 Southend
18.09.78 Ken Jones W PTS 6 London
31.10.78 Neville Estaban W PTS 6 Barnsley
14.11.78 Les McAteer DREW 8 Birkenhead
22.11.78 Glen McEwan W RSC 7 Stoke
04.12.78 Tom Collins W PTS 8 Southend
22.01.79 Bunny Johnson L PTS 10 Wolverhampton
30.01.79 Tom Collins W CO 6 Southend
05.04.79 Francis Hand W RSC 8 Liverpool
06.06.79 Bonny McKenzie W PTS 8 Burslem
17.09.79 Johnny Waldron W RTD 10 London
27.02.80 Bunny Johnson L PTS 15 Burslem (*British L. Heavyweight Title Challenge*)
17.04.80 Mustafa Wasajja L PTS 8 Copenhagen
18.06.80 Chris Lawson W RSC 8 Burslem
23.03.81 Shaun Chalcraft W PTS 10 London
16.09.81 Liam Coleman W RSC 6 Burslem
12.10.81 David Pearce L RSC 7 London
23.11.81 Alek Penarski W PTS 10 Chesterfield
15.03.82 Tom Collins L PTS 15 London (*Vacant British L. Heavyweight Title*)
10.08.82 Keith Bristol W PTS 10 London
28.02.83 Karl Canwell W CO 4 London

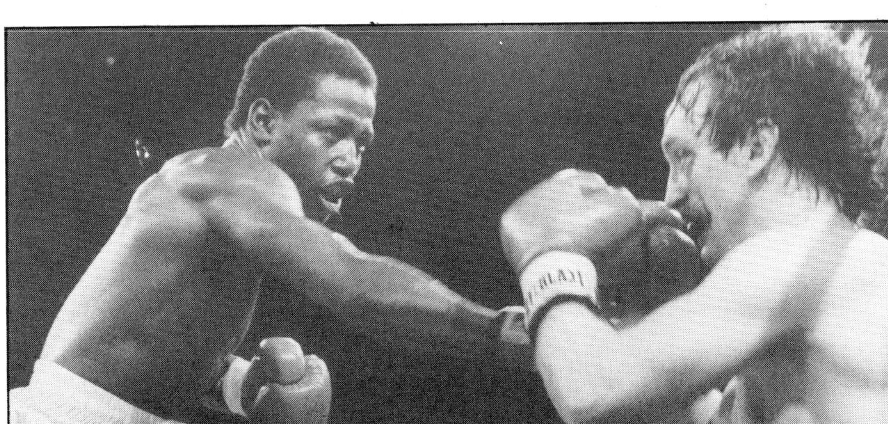

Terrence Alli (left) crosses Jeff Bumphus with the right on his way to an eighth round stoppage victory, 11 March 1987
Peter Goldfield/USA

Dennis Andries

19.05.83 Chris Lawson W CO 4 London
22.09.83 Keith Bristol W CO 4 London
26.01.84 Tom Collins W PTS 12 London
(*British L. Heavyweight Title Challenge*)
06.04.84 Tom Collins W PTS 12 Watford
(*British L. Heavyweight Title Defence*)
10.10.84 Devon Bailey W CO 12 London
(*British L. Heavyweight Title Defence*)
23.03.85 Jose Seys W RSC 3 London
07.05.85 Jeff Meachum W CO 4 New Orleans
25.05.85 Tim Broady W RSC 5 Atlantic City
06.06.85 Marcus Dorsey W CO 3 Lafayette
11.12.85 Alex Blanchard DREW 12 London
(*EBU L. Heavyweight Title Challenge*)
13.02.86 Keith Bristol W RSC 6 Longford
(*British L. Heavyweight Title Defence*)
30.04.86 J. B. Williamson W PTS 12 London
(*WBC L. Heavyweight Title Challenge*)
10.09.86 Tony Sibson W RSC 9 London
(*WBC & British L. Heavyweight Title Defence*)
07.03.87 Thomas Hearns L RSC 10 Detroit
(*WBC L. Heavyweight Title Defence*)
06.10.87 Robert Folley W PTS 10 Phoenix
20.02.88 Jamie Howe W PTS 10 Detroit
Summary: 39 contests, won 30, drew 2, lost 7.

Rufino Angulo
Floriac, France. *Born* 15.03.56
Former French L. Heavyweight Champion

24.11.78 Andre Genasi W RSC 6 Villeneuve
06.04.79 Rhida Hakimi W CO 2 Villenueve
08.12.79 Daniel Hyvon W RSC 4 Paris
21.12.79 Maurice Renaud DREW 6 Agen
01.02.80 Serge Sinelnikov W PTS 6 Agen
15.02.80 Mauro da Cruz W PTS 6 Bordeaux
28.03.80 Moussa Mukandjo L RSC 5 Chaux
18.10.80 Maurice Renaud W PTS 8 Villeneuve
06.12.80 Idrissa Konate W CO 4 Villeneuve
31.01.81 Pierre Joly DREW 10 Villeneuve
10.04.81 Joel Bonnetaz W PTS 8 Villeneuve
05.06.81 Jacques Chinon L PTS 12 Villeneuve
(*French Middleweight Title Challenge*)
23.10.81 Christian D'Helft L DIS 4 Perigueux
07.11.81 Manuel Lira W PTS 8 Villeneuve
13.11.81 Cosimo Funto W RSC 6 Rome
11.12.81 Geatano Ardito L DIS 4 Florence
12.02.82 Michel Pagani L DIS 4 Calais
05.03.82 Andre Mongalema W CO 8 Paris
19.05.82 Eric Kopec W CO 6 Villeneuve
09.10.82 Yawe Davis W PTS 8 Villeneuve
04.02.83 Carl Canwell W RSC 5 Bordeaux
19.03.83 Keith Bristol W RSC 6 Villeneuve
13.06.83 Tony Mundine W CO 5 Paris
05.08.83 Bonny McKenzie W PTS 8 Nimes
08.10.83 David Conteh W DIS 4 Villeneuve
21.11.83 Rudi Koopmans L PTS 12 Paris
(*EBU L. Heavyweight Title Challenge*)
24.02.84 Mwehu Beya L PTS 8 Bordeaux
19.04.84 Mwehu Beya W PTS 8 Paris
25.05.84 Trevor Cattouse W RSC 3 Toulouse
31.10.84 Horst Lang W CO 4 Bordeaux
07.12.84 Jonjo Green W PTS 8 Bordeaux
29.03.85 Willie Edwards L PTS 10 Bordeaux
20.12.85 Ian Lazarus W PTS 8 Bordeaux
27.01.86 Jonjo Green W PTS 8 Paris
14.03.86 Nye Williams W PTS 8 Bordeaux
10.04.86 Yombo Araka L PTS 8 Antibes
06.12.86 Abdel Moumene W RTD 3 Gailliard
05.02.87 Jean-Noel Camara W PTS 10 Bordeaux
16.04.87 Richard Caramanolis W CO 2 Marseilles
(*French L. Heavyweight Title Challenge*)
05.10.87 Roy Saffold W DIS 6 Paris
21.11.87 Virgil Hill L PTS 12 Paris
(*WBA L. Heavyweight Title Challenge*)
13.02.88 Noel Magee DREW 8 Paris
28.03.88 Richard Caramanolis L RSC 4 Paris
(*French L. Heavyweight Title Defence*)
Summary: 43 contests, won 29, drew 3, lost 11.

Azadin Anhar
Indonesia
Former Indonesian L. Flyweight Champion

03.05.85 Little Pono W CO 8 Jakarta
30.07.85 Little Holmes L PTS 8 Timor
03.08.85 Tubagus Jaya W PTS 10 Bulungan
25.08.85 Nick Dalisay L PTS 10 Jakarta
15.12.85 Little Pono W CO 10 Jakarta
(*Vacant Indonesian L. Flyweight Title*)
19.04.86 Moh Chotip W CO 6 Jakarta
16.09.86 Ray Medel L PTS 10 San Antonio
09.10.86 Jose Diaz W PTS 10 Mexicali
30.10.86 Javier Lucas L CO 4 Torreon
10.01.87 Rex Ikeda W CO 3 Semarang
09.08.87 Jum-Hwan Choi L RSC 3 Jakarta
(*IBF L. Flyweight Title Challenge*)
28.11.87 Udin Baharudin L PTS 12 Gerbandung
(*Indonesian L. Flyweight Title Defence*)
27.12.87 Jim Suyono W PTS 8 Surabaya
05.01.88 Michael Arthur W PTS 8 Malang
Summary: 14 contests, won 8, lost 6.

Lupe Aquino
Chula Vista, USA. *Born* Tijuana 23.01.63
Former WBC L. Middleweight Champion

02.04.81 Alberto Garcia W RSC 1 Los Angeles
15.05.81 Henry Drummond W PTS 4 Los Angeles
12.08.81 Rocky Cabilles W RSC 1 Las Vegas
09.09.81 Ramondo Solorzano W CO 2 Las Vegas
24.09.81 Bobby Silva W RSC 1 Las Vegas
22.10.81 Ricardo Garcia W RSC 6 Las Vegas
07.11.81 Willie McGee W CO 1 Las Vegas
17.11.81 Danny Favella W PTS 8 Phoenix
05.12.81 Barreto Hernandez W RSC 2 Las Vegas
17.12.81 Paul Gonzalez W CO 1 Phoenix
18.02.82 Andres Obregon W RSC 1 Phoenix
25.02.82 Solomon Jones W RSC 1 Las Vegas
25.03.82 Joe Moliere W PTS 8 Las Vegas
22.05.82 Eddie Nuno W PTS 8 Las Vegas
21.07.82 Clayton Hires W PTS 10 Las Vegas
07.12.82 Reinaldo Rogue W CO 2 San Diego
31.01.83 Tim Harris W PTS 10 Los Angeles
21.02.83 Rudy Hernandez L PTS 10 Los Angeles
27.05.83 Chino Bermudez W PTS 10 Los Angeles
14.06.83 Eduardo Dominguez W RSC 4 Ventura
09.08.83 David Madrid W RSC 1 Ventura
18.08.83 Victor Abraham W RSC 7 Los Angeles
10.09.83 Steve Herron W RSC 5 Atlantic City
25.11.83 Eric Martin DREW 10 Las Vegas
16.12.83 Tomas Chavez W RTD 1 Ventura
17.04.84 Marlon Starling L PTS 12 Atlantic City
(*NABF and USBA Welterweight Title Challenge*)
18.06.85 Lloyd Taylor W RSC 1 Atlantic City
30.07.85 Carl Riskus W RSC 3 Atlantic City
01.11.85 David Noel W PTS 10 Port of Spain
10.10.86 Nat Dryer W RSC 5 Las Vegas
11.11.86 Diomedes Colome W CO 5 Las Vegas
09.01.87 Anthony Wiley W RSC 2 Las Vegas
06.04.87 Davey Moore W RSC 5 Las Vegas
12.07.87 Duane Thomas W PTS 12 Bordeaux
(*WBC L. Middleweight Title Challenge*)
02.10.87 Gianfranco Rosi L PTS 12 Perugia
(*WBC L. Middleweight Title Defence*)
03.01.88 Don Curry L PTS 12 Genoa
10.04.88 Milton McCrory W PTS 10 Atlantic City
Summary: 37 contests, won 32, drew 1, lost 4.

Pascual Aranda
San Luis Potosi, Mexico. *Born* 30.11.62
Featherweight

29.10.81 Steve Cruz L CO 1 Fort Worth
28.01.82 Reggie Watson L RSC 4 Orange
02.03.82 Jose Reyna W RSC 3 Houston
19.03.82 Richard Savage L PTS 6 Houston
11.05.82 Rey Garza W PTS 6 Harlingen
14.09.82 Steve McKeyer W PTS 6 Houston
19.10.82 Elvis Daw W RSC 1 Beaumont
12.11.82 Billy White L PTS 8 Lafayette
30.11.82 Roger Trevino W RSC 3 Fort Worth
26.01.83 Alvaro Salazar W PTS 6 Alice
26.04.83 Ponciano Trevino W RSC 4 Harlingen
10.05.83 James Cooper W RSC 2 Lafayette
24.05.83 Aaron Lopez W PTS 8 San Antonio
15.07.83 Felipe Morales W CO 4 Houston
28.07.83 Leonardo Valdez W PTS 10 Las Vegas
29.09.83 Leonardo Valdez L PTS 10 Las Vegas
17.01.84 Sylvester Kennon W RSC 4 Houston
07.02.84 Alvin Fowler W RSC 2 Houston
27.03.84 Rey Garza W CO 3 Houston
19.04.84 Carlos Flores W RSC 8 Houston
24.05.84 Aaron Lopez L RSC 5 Houston
17.08.84 Jose L. Martinez W CO 1 Houston
13.09.84 Sylvester Kennon L RSC 3 Houston
13.12.84 Calvin Grove L RSC 3 Atlantic City
02.02.85 Idabeth Rojas L CO 1 Miami
17.03.85 Filberto Martinez W RSC 3 Houston
16.04.85 Cristobal Pena W RSC 7 Brownsville
09.07.85 Alvaro Salazar W RSC 4 Houston
10.09.85 Mike Ayala L PTS 12 San Antonio
(*NABF S. Bantamweight Title Challenge*)
29.05.86 James Pipps T DRAW 2 Houston
13.07.86 Jesus Ochoa W CO 2 Houston
17.08.86 Apolinar Martinez W RSC 9 Houston
29.09.86 Raphe Sims W PTS 10 Houston
09.11.86 Carlos Flores W RSC 8 Houston
01.02.87 Hector Cortez L CO 5 Houston
15.03.87 Magdelino Montoya W RSC 8 Houston
26.07.87 Antonio Esparragoza L CO 10 Houston
(*WBA Featherweight Title Challenge*)
27.03.88 Tomas Gonzalez W PTS 10 Houston
Summary: 38 contests, won 25, drew 1, lost 12.

Roger Arevalo
Merida, Mexico
Mexican S. Featherweight Champion

02.06.82 Guillermo Piste W PTS 4 Merida
07.07.82 Guillermo Piste W PTS 4 Merida
16.10.82 Rosendo Montero DREW 4 Merida
13.12.82 Fermin Zapata W PTS 4 Chetumal
09.02.83 Jose Borges W PTS 4 Merida
02.03.83 Martin Barrera DREW 6 Merida
15.04.83 Francisco Yam W CO 4 Chetumal
06.05.83 Wilberth Burgos W PTS 8 Chetumal
16.07.83 Jose Borges W PTS 6 Valladolid
15.09.83 Armin Ayala W CO 5 Motul
25.09.83 Mario Zapata W RSC 7 Chetumal
26.10.83 Alberto Chuc W PTS 10 Merida
18.11.83 Margaruto Navaez W PTS 10 Chetumal
11.02.84 Wilbert Vera W CO 3 Merida
07.04.84 Jose Medel W RSC 5 Merida
30.06.84 Marco A. Figueroa W RSC 7 Merida
27.10.84 Jorge Betancourt W RSC 7 Merida
08.12.84 William Solis W CO 5 Merida
23.03.85 Noe Gonzalez W RSC 5 Merida
02.03.85 Arturo Hernandez W RSC 6 Merida
21.04.85 Pedro Galaviz W RSC 10 Merida
22.06.85 Boni Flores W CO 3 Merida
06.08.85 Mauro Gutierrez DREW 10 Tijuana
28.09.85 Carlos Linares W RSC 6 Merida
28.12.85 Bruno Rabanales W PTS 10 Merida
15.03.86 Felipe Rocha W CO 4 Merida
26.04.86 Joaquin Acuna L PTS 10 Mexico City
21.11.86 Steve Cruz L PTS 10 Fort Worth
16.03.87 Tyrone Downes L PTS 10 Los Angeles
23.05.87 Antonio de la Paz W PTS 10 Mexico City
25.07.87 Ramon Flores W CO 5 Mexico City
(*Vacant Mexican S. Featherweight Title*)
15.08.87 Vicente Velasco W RSC 1 Mexico City
17.10.87 Jesus Rojas W CO 8 Merida
25.01.88 Mauro Gutierrez W RTD 8 Tijuana
(*Mexican S. Featherweight Title Defence*)
Summary: 34 contests, won 28, drew 3, lost 3.

Rene Arredondo (left) seen regaining his WBC light-welterweight title from Tsuyoshi Hamada

Rene Arredondo
Apatzingan, Mexico. *Born* 15.06.61
Former WBC L. Welterweight Champion

15.11.79 Zorrita Gomez W CO 1 Vera Cruz
30.12.80 Arturo Millan W RSC 3 Mexico City
31.01.81 Juan Reyes W CO 3 Mexico City
18.03.81 Pablo Santiago W CO 1 Mexico City
12.06.81 Beto Ramos W CO 5 Acapulco
11.07.81 Marcelo Vega W CO 1 Mexico City
07.08.81 Carmelo Montes W RSC 5 Acapulco
09.09.81 Ubaldo Ramirez W RSC 4 Mexico City
09.10.81 Isabel Gonzalez W CO 3 Acapulco
06.11.81 Saul Montana W RSC 4 Acapulco
11.12.81 Jose Rosas W PTS 10 Acapulco
03.02.82 Sergio Cabrera W RSC 3 Mexico City
03.03.82 Luis Rivera W CO 1 Mexico City
10.03.82 Mauricio Aceves W PTS 10 Mexico City
02.04.82 Emilio Solano W CO 3 Ciudad Valles
27.04.82 Herminio Delgado W CO 3 Mexico City
22.05.82 Jose Luis Escalante W DIS 4 Mexico City
26.06.82 Juan Carlos Alvarado W RSC 6 Mexico City
11.08.82 Leoncio Ortiz W RSC 5 Mexico City
13.10.82 Leoncio Ortiz L PTS 10 Mexico City
26.11.82 Francisco Tapia W RSC 3 Mexico City
15.12.82 Jose Luis Tapia W RSC 2 Mexico City
20.02.83 Hector Rivera W RSC 4 San Juan
09.07.83 Andre Wynn W CO 1 Los Angeles
25.08.83 Carlos Hernandez W CO 1 Los Angeles
03.09.83 Leonardo Cruz W PTS 10 Los Angeles
24.09.83 Rigoberto Ruiz W RSC 6 Los Angeles
08.12.83 Dario de Jesus W RSC 4 Los Angeles
16.02.84 Pedro Roche W CO 4 Los Angeles
12.04.84 Ricardo Lomeli W RSC 2 Los Angeles
17.05.84 Claude Noel W CO 2 Los Angeles
23.06.84 Jose Angulo W RSC 4 Los Angeles
25.09.84 Efren Olivo W RSC 5 Harlingen
02.11.84 Pedro Carbajal W RSC 1 Los Angeles
19.04.85 Hector Medina W CO 1 Los Angeles
23.05.85 Hugo Hernandez W RSC 4 Los Angeles
03.07.85 Rodolfo Gonzalez L PTS 10 Los Angeles
26.09.85 Saul Julio W RSC 4 Los Angeles
20.12.85 Eduardo Valdez W RSC 2 Los Angeles
05.05.86 Lonnie Smith W RSC 5 Los Angeles
(*WBC L. Welterweight Title Challenge*)
24.07.86 Tsuyoshi Hamada L CO 1 Tokyo
(*WBC L. Welterweight Title Defence*)
06.11.86 Saoul Mamby W PTS 10 Los Angeles
22.07.87 Tsuyoshi Hamada W RSC 6 Tokyo
(*WBC L. Welterweight Title Challenge*)
12.11.87 Roger Mayweather L RSC 6 Los Angeles
(*WBC L. Welterweight Title Defence*)
Summary: 44 contests, won 40, lost 4.

Antonio Avelar
Guadalajara, Mexico. *Born* 03.09.58
Former WBC Flyweight Champion. Former Undefeated NABF Flyweight Champion

20.06.75 Manuel Ruelas W CO 2 Guadalajara
04.07.75 Felipe Mayorga W PTS 4 Guadalajara
19.09.75 Ruperto Guevara W CO 3 Guadalajara
21.11.75 Raul Ochoa W PTS 10 Guadalajara
31.01.76 Angel Felix W PTS 10 La Paz
20.03.76 Nacho Beltran L CO 2 La Paz
09.04.76 Juanito Martinez W CO 2 Guadalajara
14.05.76 Andres Reyes L RSC 4 Guadalajara
20.08.76 Alfonso Ramirez W CO 2 Guadalajara
08.10.76 Freddy Polanco W CO 2 Guadalajara
12.11.76 Juan Guzman L CO 7 Guadalajara
17.12.76 Carlos Barbosa W RSC 6 Guadalajara
04.02.77 Freddie Castillo L PTS 10 Guadalajara
04.03.77 Pedro Camacho W RSC 6 Guadalajara
02.04.77 Tony Escobar DREW 10 La Paz
21.05.77 Gabriel Bernal L PTS 10 Mexico City
24.06.77 Refugio Rojas W CO 5 Guadalajara
24.08.77 Arturo Urrizquieta W CO 2 Mexico City
10.09.77 Victor Hugo Aguirre W RSC 5 Mexico City
12.10.77 Jose Sosa W PTS 10 Mexico City
07.01.78 Samuel Machorro L PTS 10 Mexico City
22.04.78 Freddy Hernandez W RSC 8 San Luis Poto
29.07.78 Matias Marin W CO 8 Merida
20.10.78 Freddie Castillo L RSC 10 Merida
10.02.79 Miguel Canto L PTS 15 Merida
(*WBC Flyweight Title Challenge*)
25.08.79 Samuel Machorro W PTS 10 Mexico City
01.12.79 Adelaido Galindo W CO 3 Mexico City
01.01.80 Alfredo Hernandez W CO 2 Gomez Palacio
16.02.80 Alfonso Lopez W RSC 5 Merida
01.04.80 Aniceto Vargas W CO 5 Houston
13.06.80 Rocky Mijares W CO 1 Gomez Palacio
16.08.80 Alberto Morales W RSC 10 Merida
(*NABF Flyweight Title Challenge*)
18.10.80 Rocky Mijares W CO 2 Gomez Palacio
12.05.81 Shoji Oguma W CO 7 Mito City
(*WBC Flyweight Title Challenge*)
30.08.81 Tae-Shik Kim W CO 2 Seoul
(*WBC Flyweight Title Defence*)
20.03.82 Prudencio Cardona L CO 1 Tampico
(*WBC Flyweight Title Defence*)
26.12.82 Jimmy Fernandez W RSC 6 Tuxtla
01.05.83 Fred Jackson L RSC 7 San Juan
14.05.83 Carlos de la Paz W CO 6 Tijuana
17.07.84 Diego Avila W RSC 3 Tijuana
01.01.85 Gilberto Roman W DIS 5 Mexicali
30.03.85 Gilberto Roman L RSC 7 Mexicali
11.06.85 Mario Nava W RSC 3 Tijuana
22.07.85 Jose Gallegos W CO 3 Tijuana
23.09.85 Freddie Castillo W RSC 4 Tijuana
04.02.86 Ali Solis W CO 2 La Paz
07.03.86 Arturo Mujica L RSC 4 Guadalajara
31.05.86 Wilfredo Vasquez W RSC 8 Miami
25.07.87 Miguel Lora L RSC 4 Miami
(*WBC Bantamweight Title Challenge*)
Summary: 49 contests, won 35, drew 1, lost 13.

Mike (Cyclone) Ayala
San Antonio, USA. *Born* 19.01.58
Former NABF S. Bantamweight Champion. Former Undefeated NABF Featherweight Champion

19.08.75 Raul Casarez W RSC 1 Corpus Christi
16.09.75 Beto Avila W RSC 4 Corpus Christi
03.10.75 Beto Avila W RSC 4 Piedras Negras
12.11.75 Raul Jorres W CO 1 Mobile
26.11.75 Bobby Dominguez W RSC 3 Mobile
27.02.76 Mario Castro W CO 1 Piedras Negras
13.04.76 Javier Moncivais W PTS 10 San Antonio
21.05.76 Chamaco Cuenca W CO 2 Piedras Negras
22.06.76 Tony Rocha W PTS 10 San Antonio
23.07.76 Goyo Vargas W CO 4 San Antonio
01.10.76 Chango Guillen W PTS 10 Piedras Negras
26.10.76 Ramon Elorde W PTS 10 San Antonio
18.01.77 Cesar Deciga W RSC 7 San Antonio
25.03.77 Romeo Anaya W RSC 6 San Antonio
17.05.77 Rodolfo Martinez L RSC 7 San Antonio
09.08.77 Reynaldo Hidalgo W PTS 10 San Antonio
04.10.77 Raul Tirado W PTS 10 San Antonio
06.12.77 Tarcisio Gomez W PTS 10 San Antonio
18.03.78 Ron McGarvey W CO 1 San Antonio
(*NABF Featherweight Title Challenge*)
18.07.78 Edwin Alarcon W PTS 10 San Antonio
22.08.78 Shigeo Fukuyama W RSC 6 San Antonio
22.11.78 Edel Borunda W PTS 12 San Antonio
(*NABF Featherweight Title Defence*)
24.02.79 Jose Nunez W PTS 10 Las Vegas
17.06.79 Danny Lopez L CO 15 San Antonio
(*WBC Featherweight Title Challenge*)
23.11.79 Enrique Solis W PTS 10 New York
09.05.80 Marcial Santiago W PTS 10 Commack
23.05.80 Nicky Perez W PTS 12 Clarkston
(*NABF Featherweight Title Defence*)
07.11.80 Javier Flores W PTS 10 San Antonio
26.05.81 Sergio Castro W PTS 10 San Antonio
04.08.81 Angel Lira W RSC 8 San Antonio
23.08.81 Jose Resendez W PTS 10 San Antonio
14.12.82 Tony Rocha W CO 3 Pasadena
11.02.83 Javier Flores W RSC 7 Eugene
29.04.83 Kenny Mitchell W PTS 12 San Antonio
(*Vacant NABF S. Bantamweight Title*)
30.11.83 Alejandro Garcia W CO 2 San Antonio
27.01.84 Leo Martinez W CO 12 El Paso
(*NABF S. Bantamweight Title Defence*)
22.03.84 Rodolfo Quintero W RSC 2 San Antonio
06.06.84 Jesus Lopez W RSC 4 San Antonio
09.11.84 Rodolfo Martinez W CO 6 San Antonio
19.04.85 Juan Meza L RSC 6 Los Angeles
(*WBC S. Bantamweight Title Challenge*)
10.09.85 Pascual Aranda W PTS 12 San Antonio
(*NABF S. Bantamweight Title Defence*)
02.03.86 Julian Solis W PTS 10 San Antonio
31.05.86 Hector Cortez W PTS 10 San Francisco
25.07.86 Aaron Lopez W PTS 12 San Antonio
(*NABF S. Bantamweight Title Defence*)
06.12.86 Daniel Zaragoza L CO 7 San Antonio
(*NABF S. Bantamweight Title Defence*)
01.05.87 Raul Lopez W CO 2 San Antonio
19.06.87 Arturo Tebaqui W RSC 5 San Antonio
15.07.87 Manuel Juarez W CO 1 Phoenix
15.08.87 Louie Espinosa L CO 9 San Antonio
(*WBA S. Bantamweight Title Challenge*)
Summary: 49 contests, won 44, lost 5.

Tommy Ayers
Cincinnati, USA. *Born* 27.03.63
Former Undefeated NABF Welterweight Champion

10.01.81 Gary Stallworth W RSC 1 Covington
04.09.81 Johnny Papin W RSC 1 Kansas City
21.10.81 Paul Rutledge W PTS 4 Youngstown
14.11.81 Benito Goff W CO 1 Cleveland
21.11.81 Wendell King W CO 1 Covington
27.11.81 Marshall Mackery W CO 1 Fort Mitchell
05.01.82 Mike Golden W CO 6 Atlantic City
09.01.82 Darrell Owens W RSC 1 Fort Mitchell
02.02.82 Joshua King W RSC 2 Atlantic City
05.05.82 Jerry Strickland W CO 1 Indianapolis
23.06.82 Ken Smith W RSC 1 Atlantic City
04.07.82 Mike Blunt W RSC 2 Cincinnati
20.07.82 Gary Gibson W RSC 4 Atlantic City
10.08.82 Marvin Jenkins W PTS 8 Atlantic City
06.10.82 Phil Beattie W CO 1 Youngstown
11.11.82 Johnny Sanchez W RSC 1 Atlantic City
07.01.83 Adriano Marrero W PTS 10 Cincinnati
25.02.83 Pete Seward W CO 2 Cincinnati
27.03.83 Dominic Fox W CO 1 Scranton
21.05.83 Bruce Finch W CO 2 Cincinnati
24.07.83 Marlon Starling L PTS 12 Atlantic City
(*NABF and USBA Welterweight Title Challenge*)
31.01.84 Bobby Graddy W RSC 6 Atlantic City
15.04.84 Lanny Edmonds W RSC 3 Detroit
14.08.84 Don King W RSC 8 Atlantic City
22.09.84 Roger Stafford W PTS 10 Cincinnati
18.12.84 Reymundo Valdez W RSC 5 Atlantic City
05.03.85 Robert Adams W RSC 7 Atlantic City
25.05.85 Tony Ojo W PTS 10 Washington
04.08.85 Marvin Jenkins W CO 6 Charleston
19.11.85 Dexter Smith W RSC 3 Atlantic City
01.03.86 Leland Hart W PTS 10 Washington
09.01.87 Rigoberto Lopez W RSC 5 Las Vegas

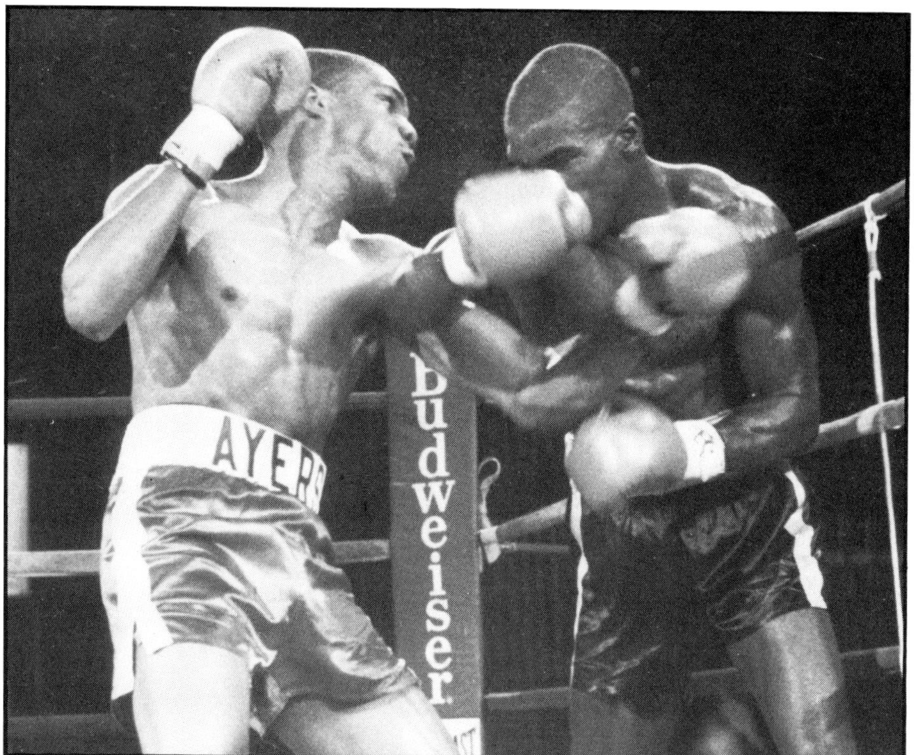

Tommy Ayers (left) mixes it with Rollin Williams during his losing battle for the vacant USBA welterweight title
IBF/Bill Baron

05.03.87 Luis Santana W RSC 4 Las Vegas
(NABF Welterweight Title Challenge)
24.05.87 Anibal Ortiz W RSC 3 Alexandria
30.06.87 Rollin Williams L PTS 12 Atlantic City
(Vacant USBA Welterweight Title)
Summary: 35 contests, won 33, lost 2.

In-Chul Baek

Ko Hung, South Korea. *Born* 20.12.61
OPBF Middleweight Champion. Former Undefeated OPBF L. Middleweight Champion

09.05.80 Sung-Jong Park W CO 2 Seoul
08.06.80 Yung-Chil Yang W RSC 2 Seoul
25.09.80 Jong-Hyun Park W CO 1 Seoul
21.11.80 Byung-Chun Choi W CO 3 Seoul
22.11.80 Sun-Kap Choi W CO 4 Seoul
29.11.80 Jang-Ho Choi W CO 3 Seoul
07.12.80 Bok-Kyu Lim W RSC 3 Seoul
14.02.81 Yung-Sil Chung W RSC 4 Seoul
19.04.81 Hiroshi Izumiya W RSC 3 Seoul
23.06.81 Conrado Salinas W CO 2 Seoul
21.08.81 Alberto Cruz W CO 1 Daejon
11.10.81 Jin-Nam Kim W RSC 3 Daejon
25.10.81 Aquilino Nicolas W CO 2 Seoul
28.11.81 Joe Wilisco W CO 3 Seoul
27.12.81 Sung-Ho Lee W RSC 12 Seoul
(Vacant OPBF L. Middleweight Title)
14.02.82 Alberto Cruz W CO 1 Daejon
(OPBF L. Middleweight Title Defence)
21.03.82 Kenji Miyata W RSC 9 Pusan
24.04.82 Muhammad Ibrahim W RSC 3 Kwangju
(OPBF L. Middleweight Title Defence)
13.06.82 Michihiro Horihata W RSC 2 Pusan
(OPBF L. Middleweight Title Defence)
03.07.82 Antonio Reyna W CO 2 Daejon
26.09.82 Fred Galang W CO 3 Taegu
23.10.82 Yohi Ari W CO 10 Chungju
(OPBF L. Middleweight Title Defence)
11.12.82 Kongrag Vorchareenrat W CO 3 Seoul
(OPBF L. Middleweight Title Defence)
02.01.83 Romy Angeles W CO 3 Daejon
(OPBF L. Middleweight Title Defence)
27.02.83 Jesus Gonzalez W CO 3 Daejon
27.03.83 Chong-Ho Kim W CO 7 Chinju
(OPBF L. Middleweight Title Defence)
19.05.83 Sean Mannion L PTS 10 Atlantic City
10.07.83 Yohi Arai W CO 5 Daejon
(OPBF L. Middleweight Title Defence)
13.11.83 Satenfa Pratip W CO 3 Cheju
07.01.84 Sakaria Ve W CO 6 Daejon
24.03.84 Mike de Guzman W CO 3 Ryoisan
(OPBF L. Middleweight Title Defence)
23.07.84 Alberto Bapaimo W CO 4 Osan
(OPBF L. Middleweight Title Defence)
12.01.85 Hendris Salmon W RSC 2 Kwangju
(OPBF L. Middleweight Title Defence)
20.04.85 Jaeh-Yung Yuh W RSC 5 Seoul
(OPBF L. Middleweight Title Defence)
13.07.85 Alberto Bapaimo W CO 3 Chungju
(OPBF L. Middleweight Title Defence)
27.10.85 Fred Hutchings W CO 9 Pusan
15.03.86 Troy Waters W PTS 12 Seoul
(OPBF L. Middleweight Title Defence)
28.06.86 Sang-Do Chung W PTS 12 Pohang
(OPBF L. Middleweight Title Defence)
27.07.86 Chun-Hwan Noh W RSC 5 Chungju
18.10.86 Jun-Sok Hwang W PTS 12 Inchon
(OPBF L. Middleweight Title Defence)
15.03.87 Paul James W PTS 10 Seoul
12.07.87 Hideo Kawamoto W CO 2 Ahnyang
21.11.87 Julian Jackson L RSC 3 Las Vegas
(Vacant WBA L. Middleweight Title)
17.04.88 Ketut Udiyana W CO 2 Nonsan
(Vacant OPBF Middleweight Title)
Summary: 44 contests, won 42, lost 2.

Gustavo Ballas

Villa Maria, Argentine. *Born* 10.02.58
South American S. Flyweight Champion. Former WBA & Argentinian S. Flyweight Champion

03.12.76 Raul Anchagno W RTD 5 Mendoza
27.04.77 Felix Ruarte W PTS 6 Mendoza
15.07.77 Manuel Quinteros W PTS 8 Mendoza
12.08.77 Ramon Baez W PTS 8 Mendoza
02.09.77 Rodolfo Trujillo W RTD 2 Mendoza
07.10.77 Hector Lopez W PTS 8 Mendoza
04.11.77 Alberto Martin W PTS 10 Villa Maria
18.11.77 Martin Devia W RTD 5 Mendoza
02.12.77 Felipe Rojas W PTS 10 Villa Maria
20.12.77 Manuel Quinteros W CO 3 Godoy Cruz
07.04.78 Reynaldo Romero W PTS 10 Villa Maria
21.04.78 Enrique Navarro W PTS 10 Mendoza
12.05.78 Hector Barreto W PTS 10 Mendoza
07.07.78 Hugo Emer W PTS 10 Villa Maria
04.08.78 Luis A. Gerez W PTS 10 Villa Maria
01.09.78 Angel Fernandez W PTS 10 Mendoza
14.09.78 Juan Carlos Rios W PTS 10 Villa Maria
21.10.78 Jose Ibiris W PTS 10 Buenos Aires
03.11.78 Carlos Escalante W PTS 10 Villa Maria
16.12.78 Angel Fernandez W PTS 10 Buenos Aires
02.02.79 Miguel A. Lazarte W PTS 10 Mar del Plata
03.05.79 Jose Lopez W PTS 10 Mendoza
18.05.79 Esteban Bustos W PTS 10 Villa Maria
06.07.79 Carlos Huilli W CO 3 Villa Maria
24.08.79 Jose Narvaez DREW 10 Mendoza
07.09.79 Hector Velazquez W PTS 10 Villa Maria
05.10.79 Jose Cardozo W CO 3 Villa Maria
19.10.79 Paulo Ribeiro W RTD 8 Mendoza
03.11.79 Santos Laciar W PTS 10 Buenos Aires
16.11.79 Johnny Mesa W CO 3 Mendoza
06.12.79 Miguel Lazarte W PTS 10 Villa Maria
08.02.80 Jose Ricord W CO 6 Mar del Plata
07.03.80 Rigoberto Marcano W PTS 10 Buenos Aires
03.04.80 Juan Aravena W RTD 5 Villa Maria
19.04.80 Rodolfo Rodriguez W PTS 10 Buenos Aires
16.05.80 Jorge Aguilar W PTS 10 Mendoza
06.06.80 Ramon Rodriguez W DIS 9 Villa Maria
27.06.80 Hector Velasquez W CO 2 San Juan
05.09.80 Ramon Rodriguez W RTD 10 Cordoba
19.09.80 Miguel Lazarte W PTS 10 Mendoza
04.10.80 Rafael Pedroza W PTS 10 Buenos Aires
22.11.80 Alfonso Lopez W PTS 10 Buenos Aires
11.12.80 Ramon Rodriguez W RTD 8 Mendoza
23.01.81 Jorge Vargas W CO 5 Villa Carlos
05.02.81 Jaime Miranda W PTS 10 Villa Maria
06.03.81 Ramon Rodriguez W RSC 6 Villa Carlos
21.03.81 Jaime Miranda W RSC 8 Buenos Aires
03.04.81 Felix Colman W PTS 10 Cordoba
09.05.81 Jackal Maruyama W RSC 11 Buenos Aires
12.06.81 Luis Gerez W PTS 10 Cordoba
26.06.81 Hector Barreto W PTS 10 Tucuman
24.07.81 Roberto Condori W RSC 9 La Banda
14.08.81 Hector Barreto W PTS 10 Cordoba
12.09.81 Suk-Chul Baek W RSC 8 Buenos Aires
(Vacant WBA S. Flyweight Title)
05.12.81 Rafael Pedroza L PTS 15 Panama City
(WBA S. Flyweight Title Defence)
26.03.82 Hector Barreto W RSC 10 VC Paz
23.04.82 Jose Gomez W PTS 10 Tucuman
07.05.82 Froilan Nievas W CO 3 Mendoza
22.05.82 Rodolfo Rodriguez W PTS 10 Buenos Aires
29.07.82 Jiro Watanabe L RSC 9 Osaka
(WBA S. Flyweight Title Challenge)
11.12.82 Adrian Roman W PTS 10 Buenos Aires
05.03.83 Raul Cuevas W PTS 10 San Luis
15.04.83 Roberto Condori W PTS 10 San Juan
12.05.83 Felix Colman W PTS 10 Posadas
03.06.83 Armando Romero W PTS 10 Santa Rosa
17.06.83 Roberto Condori W PTS 10 Rosario
02.07.83 Luis Gerez W RSC 2 Buenos Aires
15.07.83 Armando Romero W PTS 10 Cordoba
19.08.83 Juan Cortez L PTS 10 Cordoba
16.09.83 Alberto Pereyra W PTS 10 Corrientes
12.11.83 Luis Ocampo W PTS 12 Posadas
(Vacant Argentinian S. Flyweight Title)
17.02.84 Juan Ivalo W RTD 7 Mar del Plata
16.03.84 Luis Gerez W PTS 10 Mar del Plata
07.04.84 Juan Cortez W PTS 12 Buenos Aires
(Argentinian S. Flyweight Title Defence)
06.09.84 Felix Colman W PTS 12 Mendoza
(Argentinian S. Flyweight Title Defence)
13.10.84 Jose Narvaez W PTS 10 Buenos Aires
10.11.84 Rodolfo Rodriguez W PTS 10 Mendoza
23.11.84 Luis Gerez W CO 4 Mendoza
16.02.85 Juan Ivalo W PTS 10 Mar del Plata
09.03.85 Juan Cortez DREW 12 Rivadavia
(Argentinian S. Flyweight Title Defence)
03.05.85 Guillermo Mariquez W RTD 7 Mendoza
17.05.85 Ruben Condori W PTS 10 Villa Maria
08.06.85 Lucio Lopez L RTD 5 Buenos Aires
15.11.85 Juan Cortez W PTS 12 Villa Maria
(Argentinian S. Flyweight Title Defence)
13.12.85 Ramon Alberts W RSC 4 Villa Maria
28.02.86 Patricio Jesus Gil W PTS 10 Mar del Plata
14.03.86 Ramon Alberts W PTS 10 Justino Posse
11.04.86 Ruben Condori L PTS 12 Salta
(Argentinian S. Flyweight Title Defence)
11.07.86 Adrian Roman DREW 10 Cordoba
15.08.86 Ramon Alberts W PTS 10 Concepcion
30.08.86 Juan Cortez DREW 10 Cordoba
14.11.86 Paulo Ribeiro W RSC 6 Villa Maria
(Vacant South American S. Flyweight Title)
06.12.86 Ruben Condori W PTS 12 Buenos Aires
(South American S. Flyweight Title Defence)
06.02.87 Jaime Miranda W RSC 5 Mar del Plata
21.03.87 Jose Badilla W PTS 10 Buenos Aires
10.04.87 Jose Badilla W PTS 10 La Rioza

15.05.87 Eloy Alca W PTS 12 San Juan
13.06.87 Ruben Condori L PTS 10 Buenos Aires
14.08.87 Jose Narvaez W PTS 10 Villa Maria
24.10.87 Jesus Rojas L RSC 4 Miami
(WBC S. Flyweight Title Challenge)
Summary: 100 contests, won 89, drew 4, lost 7.

Iran (The Blade) Barkley
New York, USA. *Born* 09.05.60
Former Undefeated Con. Am. Middleweight Champion

09.12.82 Larry Jordan W RSC 2 Atlantic City
06.01.83 Bruce Starling W CO 1 Atlantic City
29.01.83 Dominique Williams W.RSC 1 Atlantic City
18.02.83 Don Franklin W PTS 4 Atlantic City
31.03.83 Osley Silas L PTS 6 Atlantic City
18.06.83 Jose Torres W PTS 6 Atlantic City
18.08.83 Frank Minton W RSC 5 Atlantic City
05.12.83 Marciano Bernardi W RSC 1 Atlantic City
06.01.84 Robbie Sims L RSC 6 Atlantic City
05.07.84 Esteban Pizzaro W PTS 8 Atlantic City
23.08.84 John Ford W RSC 4 Atlantic City
01.11.84 Ed Hall L PTS 8 Atlantic City
21.02.85 Osley Silas W RSC 6 Atlantic City
26.04.85 Norberto Sabater W RSC 2 New York
24.05.85 Randy Smith W PTS 10 New York
11.07.85 Carlos Betancourt W RSC 1 New York
08.08.85 Bill Lee W RSC 3 New York
29.08.85 Norberto Sabater W CO 2 New York
01.11.85 Wilford Scypion W CO 8 New York
06.12.85 Mike Tinley W PTS 12 New York
(Vacant Con. Am. Middleweight Title)
19.06.86 Tony Harrison W RSC 3 New York
(Con. Am. Middleweight Title Defence)
24.07.86 Bastante Blanco W RTD 3 New York
17.10.86 James Kinchen W PTS 10 Detroit
20.02.87 Stacy McSwain W PTS 10 Atlantic City
03.04.87 Jorge Amparo W PTS 10 Las Vegas
23.10.87 Sumbu Kalambay L PTS 15 Livorno
(Vacant WBA Middleweight Title)
29.01.88 Sanderline Williams W PTS 10 Atlantic City
06.03.88 Michael Olajide W RSC 5 New York
Summary: 28 contests, won 24, lost 4.

Fidel Bassa
Colombia. *Born* 18.12.62
WBA Flyweight Champion. Former Undefeated Fecarbox & Colombian Flyweight Champion

23.12.83 Emilio Tamarillo W CO 2 Barranquilla
27.01.84 Juan Gomez W PTS 4 Barranquilla
11.05.84 Jairo Bedoya W CO 2 Barranquilla
10.06.84 Bernardo Ceballos W RSC 1 Barranquilla
31.08.84 Felipe Medrano W CO 5 Barranquilla
21.09.84 Eugenio Oviedo W CO 2 Cartagena
01.03.85 Jorge Lugo W CO 4 Barranquilla
(Colombian Flyweight Title Challenge)
29.03.85 Rafael Julio W RSC 3 Barranquilla
(Colombian Flyweight Title Defence)
04.05.85 Antonio Mitre W RSC 4 Barranquilla
21.06.85 Leonardo Paredes W RTD 6 Cartagena
(Fecarbox Flyweight Title Challenge)
30.08.85 Victor Tejedor W CO 1 Barranquilla
28.09.85 Ernesto Sanchez W PTS 10 Barranquilla
31.01.86 Victor Sierra W PTS 10 Cartagena
14.03.86 Jose Castillo W RSC 2 Bogota
30.04.86 Manuel Sallago W RSC 8 Barranquilla
17.10.86 Pedro Nieves W CO 1 Barranquilla
13.02.87 Hilario Zapata W PTS 15 Barranquilla
(WBA Flyweight Title Challenge)
25.04.87 Dave Boy McAuley W CO 13 Belfast
(WBA Flyweight Title Defence)
15.08.87 Hilario Zapata DREW 15 Panama City
(WBA Flyweight Title Defence)
18.12.87 Felix Marty W PTS 12 Cartagena
(WBA Flyweight Title Defence)
26.03.88 Dave McAuley W PTS 12 Belfast
(WBA Flyweight Title Defence)
Summary: 21 contests, won 20, drew 1.

Jackie Beard
Jackson, Tennessee, USA. *Born* 10.09.61
Former Undefeated NABF Featherweight Champion

25.04.81 Reyes Polanco W CO 2 Phoenix
11.06.81 Gilbert Favella W CO 2 Detroit
26.06.81 Dave Green W CO 1 Nashville
29.09.81 Robert Anderson W PTS 8 Phoenix

Jackie Beard
Peter Goldfield/USA

13.10.81 Mike Rodriguez W RSC 2 Phoenix
29.10.81 Jeff Long W CO 1 Plainfield
19.11.81 Sylvester Kennon W PTS 8 Detroit
03.12.81 Al Fowler W PTS 10 Jackson
17.12.81 Rafael Rodriguez W RSC 2 Phoenix
23.01.82 Manuel Santos W RSC 6 Detroit
11.02.82 Carlos Santana W RSC 2 Jackson
28.02.82 Reyes Gonzalez W RSC 5 Las Vegas
01.05.82 Jose Caba L PTS 10 Miami
22.06.82 Nicky Perez W RSC 7 Phoenix
(NABF Featherweight Title Challenge)
27.08.82 Joe Mayes W CO 2 Detroit
15.09.82 Ruben Moreno W RSC 6 New York
20.02.83 Bernabe Montanez W PTS 10 San Juan
25.04.83 Victor Flores W PTS 10 Chicago
15.07.83 Margarito Marquez W PTS 12 Las Vegas
(NABF Featherweight Title Defence)
19.11.83 Paul de Vorce W PTS 12 Las Vegas
(NABF Featherweight Title Defence)
18.01.84 Carlos Flores W RSC 5 Corpus Christi
31.05.84 Ray Garza W RSC 1 Detroit
18.07.84 Refugio Rojas W PTS 12 Las Vegas
(NABF Featherweight Title Defence)
27.10.84 Carlos Albuerne W PTS 10 Jackson
20.12.84 Paul Graham W PTS 10 Chicago
31.01.85 Paul Graham W RSC 6 Detroit
09.05.85 Anthony English W PTS 10 Atlantic City
15.02.86 Nedric Simmons W RSC 4 Montreal
10.07.86 Johnny de la Rosa L PTS 12 New York
(Con. Am. S. Featherweight Title Challenge)
08.01.87 Dennis Cruz L RTD 7 New York
18.06.87 Richie Otero W PTS 8 New York
09.07.87 Donnie Parker W RSC 9 New York
17.09.87 Angel Hernandez W RSC 4 New York
05.02.88 Ray Doughty W CO 1 Atlantic City
14.04.88 Pedro Montero W RSC 5 New York
Summary: 35 contests, won 32, lost 3.

Oscar (Negro) Bejinez
Guadalajara, Mexico. *Born* 05.12.63
S. Featherweight

07.05.79 Jorge Vera W CO 1 Guadalajara
.06.79 Arturo Mojica W CO 3 Guadalajara
22.06.79 Jorge Martinez W CO 1 Guadalajara
06.07.79 Jesus de la Cruz W RSC 3 Guadalajara
10.08.79 Efrain Rosas W RSC 2 Guadalajara
12.10.79 Jose Acosta L RSC 6 Guadalajara
15.02.80 Arturo Hernandez W RSC 4 Guadalajara
02.05.80 Enrique Romero W CO 1 Guadalajara
23.05.80 Juan Zarate W RSC 2 Guadalajara
20.06.80 Fermin Urisquieta W CO 7 Guadalajara
17.10.80 Victor Hernandez W CO 1 Guadalajara
21.11.80 Rosendo Alonso W CO 5 Guadalajara
20.12.80 Manuel Hong W RTD 6 Merida
22.02.81 Antonio de la Paz DREW 10 Merida
25.04.81 Ray Pelon Rodriguez W CO 5 Mexico City
01.08.81 Gustavo Garcia W CO 4 Los Angeles
20.08.81 Francisco Torregoza T DRAW 1 Los Angeles
08.10.81 Tony Guido W CO 3 Los Angeles
12.11.81 Herminio Adorno W CO 2 Los Angeles
17.12.81 Rodolfo Perez W PTS 10 Los Angeles
21.01.82 Jose Resendez W RSC 9 Los Angeles
05.03.82 Rodolfo Perez W PTS 10 Los Angeles
17.06.82 Gaby Cantera W RSC 7 Los Angeles
29.06.82 Ruben Moreno W CO 4 Los Angeles
12.08.82 Adrian Arreola W PTS 10 Los Angeles
09.12.82 Rocky Garcia W PTS 10 Los Angeles
02.06.83 Bobby Castillo W RSC 2 Los Angeles
25.08.83 Ruben Solorio W PTS 10 Los Angeles
17.05.84 Kelvin Lampkin W PTS 10 Los Angeles
14.06.84 Ruben Castillo L PTS 10 Los Angeles
27.09.84 Lupe Suarez L PTS 10 Corpus Christi
23.03.85 Martin Castro W RSC 2 Zapopan
18.04.85 Manuel Juarez W CO 4 Los Angeles
15.07.85 Santos Moreno W RSC 7 Tijuana
23.10.85 Jorge Ramirez W RSC 9 Tijuana
19.12.85 Mario Miranda W PTS 10 Los Angeles
05.05.86 Rafael Limon W RSC 4 Los Angeles
03.07.86 Roger Mayweather L RTD 8 Los Angeles
29.08.87 Andre Smith W RSC 7 Los Angeles
12.11.87 Ramon Marchena W RSC 3 Los Angeles
24.03.88 Mark Fernandez W CO 2 Los Angeles
Summary: 41 contests, won 35, drew 2, lost 4.

Vincenzo Belcastro
Fuscaldo, Italy. *Born* 02.02.61
EBU Bantamweight Champion. Former Italian Bantamweight Champion

29.12.84 Claudio Tanda W PTS 6 Casoria
27.04.85 German Nunez W PTS 6 Avellino
17.05.85 Alessandro de Santis L PTS 6 Marotta
04.06.85 Alessandro de Santis DREW 6 Genoa
13.09.85 Alessandro de Santis W PTS 6 Marotta
29.10.85 Thierry Jacob L PTS 6 Paris
26.12.85 Raso Tigan W RTD 2 Pavia
21.03.86 Jean-Paul Guillard W PTS 6 Pavia
08.05.86 Makaya Kotey W PTS 4 Salerno
02.08.86 Makaya Kotey W PTS 6 Postiglione
11.10.86 Maurizio Lupino W PTS 12 Cefalu
(Italian Bantamweight Title Challenge)
06.12.86 Maurizio Lupino W DIS 7 Lamezia
(Italian Bantamweight Title Defence)
27.02.87 Alessandro de Santis DREW 12 Villariccio
(Italian Bantamweight Title Defence)
02.06.87 Antonio Picardi L PTS 12 Casoria
(Italian Bantamweight Title Defence)
07.11.87 Ley Umba Sengi W PTS 8 Salerno
08.01.88 Bofungo Eymono W PTS 6 Casoria
05.03.88 Ley Umba Sengi W PTS 6 Pesaro
13.04.88 Fabrice Benichou W CO 3 Busalia
(EBU Bantamweight Title Challenge)
Summary: 18 contests, won 13, drew 2, lost 3.

Fernando (Guary) Beltran
Culiacan, Mexico. *Born* 29.07.61
Bantamweight

27.06.80 Francisco Aguilar W CO 6 Obregon
14.11.80 Marco Santos NC 3 Culiacan
20.03.81 Hector Narvaez W RSC 6 Culiacan
13.07.81 Hector Narvaez W CO 3 Tijuana
30.07.82 Oscar Burgos W CO 2 Culiacan
26.02.83 Tony Villegas W RSC 3 Culiacan
04.03.83 Roberto Dominguez DREW 10 Ensenada
22.04.83 Conrado Lopez W PTS 10 Navojoa
08.07.83 Manuel Lara W CO 6 Culiacan
01.10.83 Jorge de Jesus W PTS 10 Culiacan
04.05.84 Rodolfo Martinez W PTS 10 Culiacan
19.12.84 Zorrita Lopez W CO 5 Culiacan
08.03.85 Bobby Dominguez W CO 4 Culiacan
18.04.85 Jaime Polo W RSC 5 Los Angeles
13.09.85 Rigoberto Estrada L PTS 10 Juarez
04.02.86 Moises Martinez W CO 3 Tijuana
19.04.86 Antonio Gonzalez L CO 10 Tijuana
15.09.86 Fabrice Benichou W PTS 8 Paris
03.10.86 Haidar Nourredine W PTS 6 La Rochelle
07.11.86 Alain Limarola W PTS 8 Bordeaux
15.08.87 Edgar Roman W PTS 10 St Tropez
14.11.87 Arvel Campbell W RSC 3 Calais
06.02.88 Kelvin Seabrooks L RSC 2 Paris
(IBF Bantamweight Title Challenge)
Summary: 23 contests, won 18, drew 1, lost 3, nc 1.

Jesse Benavides
Peter Goldfield/USA

Jesse Benavides
Corpus Christi, Texas. *Born* 08.11.63
USBA S. Bantamweight Champion

27.09.84 Tommy Valdez W CO 1 Corpus Christi
14.11.84 Ray Espinoza W CO 2 Detroit
31.01.85 Bobby Adams W RSC 3 Detroit
08.02.85 Agustin Soberanes W PTS 4 Stateline
31.03.85 Adolfo Lopez W PTS 6 Laughlin
21.05.85 Rogelio Leanos W RSC 7 Corpus Christi
10.07.85 Pedro Rodriguez W PTS 8 Corpus Christi
25.09.85 Eddie Gonzales W RSC 2 Corpus Christi
24.10.85 Eddie Petty W RSC 3 Detroit
13.12.85 Juan Armienta W RSC 1 San Antonio
10.02.86 Eugenio Morgan W RSC 3 Laughlin
11.05.86 Gerardo Velasquez W CO 1 Corpus Christi
15.06.86 Alvaro Rosquero W CO 2 Corpus Christi
28.07.86 Tony Escobar W RSC 6 Phoenix
23.08.86 David Johnson W PTS 10 Corpus Christi
10.03.87 John Boyd W RSC 10 Corpus Christi
29.05.87 Hector Cortez W CO 5 Detroit
15.08.87 Arturo Tebaqui W RSC 3 San Antonio
25.09.87 Hugo Partida W RSC 4 Tucson
31.10.87 Mike Moreno W CO 4 Phoenix
20.11.87 Greg Richardson W PTS 12 Atlantic City
(*Vacant USBA S. Bantamweight Title*)
Summary: 21 contests, won 21.

Nigel Benn
John McDonald

Nigel Benn
West Ham, England. *Born* Ilford 22.01.64
Commonwealth Middleweight Champion

28.01.87 Graeme Ahmed W RSC 2 London
04.03.87 Kevin Roper W RSC 1 Basildon
22.04.87 Bob Niewenhuizen W RSC 1 London
09.05.87 Winston Burnett W RSC 4 London
17.06.87 Reggie Marks W RSC 1 London
01.07.87 Leon Morris W CO 1 London
09.08.87 Eddie Smith W CO 1 Windsor
16.09.87 Winston Burnett W RSC 3 London
13.10.87 Russell Barker W RSC 1 Windsor
03.11.87 Ronnie Yeo W RSC 1 London
24.11.87 Ian Chantler W CO 1 Wisbech
02.12.87 Reggie Miller W CO 7 London
27.01.88 Fermin Chirinos W CO 2 London
07.02.88 Byron Prince W RSC 2 Stafford
24.02.88 Greg Taylor W RSC 2 Aberavon
14.03.88 Darren Hobson W CO 1 Norwich
20.04.88 Abdul Amoru Sanda W RSC 2 London
(*Vacant Commonwealth Middleweight Title*)
Summary: 17 contests, won 17.

Trevor (The Preacher) Berbick
Miami, USA. *Born* Jamaica 01.08.53
Former WBC Heavyweight Champion. Former Undefeated Canadian, Commonwealth & USBA Heavyweight Champion

20.11.76 Wayne Martin W RSC 5 Shediac
07.12.76 Bobby Halpern W RSC 3 Halifax
09.01.77 Ace Lucas W CO 2 New Glasgow
25.01.77 Joe Maye W RSC 7 Halifax
18.08.77 William Moore W CO 4 Halifax
08.09.77 Eddie Owens W RSC 5 Halifax
08.12.77 Eugene Green W PTS 10 Halifax
28.06.78 Horst Geisler W RSC 1 Halifax
01.08.78 Tony Moore W RSC 5 Halifax
12.09.78 Greg Johnson W RSC 4 Halifax
08.10.78 Greg Sorrentino W RTD 7 Halifax
03.04.79 Bernardo Mercado L CO 1 Halifax
26.05.79 Earl McLeay W CO 7 Glace Bay
(*Vacant Canadian Heavyweight Title*)
14.06.79 Leroy Caldwell DREW 10 Winnipeg
11.12.79 Ngozika Ekwelum W RSC 4 Halifax
11.03.80 Johnny Warr W PTS 10 Halifax
20.06.80 John Tate W CO 9 Montreal
27.08.80 Ron Rousselle W CO 1 Edmonton
(*Canadian Heavyweight Title Defence*)
11.11.80 Chuck Findlay W CO 1 Halifax
(*Canadian Heavyweight Title Defence*)
31.01.81 Chuck Gardner W RSC 4 Kingston
11.04.81 Larry Holmes L PTS 15 Las Vegas
(*WBC Heavyweight Title Challenge*)
21.07.81 Conroy Nelson W RSC 2 Halifax
(*Canadian Heavyweight Title Defence & Vacant Commonwealth Heavyweight Title*)
11.12.81 Muhammad Ali W PTS 10 Nassau
05.03.82 Gordie Racette W RSC 11 Nandimo
(*Commonwealth & Canadian Heavyweight Title Defence*)
24.04.82 Leroy Caldwell W PTS 10 Las Vegas
11.06.82 Greg Page W PTS 10 Las Vegas
02.10.82 Renaldo Snipes L PTS 10 Atlantic City
28.05.83 S. T. Gordon L PTS 10 Las Vegas
09.09.83 Ken Lakusta W CO 10 Edmonton
(*Commonwealth & Canadian Heavyweight Title Defence*)
19.02.84 Mike Cohen W CO 4 Tampa
13.03.84 Mark Lee W PTS 10 London
01.09.84 Ernie Barr W RSC 4 Nassau
(*Commonwealth Heavyweight Title Defence*)
28.11.84 Walter Santemore W PTS 10 Atlantic City
15.06.85 David Bey W RSC 11 Las Vegas
(*USBA Heavyweight Title Challenge*)
10.08.85 Mitchell Green W PTS 12 Las Vegas
(*USBA Heavyweight Title Defence*)
17.01.86 Mike Perkins W RSC 10 Atlanta
22.03.86 Pinklon Thomas W PTS 12 Las Vegas
(*WBC Heavyweight Title Challenge*)
22.11.86 Mike Tyson L RSC 2 Las Vegas
(*WBC Heavyweight Title Defence*)
31.07.87 Art Terry W RSC 5 Fort Myers
29.10.87 Lorenzo Boyd W RSC 3 Sunrise
24.11.87 Robert Evans W PTS 10 Halifax
Summary: 41 contests, won 35, drew 1, lost 5.

Tyrell Biggs
Philadelphia, USA. *Born* 22.12.60
Heavyweight

15.11.84 Mike Evans W PTS 6 New York
20.04.85 Mike Perkins W RSC 1 Corpus Christi
17.05.85 Grady Daniels W RSC 2 Stateline
13.07.85 Eddie Richardson W RSC 3 Atlantic City
29.08.85 Sterling Benjamin W RSC 7 Atlanta
19.11.85 Danny Sutton W RSC 7 Metairie
21.12.85 Tony Anthony W CO 1 Virginia Beach
25.01.86 James Tillis W PTS 8 Lancaster
23.03.86 Jeff Sims W PTS 10 Reno
14.08.86 Rod Smith W RSC 6 New York
14.09.86 Percell Davis W PTS 10 Atlantic City
29.10.86 Robert Evans W RSC 5 London
12.12.86 Renaldo Snipes W PTS 10 New York
07.03.87 David Bey W RSC 6 Las Vegas
31.07.87 Lorenzo Boyd W RSC 3 Corpus Christi
16.10.87 Mike Tyson L RSC 7 Atlantic City
(*World Heavyweight Title Challenge*)
Summary: 16 contests, won 15, lost 1.

Alex Blanchard
Amsterdam, Holland. *Born* Surinam 03.01.58
Former EBU L. Heavyweight Champion. Former Undefeated Benelux L. Heavyweight Champion

08.01.79 Klaus Hein W CO 4 Rotterdam
07.03.79 Rainer Gutekunst W RTD 3 Rotterdam
26.03.79 Sonny Kamunga W PTS 6 Groningen
28.05.79 Jean-Luc Lami W CO 2 Amsterdam
05.11.79 Etienne Bayadikilla W RSC 4 Rotterdam
26.11.79 Josef Kossman W RTD 1 Rotterdam
28.01.80 Mike McCoy W CO 2 Rotterdam
31.03.80 Oscar Angus W RSC 2 Rotterdam
28.04.80 Billy Lauder W CO 4 Amsterdam
19.05.80 Michel Chapier W RSC 6 Rotterdam
13.06.80 Gregory Marshall W CO 2 Lubeck
01.09.80 Franz Dorfer W RSC 3 Rotterdam
29.09.80 Bonny McKenzie W PTS 8 Rotterdam
20.10.80 Michel Pagani W CO 1 Rotterdam
03.03.81 Jose Lozano W PTS 8 Rotterdam
15.03.81 Earl Edwards W RSC 4 The Hague
07.09.81 Doug Demming W RSC 6 Rotterdam
05.10.81 Andre Mongalema W RSC 5 Rotterdam
02.11.81 Ennio Cometti W RSC 6 Rotterdam
24.05.82 Rudy Robles W CO 6 Rotterdam
06.09.82 Hendrik Seys W RSC 2 Rotterdam
(*Benelux L. Heavyweight Title Challenge*)
15.11.82 Rudi Koopmans L RSC 8 Rotterdam
(*EBU L. Heavyweight Title Challenge*)
18.06.83 Jose Seys W RSC 10 Izegem
(*Benelux L. Heavyweight Title Defence*)
17.10.83 James Churn W CO 4 The Hague
18.11.83 Sergio Bosio W CO 3 Middlekerke

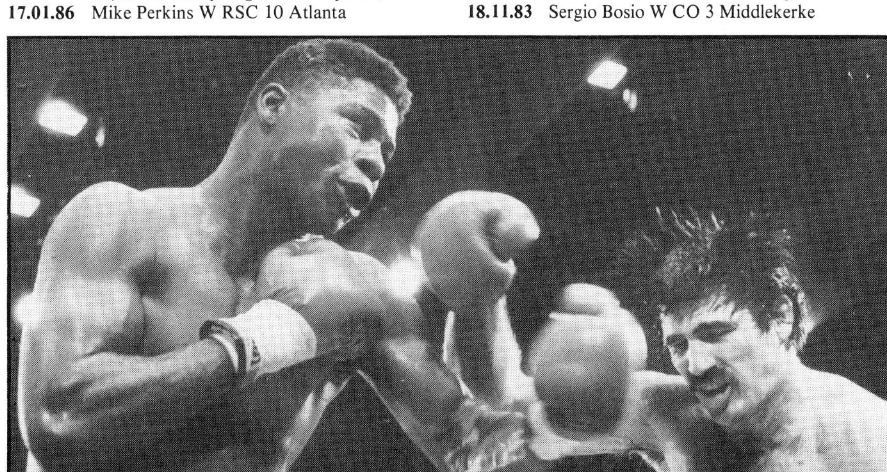

Tyrell Biggs (left) sets up Rod Smith for a sixth round stoppage win on 14 August 1986 Tom Casino

28.05.84 Richard Caramanolis W RSC 6 Amsterdam
(EBU L. Heavyweight Title Challenge)
15.09.84 Manfred Jassman W RTD 4 Dortmund
(EBU L. Heavyweight Title Defence)
11.02.85 Jerry Reddick W CO 2 Amsterdam
22.04.85 Richard Caramanolis DREW 12 Rotterdam
(EBU L. Heavyweight Title Defence)
11.12.85 Dennis Andries DREW 12 London
(EBU L. Heavyweight Title Defence)
26.03.86 Tarmo Uusivirta DREW 10 Amsterdam
03.10.86 Ralf Rocchigiani W PTS 12 Berlin
(EBU L. Heavyweight Title Defence)
01.12.86 Tom Collins W PTS 10 Arnhem
23.07.87 Mwehu Beya W RSC 7 Paris
15.08.87 Enrico Scacchia W RSC 9 Berne
(EBU L. Heavyweight Title Defence)
11.11.87 Tom Collins L CO 2 Wembley
(EBU L. Heavyweight Title Defence)
14.03.88 James Shavers W PTS 8 Arnhem
Summary: 37 contests, won 32, drew 3, lost 2.

Rodolfo Blanco
Colombia
Former Undefeated Colombian L. Flyweight Champion

05.03.82 Jose Iriarte L PTS 4 Cartagena
20.03.82 Urbano Saltarin W CO 2 San Onofre
17.04.82 Arnold Velasquez L PTS 4 Cartagena
11.03.83 Manuel Ariza L PTS 4 Sincelejo
16.06.83 Jaime Paternina W PTS 6 Sincelejo
30.07.83 Manuel Julio W RSC 5 Sincelejo
16.09.83 Nelson Polanco W PTS 8 Sincelejo
11.03.84 Leonardo Paredes W PTS 10 Barranquilla
27.07.84 Agustin Garcia L PTS 10 Cartagena
(Colombian L. Flyweight Title Challenge)
01.03.85 Elvis Alvarez W PTS 8 Barranquilla
21.03.85 Jose Iriarte W CO 3 Barranquilla
21.06.85 Arnold Velasquez W CO 5 Barranquilla
30.08.85 Alfredo Cardales W RSC 5 Barranquilla
27.09.85 Benedicto Murillo DREW 10 Barranquilla
18.10.85 Joselo Perez W RSC 4 Cartagena
31.01.86 Agustin Garcia W PTS 10 Cartagena
(Colombian L. Flyweight Title Challenge)
20.03.86 Felix Berrios W CO 2 Barranquilla
30.04.86 Hermogenes Murillo W PTS 10 Barranquilla
21.06.86 Rafael Julio W PTS 8 San Onofre
04.04.87 Alfredo Gomez W RSC 3 San Andres
19.06.87 Rafael Ramos W RSC 3 Barranquilla
20.09.87 Myung-Woo Yuh L CO 8 Inchon
(WBA L. Flyweight Title Challenge)
04.03.88 Jose Iriarte W RSC 2 Santa Marta
25.03.88 Eduardo Tunon W CO 2 Barranquilla
Summary: 24 contests, won 18, drew 1, lost 5.

Rolando Bohol
Himalayan, Philippines. *Born* 25.12.66
IBF Flyweight Champion

18.01.84 Bert Baco DREW 4 Paranaque
29.02.84 Ely Tabucol W RSC 2 Paranaque
21.03.84 Moirby Evasco W PTS 4 Paranaque
04.04.84 Ruben Portugues W PTS 4 Paranaque
02.05.84 Danny Duran W PTS 6 Paranaque
30.05.84 Bert Baco W PTS 6 Paranaque
11.07.84 John Calanogan W PTS 6 Paranaque
01.08.84 Jun Villacerna W RSC 2 Sucat
26.08.84 Junior Capino W PTS 8 Paranaque
17.10.84 Joel Advincula W PTS 8 Paranaque
14.11.84 Ric Bajelot DREW 8 Paranaque
16.01.85 John Calanogan W PTS 8 Paranaque
06.03.85 Cecilio Tutor W PTS 10 Paranaque
19.04.85 Henry Balina W PTS 10 Paranaque
03.07.85 Dommy Ursua W PTS 10 Paranaque
29.09.85 Dadoy Andujar L PTS 10 Santos City
30.10.85 Paul Torres W PTS 10 Paranaque
05.02.86 Titino Dignos W PTS 10 Paranaque
16.04.86 Ric Santiago W RSC 7 Paranaque
05.07.86 Rey Cogonon W PTS 10 Manila
20.07.86 Chun Huh L PTS 10 Sokcho
10.09.86 Allan Makitoki W PTS 10 Paranaque
15.11.86 Manasseh Base W PTS 10 Paranaque
20.02.87 Faustino Simbajon W PTS 10 Paranaque
18.05.87 Ademar Amad W PTS 10 Manila
30.08.87 Rod Naiconi W PTS 10 Paranaque
16.01.88 Chang-Ho Choi W PTS 15 Manila
(IBF Flyweight Title Challenge)
Summary: 27 contests, won 23, drew 2, lost 2.

Salvatore Bottiglieri
Naples, Italy. *Born* 30.01.60
WBC International Featherweight Champion. Former Undefeated Italian Featherweight Champion

11.02.82 Antonio Pocai W RSC 2 Naples
19.02.82 Eloi da Sylva W PTS 6 Naples
11.04.82 David Mahmutovic W CO 1 Ischia
14.05.82 Luciano Frasca W RTD 2 Naples
29.05.82 Andrea Ricci W PTS 4 Milan
08.08.82 Antonio Franca W RTD 4 Camerota
06.10.82 Museta Bingunia W PTS 6 Gragnano
29.12.82 Jofre II W PTS 8 Amalfi
24.02.83 Andrea Ricci W PTS 6 Bologna
19.03.83 Luis de la Sagra W RSC 4 Naples
24.04.83 Carlo Compiani W RTD 1 San Remo
24.07.83 Luciano Frasca L DIS 1 Rome
21.09.83 Jose Luis Vicho L PTS 8 Caserta
22.10.83 Pasquale Mazza W PTS 8 St Vincent
03.03.84 Salvatore Melluzzo W RSC 10 Riva Garda
(Italian Featherweight Title Challenge)
10.06.84 Pasquale Mazza W PTS 12 San Giuseppe
(Italian Featherweight Title Defence)
28.09.84 Salvatore Melluzzo W RSC 12 Vietri
(Italian Featherweight Title Defence)
27.03.85 Joseph Sekisambu W PTS 6 Nocera
06.07.85 Santiago Machin W PTS 6 Lerici
31.10.85 Joseph Sekisambu W PTS 8 Viterbo
08.02.86 Vicente Jorge W PTS 8 Eboli
19.07.86 Jim McDonnell L PTS 12 Wembley
(EBU Featherweight Title Challenge)
06.09.86 Ley Umba Sengi W PTS 6 Naples
21.11.86 Carlo Quintano W PTS 12 Campione
(Vacant Italian Featherweight Title)
22.03.87 Osmar Avila W RSC 7 Ischia
(Vacant WBC International Featherweight Title)
15.07.87 Alvaro Bohorquez W PTS 12 Capo D'Orlando
(WBC International Featherweight Title Defence)
09.04.88 Alvaro Bohorquez W PTS 12 Casigno
(WBC International Featherweight Title Defence)
Summary: 27 contests, won 24, lost 3.

Kamel Bou Ali
Somrane, Tunisia. *Born* 06.12.58
S. Featherweight

15.12.77 Angelo Emili W PTS 4 Bologna
13.07.79 Daniel Passeyrand W RSC 3 Valence
23.02.81 Pasquale Mazza DREW 6 Rome
09.03.81 Michel Siracusa W RSC 5 Rome
07.05.82 Hugo Carrizo W RSC 1 Bologna
02.06.82 Richard Saka W RSC 1 Chianciano
04.08.82 Tanio II W RSC 5 Rimini
08.10.82 Simadilu Lubaki W RSC 3 Rimini
17.03.83 Sammy Meck W RSC 6 Capo Orlando
05.11.83 Isidoro Cabeza W PTS 10 Tunis
13.01.84 Marcial Santiago W PTS 8 Riva del Garda
22.02.84 Roberto Pineiro W RSC 6 Milan
17.03.84 Robert Mullins W CO 2 Tunis
13.04.84 Hector Cortes W DIS 10 Milan
12.06.84 Angel Mendiola W RSC 4 Anchorage
29.07.84 Roberto Castanon W RSC 2 Milan
05.09.84 Victor Acosta W PTS 10 Tunis
17.11.84 Alfredo Layne W DIS 6 Riva del Garda
27.01.85 Rocky Lockridge L RSC 6 Riva del Garda
(WBA S. Featherweight Title Challenge)
13.12.85 Trevor Evelyn W RSC 5 Cesena
01.03.86 Paul Graham W CO 6 Tunis
28.11.86 Carlos Rodriguez W CO 2 Abano Terme
19.12.86 Sam Johnson W DIS 3 Ancona
30.12.86 Kamel Djadda W PTS 8 Cagliari
13.03.87 Idabeth Rojas W RSC 2 Forli
11.04.87 Ray Doughty W RSC 6 Bologna
22.05.87 Jose Vasquez W RTD 5 Jesi
24.07.87 Troy Davis W RSC 1 Silvi Marina
25.09.87 Richie Fowler W RSC 2 Quarto St Eleno
28.11.87 Luis Rodriguez W CO 2 Oristano
11.12.87 Gil Maldonado W CO 3 Livorno
27.02.88 Julio Gonzalez W CO 1 San Juan
10.04.88 Rafael Gandarilla W PTS 8 Iglesias
22.04.88 Jose Mosqueda W DIS 3 Milan
Summary: 34 contests, won 32, drew 1, lost 1.

Donovan Boucher
Toronto, Canada. *Born* Jamaica 1962
Canadian Welterweight Champion

15.08.85 Zest Holmes W PTS 6 Sarnia
19.09.85 Marco Carella W CO 1 Toronto
16.11.85 John Shepherd W PTS 6 Reno
19.12.85 Terry Francis W PTS 6 Ottowa
10.02.86 Ray Green W CO 1 Toronto
27.03.86 Benoit Boudreau W PTS 6 Dartmouth
08.06.86 Jim Sudberry W PTS 6 Toronto
25.08.86 Cortez Treadwell W PTS 8 Toronto
30.09.86 Gerry Meekison W PTS 8 Halifax
10.11.86 Chris Clarke L PTS 10 Halifax
27.01.87 Ira Hathaway W PTS 6 Toronto
10.02.87 Dennis Sigouin W PTS 10 Montreal
16.03.87 Robin Smith W RSC 4 Toronto
22.04.87 Jacques de Blois W RSC 2 Toronto
30.04.87 Arnie Wells W RSC 6 Detroit
07.07.87 Danny Winters W CO 7 Halifax
(Vacant Canadian Welterweight Title)
19.11.87 Wayne Gordon W RSC 11 Windsor
(Canadian Welterweight Title Defence)
25.03.88 Shawn O'Sullivan W RSC 2 Toronto
(Canadian Welterweight Title Defence)
Summary: 18 contests, won 17, lost 1.

Vince (Slim) Boulware
Harrisburg, USA. *Born* 03.09.63
S. Middleweight

07.12.84 Curtis Taylor W PTS 4 Houston
18.01.85 Jack Lucious W RSC 2 Houston
17.02.85 Ed Estrada W RSC 6 Houston
01.03.85 Greg Haley W RSC 2 Atlantic City
09.04.85 David Franklin W RSC 2 Houston
07.08.85 Tony Harrell W RSC 2 Houston
23.08.85 Dave Barrows W PTS 6 Atlantic City
11.09.85 Eric Williams W RSC 5 Houston
01.10.85 Lloyd Richardson W RSC 3 Harrisburg
13.11.85 Don Varnado W RSC 4 Houston
11.12.85 Tony Harrison W RSC 8 Houston
28.02.86 Khalid Shabazz W RSC 1 Atlantic City
12.03.86 Tommy Smith W CO 1 Houston
29.05.86 Orlando Paulding L CO 1 Houston
07.08.86 James Greene W RSC 2 Houston
11.09.86 Louis Coleman W RSC 2 Houston
13.11.86 Ronald Martin W CO 2 Houston
12.02.87 Everett Martin W PTS 12 Houston
12.11.87 Matt Brooks W RSC 8 Houston
18.12.87 Stacy McSwain W PTS 10 Hallandale
12.03.88 Graciano Rocchigiani L RSC 8 Dusseldorf
(Vacant IBF S. Middleweight Title)
Summary: 21 contests, won 19, lost 2.

Cornelius Boza-Edwards
USA. *Born* Uganda 27.05.56.
Former WBC S. Featherweight Champion. Former Undefeated EBU S. Featherweight Champion

13.12.76 Barry Price W CO 6 London
20.12.76 Paul Clemit W RSC 3 London
25.01.77 Tommy Wright W RSC 1 London
01.02.77 Danny Connolly W RSC 2 London
14.02.77 George McGurk W RSC 1 London
16.03.77 Godfrey Butler W CO 2 Solihull
18.04.77 Billy Vivian W CO 1 London
31.05.77 Tommy Glencross W RSC 2 London
14.06.77 Mario Oliveira W RSC 2 Wembley
27.09.77 Des Gwilliam L RSC 6 Wembley
08.11.77 Bingo Crooks W PTS 8 Wembley
06.12.77 Dil Collins W CO 5 London
21.02.78 Carlos Foldes W DIS 5 London
19.07.78 Ethem Ozekalin W RSC 3 Bellaria
26.09.78 George Feeney W PTS 8 Wembley
04.11.78 Godfrey Mwamba W CO 3 Lusaka
18.12.78 Georges Cotin W RSC 1 London
13.01.79 Frank Moultry W PTS 8 Miami
04.03.79 Nino Jiminez W PTS 8 San Remo
31.03.79 Godfrey Mwamba W RSC 2 Lusaka
24.06.79 Fernando Gimenez W RTD 5 Monte Carlo
03.11.79 Jose Gonzales W CO 3 Glasgow
16.03.80 Fili Ramirez W RSC 7 Las Vegas
01.04.80 Jimmy Washington W RSC 2 Wembley
22.04.80 Benny Marques W RSC 4 London
07.06.80 Jerome Artis W RSC 3 Glasgow
28.06.80 Ron Green W RSC 6 Wembley
12.07.80 Manuel Velasquez W RSC 3 Wembley
09.08.80 Alexis Arguello L RTD 8 Atlantic City

14.10.80 Roberto Torres W RSC 2 London
28.11.80 Roman Contreras W PTS 10 San Diego
08.03.81 Rafael Limon W PTS 15 Stockton
(WBC S. Featherweight Title Challenge)
30.05.81 Bobby Chacon W RTD 13 Las Vegas
(WBC S. Featherweight Title Defence)
29.08.81 Rolando Navarrete L CO 5 Via Reggio
(WBC S. Featherweight Title Defence)
24.11.81 Santiago Alvarez W RSC 3 Wembley
09.02.82 Arturo Leon W RTD 4 London
17.03.82 Carlos Hernandez W RTD 4 London
(EBU S. Featherweight Title Challenge)
24.04.82 Johnny Verderosa W RSC 3 Atlantic City
26.06.82 Robert Elizondo W PTS 10 Las Vegas
09.10.82 Blaine Dickson W PTS 10 Las Vegas
27.02.83 Pedro Laza W RSC 9 Las Vegas
15.05.83 Bobby Chacon L PTS 12 Las Vegas
09.09.83 Rocky Lockridge L PTS 10 Las Vegas
19.02.84 Trevor Evelyn W RSC 2 Tampa
17.06.84 Guy Villegas W RSC 7 Tampa
13.10.84 Charlie Choo Choo Brown W RSC 3 Belfast
17.03.85 Gary Gamble W RSC 4 Tampa
14.04.85 Melvin Paul W CO 2 London
14.07.85 John Montes W PTS 10 Tampa
30.03.86 Terrence Alli DREW 10 Las Vegas
26.09.86 Hector Camacho L PTS 12 Miami
(WBC Lightweight Title Challenge)
09.07.87 Ali Karim Muhammad W PTS 10 New York
10.10.87 Jose Luis Ramirez L CO 5 Paris
(WBC Lightweight Title Challenge)
Summary: 53 contests, won 45, drew 1, lost 7.

Livingstone Bramble
New Jersey, USA. *Born* St Croix 03.03.60
Former WBA Lightweight Champion

16.10.80 Jesus Serrano W RSC 1 Totowa
04.12.80 Bruce Williams DREW 4 Atlantic City
19.01.81 Jesus Serrano W PTS 6 Atlantic City
18.03.81 Jorge Nina W DIS 2 Totowa
16.04.81 Andre Jimenez W CO 2 Totowa
21.05.81 John Byrd W RSC 4 Totowa
04.06.81 Ken Bogner W RSC 7 Atlantic City
20.08.81 Quadir Hart W RSC 1 Totowa
31.08.81 Anthony Fletcher L PTS 8 Atlantic City
08.10.81 Alejandro Arias W PTS 8 Totowa
19.01.82 Jerome Artis W PTS 10 Atlantic City
19.04.82 Emilio Diaz W RSC 1 Atlantic City
03.07.82 Manuel Madera W RSC 4 Totowa
22.08.82 Miguel Meza W RSC 4 McAfee
27.10.82 James Busceme W PTS 10 Atlantic City
22.01.83 Romeo Sandoval W RSC 9 Atlantic City
23.02.83 Teddy Hatfield W RSC 7 Totowa
26.04.83 Gaetan Hart W PTS 10 Atlantic City
13.09.83 Juan Hernandez W RSC 5 Atlantic City
23.11.83 Tom Crowley W RSC 5 Atlantic City
15.12.83 Lorenzo Guzman W CO 2 Totowa
22.01.84 Rafael Williams W PTS 10 Atlantic City
01.06.84 Ray Mancini W RSC 14 Buffalo
(WBA Lightweight Title Challenge)
24.10.84 Edwin Curet W PTS 10 Atlantic City
16.02.85 Ray Mancini W PTS 15 Reno
(WBA Lightweight Title Defence)
16.02.86 Tyrone Crawley W RSC 13 Reno
(WBA Lightweight Title Defence)
26.09.86 Edwin Rosario L CO 2 Miami
(WBA Lightweight Title Defence)
03.04.87 Fred Pendleton DREW 10 Atlantic City
15.06.87 John Kalbhenn W RSC 5 Atlantic City
30.03.88 Edwin Curet W RSC 8 Atlantic City
Summary: 30 contests, won 26, drew 2, lost 2.

Harold Brazier
South Bend, USA. *Born* 22.10.55
NABF L. Welterweight Champion

18.05.82 Lester Groves W PTS 6 Memphis
24.06.82 Tim Hall W RSC 3 Indianapolis
08.07.82 Chris Mazzola L PTS 4 Atlantic City
17.07.82 Joe Silverberg W PTS 6 Frankfort
20.08.82 Tom Tarantino W RSC 4 Chicago
25.08.82 Mike Essett W PTS 4 Indianapolis
11.09.82 Billy Collins L PTS 6 Atlantic City
20.09.82 Dave Martin W RSC 8 Toronto
28.09.82 Pete Podgurski W PTS 6 Merriville
13.10.82 Emil Gottardo W RSC 3 Chicago
08.11.82 Toby Tyler W RSC 4 St Paul
04.02.83 Gil Miconda W RSC 3 Meridan

Harrold Brazier
Peter Goldfield/USA

11.02.83 Brian Anderson W PTS 6 Winnipeg
03.03.83 Jeff Gettemey W RSC 3 Hammond
16.03.83 Cesar Guzman W PTS 6 Atlantic City
14.05.83 Ken Saale W RSC 4 St Ann
21.06.83 Mario Cusson L PTS 8 Montreal
25.07.83 Andre Martinez W CO 2 St Paul
06.08.83 Kel Robin L PTS 8 Tampa
24.10.83 Lloyd Honeyghan L PTS 10 London
28.11.83 Brian Baronet L PTS 10 Durban
10.01.84 Tom Lally W CO 3 Highland
07.02.84 Grover Washington W PTS 6 Highland
13.03.84 Tony Taylor W CO 5 Highland
10.04.84 Curtis Gholston W PTS 6 Highland
08.05.84 Kent Acuff W RSC 4 Highland
16.05.84 Tony Taylor W PTS 6 Fort Wayne
12.06.84 Henry Mobley W PTS 6 Highland
13.07.84 Ken Larson W RSC 2 Michigan City
24.07.84 Kenny Heflin W PTS 10 Birmingham
21.08.84 Santos Rodriguez W RSC 2 South Bend
13.12.84 Anthony Travis W CO 1 Merrillville
11.01.85 Mike Essett W PTS 10 Hammond
11.03.85 Ron Chambers W PTS 10 South Bend
20.03.85 Charlie Brown W RSC 8 Lake Tahoe
16.04.85 Mike Willis W RSC 1 Highland
10.06.85 Danny Miller W CO 6 South Bend
25.06.85 Roosevelt Jones W CO 6 Birmingham
17.10.85 Joey Ruiz W PTS 10 Merrillville
01.11.85 Rocky Trampler W CO 4 Louisville
09.02.86 Ken Snider W RSC 5 Indianapolis
11.05.86 Meldrick Taylor L PTS 10 Corpus Christi
27.06.86 Ozzie O'Neal W RSC 10 French Lick
01.08.86 Willie McIntosh W CO 3 Laporte
05.09.86 John Meekins T DRAW 2 Atlantic City
(Vacant NABF L. Welterweight Title)
31.10.86 Brian Baronet W RSC 10 Atlantic City
(Vacant NABF L. Welterweight Title)
24.01.87 Bobby Brown W CO 6 Springfield
09.02.87 Ray Myers W CO 2 Bowling Green
24.02.87 John Meekins W PTS 12 Atlantic City
(NABF L. Welterweight Title Defence)
14.03.87 Jimmy Baker W RTD 6 Columbus
31.03.87 Billy Wills W CO 3 Richmond
17.04.87 Roosevelt Jones W RSC 4 Springfield
16.05.87 Jose Martinez W RSC 4 Hammond
12.06.87 Donnie Marshall W CO 5 Lincoln
09.07.87 Willie Barnes W RSC 8 Louisville
28.07.87 Leroy Jones W RSC 6 Lexington
31.07.87 Dave Reynolds W PTS 8 Fort Knox
26.09.87 Jorge Acosta W RSC 5 Lowell
05.11.87 Rafael Sanchez W CO 2 Indianapolis
05.12.87 Ray Sparks W CO 3 Davenport
28.01.88 Willie Ray W RSC 4 Omaha
04.03.88 Robin Blake W RSC 9 Las Vegas
(NABF L. Welterweight Title Defence)
12.04.88 Billy Moore W CO 2 Springfield
Summary: 63 contests, won 55, drew 1, lost 7.

Mark Breland
Brooklyn, USA. *Born* 11.05.63
Former WBA Welterweight Champion

15.11.84 Dwight Williams W PTS 6 New York
05.01.85 Marlon Palmer W PTS 6 Atlantic City
06.04.85 Steve Little W PTS 6 San Angelo
17.05.85 Vince Dunfee W RSC 2 Stateline
19.06.85 Dario de Jesus W RSC 2 Totowa
20.07.85 Don Shiver W RSC 1 Norfolk
18.10.85 Donald Gwinn W RSC 2 New York
21.12.85 Hedgemon Robertson W PTS 8 Virginia Beach
25.01.86 Troy Wortham W PTS 10 Lancaster
02.03.86 Richard Aguirre W CO 1 Lancaster
12.04.86 Darryl Anthony W RSC 3 Totowa
15.05.86 Ricardo Avendano W CO 1 New York
21.06.86 John Munduga W CO 6 Atlantic City
14.09.86 Reggie Miller W RSC 2 Atlantic City
15.10.86 Ralph Twinning W RSC 2 Columbia
13.11.86 Orlando Orozco W RSC 2 New York
06.02.87 Harold Volbrecht W CO 7 Atlantic City
(Vacant WBA Welterweight Title)
10.07.87 Juan Rondon W PTS 10 Santa Margherita
22.08.87 Marlon Starling L CO 11 Columbia
(WBA Welterweight Title Defence)
05.12.87 Javier Suazo W PTS 10 Atlantic City
05.02.88 Juan Villa W RSC 3 Atlantic City
16.04.88 Marlon Starling DREW 12 Las Vegas
(WBA Welterweight Title Challenge)
Summary: 22 contests, won 20, drew 1, lost 1.

Simon Brown
Washington, DC, USA. *Born* Jamaica 15.08.63
IBF Welterweight Champion

16.02.82 Rick Williams W PTS 4 Atlantic City
02.03.82 Vito Maselli W PTS 6 Atlantic City
10.04.82 Willie White W RSC 2 Atlantic City
27.04.82 Cookie James W RSC 5 Atlantic City
22.06.82 Cliff Lee W RSC 2 Atlantic City
18.07.82 Gene Ellington W RSC 1 Atlantic City
03.08.82 Carlos Santana W RSC 3 Atlantic City
23.08.82 Sergio Bautista W RSC 7 Atlantic City
05.10.82 George Burton W RSC 6 Atlantic City
09.11.82 Allen Braswell W CO 1 Atlantic City
14.12.82 Ruby Ortiz W CO 1 Washington
25.01.83 Ricardo Bryant W RSC 7 Atlantic City
15.03.83 Tom Moody W RSC 3 Atlantic City
26.04.83 Pete Seward W RSC 8 Atlantic City
04.06.83 Domingo Ayala W RSC 1 Atlantic City

Mark Breland (left) keeps his defences in order as Javier Suazo charges in. Mark won on points Tom Casino

01.11.83 Darryl Penn W PTS 10 Atlantic City
13.12.83 Robert Adams W PTS 10 Atlantic City
02.06.84 Clayton Hires W PTS 10 Washington
17.07.84 Jerome Johnson W PTS 10 Atlantic City
30.04.85 Martin Rojas W RSC 8 Atlantic City
23.07.85 Randy Mitchum W RSC 1 Washington
22.11.85 Marlon Starling L PTS 12 Atlantic City
(USBA Welterweight Title Challenge)
21.03.86 Kevin Howard W RSC 7 Washington
08.06.86 Shawn O'Sullivan W RSC 3 Toronto
25.09.87 Dexter Smith W RSC 6 Kingston
23.04.88 Tyrone Trice W RSC 14 Berck sur Mer
(Vacant IBF Welterweight Title)
Summary: 26 contests, won 25, lost 1.

Frank (Bomber) Bruno

Wandsworth, England. *Born* 16.11.61
Former Undefeated EBU Heavyweight Champion

17.03.82 Lupe Guerra W CO 1 London
30.03.82 Harvey Steichen W RSC 2 Wembley
20.04.82 Tom Stevenson W CO 1 London
04.05.82 Ron Gibbs W RSC 4 Wembley
01.06.82 Tony Moore W RSC 2 London
14.09.82 George Scott W RSC 1 Wembley
23.10.82 Ali Lukusa W CO 2 Berlin
09.11.82 Rudi Gauwe W CO 2 London
23.11.82 George Butzbach W RTD 1 Wembley
07.12.82 Gilberto Acuna W RSC 1 London
18.01.83 Stewart Lithgo W RTD 4 London
08.02.83 Peter Mulendwa W CO 3 London
01.03.83 Winston Allen W RSC 2 London
05.04.83 Eddie Neilson W RSC 3 London
03.05.83 Scott Ledoux W RSC 3 Wembley
31.05.83 Barry Funches W RSC 5 London
09.07.83 Mike Jameson W CO 2 Chicago
27.09.83 Bill Sharkey W CO 1 Wembley
11.10.83 Floyd Cummings W RSC 7 London
06.12.83 Walter Santemore W CO 4 London
13.03.84 Juan Figueroa W CO 1 Wembley
13.05.84 James Smith L CO 10 Wembley
25.09.84 Ken Lakusta W CO 2 Wembley
06.11.84 Jeff Jordan W RSC 3 London
27.11.84 Phil Brown W PTS 10 Wembley
26.03.85 Lucien Rodriguez W RSC 1 Wembley
01.10.85 Anders Eklund W CO 4 Wembley
(EBU Heavyweight Title Challenge)
04.12.85 Larry Frazier W CO 2 London
04.03.86 Gerrie Coetzee W CO 1 Wembley
19.07.86 Tim Witherspoon L RSC 11 Wembley
(WBA Heavyweight Title Challenge)
24.03.87 James Tillis W RSC 5 Wembley
27.06.87 Chuck Gardner W CO 1 Cannes
30.08.87 Reggie Gross W RSC 8 Marbella
24.10.87 Joe Bugner W RSC 8 London
Summary: 34 contests, won 32, lost 2.

Danilo Cabrera

Santiago, Dominican Republic. *Born* 23.09.63
Dominican S. Featherweight Champion. Former Dominican Featherweight Champion

14.03.83 Luis Ramos W CO 2 Santiago
25.04.83 Francisco Mieses W PTS 4 Santiago
10.05.83 Bernardo Zayas W RSC 5 Santiago
30.06.83 Luis Perez W RSC 1 Santiago
25.07.83 Efrain Lopez W CO 2 Santiago
20.08.83 Leopoldo Frias W PTS 8 Santiago
26.09.83 Jose Guerrero W RSC 3 Santiago
17.10.83 Antonio Rodriguez W RSC 4 Santiago
16.11.83 Emilio Hernandez W RSC 6 Santiago
07.12.83 Manuel Batista W PTS 10 Santiago
20.01.84 Manuel Garcia W CO 1 La Vega
06.02.84 Pascual Polanco W PTS 10 Santo Domingo
12.03.84 Jose de Jesus W RSC 4 Santiago
31.05.84 Manuel Batista L RSC 3 Santiago
19.06.84 Angel Rodriguez W RSC 3 Santiago
20.07.84 Bernabe Montanez W RSC 5 Carolina
15.09.84 Erskine Wade L PTS 10 Detroit
24.10.84 Ramon Santana W RSC 5 Santiago
07.12.84 Alberto Parra W PTS 10 Santo Domingo
23.02.85 Carlos Romero W PTS 10 Santo Domingo
23.03.85 Carlos Pinango W CO 8 Santo Domingo
25.05.85 Metralla Ramirez W RSC 2 Santiago
06.08.85 Rafael Arias W CO 3 Santiago
25.11.85 Jose Jimenez W PTS 12 Santiago
(Dominican Featherweight Title Challenge)
21.12.85 Radhames Bido W RSC 3 Mao
15.02.86 Barry McGuigan L RSC 14 Dublin
(WBA Featherweight Title Challenge)
22.06.86 Azumah Nelson L RSC 10 San Juan
(WBC Featherweight Title Challenge)
29.09.86 Antonio Rodriguez W RSC 4 Santo Domingo
(Dominican Featherweight Title Defence)
30.10.86 Alejandro Garcia W RSC 7 Santiago
18.12.86 Jose Bautista W RSC 2 Santiago
16.02.87 Roberto Nunez W CO 6 Santiago
(Dominican S. Featherweight Title Challenge)
14.03.87 Rafael Marichal W CO 2 Navarette
11.05.87 Jose Jimenez L PTS 12 Santiago
(Dominican Featherweight Title Defence)
08.06.87 Rafael Arias W CO 5 Santiago
21.08.87 Julio Cesar Chavez L PTS 12 Tijuana
(WBC S. Featherweight Title Challenge)
07.03.88 Francisco Diaz W PTS 12 Santiago
(Dominican S. Featherweight Title Defence)
Summary: 36 contests, won 30, lost 6.

Jack (Kid) Callahan

Indianapolis, USA
L. Middleweight

12.06.84 Jimmy McClean W RSC 4 Highland
28.06.84 Billy Doyle W RSC 2 Merrillville
10.07.84 Billy Evans W CO 2 Highland
16.08.84 George Reedy W RSC 3 Merrillville
18.09.84 Jim Farr W PTS 4 Highland
23.10.84 Bruce Strauss W PTS 6 Highland
08.11.84 Terry Jesmer W PTS 6 Indianapolis
20.11.84 John Bell W CO 2 Highland
04.12.84 George Randolph W CO 2 Birmingham
13.12.84 Floyd Smith W CO 1 Merrillville
11.01.85 Jeff Farr W RSC 3 Hammond
17.01.85 George Reedy W RSC 4 Merrillville
22.02.85 Pete Podgorski W PTS 6 Hammond
26.04.85 Skip Hansford W PTS 6 Hammond
28.05.85 Jesse Abrams W PTS 6 Merrillville
17.10.85 Frank Lux W PTS 6 Merrillville
03.12.85 Danny Miller W PTS 10 Highland
15.05.86 Mike Pollitt W PTS 10 Merrillville
22.07.86 Casey McGonigle W RSC 3 Highland
02.12.86 Brian Young W PTS 8 Highland
17.02.87 Jimmy Baker W PTS 12 Highland
26.03.87 Bob Sands W RSC 8 Fayettville
16.05.87 Raul Aguirre W RSC 2 South Bend
24.08.87 Terry Jesmer W PTS 8 Highland
16.10.87 Matthew Hilton L RTD 2 Atlantic City
(IBF L. Middleweight Title Challenge)
26.01.88 Larry Mayes W RSC 5 Highland
Summary: 26 contests, won 25, lost 1.

Victor (Luvy) Callejas

Guaynabo, Puerto Rico. *Born* 12.11.60
Former Undefeated WBA S. Bantamweight Champion

18.02.79 Jose Parrilla L PTS 4 San Juan
20.04.79 Jose Parrilla W PTS 6 St Croix
04.08.79 Wilt Jones W CO 1 St Martin
26.11.79 Albert Pagan W CO 3 St Martin
20.09.80 Noel Rivera W CO 2 San Juan
08.11.80 Pedro Garcia W RSC 2 Detroit
03.12.80 Ralph Ortiz W CO 1 St Martin
02.05.81 Milton Torres W RSC 2 Ponce
02.10.81 Victor Bultron W CO 4 Arroyo
21.11.81 Lazaro Fabian W RSC 3 San Juan
10.12.81 Juan Pimentel W CO 2 San Juan
31.03.82 Elvin Gonzalez W RSC 2 Rio Piedras
20.05.82 Carlos Alcibar W CO 3 San Juan
12.06.82 Felix Sagredo W CO 2 Miami
13.11.82 Vicente Garza W RSC 4 San Juan
15.12.82 Neil Rubio W RSC 3 Chicago
19.01.83 Manuel Santos W CO 2 San Juan
16.03.83 Jose Ortiz T DRAW 2 San Juan
07.05.83 Juan Bazan W CO 3 Guaynabo
15.02.84 Bernardo Checa W RSC 3 San Juan
26.05.84 Loris Stecca W RSC 8 Guaynabo
(WBA S. Bantamweight Title Challenge)
02.02.85 Seung-Hoon Lee W PTS 15 San Juan
(WBA S. Bantamweight Title Defence)
08.11.85 Loris Stecca W RTD 6 Rimini
(WBA S. Bantamweight Title Defence)
27.03.87 Cleo Garcia W PTS 10 San Juan
21.11.87 Pedro Nolasco W CO 1 Las Vegas
07.03.88 Jeff Fenech L RSC 10 Sydney
(Vacant WBC Featherweight Title)
Summary: 26 contests, won 23, drew 1, lost 2.

Hector (Macho) Camacho

New York, USA. *Born* Bayamon, Puerto Rico 24.05.62
Former Undefeated WBC & NABF Lightweight Champion. Former Undefeated WBC & NABF S. Featherweight Champion.

12.09.80 David Brown W PTS 4 New York
12.12.80 Benny Llanos W CO 1 New York
12.03.81 Herman Ingram W PTS 6 New York
27.03.81 Robert Johnson W CO 1 New York
24.04.81 Jerry Strickland W RSC 2 New York
02.05.81 Tomas Diaz W PTS 6 New York
16.05.81 Kato Ali W RSC 7 Kiamesha Lake
25.06.81 Marcial Santiago W PTS 8 New York
24.07.81 Jose Figueroa W CO 1 New York
16.09.81 Robert Mullins W RSC 6 New York
05.11.81 Tony Murray W PTS 10 New York
11.12.81 Blaine Dickson W PTS 12 New York
(NABF S. Featherweight Title Challenge)
15.02.82 Jorge Nina W PTS 8 New York
31.03.82 Rafael Lopez W RSC 3 New York
21.05.82 Refugio Rojas W RSC 1 New York
(NABF S. Featherweight Title Defence)
11.07.82 Louie Loi W RSC 7 New York
28.08.82 Johnny Sato W CO 4 Atlantic City
30.10.82 Melvin Paul W PTS 10 Atlantic City
20.11.82 Greg Coverson W PTS 10 Las Vegas
12.02.83 John Montes W CO 1 Anchorage
03.04.83 Irleis Perez W PTS 10 Phoenix
07.08.83 Rafael Limon W RSC 5 San Juan
(Vacant WBC S. Featherweight Title)
18.11.83 Rafael Solis W CO 5 San Juan
(WBC S. Featherweight Title Defence)
20.05.84 Rafael Williams W RSC 7 Corpus Christi
19.01.85 Louie Burke W RSC 5 Atlantic City
29.04.85 Roque Montoya W PTS 12 Buffalo
(Vacant NABF Lightweight Title)
10.08.85 Jose Luis Ramirez W PTS 12 Las Vegas
(WBC Lightweight Title Challenge)
18.12.85 Freddie Roach W PTS 10 Sacramento

Frank Bruno (right) moves in on the bulky Joe Bugner, prior to the finish John McDonald

Hector Camacho (left) made a successful defence of his WBC lightweight title against Edwin Rosario on 13 June 1986. He then beat Cornelius Boza-Edwards three months later, before handing the belt back Tom Casino

13.06.86 Edwin Rosario W PTS 12 New York (*WBC Lightweight Title Defence*)
26.09.86 Cornelius Boza-Edwards W PTS 12 Miami (*WBC Lightweight Title Defence*)
02.05.87 Howard Davis W PTS 10 Atlantic City
Summary: 31 contests, won 31.

Felipe (The Colton Comet) Canela
Los Angeles, USA. *Born* 03.11.61
Welterweight

08.02.80 Willie Hall W RSC 5 San Bernardino
22.02.80 Eric Bonilla W PTS 6 San Bernardino
07.03.80 Eric Bonilla T DRAW 2 San Bernardino
31.03.80 Eric Bonilla W CO 5 San Bernardino
02.05.80 Memo Arreola W PTS 6 San Bernardino
30.05.80 Eric Bonilla W RSC 5 San Bernardino
13.06.80 Alfredo Carranza W CO 7 San Bernardino
01.07.80 Henry Gill, W RSC 5 San Bernardino
06.11.80 Petrovillo Vasquez W RSC 5 Los Angeles
17.02.81 Carlos Bryant W RSC 3 Los Angeles
03.03.81 Eric Bonilla W RSC 5 Los Angeles
04.04.81 Barritos Hernandez W CO 3 Los Angeles
04.06.81 Rudy Hernandez W CO 9 Los Angeles
09.09.81 Reinaldo Rogue W RSC 6 Las Vegas
02.02.82 Tim Harris L PTS 12 Sacramento
03.06.82 Reinaldo Rogue W CO 6 San Bernardino
09.07.82 Eddie Nuno W PTS 10 San Bernardino
19.08.82 Jerry Cheatham W PTS 10 Las Vegas
21.10.82 Frankie Davis W PTS 10 Las Vegas
06.05.83 Hector Rivera W RSC 8 Chino
30.09.83 Hedgemon Robertson W RSC 11 Los Angeles
12.10.83 Victor Abraham W PTS 10 Los Angeles
05.03.84 Victor Abraham W PTS 10 Los Angeles
30.03.84 Nino la Rocca L PTS 10 Las Vegas
21.05.84 Derrick Kelly L PTS 10 Los Angeles
12.07.84 Luis Santana L PTS 10 Las Vegas
21.09.84 Glen Corbus DREW 12 San Jose
20.12.84 Derrick Kelly DREW 10 Los Angeles
16.05.85 Mitchell Julien L PTS 10 San Jose
27.05.86 Alfonso Long W RSC 8 Irvine
25.07.86 Richard Aguirre W CO 1 San Diego
04.09.86 Alfonso Long W PTS 10 San Jose
14.11.86 Charles Nwokolo W PTS 12 Universal City
05.02.87 Russell Mitchell L RTD 7 Riverside
07.07.87 Roman George W RSC 3 Los Angeles
01.10.87 Derwin Richards W PTS 10 Los Angeles
07.03.88 Derrick Kelly L PTS 12 Los Angeles
Summary: 37 contests, won 27, drew 3, lost 7.

Gaby Canizales
Laredo, USA. *Born* 01.05.60
Former WBA & USBA Bantamweight Champion

30.04.79 Jose Perez W CO 1 Monclova
07.05.79 Juanio Bernal W CO 1 Monclova
06.06.80 Polin Flores W CO 1 Laredo
15.06.80 Jose Salas W CO 2 Laredo
02.09.80 Miguel Meza W CO 2 Laredo
13.09.80 Oscar Gomez W CO 6 San Antonio
14.10.80 Memo Velazquez W CO 1 Laredo
05.12.80 Miguel Medina W CO 6 Corpus Christi
10.03.81 Cecilio Ostos W CO 1 Laredo
05.05.81 Mario Nava L PTS 10 Laredo
14.05.81 Calvin Sheppard W PTS 10 Dallas
15.06.81 Elias de Leon W CO 2 Laredo
27.06.81 Jorge Cruz W CO 1 Laredo
01.09.81 Francisco Bejines W RSC 2 Laredo
31.10.81 Mario Gomez W RSC 10 Laredo
02.12.81 Mario Nava W PTS 10 Laredo
11.02.81 Ed Bonilla W CO 2 Laredo
10.03.82 Juan Castellanos W PTS 12 Laredo
22.04.82 Ramon Guillen W CO 5 Laredo
16.05.82 Ricardo Varela W PTS 10 San Antonio
24.06.82 Diego Rosario W RSC 5 Atlantic City (*Vacant USBA Bantamweight Title*)
01.08.82 Jose Torres W PTS 10 San Antonio
22.09.82 Franco Torregoza W CO 10 Atlantic City (*USBA Bantamweight Title Defence*)
19.10.82 Jose L. Soto W CO 2 Laredo
23.11.82 Gustavo Martinez W CO 3 Laredo
13.03.83 Jeff Chandler L PTS 15 Atlantic City (*WBA Bantamweight Title Challenge*)
13.05.83 Ron Cisneros W RSC 10 Laredo (*USBA Bantamweight Title Defence*)
19.10.83 Norberto Castellanos W RSC 1 Laredo
12.11.83 James Pipps W RSC 6 Beaumont (*USBA Bantamweight Title Defence*)
07.02.84 Pedro Rodriguez W RSC 3 Houston
06.06.84 Javier Diaz W CO 2 San Antonio
25.08.84 Kelvin Seabrooks W PTS 12 Laredo (*USBA Bantamweight Title Defence*)
30.01.85 Jeff Whaley W PTS 10 Atlantic City
22.05.85 Troy Townsend W RSC 10 Atlantic City
10.03.86 Richard Sandoval W RSC 7 Las Vegas (*WBA Bantamweight Title Challenge*)
04.06.86 Bernardo Pinango L PTS 15 East Rutherford (*WBA Bantamweight Title Defence*)
11.12.86 Armando Morales W CO 2 Houston
30.01.87 Mauro Diaz W PTS 10 San Antonio
29.03.87 Mike Moreno W RSC 3 Tucson
05.05.87 Julio Blanco W PTS 10 San Antonio
06.07.87 Raul Perez L RSC 9 Tijuana
18.09.87 Alejandro Valenzuela W CO 3 Phoenix
27.11.87 Louis Curtis W PTS 12 Atlantic City (*Vacant USBA Bantamweight Title*)
25.03.88 Kenny Mitchell L PTS 12 Houston (*USBA Bantamweight Title Defence*)
Summary: 44 contests, won 39, lost 5.

Orlando Canizales

Orlando Canizales
Laredo, USA. *Born* 25.11.65
NABF Flyweight Champion. USBA S. Flyweight Champion

25.08.84 Juan Perez W RSC 2 Laredo
09.11.84 Rey Euresti W CO 1 San Antonio
05.03.85 Rogelio Leanos DREW 4 Houston
09.04.85 John Camaro W RSC 1 Houston
09.05.85 Nelson Garcia W RSC 1 Houston
26.07.85 Manuel Sago W RSC 2 Atlantic City
09.10.85 Roland Luna W RSC 1 Houston
18.10.85 Armando Quiroz W PTS 6 Laredo
20.11.85 Steve Whetstone W RSC 3 Houston
12.12.85 Jorge Fuentes W RSC 5 Houston
12.03.86 Timo Villaneuva W RSC 2 Houston
06.05.86 Javier Diaz W PTS 10 San Antonio
20.07.86 Paul Gonzales L PTS 12 Stateline (*NABF Flyweight Title Challenge*)
27.09.86 Juan Garcia W CO 1 Victoria
11.12.86 Jorge Vazquez W CO 2 Houston
30.01.87 Prudencio Cardona W RSC 6 San Antonio
20.02.87 Javier Lucas W RSC 9 San Jose
03.06.87 Alonzo Gonzalez W PTS 10 San Jose
25.09.87 Jose Olivares W CO 4 San Antonio
12.11.87 Armando Velasco W RSC 4 Houston (*Vacant NABF Flyweight Title*)
15.04.88 Louis Curtis W RSC 2 Atlantic City (*Vacant USBA S. Flyweight Title*)
Summary: 21 contests, won 19, drew 1, lost 1.

Jorge Cano
Yucatan, Mexico. *Born* 19.07.60
Former Mexican L. Flyweight Champion

27.01.78 Arsenio Euan W RSC 4 Uman
15.03.78 Fernando Chavez W PTS 4 Merida
05.04.78 Jorge Pech W PTS 4 Merida
02.11.78 Raul Armando L DIS 3 Cozumel
17.12.78 Jorge Cruz W PTS 8 Cozumel
11.04.79 Jorge Lopez W RSC 5 Merida
29.11.79 Eloy Cardenas W RSC 9 Merida
21.12.79 Eloy Cardenas W PTS 10 Chetumal
05.03.80 Arturo Gonzalez L RSC 8 Merida
18.05.80 Ramon Concha W RSC 6 Merida
31.07.82 Ben Martin W RSC 4 Can Cun
12.11.82 Raton Perez W PTS 10 Tuxtla
17.12.82 Jorge Gutierrez W PTS 10 Tuxtla
13.02.83 Miguel Juarez W RSC 10 Tuxtla
23.03.83 Margarito Narvaez W RSC 8 Merida
13.05.83 Javier Alonzo W PTS 10 Chetumal
17.06.83 Javier Varquez W TD 10 Chetumal
22.11.83 Alejandro Flores W RSC 4 Cordova
11.02.84 Finito Lopez W RSC 4 Merida
10.03.84 Jorge Tzuc W RSC 5 Campeche
07.04.84 Rafael Alonzo W PTS 10 Mexico City
11.08.84 Juan Herrera W PTS 10 Mexico City
29.09.84 Babe Luis W PTS 12 Merida (*Vacant Mexican L. Flyweight Title*)
30.11.84 Antoine Montero L RSC 9 Grenoble
02.03.85 Efren Pinto L PTS 12 Mexico City (*Mexican L. Flyweight Title Defence*)
08.04.85 Teraporn Saengano L PTS 10 Bangkok
18.08.85 German Torres W PTS 10 Mexico City
10.11.85 Jung-Koo Chang L PTS 12 Daejon (*WBC L. Flyweight Title Challenge*)
22.03.86 Emilio Santos W PTS 10 Mexico City (*Vacant Mexican L. Flyweight Title*)
24.05.86 Isidro Perez L PTS 12 Mexico City (*Mexican L. Flyweight Title Defence*)
29.11.86 Ruben Padilla W PTS 10 Merida
27.02.87 Emilio Santos W RSC 4 Acapulco (*Vacant Mexican L. Flyweight Title*)
25.04.87 Babe Luis W RSC 8 Mexico City (*Mexican L. Flyweight Title Defence*)
12.07.87 Yong-Kang Kim L PTS 10 Buchon
26.09.87 Humberto Gonzalez L PTS 12 Cancun (*Mexican L. Flyweight Title Defence*)
14.11.87 Rodolfo Alvarado W RSC 2 Merida
Summary: 36 contests, won 27, lost 9.

Richard Caramanolis
Marseilles, France. *Born* 07.03.58
French L. Heavyweight Champion. Former EBU L. Heavyweight Champion

29.02.80 Bojan Sverzina W PTS 6 Marseilles
21.03.80 Darko Barakovic W CO 1 Montpellier
18.04.80 Gabriel Lazzari W PTS 6 Paris
09.05.80 Bruno Arati W RSC 6 Marseilles

06.06.80 Jose Centa W RTD 3 Marseilles
04.10.80 Boyd Farrar W RTD 7 Marseilles
28.11.80 Maurice Trepant W PTS 8 Marseilles
30.01.81 Robert Desnouck W PTS 8 Marseilles
27.02.81 Ibelo Moano W PTS 8 Marseilles
03.04.81 Robert Powell W CO 1 Marseilles
21.04.81 Bonny McKenzie W PTS 8 Marseilles
19.06.81 Carlton Benoit W PTS 8 Marseilles
10.10.81 Trevor Cattouse W CO 2 Marseilles
23.10.81 Gino Freo W CO 5 Marseilles
11.12.81 Avenamar Peralta W CO 9 Marseilles
21.01.82 Alek Penarski W CO 1 Paris
19.02.82 John Cox W RTD 7 Marseilles
05.03.82 Pierre Kabassu W PTS 10 Nice
02.04.82 Eric Kopec W RSC 4 Marseilles
08.10.82 Dave Conteh W PTS 10 Marseilles
04.12.82 Fred Serres W PTS 10 Marseilles
10.02.83 Hocine Tafer W CO 6 Marseilles
(French L. Heavyweight Title Challenge)
29.04.83 Manuel Lira W CO 1 Aix
19.05.83 Cordwell Hylton W CO 4 Paris
10.10.83 Vedat Akova W RSC 5 Paris
02.02.84 Rudi Koopmans W RTD 8 Marseilles
(EBU L. Heavyweight Title Challenge)
28.05.84 Alex Blanchard L RSC 6 Amsterdam
(EBU L. Heavyweight Title Defence)
12.10.84 Sergio Bosio W RSC 2 Antibes
22.04.85 Alex Blanchard DREW 12 Rotterdam
(EBU L. Heavyweight Title Challenge)
14.07.85 Arthel Lawhorne DREW 7 Monte Carlo
21.02.86 Stuart Robinson W RTD 4 Marseilles
18.04.86 Pierre Kabassu W RTD 6 Marseilles
(French L. Heavyweight Title Defence)
30.05.86 Jean-Max Delnard W RSC 5 Avignon
(French L. Heavyweight Title Defence)
20.12.86 Lennie Howard W RSC 1 St Ouen
31.01.87 Jose Seys W RSC 4 Montpelier
16.04.87 Rufino Angulo L CO 2 Marseilles
(French L. Heavyweight Title Defence)
22.05.87 Jerry Brown W CO 1 La Seyne
21.11.87 Terry Walker W RSC 3 Paris
28.03.88 Rufino Angulo W RSC 4 Paris
(French L. Heavyweight Title Challenge)
Summary: 39 contests, won 35, drew 2, lost 2.

Juan Carazo
Caguas, Puerto Rico. *Born* 1964
S. Bantamweight

17.03.84 Marcos Claudia W RSC 2 San Juan
23.06.84 Israel Santiago W RSC 3 San Juan
08.12.84 Martin Lantigua W CO 1 San Juan
02.02.85 Julio Guerrero W PTS 8 Hato Rey
28.02.85 Jose Pena W CO 3 Santo Domingo
23.03.85 Fernando Mateo W CO 1 Santiago
18.11.85 Julio Osoro W RSC 2 Caguas
21.12.85 Edwin Calix W CO 2 Caguas
03.05.86 Tom Elston W RSC 5 Guaynabo
30.05.86 Jesus Bastardo W PTS 10 Curacao
12.09.86 Luis Navarro W RSC 3 Chicago
28.11.86 Jesus Bastardo W RSC 6 Curacao
14.03.87 Wilfredo Vasquez L CO 1 San Juan
30.07.87 William Ramos W PTS 10 San Juan
11.08.87 Jose Luis Vegagil W RSC 3 Chicago
20.11.87 Diego Avila W PTS 10 Chicago
09.04.88 Tim Silva W RSC 6 Las Vegas
Summary: 17 contests, won 16, lost 1.

Romolo Casamonica
Rome, Italy. *Born* 23.12.62
Former Undefeated Italian Welterweight Champion

05.01.85 Felix di Ciocco W PTS 6 Perugia
08.03.85 Alaoui Aziz W RSC 4 Caserta
29.03.85 Ngindola Engote W PTS 6 Rome
14.05.85 Moktar Djelassi W PTS 6 Rome
08.06.85 Ambrose Mendy W RSC 1 Castellar
29.06.85 Ngindola Engote W RTD 3 Bellaria
27.07.85 Moktar Djelassi W PTS 6 Carrara
12.10.85 Sinisa Popovich W PTS 6 Cesena
13.12.85 Giuseppe Mercuri W RSC 6 Cesena
22.02.86 Oronzo Oggiano W RSC 2 Montecatino
07.03.86 Rafael Fuentes W RTD 3 Rimini
30.05.86 Tanio II W RTD 2 Abano Terme
04.07.86 Hassen Maghraoui W RSC 4 Porlezza
13.08.86 Chaoachi Lofti W RSC 2 Sarzana
15.09.86 Pete Podgorski W RTD 2 Paris
10.10.86 Lee McKenzie W CO 1 Cesena
14.11.86 Ed Brinoles W CO 2 San Giuseppe

Romolo Casamonica

14.02.87 Frank Sheehan W RSC 2 Lucca
27.03.87 Sammy Young W RSC 4 Cagliari
22.04.87 Ricky Kaiser W CO 4 Catania
10.07.87 Lorenzo Giappone W RTD 10 San Margherita
(Vacant Italian Welterweight Title)
25.09.87 Harlein Holden W RSC 2 San Elena
17.10.87 Luciano Navarra W RTD 8 San Gavino
(Italian Welterweight Title Defence)
12.03.88 Tomas Garcia W PTS 8 Lerici
Summary: 24 contests, won 24.

Amancio Castro
Monteria, Colombia. *Born* 26.09.58
Former Fecarbox Lightweight Champion

27.06.79 Amalio Salgado W CO 4 Monteria
21.09.79 Latigo Montes W PTS 6 Monteria
27.10.79 Juan Cuello W PTS 8 Monteria
.80 Manuel Escamilla W PTS 10 Monteria
.80 Rocky Wilson DREW 10 Monteria
27.02.80 Fernando Ochoa W PTS 10 Monteria
10.06.80 Diego Ortiz W RSC 5 Monteria
21.09.80 Sergio Alvarez L PTS 10 Monteria
07.03.81 Sergio Alvarez W CO 10 Cartagena
24.04.81 Victor Pacheco W PTS 10 Monteria
15.01.82 Luis Godoy W RSC 6 Cartagena
(Fecarbox Lightweight Title Challenge)
20.08.82 Eduardo Valdez L PTS 12 Barranquilla
(Fecarbox Lightweight Title Defence)
26.03.83 Antonio Cervantes L PTS 12 Cartagena
(Fecarbox L. Welterweight Title Challenge)
20.08.83 Saul Julio L PTS 10 Cartagena
17.12.83 Saul Julio L PTS 8 Monteria
27.04.84 Jorge Alvarado NC 3 Panama City
05.07.84 Jorge Delgado L PTS 10 San Jose
31.05.86 Francisco Fernandez DREW 10 Panama City
18.11.86 Bartolo Perez W CO 1 Monteria
28.02.87 Francisco Martinez W CO 2 Miami
30.04.87 Jimmy Paul W RSC 2 Detroit
25.07.87 Nick Parker W RSC 5 Miami
27.11.87 Alfredo Layne W PTS 10 Miami
18.03.88 Billy Wooten W CO 7 Miami
Summary: 24 contests, won 15, drew 2, lost 6, nc 1.

Armando Castro
Mexico City, Mexico
Mexican S. Flyweight Champion

13.10.84 Antonio Escamilla W PTS 4 Mexico City
11.05.85 Esteban Ayala L DIS 1 Mexico City
20.07.85 Martin Villaneuva W PTS 4 Mexico City
20.09.85 Domingo Dominguez W RSC 2 Mexico City
10.10.85 Jesse Martinez W RSC 2 Nuevo Laredo
23.11.85 Fernando Hernandez W PTS 6 Mexico City
14.05.86 Pablo Gomez W RSC 1 Mexico City
17.05.86 Eduardo Ramirez L PTS 6 Mexico City
26.07.86 Aquilino Lopez W CO 4 Mexico City
12.11.86 Raul Quiroga W PTS 10 Mexico City
06.12.86 Oscar Ortiz W RSC 7 Mexico City
19.12.86 Ismael Benitez W CO 4 Acapulco
18.02.87 Oscar Ortiz W RSC 5 Mexico City
28.03.87 Fernando Varguez L PTS 10 Merida
17.04.87 Francisco Gonzalez L PTS 10 Cancun
11.07.87 Carlos de la Paz W RSC 1 Mexico City
08.08.87 Mijailo Hernandez W RSC 5 Mexico City
03.10.87 Victor Rabanales L RSC 1 Mexico City
14.11.87 Artemio Ruiz W CO 4 Mexico City
19.12.87 Jimmy Fernandez W RSC 5 Mexico City
(Mexican S. Flyweight Title Challenge)
13.02.88 Jose Montiel W RSC 4 Mexico City
Summary: 21 contests, won 16, lost 5.

Ernie Cataluna
Tapaz, Philippines. *Born* 18.08.60
Former OPBF Bantamweight Champion & Former Undefeated Philippines Bantamweight Champion

18.03.81 Raul Pipino W PTS 4 Ilocos
18.07.81 Fighting Cornejo W CO 3 Baguio
14.08.81 Alex So W PTS 6 Quezon City
03.10.81 Little Puncher DREW 6 Baguio
24.10.81 Joe Hiyas L PTS 8 Paranaque
20.11.81 Fel Cabrera W PTS 8 Dapitan
17.12.81 Amado Cabato DREW 8 Manila
27.03.82 Amado Cabato L PTS 8 Meycuayan
10.09.82 Audy Murphy W RSC 7 Quezon City
15.10.82 Larry Enriquez W PTS 8 Paranaque
26.11.82 Cris Cogono W PTS 6 Baguio
11.12.82 John Castro W PTS 10 Garmen
15.01.83 Jimmy Boy W RSC 7 Baguio
04.02.83 Fred Iglesias W PTS 10 Pasay
04.03.83 Amado Cabato DREW 10 Manila
25.03.83 Rico Lequin W PTS 10 Manila
30.05.83 Flash Emmanuel DREW 10 Manila
18.06.83 Audy Murphy W PTS 10 Baguio
19.11.83 Jun Arbas W PTS 10 Cagayan
03.02.84 Rene Brugada W RSC 8 Pasay
23.02.84 Dommy Circulado W PTS 10 Manila
30.03.84 Ernie Mata W RSC 8 Manila
(Vacant Philippines Bantamweight Title)
23.06.84 Celso Areglo W PTS 12 Baguio
(Philippines Bantamweight Title Defence)
15.08.84 Joe Hiyas T DRAW 9 Paranaque
04.11.84 Boy Abuela W PTS 10 Manila
04.12.84 Chan-Young Park L PTS 10 Seoul
15.03.85 Boy Blanca L RSC 10 Manila
(Philippines Bantamweight Title Defence)
03.05.85 Boy Abuela W RSC 2 Pasay
20.06.85 Boy Blanca W PTS 12 Manila
(Philippines Bantamweight Title Challenge)
02.10.85 Gil Ragas W RSC 2 Pasay
29.12.85 Flash Emmanuel W PTS 12 Gen Santos
(Philippines Bantamweight Title Defence)
05.04.86 Ki-Yul Kang L PTS 12 Masan
(OPBF Bantamweight Title Challenge)
16.07.86 Rodrigo Loferez W RSC 5 Ozamis
(Philippines Bantamweight Title Defence)
07.09.86 Sambung W PTS 10 Jember
08.02.87 Ki-Yul Kang W RSC 2 Masan
(OPBF Bantamweight Title Challenge)
09.10.87 Sam-Yong Kim DREW 10 Anyang
18.11.87 Kelvin Seabrooks L RSC 4 San Cataldo
(IBF Bantamweight Title Challenge)
19.12.87 Chun Huh L PTS 12 Chinju
(OPBF Bantamweight Title Defence)
Summary: 38 contests, won 25, drew 6, lost 7.

Herman Cavesuela
Watsonville, USA. *Born* 02.10.64
L. Middleweight

31.03.84 Edwin Keller W PTS 4 San Jose
14.04.84 Ruben Posadas W PTS 4 Carson City
13.07.84 Joe Lewis W RSC 1 San Jose
13.12.84 Clinton Reymus W PTS 4 Lake Tahoe
30.01.85 Frank White W PTS 6 San Jose
23.02.85 Joe Lewis W PTS 6 Carson City
16.03.85 Clinton Reymus L PTS 8 Tenopah
16.05.85 Joe Lewis W RSC 2 San Jose
29.06.85 Sam Sanchez W RSC 2 Salinas
05.07.85 Perry Levoe W RSC 1 Gardnerville
28.07.85 Sam Huston W PTS 8 Salinas
26.10.85 Darryl Penn W PTS 8 Lake Tahoe
25.01.86 Jake Torrance W PTS 8 Carson City
01.03.86 Carl Owens W CO 2 Carson City
28.03.86 Tom Covington W RSC 4 Stateline
04.07.86 Clinton Reymus W PTS 10 Gardnerville
23.07.86 Israel Cole L PTS 10 Watsonville
27.02.87 Ricky Locke W PTS 10 Pleasanton
21.03.87 Clive Chamberlain W PTS 10 Carson City

07.06.87 James Williams W CO 9 Monterey
16.06.87 Mardo Roybal W PTS 10 Reno
14.08.87 Fred Hutchings W PTS 10 Stockton
02.10.87 Ron Daniels W CO 2 Monterey
28.10.87 Milton McCrory L PTS 12 Las Vegas
(NABF L. Middleweight Title Challenge)
06.02.88 Kenny Lopez W PTS 10 Monterey
19.03.88 Charles Allen W RSC 7 Monterey
Summary: 26 contests, won 23, lost 3.

Frank Cedeno
Mohon, Philippines. *Born* 16.03.58
Former WBC Flyweight Champion. Former Undefeated Philippines Flyweight Champion

20.11.76 Rey de los Santos L PTS 8 Cebu City
05.01.77 Eduardo Dacuno DREW 8 Cagayan
29.01.77 Pete Alda W RSC 6 Cebu City
26.02.77 Rey de los Santos DREW 8 Cebu City
14.05.77 Angel Jonathan W RSC 8 Cebu City
18.06.77 Salvador Perez W PTS 10 Cebu City
23.07.77 Glen Orlanos L RSC 10 Cebu City
15.10.77 George Nunal W PTS 10 Cebu City
02.12.77 Peter Noble W PTS 10 Cebu City
01.04.78 Fred Villanueva W RSC 6 Cebu City
29.04.78 Gil Aguilar W RSC 8 Zamboanga
18.06.78 Henry Balinas W RSC 4 Manila
30.09.78 Little Aguilar W PTS 10 Caluagua
04.11.78 Brigildo Canada W RSC 7 Caluagua
30.11.78 Eric Blancia L PTS 10 Bukidnon
23.02.79 Franco Torregoza W PTS 10 Manila
20.04.79 Lino Boy Base W PTS 10 Manila
26.05.79 William Develos L PTS 10 Caluagua
15.06.79 Robinson Abato W PTS 10 Manila
09.07.79 Wilson Castillon W RSC 8 Iloilo
05.10.79 Pablo Pepito W PTS 10 Manila
23.12.79 Flash Jagdon W RSC 5 Cebu City
29.03.80 Melchor Degsi W PTS 12 Baguio
(Vacant Philippines Flyweight Title)
16.05.80 Arnel Arrozal W PTS 10 Manila
16.07.80 Siony Carupo W PTS 12 Paranaque
(Philippines Flyweight Title Defence)
17.09.80 Monsyram Mahachai W RSC 7 Pasay
29.11.80 Brigildo Canada W PTS 10 Davao
19.02.81 Lito Cortez W RSC 7 Manila
(Philippines Flyweight Title Defence)
02.05.81 Dan Pisalchai W PTS 10 Cebu City
04.07.81 Ric Diamale W PTS 10 Cebu City
20.12.81 Vel Libradilla W PTS 10 Baguio
23.01.82 Ramon Chan T DRAW 12 Baguio
(Philippines Flyweight Title Defence)
27.03.82 Chong-Chull Park W RSC 8 Pasay
27.06.82 Hong-Soo Yang L PTS 12 Wonjoo
(OPBF Flyweight Title Challenge)
14.08.82 William Develos L PTS 10 Paranaque
26.11.82 Chan-Soo Chung W PTS 10 Quezon City
21.01.83 Allen Makitoki W RSC 6 Manila
(Philippines Flyweight Title Defence)
18.03.83 Bobby Williams W RSC 4 Manila
03.07.83 Ok-Kyun Yuh W PTS 10 Seoul
27.09.83 Charlie Magri W RSC 6 London
(WBC Flyweight Title Challenge)
18.01.84 Koji Kobayashi L RSC 2 Tokyo
(WBC Flyweight Title Defence)
23.06.84 Nestor Miraflor W RSC 1 Baguio
16.11.84 Choong-Suk Kim W CO 7 Manila
01.03.85 Makoto Taguchi W RSC 3 Manila
11.04.85 Zaldy Adrayan W RSC 2 Cebu City
25.05.85 Lito Zarda W RSC 6 Baguio
19.07.85 Hugo Partida W PTS 10 Manila
06.10.85 Yeung-Yong Sithprasong W CO 5 Bangkok
20.12.85 Deo Ravalo W RSC 6 Cebu City
16.08.86 Fel Malatag W CO 7 Toledo
29.11.86 Flash Jordan W CO 2 Ozamis
19.03.87 Gilberto Roman L PTS 12 Mexicali
(WBC S. Flyweight Title Challenge)
14.12.87 Tanomsak Singboebae L PTS 10 Bangkok
27.03.88 Yung-Chun Min L TD 5 Seoul
Summary: 54 contests, won 41, drew 3, lost 10.

Jung-Koo (The Hawk) Chang
Pusan, South Korea. *Born* 04.02.63
WBC L. Flyweight Champion

17.11.80 Jong-Yul Suh W CO 3 Seoul
19.11.80 Jin-Hyong Park W CO 3 Seoul
22.11.80 Eu-Kwan Lee W PTS 4 Seoul
23.11.80 Ho-Chol Pyun W PTS 4 Seoul
29.11.80 Hi-Sup Shin W PTS 4 Seoul
09.12.80 Nam-Keun Kang W PTS 6 Seoul
11.01.81 Jin-Hyong Park W CO 2 Pusan
23.01.81 Chang-Pyo Hong W PTS 8 Pusan
29.03.81 Yo-Dong Kim W PTS 6 Pusan
25.04.81 Michael Bulka W PTS 10 Pusan
07.06.81 Oscar Bolivar W PTS 10 Daejon
04.09.81 Rod Esmero W PTS 10 Pusan
11.10.81 Leonardo Paredes W CO 6 Daejon
18.11.81 Chut Thairungriang W CO 2 Pusan
26.12.81 Alfonso Lopez W CO 3 Seoul
10.02.82 Jong-Kwan Chung W RSC 6 Taegu
04.04.82 Luk-Odd Phitiporn W CO 5 Pusan
06.06.82 Amado Ursua W PTS 10 Seoul
18.09.82 Hilario Zapata L PTS 15 Chonju
(WBC L. Flyweight Title Challenge)
05.12.82 Rodrigo Saonoy W PTS 10 Chungju
06.02.83 Tito Abella W CO 2 Chungju
26.03.83 Hilario Zapata W RSC 3 Daejon
(WBC L. Flyweight Title Challenge)
11.06.83 Masaharu Iha W RSC 2 Taegu
(WBC L. Flyweight Title Defence)
10.09.83 German Torres W PTS 12 Daejon
(WBC L. Flyweight Title Defence)
31.03.84 Sot Chitalada W PTS 12 Pusan
(WBC L. Flyweight Title Defence)
18.08.84 Katsuo Tokashiki W RSC 9 Pohang
(WBC L. Flyweight Title Defence)
15.12.84 Tadashi Kuramochi W PTS 12 Pusan
(WBC L. Flyweight Title Defence)
27.04.85 German Torres W PTS 12 Ulsan
(WBC L. Flyweight Title Defence)
03.08.85 Francisco Montiel W PTS 12 Seoul
(WBC L. Flyweight Title Defence)
10.11.85 Jorge Cano W PTS 12 Daejon
(WBC L. Flyweight Title Defence)
13.04.86 German Torres W PTS 12 Kwangju
(WBC L. Flyweight Title Defence)
13.09.86 Francisco Montiel W PTS 12 Seoul
(WBC L. Flyweight Title Defence)
14.12.86 Hideyuki Ohashi W RSC 5 Inchon
(WBC L. Flyweight Title Defence)
19.04.87 Efren Pinto W RSC 6 Seoul
(WBC L. Flyweight Title Defence)
28.06.87 Agustin Garcia W RSC 10 Seoul
(WBC L. Flyweight Title Defence)
13.12.87 Isidro Perez W PTS 12 Seoul
(WBC L. Flyweight Title Defence)
Summary: 36 contests, won 35, lost 1.

Tae-Il Chang
South Korea. *Born* 10.04.65
OPBF S. Flyweight Champion. Former IBF & South Korean S. Flyweight Champion

18.10.81 Byung-Kyu Lee DREW 4 Seoul
08.11.81 Rae-Ki Ahn W PTS 4 Seoul
06.12.81 Jae-Min Shin W PTS 6 Seoul
14.02.82 Yong-Bon Yun W CO 1 Seoul
20.03.82 Yun-Sik Chae W PTS 6 Seoul
28.03.82 Jae-Sung Uhm L PTS 6 Seoul
18.09.83 Sang-Suk Bang W PTS 6 Seoul
23.10.83 Chung-Dae Lee W PTS 6 Seoul
04.12.83 Won-Keun Chae W PTS 6 Seoul
25.12.83 Joong-Suk Kwon W PTS 8 Seoul
12.02.84 Hoi-Yul Yang W PTS 8 Seoul
08.04.84 Chang-Kyun Oh W PTS 8 Seoul
13.05.84 Yun-Kuk Lee W PTS 8 Seoul
13.07.84 Masaharu Inami W CO 9 Yokohama
09.09.84 Ok-Kyun Yuh W RSC 9 Seoul
(South Korean S. Flyweight Title Challenge)
03.11.84 Seung-Hyun Bang L PTS 10 Seoul
(South Korean S. Flyweight Title Defence)
24.03.85 Byung-Yum Choi W CO 2 Mokpo
01.06.85 Edel Geronimo W PTS 12 Inchon
(Vacant OPBF S. Flyweight Title)
31.05.86 Wongso Indrajit W CO 5 Seoul
17.10.86 Ruben de la Cruz W CO 7 Suwon
15.02.87 Hi-Suk Kim W RSC 5 Buju
17.05.87 Soon-Chun Kwan W PTS 15 Pusan
(Vacant IBF S. Flyweight Title)
17.10.87 Elly Pical L PTS 15 Jakarta
(IBF S. Flyweight Title Defence)
24.01.88 Byong-Kwan Chung W PTS 12 Chungbok
(OPBF S. Flyweight Title Challenge)
26.03.88 Yossi Amnifu W PTS 12 Namhae
(OPBF S. Flyweight Title Defence)
Summary: 25 contests, won 21, drew 1, lost 3.

Julio Cesar Chavez
Ciudad Obregon, Mexico. *Born* 12.07.62
WBA Lightweight Champion. Former Undefeated WBC S. Featherweight Champion

05.02.80 Andres Felix W CO 6 Culiacan
08.04.80 Ramon Flores W CO 3 Navojoa
20.05.80 Roberto Garcia W CO 6 Guaymas
18.07.80 Tito Geraldo W PTS 6 Guamuchil
05.09.80 Miguel Cebrero W PTS 10 Culiacan
22.09.80 Jesus Lara W PTS 10 Culiacan
13.10.80 Jesus Martinez W CO 1 Culiacan
26.11.80 Andres Felix W CO 2 Culiacan
15.12.80 Roberto Flores W CO 3 Culiacan
02.02.81 Julio Gaxiola W RSC 4 Tijuana
03.04.81 Miguel Ruiz W CO 1 Culiacan
08.05.81 Eduardo Acosta W CO 2 Culiacan
05.06.81 Victor Games W CO 1 Culiacan
26.06.81 Fidel Navarro W CO 1 Culiacan
10.07.81 Bobby Dominguez W CO 3 Culiacan
27.07.81 Daniel Martinez W RSC 1 Tijuana
07.08.81 Jesus Lara W RSC 2 Culiacan
31.08.81 Daniel Felizardo W CO 3 Tijuana
25.09.81 Jorge Ramirez W CO 2 Culiacan
19.10.81 Jose Medina W CO 6 Tijuana
18.12.81 Manuel Vasquez W RSC 7 Culiacan
12.01.82 Ramon Lucas W CO 1 Tijuana
29.01.82 Jesus Garcia W RSC 2 Guamuchil
04.02.82 Ramon Peraza W CO 1 Tijuana
19.02.82 Carlos Bryant W CO 2 Culiacan
11.03.82 Johnny Jensen W CO 3 Tijuana
26.04.82 Ben Abarca W PTS 10 Mexicali
08.05.82 Juan C. Alvarado W CO 3 Culiacan
19.07.82 Gustavo Salgado W CO 2 Tijuana
20.08.82 Santos Rodriguez W RSC 8 Culiacan
28.09.82 Jose Resendez W RSC 6 Tijuana
23.10.82 Jerry Lewis W RSC 5 Tijuana
11.12.82 Jerry Lewis W DIS 6 Sacramento
04.03.83 Otoniel Lopez W CO 5 Ensenada
04.04.83 Ernesto Herrera W CO 2 Tijuana
01.05.83 Javier Fragoso W CO 4 San Juan
15.06.83 Romeo Sandoval W RSC 2 Los Angeles
16.07.83 Ben Abarca W RSC 5 Culiacan
01.09.83 Adrian Arreola W PTS 10 Los Angeles
30.12.83 Armando Flores W RSC 3 Mazatlan
04.05.84 Ramon Avitia W CO 6 Culiacan
13.07.84 Delfino Martinez W CO 3 Hermosillo
13.09.84 Mario Martinez W RSC 8 Los Angeles
(Vacant WBC S. Featherweight Title)
01.01.85 Manny Hernandez W RSC 3 Mexico City
19.04.85 Ruben Castillo W RSC 6 Los Angeles
(WBC S. Featherweight Title Defence)
07.07.85 Roger Mayweather W RSC 2 Las Vegas
(WBC S. Featherweight Title Defence)
22.09.85 Dwight Pratchett W PTS 12 Las Vegas
(WBC S. Featherweight Title Defence)
19.12.85 Jeff Bumphus W TD 5 Los Angeles
22.03.86 Roberto Collins W CO 2 Las Vegas
15.05.86 Faustino Barrios W RSC 5 Paris
(WBC S. Featherweight Title Defence)
13.06.86 Refugio Rojas W RSC 7 New York
(WBC S. Featherweight Title Defence)
03.08.86 Rocky Lockridge W PTS 12 Monte Carlo
(WBC S. Featherweight Title Defence)
12.12.86 Juan Laporte W PTS 12 New York
(WBC S. Featherweight Title Defence)
18.04.87 Francisco Tomas Cruz W RSC 3 Nimes
(WBC S. Featherweight Title Defence)
21.08.87 Danilo Cabrera W PTS 12 Tijuana
(WBC S. Featherweight Title Defence)
21.11.87 Edwin Rosario W RSC 11 Las Vegas
(WBA Lightweight Title Challenge)
05.03.88 Nicky Perez W RSC 3 Tijuana
16.04.88 Rodolfo Aguilar W RSC 6 Las Vegas
(WBA Lightweight Title Defence)
Summary: 58 contests, won 58.

Spencer (The Warrior) Chavis
Dearborn, USA. *Born* 16.05.65
Cruiserweight

05.08.82 Clyde Alexander W CO 1 Detroit
18.09.82 Charles Presswood W CO 1 Dearborn
17.11.82 Leo Brandon W RSC 3 Ann Arbor
28.01.83 Bill Hollis W PTS 4 Wyandotte
23.02.83 Ed Temple W CO 4 Romulus
16.04.83 Frank Farmer W PTS 6 Detroit
22.04.83 James Churn W PTS 6 Detroit
21.12.83 Sonny Mason W CO 1 Detroit
23.03.84 Asim Abdul W PTS 6 Allen Park

19.04.84 Stan Johnson W CO 1 Detroit
10.05.84 Don Townsend W PTS 6 Allen Park
31.05.84 James Holly W CO 1 Detroit
27.09.84 Stan Johnson W CO 1 Detroit
24.10.84 Vernon Bridges W PTS 6 Detroit
21.02.85 Roy Saffold W PTS 8 Detroit
08.05.85 Rick Ennis W PTS 6 Detroit
16.07.85 Curtis Isaac L PTS 10 Detroit
01.04.86 Dick Silas W RSC 1 Memphis
21.05.86 Earl Lewis W RSC 3 Mount Clemens
30.09.86 Willie Mayberry W RSC 1 Detroit
10.10.86 Bert Cooper L CO 3 Las Vegas
(*NABF Cruiserweight Title Challenge*)
27.01.87 Trent Surratt W RSC 3 Detroit
31.03.87 Curtis Isaac W PTS 10 Detroit
28.04.87 Antonio Arvizu W CO 1 Detroit
19.05.87 Dawud Shaw W RSC 5 Detroit
30.06.87 Joey Parker W PTS 10 Detroit
29.09.87 Young Joe Louis W RSC 6 Detroit
27.10.87 Terry Denny W RSC 3 Detroit
28.01.88 Paul Madison W PTS 10 Detroit
23.02.88 Pat Strachan W PTS 10 Detroit
Summary: 30 contests, won 28, lost 2.

Sot Chitalada
Thailand. *Born* 24.05.62
WBC Flyweight Champion

05.12.82 Srithunchai Sithsanae W CO 2 Bangkok
23.01.83 Suriya Pratumvadee W PTS 6 Bangkok
18.12.83 Niphonyuth Sakadam W CO 3 Bangkok
30.01.84 Jownaranoi Chomkatha W CO 2 Bangkok
31.03.84 Jung-Koo Chang L PTS 12 Pusan
(*WBC L. Flyweight Title Challenge*)
05.06.84 Wick Tengam W RSC 6 Bangkok
02.07.84 Rudy Palicua W RSC 7 Bangkok
08.10.84 Gabriel Bernal W PTS 12 Bangkok
(*WBC Flyweight Title Challenge*)
20.02.85 Charlie Magri W RTD 4 London
(*WBC Flyweight Title Defence*)
22.06.85 Gabriel Bernal DREW 12 Bangkok
(*WBC Flyweight Title Defence*)
22.02.86 Freddie Castillo W PTS 12 Kuwait
(*WBC Flyweight Title Defence*)
30.08.86 Moon-Jin Choi W RSC 9 Bangkok
12.10.86 Narkalart Kiatsontaya W CO 2 Bangkok
10.12.86 Gabriel Bernal W PTS 12 Bangkok
(*WBC Flyweight Title Defence*)
05.09.87 Rae-Ki Ahn W CO 4 Bangkok
(*WBC Flyweight Title Defence*)
31.01.88 Hideaki Kamishiro W RSC 7 Osaka
(*WBC Flyweight Title Defence*)
Summary: 16 contests, won 14, drew 1, lost 1.

Chang-Ho Choi
South Korea. *Born* 10.02.64
Former IBF Flyweight Champion. Former Undefeated South Korean Flyweight Champion

01.12.82 Chang-Yung Chung L PTS 4 Seoul
13.07.85 Hwang-Sik Wang W RSC 3 Chungju
22.09.85 Chun-Chi Hyun W PTS 4 Chungju
05.12.85 Ki-Bong Lee W RSC 1 Seoul
08.12.85 Ki-Sang Kim W PTS 4 Seoul
10.12.85 Byung-Nam Park W RSC 3 Seoul
12.01.86 Yung-Hyon Kang W CO 2 Seoul
22.02.86 Chung-Dong Kim W RSC 3 Daejon
13.04.86 Ro-Seung Choi W CO 1 Kwangju
18.05.86 Ha-Sik Lim L PTS 8 Taegu
29.06.86 Chung-Seop Chun W RSC 6 Seoul
02.08.86 Bok-Kyu Choi W RSC 1 Inchon
18.10.86 Chu-Shik Cho W RSC 5 Inchon
14.12.86 Sung-Dae Park W RSC 2 Inchon
22.02.87 Heun-Kuk Chae W PTS 10 Inchon
(*Vacant South Korean Flyweight Title*)
05.09.87 Dodie Penalosa W CO 11 Manila
(*IBF Flyweight Title Challenge*)
16.01.88 Rolando Bohol L PTS 15 Manila
(*IBF Flyweight Title Defence*)
Summary: 17 contests, won 14, lost 3.

Jum-Hwan Choi
Pusan, South Korea. *Born* 09.06.63
IBF L. Flyweight Champion

13.03.83 Chong-Don Kim W PTS 6 Seoul
03.04.83 Sung-Kyu Kim W PTS 6 Seoul
17.04.83 Yong-Soo Kim W PTS 6 Seoul
08.05.83 Won-Soo Chung W PTS 6 Seoul
29.05.83 Hyung-Soo Choi W PTS 6 Seoul
12.06.83 Byung-Dae Yuh W PTS 6 Seoul
10.07.83 Ha-Sik Lim W PTS 8 Seoul
14.08.83 Sung-Kwan Chun W PTS 8 Seoul
23.10.83 Chang-Yung Chang W PTS 10 Seoul
25.12.83 Ha-Sik Lim W PTS 10 Seoul
13.05.84 Jung-Hyun Kim W CO 2 Seoul
15.07.84 Kyung-Jae Chang W PTS 10 Pohang
16.11.84 Dodie Penalosa L PTS 15 Manila
(*IBF L. Flyweight Title Challenge*)
30.03.85 Kyung-Jae Chang W PTS 10 Suwon
23.01.86 Yung-Il Choi W PTS 10 Seoul
07.12.86 Cho-Woon Park W PTS 15 Pusan
(*Vacant IBF L. Flyweight Title*)
29.03.87 Tacy Macalos W PTS 15 Seoul
(*IBF L. Flyweight Title Defence*)
05.07.87 Toshihiko Matsuta W RSC 4 Seoul
(*IBF L. Flyweight Title Defence*)
09.08.87 Azadin Anhar W RSC 3 Jakarta
(*IBF L. Flyweight Title Defence*)
30.01.88 Rolando Pascua W PTS 10 Masan
Summary: 20 contests, won 19, lost 1.

Chil-Sung Chun

Chil-Sung Chun
Sinan, South Korea. *Born* 07.07.61
Lightweight

01.03.86 Chong-Ha Chin W CO 3 Mokpo
28.06.86 Oh-Yong Kim W CO 2 Kunsan
26.07.86 Thungberm Lukmatulee W CO 3 Osan
17.10.86 Lulu Villaverde W PTS 10 Hongchun
17.01.87 Ayuthaya Sithphakamron W CO 1 Hongchun
04.03.87 Louis Ilago W CO 8 Chunchon
14.06.87 Darryl Tyson W PTS 10 Bukok
30.08.87 Yoshimitsu Azato W TD 4 Kumi
08.10.87 Rico Velasquez L RTD 4 Los Angeles
20.12.87 Juhari W PTS 10 Pyongtaek
26.03.88 Leo Sabanal W RSC 3 Seoul
Summary: 11 contests, won 10, lost 1.

Bi-Won Chung
South Korea. *Born* 15.01.60
Former IBF Flyweight Champion. Former South Korean L. Flyweight Champion

28.02.82 Soon-Jae Lee W PTS 4 Seoul
28.03.82 Byung-Hwa Chung W RSC 2 Seoul
26.04.82 Keun-Pil Chung W RSC 2 Seoul
21.05.82 Ki-Man Yuh W PTS 4 Seoul
23.05.82 Kang-Hwan Kim W PTS 4 Seoul
24.05.82 Chul Hyun W PTS 4 Seoul
05.06.82 Chong-Bong Choi W PTS 4 Seoul
31.07.82 Ki-Yung Kim W PTS 6 Seoul
31.10.82 Yun-Ree Moon DREW 6 Seoul
22.01.83 Keum-Sup Han W PTS 8 Seoul
19.02.83 Tatsuya Sugi W RTD 5 Seoul
03.04.83 Soon-Yun Mah DREW 10 Seoul
06.05.83 Soon-Yun Mah W CO 8 Seoul
(*South Korean L. Flyweight Title Challenge*)
26.07.83 Jae-Hong Kim L PTS 10 Seoul
(*South Korean L. Flyweight Title Defence*)
29.03.84 Sung-Kyu Kim W PTS 10 Seoul
27.05.84 Myung-Woo Yuh L PTS 10 Seoul
09.07.84 German Torres L PTS 10 Seoul
08.09.84 Dosa Kim L PTS 10 Seoul
08.12.84 Soon-Jung Kang W PTS 10 Chinju
16.02.85 Keum-Sup Han W PTS 10 Seoul
14.04.85 Soon-Jung Kang W PTS 10 Pohang
25.05.85 Benjie Miole W PTS 10 Buhan
20.10.85 Boy Samson W CO 2 Nonsan
28.12.85 Oh-Kong Son W PTS 10 Suwon
27.04.86 Chong-Kwan Chung W PTS 15 Pusan
(*IBF Flyweight Title Challenge*)
02.08.86 Hi-Sup Shin L RSC 15 Inchon
(*IBF Flyweight Title Defence*)
20.12.86 Rolando Protacio W RSC 5 Seoul
14.03.87 Ronnie Vallescas W CO 3 Chunchon
27.06.87 Downrung Technicutaradit W PTS 10 Chochiwon
13.09.87 Chung-Sup Chun W CO 4 Jinju
20.12.87 Ritchai Lukmingkwan W RSC 8 Pyungtaek
21.02.88 Dev Chuvatana W PTS 10 Seoul
Summary: 32 contests, won 25, drew 2, lost 5.

Byong-Kwan Chung
South Korea
Former OPBF S. Flyweight Champion. Former Undefeated South Korean S. Flyweight Champion

08.10.83 Nam-Chul Park W PTS 4 Hongseong
20.11.83 Sam-Ki Ro W PTS 4 Seoul
12.12.83 Yung-Kil Park W PTS 4 Seoul
14.12.83 Chong-Pil Kim L PTS 6 Seoul
14.01.84 Soon-Il Guy L PTS 6 Seoul
25.02.84 Eul-Chul Chung W PTS 6 Seoul
01.04.84 Kyung-Soo Choi L RSC 5 Seoul
17.07.84 Chun-Won Kang DREW 6 Mokpo
24.11.84 Bong-Chun Kim DREW 8 Gunsan
30.06.85 Sang-Don Kim W PTS 6 Seoul
22.09.85 Jae-Yun Lee L PTS 6 Chungju
17.11.85 Ki-Yung Ahn W CO 1 Seoul
20.12.85 Seung-Kwan Lee W PTS 6 Pusan
15.03.86 Joong-Seob Cheon W PTS 6 Kangneung
28.06.86 Chul-Ho Chung W CO 2 Pohang
02.08.86 Yun-Ho Park W PTS 10 Inchon
(*Vacant South Korean S. Flyweight Title*)
16.11.86 Ki-Chang Kim W RSC 3 Seoul
(*OPBF S. Flyweight Title Challenge*)
17.01.87 Dae-Yong Park DREW 10 Kwangwonjo
(*OPBF S. Flyweight Title Defence*)
26.04.87 Wongso Indrajit W PTS 12 Jinju
(*OPBF S. Flyweight Title Defence*)
29.08.87 Shunichi Nakajima W PTS 12 Chungju
(*OPBF S. Flyweight Title Defence*)
12.10.87 Kaosai Galaxy L RSC 3 Bangkok
(*WBA S. Flyweight Title Challenge*)
24.01.88 Tae-Il Chang L PTS 12 Chungbok
(*OPBF S. Flyweight Title Defence*)
Summary: 22 contests, won 13, drew 3, lost 6.

Hi-Yun Chung
South Korea
OPBF S. Bantamweight Champion. Former Undefeated South Korean S. Flyweight & S. Bantamweight Champion

02.12.81 Hyo-Myung Yuh L PTS 4 Seoul
21.02.82 Sun-Bin Lim W PTS 4 Seoul
07.03.82 Yun Yong W PTS 4 Seoul
23.05.82 Choon-Sung Yuh W PTS 4 Seoul
25.05.82 Cha-Suk Oh W PTS 4 Seoul
05.06.82 Rang-Soo Park W PTS 4 Seoul
31.07.82 Yun-Kap Choi W PTS 6 Seoul
19.10.82 Chong-Hyuk Lim W PTS 6 Seoul
27.11.82 Yuerk Choo W PTS 8 Seoul
26.12.82 Ok-Kyun Yuh W PTS 10 Seoul
(*South Korean S. Flyweight Title Challenge*)
27.02.83 Jae-Myung Choi DREW 10 Seoul
(*South Korean S. Flyweight Title Defence*)
06.05.83 Diego de Villa W CO 8 Seoul
26.06.83 Joo-Do Chun L PTS 10 Seoul
(*South Korean S. Flyweight Title Defence*)
03.09.83 Ho-Chung Kim W PTS 8 Seoul
26.11.83 Baek-Man Lee W PTS 10 Seoul
05.02.84 Kyu-Chan Cho W PTS 10 Seoul
(*South Korean S. Flyweight Title Challenge*)
25.03.84 Hyung-Sik Lim DREW 10 Seoul
(*South Korean S. Flyweight Title Defence*)

19.05.84 Elly Pical L TD 4 Seoul
(*OPBF S. Flyweight Title Challenge*)
29.11.85 Tae-Yul Suh W CO 4 Chungju
18.01.86 Yung-Kil Choi W PTS 8 Seoul
14.06.86 Hong-Kyu Yang W CO 2 Inchon
17.08.86 Kyu-Chang Cho DREW 10 Seoul
07.11.86 Hun-Yung Park W PTS 10 Seoul
(*South Korean S. Bantamweight Title Challenge*)
27.12.86 Jung-Man Park W PTS 10 Taeju
(*South Korean S. Bantamweight Title Defence*)
24.03.87 Prayoonsak Muangsurin W TD 7 Samutprakarn
(*OPBF S. Bantamweight Title Challenge*)
16.05.87 Joe Hiyas L PTS 12 Manila
(*Vacant WBC International S. Bantamweight Title*)
18.07.87 Flash Emmanuel W TD 6 Boeun
(*OPBF S. Bantamweight Title Defence*)
24.10.87 Takashi Shuto W CO 5 Joungsun
(*OPBF S. Bantamweight Title Defence*)
13.02.88 Chung-Woo Park DREW 12 Seoul
(*OPBF S. Bantamweight Title Defence*)
Summary: 29 contests, won 21, drew 4, lost 4.

Yung-Kil Chung

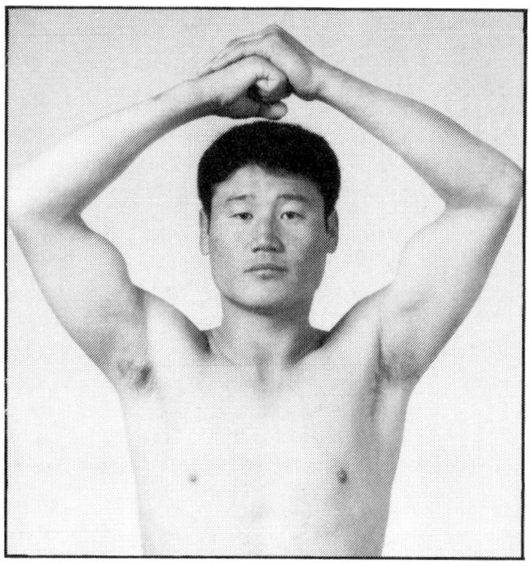

Yung-Kil Chung
South Korea. *Born* 08.09.63
OPBF Welterweight Champion. Former Undefeated South Korean Welterweight Champion

26.12.81 Ki-Nak Jung W PTS 4 Seoul
14.02.82 Jae-Hyung Lim W PTS 4 Daejon
15.04.82 Seung-Ho Kim DREW 6 Ulsan
19.06.82 Dong-Uwn Shin L PTS 8 Seoul
04.09.82 Hwa-Young Song DREW 4 Taegu
10.12.82 Byung-Soon Yuh W RSC 5 Chungju
05.02.83 Yung-Man Park W PTS 8 Daejon
21.05.83 Dong-Bok Lee W RSC 2 Seoul
17.06.83 Seung-Soon Lee L PTS 10 Seoul
(*South Korean Welterweight Title Challenge*)
03.09.83 Ki-Hae Song W RSC 5 Seoul
13.11.83 Chong-Won Park W RSC 5 Juju
05.02.84 Seung-Soon Lee L PTS 10 Seoul
(*South Korean Welterweight Title Challenge*)
21.03.84 Chong-Won Park W CO 6 Pusan
19.05.84 Tae-Wang Kang W PTS 10 Daejon
18.11.84 Jae-Young Park W CO 4 Daejon
(*Vacant South Korean Welterweight Title*)
19.01.85 Kang-Chul Choi W RSC 5 Taegu
(*South Korean Welterweight Title Defence*)
14.04.85 Young-Bae Lee W PTS 10 Pohang
(*South Korean Welterweight Title Defence*)
17.07.85 Kyung-Shik Park W RSC 7 Masan
(*South Korean Welterweight Title Defence*)
27.10.85 Joo-Kwan Chung W PTS 10 Pusan
(*South Korean Welterweight Title Defence*)
29.11.85 Young-Bae Lee W CO 10 Chungju
(*South Korean Welterweight Title Defence*)
16.02.86 Kyung-Shik Park W CO 6 Ulsan
(*South Korean Welterweight Title Defence*)
27.04.86 Kang-Chul Choi W CO 4 Pusan
(*South Korean Welterweight Title Defence*)
27.07.86 Yong-Chul Park W RSC 6 Hongchun
(*South Korean Welterweight Title Defence*)
18.10.86 In-Son Kim W CO 7 Inchon
(*South Korean Welterweight Title Defence*)
31.01.87 Noli Deguia W CO 1 Sungjung
29.03.87 Seung-Soon Lee W PTS 12 Wonju
(*OPBF Welterweight Title Challenge*)
13.06.87 Francisco Ferrer W PTS 12 Chungju
(*OPBF Welterweight Title Defence*)
23.08.87 Noboyuki Tabata W RSC 9 Jumchon
(*OPBF Welterweight Title Defence*)
14.11.87 Arman Pecar W CO 4 Seoul
(*OPBF Welterweight Title Defence*)
12.03.88 Rolando Ferrer W CO 3 Samchunpo
Summary: 30 contests, won 25, drew 2, lost 3.

Richard (Shrimpy) Clarke
Jamaica. *Born* 20.04.63
Con. Am, Fecarbox & WBC International Flyweight Champion. Former Undefeated Commonwealth Champion

31.01.81 Alejandro Perez W PTS 6 Kingston
18.05.81 Alejandro Perez W PTS 6 Kingston
16.09.81 Norman Tomlinson W CO 4 Kingston
01.12.81 Jim Bowens W CO 1 Kingston
30.01.82 William Santos W CO 4 Kingston
26.03.82 Pascual Polanco W PTS 6 Kingston
18.12.82 Juan Bisono L PTS 8 Haiti
26.04.83 Juan Bisono L PTS 8 Haiti
01.12.84 Vicente Arias W PTS 6 Haiti
04.05.85 Alfonso Lopez W PTS 10 Haiti
24.08.85 Kid Macumba W RTD 11 Haiti
(*Vacant Fecarbox Flyweight Title*)
13.11.85 Bernardo Diaz W PTS 10 Kingston
26.04.86 Wayne Mulholland W CO 4 Kingston
(*Vacant Commonwealth Flyweight Title*)
04.10.86 Amado Ursua W PTS 10 Kingston
05.12.86 Juan Herrera W PTS 12 Kingston
(*Vacant Con. Am. Flyweight Title*)
01.05.87 Jimmy Fernandez W PTS 12 Kingston
(*Vacant WBC International Flyweight Title*)
25.09.87 Prudencio Cardona W PTS 10 Kingston
03.12.87 Julio Gudino W PTS 12 Kingston
(*WBC International Flyweight Title Defence*)
Summary: 18 contests, won 16, lost 2.

Pierre Coetzer
Pretoria, South Africa. *Born* 12.06.61
South African Heavyweight Champion

05.02.83 Isaac Ndlamlege W RSC 1 Johannesburg
14.03.83 Caifas Masondo W CO 2 Durban
23.04.83 Jerry Shezi W PTS 6 Johannesburg
11.06.83 Louis Hendriks W RSC 5 Johannesburg
04.07.83 Ron Ellis W CO 4 Durban
03.09.83 Steve Gee W PTS 8 Johannesburg
28.01.84 Billy Thomas W RSC 5 Johannesburg
31.03.84 Felipe Rodriguez W RSC 2 Johannesburg
18.05.84 Leroy Caldwell W PTS 8 Johannesburg
16.07.84 Bernard Benton L PTS 10 Durban
22.09.84 Bennie Knoetze W CO 3 Johannesburg
(*Vacant South African Heavyweight Title*)
25.03.85 Mark Lee W PTS 10 Durban
13.05.85 Rick Sekorski W PTS 10 Johannesburg
08.07.85 David Jaco W CO 6 Johannesburg
07.09.85 Dion Simpson W RSC 8 Johannesburg
30.09.85 Larry Frazier W PTS 10 Johannesburg
19.02.86 Young Joe Louis W RSC 9 Johannesburg
02.04.86 Franco Thomas W CO 2 Durban
14.05.86 K. P. Porter W RSC 6 Johannesburg
27.09.86 Luis Lozano W CO 1 Sun City
08.03.87 Chris Jacobs W CO 2 Johannesburg
30.08.87 Alfredo Evangelista W PTS 10 Johannesburg
28.09.87 Bernard Benton W CO 1 Johannesburg
06.03.88 Ossie Ocasio L PTS 10 Capetown
Summary: 24 contests, won 22, lost 2.

Juan M. Coggi

Juan M. (Latigo) Coggi
Rosario, Argentine. *Born* 19.12.61
WBA L. Welterweight Champion. Former Undefeated Argentinian L. Welterweight Champion

02.04.82 Horacio Valdez W CO 4 La Plata
07.05.82 Viterman Sanchez W PTS 6 La Plata
11.06.82 Ramon Gramasco W CO 2 Brandsen
10.09.82 Felipe Baez W RSC 6 Brandsen
22.10.82 Rogelio Florentin W CO 2 Brandsen
12.11.82 Carlos Fallone W RSC 4 Brandsen
10.12.82 Roberto Villalobos W PTS 8 Brandsen
11.02.83 Osvaldo Cobros W CO 1 Brandsen
08.04.83 Carlos Fallone W CO 7 J C Paz
18.05.83 Apolinario Romero W PTS 10 Buenos Aires
15.06.83 Sergio Brites W CO 2 Buenos Aires
14.10.83 Anibal Ozuna W PTS 10 La Plata
09.11.83 Apolinario Romero W PTS 10 Buenos Aires
07.12.83 Anibal Ozuna W CO 2 Buenos Aires
23.12.83 Romulo Ibarra W PTS 10 Brandsen
10.02.84 Marcelo Villagra W PTS 10 Las Flores
09.03.84 Ricardo Espinoza W PTS 10 Mar del Plata
23.06.84 Ricardo Espinoza W RSC 2 Buenos Aires
10.08.84 Pedro A. Gutierrez W CO 1 La Plata
01.09.84 Ramon Collado W PTS 10 Buenos Aires
11.11.84 Marcelo Villagra W PTS 10 San Juan
22.02.85 Miguel Pereyra W PTS 10 Mar del Plata
09.03.85 Adolfo Rossi L PTS 10 Buenos Aires
11.05.85 Ramon Jara W CO 7 Buenos Aires
20.06.85 Ramon Collado DREW 10 Las Flores
03.08.85 Miguel Pereyra W RTD 7 Buenos Aires
31.08.85 Oscar Sosa W RTD 7 Rojas
26.10.85 Ruben Verdun W TD 7 Rojas
07.03.86 Sergio Brites W CO 5 Mar del Plata
05.04.86 Edecio Molina W PTS 10 Buenos Aires
14.06.86 Jose Saldivia W CO 2 Santa Maria
19.07.86 Ramon Collado DREW 10 La Plata
25.10.86 Hugo Hernandez W CO 3 Buenos Aires
(*Argentinian L. Welterweight Title Challenge*)
04.04.87 Jose Magarinos W CO 5 General Roca
04.07.87 Patrizio Oliva W CO 3 Ribera
(*WBA L. Welterweight Title Challenge*)
19.02.88 Mario Araya W CO 6 Catamarca
Summary: 36 contests, won 33, drew 2, lost 1.

Lion Collins
Philippines
S. Bantamweight

28.04.84 Alex de la Flor W PTS 4 Cavite City
24.06.84 Moirby Evasco DREW 4 Cavite City
01.08.84 Sonny Altarejos W PTS 4 Paranaque
31.08.84 Mohammad Raffi W PTS 4 Manila
28.09.84 Salvador Maca W PTS 4 Manila
04.11.84 Felix Enero W PTS 4 Quezon City
30.11.84 Rex Rapiso DREW 4 Manila
26.04.85 Wilson Apurado W PTS 4 Manila
06.05.85 Sam Ansig W PTS 4 Manila
15.05.85 Leo Ero L PTS 6 Paranaque
04.07.85 Felix Enero W PTS 6 Manila
26.10.85 Aki Caparuso W PTS 6 Manila
14.12.85 Leo Dozal W PTS 6 Gapan
05.02.86 Boy Granciosa DREW 8 Paranaque
05.03.86 Rodrigo Altarejos W PTS 6 Paranaque
12.04.86 Ernesto Mabagsik W PTS 8 Tanay

16.05.86 Jun Gavero T DRAW 6 Angeles
15.06.86 Sam Ansig W PTS 8 Quezon City
22.07.86 Zaldy Mira W PTS 6 Legaspi
20.08.86 Joe Hiyas L PTS 10 Paranaque
20.09.86 Fel Aporto W PTS 10 Quezon City
15.11.86 Lorenzo Formanes W PTS 10 Cabiao
27.12.86 William Develos W RSC 3 Quezon City
27.03.87 Rudy Casicas W PTS 10 Quezon City
16.05.87 Jorge Olan W RSC 6 Manila
19.07.87 Seung-Hoon Lee L CO 5 Pohang
(IBF S. Bantamweight Title Challenge)
09.10.87 Bernabe Aliping W PTS 10 Quezon City
16.11.87 Jojo Cayson L PTS 10 Quezon City
10.01.88 Little Bangoyan L PTS 10 Manila
20.02.88 Liem Tianhong W PTS 10 Jakarta
23.04.88 Byung-Soo Park L RSC 1 Buju
(OPBF Featherweight Title Challenge)
Summary: 31 contests, won 21, drew 4, lost 6.

(Elton) Tom Collins

Leeds, England. *Born* Curacao 01.07.55
EBU L. Heavyweight Champion. Former Undefeated British L. Heavyweight Champion

17.01.77 Ginger McIntyre W RSC 2 Birmingham
16.05.77 Mick Dolan W PTS 6 Manchester
01.06.77 Johnny Cox W CO 3 Dudley
23.11.77 George Gray W RSC 3 Stoke
19.01.78 Clint Jones W RSC 3 London
21.03.78 Joe Jackson W PTS 8 Luton
09.05.78 Harald Skog L PTS 8 Oslo
17.07.78 Karl Canwell L RSC 6 London
28.11.78 Carlton Benoit W CO 1 Sheffield
04.12.78 Dennis Andries L PTS 8 Southend
30.01.79 Dennis Andries L CO 6 Southend
22.10.79 Danny Lawford W RSC 7 Nottingham
28.11.79 Eddie Smith W PTS 8 Solihull
25.02.80 Greg Evans W RSC 1 Bradford
15.04.80 Chris Lawson W RSC 4 Blackpool
04.12.80 Mustafa Wasajja L PTS 8 Randers
09.03.81 Karl Canwell W PTS 10 Bradford
15.03.82 Dennis Andries W PTS 15 London
(Vacant British L. Heavyweight Title)
26.05.82 Trevor Cattouse W CO 4 Leeds
(British L. Heavyweight Title Defence)
07.10.82 John Odhiambo L RSC 5 Copenhagen
09.03.83 Antonio Harris W RSC 6 Solihull
(British L. Heavyweight Title Defence)
09.04.83 Alex Sua W PTS 12 Auckland
17.12.83 Leslie Stewart L PTS 10 Trinidad
26.01.84 Dennis Andries L PTS 12 London
(British L. Heavyweight Title Defence)
06.04.84 Dennis Andries L PTS 12 Watford
(British L. Heavyweight Title Challenge)
21.09.84 Alek Penarski L PTS 8 Alfreton
24.01.85 Jonjo Greene W RSC 7 Manchester
30.03.85 Chisanda Mutti L PTS 10 Dortmund
18.04.85 Andy Straughn L CO 1 Halifax
14.10.85 Harry Cowap W CO 4 London
29.11.85 Ralf Rocchigiani L PTS 8 Frankfurt
20.12.85 Pierre Kabassu DREW 8 Forbach
01.04.86 Winston Burnett W PTS 8 Leeds
19.04.86 Yawe Davis W CO 3 San Remo
01.12.86 Alex Blanchard L PTS 10 Arnhem
11.03.87 John Moody W RSC 10 London
(Vacant British L. Heavyweight Title)
11.11.87 Alex Blanchard W CO 2 Usk
(EBU L. Heavyweight Title Challenge)
Summary: 37 contests, won 22, drew 1, lost 14.

Diomedes Colome

Dominican Republic. *Born* 03.05.65
Welterweight

23.12.82 David Rosen W PTS 4 Las Vegas
20.01.83 Tony Montgomery L PTS 4 Los Angeles
24.02.83 Frank White W PTS 4 Los Angeles
24.03.83 Javier Ruiz W CO 2 Los Angeles
03.04.83 Roberto Leyva W CO 2 Phoenix
21.04.83 Raul Nava W RSC 1 Las Vegas
10.05.83 Mike Castro W CO 2 Phoenix
18.06.83 Howard Smith W CO 2 San Carlos
28.07.83 Eddie Wright W RTD 2 Las Vegas
07.08.83 Dexter Smith W PTS 8 Las Vegas
22.12.83 Jesse Ruiz W RSC 5 Las Vegas
20.01.84 Ken Releford W RSC 3 Las Vegas
03.02.84 Reggie Miller W PTS 10 Las Vegas
30.03.84 Gary Baca W RSC 7 Las Vegas
12.06.84 Eric Martin L PTS 12 Las Vegas
09.08.84 Eric Martin W PTS 13 Las Vegas
11.10.84 Clayton Hires W PTS 10 Las Vegas
24.01.85 Anthony Thomas W PTS 8 Las Vegas
08.07.85 Kel Robins W RSC 5 Los Angeles
15.10.85 Derrick Kelly W PTS 10 Los Angeles
17.12.85 Manning Galloway L PTS 12 Los Angeles
11.11.86 Lupe Aquino L CO 5 Las Vegas
16.09.87 Floyd Peavy W RSC 6 Los Angeles
24.11.87 Charles Nwokolo W PTS 10 Los Angeles
Summary: 24 contests, won 20, lost 4.

Ruben Condori

Ruben Condori

Salta, Argentine. *Born* 18.03.60
Argentinian S. Flyweight Champion. Former Argentinian Flyweight Champion. Former Undefeated South American Flyweight Champion

03.06.77 Damian Roman W RSC 3 Salta
05.08.77 Jose Lopez W PTS 6 Salta
19.08.77 Luis Gomez W PTS 6 Salta
02.09.77 Raul Anchanga W CO 1 Salta
23.09.77 Ramon Galarce W PTS 6 Salta
25.11.77 Jose Lopez DREW 8 Salta
17.02.78 Hectori Patri DREW 6 Salta
03.03.78 Roberto Sosa W RTD 4 Salta
07.04.78 Carlos Cortes W PTS 6 Salta
12.05.78 Jose Gutierrez W RSC 3 Salta
07.07.78 Cisco Altamirano W PTS 10 Salta
01.09.78 Luis Gomez W RSC 6 Salta
20.10.78 Jorge Mansilla W RSC 6 Salta
23.03.79 Ric Gomez W PTS 10 Salta
11.05.79 Jose Narvaez L PTS 10 La Rioja
02.06.79 Marino Suarez L PTS 10 General Pico
27.07.79 Domingo Aragon DREW 10 Rosario
28.09.79 Enrique Navarro W CO 3 Salta
19.10.79 Adrian Roman L TD 7 Cordoba
16.11.79 Hector Velasquez W PTS 10 Salta
07.12.79 Jose Ibiris W PTS 10 Salta
28.12.79 Jose Ibiris W PTS 10 Salta
18.01.80 Raul Perez W PTS 10 Salta
29.02.80 Rodolfo Rodriguez W PTS 10 Salta
28.03.80 Santos Laciar DREW 10 Cordoba
19.04.80 Adrian Roman DREW 10 Buenos Aires
16.05.80 Domingo Aragon W PTS 10 Salta
06.06.80 Jorge O. Aguilar W PTS 10 Salta
01.08.80 Miguel Lazarte W PTS 10 Salta
05.09.80 Paulo Ribeiro W PTS 10 Salta
24.10.80 Hector Barreto W PTS 10 Salta
12.12.80 Erik Vanegas W CO 4 San Pedro
15.01.81 Hector Patri T DRAW 3 Salta
18.02.81 Miguel Lazarte W PTS 10 Salta
27.02.81 Jorge Chavarria W PTS 10 Salta
16.04.81 Alfonso Lopez DREW 10 Salta
15.05.81 Felix Colman W PTS 10 Salta
04.09.81 Juan Rios W RSC 8 Salta
18.09.81 Santos Laciar DREW 10 Cordoba
09.10.81 Adrian Roman W PTS 12 Salta
(Vacant Argentinian Flyweight Title)
06.11.81 Miguel Lazarte W PTS 10 Salta
19.02.82 Adrian Roman L PTS 10 Cordoba
23.04.82 Miguel Lazarte W PTS 10 Salta
21.05.82 Domingo Aragon W PTS 10 Salta
10.09.82 Adrian Roman L RSC 7 Salta
(Argentinian Flyweight Title Defence)
17.12.82 Ramon Albers L PTS 10 Concordia
03.02.83 Felix Colman W PTS 10 Posadas
14.03.83 Welile Nkosinkulu L PTS 10 Cape Town
20.05.83 Ramon Albers W PTS 10 Salta
19.06.83 Alberto Pacheco W PTS 10 Salta
30.06.83 Jaime Miranda W PTS 12 Salta
(Vacant South American Flyweight Title)
07.10.83 Alberto Pacheco DREW 10 Reconquista
30.12.83 Adrian Roman W PTS 12 Salta
(South American Flyweight Title Defence)
10.02.84 Ramon Rodriguez W RTD 8 Jujuy
16.03.84 Adrian Roman L PTS 12 Cordoba
(Argentinian Flyweight Title Challenge)
18.04.84 Ramon Albers DREW 10 Concordia
31.08.84 Hector Fernandez W RSC 6 Salta
09.10.84 Jose Cufre W PTS 10 Salta
17.01.85 Raul Perez W RSC 6 Salta
05.02.85 Jaime Loyola W PTS 10 Salta
08.03.85 Adrian Roman W PTS 10 Salta
29.03.85 Armando Romero W PTS 10 Salta
17.05.85 Gustavo Ballas L PTS 10 Villa Maria
14.06.85 Ramon Albers W PTS 10 Salta
05.07.85 Jose Cufre W CO 10 Salta
09.08.85 Jose Cufre L PTS 10 Villa Maria
04.10.85 Alberto Pacheco W PTS 10 Salta
22.11.85 Jose Narvaez W PTS 10 Salta
13.12.85 Lucio Lopez W PTS 10 Salta
12.02.86 Juan Ivalo W RSC 7 Salta
14.03.86 Memo Manrique W RTD 5 Salta
11.04.86 Gustavo Ballas W PTS 12 Salta
(Argentinian S. Flyweight Title Challenge)
16.05.86 Hector Patri W PTS 10 Salta
18.07.86 Gilberto Roman L PTS 12 Salta
(WBC S. Flyweight Title Challenge)
04.10.86 Lucio Lopez L PTS 10 Buenos Aires
08.11.86 Lucio Lopez DREW 10 Corrientes
06.12.86 Gustavo Ballas L PTS 12 Buenos Aires
(South American S. Flyweight Title Challenge)
14.02.87 Luis Ocampo W RSC 11 Posadas
(Argentinian S. Flyweight Title Defence)
03.04.87 Guillermo Manrique W RTD 6 Salta
15.05.87 Jose Badilla W PTS 10 Salta
13.06.87 Gustavo Ballas W PTS 10 Buenos Aires
04.09.87 Francisco Quiroz W PTS 10 Salta
04.12.87 Juan Cortes W PTS 10 Salta
23.01.88 Oscar Vergara W CO 3 Salta
29.04.88 Nelson Ulrich W RTD 7 Tartagal
Summary: 85 contests, won 61, drew 11, lost 13.

Gerry Cooney

Huntington, USA. *Born* 24.08.56
Heavyweight

15.02.77 Billy Jackson W CO 1 New York
02.03.77 Jimmy Robertson W RSC 2 New York
20.03.77 Jose Rosario W CO 1 Louisville
03.08.77 Matt Robinson W PTS 4 New York
18.11.77 Joe Maye W RSC 4 New York
30.11.77 Quinnie Locklear W CO 1 White Plains
21.12.77 Jimmie Sykes W CO 1 Brooklyn
14.01.78 Terry Kidd W CO 1 Hauppauge
27.01.78 Austin Johnson W CO 1 Hempstead
11.02.78 Gary Bates W RSC 4 Las Vegas
17.03.78 S. T. Gordon W DIS 4 Las Vegas
22.06.78 G. G. Maldonado W RSC 8 New York
05.10.78 Charlie Polite W RSC 4 White Plains
01.11.78 Sam McGill W PTS 8 White Plains
15.12.78 Grady Daniels W RTD 6 New York
13.01.79 Eddie Lopez W PTS 8 Miami
26.02.79 Charlie Johnson W CO 1 New York
29.06.79 Tom Prater W CO 2 New York
22.08.79 Broderick Mason W CO 4 New York
19.10.79 Malik Dozier W RSC 6 Commack
09.11.79 Dino Dennis W RSC 3 New York
14.12.79 Leroy Boone W RSC 6 Atlantic City
25.05.80 Jimmy Young W RTD 4 Atlantic City
24.10.80 Ron Lyle W CO 1 Uniondale
11.05.81 Ken Norton W RSC 1 New York
11.06.82 Larry Holmes L RSC 13 Las Vegas
(WBC Heavyweight Title Challenge)
29.09.84 Phil Brown W RSC 4 Anchorage
08.12.84 George Chaplin W RSC 2 Phoenix
30.05.86 Eddie Gregg W RSC 1 San Francisco
15.06.87 Michael Spinks L RSC 5 Atlantic City
Summary: 30 contests, won 28, lost 2.

22.02.84	Malanda Kianda W PTS 6 Gragnano
04.03.84	Malanda Kianda W PTS 6 Sestri
07.06.84	Eloi de Souza W CO 6 Vieste
09.11.84	Luigi la Grasta W CO 1 Carbonia
14.12.84	Serge Boymond W RSC 3 Savona
01.03.85	Robert Forneris W PTS 6 Chiavari
22.06.85	Angelo Licata W RSC 4 Sestri
27.09.85	Luigi de Rosa W PTS 8 Lucca
30.05.86	Jose Maillot W RSC 5 Chiavari
06.09.86	Mwilambwe Tshikala W PTS 8 Naples
11.10.86	Marco Gallo W RSC 5 Cefalu (*Vacant Italian Lightweight Title*)
10.01.87	Francisco Rodriguez W RSC 5 Agrigento
15.07.87	Fernando Blanco W RSC 4 Capo D'Orlando
01.08.87	Bruno de Montis W RSC 1 Asiago (*Italian Lightweight Title Defence*)
23.10.87	Abdel Marbi W RSC 4 Livorno
03.01.88	Mark Brannon W CO 3 Genoa
05.03.88	Harold Romero W RSC 3 Pesaro

Summary: 21 contests, won 20, lost 1.

Tony de Luca
San Diego, USA. *Born* 08.07.62
Flyweight

24.06.83	Alberto Garcia W PTS 4 Santa Rosa
15.09.83	Jose Hernandez W PTS 4 San Rafael
28.03.85	Alberto Garcia W PTS 4 San Diego
27.06.85	Jose Morales W CO 2 San Diego
18.07.85	Rufino Lugo DREW 6 San Diego
15.08.85	Alberto Hernandez T DRAW 4 San Diego
17.10.85	Manuel Martinez W RSC 1 San Diego
21.11.85	Eduardo Pacheco W RSC 5 San Diego
11.01.86	Mauro Diaz L RSC 5 Big Bear City
17.04.86	Oscar Aguilar W CO 2 San Diego
25.07.86	Jose Hernandez W RSC 5 San Diego
26.03.87	Jose Quirino W PTS 8 San Diego
21.05.87	Abraham Garcia W PTS 10 San Diego
19.08.87	Efren Pinto W PTS 10 San Diego
19.11.87	Jose M. Diaz W PTS 10 San Diego
18.02.88	Katsumi Komiyami T DRAW 2 San Diego

Summary: 16 contests, won 12, drew 3, lost 1.

Giovanni de Marco
Alvignano, Italy. *Born* 11.12.60
WBC International L. Middleweight Champion. Former Italian Middleweight Champion.

03.04.82	Walter Borghesi W RSC 2 Piedemonte
28.05.82	Mario Loreni W RSC 3 Empoli
11.06.82	Hosanna Mobana W RSC 2 Lucca
07.08.82	Mauricio Hernandez da Cruz W PTS 6 Vairano
08.10.82	Mabobo Kamunga W PTS 6 Florence
18.12.82	Butangi Nbolameso W RSC 2 Piedemonte
12.03.83	Waluenga Nkongo W RSC 4 Piedemonte
15.04.83	Christian Chesini W RSC 7 Florence
11.06.83	Giovanni Cannizzo W CO 4 Piedemonte
16.07.83	Paul Muyodi W DIS 3 Messina
21.09.83	Mayele Mabele W PTS 6 Caserta
12.12.83	Robert Dormoy W RSC 2 Piedemonte
28.12.83	Folly Muyanga W PTS 6 Campobasso
16.03.84	Butangi Nbolameso W PTS 8 Viterbo
07.06.84	Mayele Mabele W PTS 8 Vieste
21.11.84	Tony Britton W RSC 5 Lucca
04.01.85	Aldo Buzzetti W RTD 5 Lucca (*Italian Middleweight Title Challenge*)
29.03.85	Mosimo Maeleke W PTS 8 Rome
05.06.85	Edmondo Buttiglione DREW 12 Lucca (*Italian Middleweight Title Defence*)
26.09.85	Sumbu Kalambay L PTS 12 Caserta (*Italian Middleweight Title Defence*)
19.04.86	Giovanni Martorina W PTS 8 San Remo
03.09.86	Sumbu Kalambay L RTD 11 Silvio (*Italian Middleweight Title Challenge*)
17.04.87	Mabobo Kamunga W PTS 8 Caserta
28.06.87	Inino wa Bolamba W PTS 8 San Nicola
01.08.87	Nazario Mariotti W PTS 8 Asiago
02.12.87	Ramon Abeldano W PTS 12 San Giuseppe (*WBC International L. Middleweight Title Challenge*)

Summary: 26 contests, won 23, drew 1, lost 2.

Mario de Marco
Rafaela, Argentine. *Born* 13.08.59
Former Undefeated South American & Argentinian L. Flyweight Champion

04.10.80	Tomas Gomez W PTS 6 Buenos Aires
22.11.80	Mario Fernandez DREW 6 Buenos Aires

Mario de Marco

06.02.81	Ramon Albers DREW 6 Concordia
09.05.81	Ruben Paniagua W PTS 6 Buenos Aires
06.06.81	Ramon Albers W PTS 6 Buenos Aires
29.08.81	Tomas Gomez W PTS 6 Buenos Aires
31.10.81	Ruben Paniagua L PTS 8 Buenos Aires
05.03.82	Cesar Gomez W RTD 6 JC Paz
01.05.82	Miguel Leal W RSC 10 Merida
25.08.82	Jose Ibiris W PTS 10 Buenos Aires
17.11.82	Ramon Albers W PTS 10 Buenos Aires
04.03.83	Adrian Roman L PTS 10 Cordoba
29.06.83	Miguel Lazarte W PTS 12 Buenos Aires (*Argentinian L. Flyweight Title Challenge*)
05.08.83	Alberto Fernandez W CO 2 Rafaela
09.09.83	Ustacio Zaracho W CO 3 Rafaela
19.11.83	Hector Patri W PTS 12 Buenos Aires (*Argentinian L. Flyweight Title Defence*)
28.01.84	Eduardo Acosta W PTS 6 Marsala
06.04.84	Rodolfo Rodriguez W RTD 10 Concordia (*S. American L. Flyweight Title Challenge*)
08.06.84	Hector Patri W PTS 10 Rio Gallegos
04.08.84	Miguel Lazarte DREW 12 General Pico (*Argentinian L. Flyweight Title Defence*)
20.09.84	Hector Patri W PTS 10 Rio Grande
14.12.84	Juan Ivalo T DRAW 5 La Plata (*Argentinian L. Flyweight Title Defence*)
28.06.85	Hector Patri W PTS 12 Ceres (*Argentinian L. Flyweight Title Defence*)
15.09.85	Ustacio Zaracho W RSC 3 Ayacucho
06.12.85	Julio Juarez W RTD 7 San Martin
06.06.86	Enrique Caro W CO 3 Tres de Febrero
30.11.86	Myung-Woo Yuh L PTS 15 Seoul (*WBA L. Flyweight Title Challenge*)
13.02.87	Jose Badilla W PTS 12 Mar del Plata (*South American L. Flyweight Title Defence*)
09.05.87	Ricardo Escobar W PTS 10 Bovril
08.06.87	Roberto Ledesma W PTS 10 San Martin
31.10.87	Ricardo Escobar W PTS 10 Villaguay
19.03.88	Ricardo Escobar W PTS 10 Longchamps

Summary: 32 contests, won 25, drew 4, lost 3.

Doug (Cobra) de Witt
Youngstown, USA. *Born* 13.08.61
USBA Middleweight Champion

28.03.80	Peter Pennello W PTS 4 Tarrytown
14.05.80	Charles Hecker W CO 3 White Plains
11.06.80	Calvin Clark W PTS 4 White Plains
17.09.80	Larry Davis W PTS 6 White Plains
15.10.80	Terry Duncan W PTS 6 White Plains
17.12.80	Derrick Doughty W CO 1 White Plains
21.01.81	Larry Davis W PTS 6 White Plains
18.02.81	Pop Nance W PTS 8 White Plains
08.03.81	Ben Serrano L PTS 8 Atlantic City
24.04.81	Kevin Cheatham W CO 1 White Plains
25.06.81	Lenny Villers W RSC 8 Tarrytown
09.10.81	Danny McAloon W RSC 3 White Plains
24.11.81	Tony Suero DREW 8 White Plains
22.12.81	Charles Hecker W RSC 5 Atlantic City
04.02.82	Danny Long W PTS 8 Atlantic City
04.03.82	Bill Medei W RSC 1 Atlantic City
21.03.82	Ben Serrano DREW 8 Atlantic City
04.08.82	Mike Hyman W RSC 6 White Plains
02.10.82	Billy Page W CO 1 Atlantic City
20.10.82	Teddy Mann W RSC 5 White Plains
16.02.83	Vernon Reed W CO 1 East Rutherford
09.08.83	Kane Starling W RSC 8 White Plains
09.09.83	Hector Rosario W RSC 4 White Plains
13.01.84	Fred Boynton W RTD 5 White Plains
17.02.84	Mike Tinley W PTS 12 Atlantic City
19.04.84	Rico Hoye W PTS 10 Atlantic City
04.10.84	Jimmy Sykes W RSC 1 Atlantic City
08.03.85	Don Lee DREW 10 Atlantic City
30.08.85	Robbie Sims L PTS 10 Atlantic City
18.01.86	Louis Rivera W RSC 7 Atlantic City
06.05.86	Charlie Boston W PTS 10 Atlantic City
13.07.86	Milton McCrory L PTS 10 Las Vegas
17.10.86	Thomas Hearns L PTS 12 Detroit (*NABF Middleweight Title Challenge*)
20.02.87	Jose Quinones L RSC 3 Atlantic City
18.08.87	Lenny Lapaglia W PTS 10 Atlantic City
06.11.87	Tony Thornton W PTS 13 Atlantic City (*Vacant USBA Middleweight Title*)
29.01.88	Ron Essett DREW 10 Atlantic City

Summary: 37 contests, won 28, drew 4, lost 5.

Jorge Urbina Diaz
Patzcuaro, Mexico. *Born* 02.01.66
S. Bantamweight

23.04.82	Sergio Jimenez W CO 4 Guadalajara
21.05.82	Antonio Ramos W CO 3 Guadalajara
26.06.82	Raul Martinez W RSC 2 Guadalajara
20.01.83	Luis Fernando W CO 5 Uruapan
04.02.83	Alejandro Sosa W PTS 10 Colima
17.02.83	Jesus Mayorga W PTS 10 Guadalajara
11.03.83	Javier Hernandez L RSC 2 Mexico City
13.05.83	Ricardo Gonzalez W CO 4 Guadalajara
03.06.83	Mario Rivera W RSC 1 Guadalajara
05.08.83	Roberto Ramos W CO 5 Guadalajara
16.09.83	Lupe Torres W PTS 10 Guadalajara
12.11.83	Damian Hernandez W RSC 7 Mexico City
16.12.83	Roberto Martinez W CO 2 Guadalajara
13.01.84	Oscar Guzman W CO 3 Guadalajara
17.02.84	Jesus Mayorga W PTS 10 Guadalajara
06.04.84	Julio Duendano W RSC 5 Guadalajara

Doug de Witt (left) looks apprehensive here, but at the end of the ten-rounder he shared the spoils with Don Lee, back in March 1985

Tom Casino

11.05.84 Fidel Martinez DREW 10 Guadalajara
08.06.84 Jose Valdez W RSC 8 Guadalajara
13.07.84 Felipe Fernandez W RSC 6 Guadalajara
23.08.84 Carlos de la Paz L CO 2 Guadalajara
02.11.84 Lupe Torres W CO 4 Guadalajara
19.01.85 Hilario Manjarrez W CO 4 Mexico City
01.03.85 Javier Hernandez L RSC 4 Zihuatanejo
30.03.85 Angel Faz W CO 2 Monterrey
17.05.85 Enrique Ursua W RSC 7 Guadalajara
06.07.85 Jose Pineda L PTS 10 Ciudad Valles
06.09.85 Jorge Ramirez L PTS 10 Monterrey
18.10.85 Martin Garcia W PTS 10 Guadalajara
10.02.86 Paul Lucas DREW 8 Los Angeles
05.04.86 Jaime Garza L RSC 3 Palm Springs
05.06.86 Gaby Gutierrez W RSC 7 Sacramento
03.07.86 Eddie Rodriguez W PTS 8 San Jose
13.08.86 Darryl Thigpen W RSC 6 Los Angeles
04.09.86 Alex Madrid W RSC 1 San Jose
02.10.86 Adrian Arreola W PTS 10 San Jose
13.11.86 Hector Cortez W PTS 12 San Jose
11.12.86 Tony Montoya W RSC 5 San Jose
12.02.87 Jorge Rodriguez W PTS 10 San Jose
05.04.87 Seung-Hoon Lee L CO 10 Seoul
(IBF S. Bantamweight Title Challenge)
07.08.87 Harold Petty W PTS 10 San Jose
28.03.88 Jorge Ramirez L RSC 5 Los Angeles
Summary: 41 contests, won 31, drew 2, lost 8.

Raul Diaz
Bucaramanga, Colombia
Former Undefeated Fecarbox & Colombian S. Flyweight Champion

21.10.78 Gonzalo Rios W RSC 4 Bucaramanga
19.11.78 William Salgado W PTS 6 Bucaramanga
03.12.78 Abdon Peralta W CO 1 Bucaramanga
18.02.79 Oliveiro Mahecha W PTS 8 Bucaramanga
18.03.79 Juan Herrera W PTS 8 Bucaramanga
10.06.79 Urbano Saltarin W PTS 10 Bucaramanga
15.07.79 Hector Pinto W RSC 4 Bucaramanga
09.08.79 Felipe Hernandez W RSC 9 Bucaramanga
17.09.79 Manuel Rios W PTS 10 Bucaramanga
02.12.79 Sofanor Rodriguez W RSC 7 Bucaramanga
23.12.79 Sofanor Rodriguez W CO 6 Cucuta
10.02.80 Carlos Osorio W RSC 4 Bucaramanga
(Colombian S. Flyweight Title Challenge)
15.06.80 John Jandris W RSC 8 Bucaramanga
26.06.80 Luis Tapias W PTS 10 Cartagena
23.08.80 Henry Diaz W PTS 12 Bucaramanga
(Colombian S. Flyweight Title Defence)
26.02.81 Julio S. Solano L PTS 12 Santo Domingo
(Latin American S. Flyweight Title Challenge)
11.04.81 Pascual Polanco W DIS 3 Cartagena
17.06.81 Henry Diaz W CO 10 Cartagena
21.07.81 Luis Tapias L PTS 10 Monteria
26.02.82 Jorge Ortiz W RSC 9 Bucaramanga
17.04.82 Miguel Perez L RSC 7 Cartagena
(Colombian S. Flyweight Title Defence)
03.06.83 Joaquin Carballo W RSC 3 Barranquilla
(Vacant Colombian S. Flyweight Title)
12.08.83 Alfredo Herrera W RSC 4 Bucaramanga
(Colombian S. Flyweight Title Defence)
01.10.83 Luis Newman W PTS 10 Monteria
07.04.84 Pedro Romero W RSC 10 Bucaramanga
(Fecarbox S. Flyweight Title Challenge)
30.06.84 Jorge Echavarria W RSC 5 Bucaramanga
02.03.85 Juan Polo Perez L PTS 10 Cartagena
30.03.85 Miguel Perez W PTS 10 Bucaramanga
05.10.85 Toribio Riasco W CO 10 Bucaramanga
28.02.86 Rafael Betancourt W RSC 5 Bucaramanga
30.05.86 Jorge Monar W PTS 10 Bucaramanga
24.10.86 Don Brockington W RSC 3 Fort Lauderdale
14.11.86 Karry Allen W PTS 10 Fort Lauderdale
17.01.87 Juan Camero W RSC 3 Miami
02.08.87 Luis Chanis W PTS 10 Barrancabermeja
20.02.88 Elly Pical L PTS 15 Pontianak
(IBF S. Flyweight Title Challenge)
Summary: 36 contests, won 31, lost 5.

Robert Dickie
Swansea, Wales. *Born* Carmarthen 23.06.64
WBC International S. Featherweight Champion. Former Undefeated British Featherweight Champion

12.03.83 Billy Hough W PTS 6 Swindon
25.04.83 Charlie Brown W RSC 4 Aberdeen
16.05.83 George Bailey W RSC 3 Birmingham
27.05.83 Howard Williams W RSC 3 Swansea
13.06.83 Danny Flynn DREW 8 Glasgow
10.10.83 Danny Flynn L RSC 5 Glasgow
14.05.84 Dave Pratt W PTS 8 Nottingham
24.10.84 Charlie Coke W RSC 3 Mayfair
21.11.84 John Sharkey W DIS 4 Solihull
08.12.84 Steve Enright W RSC 1 Swansea
25.02.85 John Sharkey W CO 2 Glasgow
20.03.85 John Maloney W RSC 3 Solihull
08.05.85 Mark Reefer W RSC 1 Solihull
31.07.85 Dean Bramhald W RSC 7 Porthcawl
07.10.85 Frank Khonkhobe DREW 10 Kimberley
09.04.86 John Feeney W PTS 12 London
(Vacant British Featherweight Title)
30.07.86 Steve Sammy Sims W CO 5 Ebbw Vale
(British Featherweight Title Defence)
29.10.86 John Feeney W PTS 12 Ebbw Vale
(British Featherweight Title Defence)
20.10.87 Rocky Lawlor W DIS 2 Stoke
18.01.88 Arvell Campbell W PTS 8 Cardiff
28.03.88 Hengky Gun W RSC 5 Stoke
(WBC International S. Featherweight Title Challenge)
Summary: 21 contests, won 18, drew 2, lost 1.

Marcello di Crocce
Benito Juarez, Argentine. *Born* 11.08.63
Argentinian Welterweight Champion

13.01.84 Claudio Alvarez W CO 1 Villa Huidobro
19.05.84 Norberto Ruiz W RSC 3 Buenos Aires
13.07.84 Roberto Yonni W CO 2 Concordia
17.08.84 Alberto Alvarado W CO 6 Rivadavia
07.09.84 Juan Burgues W RSC 5 Montevideo
11.10.84 Manuel Ledesma W CO 1 Rivadavia
09.11.84 Juan A. Merlo W CO 7 Concordia
08.12.84 Luis Sanchez W RTD 4 Buenos Aires
06.03.85 Juan Barbosa W PTS 10 Rio Gallegos
30.03.85 Carlos Prieto L PTS 10 Buenos Aires
15.06.85 Hector Gonzalez W CO 2 Buenos Aires
31.07.85 Jose Luduena W RSC 8 Buenos Aires
04.09.85 Hector Gonzalez W PTS 10 Buenos Aires
02.11.85 Hugo Luero W TD 3 Buenos Aires
07.12.85 Hector Gonzalez W CO 1 Buenos Aires
25.01.86 Hugo Luero DREW 10 Mar del Plata
12.04.86 Hugo Luero DREW 10 Buenos Aires
09.05.86 Simon Escobar W PTS 10 Rivadavia
11.07.86 Hugo Luero W RSC 9 Rivadavia
27.08.86 Ramon Abeldano L PTS 10 Buenos Aires
10.10.86 Mario Matthysse W PTS 10 Viedma
31.10.86 Juan O. Barbosa W PTS 10 Mar del Plata
22.11.86 Antonio Juarez W PTS 10 Buenos Aires
02.02.87 Luciano Ploner W CO 5 Las Grutas
20.02.87 Ramon Collado W PTS 10 Mar del Plata
28.03.87 Ramon Jara W PTS 10 Buenos Aires
04.07.87 Antonio Dacosta W RTD 10 Buenos Aires
13.11.87 Simon Escobar W PTS 12 Villa Mercedes
(Argentinian Welterweight Title Challenge)
04.03.88 Antonio Juarez W PTS 10 Rio Gallegos
02.04.88 Jose Ludvena W RSC 9 Buenos Aires
Summary: 30 contests, won 26, drew 2, lost 2.

Othal (Choo Choo) Dixon
Houston, USA. *Born* 22.10.60
L. Welterweight

28.08.81 Ken Releford W PTS 6 Beaumont
11.07.83 Kean McGill W CO 2 Houston

Othal Dixon
Peter Goldfield/USA

26.07.83 Marvin Freeman W CO 1 Beaumont
12.11.83 Nacho Acosta W CO 3 Beaumont
17.01.84 Anthony Bryant W RSC 4 Houston
07.02.84 Calvin Prejan W RSC 4 Houston
27.03.84 Ricky Henderson W RSC 7 Houston
19.04.84 Ruben Gallardo W RSC 5 Houston
24.05.84 Dwayne Primm W CO 2 Houston
15.06.84 Teddy Hatfield W RSC 5 Houston
11.10.84 Arthur Clarke W RSC 2 Houston
16.11.84 Charles Allen W RSC 5 Houston
18.03.85 Efren Olivo W RSC 2 Houston
26.04.85 Sammy Young W RSC 4 Atlantic City
19.06.85 Sammy Fuentes L PTS 10 Atlantic City
20.11.85 Jeff Goodwin W RSC 2 Houston
11.12.85 Steve Mitchell W PTS 10 Houston
09.10.86 J. D. Dobbins W CO 2 Houston
13.11.86 Dwayne Primm W RSC 5 Houston
27.02.87 Howard Davis L PTS 10 Atlantic City
22.05.87 Ricky Henderson W RSC 3 Houston
13.08.87 Ruben Munoz W CO 1 Houston
17.10.87 Jimmy Paul W CO 4 Atlantic City
15.01.88 John Meekins L RSC 2 Atlantic City
Summary: 24 contests, won 21, lost 3.

Michael (Dynamite) Dokes
Akron, USA. *Born* 10.08.58
Former WBA Heavyweight Champion. Former Undefeated NABF & Con. Am. Heavyweight Champion

15.10.76 Al Byrd W RSC 4 Los Angeles
14.01.77 Sergio Rodriguez W RSC 2 Pensacola
29.01.77 Dave Wilson W PTS 4 Miami
06.03.77 Charlie Jordan W RSC 4 Marion
10.04.77 Ed Turner W PTS 6 Miami
03.03.78 George Holden W CO 3 Curacao
25.03.78 Abdul Khan W PTS 8 Las Vegas
29.04.78 Dan Johnson W PTS 6 Los Angeles
26.09.78 Terry Mims W PTS 8 Miami
27.10.78 Eugene Green W PTS 8 New York
08.12.78 Ira Martin W RSC 8 New York
23.03.79 Wendell Bailey W PTS 10 Las Vegas
12.05.79 Greg Sorrentino W RSC 3 Las Vegas
20.07.79 Willie McIntyre W CO 2 Miami

Michael Dokes (right) shoots a right over the top of Eddie Richardson's left lead, before stopping him in the tenth and final round
Tom Casino

28.09.79 Jimmy Young W PTS 10 Las Vegas
13.01.80 Earl Tripp W RSC 1 Las Vegas
10.02.80 Lucien Rodriguez W PTS 10 Miami
19.04.80 Ossie Ocasio DREW 10 San Juan
28.06.80 Ossie Ocasio W RSC 1 San Juan
02.10.80 Tom Fischer W CO 7 Las Vegas
22.03.81 Randy Cobb W PTS 10 Las Vegas
12.06.81 John L. Gardner W CO 4 Detroit
09.08.81 Harry Terrell W CO 1 Cleveland
06.11.81 George Chaplin W PTS 10 Pittsburgh
30.01.82 Lynn Ball W RSC 1 Las Vegas
(Vacant NABF Heavyweight Title)
20.03.82 Franco Thomas W RSC 5 Atlantic City
(NABF Heavyweight Title Defence)
10.12.82 Mike Weaver W RSC 1 Las Vegas
(WBA Heavyweight Title Challenge)
20.05.83 Mike Weaver DREW 15 Las Vegas
(WBA Heavyweight Title Defence)
23.09.83 Gerrie Coetzee L CO 10 Richfield
(WBA Heavyweight Title Defence)
31.08.84 Mike Jameson W PTS 10 Las Vegas
16.02.85 Young Joe Louis W CO 2 Kingston
15.03.85 Randy Cobb W TD 4 Las Vegas
(Vacant Con. Am. Heavyweight Title)
17.12.87 K. P. Porter W RSC 5 New York
22.01.88 Ken Lakusta W RSC 7 Atlantic City
24.02.88 Eddie Richardson W RSC 10 New York
28.04.88 James Pritchard W RSC 7 New York
Summary: 36 contests, won 33, drew 2, lost 1.

James (Buster) Douglas
Ohio, USA. *Born* 07.04.60
Heavyweight

31.05.81 Dan Banks W CO 3 Columbus
23.07.81 Michael Lear W PTS 4 Columbus
27.09.81 Mike Rodgers W CO 3 Columbus
14.10.81 Tommy Stevenson W RSC 5 Indianapolis
23.10.81 Johnny Clark W PTS 4 Toledo
06.11.81 David Bey L RSC 3 Pittsburgh
23.12.81 Donny Johnson W RSC 3 Canton
23.01.82 Hubert Adams W CO 1 McConnelsville
14.02.82 Don Townsend W PTS 6 Erie
16.02.82 Marvin Earle W CO 2 Kalamazoo
25.03.82 Rick Enis W PTS 6 Indianapolis
24.04.82 Mel Daniels W RSC 4 Johnstown
16.10.82 Steffen Tangstad DREW 8 Chicago
20.11.82 Tim Johnson W CO 1 Columbus
09.03.83 Jesse Clark W CO 2 Niles
29.03.83 Leroy Diggs W CO 7 Atlantic City
16.04.83 Jesse Clark W RSC 2 Muskegon
29.04.83 Henry Porter W CO 2 Atlantic City
05.07.83 Dave Johnson W PTS 10 Atlantic City
28.09.83 Eugene Cato W RSC 1 Atlantic City
17.12.83 Mike White L RSC 9 Atlantic City
09.07.84 Dave Starkey NC 1 Columbus
09.11.84 Randy Cobb W PTS 10 Las Vegas
27.03.85 Dion Simpson W RSC 1 Atlantic City
09.05.85 Jesse Ferguson L PTS 10 Atlantic City
17.01.86 Greg Page W PTS 10 Atlanta
19.04.86 Dave Jaco W PTS 10 Las Vegas
06.09.86 Dee Collier W PTS 10 Las Vegas
30.05.87 Tony Tucker L RSC 10 Las Vegas
(Vacant IBF Heavyweight Title)
19.11.87 Donnie Long W CO 2 Columbus
24.02.88 Percell Davis W RSC 10 Daluth
16.04.88 Jerry Halstead W RSC 9 Las Vegas
Summary: 32 contests, won 26, drew 1, lost 4, nd 1.

Tyrone Downes
Barbados. *Born* 1958
Commonwealth Featherweight Champion. Former Undefeated Barbados & Fecarbox Lightweight Champion. Former Undefeated Barbados Featherweight Champion

12.02.75 Bruce Scanterbury W PTS 6 Bridgetown
20.03.75 Bruce Scanterbury W PTS 8 Bridgetown
11.04.75 Malcolm Beckles W PTS 10 Bridgetown
24.05.76 Silford Ashley W PTS 10 Bridgetown
04.06.76 Silford Ashley W PTS 10 Bridgetown
23.06.77 Norman Yearwood W PTS 10 Bridgetown
21.07.77 Norman Yearwood W PTS 15 Bridgetown
(Barbados Featherweight Title Challenge)
03.01.78 Hurricane Jackson W PTS 15 Bridgetown
(Barbados Lightweight Title Challenge)
04.03.79 Azor Agosto W PTS 10 Bridgetown
20.03.79 Malcolm Beckles W PTS 10 Bridgetown
15.06.80 Miguel Morales L RSC 6 Port of Spain
12.08.80 Fitzroy Davidson L PTS 10 Port of Spain
20.03.81 Jesus Flores L PTS 10 Port of Spain
29.01.82 Julius Martin W PTS 8 Port of Spain
04.06.82 Ismael Santana W RSC 10 Port of Spain
27.08.82 Roberto Pineiro W PTS 10 Port of Spain
22.02.83 Nelson Cruz W RSC 5 Port of Spain
19.08.83 Geronimo Luquez W PTS 12 Port of Spain
(Vacant Fecarbox Lightweight Title)
02.12.83 Luis Rivera W RSC 5 Port of Spain
16.12.83 David Capo W RSC 7 Port of Spain
16.03.84 Denzil Surall W RSC 5 Port of Spain
17.05.84 Marcos Villasana L RSC 4 Los Angeles
27.10.84 Aurelio Benitez W PTS 10 Port of Spain
01.03.85 Terry Kemp W RSC 3 Port of Spain
10.05.85 Florentino Garcia W RSC 2 Fort Lauderdale
11.06.85 Bernard Taylor L PTS 10 Atlantic City
03.08.85 Alberto Parra W PTS 10 Port of Spain
01.11.85 Hector Cortes W RSC 3 Port of Spain
28.02.86 Snake Mandeya W PTS 12 Port of Spain
(Vacant Commonwealth Featherweight Title)
04.10.86 Edwin Pintor W PTS 10 Bridgetown
16.03.87 Roger Arevalo W PTS 10 Los Angeles
23.05.87 Ray Akwaye W RTD 5 Port of Spain
(Commonwealth Featherweight Title Defence)
02.10.87 Felix Guzman W CO 2 Port of Spain
Summary: 33 contests, won 28, lost 5.

Buster (Demon) Drayton
Philadelphia, USA. *Born* 02.03.53
Former IBF L. Middleweight Champion

09.11.78 Charles Carey DREW 4 Virginia Beach
14.12.78 Jesse Carter W PTS 6 Virginia Beach
31.05.79 Frank Moore W CO 1 Virginia Beach
03.07.79 Bob Saxton W CO 1 Atlantic City
30.08.79 Jesse Carter W CO 6 Virginia Beach
20.09.79 Julius Spell W PTS 4 Virginia Beach
18.10.79 Cliff Smith W RSC 1 Philadelphia
09.08.80 Bill Harrington W RSC 2 Atlantic City
01.10.80 Curtis Taylor ND 8 Atlantic City
06.11.80 Kevin Perry L RSC 3 Atlantic City
24.01.81 Dan Snyder W CO 4 Philadelphia
07.02.81 Mark Holmes L PTS 6 Atlantic City
14.06.81 Mario Maldonado L PTS 8 Atlantic City
25.07.81 Tyrone Demby W PTS 6 Atlantic City
23.12.81 D. C. Walker W CO 2 Providence
17.01.82 Dan Snyder W PTS 8 Atlantic City
07.03.82 Lindell Holmes L PTS 10 Atlantic City
29.04.82 Duane Thomas W RSC 7 Atlantic City
31.07.82 Bruce Johnson W RSC 9 Atlantic City
31.10.82 Sumbu Kalambay L PTS 8 San Remo
05.02.83 Bushy Bester L PTS 10 Johannesburg
12.04.83 Dave Plowden W PTS 8 Charleston
12.05.83 Clint Jackson W RSC 2 Bristol
09.06.83 Patrizio Diaz W PTS 10 Atlantic City
01.09.83 Mario Maldonado L PTS 10 Atlantic City
01.10.83 Fred Hutchings L PTS 10 Stockton
28.01.84 Greg Clark W RSC 2 Johannesburg
11.04.84 Jimmy Cable W CO 1 London
13.05.84 Mark Kaylor W RSC 7 Wembley
25.06.84 Gary Coates W CO 4 Atlantic City
26.09.84 Terry Holmes W RTD 2 Atlantic City
28.11.84 Tony Harrison W RSC 10 Atlantic City
13.02.85 Thomas Smith W PTS 10 Atlantic City
14.04.85 James Kinchen L PTS 10 London
10.06.85 Dennis Johnson W RSC 10 Metairie
14.09.85 John Jarvis W RSC 6 Atlantic City
22.01.86 Bruce Jackson W CO 5 Atlantic City
04.04.86 Sammy Leonard W RSC 4 Atlantic City
04.06.86 Carlos Santos W PTS 15 East Rutherford
(Vacant IBF L. Middleweight Title)
20.06.86 Benito Fernandez W RSC 5 Paris
24.08.86 Davey Moore W RSC 10 Juan les Pins
(IBF L. Middleweight Title Defence)
28.02.87 Juan A. Villa W CO 2 Vincennes
27.03.87 Said Skouma W RTD 10 Cannes
(IBF L. Middleweight Title Defence)
27.06.87 Matthew Hilton L PTS 15 Montreal
(IBF L. Middleweight Title Defence)
05.12.87 Leroy Jones W CO 4 Davenport
Summary: 45 contests, won 33, drew 1, lost 10, nd 1.

Frankie Duarte
Venice, USA. *Born* 03.09.54
Former Undefeated NABF Bantamweight Champion

16.08.73 Tony Ramos W CO 1 Los Angeles
27.09.73 Baby Corona W RSC 3 Los Angeles
18.10.73 Manny Gonzalez W PTS 4 Los Angeles
25.10.73 Juan Lopez W RSC 4 Los Angeles
15.11.73 Joaquin Heredia W CO 2 Los Angeles
02.01.74 Johnny Meza W RSC 1 Las Vegas
10.01.74 Gaspar Montejo W CO 3 Los Angeles
26.01.74 Jorge Rodriguez W RSC 2 Tucson
07.02.74 Pedro Torres W CO 3 Los Angeles
12.02.74 Jorge de la Rosa W RSC 1 Sacramento
21.03.74 Frank Granados W RSC 5 Los Angeles
24.05.74 Tetsuru Kawakami W PTS 10 Los Angeles
11.07.74 Rufino Hernandez W RSC 3 Los Angeles
29.08.74 Antonio Garcia W CO 5 Los Angeles
26.09.74 Tanny Amancio W RSC 5 Los Angeles
04.11.74 Cecil Escobido W RSC 2 Honolulu
03.12.74 Joe Guevara L PTS 12 Sacramento
13.03.75 Jorge Altamirano W PTS 10 Los Angeles
24.04.75 Famosito Gomez W PTS 10 Los Angeles
29.05.75 Famosito Gomez L PTS 10 Los Angeles
20.09.75 Jose Rosa W CO 6 Los Angeles
15.10.75 Al Diaz W PTS 10 Honolulu
08.01.76 Seco Luna W PTS 10 Los Angeles
13.02.76 Santiago Hernandez W CO 4 San Bernardino
17.06.76 Francisco Cruz W RSC 8 Los Angeles
11.05.76 Ernie Graf W RSC 6 Honolulu
27.06.76 Jose Cazares W RSC 4 Tijuana
11.11.76 Alfonso Gutierrez W RSC 5 Los Angeles
09.12.76 Martin Buchanan W RSC 4 Los Angeles
14.04.77 Jorge Carrasco W CO 9 Los Angeles
09.06.77 Albert Davila L RSC 5 Los Angeles
12.02.78 Chamaco Lopez W RSC 9 Mexicali
25.02.78 Danny O'Campo W RSC 9 Los Angeles
29.08.78 Peter King W PTS 10 Pico Rivera
22.02.79 Francisco Flores W PTS 12 Los Angeles
19.06.79 Rolando Navarrete L PTS 10 Honolulu
24.02.81 Neptali Alamag L PTS 10 Honolulu
30.05.84 Louis Hernandez W CO 7 Reseda
20.07.84 David Rojas W RSC 4 Culver City
20.11.84 Carlos Canchola W PTS 10 Reseda
10.04.85 Richie Sandoval L PTS 10 Sacramento
24.09.85 Ron Cisneros W RSC 7 Los Angeles
29.10.85 Fred Jackson T DRAW 2 Reseda
28.01.86 Pedro Gonzalez W RSC 1 Reseda
17.03.86 Mike Morino W PTS 10 Los Angeles
20.05.86 George Garcia W RSC 6 Los Angeles
10.07.86 Jesus Salud W RSC 9 Los Angeles
(Vacant NABF Bantamweight Title)
30.09.86 Jose Torres W RSC 9 Reseda
03.02.87 Bernardo Pinango L PTS 15 Los Angeles
(WBA Bantamweight Title Challenge)
22.06.87 Albert Davila W RSC 10 Los Angeles
(NABF Bantamweight Title Defence)
Summary: 50 contests, won 42, drew 1, lost 7.

Johnny Duplessis
Peter Goldfield/USA

Johnny (Super D) Duplessis
New Orleans, USA. *Born* 04.08.66
Former Undefeated Con. Am. Lightweight Champion

25.09.84 Willie Covington W RSC 2 Metairie
11.10.84 James Seals W PTS 4 Morgan City
16.10.84 Ken Pryor W RSC 4 Pasadena
20.11.84 Elton Sneez W CO 2 Metairie
04.12.84 Marvin Freeman W CO 1 St Bernard
16.01.85 Ray Smith W CO 2 Lafayette
21.02.85 Tony Guerrero W PTS 4 Morgan City
04.03.85 Jerome Brooks W RSC 5 Metairie
18.04.85 Tony Guerrero W RSC 3 Monroe

07.05.85 Darren Neal W RSC 4 Metairie
10.06.85 James Sanders W RSC 4 Metairie
11.07.85 Jim Martin W PTS 6 Morgan City
30.07.85 Victor McCray W CO 2 Metairie
06.09.85 Reuben Moran W CO 1 Terrytown
17.09.85 Norris Steiner W RSC 4 Metairie
15.10.85 Reese Smith W PTS 6 Metairie
26.11.85 Darryl Jacobs W PTS 6 Atlantic City
06.03.86 Joey Soler W PTS 8 Metairie
06.05.86 Joe Celestine W RSC 3 Metairie
01.07.86 Earl Sabber W RSC 3 New Orleans
26.08.86 Mark Lassien W CO 2 Metairie
11.12.86 Edwin Curet W PTS 10 Metairie
09.03.87 Nelson Bolanos W RSC 6 New Orleans (*Con. Am. Lightweight Title Challenge*)
30.06.87 Robert Dixon W RSC 5 Metairie
25.08.87 Anthony Williams W PTS 10 Atlantic City
16.12.87 Sergio Aguirre W PTS 10 New Orleans
16.04.88 Herminio Morales W RSC 2 Las Vegas
Summary: 27 contests, won 27.

Johnny du Plooy

Johannesburg, South Africa. *Born* 27.09.64
Heavyweight

27.04.85 Serfonis Naile W RSC 1 Johannesburg
10.07.85 Blessing Mbyasa W CO 1 Durban
07.09.85 Howard Mpepsi W RSC 5 Johannesburg
18.12.85 Hansie van den Berg W CO 3 Cape Town
19.02.86 Linus Wallette W RSC 1 Johannesburg
02.04.86 Ron Ellis W RSC 2 Durban
14.05.86 Stanley Ross W PTS 8 Johannesburg
01.09.86 Mike Jameson W PTS 10 Durban
07.10.86 Young Joe Louis W RTD 4 Durban
30.10.86 Steve Zouski W RSC 4 Hartford
22.11.86 David Jaco W CO 2 Johannesburg
07.02.87 K. P. Porter W CO 6 Sun City
27.04.87 David Bey W CO 9 Johannesburg
24.06.87 James Tillis W RSC 10 Johannesburg
27.07.87 Tyrone Booze W CO 2 Johannesburg
12.09.87 Bennie Knoetze W CO 1 Johannesburg
31.10.87 Rickey Parkey W RSC 10 Sun City
28.11.87 Mike Weaver L RTD 6 Johannesburg
27.02.88 James Broad W CO 4 Johannesburg
30.04.88 Mike Weaver W CO 2 Sun City
Summary: 20 contests, won 19, lost 1.

Roberto (Hands of Stone) Duran

Guarare, Panama. *Born* 16.06.51
Former Undefeated World Lightweight Champion. Former WBC Welterweight Champion. Former Undefeated WBA L. Middleweight Champion

08.03.67 Carlos Mendoza W PTS 4 Colon
04.04.67 Manuel Jimenez W CO 1 Colon
14.05.67 Juan Gondola W CO 1 Colon
30.05.67 Eduardo Morales W CO 1 Panama City
10.08.67 Enrique Jacobo W CO 1 Panama City
12.01.68 Cesar de Leon W CO 2 Panama City
20.06.68 Eduardo Morales W CO 1 Panama City
25.08.68 Leroy Cargill W CO 1 Panama City
07.12.68 Carlos Howard W CO 1 Panama City
19.01.69 Alberto Brands W RSC 4 Panama City
01.02.69 Eduardo Fruto W PTS 8 Panama City
18.05.69 Jacinto Garcia W RSC 4 Panama City
22.06.69 Adolfo Osses W RSC 7 Panama City
16.07.69 Serafin Garcia W RSC 5 Panama City
23.11.69 Luis Patino W CO 8 Panama City
05.04.70 Felipe Torres W PTS 10 Mexico City
16.05.70 Ernesto Marcel W RSC 10 Panama City
10.07.70 Clemente Mucino W CO 6 Colon
05.09.70 Marvin Castanedas W CO 1 Panama City
18.10.70 Nacho Castanedas W RSC 3 Panama City
09.01.71 Jose Angel Herrera W RSC 6 Monterrey
06.03.71 Jose Acosta W CO 1 Panama City
29.05.71 Lloyd Marshall W CO 6 Panama City
18.07.71 Fermin Soto W RSC 3 Monterrey
13.09.71 Benny Huertas W CO 1 New York
16.10.71 Hiroshi Kobayashi W CO 7 Panama City
15.01.72 Angel Robinson Garcia W PTS 10 Panama City
10.03.72 Francisco Munoz W RSC 1 Panama City
26.06.72 Ken Buchanan W RSC 13 New York (*WBA Lightweight Title Challenge*)
02.09.72 Greg Potter W CO 1 Panama City
29.10.72 Lupe Ramirez W CO 1 Panama City
17.11.72 Esteban de Jesus L PTS 10 New York
20.01.73 Jimmy Robertson W CO 5 Panama City (*WBA Lightweight Title Defence*)
22.02.73 Juan Medina W RSC 7 Los Angeles
17.03.73 Javier Ayala W PTS 10 Los Angeles
14.04.73 Gerardo Ferrat W CO 2 Panama City
02.06.73 Hector Thompson W RSC 8 Panama City (*WBA Lightweight Title Defence*)
04.08.73 Doc McClendon W PTS 10 San Juan
08.09.73 Guts Ishimatsu W RSC 10 Panama City (*WBA Lightweight Title Defence*)
01.12.73 Tony Garcia W CO 2 Santiago
21.01.74 Leonard Taverez W RSC 4 Paris
16.02.74 Armando Mendoza W RSC 3 Panama City
16.03.74 Esteban de Jesus W RSC 11 Panama City (*WBA Lightweight Title Defence*)
06.07.74 Flash Gallego W RSC 5 Panama City
02.09.74 Hector Matta W PTS 10 San Juan
31.10.74 Jose Vasquez W CO 2 San Jose
16.11.74 Adalberto Vanegas W CO 1 Panama City
21.12.74 Masataka Takayama W RSC 1 San Jose (*WBA Lightweight Title Defence*)
15.02.75 Andres Salgado W CO 1 Panama City
02.03.75 Ray Lampkin W CO 14 Panama City (*WBA Lightweight Title Defence*)
03.06.75 Jose Peterson W RSC 1 Miami
02.08.75 Pedro Mendoza W CO 1 Managua
13.09.75 Alirio Acuna W CO 3 Chitre
30.09.75 Edwin Viruet W PTS 10 Uniondale
14.12.75 Leoncio Ortiz W CO 15 San Juan (*WBA Lightweight Title Defence*)
04.05.76 Saoul Mamby W PTS 10 Miami
22.05.76 Lou Bizzarro W CO 14 Erie (*WBA Lightweight Title Defence*)
31.07.76 Emiliano Villa W RSC 7 Panama City
15.10.76 Alvaro Rojas W CO 1 Los Angeles (*WBA Lightweight Title Defence*)
29.01.77 Vilomar Fernandez W CO 13 Miami (*WBA Lightweight Title Defence*)
16.05.77 Javier Muniz W PTS 10 Landover
06.08.77 Bernardo Diaz W CO 1 Panama City
17.09.77 Edwin Viruet W PTS 15 Philadelphia (*WBA Lightweight Title Defence*)
21.01.78 Esteban de Jesus W CO 12 Las Vegas (*WBA Lightweight Title Defence. WBC Lightweight Title Challenge*)
27.04.78 Adolph Viruet W PTS 10 New York
01.09.78 Ezequiel Obando W CO 2 Panama City
08.12.78 Monroe Brooks W RSC 8 New York
08.04.79 Jimmy Heair W PTS 10 Las Vegas
22.06.79 Carlos Palomino W PTS 10 New York
28.09.79 Zeferino Gonzalez W PTS 10 Las Vegas
13.01.80 Josef Nsubuga W RSC 4 Las Vegas
24.02.80 Wellington Wheatley W RSC 7 Las Vegas
20.06.80 Sugar Ray Leonard W PTS 15 Montreal (*WBC Welterweight Title Challenge*)
25.11.80 Sugar Ray Leonard L RTD 8 New Orleans (*WBC Welterweight Title Defence*)
09.08.81 Nino Gonzalez W PTS 10 Cleveland
26.09.81 Luigi Minchillo W PTS 10 Las Vegas
30.01.82 Wilfred Benitez L PTS 15 Las Vegas (*WBC L. Middleweight Title Challenge*)
04.09.82 Kirkland Laing L PTS 10 Detroit
12.11.82 Jimmy Batten W PTS 10 Miami
29.01.83 Pipino Cuevas W RSC 4 Los Angeles
16.06.83 Davey Moore W RSC 8 New York (*WBA L. Middleweight Title Challenge*)
10.11.83 Marvin Hagler L PTS 15 Las Vegas (*World Middleweight Title Challenge*)
15.06.84 Thomas Hearns L CO 2 Las Vegas (*WBC L. Middleweight Title Challenge*)
31.01.86 Manuel Zambrano W CO 2 Panama
18.04.86 Jorge Suero W CO 2 Panama
23.06.86 Robbie Sims L PTS 10 Las Vegas
16.05.87 Victor Claudio W PTS 10 Miami
12.09.87 Juan C. Gimenez W PTS 10 Miami
05.02.87 Ricky Stackhouse W PTS 10 Atlantic City
14.04.88 Paul Thorn W RSC 6 Atlantic City
Summary: 90 contests, won 83, lost 7.

The ageless Roberto Duran (right) keeps going. Ricky Stackhouse is pictured running on to the left hand of Duran, who has now been a pro for 21 years Tom Casino

Carlos Elliott

Japan. *Born* Alabama, USA 29.04.62
OPBF L. Middleweight Champion. Former Undefeated Japanese L. Middleweight Champion

04.03.83 Masahashi Yoshida W CO 2 Tokyo
21.06.83 Nobo Chisaka W CO 2 Hachinohe
02.09.83 Won-Ki Chung W CO 4 Tokyo
19.11.83 Chung-Jae Hwang W CO 2 Daejon
03.02.84 Young Dela Cruz W CO 1 Tokyo
05.04.84 Byung-Sun Yuh W CO 5 Tokyo
30.07.84 Junya Kushikino L CO 6 Tokyo (*Japanese Welterweight Title Challenge*)
11.10.84 Ki-Keum Son W CO 3 Tokyo
10.01.85 Ki-Young Park W RSC 5 Tokyo
20.07.85 Mugen Kawasaka W CO 2 Hachinohe (*Japanese L. Middleweight Title Challenge*)
07.11.85 Mitsuo Hatano W RSC 8 Tokyo (*Japanese L. Middleweight Title Defence*)
09.01.86 Noboru Kawaguchi W RSC 1 Tokyo (*Japanese L. Middleweight Title Defence*)
24.03.86 Mitsuo Hatano W RSC 5 Tokyo (*Japanese L. Middleweight Title Defence*)
24.07.86 Tony Stockey W CO 1 Tokyo
02.12.86 Rolando Aldemir W RSC 5 Tokyo
02.04.87 Jae-Hyung Yuh W RSC 9 Tokyo (*Vacant OPBF L. Middleweight Title*)
22.07.87 Francisco Ferrer W PTS 8 Tokyo
28.11.87 San-Do Chung W PTS 12 Hachinohe (*OPBF L. Middleweight Title Defence*)
21.03.88 Renato Angulo W RSC 5 Tokyo
Summary: 19 contests, won 18, lost 1.

Lester Ellis

Melbourne, Australia. *Born* England 15.03.65
Australian L. Welterweight & Lightweight Champion. Former IBF S. Featherweight Champion. Former Undefeated Commonwealth S. Featherweight Champion

24.04.83 Ben Lappori W RSC 4 Preston
25.06.83 Roy Hughes W RSC 2 Heidelberg
06.10.83 Brian Roberts W PTS 8 Tottenham
17.11.83 Gary Williams W CO 2 Tottenham
01.12.83 Charlie Andrews W RSC 2 Shepparton
15.12.83 Kirk Blair W RSC 5 Tottenham
13.02.84 Jeff Smith W RSC 8 Melbourne
09.03.84 Dennis Talbot W RSC 3 Melbourne
20.05.84 Norm Stevens W RSC 6 Heidelberg
30.05.84 Lindsay Roberts W CO 1 Melbourne
04.07.84 Richard Fowler W RSC 10 Melbourne
14.09.84 Steve Sammy Sims W PTS 10 Melbourne
18.10.84 Kyoshi Sasaki W PTS 10 Melbourne

16.11.84 John Sichula W PTS 12 Melbourne
(Commonwealth S. Featherweight Title Challenge)
15.02.85 Hwan-Kil Yuh W PTS 15 Melbourne
(IBF S. Featherweight Title Challenge)
26.04.85 Rod Sequenan W CO 13 Melbourne
(IBF S. Featherweight Title Defence)
12.07.85 Barry Michael L PTS 15 Melbourne
(IBF S. Featherweight Title Defence)
04.11.85 Conrad Maez W RSC 2 Brisbane
02.12.85 Marvin Garris W PTS 10 Sidney
16.12.85 John Sichula L RSC 4 Melbourne
27.03.86 Rafael Solis W RSC 8 Melbourne
13.06.86 Idabeth Rojas W PTS 10 Adelaide
09.10.86 Tony Miller W PTS 10 Melbourne
13.03.87 Ernesto Espana W PTS 10 Melbourne
30.04.87 Dale Artango W RTD 6 Melbourne
(Australian Lightweight Title Challenge)
18.06.87 Babu Gounder W RSC 2 Melbourne
28.08.87 Tommy Cordova W RSC 10 Melbourne
12.02.88 Jun Tito W CO 3 Sydney
16.03.88 Pat Leglise W RTD 5 Brisbane
(Australian L. Welterweight Title Challenge)
20.04.88 Rod Sequenan W CO 1 Brisbane
Summary: 30 contests, won 28, lost 2.

Jean-Marie Emebe
France. *Born* Cameroons 17.08.55
L. Heavyweight. Former Undefeated ABU Middleweight Champion

03.07.76 Idrissia Konate W CO 5 Douala
14.08.76 Yene Dieudonne W CO 4 Douala
16.11.76 Manuel Lira W CO 3 Paris
21.05.77 Jean Grandjean W RSC 2 Douala
27.07.77 Abrahim Yovoutousso W CO 5 Douala
05.11.77 Billy Savage W CO 4 Lagos
(ABU Middleweight Title Challenge)
11.05.78 Joe Wilson W CO 5 Togo
06.10.78 Jose Hernandez W CO 7 Douala
02.03.79 Jacques Chinon W PTS 8 Douala
07.04.79 Jose Lozano W RTD 8 Douala
05.05.79 Idrissa Konate W RSC 3 Yaounde
09.11.79 Richard Ofuso W CO 1 Dakar
(ABU Middleweight Title Defence)
06.01.80 Jose Lozano L DIS 4 Libreville
19.03.81 Agamil Yilderim W RSC 9 Paris
21.05.81 Mel Dennis W RSC 3 Paris
07.11.81 Phil Keating W RSC 5 Noumea
14.12.81 Fred Reed W RSC 4 Paris
30.01.82 Bruce Strauss W CO 3 Yaounde
21.03.82 Ralph Moncrief W PTS 10 Atlantic City
14.12.82 William Brigham W RSC 2 Pasadena
18.02.83 Bob Patterson W RSC 9 New York
27.05.83 Murray Sutherland L RSC 9 Providence
10.02.84 Mauricio da Cruz W CO 1 Abidjan
06.05.85 John Davis W PTS 10 Abidjan
06.05.85 Jose Seys W RSC 3 Grenoble
13.12.85 Jonjo Green W PTS 10 Antibes
20.09.86 Marvin Johnson L RSC 13 Indianapolis
(WBA L. Heavyweight Title Challenge)
20.12.86 Tony Golden W CO 4 Yaounde
24.04.87 Jose Seys L DIS 4 Abidjan
03.04.88 Virgil Hill L RSC 11 Bismarck
(WBA L. Heavyweight Title Challenge)
Summary: 30 contests, won 25, lost 5.

Antonio Esparragoza
Venezuela. *Born* 02.09.59
WBA Featherweight Champion

24.02.81 Antony Wasa W RSC 2 Cumana
01.10.81 Ramon Bolivar W RSC 2 Maracay
31.10.81 Luis Solorzano W RSC 2 Maracay
25.01.82 David Siso W CO 2 Barquisimeto
01.02.82 Angel Torres L RSC 6 Caracas
10.05.82 Francisco Leta W RSC 5 Cumana
24.05.82 Alejandro Garcia W RSC 2 Cumana
21.06.82 Tito Roque W RSC 2 Cumana
26.07.82 Angel Torres W RSC 9 Cumana
04.10.82 Bernardo Pinango DREW 10 Caracas
06.11.82 Fred Pitalua W RSC 4 Caracas
19.02.83 Antonio Rodriguez W RSC 3 Cumana
26.03.83 Jose Mosqueda W RSC 7 Catia
13.05.83 Alberto Parra W RSC 3 Margarita
01.10.83 Fabio Mosquera W CO 3 Caracas
16.12.83 Ruben Veliz W RSC 3 Ciudad Bolivar
15.05.84 Jose de Jesus W RSC 5 Aruba
07.07.84 Eduardo Laguna W RSC 4 Maracaibo
11.08.84 Jose Guerrero W PTS 10 Aruba
10.10.84 Bernardo Checa DREW 10 Isla Margarita
02.02.85 Jeff Roberts W RSC 7 San Juan
23.02.85 Jose Rivera W RSC 2 Santo Domingo
04.05.85 Johnny de la Rosa W RSC 2 Aruba
17.02.86 Jose Ortiz W CO 2 Turmero
22.03.86 Bernardo Checa W CO 2 Caracas
19.05.86 Nelson Rodriguez DREW 10 San Juan
16.01.86 Octavio Quinonen W RSC 3 Phoenix
06.03.87 Steve Cruz W RSC 12 Fort Worth
(WBA Featherweight Title Challenge)
26.07.87 Pascual Aranda W CO 10 Houston
(WBA Featherweight Title Defence)
Summary: 29 contests, won 25, drew 3, lost 1.

Louie Espinosa
Phoenix, USA. *Born* 12.05.62
NABF S. Bantamweight Champion. Former WBA S. Bantamweight Champion

23.11.82 Adan Uribe W RSC 3 Phoenix
14.12.82 Ashby Dancy W RSC 3 Tucson
11.02.83 Leonard Ayala W CO 2 Phoenix
01.03.83 Felipe de Jesus W RSC 7 Phoenix
03.04.83 Ron Gary W PTS 6 Phoenix
10.05.83 Hector Sifuentes W PTS 6 Phoenix
27.06.83 Jose Resendez W PTS 6 Phoenix
09.09.83 Manny Juarez W RSC 5 Las Vegas
25.10.83 Dana Roston L PTS 10 Las Vegas
14.01.84 Arnold White W CO 1 Reno
15.06.84 Dwight Pratchett W PTS 8 Las Vegas
11.09.84 Ed Richardson W RSC 4 Lafayette
28.11.84 Elvin Gonzalez W RSC 5 Atlantic City
14.12.84 Raul Albaladejo W PTS 8 New York
16.02.85 Juan Romero W RSC 5 Reno

Louie Espinosa

19.07.85 Troy Townsend W RSC 8 Poughkeepsie
03.08.85 Ron Gary W RSC 6 Phoenix
24.08.85 Felipe Olivar W RSC 4 Phoenix
03.10.85 Jesse Sierra W RSC 4 Austin
30.01.86 Angel Valle W CO 2 Los Angeles
01.05.86 Carmelo Negron W RSC 4 New York
12.08.86 Jerry Davis W RSC 1 Ashland
16.01.87 Tommy Valoy W RSC 4 Phoenix
(Vacant WBA S. Bantamweight Title)
16.05.87 Capri Lipkins W CO 8 San Juan
15.07.87 Manuel Vilchez W RSC 15 Phoenix
(WBA S. Bantamweight Title Defence)
15.08.87 Mike Ayala W CO 9 San Antonio
(WBA S. Bantamweight Title Defence)
28.11.87 Juan Gervacio L PTS 12 San Juan
(WBA S. Bantamweight Title Defence)
28.01.88 Refugio Rojas W RSC 8 Tucson
29.03.88 Tony Cisneros W RSC 3 Edmonton
08.04.88 Jerome Coffee W RSC 5 Las Vegas
(Vacant NABF S. Bantamweight Title)
Summary: 30 contests, won 28, lost 2.

Luis (Luisito) Espinosa
Manila, Philippines. *Born* 26.06.68
Bantamweight

25.05.84 Vladimir Raffy W PTS 4 San Pedro
29.07.84 Ric Santiago W PTS 4 Pasay City
17.08.84 Ariel Samson L PTS 6 Tayuman
15.09.84 Manuel Corpus W RSC 3 Pasay City
22.09.84 Danny Duran W RSC 2 Pasay City

Luis Espinosa

16.11.84 Titing Dignos W PTS 6 Quezon City
22.03.85 Romy Austria W PTS 10 Pasay City
29.05.85 Roger Pilapil W PTS 10 Paranaque
19.07.85 Romy Navarrete W PTS 10 Pasig
06.12.85 Jun Resma L PTS 10 Paranaque
02.02.86 Dadoy Andujar L PTS 10 Santos City
22.03.86 Robinson Cabuaso W PTS 10 Quezon City
25.06.86 Boy Blanca W PTS 10 Paranaque
08.11.86 Bong-Ho Lee W PTS 10 Manila
07.02.87 Ruben de la Cruz W RSC 9 Davao
16.05.87 Roger Pilapil W RSC 3 Manila
05.09.87 Dadoy Andujar W PTS 10 Quezon City
27.09.87 Loremer Pontino W CO 3 Tagum
14.03.88 Juan J. Estrada L RSC 10 Tijuana
(WBC International Bantamweight Title Challenge)
Summary: 19 contests, won 15, lost 4.

Juan J. (Dinamita) Estrada
Tijuana, Mexico. *Born* 28.11.63
WBC International Bantamweight Champion

07.08.83 Victor Cuevas W CO 1 Tijuana
30.08.83 Jaime Fraile W CO 1 Tijuana
26.09.83 Jorge de Alba W CO 1 Tijuana
29.10.83 Jose L. Maytorena W CO 1 Tijuana
28.11.83 Fausto Mendoza W CO 1 Tijuana
19.12.83 Jose Alvarado W CO 1 Ensenada
05.03.84 Bonny Millan W CO 1 Tijuana
27.03.84 Jiquilpan Canedo L RSC 8 Tijuana
29.05.84 Lupe Rubin W CO 2 Tijuana
03.07.84 Jiquilpan Canedo W RSC 6 Tijuana
14.08.84 Alvino Aguilar W CO 2 Tijuana
01.10.84 Ubaldo Gonzalez W RSC 4 Tijuana
19.11.84 Angel Felix W RSC 3 Tijuana
10.12.84 Alberto Martinez L PTS 10 Tijuana
11.02.85 Julio Valle W RSC 9 Tijuana
08.03.85 Pedro Rodriguez W RSC 10 Tijuana
14.03.85 Martin Dominguez W CO 2 Ensenada
22.04.85 Felipe Mojica W CO 6 Tijuana
16.05.85 Ron Cisneros W PTS 10 Los Angeles
11.06.85 Jose Cazeres W RSC 2 Tijuana
27.07.85 Tony Escobar W PTS 10 Ensenada
26.09.85 Ramon Jimenez W CO 4 Tijuana
14.10.85 Manuel Aguilar L RSC 2 Tijuana
06.12.85 Manuel Aguilar W RSC 9 Tijuana
17.03.86 Alejandro Flores W CO 5 Tijuana
25.04.86 Lupe Torres W RSC 8 Tijuana
16.06.86 Jorge Ramirez L PTS 12 Tijuana
(Mexican Bantamweight Title Challenge)
06.09.86 Lucio Lopez L PTS 10 Buenos Aires
27.10.86 Rodolfo Ortega W CO 6 Tijuana
08.12.86 Koetha Tanaka W RSC 4 Tijuana
03.02.87 Edel Geronimo W PTS 10 Los Angeles
20.03.87 Miguel Cota W RSC 4 Mexicali
18.05.87 Jose L. Cruz W CO 3 Tijuana
22.06.87 Azael Moran W CO 2 Tijuana
10.09.87 Lucilo Nolasco L RTD 7 Los Angeles
03.11.87 Albert Davila L TD 3 Los Angeles
07.12.87 Raul Valdez W TD 10 Tijuana
(WBC International Bantamweight Title Challenge)
14.03.88 Luis Espinosa W RSC 10 Tijuana
(WBC International Bantamweight Title Defence)
Summary: 38 contests, won 31, lost 7.

Mike Evans
Illinois, USA. *Born* 1960
Heavyweight

02.06.83 Dee Dee Collier W PTS 4 Los Angeles
04.08.83 Frank Garcia DREW 4 Los Angeles
26.08.83 Ricky Reese L RSC 1 Los Angeles
02.06.84 Larry Roberson W PTS 6 Chicago
11.08.84 Jim Peat W RSC 3 Woodstock
15.11.84 Tyrell Biggs L PTS 6 New York
29.05.85 Don Townsend W RSC 4 Merrillville
28.06.85 Larry Roberson W RSC 1 Hammond
08.08.85 Wesley Smith W PTS 6 Chicago
21.09.85 Jessie Hicks W RSC 5 Chicago
20.11.85 Frank Draper W RSC 3 Erie
12.12.85 Dave Slaughter W RSC 7 Chicago
13.12.85 Mike Cohen W RSC 5 Bethlehem
30.05.87 Oscar Holman W PTS 8 Las Vegas
30.06.87 Jack Johnson W RSC 1 Detroit
01.08.87 Steve Zouski W PTS 8 Las Vegas
11.02.88 Steve Zouski W PTS 10 Chicago
Summary: 17 contests, won 14, drew 1, lost 2.

Matt (The Beta Bomber) Farrago
Syracuse, USA. *Born* 14.04.61
Middleweight

05.07.83 Kevin Daigle W PTS 6 Syracuse
30.09.83 Ron Sulem W PTS 4 Albany
21.10.83 Frank Murray W CO 2 Syracuse
09.12.83 Joaquin Rodriguez W PTS 4 Syracuse
21.12.83 Morton Johnson W RSC 3 Syracuse
02.03.84 Ray Hamilton W CO 3 Shirley
27.04.84 Robert Rivers W PTS 6 Shirley
21.07.84 Lemorrah Balding W CO 5 Swan Lake
17.01.85 Billy Joe W RSC 4 Albany
06.03.85 Billy Joe W PTS 6 Albany
21.04.85 Fred Spry W PTS 8 Syracuse
14.08.85 George Lanton W RSC 3 Atlantic City
10.09.85 Dave Cherry W RSC 4 Atlantic City
22.10.85 Mike Peoples W PTS 6 Atlantic City
17.12.85 Ron Malek W RSC 2 Atlantic City
04.03.86 Steve Sheeran W PTS 6 Atlantic City
02.04.86 Pete Seward W PTS 10 Syracuse
20.04.86 Sammy Floyd W PTS 10 Stonybrook
24.06.86 Mark Frazier W PTS 10 Syracuse
16.09.86 Bobby Joe Young DREW 10 Syracuse
13.03.87 Don Johnson W PTS 10 East Rutherford
23.07.87 Harlein Holden W RSC 3 New York
03.09.87 Kevin Brazier W PTS 10 New York
17.03.88 Pat Prisco W RSC 6 New York
Summary: 24 contests, won 23, drew 1.

Willie Featherstone

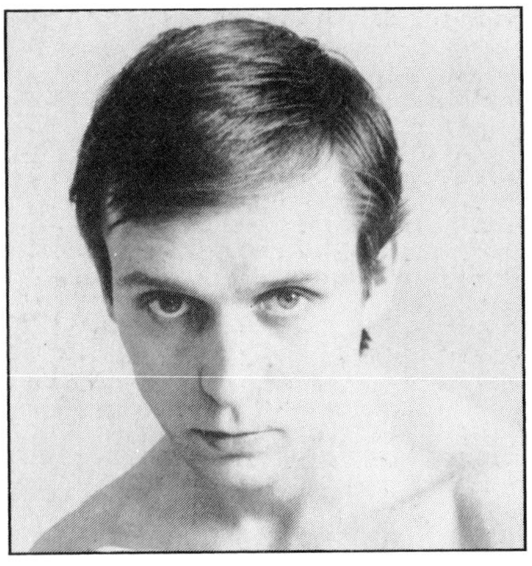

Willie Featherstone
Toronto, Canada. *Born* 14.05.59
Canadian & Commonwealth L. Heavyweight Champion

17.01.78 Murray Sutherland W RSC 3 Toronto
03.04.78 Al Bell W CO 1 Toronto
11.07.78 Harry White W RSC 1 Toronto
05.02.79 Tyrone Freeman W PTS 8 Hull
18.12.79 Bob Lalonde W CO 1 Montreal
27.01.80 Jo Jo Dent W RSC 2 Montreal
12.02.80 Elisha Obed L PTS 8 Montreal
25.03.80 Marciano Bernardi DREW 10 Montreal
27.01.81 Bill Hollis W RSC 4 Toronto
02.06.81 Wes Rowe W PTS 8 Toronto
10.12.81 Doug Demmings L PTS 10 Winnipeg
22.06.84 Tony Curovic W PTS 8 Toronto
11.12.84 Bill Hollis W CO 1 Toronto
14.02.85 Frank Minton W PTS 8 Toronto
31.05.85 Tim Long W RSC 3 Toronto
03.12.85 Darryl Spain W CO 5 Toronto
01.04.86 Jerry Harris W PTS 8 Toronto
14.06.86 Danny Lindstrom L PTS 8 Edmonton
18.08.86 Roddy MacDonald W RTD 5 Toronto
(*Canadian L. Heavyweight Title Challenge*)
14.03.87 Roddy MacDonald W PTS 12 Sydney
(*Canadian L. Heavyweight Title Defence*)
12.09.87 Enoch Chama W PTS 12 Sydney
(*Vacant Commonwealth L. Heavyweight Title*)
08.12.87 Danny Lindstrom W PTS 12 Toronto
(*Commonwealth and Canadian L. Heavyweight Title Defence*)
Summary: 22 contests, won 18, drew 1, lost 3.

Jeff Fenech
Sydney, Australia. *Born* 28.05.64
WBC & Australian Featherweight Champion. Former Undefeated WBC S. Bantamweight Champion. Former Undefeated IBF Bantamweight Champion & Australian S. Flyweight Champion

12.10.84 Bobby Williams W RSC 2 Marrickville
26.10.84 Percy Israel W RSC 7 Marrickville
30.11.84 Junior Thompson W RSC 3 Marrickville
(*Vacant Australian S. Flyweight Title*)
15.12.84 Iliesa Manila W RSC 2 Suva
01.02.85 Wayne Mulholland W RSC 5 Dapto
04.03.85 Rolly Navarro W RSC 4 Sydney
26.04.85 Satoshi Shingaki W RSC 9 Sydney
(*IBF Bantamweight Title Challenge*)
14.06.85 John Matienza W RSC 6 Sydney
26.07.85 John Farrell W CO 9 Brisbane
23.08.85 Satoshi Shingaki W CO 3 Sydney
(*IBF Bantamweight Title Defence*)
04.11.85 Kenny Butts W RTD 2 Brisbane
02.12.85 Jerome Coffee W PTS 15 Sydney
(*IBF Bantamweight Title Defence*)
11.04.86 Daniel Zaragoza W PTS 10 Sydney
18.07.86 Steve McCrory W RSC 14 Sydney
(*IBF Bantamweight Title Defence*)
03.04.87 Tony Miller W PTS 12 Melbourne
(*Australian Featherweight Title Challenge*)
08.05.87 Samart Payakarun W RSC 4 Sydney
(*WBC S. Bantamweight Title Challenge*)
10.07.87 Greg Richardson W RTD 5 Sydney
(*WBC S. Bantamweight Title Defence*)
16.10.87 Carlos Zarate W TD 4 Sydney
(*WBC S. Bantamweight Title Defence*)
11.12.87 Osmar Avila W CO 1 Sydney
07.03.88 Victor Callejas W RSC 10 Sydney
(*Vacant WBC Featherweight Title*)
Summary: 20 contests, won 20.

Francisco (Rocky) Fernandez
Panama
Panamanian S. Featherweight Champion. Former Latin American Featherweight Champion

09.02.80 Rafael Montero W RSC 1 Panama City
03.03.80 Angel Asprilla L PTS 4 Panama City
28.06.80 Ernesto Arce L CO 1 Panama City
20.09.80 Angel Asprilla W PTS 4 Panama City
29.11.80 Cecilio Garibaldi W PTS 6 Panama City
04.04.81 Alcibiades Blandon L PTS 10 Panama City
23.03.81 Victor Samudio L CO 1 Panama City
10.10.81 Juan Mayoral W CO 8 San Andres
28.11.81 Francisco Perez W PTS 10 Colon
03.04.82 Humberto Mejia W RSC 10 Colon
30.04.82 Jose Santana W RSC 3 Panama City
03.07.82 Victor Samudio W CO 1 Panama City
04.09.82 Victor Torres W RSC 3 Colon
30.10.82 Mario Wilson W CO 2 Colon
18.12.82 Jorge Lujan L PTS 10 Panama City
05.02.83 Mario Miranda L PTS 10 Panama City
16.04.83 Humberto Mejia W RSC 7 Panama City
12.08.83 Idabeth Rojas W PTS 10 Miami
(*Vacant Latin American Featherweight Title*)
11.09.83 Eduardo Prieto L PTS 12 Miami
08.10.83 Bernard Taylor L PTS 10 Los Angeles
17.12.83 Mario Wilson W RSC 5 Panama City
27.01.84 Felipe Orozco L RSC 6 Barranquilla
08.06.84 Roberto Diaz W CO 5 Lima
29.06.84 Jose Marmolejo L PTS 12 Panama City
(*Latin American Featherweight Title Defence*)
06.10.84 Julio Ruiz W RSC 6 Panama City
24.11.84 Jose Williams W RSC 10 Panama City
18.01.85 Pascual Patterson W RSC 1 Panama City
(*Vacant Panamanian S. Featherweight Title*)
20.04.85 Ezequiel Mosquera W CO 2 Panama City
18.05.85 Bernardo Checa W RSC 2 Panama City
28.07.85 Angel Mayor W CO 1 Miami
05.10.85 Bernardo Checa W RSC 4 Panama City
31.01.86 Manuel Batista L PTS 10 Panama City
31.05.86 Amancio Castro DREW 10 Panama City
20.12.86 Luis Portocarrero W RSC 8 Panama City
21.02.87 Edgar Castro W CO 7 Panama City
22.05.87 Libardo Herrera W RSC 1 Panama City
31.07.87 Brian Mitchell L RSC 14 Panama City
(*WBA S. Featherweight Title Challenge*)
18.12.87 Rafael Pineda L RSC 5 Cartagena
Summary: 38 contests, won 24, drew 1, lost 13.

Jose Mario Flores
Pergamino. *Born* Uruguay 01.02.55
Former Undefeated South American Middleweight, L. Heavyweight & Cruiserweight Champion

06.02.76 Alejandro Garcia W PTS 6 Pergamino
20.02.76 Celso Sosa W RSC 3 Pergamino
12.03.76 Gregorio Navarro W CO 3 Pergamino
30.04.76 Hector Altamirand W PTS 8 Pergamino
24.05.76 Victor Pereyra W RSC 3 Pergamino
04.06.76 Octavio Escauriza W PTS 8 Pergamino
18.06.76 Jose Pinto W CO 3 Pergamino
16.07.76 Juan Paz W RSC 8 Pergamino
07.08.76 Alberto Almiron W PTS 10 Pergamino
03.09.76 Hugo Obregon W PTS 10 Pergamino
17.09.76 Segundo Miguel Paiz DREW 10 Pergamino
05.11.76 Segundo Miguel Paiz W CO 6 Pergamino
25.11.76 Hugo Obregon W PTS 10 Pergamino
17.12.76 Juan Carlos Artaza W PTS 10 Pergamino
27.01.77 Raul Paez W PTS 10 Arrecifes
10.03.77 Raul Paez W RTD 4 Pergamino
09.04.77 Esteban Osuna W PTS 10 Pergamino
07.05.77 Camilo Gaitan DREW 10 Pergamino
20.05.77 Hugo Saavedra W CO 2 Cordoba
03.06.77 Ramon Mendez W PTS 10 Pergamino
09.07.77 Hugo Obregon W PTS 10 Junin
05.08.77 Camilo Gaitan W PTS 10 Pergamino
29.08.77 Rodolfo Rosales W PTS 10 Buenos Aires
16.09.77 Antonio Lopez W RSC 8 Pergamino
01.10.77 Cesar Duarte W CO 10 Buenos Aires
22.10.77 Alberto Almiron W PTS 10 Buenos Aires
11.11.77 Roque Roldan W PTS 10 Pergamino
23.12.77 Cesar Duarte W PTS 10 Pergamino
20.01.78 Rogelio Zarza W PTS 10 Azul
03.03.78 Cesar Duarte L PTS 10 San Luis
06.04.78 Ricardo Arce L PTS 10 Posadas
05.05.78 Alberto Almiron T DRAW 7 Pergamino
27.05.78 Ruben Pardo W PTS 10 Buenos Aires
07.07.78 Roque Roldan W PTS 10 Pergamino
12.08.78 Marcelo Quinones W PTS 12 Montevideo
(*South American Middleweight Title Challenge*)
08.09.78 Jose Vega W PTS 10 Pergamino
24.09.78 Alberto Almiron W PTS 10 Salta
13.10.78 Oscar Aguero W CO 8 Azul
25.11.78 Hugo Obregon DREW 10 Olavarria
12.01.79 Ruben Prado L RTD 4 Mar del Plata
(*South American Middleweight Title Defence*)
13.07.79 Jose Vega L PTS 10 Rosario
10.08.79 Rogelio Zarza DREW 10 Salta
31.08.79 Antonio Lopez W RSC 10 Rosario
05.10.79 Alberto Almiron W PTS 10 San Miguel
02.11.79 Rogelio Zarza L CO 9 Concordia
24.04.80 Aldo Carmona W RTD 8 Pergamino
09.05.80 Roberto Ortiz W RTD 4 Viamonte
24.05.80 Rogelio Zarza W PTS 10 Pergamino
14.06.80 Crispin de Oliveira W RSC 6 Pergamino
12.09.80 Hugo Salega W RTD 3 San Miguel
10.10.80 Manuel Flores W RTD 2 Pergamino
19.12.80 Rogelio Zarza W PTS 10 Tapiales
23.01.81 Jose Duran W RTD 8 Pergamino
13.03.81 Cesar Duarte W PTS 10 Tucuman
25.04.81 Ruben Pardo W PTS 12 Buenos Aires
(*South American Middleweight Title Challenge*)
15.05.81 Natalio Ibarra W CO 6 Pergamino

29.05.81 Juan Ibanez W PTS 10 Tucuman
13.06.81 Juan Domingo Roldan L CO 3 Buenos Aires
08.08.81 Jorge Servin W RSC 5 San Miguel
04.09.81 Jesus Ibanez W PTS 10 Montevideo
06.11.81 Juan Fernandez W CO 6 Pergamino
20.11.81 Norberto Cabrera W PTS 10 Montevideo
18.12.81 Angel Salinas W PTS 10 Montevideo
19.02.82 Angel Salinas W PTS 10 Buenos Aires
12.03.82 Jesus Ibanez W RSC 9 Pergamino
10.04.82 Abel C. Bailone W PTS 10 Buenos Aires
07.05.82 Alfredo Morales W CO 2 San Nicolas
24.05.82 Jose Vega W RSC 2 Pergamino
26.06.82 Norberto Cabrera W RSC 8 Pergamino
06.08.82 Chris Wells W RSC 8 Montevideo
08.10.82 Ricardo Molina W PTS 10 Montevideo
23.12.82 Aldo Carmona W PTS 10 Pergamino
18.03.83 Don Wigfall W RSC 6 Atlantic City
13.04.83 Rogelio Zarza W RTD 5 Montevideo
06.05.83 Ruben Paredes W CO 1 Rojas
21.05.83 Aldo Carmona W RSC 2 General Pico
01.07.83 Juan Rodriguez W CO 7 Pergamino
30.07.83 Cesar Romero L CO 2 Buenos Aires
17.09.83 Irineo Cabrera W CO 2 Pergamino
06.10.83 Andres Olmedo W CO 6 Asuncion
13.11.83 Juan C. Gimenez L CO 1 Asuncion
(*Vacant South American L. Heavyweight Title*)
16.03.84 Andres Olmedo W PTS 10 Parana
16.08.84 Jorge Salgado L PTS 10 Mendoza
07.09.84 Angel Caro DREW 10 Mar del Plata
10.11.84 Victor Robledo W PTS 12 Buenos Aires
(*South American L. Heavyweight Title Challenge*)
17.05.85 Juan Leiva W RTD 7 Daireaux
12.07.85 Juan Rodriguez W PTS 10 Villa Angela
24.08.85 Clarismundo Silva W RSC 5 Pergamino
(*South American L. Heavyweight Title Defence*)
27.09.85 Roberto Cardozo W RSC 5 Rosario
23.11.85 Pedro Cichero W RTD 7 Pergamino
21.12.85 Hector Rohr W PTS 10 Pergamino
18.04.86 Hugo Rufino W RTD 3 Pergamino
24.05.86 Hector Rohr W CO 4 Necochea
(*South American Cruiserweight Title Challenge*)
08.08.86 Marvin Camel W PTS 10 Pergamino
22.11.86 Jimmy Bills W PTS 10 Pergamino
06.02.87 Juan Fernandez DREW 10 Parana
14.08.87 Alberto Ubelart W PTS 10 Pergamino
18.09.87 Eduardo Contreras W PTS 10 Pergamino
22.01.88 Carlos de Leon L PTS 12 Atlantic City
(*WBC Cruiserweight Title Challenge*)
Summary: 99 contests, won 82, drew 7, lost 10.

George Foreman
Marshall, USA. *Born* 22.01.48
Former World Heavyweight Champion

23.06.69 Don Waldhelm W RSC 3 New York
01.07.69 Fred Askew W CO 1 Houston
14.07.69 Sylvester Dulaire W RSC 1 Washington
18.08.69 Chuck Wepner W RSC 3 NewYork
18.09.69 John Carroll W CO 1 Seattle
23.09.69 Cookie Wallace W CO 2 Houston
07.10.69 Vernon Clay W CO 2 Houston
31.10.69 Roberto Davila W PTS 8 New York
05.11.69 Leo Peterson W CO 4 Scranton
18.11.69 Max Martinez W CO 2 Houston
06.12.69 Bob Hazleton W CO 1 Las Vegas
16.12.69 Levi Forte W PTS 10 Miami
18.12.69 Gary Wiler W CO 1 Seattle
06.01.70 Charlie Polite W CO 4 Houston
26.01.70 Jack O'Halloran W CO 5 New York
16.02.70 Greg Peralta W PTS 10 New York
31.03.70 Rufus Brassell W CO 1 Houston
17.04.70 James J. Woody W RSC 3 New York
29.04.70 Aaron Eastling W CO 4 Cleveland
16.05.70 George Johnson W RSC 7 Los Angeles
20.07.70 Roger Russell W CO 1 Philadelphia
04.08.70 George Chuvalo W RSC 3 New York
03.11.70 Lou Bailey W CO 3 Oklahoma City
18.11.70 Boone Kirkman W RSC 2 New York
19.12.70 Mel Turnbow W RSC 1 Seattle
08.02.71 Charlie Boston W CO 1 St Paul
03.04.71 Stanford Harris W CO 2 Lake Geneva
10.05.71 Greg Peralta W RSC 10 Oakland
14.09.71 Vic Scott W RSC 1 El Paso
21.09.71 Leroy Caldwell W CO 3 Beaumont
07.10.71 Ollie Wilson W CO 2 San Antonio
29.10.71 Luis Pires W RSC 4 New York
29.02.72 Murphy Goodwin W CO 2 Austin
07.03.72 Clarence Boone W CO 2 Beaumont
10.04.72 Ted Gullick W CO 2 Los Angeles
11.05.72 Miguel Paez W CO 2 Oakland
10.10.72 Terry Sorrells W CO 2 Salt Lake City
22.01.73 Joe Frazier W RSC 2 Kingston
(*World Heavyweight Title Challenge*)
01.09.73 Joe Roman W CO 1 Tokyo
(*World Heavyweight Title Defence*)
26.03.74 Ken Norton W RSC 2 Caracas
(*World Heavyweight Title Defence*)
30.10.74 Muhammad Ali L CO 8 Kinshasa
(*World Heavyweight Title Defence*)
24.01.76 Ron Lyle W CO 5 Las Vegas
15.06.76 Joe Frazier W RSC 5 New York
14.08.76 Scott le Doux W CO 3 Utica
15.10.76 Dino Dennis W RSC 4 Los Angeles
22.01.77 Pedro Agosta W CO 4 Pensacola
17.03.77 Jimmy Young L PTS 12 San Juan
09.03.87 Steve Zouski W RSC 4 Sacramento
09.07.87 Charlie Hostetter W CO 3 Oakland
15.09.87 Bobby Crabtree W RSC 6 Springfield
21.11.87 Tim Anderson W RSC 4 Orlando
18.12.87 Rick Sekorski W RSC 3 Las Vegas
23.01.88 Tom Trimm W CO 1 Orlando
05.02.88 Guido Trane W RSC 5 Las Vegas
19.03.88 Dwight Muhammad Qawi W RSC 7 Las Vegas
Summary: 55 contests, won 53, lost 2.

Miguel Francia
Buenos Aires, Argentine. *Born* 19.09.61
Argentinian Featherweight Champion

18.11.83 Eduardo Bagala W PTS 6 Tres Arroyos
24.03.84 Eduardo Bagala W TD 5 Buenos Aires
02.06.84 Eduardo Bagala W PTS 6 Buenos Aires
21.07.84 Fidel Avila L RSC 5 Buenos Aires
01.09.84 Antonio Aguirre W RSC 3 Buenos Aires
06.10.84 Jorge Fernandez W PTS 8 Buenos Aires
16.03.85 Julio Ramirez W PTS 8 Buenos Aires
12.04.85 Luis Rodriguez W PTS 10 Rosario
07.06.85 Julio Ramirez L PTS 10 San Nicolas
02.08.85 Carlos Velazquez DREW 10 Caleta Oliva
30.08.85 Esteban Bustos DREW 10 Salta
18.09.85 Pedro Decima L CO 3 Buenos Aires
14.12.85 Osmar Avila L RSC 8 Lincoln
14.03.86 Carlos Velazquez W PTS 10 Rivadavia
06.06.86 Ramon Dominguez W DIS 10 Rosario
07.11.86 Osmar Avila L PTS 12 Mar del Plata
25.07.87 Jose Mario Lopez W PTS 12 Buenos Aires
(*Argentinian Featherweight Title Challenge*)
09.10.87 Ruben Astorga W PTS 10 Montevideo
18.12.87 Fidel Avila W PTS 10 Temperley
02.03.88 Ruben Astorga W PTS 10 Buenos Aires
Summary: 20 contests, won 13, drew 2, lost 5.

Jeff Franklin
Las Vegas, USA. *Born* 30.09.62
USBA Featherweight Champion

29.09.83 Roberto Cantu W PTS 6 Las Vegas
25.10.83 Manny Juarez W PTS 6 Las Vegas
22.12.83 Tito Arazte W RSC 3 Las Vegas
20.01.84 David Vela W PTS 4 Las Vegas
03.02.84 John Rivera W RTD 3 Las Vegas
11.10.84 Candid Partida W PTS 6 Las Vegas
13.12.84 Roy Muniz W PTS 4 Stateline
24.05.85 Andy Minsker L PTS 6 Las Vegas
25.09.85 Evelio Perez DREW 6 Las Vegas
30.03.86 Gus Lopez W RSC 4 Las Vegas
22.04.86 Danny Garcia W PTS 6 Las Vegas
23.06.86 Evelio Perez W PTS 4 Las Vegas
13.07.86 Don Porter W RSC 3 Las Vegas
25.07.86 Lupe Gutierrez L PTS 8 Las Vegas
17.10.86 Sylvester Kennon W CO 4 Bismark
11.11.86 Alex Vega W CO 1 Las Vegas
26.12.86 Mark Perea W PTS 8 Las Vegas
05.03.87 Adam Garcia W RSC 4 Las Vegas
20.03.87 Jesus Pool DREW 8 Las Vegas
18.07.87 Adam Garcia W PTS 10 Las Vegas
09.10.87 Tracey Patterson W PTS 10 Las Vegas
18.12.87 Steve Cruz W PTS 10 Las Vegas
05.02.88 Bernard Taylor DREW 12 Las Vegas
(*NABF Featherweight Title Challenge*)
08.04.88 Aaron Lopez W PTS 12 Las Vegas
(*Vacant USBA Featherweight Title*)
Summary: 24 contests, won 19, drew 3, lost 2.

Moises Fuentes
Bucaramanga, Colombia
Former Colombian S. Bantamweight Champion

11.03.83 Jorge Acosta W PTS 4 Barranquilla
29.10.83 Augusto Borge W CO 5 Bucaramanga
26.11.83 Kadid Prada W CO 3 Bucaramanga
30.04.84 Gustavo Dixon W CO 6 Bucaramanga
09.03.85 Juan Estupinan W PTS 8 Bucaramanga
27.04.85 Jesus Espitia W RSC 5 Bucaramanga
17.08.85 Mario Livingstone W CO 5 Bucaramanga
(*Colombian S. Bantamweight Title Challenge*)
05.10.85 Ezequiel Hernandez W PTS 10 Bucaramanga
30.11.85 Marcelino Gelez W CO 6 Bucaramanga
(*Colombian S. Bantamweight Title Defence*)
22.03.86 Ezequiel Hernandez W PTS 10 Bucaramanga
(*Colombian S. Bantamweight Title Defence*)
09.05.86 Manuel Salgado W PTS 10 San Vincente
(*Colombian S. Bantamweight Title Defence*)
03.10.86 Alejandro Galvis W RSC 5 Bucaramanga
(*Colombian S. Bantamweight Title Defence*)
08.11.86 Jaime Castellon W RSC 7 Bucaramanga
(*Colombian S. Bantamweight Title Defence*)
13.03.87 Joaquin Caraballo W CO 6 Bucaramanga
(*Colombian S. Bantamweight Title Defence*)
03.04.87 Alvaro Narvaez W PTS 10 Bucaramanga
(*Colombian S. Bantamweight Title Defence*)
15.05.87 Luis Mendoza L PTS 10 Cartagena
(*Colombian S. Bantamweight Title Defence*)
02.08.87 Francisco Arroyo W PTS 10 Barranquilla
19.12.87 Gabriel Narvaez W PTS 8 Bucaramanga
05.02.88 Robinson Garcia W PTS 10 Medellin
Summary: 19 contests, won 18, lost 1.

Tony (Torpedo) Fulilangi
Australia. *Born* Tonga 1960
South Pacific Heavyweight Champion

17.06.81 Pake Dudoit W RSC 1 Honolulu
03.08.81 Memo Soto W CO 2 Tucson
19.08.81 Tim Lampkin W RSC 2 Las Vegas
02.09.81 Brady Wills W RSC 2 Las Vegas
13.10.81 Charley Smith W CO 2 Phoenix
17.11.81 Tim Lampkin W CO 3 Phoenix
05.12.81 Larry Ware W RSC 2 Las Vegas
07.01.82 J. D. Hall W CO 1 Phoenix
03.02.82 Otis Bates W PTS 6 Las Vegas
18.02.82 Rubin Williams W CO 4 Phoenix
16.03.82 Charlie Wade W CO 1 Phoenix
20.04.82 Arnold Sam W RSC 3 Phoenix
04.05.82 Mark Wills W CO 1 Las Vegas
13.05.82 Teskac Dragutin W CO 1 Los Angeles
20.05.82 Rocky Young W RSC 1 Phoenix
06.06.82 Mike Jameson W RSC 10 Laughlin
22.06.82 Johnny Scott W RSC 1 Phoenix
10.07.82 Harvey Steichen W CO 1 Phoenix
03.08.82 Fernando Montes W RSC 8 Phoenix
25.11.82 Ron Gibbs W RSC 6 Las Vegas
27.01.83 Bruce Grandham W RSC 2 Las Vegas
21.04.83 Nick Wells W RSC 2 Las Vegas
16.05.83 Tony Perea DREW 10 Houston
22.09.83 Monte Masters L RSC 14 Phoenix
26.06.84 Hector Fernandez W CO 1 Phoenix
10.07.84 Charley Smith W CO 5 Phoenix
08.12.84 John White W CO 1 Phoenix
21.05.85 Ben Griffin W RSC 2 Laughlin
29.07.85 Hector Garcia W CO 4 Phoenix
01.11.85 Jimmy Young DREW 10 Phoenix
09.08.86 Rocky Salanoa W PTS 12 Auckland
(*Vacant South Pacific Heavyweight Title*)
22.08.86 Geoff Pate W RTD 1 Auckland
14.11.86 Lucius Kirkley W RSC 4 Sydney
11.12.86 Dean Waters W PTS 10 Sydney
20.02.87 Luke Tui W CO 2 Auckland
13.03.87 Niko Degai W RSC 3 Auckland
17.08.87 Terry Walker W RSC 4 Phoenix
12.12.87 Mickey Pryor W RSC 2 Phoenix
19.03.88 Bert Cooper L RSC 4 Las Vegas
(*NABF Cruiserweight Title Challenge*)
Summary: 39 contests, won 35, drew 2, lost 2.

Kaokor Galaxy
Petchaboon, Thailand. *Born* 15.05.59
Former Undefeated Thai Bantamweight Champion

09.10.85 Kwanarong Savadivaree W CO 3 Bangkok
30.10.85 Kiat Kiatsonthaya W CO 4 Bangkok
27.11.85 Rakchai Kiatsontaya W PTS 6 Bangkok
08.01.86 Mansor Jitpatana W CO 4 Bangkok
19.02.86 Panchai Kiatsontaya W PTS 6 Bangkok
26.03.86 Nakalart Kiatsontaya W PTS 6 Bangkok
11.06.86 Rakchai Kiatsontaya W CO 5 Bangkok
09.07.86 Kwan Sisamnuay W CO 4 Bangkok
(*Vacant Thai Bantamweight Title*)
13.08.86 Narkalart Kiatsontaya W CO 5 Bangkok
25.09.86 Singnoi Singkrungtorn W CO 5 Bangkok
(*Thai Bantamweight Title Defence*)
14.01.87 Keiichi Ozaki W PTS 10 Bangkok
05.04.87 Yon-Man Cha W RSC 6 Bangkok
07.05.87 Ben Capaggan W RSC 2 Bangkok
25.06.87 Tony Pruitt W RSC 8 Bangkok
06.09.87 Russell Finn W RSC 3 Bangkok
12.10.87 Constancio Dangla W CO 4 Bangkok
14.12.87 Do-Buk Cha W CO 2 Bangkok
Summary: 17 contests, won 17.

Kaosai Galaxy
Petchaboon, Thailand. *Born* 15.05.59
WBA S. Flyweight Champion. Former Undefeated Thai Bantamweight Champion

17.12.80 Pukk Srithum W CO 5 Bangkok
31.12.80 Prasong Sithkempetch W CO 3 Bangkok
26.01.81 Prasong Sithkempetch W CO 1 Bangkok
13.05.81 Terdsakdi Pornthavee W CO 3 Bangkok
10.06.81 Tanee Singchaowang W CO 1 Bangkok
24.06.81 Phichitsuk Kor-u-Sayarm W PTS 6 Bangkok
29.07.81 Sakda Saksuree L PTS 10 Bangkok
(*Thai Bantamweight Title Challenge*)
29.08.81 Monsak Muangsurin W RSC 3 Bangkok
10.09.81 Sakda Saksuree W CO 6 Bangkok
14.10.81 Tsuguyuki Toma W CO 4 Bangkok
25.01.82 Sak Chorsirirat W CO 7 Bangkok
(*Thai Bantamweight Title Challenge*)
10.03.82 Katsuyuki Ohashi W CO 7 Bangkok
14.04.82 Yu-Ok Joo W RSC 4 Bangkok
24.05.82 Ali Formentera W RSC 5 Bangkok
14.07.82 Agus Suyanto W RSC 4 Bangkok
26.08.82 Adan Uribe W CO 4 Bangkok
13.10.82 Willie Jensen W CO 2 Bangkok
27.11.82 Mun-Kyun Joo W RSC 4 Nakorn
24.12.82 Marciano Sekiyama W CO 4 Bangkok
23.02.83 Jose Luis Soto W CO 2 Bangkok
10.05.83 Luis Ibanez W CO 3 Bangkok
30.06.83 Montsayarm Mahacha W RSC 3 Bangkok
03.08.83 Chang-Yung Park W PTS 10 Bangkok
12.10.83 Gil Ragas W RSC 7 Bangkok
13.12.83 Noritetsu Kato W RTD 4 Bangkok
14.03.84 Sung-Um Jae W PTS 10 Bangkok
11.07.84 Val de Vera W RSC 7 Bangkok
02.09.84 Yun-Lee Moon W RSC 2 Bangkok
21.11.84 Eusebio Espinal W CO 6 Bangkok
(*Vacant WBA S. Flyweight Title*)
06.03.85 Dong-Chun Lee W CO 7 Bangkok
(*WBA S. Flyweight Title Defence*)
17.07.85 Rafael Orono W RSC 5 Bangkok
(*WBA S. Flyweight Title Defence*)
23.12.85 Edgar Monserrat W RSC 2 Bangkok
(*WBA S. Flyweight Title Defence*)
01.11.86 Israel Contreras W CO 5 Curacao
(*WBA S. Flyweight Title Defence*)
28.02.87 Elly Pical W CO 14 Jakarta
(*WBA S. Flyweight Title Defence*)
25.06.87 Joung-Sup Chun W CO 3 Bangkok
12.10.87 Byong-Kwan Chung W RSC 3 Bangkok
(*WBA S. Flyweight Title Defence*)
26.01.88 Kongtoranee Payakarun W PTS 12 Bangkok
(*WBA S. Flyweight Title Defence*)
Summary: 37 contests, won 36, lost 1.

Efisio Galici
Cagliari, Italy. *Born* 04.07.57
WBC International Welterweight Champion & Former Undefeated Italian Welterweight Champion

27.07.83 Franco Callegari W PTS 6 Soleminis
19.08.83 Giuseppe Agate W RSC 3 Bessude
30.09.83 Sandro Crisafulli W RSC 1 Modena
14.10.83 Folly Muyanga W CO 2 Milan
13.01.84 Mayebe Mabele W PTS 6 Riva del Garda
13.04.84 Folly Muyanga W RSC 1 Sassari

Efisio Galici

27.04.84 George Ssonko W CO 3 Cagliari
04.06.84 Nazario Mariotti W PTS 6 Milan
24.08.84 Guido di Rocco W RSC 5 Cagliari
26.10.84 Mauro da Cruz W PTS 6 Cagliari
08.03.85 Sami Barra W RSC 4 Modena
20.04.85 Ngindola Engote W PTS 4 Ceriale
27.07.85 Raphael Salamone W RSC 3 Carraca
13.12.85 Francesco Gallo W RSC 2 Cesena
17.01.86 Charles Ssali W RTD 7 Empoli
31.01.86 Piero Spadaccini W DIS 7 Abiate
07.03.86 Claude Lancastre W RSC 3 Rimini
24.04.86 Hugoes Samo W CO 2 Garbagnate
09.05.86 Jose Castillo W RSC 2 Sassari
11.07.86 Daniele Zappaterra W RTD 2 Spagnoli
(*Vacant Italian Welterweight Title*)
10.10.86 Martin Rojas W CO 2 Cesena
28.11.86 Sergio Aguirre W CO 2 Abano
27.03.87 Orlando Orozco W CO 5 Cagliari
(*WBC International Welterweight Title Challenge*)
29.05.87 Dario de Jesus W RSC 1 Cento
12.06.87 Ken Releford W RSC 1 Pula
25.09.87 Ricky Stoner W PTS 12 Quartu
(*WBC International Welterweight Title Defence*)
28.11.87 Eduardo Batista W CO 2 Oristano
(*WBC International Welterweight Title Defence*)
10.04.88 Francisco Bobadilla W RSC 5 Iglesias
(*WBC International Welterweight Title Defence*)
Summary: 28 contests, won 28.

Jesus Gallardo

Jesus (Bebe) Gallardo
Tijuana, Mexico. *Born* 16.02.64
S. Middleweight

.03.84 Eusebio Urias W CO 1 Tijuana
.06.84 Olegario Beltran W CO 4 Tijuana
29.08.84 Jonias Suastegui W CO 2 Tijuana
23.09.84 Manuel Leyva W CO 1 Tijuana
29.10.84 Tomas Garcia W CO 2 Tijuana
.02.85 Jaime Montano W CO 1 Tijuana
.05.85 Jorge Gonzalez W CO 1 Tijuana
14.10.85 Ramon Cardoso W CO 6 Tijuana
25.11.85 Jorge Miranda W CO 6 Tijuana
04.02.86 Antonio Verduzco W CO 1 Tijuana
21.02.86 Gil Canchola W CO 1 Tijuana
05.04.86 Juan Elizondo W CO 1 Tijuana
02.05.86 Dave Franklin L RSC 4 Tijuana
20.10.86 Tommy Lozano W CO 1 Tijuana
24.11.86 Ismael Quintas W CO 1 Tijuana
19.12.86 Andres Uribe W RSC 2 Tijuana
04.04.87 Jose Luis Millan W RSC 6 Tijuana
26.05.87 Dave Franklin W PTS 10 Tijuana
21.08.87 Marcos Geraldo W CO 2 Tijuana
19.10.87 Olegario Beltran W RSC 2 Tijuana
06.12.87 Chong-Pal Park L RSC 2 Seoul
(*Vacant WBA S. Middleweight Title*)
05.03.88 Andres Ramirez W PTS 10 Tijuana
Summary: 22 contests, won 20, lost 2.

Luis Gamez
Venezuela
WBA M. Flyweight Champion. Former Undefeated Venezuelan L. Flyweight Champion

14.06.85 Francisco Garcia W PTS 4 Maracay
13.09.85 Alcides Hernandez W PTS 4 Maracay
.85 Jose Castillo W CO 5 Maracay
05.11.85 Alberto Pimienta W CO 3 Maracaibo
23.11.85 Angel Escorcia W RSC 2 Guayamo
12.02.86 Jose Castillo W PTS 8 Maracay
19.04.86 Rafael Lara W CO 6 Maracay
26.07.86 Fidel Gonzalez W CO 5 Maracay
31.10.86 Rafael Lara W CO 3 Pascua
28.11.86 Alberto Escorcia W CO 4 Maracaibo
02.02.87 Rafael Bolivar W TD 2 Maracay
21.03.87 Jose Castillo W RSC 5 Maracay
30.04.87 Pedro Nieves W PTS 10 Turmero
(*Vacant Venezuelan L. Flyweight Title*)
23.06.87 Leonardo Paredes W RSC 4 Maracay
22.08.87 Alfredo Reyes W CO 2 Turmero
(*Venezuelan L. Flyweight Title Defence*)
10.10.87 Victoriano Hernandez W PTS 10 Turmero
11.11.87 Victoriano Hernandez W PTS 10 Maracay
10.01.88 Bung-Jung Kim W PTS 12 Pusan
(*Vacant WBA M. Flyweight Title*)
24.04.88 Kenji Yokozawa W RSC 3 Tokyo
(*WBA M. Flyweight Title Defence*)
Summary: 19 contests, won 19.

Agustin (Baby) Garcia
Colombia
Former Colombian L. Flyweight Champion

28.06.80 Jairo Bedoya W PTS 6 Cartagena
22.08.80 John Jaramillo W PTS 8 Maicao
22.11.80 Rodolfo Rodriguez L RSC 3 Maracaibo
30.01.81 Felipe Medrano W CO 2 Cartagena
(*Vacant Colombian L. Flyweight Title*)
27.03.81 Orlando Maestre DREW 12 Barranquilla
(*Colombian L. Flyweight Title Defence*)
06.07.81 Reinaldo Becerra L PTS 12 Caracas
(*Con. Am. L. Flyweight Title Challenge*)
22.08.81 Nelson Polanco W CO 10 Apartado
(*Colombian L. Flyweight Title Defence*)
19.06.82 Homer Meza L RSC 8 Cartagena
27.08.82 Felipe Medrano W PTS 12 Maicao
(*Colombian L. Flyweight Title Defence*)
27.11.82 Agustin Higirino L RSC 3 Santa Marta
12.05.83 Uriel Londono W PTS 10 Cerete
(*Colombian L. Flyweight Title Defence*)
18.06.83 Nelson Polanco W PTS 10 Cartagena
(*Colombian L. Flyweight Title Defence*)
20.08.83 Jose Iriarte W PTS 10 Cartagena
(*Colombian L. Flyweight Title Defence*)
18.02.84 Jorge Lugo W PTS 8 Cartagena
14.04.84 Alfredo Gomez W PTS 10 Cartagena
27.07.84 Rodolfo Blanco W PTS 10 Cartagena
(*Colombian L. Flyweight Title Defence*)
21.09.84 Juan Gomez W RSC 3 Cartagena
06.10.84 Bernardo Gonzalez W PTS 8 Cartagena
29.03.85 Prudencio Cardona W PTS 10 Cartagena
03.05.85 Victor Sierra W PTS 10 Cartagena
21.06.85 Santos Hoo W PTS 10 Cartagena
20.07.85 Francisco Quiroz W PTS 10 Cartagena
18.10.85 Benedicto Murillo DREW 10 Cartagena
31.01.86 Rodolfo Blanco L PTS 10 Cartagena
(*Colombian L. Flyweight Title Defence*)
08.08.86 Rafael Julio DREW 8 Santa Marta
12.09.86 Manuel Julio W RSC 2 Cartagena
31.10.86 Ruben Veraga W PTS 6 Monteria
21.12.86 Alfredo Cardales W RSC 4 Cartagena
13.02.87 Jose Castillo W CO 5 Barranquilla

13.03.87 Arnold Velasquez W PTS 8 Cartagena
03.04.87 Jose Iriarte W PTS 8 Barranquilla
28.06.87 Jung-Koo Chang L RSC 10 Seoul
(WBC L. Flyweight Title Challenge)
11.09.87 Manuel Julio W PTS 10 Barranquilla
30.10.87 Felipe Medrano W CO 3 Cartagena
19.02.88 Luis Salazar W CO 5 Cartagena
04.03.88 Bernardo Ceballos W RTD 2 Santa Marta
25.03.88 Orlando Maestre W PTS 10 Barranquilla
Summary: 37 contests, won 28, drew 3, lost 6.

Jaime Garza
Santa Cruz, USA. *Born* 10.09.59
Former WBC S. Bantamweight Champion

07.02.78 Eduardo Villareal W CO 1 Reynosa
02.03.78 Francisco Silva W CO 1 Reynosa
30.11.78 Miguel Bejarano W CO 1 Los Angeles
14.12.78 Augustin Sanchez W RSC 2 Los Angeles
11.01.79 Delfino Cornejo W RSC 2 Los Angeles
18.01.79 Jose Villegas W CO 4 Los Angeles
23.08.79 Jose Villegas W PTS 6 Los Angeles
25.09.79 Ramon Barrera W CO 3 Los Angeles
02.11.79 Fernando Reyes W RSC 2 San Diego
08.12.79 Ernesto Rios W CO 3 Los Angeles
14.12.79 Jose Lopez W CO 1 San Bernardino
02.02.80 Joe Lopez W CO 1 Phoenix
22.02.80 Jose Hernandez W RSC 2 San Bernardino
21.03.80 Luis Avila W CO 8 San Bernardino
12.04.80 Pedro Gonzales W RSC 2 Tucson
02.05.80 Jose Reyna W CO 1 San Bernardino
13.05.80 Luis Avila W PTS 10 Bakersfield
21.06.80 Augustin Granados W CO 1 Las Vegas
17.07.80 Luis Sandoval W CO 3 Los Angeles
07.08.80 Lorenzo Ramirez W CO 4 Los Angeles
13.09.80 Calvin Sheppard W CO 4 San Antonio
30.10.80 Jose Valente W RSC 3 Los Angeles
13.12.80 Manuel Ruelas W CO 1 El Paso
17.02.81 Robert Anderson W CO 1 Los Angeles
04.04.81 Hector Cortez W CO 1 Los Angeles
15.05.81 Alex Garcia W CO 2 Los Angeles
19.06.81 Franco Torregoza W CO 1 Las Vegas
26.07.81 Lupe Martinez W RSC 3 Las Vegas
20.08.81 Carlos Zuniga W RSC 2 Los Angeles
03.09.81 Rodolfo Quintero W RSC 2 Los Angeles
15.10.81 Romeo Lira W CO 3 Los Angeles
19.11.81 Antonio de la Paz W CO 2 Los Angeles
17.12.81 Joaquin Acuna W CO 4 Los Angeles
04.02.82 Carlos Mendoza W RSC 10 Los Angeles
19.06.82 Carmelo Negron W RSC 5 Las Vegas
06.11.82 Hugo Partida W RSC 1 Los Angeles
03.03.83 Ruben Moreno W CO 1 Los Angeles
15.06.83 Bobby Berna W RSC 2 Los Angeles
(Vacant WBC S. Bantamweight Title)
17.11.83 Beto Perez W CO 5 Los Angeles
26.05.84 Felipe Orozco W CO 3 Miami
(WBC S. Bantamweight Title Defence)
03.11.84 Juan Meza L CO 1 Kingston
(WBC S. Bantamweight Title Defence)
24.02.86 Arnel Arrozal W RSC 3 Irvine
05.04.86 Jorge Urbina Diaz W RSC 3 Palm Springs
29.04.86 Mario Gomez W RSC 4 Irvine
10.12.86 Carlos Linares W RSC 5 Long Beach
26.01.87 Darryl Thigpen L RSC 6 Irvine
09.04.87 Dwight Pratchett W PTS 10 Los Angeles
18.05.87 Joe Ruelas W PTS 10 Los Angeles
30.06.87 George Navarro L PTS 10 Los Angeles
09.12.87 James Manning W RSC 6 Long Beach
24.03.88 Marcos Villasana L CO 5 Los Angeles
Summary: 51 contests, won 47, lost 4.

Loreto Garza
Sacramento, USA. *Born* 23.05.62
Con. Am. L. Welterweight Champion

01.02.83 Don Canada W CO 2 Sacramento
05.04.83 James Sowell W CO 2 Sacramento
21.06.83 Francisco Estrella W CO 1 Sacramento
21.10.83 Howard Smith W RSC 4 Sacramento
25.10.83 Jose Resendez W CO 3 Sacramento
15.11.83 Francisco Tomas Cruz L RSC 4 Sacramento
06.03.84 Peter Cunningham W PTS 6 Sacramento
03.04.84 Jerry Lewis W RSC 3 Sacramento
03.07.84 Mario Castro W RSC 2 Sacramento
18.06.85 Ernie Landeros DREW 6 Sacramento
15.08.85 Rene Hedman W RSC 1 Sacramento
23.02.86 Chauncey Hayes W PTS 8 Richmond
05.06.86 Erwin Brown W RSC 3 Sacramento
20.07.86 Roberto Garcia W RSC 2 Stateline
27.09.86 Roberto Garcia W CO 7 Stateline
09.03.87 Mucio Nava W CO 1 Sacramento
21.05.87 Willie Montana W RSC 6 Sacramento
01.07.87 Gary Williams W RSC 1 Sacramento
01.09.87 Amy Pacana W RSC 2 Sacramento
25.09.87 Javier Juarez W RSC 1 Sacramento
12.02.88 Charlie Choo Choo Brown W RSC 4 Sacramento
22.04.88 Harry Arroyo W RSC 1 Sacramento
(Con. Am. L. Welterweight Title Challenge)
Summary: 22 contests, won 20, drew 1, lost 1.

Juan Gervacio
La Romana, Dominican Republic. *Born* 17.10.67
Former WBA S. Bantamweight Champion

21.12.85 Felix Llanos W CO 1 Caguas
05.03.86 Jose Vega DREW 4 Aguadilla
03.05.86 Wilfredo Lanza W CO 2 Guaynabo
30.05.86 Jesus Pool DREW 6 Curacao
22.06.86 Pedro Arroyo W RSC 3 San Juan
05.07.86 Javier Arce W CO 1 San Juan
06.09.86 Jose Rivera W RSC 1 San Juan
04.10.86 Atilano Quinones W PTS 6 San Juan
08.11.86 Jesus Filomeno W RSC 3 San Juan
06.12.86 Edwin Salgado W PTS 8 San Juan
10.01.87 Jorge Ortiz W RSC 3 San Juan
21.02.87 Jaime Polo W CO 2 San Juan
19.03.87 Manuel Miranda W RSC 2 San Juan
16.05.87 Rafael Forte W CO 2 San Juan
06.06.87 Jeff Hanna W RSC 4 San Juan
08.08.87 Carlos Flores W RSC 5 San Juan
03.09.87 Ramon Cruz W RSC 10 San Juan
28.11.87 Louie Espinosa W PTS 12 San Juan
(WBA S. Bantamweight Title Challenge)
27.02.88 Bernardo Pinango L PTS 12 San Juan
(WBA S. Bantamweight Title Defence)
02.04.88 Paul Mingo W CO 2 San Juan
Summary: 20 contests, won 17, drew 2, lost 1.

Juan C. (Puma) Gimenez
Asuncion, Paraguay. *Born* 20.12.60
WBC International Middleweight Champion. Former South American L. Heavyweight Champion

02.07.82 Delfin Olivera W RSC 2 Asuncion
06.08.82 Clarismundo Silva W CO 4 Asuncion
17.09.82 Helmut Ulka W CO 6 Asuncion
14.10.82 Freddie Brown W PTS 10 Asuncion
04.02.83 Andres Olmedo W PTS 10 Asuncion
12.07.83 Luis Vega W RSC 4 Asuncion
12.08.83 Andres Olmedo W PTS 10 Asuncion
28.09.83 Alfredo Morales W CO 1 Asuncion
13.11.83 Jose Maria Flores W CO 1 Asuncion
(Vacant South American L. Heavyweight Title)
13.01.84 Juan Leiva W PTS 10 Asuncion
25.02.84 Jorge Servin W RTD 4 Asuncion
(South American L. Heavyweight Title Defence)
06.04.84 Jorge Salgado DREW 12 Asuncion
(South American L. Heavyweight Title Defence)
09.06.84 Cesar Romero L PTS 10 Buenos Aires
02.08.84 Juan Leiva W RTD 4 Posadas
08.09.84 Victor Robledo L PTS 12 Buenos Aires
(South American L. Heavyweight Title Defence)
14.12.84 Jorge Salgado W RSC 10 Asuncion
15.02.85 Ed Contreras W PTS 10 Asuncion
20.04.85 Roberto Ruiz W RSC 7 Buenos Aires
17.05.85 Enrique Coronel W PTS 10 Asuncion
04.08.85 Joao Tavares W CO 4 Asuncion
26.09.85 Antonio Caro W RTD 4 Asuncion
11.10.85 Enrique Coronel W CO 5 Obera
25.11.85 Osmar Ochoa W PTS 10 Asuncion
07.06.86 Carlos Herrera W CO 3 Buenos Aires
13.09.86 Juan Domingo Roldan L PTS 10 Buenos Aires
15.11.86 Pompilio Salgado DREW 10 Barranquilla
20.02.87 Mauro F. Cruz W RTD 8 Asuncion
20.03.87 Julio Gonzalez W PTS 10 Asuncion
08.05.87 Enrique Coronel W PTS 10 Asuncion
29.05.87 Hugo Vera W RSC 10 Asuncion
12.09.87 Roberto Duran L PTS 10 Miami
23.10.87 Jimmy Smith W CO 1 Miami
23.01.88 Jorge Amparo W PTS 12 Asuncion
(WBC International Middleweight Title Challenge)
22.03.88 Horacio Silva W PTS 10 Asuncion
Summary: 34 contests, won 28, drew 2, lost 4.

Nestor Giovannini
Rafaela, Argentine. *Born* 07.02.61
WBC International L. Heavyweight Champion. Former Argentinian L. Heavyweight Champion

06.07.84 Mario Melo L PTS 6 Morteros
25.08.84 Miguel Mosna W PTS 6 Buenos Aires
06.10.84 Anibal Romero W PTS 6 Buenos Aires
03.11.84 Mario Melo W PTS 6 Buenos Aires
08.12.84 Miguel Mosna W PTS 8 Buenos Aires
22.03.85 Daniel Guibaudo W CO 5 Rafaela
11.04.85 Anibal Romero W PTS 10 Rafaela
18.05.85 Mario Melo L RSC 5 Buenos Aires
25.07.85 Juan Leiva W RTD 1 Rafaela
23.08.85 Anibal Romero W PTS 10 San Vicente
13.09.85 Victor Robledo W PTS 10 Rafaela
05.10.85 Sergio Merani DREW 8 Buenos Aires
21.11.85 Juan Rodriguez W PTS 10 Rafaela
20.12.85 Juan Fernandez W PTS 12 Rafaela
11.04.86 Miguel Cea W RSC 7 Rafaela
04.07.86 Pedro Ferraro W CO 8 Rafaela
23.08.86 Jorge Salgado W TD 11 Buenos Aires
(Argentinian L. Heavyweight Title Challenge)
13.11.86 Anibal Romero W PTS 10 Rafaela
12.12.86 Jorge Salgado DREW 12 Rafaela
(South American L. Heavyweight Title Challenge)
06.02.87 Clarismundo Silva W PTS 10 Rafaela
13.03.87 Eduardo Contreras W PTS 12 Rafaela
(Argentinian L. Heavyweight Title Defence)
09.06.87 Miguel Steinbach W PTS 10 Rafaela
10.07.87 Miguel Maldonado W RTD 7 Tandil
21.08.87 Angel Caro W PTS 10 Rafaela
25.09.87 Angel Caro W RTD 3 Resistencia
09.10.87 Nestor Albarracin W CO 4 Ceres
13.11.87 Eduardo Contreras W PTS 10 Rosario
12.12.87 Jorge Salgado L PTS 12 Ushuaia
(Argentinian L. Heavyweight Title Defence)
31.03.88 Noe Cruciani W CO 1 Spoleto
(WBC International L. Heavyweight Title Challenge)
Summary: 29 contests, won 24, drew 3, lost 2.

Paul Gonzales
Pecos, USA. *Born* 18.04.64
Former Undefeated NABF Flyweight Champion

10.08.85 Jose Torres W PTS 6 Reseda
05.12.85 Joey Roach W PTS 8 Hollywood
02.02.86 Alonzo Gonzales W PTS 12 Hollywood
(NABF Flyweight Title Challenge)
17.04.86 Javier Barajas W PTS 10 Bakersfield
20.07.86 Orlando Canizales W PTS 12 Stateline
(NABF Flyweight Title Defence)
07.07.87 Lucilo Nolasco W PTS 10 Los Angeles
18.10.87 Ron Cisneros W PTS 10 Stateline
Summary: 7 contests, won 7.

Humberto (Chiquita) Gonzalez
Netzahualcoyotl, Mexico. *Born* 22.03.67
Mexican L. Flyweight Champion

01.09.84 Jorge Ortega W PTS 4 Mexico City
19.12.84 Narciso Perez W RSC 1 Mexico City
20.02.85 Carmelo Perez W RSC 1 Mexico City
20.04.85 Francisco Villa Gomez W RSC 1 Mexico City
08.06.85 Martin Alvarez W RSC 2 Mexico City
27.07.85 Otilio Gallegos W RSC 2 Mexico City
07.09.85 Eduardo Ramirez W CO 4 Mexico City
09.11.85 Javier Alvarez W RSC 1 Mexico City
14.12.85 Carlos Rezago W CO 5 Mexico City
15.03.86 Martin Perez W RSC 2 Mexico City
22.05.86 Sergio Medina W CO 3 Neza
18.06.86 Alcie Hernandez W RSC 2 Mexico City
08.10.86 Agustin Macias W RSC 4 Mexico City
06.12.86 Jorge Gutierrez W RSC 5 Mexico City
22.02.87 Javier Alonso W CO 1 Acapulco
09.05.87 Ruben Padilla W RSC 7 Mexico City
13.06.87 Santiago Mendez W RSC 8 Mexico City
25.07.87 Jose M. Diaz W CO 2 Mexico City
26.09.87 Jorge Cano W PTS 12 Cancun
(Mexican L. Flyweight Title Challenge)
05.03.88 Jose L. Zepeda W CO 6 Tijuana
Summary: 20 contests, won 20.

Rodolfo (Gato) Gonzalez
Mexico City, Mexico. *Born* 02.07.59
L. Welterweight

21.10.78 Manuel Ferrer W RSC 5 Mexico City
23.12.78 Jose Tolosa W CO 1 Mazatlan
10.02.79 Juan Hernandez W RSC 4 Merida
16.03.79 Chucho Saucedo W CO 3 Mazatlan
26.05.79 Lupe Perez W RSC 6 Merida
07.07.79 Rafael Rojas W RSC 3 Mazatlan
22.07.79 Jose Escalante W CO 4 San Luis Potosi
25.08.79 Juan Elizondo W CO 6 Tijuana
06.10.79 Humberto Caicedo W CO 1 McAllen
10.11.79 Salvador Torres W CO 1 Guadalajara
08.12.79 Curtis Ramsey W RSC 2 Los Angeles
16.02.80 Alfredo Pitalua W RSC 10 Mexico City
02.04.80 Nacho Jiminez W CO 3 Los Angeles
03.07.80 Modesto Concepcion W CO 2 Los Angeles
26.07.80 Herman Montes T DRAW 3 Los Angeles
04.10.80 Celso Limon W PTS 10 Guadalajara
16.12.80 Norman Goins W RSC 1 Los Angeles
16.03.81 Vilomar Fernandez W RSC 2 Los Angeles
13.06.81 Andy Ganigan W PTS 10 Los Angeles
25.07.81 Tae-Jin Moon W PTS 10 Los Angeles
12.09.81 Claude Noel L PTS 15 Atlantic City
(*Vacant WBA Lightweight Title*)
09.09.82 Robert Turner W CO 1 Fort Worth
02.10.82 Vicente Mijares L RSC 9 Torreon
11.12.82 Cayetano Correa L PTS 10 Mexico City
11.05.83 Carlos Villacana W RSC 4 Corpus Christi
24.06.83 Daniel Felizardo W RSC 2 Forth Worth
26.07.83 James Martinez W PTS 10 Houston
19.08.83 Agustin Estrada W PTS 10 Juarez
22.10.83 Bennie Abarca W PTS 10 Tijuana
27.01.84 Vicente Mijares L PTS 10 Torreon
01.03.84 Roberto Collins W RSC 3 Los Angeles
31.05.84 Roque Montoya W TD 8 Los Angeles
12.07.84 See-Kwon Lee W CO 1 Los Angeles
14.12.84 Javier Barcenas W RSC 1 Acapulco
18.02.85 Jose Luis Castillo W CO 4 Tijuana
29.03.85 Juan Cruces W RSC 3 Miami
23.05.85 Darrell Cottrell W CO 5 Los Angeles
03.07.85 Rene Arredondo W PTS 10 Los Angeles
26.09.85 Luis Urraca W RSC 5 Los Angeles
20.11.85 Lorenzo Garcia W PTS 10 Los Angeles
25.02.86 Rollin Williams W PTS 4 Los Angeles
03.03.86 Jamey Ollenberger W PTS 10 Sacramento
15.08.86 Jorge Hernandez W PTS 10 Guadalajara
10.01.87 Patrizio Oliva L PTS 15 Agrigento
(*WBA L. Welterweight Title Challenge*)
25.07.87 Rigoberto Lopez W CO 6 Mexico City
09.10.87 Ronnie Shields L PTS 10 Los Angeles
22.12.87 Roberto Collins W CO 2 Obregon
Summary: 47 contests, won 40, drew 1, lost 6.

Herol (Bomber) Graham
Sheffield, England. *Born* 13.09.59
Former EBU Middleweight Champion. Former Undefeated British Middleweight Champion. Former Undefeated British, Commonwealth & EBU L. Middleweight Champion

28.11.78 Vivian Waite W PTS 6 Sheffield
04.12.78 Curtis Marsh W RTD 1 Southend
22.01.79 Jimmy Roberts W RSC 2 Bradford
12.02.79 Dave Southwell W PTS 8 Reading
28.02.79 Dave Southwell W PTS 8 Burslem
27.03.79 George Walker W PTS 8 Southend
27.04.79 Mac Nicholson W PTS 8 Newcastle
16.05.79 Gordon George W PTS 8 Sheffield
26.09.79 Lloyd James W PTS 8 Sheffield
27.10.79 Billy Ahearne W RSC 3 Barnsley
27.11.79 Errol McKenzie W PTS 8 Sheffield
12.02.80 Glen McEwan W PTS 8 Sheffield
22.04.80 George Danahar W PTS 8 Sheffield
09.09.80 Joey Mack W PTS 8 Sheffield
30.10.80 Larry Mayes W RSC 4 Liverpool
22.01.81 Lancelot Innes W PTS 10 Liverpool
24.03.81 Pat Thomas W PTS 15 Sheffield
(*British L. Middleweight Title Challenge*)
17.06.81 Prince Rodney W RSC 1 Sheffield
25.11.81 Kenny Bristol W PTS 15 Sheffield
(*Commonwealth L. Middleweight Title Challenge*)
24.02.82 Chris Christian W RSC 9 Sheffield
(*British & Commonwealth L. Middleweight Title Defence*)
22.04.82 Fred Coranson W PTS 10 Liverpool
30.09.82 Hunter Clay W PTS 15 Lagos
(*Commonwealth L. Middleweight Title Defence*)
15.03.83 Tony Nelson W RTD 5 Wembley
23.05.83 Clemente Tshinza W CO 2 Sheffield
(*Vacant EBU L. Middleweight Title*)
11.10.83 Carlos Betancourt W CO 1 London
09.12.83 Germain le Maitre W RSC 8 St Nazaire
(*EBU L. Middleweight Title Defence*)
22.07.84 Lindell Holmes W RSC 5 Sheffield
25.09.84 Irwin Hines W CO 2 Wembley
16.10.84 Jose Seys W RSC 6 London
26.11.84 Liam Coleman W RSC 3 Sheffield
06.03.85 Jose Rosemain W CO 5 London
24.04.85 Jimmy Price W CO 1 London
(*Vacant British Middleweight Title*)
16.10.85 Roberto Ruiz W RSC 2 London
03.12.85 Sanderline Williams W PTS 10 Belfast
05.02.86 Ayub Kalule W RSC 10 Sheffield
(*EBU Middleweight Title Challenge*)
23.06.86 Ernie Rabotte W RSC 1 Las Vegas
04.11.86 Mark Kaylor W RTD 8 Wembley
(*EBU Middleweight Title Defence*)
17.01.87 Charlie Boston W RTD 7 Belfast
26.05.87 Sumbu Kalambay L PTS 12 Wembley
(*EBU Middleweight Title Defence*)
05.12.87 Ricky Stackhouse W RSC 8 Doncaster
Summary: 40 contests, won 39, lost 1.

Uriah Grant
Jamaica. *Born* 1961
L. Heavyweight

22.06.84 Rogelio Bolanos W RSC 3 Palm Beach
07.12.84 Henry Tillman L RSC 2 Houston
10.05.85 Keith Allen W RSC 5 Fort Lauderdale
23.07.85 Fred Jenkins W RTD 1 Miami
17.10.85 Ricky Womack L PTS 6 Merrillville
25.10.85 James Sisco W RSC 2 Miami
26.11.85 Gary Clarke W CO 4 Miami
26.12.85 Dean Moore W RSC 6 Miami
31.01.86 Reg Neal W CO 1 Miami
21.02.86 Matt Saad Muhammad W PTS 10 Fort Lauderdale
06.05.86 Leslie Stewart L PTS 8 Atlantic City
28.08.86 Grover Robinson W RSC 7 Los Angeles
19.10.86 Abdul Muhammad W RSC 1 Fort Pierce
18.11.86 Arthel Lawhorne W RSC 10 Los Angeles
19.12.86 Manuel Murillo W RSC 6 Miami
22.01.87 Robert Folley W RTD 4 Los Angeles
09.04.87 Ramzi Hassan L PTS 12 Los Angeles
08.08.87 Abdul Muhammad W CO 1 Sunrise
23.10.87 Eric Holly W RSC 5 Miami
28.11.87 Louis Coleman W CO 1 New Haven
Summary: 20 contests, won 16, lost 4.

Michael Greer
Memphis, USA. *Born* 09.09.55
Con. Am. Cruiserweight Champion

22.04.80 Steve Mormino W PTS 4 Memphis
13.05.80 Phil Brown DREW 6 Memphis
01.07.80 John Pinney W CO 6 Memphis
26.07.80 George Goforth W PTS 8 Jenkins
09.09.80 Art Pruitt W RSC 6 Memphis
27.09.80 George Goforth W CO 5 Jenkins
08.02.81 Ed Turner W RSC 5 Sedalia
04.04.81 Fred Miller W CO 2 Owensboro
22.04.81 Willie Goodman W PTS 6 Birmingham
26.06.81 Tony James W RSC 1 Blythville
13.10.81 Henry Porter W PTS 8 Memphis
24.11.81 James Dixon W PTS 10 Memphis
16.02.82 Demetrius Edwards W PTS 10 Memphis
07.04.82 Charles Bryant W CO 2 Nashville
18.05.82 Tom Stevenson L CO 1 Memphis
18.07.82 Charles Allen W CO 1 Pensacola
17.08.82 Larry Strogen W RSC 4 Memphis
22.10.82 Carl Williams L RSC 3 New York
08.01.83 Henry Porter DREW 8 St Ann
16.02.83 Jeff Sims L RSC 3 East Rutherford
28.04.83 Otis Bates W PTS 12 Little Rock
24.09.83 Pinklon Thomas L RSC 5 Totowa
06.12.83 Keith Allen W PTS 6 Memphis
24.01.84 Larry Jones W RSC 1 Memphis
03.02.84 Dick Scott DREW 6 Memphis
10.09.84 Mike Rollins W CO 2 Helena
22.11.84 Pisai Finai W RSC 3 St Paul
22.01.85 Nick Smith W CO 1 Memphis
27.02.85 Dwight Muhammad Qawi L PTS 10 Atlantic City
13.03.85 Andy Stokes W PTS 8 Las Vegas
03.09.85 Rick Willis W RSC 5 Memphis
05.11.85 Keith Allen W RSC 8 Memphis
07.01.86 Paul Madison W PTS 10 Memphis
04.03.86 Willard Dumas W CO 1 Memphis
03.06.86 Alan Whitfield W CO 3 Memphis
10.08.86 Carlos de Leon L RSC 8 Giardini Naxos
(*WBC Cruiserweight Title Challenge*)
07.10.86 Lupe Guerra W CO 4 Memphis
08.11.86 David Harvey W CO 2 Greenville
02.12.86 David Kliewer W RSC 3 Memphis
03.03.87 Aaron Brown W RSC 6 Memphis
21.05.87 Johnny Davis W PTS 12 Memphis
(*Vacant Con. Am. Cruiserweight Title*)
01.09.87 Curtis Isaac W PTS 12 Memphis
(*Con. Am. Cruiserweight Title Defence*)
05.01.88 Keith Allen W RSC 4 Memphis
02.02.88 Pat Strachan W PTS 12 Memphis
(*Con. Am. Cruiserweight Title Defence*)
Summary: 44 contests, won 35, drew 3, lost 6.

Calvin (Silky) Grove
Coatsville, USA. *Born* 05.08.62
IBF Featherweight Champion & Former Unbeaten USBA Featherweight Champion

03.06.82 Mike Davis W CO 2 Conshohocken
13.06.82 Greg Turner W RSC 1 Atlantic City
19.07.82 Jose Abru W RSC 2 Atlantic City
04.08.82 Sylvester Kennon W PTS 6 Atlantic City
22.09.82 Rick Stinnie W CO 1 Atlantic City
27.10.82 Leon Drummond W CO 2 Atlantic City
24.11.82 Tony Rutledge W PTS 6 Atlantic City
13.01.83 Ray Evans W PTS 6 Atlantic City
12.03.83 Jose Figueroa W PTS 6 Atlantic City
15.06.83 Santos Cruz W PTS 8 Atlantic City
17.07.83 Juan Figueroa W PTS 8 Atlantic City
22.09.83 Vic del Rio W RSC 3 Atlantic City
23.11.83 William Martinez W RSC 3 Atlantic City
17.01.84 Harrison Azari W RSC 1 Philadelphia
06.03.84 Sylvester Price W RSC 4 Atlantic City
07.04.84 Pedro Montero W PTS 10 Atlantic City
21.05.84 Satos Moreno W PTS 10 Atlantic City
21.08.84 Margarito Marquez W RSC 5 Atlantic City
13.12.84 Pascual Aranda W RSC 3 Atlantic City
04.02.85 Kelvin Seabrooks W PTS 10 Atlantic City
24.04.85 Idabeth Rojas W PTS 10 Atlantic City
28.06.85 Irving Mitchell W PTS 12 Atlantic City
(*USBA Featherweight Title Challenge*)
19.09.85 Paul Devorce W PTS 10 Atlantic City
25.10.85 Dana Roston W PTS 12 Atlantic City
(*USBA Featherweight Title Defence*)
16.02.86 Jeff Roberts W PTS 10 Troy
03.05.86 Pepe Vazquez W PTS 10 Glens Falls
04.09.86 Billy White W RSC 6 Atlantic City
(*USBA Featherweight Title Defence*)
28.11.86 Aristides Acevedo W PTS 10 Atlantic City
26.03.87 Angel Hernandez W PTS 10 Atlantic City
10.09.87 Tony Cisneros W PTS 10 Houston
12.11.87 Capri Lipkins W PTS 8 Houston
23.01.88 Antonio Rivera W RSC 4 Gamaches
(*IBF Featherweight Title Challenge*)
Summary: 32 contests, won 32.

Jerry (Wimpy) Halstead
Oklahoma City, USA. *Born* 12.09.63
Heavyweight

10.06.80 Leon Patterson W CO 3 Oklahoma City
17.06.80 Fred Williams W CO 3 Oklahoma City
01.07.80 Tim Moore W CO 1 Oklahoma City
15.07.80 Russell Fitzgerald W PTS 4 Oklahoma City
05.08.80 Pete Lewis W PTS 4 Oklahoma City
19.08.80 Dick Chesio W CO 1 Oklahoma City
09.09.80 Ron Brown W CO 1 Oklahoma City
25.09.80 James Brown W RSC 2 Oklahoma City
20.11.80 Andy McNeil W CO 3 Oklahoma City
06.01.81 James Logan W CO 2 Oklahoma City
27.01.81 Joe Miller W RSC 2 Oklahoma City
17.02.81 Archie Birch W CO 1 Oklahoma City
17.03.81 Earl McFadden W PTS 4 Oklahoma City
03.07.81 Earl McFadden W PTS 6 Hugo
04.08.81 Dick Silas W CO 5 Oklahoma City
02.09.81 Jim Green W PTS 6 Oklahoma City
09.02.82 Ron Ackerson W CO 5 Oklahoma City
18.03.82 Jim Green W PTS 6 Oklahoma City
03.04.82 Ron Brown W CO 6 Denver
29.05.82 Darren Encline W CO 1 Oklahoma City
05.11.82 Joe Byrd W PTS 4 Atlantic City
07.01.83 Mike Costello L PTS 6 Hartford
24.03.83 Abdul Makin W PTS 8 Bridgeport
05.05.83 Mike Costello L CO 2 Atlantic City
13.01.84 Tyrone Booze DREW 8 Hartford

22.02.84 Walter Cevoli L PTS 10 Milan
20.03.84 Alvino Manson L CO 5 Atlantic City
20.09.85 Fred Muhammad W CO 1 Kemmerer
08.10.85 Alan Jamieson W CO 2 Oklahoma City
23.10.85 Ken Penn W RSC 2 Oklahoma City
05.11.85 Danny Davis W CO 2 Oklahoma City
03.12.85 James Young W CO 1 Oklahoma City
21.01.86 Lupe Guerra W CO 2 Oklahoma City
04.03.86 Larry Frazier W PTS 10 Bakersfield
01.04.86 Otis Hardy Bates W CO 3 Oklahoma City
12.06.86 Steve Eisenbarth W RSC 2 Los Angeles
02.09.86 Bill Findley W CO 2 Oklahoma City
16.09.86 Joe Brewer W CO 3 Oklahoma City
26.09.86 Aaron Brown W CO 2 Wichita
07.10.86 Ricky Keller W CO 4 Oklahoma City
21.10.86 Charles Atlas W RSC 4 Oklahoma City
04.11.86 Ken Elliott W PTS 10 Oklahoma City
22.11.86 Greg Page L RSC 8 Las Vegas
20.01.87 Greg Murray W CO 2 Oklahoma City
03.02.87 Mickey Pryor W CO 3 Oklahoma City
17.02.87 Aaron Brown W CO 5 Oklahoma City
21.02.87 Earl Cobbins W CO 2 Kansas City
24.03.87 Michael Tyson W CO 5 Oklahoma City
20.04.87 Percell Davis W RSC 8 Santa Monica
30.05.87 Tony Tubbs L PTS 10 Las Vegas
07.07.87 Ron Draper W CO 1 Oklahoma City
21.07.87 Rocky Young W CO 2 Oklahoma City
04.08.87 Joe Adams W CO 4 Oklahoma City
18.08.87 Wilson Douglas W CO 2 Oklahoma City
01.09.87 Lorenzo Boyd W CO 1 Oklahoma City
15.09.87 Danny Ross W RSC 3 Oklahoma City
06.10.87 Wes Smith W PTS 10 Oklahoma City
20.10.87 Al Jones W CO 6 Oklahoma City
03.11.87 Stan Johnson W CO 1 Oklahoma City
17.11.87 Keith McMurray W PTS 10 Oklahoma City
01.12.87 Bobby Crabtree W PTS 12 Oklahoma City
02.02.88 Walter Santemore W PTS 10 Oklahoma City
16.04.88 James Douglas L RSC 9 Las Vegas
Summary: 63 contests, won 55, drew 1, lost 7.

Tsuyoshi Hamada
Nakagusuku, Japan. *Born* 29.11.60
Former WBC L. Welterweight Champion. Former Undefeated OPBF & Japanese Lightweight Champion

21.05.79 Norimasa Kakegawa W CO 1 Tokyo
04.10.79 Masahiko Murayama W CO 1 Tokyo
23.10.79 Fusao Imai L PTS 4 Tokyo
22.02.80 Kunio Taga W CO 5 Tokyo
29.04.80 Katsuo Kazama W CO 1 Tokyo
01.07.80 Shizuo Tosaka W CO 6 Tokyo
29.08.80 Minhiko Okuyama W CO 1 Tokyo
23.11.80 Takeshi Mine W CO 1 Tokyo
10.02.81 Takeshi Fukui W CO 8 Tokyo
10.05.81 Verachart Mahachai W CO 2 Tokyo
18.07.81 Deo Rabago W RSC 9 Tokyo
05.08.83 Max Boy Toyogon W CO 2 Tokyo
14.10.83 Domy Soriano W CO 1 Tokyo
01.03.84 Jose Resendez NC 6 Los Angeles
03.04.84 Greg Triplett W RSC 3 Reseda
12.07.84 Rommy Cunanam W CO 1 Tokyo
09.09.84 Claude Noel W CO 4 Tokyo
02.12.84 Hikaru Tomonari W RSC 7 Tokyo
(*Japanese Lightweight Title Challenge*)
04.04.85 Downthong Chuvatana W RSC 2 Tokyo
07.07.85 Jong-Jong Pacquing W PTS 12 Tokyo
(*OPBF Lightweight Title Challenge*)
04.11.85 Suwarno Perico W CO 1 Naha
(*OPBF Lightweight Title Defence*)
24.07.86 Rene Arredondo W CO 1 Tokyo
(*WBC L. Welterweight Title Challenge*)
02.12.86 Ronnie Shields W PTS 12 Tokyo
(*WBC L. Welterweight Title Defence*)
22.07.87 Rene Arredondo L RSC 6 Tokyo
(*WBC L. Welterweight Title Defence*)
Summary: 24 contests, won 21, lost 2, nc 1.

Ramzi Hassan
California, USA. *Born* Palestine 07.12.62
L. Heavyweight

01.09.82 Nova Garcia W PTS 4 Merrillville
16.10.82 Clarence Osby W PTS 4 Chicago
17.11.82 Anton Hibbler W PTS 4 Hammond
03.01.83 Gary Jones W PTS 4 Chicago
07.02.83 Kirk Bell W CO 1 Chicago
07.03.83 James Churn W PTS 6 Chicago
20.03.83 John Cox W PTS 4 Chicago
28.04.83 Clarence Osby L PTS 6 Hammond
20.06.83 Francis Sargent W RSC 1 Chicago
13.10.83 Jimmie Bills W PTS 6 San Jose
04.11.83 Larry Musgrove W PTS 6 San Jose
23.02.84 Larry Musgrove W PTS 6 San Jose
11.08.84 Eddie Bell W PTS 4 Woodstock
22.09.84 Jerry Harris W PTS 4 Arlington Heights
02.11.84 Jim Wilder W PTS 6 Chicago
20.12.84 James Churn W PTS 6 Chicago
25.02.85 Roy Saffold W CO 4 Chicago
22.03.85 Al Rankin W PTS 8 Hammond
28.06.85 Steve Alread W CO 1 Hammond
08.08.85 Slobodan Kacar L PTS 10 Chicago
19.06.86 Danny Blake W PTS 8 San Diego
28.08.86 Jerry Okorodudu W PTS 10 Los Angeles
03.12.86 Kelvin Kelly W PTS 10 Los Angeles
23.02.87 Jeff Lampkin W PTS 10 Los Angeles
09.04.87 Uriah Grant W PTS 12 Los Angeles
16.06.87 Jimmy Bills W PTS 10 Reno
30.06.87 Glenn Kennedy W PTS 12 Los Angeles
24.11.87 Tony Willis L RSC 12 Los Angeles
(*Vacant USBA L. Heavyweight Title*)
Summary: 28 contests, won 25, lost 3.

Kiyoshi Hatanaka
Aichi, Japan. *Born* 07.03.67
Former Undefeated Japanese S. Flyweight Champion

27.11.84 Harelya Yamauchi W CO 1 Nagoya
05.02.85 Chuji Sanuki W RSC 1 Osaka
29.04.85 Shigehito Hayashe W CO 1 Osaka
26.06.85 Shuichi Sakakibara W CO 1 Nagoya
28.07.85 Shinpei Sato W CO 1 Okazaki
08.10.85 Takuji Hijiri W PTS 4 Nagoya
30.11.85 Akio Kawamata W PTS 6 Hamamatsu
04.03.86 Hiromitsu Tatsuki W CO 1 Osaka
09.05.86 Takashi Hirata W PTS 8 Nagoya
14.07.86 Tadashi Maruo W PTS 10 Tokyo
18.10.86 Masaki Sono W CO 2 Nagoya
23.02.87 Tadashi Maruo W RSC 3 Tokyo
(*Japanese S. Flyweight Title Challenge*)
10.07.87 Teruaki Miyasato W PTS 10 Nagoya
(*Japanese S. Flyweight Title Defence*)
29.10.87 Surasith Meeprasert W CO 1 Nagoya
16.02.88 Constancio Dangla W CO 3 Nagoya
Summary: 15 contests, won 15.

Gene (Mad Dog) Hatcher
Fort Worth, USA. *Born* 28.06.59
Former Undefeated Con. Am. Welterweight Champion. Former WBA L. Welterweight Champion

30.04.81 Ken Sheppard W RSC 1 Fort Worth
28.05.81 Victor Hernandez W PTS 6 Las Vegas
16.06.81 Clyde Spencer W CO 1 Fort Worth
07.07.81 Ali Husson W PTS 6 Fort Worth
17.07.81 Ramiro Pruneda W RSC 3 Beaumont
04.08.81 Dwaine Prim W RSC 6 Fort Worth
22.08.81 Milton Hall W RSC 4 Las Vegas
07.10.81 Bobby McMillan W CO 4 Beaumont
29.10.81 Raul Trujillo W RSC 2 Fort Worth
26.11.81 Ricardo Garcia W CO 3 Las Vegas
10.03.82 Charles Allen W RSC 2 Lake Charles
10.04.82 Alfredo Escalera W PTS 10 Fort Worth
10.06.82 Danny Favella W RSC 3 Las Vegas
14.07.82 Jermoe Artis W RTD 7 Fort Worth
17.10.82 Tyrone Crawley L PTS 10 Atlantic City
11.11.82 Anthony Bryant W RSC 3 Brownwood
23.12.82 Darryl Cottrell W RSC 7 Las Vegas
25.02.83 Romeo Sandoval W RSC 5 Las Vegas
16.06.83 Alfredo Escalera L PTS 10 New York
08.08.83 Luis Rivera W CO 5 Houston
13.10.83 Ed Lugo W CO 4 Dallas
12.11.83 Joe Manley W PTS 12 Las Vegas
21.04.84 Hector Sifuentes W PTS 10 Fort Worth
01.06.84 Johnny Bumphus W RSC 11 Buffalo
(*WBA L. Welterweight Title Challenge*)
15.12.84 Ubaldo Sacco W PTS 15 Fort Worth
(*WBA L. Welterweight Title Defence*)
21.07.85 Ubaldo Sacco L RSC 9 Campione
(*WBA L. Welterweight Title Defence*)
04.02.86 Kevin Austin W PTS 10 San Antonio
08.08.86 Sergio Valles W RSC 4 El Paso
23.09.86 Ric Lomeli W CO 3 Fort Worth
24.10.86 Darryl Anthony W RSC 11 Atlantic City
(*Vacant Con. Am. Welterweight Title*)
15.02.87 Frankie Warren L PTS 10 Sacramento
30.08.87 Lloyd Honeyghan L RSC 1 Marbella
(*WBC Welterweight Title Challenge*)
Summary: 32 contests, won 27, lost 5.

Greg (Mutt) Haugen
Auburn, USA. *Born* 31.08.60
IBF Lightweight Champion. Former Undefeated NABF Lightweight Champion

04.11.82 Noel Arriesgado W PTS 8 Anchorage
04.12.82 Noel Arriesgado W RSC 7 Anchorage
13.01.83 Joe Perez W PTS 10 Seattle
23.02.83 Max Cervantes W RSC 4 Seattle
29.03.83 Larry Yazee W RSC 2 Seattle
26.04.83 Chuck Peralta W PTS 10 Seattle
12.07.83 Roosevelt Booth W PTS 4 Miami
20.09.83 Ted Michaeliszyn W PTS 6 Las Vegas
27.09.84 Tony Villa W RSC 2 Las Vegas
07.02.85 Ted Michaeliszyn W RSC 7 Seattle
07.03.85 Juan del Toro T DRAW 1 Seattle
17.07.85 Jeff Bumphus W PTS 8 Atlantic City
22.08.85 Freddie Roach W RSC 7 Las Vegas
06.11.85 Chris Calvin W RSC 6 Las Vegas
06.01.86 Charlie Brown W RSC 1 Las Vegas
16.02.86 Juan Alvarado W RSC 9 Reno
26.03.86 Ken Willis W PTS 10 Las Vegas
24.05.86 Edwin Curet W PTS 12 Las Vegas
(*Vacant NABF Lightweight Title*)
19.08.86 Ernie Landeros W PTS 10 Las Vegas
05.12.86 Jimmy Paul W PTS 15 Las Vegas
(*IBF Lightweight Title Challenge*)
07.06.87 Vinny Pazienza L PTS 15 Providence
(*IBF Lightweight Title Defence*)
16.12.87 Derrick McGuirre W RSC 6 Las Vegas
06.02.88 Vinny Pazienza W PTS 15 Atlantic City
(*IBF Lightweight Title Challenge*)
11.04.88 Miguel Santana W TD 11 Tacoma
(*IBF Lightweight Title Defence*)
Summary: 24 contests, won 22, drew 1, lost 1.

Thomas (Hit Man) Hearns
Detroit, USA. *Born* 18.10.58
WBC Middleweight Champion. Former Undefeated WBC L. Heavyweight Champion. Former WBA Welterweight Champion. Former Undefeated USBA Welterweight Champion. Former Undefeated WBC L. Middleweight Champion. Former Undefeated NABF Middleweight Champion

25.11.77 Jerome Hill W CO 2 Detroit
07.12.77 Jerry Strickland W CO 3 Mount Clemens
16.12.77 Willie Wren W RSC 3 Detroit
29.01.78 Anthony House W CO 2 Detroit

Greg Haugen (right) regained his IBF lightweight title after a rousing battle with the never-say-die Vinny Pazienza
Tom Casino

10.02.78 Robert Adams W CO 3 Detroit
17.02.78 Billy Goodwin W RSC 2 Saginaw
17.03.78 Ray Fields W RSC 2 Detroit
31.03.78 Tyrone Phelps W CO 3 Saginaw
08.06.78 Jimmy Rothwell W CO 1 Detroit
20.07.78 Raul Aguirre W CO 2 Detroit
03.08.78 Eddie Marcelle W CO 2 Detroit
07.09.78 Bruce Finch W CO 3 Detroit
26.10.78 Pedro Rojas W RSC 1 Detroit
09.12.78 Rudy Barro W CO 4 Detroit
13.01.79 Clyde Gray W RSC 10 Detroit
31.01.79 Sammy Ruckard W RSC 8 Detroit
03.03.79 Segundo Murillo W RSC 8 Detroit
03.04.79 Alfonso Hayman W PTS 10 Philadelphia
20.05.79 Harold Weston W RTD 6 Las Vegas
28.06.79 Bruce Curry W CO 3 Detroit
23.08.79 Mao de la Rosa W RSC 2 Detroit
22.09.79 Jose Figueroa W CO 3 Los Angeles
18.10.79 Saensak Muangsurin W RSC 3 Detroit
30.11.79 Mike Colbert W PTS 10 New Orleans
03.02.80 Jim Richard W CO 3 Las Vegas
02.03.80 Angel Espada W RSC 4 Detroit (*Vacant USBA Welterweight Title*)
31.03.80 Santiago Valdez W RSC 1 Las Vegas
03.05.80 Eddie Gazo W CO 1 Detroit
02.08.80 Pipino Cuevas W RSC 2 Detroit (*WBA Welterweight Title Challenge*)
06.12.80 Luis Primera W CO 6 Detroit (*WBA Welterweight Title Defence*)
25.04.81 Randy Shields W RSC 12 Phoenix (*WBA Welterweight Title Defence*)
25.06.81 Pablo Baez W RSC 4 Houston (*WBA Welterweight Title Defence*)
16.09.81 Ray Leonard L RSC 14 Las Vegas (*WBA Welterweight Title Defence & WBC Welterweight Title Challenge*)
11.12.81 Ernie Singletary W PTS 10 Nassau
27.02.82 Marcos Geraldo W CO 1 Las Vegas
25.07.82 Jeff McCracken W RSC 8 Detroit
03.12.82 Wilfred Benitez W PTS 15 New Orleans (*WBC L. Middleweight Title Challenge*)
10.07.83 Murray Sutherland W PTS 10 Atlantic City
11.02.84 Luigi Minchillo W PTS 12 Detroit (*WBC L. Middleweight Title Defence*)
15.06.84 Roberto Duran W CO 2 Las Vegas (*WBC L. Middleweight Title Defence*)
15.09.84 Fred Hutchings W RSC 3 Saginaw (*WBC L. Middleweight Title Defence*)
15.04.85 Marvin Hagler L RSC 3 Las Vegas (*World Middleweight Title Challenge*)
10.03.86 James Shuler W CO 1 Las Vegas (*NABF Middleweight Title Challenge*)
23.06.86 Mark Medal W RSC 8 Las Vegas (*WBC L. Middleweight Title Defence*)
17.10.86 Doug de Witt W PTS 12 Detroit (*NABF Middleweight Title Defence*)
07.03.87 Dennis Andries W RSC 10 Detroit (*WBC L. Heavyweight Title Challenge*)
29.10.87 Juan Domingo Roldan W CO 4 Las Vegas (*Vacant WBC Middleweight Title*)
Summary: 47 contests, won 45, lost 2.

Angel Hernandez
Puerto Rico. *Born* 21.02.61
Con. Am. Lightweight Champion

13.10.79 Jose Torres W PTS 4 San Juan
18.02.80 Luis Mejias W PTS 4 San Juan
03.03.80 Luis Adorno W PTS 4 San Juan
21.04.80 Reinaldo Gonzalez DREW 4 San Juan
29.05.80 Hector Cruz W RSC 3 San Juan
04.07.80 Mike Drayton W PTS 8 Martinique
24.07.80 Efrain Acosta W PTS 6 San Juan
04.09.80 Reinaldo Gonzalez W PTS 6 San Juan
18.09.80 Victor Torres W PTS 8 Dorado
13.12.80 Raul Morales W PTS 8 El Paso
05.02.81 Jose Alejandro DREW 10 Trujillo
20.06.81 Raul Hernandez W RSC 4 San Juan
05.10.81 Roberto Hernandez W RSC 8 San Juan
30.11.81 Sergio Bautista W PTS 10 San Juan
18.09.82 Oscar Huertas W PTS 10 Miami
11.03.83 Ed Lugo W CO 5 Miami
25.06.83 Jose Renta W RSC 6 San Juan
26.05.84 Hector Sifuentes W RSC 1 Guaynabo
02.02.85 Jose Rivera W RSC 6 San Juan
05.10.85 Orlando Romero Uribe W RSC 6 San Juan
07.06.86 Jose Benitez W RSC 2 San Juan
26.09.86 Ray Estades W RSC 1 Miami
06.12.86 Junuel Rodriguez W RSC 3 San Juan
21.02.87 Roberto Medina W RSC 8 San Juan
27.03.87 Victor Belcher W PTS 10 San Juan
28.09.87 Juan Minaya W RSC 5 Santo Domingo (*Vacant Con. Am. Lightweight Title*)
24.03.88 Miguel Alvarado W RSC 2 San Juan
14.04.88 Tim Burgess W PTS 10 New York
Summary: 28 contests, won 26, drew 2.

Hugo Hernandez

Hugo (Little Bird) Hernandez
Bahia Blanca, Argentine. *Born* 10.04.60
Argentinian L. Welterweight Champion

13.06.80 Raul Gonzalez W CO 1 Bariloche
11.07.80 Roberto Maciel W RTD 4 Bariloche
15.08.80 Angel Olea W PTS 8 Mendoza
12.09.80 Carlos Canete W RSC 8 Mendoza
10.10.80 Juan Huale W CO 1 Bariloche
07.11.80 Ramon Allende W CO 2 Bariloche
21.11.80 Angel Olea W TD 3 Bariloche
05.12.80 Cirilo Ruiz W CO 7 Bariloche
10.01.81 Felipe Baez W RTD 9 Bariloche
13.03.81 Ramon Abeldano DREW 10 Bariloche
23.05.81 Marcelo Romero W RSC 5 Buenos Aires
19.06.81 Felipe Baez W PTS 10 Allen
14.08.81 Nicolas Arkuszyn W PTS 10 Bariloche
06.11.81 Romulo Ibarra W DIS 9 Bariloche
18.12.81 Romulo Ibarra W RSC 5 Buenos Aires
05.02.82 Juan A. Merlo W DIS 10 Bariloche
12.05.82 Ricardo Espinosa W RSC 8 Buenos Aires
04.06.82 Julio Melone W PTS 10 Cordoba
30.06.82 Ramon Collado W CO 4 Buenos Aires
23.07.82 Carlos Canete W RSC 7 Cordoba
20.08.82 Juan Zuniga W RSC 5 Cordoba
10.09.82 Jose Funes W PTS 10 Cordoba
18.02.83 Alfredo Moyano W CO 1 Cordoba
08.04.83 Gabriel Sanchez W CO 3 Neuquen
03.06.83 Jose Funes W RTD 1 San Rafael
08.07.83 Julio Melone ND 3 Cordoba
13.08.83 Hugo Luero W RSC 2 Buenos Aires
15.10.83 Ramon Collado W PTS 10 Buenos Aires
19.05.84 Adolfo Arce W RSC 3 Buenos Aires
22.06.84 Romulo Ibarra W RTD 7 Mendoza
20.07.84 Mario Mattus W CO 2 Bariloche
06.10.84 Kevin Austin W CO 3 Buenos Aires
17.11.84 Carlos Prieto W PTS 10 Buenos Aires
14.12.84 Pedro Vargas W CO 1 San Juan
15.02.85 Jimmy Blevins W CO 2 Bariloche
16.03.85 Antonio Vicente W RSC 10 Buenos Aires
12.04.85 Sergio Loyola W RTD 3 Cipolett
23.05.85 Rene Arredondo L RSC 4 Los Angeles
07.09.85 Lorenzo Garcia W PTS 12 Buenos Aires (*Vacant Argentinian L. Welterweight Title*)
18.10.85 Antonio Vicente W PTS 10 Bariloche
18.04.86 Adolfo Rossi W CO 3 Buenos Aires (*Argentinian L. Welterweight Title Defence*)
17.05.86 Ramon Jara W CO 7 Buenos Aires (*Argentinian L. Welterweight Title Defence*)
15.08.86 Jose Luduena W CO 6 Mendoza
25.10.86 Juan M. Coggi L CO 3 Buenos Aires (*Argentinian L. Welterweight Title Defence*)
04.04.87 Eduardo Benevent W PTS 10 Buenos Aires
22.05.87 Ramon Collado W PTS 10 Mendoza
20.06.87 Eduardo Benevent W RSC 2 Buenos Aires
14.08.87 Jorge Tejeda W PTS 10 Mendoza
11.12.87 Juan Ceballos W PTS 10 Salta
05.02.88 Jorge Tejeda W CO 2 San Rafael
02.04.88 Eduardo Benevent W PTS 12 Lincoln (*Argentinian L. Welterweight Title Defence*)
Summary: 51 contests, won 47, drew 1, lost 2, nc 1.

Virgil (Sugar) Hill
Williston, USA. *Born* 18.01.64
WBA L. Heavyweight Champion. Former Undefeated Con. Am. L. Heavyweight Champion

15.11.84 Arthur Wright W RSC 2 New York
05.01.85 John Tyrrell W RSC 1 Atlantic City
16.02.85 Dave Vedder W PTS 6 Reno
13.07.85 Dawud Shaw W PTS 6 Atlantic City
22.01.86 Fred Jordan W RSC 4 Atlantic City
02.03.86 James Williamson W RSC 6 Lancaster
30.04.86 Abdul Hakim W RSC 4 Atlantic City
30.06.86 Santiago Valdez W RSC 1 Everett
10.07.86 Mike Sedillo W PTS 8 Los Angeles
02.08.86 Willie Mayberry W RSC 1 Detroit
14.08.86 Marcus Dorsey W RSC 2 Lynnwood
04.10.86 Wayne Caplette W CO 1 Williston
17.10.86 Eric Winbush W PTS 10 Bismark
11.12.86 Clarence Osby W PTS 12 New York (*Vacant Con. Am. L. Heavyweight Title*)
03.03.87 James Williams W CO 4 Fargo
01.05.87 Marvin Camel W CO 1 Grand Forks
13.06.87 Marcos Geraldo W RSC 2 Lake Tahoe
22.07.87 Junior Edmond W PTS 10 Minot
05.09.87 Leslie Stewart W RSC 4 Atlantic City (*WBA L. Heavyweight Title Challenge*)
21.11.87 Rufino Angulo W PTS 12 Paris (*WBA L. Heavyweight Title Defence*)
03.04.88 Jean-Marie Emebe W RSC 11 Bismarck (*WBA L. Heavyweight Title Defence*)
Summary: 21 contests, won 21.

Dave Hilton
Peter Goldfield/USA

Dave Hilton
Montreal, Canada. *Born* 09.12.63
Middleweight. Former Undefeated Con. Am. & Canadian Welterweight Champion

10.02.81 Noel Torres W RSC 2 Montreal
10.03.81 Kevin Coffee W CO 1 Montreal
14.06.81 Denis Brisson W PTS 4 Montreal
26.06.81 Eddie Ortiz W CO 2 Halifax
29.09.81 Brian Anderson W PTS 4 Montreal
03.11.81 Daniel Gagnon W RSC 4 Montreal
15.12.81 Ray Rosa W RSC 1 Montreal
04.03.82 Henry Rosa W CO 1 Montreal
22.06.82 Daniel Gagnon W PTS 6 Montreal
21.09.82 Bobby Green W CO 1 Montreal
19.10.82 Tim Elliott W CO 2 Montreal
12.11.82 Jean-Paul Petrin W CO 6 Montreal
14.12.82 Mike Blunt W RSC 1 Montreal
25.01.83 Bob Harvey W RSC 3 Montreal
15.02.83 Sam Gervins W PTS 8 Montreal
21.06.83 Pedro Acosta W CO 2 Montreal
29.07.83 Bruce Strauss W CO 3 Cornwall
04.12.83 Mario Cusson T DRAW 3 Montreal (*Canadian Welterweight Title Challenge*)
25.03.84 Mario Cusson W RSC 1 Montreal (*Canadian Welterweight Title Challenge*)
10.07.84 Dennis Sigouin W RSC 10 Montreal (*Vacant Con. Am. Welterweight Title*)
11.12.84 Pete Padilla W RSC 2 Montreal (*Con. Am. Welterweight Title Defence*)
22.01.85 Sammy Horne W RSC 3 Montreal
15.03.85 Dennis Fain W RSC 2 Las Vegas

01.02.87 Yong-Man Cha W RSC 2 Sungnam
(*South Korean S. Flyweight Title Challenge*)
26.04.87 Yun-Ho Park W CO 5 Chungbok
(*South Korean S. Flyweight Title Defence*)
30.06.87 Dae-Yong Park W CO 5 Seoul
(*South Korean S. Flyweight Title Defence*)
19.12.87 Ernie Cataluna W PTS 12 Chinju
(*OPBF Bantamweight Title Challenge*)
06.03.88 Gilbert Albay W RSC 5 Seoul
(*OPBF Bantamweight Title Defence*)
Summary: 23 contests, won 22, lost 1.

Hiroki Ioka

Sakai City, Japan. *Born* 08.01.69
WBC M. Flyweight Champion. Former Undefeated Japanese M. Flyweight Champion

23.01.86 Yukio Yorimochi W CO 3 Tokyo
10.02.86 Hiroshi Udo W CO 2 Kochi City
05.03.86 Osamu Ueomoto W CO 2 Osaka
13.09.86 Masao Kasai W PTS 4 Matsumoto
07.10.86 Yoshihide Tobo W RSC 2 Osaka
22.02.87 Hisashi Nakatomi W RTD 1 Tokyo
28.04.87 Akira Kiyono W PTS 8 Osaka
08.07.87 Kenji Ono W PTS 10 Osaka
(*Japanese M. Flyweight Title Challenge*)
18.10.87 Mai Thornburifarm W PTS 12 Osaka
(*Vacant WBC M. Flyweight Title*)
31.01.88 Kyung-Yung Lee W RSC 12 Osaka
(*WBC M. Flyweight Title Defence*)
Summary: 10 contests, won 10.

John D. Jackson

Stanford, USA. *Born* 17.05.63
L. Middleweight

11.03.84 Kim Brady W RSC 1 Atlantic City
11.04.84 Keith Todd W RSC 3 Scranton
10.05.84 Bob Thomas W PTS 6 Philadelphia
26.06.84 Louis Owens W PTS 4 Atlantic City
17.10.84 Felipe Montellano W PTS 6 Atlantic City
20.03.85 Gary Tibbs W CO 4 Atlantic City
13.06.85 Billy Ray Joe W RSC 1 Atlantic City
18.07.85 Robert Thomas W PTS 8 Philadelphia
04.09.85 Vince Mays W RSC 5 Atlantic City
25.02.86 Orlando Montalvo W CO 2 Atlantic City
14.06.86 Mike Castronova W RSC 1 Shillington
31.07.86 Milton Leaks W PTS 8 Atlantic City
28.10.86 Tony Ojo W RSC 3 Pennsauken
25.11.86 John B. Walker W RSC 1 Atlantic City
13.01.87 Sidney Outlaw W RSC 6 Philadelphia
21.07.87 Davey Moore W PTS 10 Atlantic City
Summary: 16 contests, won 16.

Julian Jackson

St Thomas, Virgin Islands. *Born* 12.09.60
WBA L. Middleweight Champion. Former Undefeated Con. Am. L. Middleweight Champion

12.02.81 Inocencio Carmona W PTS 6 San Juan
05.03.81 Rafael Ayala W RSC 1 Trujillo Alto
09.04.81 Marcelino Flores W CO 2 San Juan
16.05.81 Reyes Escalera W RSC 3 St Thomas
15.08.81 Edwin Rodriguez W RSC 1 San Juan
26.09.81 Dario D'Asa W CO 3 Miami
20.03.82 Billy Page W PTS 6 Atlantic City
06.06.82 Al Cook W CO 2 Miami
18.08.82 Miguel Sepulveda W RSC 3 San Juan
17.11.82 Mack Heimbaugh W RSC 4 St Joseph
19.01.83 Domenic Fox W CO 2 San Juan
06.03.83 Jake Torrence W RSC 5 Atlantic City
18.05.83 Renaldo Rogue W RSC 1 Las Vegas
25.06.83 David Plowden W RSC 3 San Juan
15.10.83 Jeff Nelson W RSC 3 Miami
20.01.84 Carlton Brown W RSC 1 New York
17.03.84 Eddie Gazo W CO 2 Hato Rey
16.05.84 J. J. Cottrell W RSC 5 Las Vegas
20.06.84 Ron Warrior W CO 3 San Juan
(*Vacant Con. Am. L. Middleweight Title*)
15.08.84 Curtis Ramsey W RSC 12 Las Vegas
(*Con. Am. L. Middleweight Title Defence*)
03.11.84 Santos Solis W RSC 8 San Juan
21.11.84 Tim Harris W RSC 8 Las Vegas
(*Con. Am. L. Middleweight Title Defence*)
12.07.85 Rafael Corona W RSC 3 Santa Clara
10.08.85 Jose Padilla W RSC 3 Las Vegas
15.11.85 Raul Hernandez W RSC 1 Miami
28.02.86 Lopez McGee W CO 2 St Thomas
22.03.86 Mark Allman W RSC 1 Las Vegas
19.04.86 Pancho del Toro W CO 2 Las Vegas
20.05.86 Derrick Drane W RSC 2 New York
23.08.86 Mike McCallum L RSC 2 Miami
(*WBA L. Middleweight Title Challenge*)
19.12.86 Khalif Shabazz W CO 1 Virgin Islands
24.04.87 Milton Leaks W CO 1 Hartford
(*Vacant Con. Am. L. Middleweight Title*)
21.11.87 In-Chul Baek W RSC 3 Las Vegas
(*Vacant WBA L. Middleweight Title*)
16.04.88 Reggie Barnes W CO 1 Las Vegas
Summary: 34 contests, won 33, lost 1.

Tyrone (Harlem Butcher) Jackson

New York, USA. *Born* 23.10.60
Con. Am. S. Featherweight Champion

04.06.81 Glenn Richardson W RSC 4 New York
25.06.81 Gilbert de Jesus W RSC 2 New York
08.08.81 Vergon Hill W PTS 4 New York
03.09.81 Jose Espada W RSC 3 Atlantic City
12.09.81 Cheo Ortiz W CO 3 New York
25.09.81 Glenn Guy W CO 1 New York
05.11.81 Darryl Graham W RSC 3 Atlantic City
05.02.82 Emilio Rodriguez W RSC 1 New York
26.02.82 Cheo Ortiz W PTS 6 New York
24.04.82 Fernando Ortiz W CO 2 Atlantic City
07.11.82 Robert Mullins W CO 3 New York
19.11.82 Jeff Roberts W PTS 8 New York
26.03.83 Tim Daniels W RSC 5 New York
01.05.83 Felix Cortes W CO 1 Atlantic City
28.05.83 Victor Acosta W PTS 10 New York
28.09.83 Willy Martinez W RSC 4 New York
13.12.83 Elvin Gonzalez W RSC 5 Atlantic City
17.04.84 Clarence Hudson W RSC 4 Atlantic City
08.03.85 Felix Thereaux W RSC 3 New York
10.05.85 Juan Torres W CO 2 New York
28.06.85 Paul de Vorce W PTS 12 New York
19.09.85 Rosendo Alonso W CO 1 New York
(*Con. Am. S. Featherweight Title Challenge*)
16.02.86 Ki-Yung Chung L RTD 6 Ulsan
(*IBF Featherweight Title Challenge*)
23.04.87 Floyd Favors W RSC 10 New York
(*Con. Am. S. Featherweight Title Defence*)
12.08.87 Mario Salazar W CO 2 New York
03.09.87 Wilmer Ruiz W CO 6 New York
(*Con. Am. S. Featherweight Title Defence*)
29.10.87 Darryl Sampy W RSC 2 New York
(*Con. Am. S. Featherweight Title Defence*)
24.02.88 Robinson Sanchez W RSC 3 New York
Summary: 28 contests, won 27, lost 1.

Thierry Jacob

Calais, France. *Born* 08.03.65
French Bantamweight Champion

29.10.85 Vincenzo Belcastro W PTS 6 Paris
09.11.85 Eloi Kiroffo W RSC 2 Lille
14.12.85 Jean-Paul Guillard W RTD 1 Calais
08.02.86 Eloi Kiroffo W RSC 2 Lille
08.03.86 Francisco Garcia W CO 4 Calais
17.03.86 German Nunez W CO 1 Paris
05.04.86 Kevin Downer W CO 5 Boulogne
26.04.86 Mohamed Bouras W RTD 3 Calais
10.05.86 Freddy Cruz W PTS 8 Gravelines
30.05.86 Jean Chartier W RSC 3 Grande Synthe
12.09.86 Blas Canovas W RSC 4 Paris
04.10.86 Kelvin Smart W PTS 8 Calais
27.10.86 Bobby McDermott W RSC 3 Paris
29.11.86 Manuel Carrasco W RSC 2 Calais
24.01.87 Alain Limarola W RSC 5 Calais
(*French Bantamweight Title Challenge*)
18.04.87 Ezequiel Hernandez W PTS 8 Calais
23.05.87 Sammy Ruiz W RSC 4 Calais
04.07.87 Kelvin Seabrooks NC 9 Calais
(*IBF Bantamweight Title Challenge*)
03.10.87 Juan Castellanos W PTS 8 Gravelines
14.11.87 Ricky West W CO 2 Calais
30.01.87 Fabrice Benichou L CO 9 Calais
(*Vacant EBU Bantamweight Title*)
Summary: 21 contests, won 19, lost 1, nc 1.

Gert Bo Jacobsen

Oestrup, Denmark. *Born* 18.12.61
WBC International Lightweight Champion. Former Undefeated EBU Lightweight Champion

07.10.82 Chris McCallum W CO 1 Copenhagen
05.11.82 Gilbert Heluin W PTS 6 Copenhagen
02.12.82 Benito Murillo W PTS 4 Randers
11.02.83 Eddie Morgan W RSC 3 Copenhagen
08.04.83 Hugo Carrizo W PTS 6 Copenhagen
06.10.83 Gary Lucas W CO 4 Copenhagen
01.12.83 Aldo di Benedetto W CO 2 Copenhagen
13.01.84 Charles Jurietti W RSC 1 Randers
18.02.84 Jose Luis Vicho W PTS 8 Copenhagen
05.10.84 Jesus Matilla W RSC 3 Randers
09.11.84 Vicente Jorge W PTS 8 Copenhagen
08.03.85 Jose Ortiz W CO 2 Copenhagen
20.06.85 Claude Lancastre W RSC 4 Copenhagen
01.11.85 Jose Garcia W RSC 2 Copenhagen
07.12.85 Nelson Trujillo W RSC 10 Copenhagen
10.01.86 Rene Weller W RSC 8 Randers
(*EBU Lightweight Title Challenge*)
18.04.86 Alfredo Raininger W PTS 12 Randers
(*EBU Lightweight Title Defence*)
17.10.86 Fernando Blanco W PTS 12 Randers
(*EBU Lightweight Title Defence*)
06.02.87 Joey Joynson W CO 1 Herning
27.02.87 Jose A. Hernandez W PTS 12 Randers
(*EBU Lightweight Title Defence*)
28.03.87 Felipe Julio W RSC 5 Copenhagen
(*Vacant WBC International Lightweight Title*)
08.06.87 Alain Simoes W RSC 8 Merignac
(*EBU Lightweight Title Defence*)
02.10.87 Claudio Nitti W RSC 4 Copenhagen
(*EBU Lightweight Title Defence*)
15.01.88 Herbie Bivalacqua W CO 4 Skive
05.02.88 Joey Medina W RSC 6 Atlantic City
Summary: 25 contests, won 25.

Rene Jacquot

Toul, France
EBU L. Middleweight Champion. Former Undefeated French L. Middleweight Champion

25.02.83 Richard Bankeu W PTS 6 Nancy
26.03.83 Mohatar Bekheira W PTS 6 Moirans
07.01.84 Stephane Walter L PTS 6 Besancon
13.02.84 Patrick Grisot W PTS 6 Paris
20.02.84 Jean-Pierre Calvez W PTS 6 Paris
27.02.84 Victor Santoncini L PTS 6 Paris

Tyrone Jackson wins yet again and celebrates Tom Casino

28.04.84 Alphonse Matoubella L PTS 6 St Malo
26.10.84 Thierry Pierluigi W RSC 4 Echirolles
30.11.84 Felix di Ciocco L PTS 6 Grenoble
22.12.84 Angelo Liquori W RSC 6 Muggio
05.01.85 Salvatore Pisani W PTS 6 Voiron
22.03.85 Abdelkader Souhihi L RTD 5 Nice
07.06.85 Andrea Scardigli L PTS 6 Scandicci
29.06.85 Luciano Bruno L PTS 6 Bellaria
26.10.85 Hugues Samo W RSC 6 Grenoble
06.12.85 Helier Custos W PTS 8 Echirolles
25.01.86 Rafael Salamone W PTS 8 Grenoble
28.02.86 Yvon Segor L PTS 10 Pointe a Pitre
(French L. Middleweight Title Challenge)
16.05.86 Giovanni Chirra W PTS 8 Mulhouse
27.06.86 Nino la Rocca W DIS 3 Modena
03.10.86 Mauro Martelli L PTS 10 Geneva
06.12.86 Jean-Yves Piperol W RTD 5 Pointe a Pitre
23.01.87 Jean-Paul Roux W PTS 10 Echirolles
10.04.87 Yvon Segor W RSC 7 Echirolles
(French L. Middleweight Title Challenge)
23.06.87 Joel Brival W PTS 8 Paris
03.10.87 Serge Meyers W RTD 3 Echirolles
09.10.87 John van Elteren W RSC 5 Morges
05.12.87 Miodrag Perunovic W RTD 6 Gaillard
29.01.88 Luigi Minchillo W RSC 4 Rimini
(Vacant EBU L. Middleweight Title)
09.04.88 Eric Taton W RSC 12 Echirolles
(EBU L. Middleweight Title Defence)
Summary: 30 contests, won 21, lost 9.

Marvin (Pops) Johnson
Indianapolis, USA. *Born* 12.04.54
Former WBA L. Heavyweight Champion. Former WBC L. Heavyweight Champion. Former Undefeated USBA L. Heavyweight Champion

23.05.73 Sylvester Wilder W RSC 2 Indianapolis
17.09.73 Al Byrd W RSC 1 Fort Wayne
30.10.73 Chuck Warfield W RTD 5 Fort Wayne
17.07.74 Ted Paxton W CO 2 Chicago
12.11.74 Johnny Words W RSC 6 Indianapolis
11.12.74 Jim Adams W RSC 1 Indianapolis
29.01.75 Gary Summerhayes W PTS 10 Indianapolis
17.04.75 Paul Cardoza W RSC 5 Indianapolis
13.11.75 Eddie Owens W RSC 3 Indianapolis
03.04.76 Ray Anderson W RTD 5 Indianapolis
15.04.76 Harold Carter W RSC 2 Indianapolis
14.09.76 Wayne Magee W RSC 1 Philadelphia
30.11.76 Vandell Woods W PTS 10 Philadelphia
21.02.77 Johnny Townsend W PTS 10 Philadelphia
22.04.77 Tom Bethea W RSC 4 Indianapolis
26.07.77 Matt Saad Muhammad L CO 12 Philadelphia
(NABF L. Heavyweight Title Challenge)
28.09.77 Johnny Fields W CO 1 Cleveland
01.11.77 Billy Douglas W RSC 5 Philadelphia
25.01.78 Roberto Reynosa W CO 1 Indianapolis
03.04.78 Eddie Davis W RSC 7 Indianapolis
24.05.78 Johnny Baldwin W PTS 10 Philadelphia
17.06.78 Lottie Mwale L PTS 8 Belgrade
15.09.78 Jerry Celestine W PTS 10 New Orleans
02.12.78 Mate Parlov W RSC 10 Marsala
(WBC L. Heavyweight Title Challenge)
22.04.79 Matt Saad Muhammad L RSC 8 Indianapolis
(WBC L. Heavyweight Title Defence)
20.09.79 Carlos Marks W PTS 10 Indianapolis
30.11.79 Victor Galindez W RSC 11 New Orleans
(WBA L. Heavyweight Title Challenge)
31.03.80 Mustapha Muhammad L RSC 11 Knoxville
(WBA L. Heavyweight Title Defence)
09.09.80 Lee Royster W CO 4 Atlantic City
16.01.81 Eddie Straight W RSC 1 Indianapolis
28.01.81 Rick Nash W RSC 3 Indianapolis
28.03.81 Michael Spinks L CO 4 Atlantic City
06.04.82 Darnell Hayes W RSC 2 Danville
14.10.82 Alvin Manson W CO 1 Indianapolis
25.02.83 Ernie Barr W CO 8 Nassau
21.11.83 Michael Brothers W RSC 10 Chicago
18.01.84 Elvis Parks W RSC 4 Indianapolis
26.03.84 Eddie Gonzalez W CO 4 Atlantic City
14.06.84 Jerome Clouden W RSC 5 Atlantic City
30.08.84 Johnny Davis W PTS 10 Atlantic City
08.11.84 Charles Williams W PTS 10 Indianapolis
13.12.84 Eddie Collins W RSC 2 Atlantic City
17.01.85 Charles Henderson W RSC 2 Merrillville
21.04.85 Eddie Davis W RSC 6 Atlantic City
(USBA L. Heavyweight Title Challenge)
11.10.85 Raliegh Searcey W CO 4 Terre Haute
04.12.85 Frank Lux W RSC 7 Indianapolis
09.02.86 Leslie Stewart W RSC 7 Indianapolis
(Vacant WBA L. Heavyweight Title)
20.09.86 Jean-Marie Emebe W RSC 13 Indianapolis
(WBA L. Heavyweight Title Defence)
23.05.87 Leslie Stewart L RTD 8 Port of Spain
(WBA L. Heavyweight Title Defence)
Summary: 49 contests, won 43, lost 6.

Sumbu Kalambay
Italy. *Born* Zaire 10.04.56
WBA Middleweight Champion. Former Undefeated EBU Middleweight Champion. Former Undefeated Italian Middleweight Champion

10.10.80 Esperno Postl W RSC 7 Wolkersdorf
24.10.80 Luigi Marini W RSC 6 Ancona
05.12.80 Aldo Buzzetti L PTS 8 Piacenza
08.01.81 Stephane Ferrara DREW 6 Paris
05.02.81 Christian D'Helft W PTS 8 Paris
09.03.81 Cosimo Carbone W RSC 3 Rome
20.03.81 Giovanni Martorina W PTS 6 Ancona
17.04.81 Damiano Lassandro W RSC 8 Pesaro
15.05.81 Christian D'Helft W RTD 1 Pesaro
25.05.81 Giovanni Martorina W RSC 1 Milan
27.06.81 Christian D'Helft W RSC 3 Pesaro
25.09.81 Jose Duran W RSC 4 Pesaro
23.10.81 Sonny Kamunga W CO 7 Pesaro
13.11.81 Michel Pagani W CO 2 Rome
11.12.81 Jose Lozano W PTS 8 Milan
26.12.81 Gabriele Lazzari W RSC 6 Bologna
05.02.82 Steve Williams W RSC 2 Bologna
02.04.82 Costello King W RSC 2 Milan
29.05.82 Jose Quinones W CO 2 Milan
01.09.82 Joe Ouru W DIS 1 Ischia
31.10.82 Buster Drayton W PTS 8 San Remo
10.12.82 Salvatore Perez W RSC 2 Pesaro
22.12.82 Stacey McSwain W PTS 8 St Vincent
24.02.83 Bruce Johnson W RTD 6 Bologna
10.04.83 Wilson Bell W CO 1 San Remo
24.07.83 Jimmy Sykes W PTS 8 Rome
03.09.83 Guy Kennedy W RSC 6 Marsala
13.10.83 James Williams W CO 1 Pesaro
29.10.83 Ralph Moncrief W PTS 10 San Remo
09.12.83 Irwin Hines W RSC 8 Fano
19.02.84 Al Styles W RSC 2 Capo D'Orlando
13.04.84 Allen Alexander W PTS 8 Pesaro
07.07.84 Rico Hoye W PTS 8 Perugia
22.09.84 Tony Cerda W PTS 8 Monte Carlo
10.12.84 Clinton Jackson W PTS 8 Paris
08.03.85 Tony Harrison W RSC 4 Piagge
06.04.85 Duane Thomas L PTS 10 Atlantic City
27.04.85 Jose Duarte W PTS 8 Avelino
14.07.85 Don Bowers W PTS 8 Monte Carlo
26.09.85 Giovanni de Marco W PTS 12 Caserta
(Italian Middleweight Title Challenge)
19.12.85 Ayub Kalule L PTS 12 Ancona
(EBU Middleweight Title Challenge)
15.03.86 Cliff Gilpin W PTS 8 Monte Carlo
03.09.86 Giovanni de Marco W RTD 11 Silvio Marina
(Italian Middleweight Title Defence)
13.12.86 Cecil Pettigrew W PTS 8 Ragusa
21.03.87 Bastante Blanco W RTD 5 Ischia
26.05.87 Herol Graham W PTS 12 Wembley
(EBU Middleweight Title Challenge)
23.10.87 Iran Barkley W PTS 15 Livorno
(Vacant WBA Middleweight Title)
01.03.88 Mike McCallum W PTS 12 Pesaro
(WBA Middleweight Title Defence)
Summary: 48 contests, won 44, drew 1, lost 3.

Akio Kameda
Tokyo, Japan
Former Undefeated Japanese Welterweight & L. Welterweight Champion

15.03.77 Edmundo Govea W CO 2 Honolulu
22.05.77 Shigeru Goda W RSC 2 Sapporo
23.07.77 Senju Yamaguchi W RSC 5 Tokyo
29.10.77 Kazunori Shiratori W RSC 5 Tokyo
23.01.78 Mamoru Taira W CO 3 Nagoya
03.03.78 Hyung-Il Lee W RSC 6 Tokyo
28.04.78 Shoji Tsujimoto W RSC 5 Tokyo
(Japanese Welterweight Title Challenge)
27.10.78 Yohi Ari W PTS 10 Tokyo
(Japanese Welterweight Title Defence)
26.01.79 Young-Taek Kim W RSC 6 Tokyo
22.04.79 Kazumi Nakao W CO 2 Tokyo
(Japanese Welterweight Title Defence)
12.07.79 Katsuhiro Sawada W RSC 2 Tokyo
29.11.79 Tatsuo Ohara W CO 2 Tokyo
(Japanese Welterweight Title Defence)
18.03.80 Kazunori Shiratori W RSC 8 Tokyo
(Japanese Welterweight Title Defence)
01.07.80 Mitsuo Kushikino W RSC 8 Tokyo
12.11.80 Kazumi Nakao W RSC 4 Tokyo
(Japanese Welterweight Title Defence)
21.04.81 Dynamite Matsuo W PTS 10 Tokyo
(Japanese Welterweight Title Defence)
07.09.81 Mitsuo Kushikino W PTS 10 Tokyo
(Japanese Welterweight Title Defence)
04.07.82 Aaron Pryor L RSC 6 Cincinnati
(WBA L. Welterweight Title Challenge)
02.11.82 Tatsuya Moriyasu W PTS 10 Tokyo
(Japanese L. Welterweight Title Challenge)
09.01.83 Shoji Okishima W PTS 10 Kyoto
(Japanese L. Welterweight Title Defence)
25.04.83 Yutaka Itoi W CO 4 Tokyo
(Japanese L. Welterweight Title Defence)
05.09.83 Ryo Asuka W CO 3 Tokyo
(Japanese L. Welterweight Title Defence)
14.11.83 Taijiro Niyama W CO 5 Tokyo
(Japanese L. Welterweight Title Defence)
20.02.84 Sang-Moon Suh W CO 7 Tokyo
27.05.84 Eung-Shik Kim L CO 4 Seoul
(OPBF L. Welterweight Title Challenge)
07.10.84 Eung-Shik Kim L RSC 7 Seoul
(OPBF L. Welterweight Title Challenge)
27.10.85 Kei Tsukata W CO 5 Peking
18.08.86 Francisco Ferrer W PTS 10 Nara
27.10.86 Kei Tsukata W CO 5 Kashiwara
28.04.87 Pastor Arcaya W CO 5 Nagoya
01.07.87 Terry Marsh L RTD 6 London
(IBF L. Welterweight Title Challenge)
Summary: 31 contests, won 27, lost 4.

Hideaki Kamishiro
Fukuoka, Japan. *Born* 28.03.62
Flyweight

05.09.84 Katsunori Kaneshima W CO 2 Osaka
29.04.85 Takuya Tsuji W RSC 2 Osaka
27.11.85 Gonzaburo Nobu W RSC 6 Osaka
05.03.86 Masakatsu Sakuma W PTS 10 Osaka
02.06.86 Sakdisamuth Singsamang W RSC 8 Osaka
07.10.86 Makoto Sawamura W RSC 3 Osaka
08.07.87 Masaki Sono W RSC 4 Osaka
31.01.88 Sot Chitalada L RSC 7 Osaka
(WBC Flyweight Title Challenge)
Summary: 8 contests, won 7, lost 1.

Sumbu Kalambay Peter Goldfield/USA

Soon-Jung Kang
South Korea. *Born* 15.01.62
South Korean Flyweight Champion

18.11.80 Jun-Woo Lee W PTS 4 Seoul
19.11.80 Sam-Joo Sun L PTS 4 Seoul
23.01.81 San-Moon Lee W PTS 4 Pusan
25.04.81 Jae-Huan Cho W PTS 4 Pusan
06.05.81 Yau-Kyang How W PTS 4 Seoul
09.05.81 Ki-Ho Shin L PTS 4 Seoul
29.07.81 Jung-Sok Park W PTS 4 Pusan
23.08.81 Ki-Joung Kim W PTS 6 Pusan
25.09.81 Yun-Ho Park W PTS 4 Pusan
18.11.81 Ok-Shik Kim W PTS 4 Pusan
10.02.82 Sang-Moon Lee W PTS 8 Taegu
26.06.82 Dong-Chun Lee W PTS 10 Seoul
04.09.82 Juanito Abraca W PTS 10 Taegu
09.10.82 Chan-Soo Chung W PTS 10 Seoul
(*Vacant South Korean Flyweight Title*)
02.01.83 Youn-Ri Moon W PTS 10 Daejon
26.02.83 Ki-Ho Shin W PTS 10 Seoul
(*South Korean Flyweight Title Defence*)
21.03.83 German Torres L PTS 10 Tokyo
02.04.83 Prudencio Cardona DREW 10 Seoul
17.07.83 Noel Tibay W PTS 10 Chinju
29.10.83 Sang-Moon Lee W PTS 10 Daejon
24.12.83 Chang-Young Chang W RSC 8 Seoul
26.02.84 Yun-Ho Park W PTS 10 Namhae
26.05.84 Do-Sa Kim W PTS 10 Wonju
08.12.84 Bi-Won Chung L PTS 10 Chinju
14.04.85 Bi-Won Chung L PTS 10 Pohang
22.09.85 Titing Dignos W PTS 10 Chungju
24.11.85 Houn-Kuk Chae L PTS 10 Seoul
(*Vacant South Korean Flyweight Title*)
21.02.86 Dodie Penalosa L PTS 10 Manila
27.04.86 In-Soo Kim W PTS 8 Pusan
01.06.86 Houn-Kuk Chae W PTS 10 Inchon
(*South Korean Flyweight Title Challenge*)
30.08.86 Suk-Bong Kim W PTS 10 Osan
(*South Korean Flyweight Title Defence*)
14.12.86 Han-Bong Kang W RSC 4 Inchon
(*South Korean Flyweight Title Defence*)
01.03.87 Tanomsak Singboebae L PTS 12 Bangkok
(*OPBF Flyweight Title Challenge*)
26.04.87 Moon-Jin Choi W PTS 10 Chinju
(*South Korean Flyweight Title Defence*)
28.06.87 Houn-Kuk Chae W PTS 10 Inchon
(*South Korean Flyweight Title Defence*)
09.10.87 Duk-Hyun Kim W RSC 5 Anyang
(*South Korean Flyweight Title Defence*)
24.01.88 Trifon Torralba W RSC 4 Seoul
Summary: 37 contests, won 28, drew 1, lost 8.

Derrick (Hurricane) Kelly
Gary, USA. *Born* 03.01.61
Welterweight

22.04.83 Rodolfo Villegas W RSC 2 Los Angeles
06.05.83 Johnny Gonzales W PTS 6 Los Angeles
10.06.83 Greg Starks W CO 2 Los Angeles
17.06.83 Bob Manous W PTS 4 Los Angeles
01.07.83 Joe Molier W RSC 1 Los Angeles
13.07.83 Alfonso Long W PTS 8 Ventura
11.08.83 Juan Veloz W CO 6 Los Angeles
15.09.83 Marcos Jacobo W PTS 6 Los Angeles
06.10.83 Bertram Buchanan W PTS 6 Los Angeles
21.05.84 Felipe Canela W PTS 10 Los Angeles
27.09.84 Tomas Perez W PTS 10 Los Angeles
20.12.84 Felipe Canela DREW 10 Los Angeles
21.02.85 Glen Corbus W RSC 6 Los Angeles
10.06.85 Roberto Mendez W RSC 7 Los Angeles
20.08.85 Nelson Ortiz W PTS 10 Los Angeles
15.10.85 Diomedes Colome L PTS 10 Los Angeles
08.04.87 Tomas Perez W PTS 12 Los Angeles
18.05.87 Lorenzo Guzman W RSC 6 Los Angeles
15.07.87 Alfonso Long DREW 12 Riverside
13.08.87 Terry Norris W PTS 10 Los Angeles
01.10.87 Anthony Pearson W PTS 10 Los Angeles
03.11.87 Luis Santana W PTS 10 Los Angeles
07.03.88 Felipe Canela W PTS 12 Los Angeles
Summary: 23 contests, won 20, drew 2, lost 1.

Eung-Shik Kim
Kangshin, South Korea. *Born* 06.07.58
Former OPBF L. Welterweight Champion. Former Undefeated South Korean L. Welterweight Champion

12.09.82 Chul-Won Yang W CO 4 Seoul
03.10.82 Myung-Soo Park W RSC 8 Seoul
18.01.83 Chul-Ho Yun W RSC 6 Seoul
20.03.83 Gar Atayde W CO 2 Seoul
08.05.83 Jose Torres W CO 4 Seoul
12.06.83 Hwang Woo W PTS 10 Seoul
(*South Korean L. Welterweight Title Challenge*)
04.09.83 Ruben Rabago W PTS 12 Seoul
(*Vacant OPBF L. Welterweight Title*)
16.10.83 Flash Romero W RSC 3 Seoul
(*OPBF L. Welterweight Title Defence*)
22.01.84 Fernando Gloria W CO 8 Seoul
(*OPBF L. Welterweight Title Defence*)
27.05.84 Akio Kameda W CO 4 Seoul
(*OPBF L. Welterweight Title Defence*)
07.10.84 Akio Kameda W RSC 7 Seoul
(*OPBF L. Welterweight Title Defence*)
20.01.85 Cisco Ferrer W RSC 3 Seoul
(*OPBF L. Welterweight Title Defence*)
26.05.85 Cris Ladera W CO 3 Seoul
(*OPBF L. Welterweight Title Defence*)
02.10.85 Kyung-Duk Ahn L PTS 12 Seoul
(*OPBF L. Welterweight Title Defence*)
24.11.85 Hwa-Yung Song W PTS 10 Inchon
10.08.86 Tricky Kawaguchi W CO 4 Seoul
15.03.87 Jun Ramos W CO 3 Seoul
07.06.87 Tae-Wang Kang W PTS 10 Pusan
25.10.87 Elmer Leonardo W CO 6 Seoul
Summary: 19 contests, won 18, lost 1.

Yong-Kang Kim
Hwasoon-Kun, South Korea. *Born* 03.01.65
OPBF L. Flyweight Champion. Former Undefeated South Korean L. Flyweight Champion

06.04.85 Byung-Sik Bae W RSC 4 Taegu
01.06.85 Jun-Won Kang W PTS 4 Inchon
29.06.85 Yung-Suk Ahn W RSC 4 Seoul
17.08.85 Hyung-Man Lee W PTS 4 Buchon
20.10.85 Noh-Yun Hwan W CO 2 Nonsan
23.11.85 Ke-Yun Chung W PTS 8 Inchon
12.04.86 Sung-Kyu Kim W PTS 8 Yungchun
28.06.86 Su-Yung Lee W CO 2 Kunsan
26.07.86 Eul-Chul Jung W PTS 8 Osan
17.10.86 Han-Bong Kang W CO 7 Suwon
17.01.87 Ha-Sik Lim W PTS 10 Hongchun
(*South Korean L. Flyweight Title Challenge*)
08.03.87 Sung-Kyu Kim W PTS 10 Seoul
30.05.87 William Belan W CO 1 Osan
12.07.87 Jorge Cano W PTS 10 Buchon
11.12.87 Putt Ohyuthanakorn W RSC 10 Kwangju
(*Vacant OPBF L. Flyweight Title*)
20.02.88 Sonny Vidal W PTS 12 Kimpo
(*OPBF L. Flyweight Title Defence*)
Summary: 16 contests, won 16.

James (The Heat) Kinchen
San Diego, USA. *Born* 01.03.57
Former Undefeated USBA Middleweight Champion

08.08.80 Daniel Marks W CO 1 Dallas
23.09.80 Larry Rayford W CO 3 New Orleans
22.01.81 Henry Drummond W PTS 4 Las Vegas
28.01.81 Fred Garcia W CO 2 San Diego
18.02.81 Danny Kirk W RSC 1 Las Vegas
25.03.81 Jimmy Owens W PTS 6 Las Vegas
15.04.81 Larry Myers W RSC 2 Las Vegas
01.05.81 Mike Hutchinson W CO 2 San Diego
03.06.81 Eddie Casper W CO 2 Las Vegas
12.06.81 James Williams W CO 2 San Diego
17.06.81 Reuben Rascone W RSC 1 Las Vegas
08.07.81 Darryl Womack W CO 2 Las Vegas
29.07.81 Juan Rivas W RSC 2 Las Vegas
21.08.81 Everett Conklin DREW 8 Las Vegas
30.09.81 Everett Conklin W CO 6 Las Vegas
04.11.81 Ron Brown W CO 6 Las Vegas
25.11.81 Jesse Avila W RSC 6 Las Vegas
13.01.82 Marvis Sanders W CO 10 Las Vegas
17.02.82 Rudy Robles W PTS 10 Las Vegas
27.03.82 Leroy Green W RSC 9 Atlantic City
23.05.82 Alejos Rodriguez W CO 4 Las Vegas
27.08.82 Joe Gonsalves W CO 5 San Jose
05.09.82 Odell Hadley W PTS 10 St Joseph
30.09.82 Tommy Howard W RSC 10 San Diego
31.10.82 Ralph Moncrief W PTS 10 McAfee
20.01.83 Mike Clark W PTS 10 San Diego
07.04.83 Ernesto Caballero W RSC 8 San Diego
19.05.83 Fred Reed W RSC 1 San Diego
28.05.83 Felton Marshall W RSC 9 Las Vegas
16.07.83 Jose Mireles W CO 1 Dallas
13.08.83 Juan Diaz W RSC 2 Las Vegas
19.11.83 Murray Sutherland W PTS 10 St Joseph
26.02.84 Al Rankin W RSC 3 Beaumont
25.04.84 Erwin Williams W CO 9 San Jose
26.09.84 Jorge Amparo DREW 10 Atlantic City
24.11.84 Alex Ramos W RSC 9 Stateline
(*USBA Middleweight Title Challenge*)
16.02.85 James Shuler L PTS 12 Atlantic City
(*NABF Middleweight Title Challenge*)
14.04.85 Buster Drayton W PTS 10 London
30.07.85 Frank Minton W RSC 9 Atlantic City
11.07.86 Frank Minton W CO 7 Las Vegas
17.10.86 Iran Barkley L PTS 10 Detroit
06.04.87 Juan Domingo Roldan L RSC 9 Las Vegas
18.06.87 Randy Smith W PTS 10 San Diego
25.08.87 Larry Musgrove L TD 3 Reseda
19.11.87 Milford Kemp W PTS 10 San Diego
27.01.88 Tim Williams W PTS 12 San Diego
26.02.88 Antonio Adame W CO 2 Tijuana
17.03.88 Ricky Locke W CO 3 San Diego
Summary: 48 contests, won 42, drew 2, lost 4.

Tomohiro Kiyuna
Okinawa, Japan. *Born* 28.04.62
Former Japanese L. Flyweight Champion

18.11.81 Susumu Arina W RSC 1 Tokyo
08.03.82 Kazuo Sawada W PTS 4 Okinawa
23.07.82 Toshio Oki W CO 2 Tokyo
06.09.82 Ryuji Ikeda W PTS 4 Tokyo
18.10.82 Masato Tanaka W PTS 4 Tokyo
12.11.82 Tadashi Kuramochi L PTS 4 Tokyo
26.03.83 Katsumi Takeshita W PTS 6 Tokyo
02.06.83 Kaigara Ira W PTS 6 Okinawa
30.01.84 Hiroyuki Aikata W RSC 1 Tokyo
06.05.84 Masate Kudo W PTS 10 Tokyo
29.10.84 Masato Tanaka W RSC 1 Tokyo
10.12.84 Yukito Tamakuma W RSC 10 Tokyo
25.02.85 Kazuyoshi Kurashita W CO 4 Tokyo
19.05.85 Yuto Kazaki W CO 7 Okinawa
26.08.85 Yoshiaki Nojima W PTS 10 Tokyo
(*Japanese L. Flyweight Title Challenge*)
27.01.86 Yoshiaki Nojima W PTS 10 Tokyo
(*Japanese L. Flyweight Title Defence*)
14.06.86 Myung-Woo Yuh L RSC 12 Inchon
(*WBA L. Flyweight Title Challenge*)
17.11.86 Katsumi Komiyami W PTS 10 Tokyo
12.01.87 Yukinari Oshiro W PTS 10 Tokyo
(*Vacant Japanese L. Flyweight Title*)
27.04.87 Seiji Tomari W PTS 10 Tokyo
(*Japanese L. Flyweight Title Defence*)
26.07.87 Masaru Yoshimoto W CO 6 Okinawa
(*Japanese L. Flyweight Title Defence*)
19.10.87 Missile Kudo W PTS 10 Tokyo
11.01.88 Hideyuki Ohashi L PTS 10 Tokyo
(*Japanese L. Flyweight Title Defence*)
Summary: 23 contests, won 20, lost 3.

Harold (The Shadow) Knight
Plainfield, USA. *Born* 20.12.63
USBA S. Featherweight Champion

05.07.83 Tom Mason W RSC 1 Atlantic City
02.08.83 Derrick Swinney W PTS 4 Atlantic City
30.11.83 Kelvin Louis W RSC 1 Atlantic City
14.01.84 Darrell Jacobs W RSC 3 Atlantic City
07.02.84 Larry Highsmith W RSC 1 Atlantic City
03.03.84 Jose Ortiz W RSC 3 Atlantic City
13.04.84 Dan Rivera W PTS 6 New York
29.06.84 Frank Mackey W RSC 1 Hampstead
23.08.84 Tim Daniels W PTS 8 Malboro
07.05.85 Mauri Saalakhan W PTS 6 Atlantic City
30.06.85 Eduardo Miranda W RSC 1 Atlantic City
16.10.85 Tomas Otero W CO 1 New Brunswick
24.02.87 Rene Resto W RSC 2 Atlantic City
25.03.87 Darrell Savoy W RSC 4 Atlantic City
30.04.87 Kenny Baysmore W RSC 7 Atlantic City
(*USBA S. Featherweight Title Challenge*)
30.06.87 Rafael Gandarilla W RSC 6 Atlantic City
28.07.87 Sylvester Kennon W RSC 7 Atlantic City
25.09.87 Anthony English W RSC 4 Atlantic City
(*USBA S. Featherweight Title Defence*)
11.11.87 Erskine Wade W RSC 11 Atlantic City
(*USBA S. Featherweight Title Defence*)
02.04.88 Rocky Lockridge L PTS 15 Atlantic City
(*IBF S. Featherweight Title Challenge*)
Summary: 20 contests, won 19, lost 1.

Harold Knight (left) looks on as the referee rescues his opponent, Erskine Wade, in the 11th round of their USBA super-featherweight title bout

Tom Casino

Nana Yaw Konadu
Ghana
Commonwealth & ABU Flyweight Champion

25.05.85 George Freeman W PTS 6 Accra
29.06.85 Ebo Danquah DREW 6 Accra
07.12.85 Flash Conteh W CO 1 Accra
08.03.86 Joe Power W CO 3 Sunyani
27.06.86 Osei Owusu W CO 2 Kumasi
30.08.86 Ramon Agyare W RSC 6 Accra
25.10.86 Ray Amoo W CO 3 Accra
13.12.86 Steve Muchoki W CO 12 Accra
(ABU Flyweight Title Challenge)
28.08.87 Ramon Pichardo W RSC 2 Las Vegas
10.10.87 Albert Musankabala W CO 6 Accra
(Vacant Commonwealth Flyweight Title)
23.12.87 Pat Nkwo W CO 2 Accra
Summary: 11 contests, won 10, drew 1.

Soon-Chun Kwon
S. Korea. *Born* 24.04.59
Former IBF Flyweight Champion. Former Undefeated OPBF S. Flyweight Champion

16.10.77 Sang-Koo Lee W CO 2 Seoul
11.08.79 Chung-Kun Choi L PTS 4 Seoul
18.11.80 Yung-Bon Song W PTS 4 Seoul
19.11.80 Chun-Jae Lee W RSC 4 Seoul
23.11.80 Sang-Moon Lee W PTS 4 Seoul
30.11.80 Chang-Soo Chung W PTS 4 Seoul
07.12.80 Yang-Lim Lee W RSC 2 Seoul
14.02.81 Shin-Hyun Cho W RSC 2 Seoul
04.04.81 Tsuguyuki Toma W CO 2 Wonju
19.04.81 Yoshiyuki Uchikoshi L DIS 1 Seoul
27.06.81 Frankie Granados W CO 1 Pusan
31.07.81 Rudy Esmero DREW 10 Pusan
17.10.81 William Develos W PTS 12 Seoul
(OPBF S. Flyweight Title Challenge)
06.12.81 Hiroyuki Kobayashi W PTS 10 Kwangju
03.01.82 Diego de Villa W CO 7 Pusan
07.03.82 Ali Formentera W RSC 6 Taegu
(OPBF S. Flyweight Title Defence)
08.05.82 Payao Pooltarat W PTS 12 Seoul
(OPBF S. Flyweight Title Defence)
20.06.82 Jimmy Fernandez W RSC 3 Kwangju
19.09.82 Joe Hiyas W PTS 12 Pusan
(OPBF S. Flyweight Title Defence)
30.10.82 Flash Jagdon W CO 1 Taegu
02.01.83 Phaktai Osodsapha W CO 1 Daejon
(OPBF S. Flyweight Title Defence)
12.03.83 Rene Aroy W RSC 9 Masan
14.05.83 Pat Bracero W CO 2 Pusan
(OPBF S. Flyweight Title Defence)
24.07.83 Ruben de la Cruz W CO 4 Kwangju
06.10.83 Jiro Watanabe L TD 11 Osaka
(WBA S. Flyweight Title Challenge)
24.12.83 Rene Busayong W CO 5 Seoul
(Vacant IBF Flyweight Title)
25.02.84 Roger Castillo W CO 12 Seoul
(IBF Flyweight Title Defence)
19.05.84 Ian Clyde W PTS 15 Daejon
(IBF Flyweight Title Defence)
07.09.84 Joaquin Caraballo NC 12 Chungju
(IBF Flyweight Title Defence)
25.01.85 Chong-Kwan Chung DREW 15 Daejon
(IBF Flyweight Title Defence)
14.04.85 Shinobu Kawashima W CO 3 Pohang
(IBF Flyweight Title Defence)
17.07.85 Chong-Kwan Chung DREW 15 Masan
(IBF Flyweight Title Defence)
20.12.85 Chong-Kwan Chung L RSC 4 Pusan
(IBF Flyweight Title Defence)
17.05.87 Tae-Il Chang L PTS 15 Pusan
(Vacant IBF S. Flyweight Title)
Summary: 34 contests, won 25, drew 3, lost 5, nc 1.

Santos (Falucho) Laciar
Huinca Renanco, Argentine. *Born* 31.01.59
Former WBC S. Flyweight Champion. Former Undefeated WBA, South American & Argentinian Flyweight Champion

03.12.76 Carlos Maliene W CO 4 Huinca Renanco
13.01.77 Angel Pereyra W RTD 4 Huinca Renanco
05.02.77 Amado Chavez W RTD 5 Realico
25.02.77 Jose Flores W CO 4 Huinca Renanco
26.03.77 Alejandro Olguin DREW 10 Luiggi
22.04.77 Alberto Martin W PTS 10 Huinca Renanco
07.05.77 Jose Izquierdo W PTS 10 Realico
18.06.77 Jose Zarate W CO 1 Huinca Renanco
08.07.77 Jose Ibiris DREW 10 Huinca Renanco
09.09.77 Carlos Sosa W PTS 12 Villa Maria
30.09.77 Manuel Quinteros W RTD 8 Huinca Renanco
22.10.77 Carlos Reyes Sosa W RTD 6 Villa Carlos
04.11.77 Jose Izquierdo W PTS 10 Huinca Renanco
17.12.77 Enrique Navarro W RTD 6 Realico
13.01.78 Luis Gerez W PTS 10 Huinca Renanco
10.02.78 Jose Ibiris W PTS 10 Huinca Renanco
14.04.78 Ramon Soria DREW 10 Huinca Renanco
19.05.78 Carlos Aguero W PTS 10 Huinca Renanco
02.06.78 Reynaldo Romero W PTS 10 Huinca Renanco
08.07.78 Hector Barreto W PTS 10 Huinca Renanco
06.09.78 Jose Izquierdo W PTS 10 Villa Carlos
20.09.78 Jose Luis Lopez W RTD 4 Villa Carlos
06.10.78 Luis Gerez DREW 10 Villa Maria
21.10.78 Angel Fernandez W PTS 10 Buenos Aires
09.11.78 Felipe Rojas W CO 5 Villa Carlos
01.12.78 Ramon Soria L PTS 10 Mendoza
14.12.78 Raul Perez W PTS 10 Villa Carlos
26.01.79 Jose Ibiris W PTS 10 Villa Carlos
14.02.79 Juan Rios W PTS 10 Villa Carlos
16.03.79 Raul Perez L PTS 10 Huinca Renanco
11.04.79 Gilberto Lopez W PTS 10 Villa Carlos
26.04.79 Jose Flores W RSC 7 Villa Carlos
25.05.79 Raul Perez L PTS 10 Villa Carlos
22.06.79 Juan Espindola W PTS 10 Cordoba
02.08.79 Miguel Lazarte DREW 10 Villa Carlos
06.09.79 Luis Gomez W PTS 10 Villa Carlos
12.10.79 Hector Velasquez W PTS 10 Villa Carlos
03.11.79 Gustavo Ballas L PTS 10 Buenos Aires
07.12.79 Federico Condori W PTS 10 Buenos Aires
27.02.80 Miguel Lazarte W PTS 12 Villa Carlos
(Vacant Argentinian Flyweight Title)
28.03.80 Ruben Condori DREW 10 Cordoba
18.04.80 Domingo Aragon W PTS 10 Cordoba
09.05.80 Juan Brizuela W PTS 10 Cordoba
06.06.80 Adrian Roman W CO 3 Cordoba
23.07.80 Miguel Velez W RTD 6 Villa Carlos
30.08.80 Jaime Miranda T DRAW 8 Santiago
(South American Flyweight Title Challenge)
06.11.80 Federico Condori W PTS 10 Huinca Renanco
22.11.80 Jaime Miranda W PTS 12 Villa Carlos
(South American Flyweight Title Challenge)
08.12.80 Charlie Magri L PTS 10 London
30.01.81 Jose de la Cruz W CO 8 Mar del Plata
28.03.81 Peter Mathebula W RSC 7 Soweto
(WBA Flyweight Title Challenge)
08.05.81 Miguel Lazarte W PTS 10 Cordoba
06.06.81 Luis Ibarra L PTS 15 Buenos Aires
(WBA Flyweight Title Defence)
22.08.81 Rodolfo Rodriguez DREW 10 Buenos Aires
04.09.81 Santos Aragon W PTS 10 Morteros
18.09.81 Ruben Condori DREW 10 Cordoba
02.10.81 Miguel Lazarte W PTS 10 Tucuman
07.11.81 Rodolfo Rodriguez DREW 10 Buenos Aires
01.05.82 Juan Herrera W RSC 13 Merida
(WBA Flyweight Title Challenge)
11.06.82 Domingo Aragon W PTS 10 Huinca Renanco
08.07.82 Ruben Paniagua W PTS 10 Cordoba
22.07.82 Jose Gomez W PTS 10 Villa Carlos
14.08.82 Betulio Gonzalez W PTS 15 Maracaibo
(WBA Flyweight Title Defence)
09.10.82 Ramon Albers W RTD 5 Morteros
05.11.82 Steve Muchoki W RSC 13 Copenhagen
(WBA Flyweight Title Defence)
18.12.82 Rodolfo Rodriguez W PTS 10 Buenos Aires
04.03.83 Ramon Neri W CO 9 Cordoba
(WBA Flyweight Title Defence)
05.05.83 Shuichi Hozumi W RSC 2 Shizuoka
(WBA Flyweight Title Defence)
17.07.83 Hi-Sup Shin W CO 1 Cheju
(WBA Flyweight Title Defence)
16.12.83 Juan Cortes W PTS 10 Cordoba
28.01.84 Juan Herrera W PTS 15 Marsala
(WBA Flyweight Title Defence)
15.09.84 Prudencio Cardona W CO 10 Cordoba
(WBA Flyweight Title Defence)
08.12.84 Hilario Zapata W PTS 15 Buenos Aires
(WBA Flyweight Title Defence)
06.05.85 Antoine Montero W PTS 15 Grenoble
(WBA Flyweight Title Defence)
07.06.86 Jaime Miranda W PTS 10 Rio Tercero
17.07.86 Alberto Pacheco W CO 8 Santa Fe
30.08.86 Gilberto Roman DREW 12 Cordoba
(WBC S. Flyweight Title Challenge)
24.10.86 Jose Narvaez W PTS 10 Concepcion
08.11.86 Oscar Bolivar W PTS 10 Buenos Aires
30.01.87 Hector Patri W PTS 10 Mar del Plata
05.03.87 Jose Narvaez W PTS 10 La Rioja
21.03.87 Isaias Carvacho W CO 4 Esquel
03.04.87 Alejandro Vazquez W CO 2 Trelew
16.05.87 Gilberto Roman W RSC 11 Reims
(WBC S. Flyweight Title Challenge)
08.08.87 Jesus Rojas L PTS 12 Miami
(WBC S. Flyweight Title Defence)
10.12.87 Jose Narvaez W PTS 10 Bahia Blanca
17.02.88 Juan Ivalo W RTD 6 Mar del Plata
05.03.88 Bernardo Mendoza W CO 3 Buenos Aires
02.04.88 Jose Narvaez W PTS 10 San Luis
15.04.88 Ricardo Escobar W PTS Pico Truncado
Summary: 90 contests, won 72, drew 12, lost 6.

Kirkland Laing
Nottingham, England. *Born* Jamaica 20.06.54
British Welterweight Champion

14.04.75 Joe Hannaford W CO 2 Nottingham
12.05.75 Liam White W PTS 8 Nottingham
29.09.75 Derek Simpson W PTS 8 Nottingham
25.11.75 Oscar Angus W PTS 6 London

28.09.80 Tsuguyuki Toma W RSC 7 Pusan
16.11.80 Flash Jagdon W CO 7 Pusan
22.02.81 Carlos Alcibar W PTS 10 Pusan
31.07.81 Neptali Alamag W PTS 10 Pusan
22.09.81 Sakad Saksuree W CO 6 Seoul
25.10.81 Suvan Muansgurin W PTS 10 Taegu
31.01.82 Hitoshi Ohashi W CO 1 Pusan
04.04.82 Arcades Sing-Jom Thong W CO 8 Pusan
03.06.82 Lupe Pintor L RSC 11 Los Angeles
(WBC Bantamweight Title Challenge)
13.11.82 Poker Pelegrino W RSC 9 Seoul
23.01.83 Manachai Sorvatana W CO 2 Daejon
21.03.83 Ricardo Cardona W CO 6 Masan
07.05.83 Martin Hernandez W CO 4 Seoul
18.06.83 Efren Guineta W CO 4 Taegu
21.08.83 Poker Pelegrino W RSC 7 Taegu
09.10.83 Renato Paulino W PTS 10 Taegu
18.12.83 Morsak Muangsurin W CO 1 Daejon
04.02.84 Morris Pastor W CO 2 Seoul
01.04.84 Kid Sumaila W PTS 10 Yosu
09.09.84 Ernie Sanico W RSC 4 Inchon
15.12.84 Dajvarin Hollywood W PTS 10 Pusan
02.02.85 Victor Callejas L PTS 15 San Juan
(WBA S. Bantamweight Title Challenge)
22.06.85 Pablo Pepito W PTS 10 Seoul
19.10.85 Flash Rockman W CO 1 Pohang
25.01.86 Rudy Casicas L RSC 8 Daejon
24.05.86 Majie Bona W RSC 6 Sunchon
13.09.86 Little Bangoyan W PTS 10 Daejon
18.01.87 Prayurasak Muangsurin W CO 9 Pohang
(Vacant IBF S. Bantamweight Title)
05.04.87 Jorge Urbina Diaz W CO 10 Seoul
(IBF S. Bantamweight Title Defence)
19.07.87 Lion Collins W CO 5 Pohang
(IBF S. Bantamweight Title Defence)
27.12.87 Jose Sanabria W PTS 15 Pohang
(IBF S. Bantamweight Title Defence)
20.03.88 Julian Solis W PTS 10 Ulsan
Summary: 48 contests, won 42, lost 6.

Seung-Soon Lee
South Korea
Former OPBF Welterweight Champion. Former Undefeated South Korean Welterweight Champion

21.11.79 Hyong-Dok Choi L PTS 4 Seoul
03.02.80 Young-Ki Yuh W PTS 4 Seoul
21.06.80 Myung-Ki Lee W RSC 1 Seoul
24.09.80 Hyon-Sok Lee W RSC 3 Seoul
17.10.80 Che-Kwon Yuh W CO 1 Seoul
18.11.80 Che-Il Yang W RSC 2 Seoul
21.11.80 Dae-Woo Han W PTS 4 Seoul
23.11.80 Sok-Sun Lim W RSC 3 Seoul
30.11.80 Mu-Sok Hwang W PTS 4 Seoul
07.12.80 Daek-Chang Chong W RSC 3 Seoul
15.03.81 Sok-Sun Lim W RSC 3 Seoul
26.04.81 Soo-Hyung Yuh W RSC 2 Taegu
16.08.81 Joe Lim W PTS 10 Seoul
27.09.81 Leo Casino W RSC 4 Seoul
21.02.82 Koru Jokker W RSC 7 Seoul
21.08.82 Yung-Sop Seo W RSC 6 Seoul
18.01.83 Jae-Yong Park W CO 7 Seoul
(South Korean Welterweight Title Challenge)
17.06.83 Yung-Kil Chung W PTS 10 Seoul
(South Korean Welterweight Title Defence)
04.09.83 Chung-Won Park W CO 9 Seoul
(South Korean Welterweight Title Defence)
05.02.84 Yung-Kil Chung W PTS 10 Seoul
(South Korean Welterweight Title Defence)
25.03.84 Mar Simbajon W CO 5 Seoul
17.06.84 Keun-Soo Park W RSC 1 Seoul
12.07.84 Sergio Sanchez W RSC 3 Los Angeles
23.09.84 Nilo Acido W RSC 4 Seoul
04.01.85 Lito Vazquez W CO 4 Seoul
24.03.85 Willie Makitoki W RSC 2 Seoul
07.07.85 Sil Sarana W CO 3 Seoul
27.10.85 Fernando Gloria W PTS 10 Seoul
14.02.86 Petch Petcharern W CO 2 Seoul
09.08.86 Dionisio Castillo W CO 4 Seoul
15.02.87 Yung-Sok Hwang W RSC 6 Wonju
(OPBF Welterweight Title Challenge)
29.03.87 Yung-Kil Chung L PTS 12 Wonju
(OPBF Welterweight Title Defence)
01.08.87 Boy Romero W CO 4 Suwon
24.04.88 Francisco Ferrer W PTS 10 Seoul
Summary: 34 contests, won 32, lost 2.

Sung-Woo Lee
South Korea. *Born* 06.10.66
Former Undefeated South Korean M. Flyweight Champion

01.06.86 Ku-Yun Baek DREW 4 Seoul
17.08.86 Byung-Oh Choi W RSC 4 Seoul
02.11.86 Kwang-Sik Lee W RSC 2 Sunchun
08.12.86 Je-Man Lee W PTS 4 Seoul
11.12.86 Kwang-Suk Kim W PTS 4 Seoul
14.12.86 Hi-Chung Noh L PTS 4 Seoul
25.01.87 Kee-Sik Yang W RSC 2 Seoul
28.03.87 Chung-Keun Lim W PTS 8 Seoul
06.06.87 Soo-Yong Shim W PTS 10 Hongchun
(Vacant South Korean M. Flyweight Title)
15.08.87 Sang-Shik Kang W RSC 2 Eijongbu
(South Korean M. Flyweight Title Defence)
13.02.88 In-Kyu Hwang W PTS 10 Seoul
Summary: 11 contests, won 9, drew 1, lost 1.

Yul-Woo Lee
South Korea
Flyweight

13.07.85 Dong-Pil Yeom W PTS 4 Chungju
05.12.85 Ros-Eong Choi W PTS 4 Seoul
08.12.85 Sang-Chun Lee W PTS 4 Seoul
10.12.85 Chong-Hwa Park W CO 2 Seoul
28.06.86 Chun-Byun Kim W RSC 5 Pohang
21.07.86 Chan-Yub Chun W CO 2 Hongchun
30.08.86 Sang-Hyon Kim W PTS 10 Pohang
01.11.86 Keun-Soo Choi W PTS 10 Pohang
18.01.87 Sang-Hyun Han W PTS 10 Pohang
19.04.87 Romy Navarrete W CO 7 Inchon
28.06.87 Julio Gudino W PTS 10 Inchon
14.11.87 Arnulfo Melencion W RSC 4 Seoul
13.12.87 Amado Ursua W CO 5 Daejon
20.03.88 Duk-Hyun Kim W CO 7 Ulson
Summary: 14 contests, won 14.

Rocky Lockridge
Tacoma, USA. *Born* 30.01.59
IBF S. Featherweight Champion. Former WBA S. Featherweight Champion. Former USBA Featherweight Champion

09.08.78 Tony Reed W RSC 2 Seattle
05.10.78 Jose Lara W PTS 6 Seattle
14.11.78 Tony Hernandez W RSC 1 Totowa
13.03.79 Melvin Bethea W CO 1 Totowa
17.04.79 Melvin Boynton W RSC 2 Totowa
27.04.79 Francisco Maldonado W CO 2 Newark
31.05.79 Ronnie Green W CO 1 Philadelphia
18.09.79 Gerald Hayes W PTS 12 East Rutherford
30.10.79 Jose Ortiz W CO 2 Totowa
08.01.80 Sammy Goss W RSC 5 Totowa
19.02.80 Fel Clemente W RSC 7 Totwa
(Vacant USBA Featherweight Title)
08.03.80 Richard Rozelle W CO 2 McAfee
01.04.80 Joey Mayes W RSC 2 Totowa
19.06.80 Marcial Santiago W RSC 3 Totowa
13.07.80 Alfonso Evans W RSC 5 McAfee
21.08.80 Livio Nolasco W RSC 4 Totowa
04.10.80 Eusebio Pedroza L PTS 15 McAfee
(WBA Featherweight Title Challenge)
18.12.80 Benny Marquez W RSC 3 Totowa
22.01.81 Ernesto Gonzalez W CO 1 Totowa
06.04.81 Edwin Rivera W PTS 12 Atlantic City
21.05.81 Sergio Reyes W RSC 3 Totowa
22.08.81 Juan Laporte L CO 2 Las Vegas
(USBA Featherweight Title Defence)
12.11.81 Refugio Rojas W PTS 10 East Rutherford
10.12.81 Tony Tris W PTS 10 Totowa
14.03.82 Jose Resendez W RSC 5 Atlantic City
10.04.82 Robert Mullins W RSC 5 Atlantic City
23.05.82 Jose Nieto W RSC 8 Atlantic City
24.06.82 Daniel Felizardo W CO 2 Atlantic City
22.08.82 Miguel Hernandez W RSC 3 McAfee
25.09.82 Angel Lira W RSC 6 McAfee
24.11.82 Alberto Collazo W RSC 9 Atlantic City
24.04.83 Eusebio Pedroza L PTS 15 Liguma
(WBA Featherweight Title Challenge)
14.07.83 Danny Cruz W RSC 1 Totowa
09.09.83 Cornelius Boza-Edwards W PTS 10 Las Vegas
23.11.83 Jeff Goodwin W RSC 3 Atlantic City
26.02.84 Roger Mayweather W CO 1 Beaumont
(WBA S. Featherweight Title Challenge)
12.06.84 Tae-Jin Moon W RSC 11 Anchorage
(WBA S. Featherweight Title Defence)
29.07.84 Julio Llerena W CO 6 Milan
27.01.85 Kamel Bou Ali W RSC 6 Riva del Garda
(WBA S. Featherweight Title Defence)
19.05.85 Wilfredo Gomez L PTS 15 San Juan
(WBA S. Featherweight Title Defence)
18.12.85 Fernando Segura W RSC 4 Atlantic City
12.03.86 Efrain Nieves W RSC 3 Atlantic City
03.08.86 Julio Cesar Chavez L PTS 12 Monte Carlo
(WBC S. Featherweight Title Challenge)
22.10.86 Felipe Orozco W PTS 10 Atlantic City
24.05.87 Dennis Cruz W CO 7 Corpus Christi
09.08.87 Barry Michael W RTD 8 Windsor
(IBF S. Featherweight Title Challenge)
25.10.87 Johnny de la Rosa W RSC 10 Tucson
(IBF S. Featherweight Title Defence)
02.04.88 Harold Knight W PTS 15 Atlantic City
(IBF S. Featherweight Title Defence)
Summary: 48 contests, won 43, lost 5.

Daniel Londas
Forte de France, Martinique. *Born* 17.05.54
French S. Featherweight Champion

28.11.80 Rene Kowalski W RSC 4 Reims
06.12.80 Patrick Drelon W RSC 4 Epernay
20.12.80 Abdel Kerzazi W PTS 6 Reims
05.02.81 Slaedine Gardachi W RSC 2 Paris
26.02.81 Antonio Secci W RSC 3 Paris
07.03.81 Daniel Passeyrand W RSC 3 Reims
14.03.81 George Sutton W PTS 6 Sur Marne
04.04.81 Orlando Ramos W PTS 6 Fort de France
09.05.81 Angel Monstavo W CO 3 Fort de France
12.09.81 Harold Bernard W PTS 8 Fort de France
03.10.81 Elmer Sutington W RSC 4 Fort de France
17.10.81 Gerard Jacob W PTS 8 Reims
31.10.81 Vernon Penprase W PTS 8 Chalons
05.02.82 Maldo Maldonado W PTS 8 Fort de France
05.03.82 Mohammed Boundka W CO 4 Paris
27.03.82 Roberto Bido W PTS 8 Fort de France
26.04.82 Francis Bailleua W CO 2 Paris
(French S. Featherweight Title Challenge)
29.05.82 Alain Lefiol W RSC 8 Fort de France
(French S. Featherweight Title Defence)
07.06.82 Carlos Hernandez W PTS 8 Paris
06.11.82 Roberto Castanon L RTD 9 Leon
(EBU S. Featherweight Title Challenge)

Rocky Lockridge (right) surprised quite a few scribes when he outboxed and outpunched Harold Knight to retain his IBF super-featherweight title
Tom Casino

28.12.82 Michel Siracusa L PTS 8 Aix
25.03.83 Carlos Foldes W PTS 8 Paris
07.05.83 Francis Tripp W RSC 9 Pontarlier
(French S. Featherweight Title Defence)
13.07.83 Nelson Cruz Tamariz W PTS 10 Fort de France
10.10.83 Sammy Meck W PTS 8 Paris
18.11.83 Michel Siracusa L RSC 10 Reims
(French S. Featherweight Title Defence)
14.01.84 Vicente Macias W PTS 8 Epernay
03.02.84 Farid Gallouze W RSC 4 Chalons
14.04.84 Amalio Galan W PTS 8 Epernay
26.05.84 Rene Weller L PTS 12 Dusseldorf
(EBU Lightweight Title Challenge)
14.12.84 Francis Tripp W RSC 4 Fort de France
26.01.85 Jose Maillot W RSC 4 Valence
22.03.85 Michel Siracusa W PTS 10 Reims
(French S. Featherweight Title Challenge)
26.04.85 Steve Griffith W RSC 8 Thionville
06.05.85 Carlos Laciar W PTS 8 Grenoble
15.06.85 Paul Tiziwana W CO 4 Reims
27.10.85 Sammy Meck W PTS 10 Rouen
12.12.85 Vicente Sendin W PTS 8 Reims
25.01.86 Hugo Carrizo W PTS 8 Rouen
21.02.86 Jose Garcia W RSC 8 Paris
28.04.86 Maurice Vivies W PTS 10 St Ouen
(French S. Featherweight Title Defence)
04.07.86 Fosa Coadrado W CO 1 Fort de France
12.09.86 Carlos Rodriguez W PTS 8 Paris
27.10.86 Paul Downie W CO 2 Paris
20.12.86 Jean-Marc Renard DREW 12 St Ouen
(EBU S. Featherweight Title Challenge)
16.05.87 Salvatore Curcetti L RSC 1 Reims
(Vacant EBU S. Featherweight Title)
04.07.87 Sammy Meck W PTS 10 Calais
(French S. Featherweight Title Defence)
03.10.87 Brian Mitchell L PTS 15 Gravelines
(WBA S. Featherweight Title Challenge)
09.01.88 Joe Alexander W PTS 8 Abidjan
05.02.88 Orlando Fernandez W PTS 8 Point a Pitre
11.03.88 Brian Roche W DIS 5 Paris
Summary: 51 contests, won 44, drew 1, lost 6.

Alfonso (Bumblebee) Long
Los Angeles, USA. *Born* 11.05.62
Welterweight

13.04.82 Leland Hart W PTS 6 Sacramento
23.07.82 Rod Stevens W PTS 4 Culver City
08.12.82 Johnny Gonzalez W PTS 6 Ventura
09.02.83 Jose Morado W RSC 2 Ventura
11.03.83 Romeo Bellis W RSC 2 Culver City
23.04.83 Roberto Veta W RSC 3 Culver City
27.05.83 Juan J. Ramirez W RSC 5 Culver City
28.06.83 Jose Serna W RSC 1 Culver City
13.07.83 Derrick Kelly L PTS 8 Ventura
02.08.83 Ignacio Acosta W RSC 1 Culver City
02.09.83 Glen Corbus W PTS 8 San Jose
01.11.83 J. D. Williams W RSC 4 Reseda
30.11.83 Joe Moliere W RSC 6 Reseda
07.05.84 Dennis Mulholland W PTS 10 Bakersfield
12.07.84 Jorge Vaca L PTS 10 Los Angeles
07.11.84 Billy Smith W RSC 1 Los Angeles
09.01.85 Robert Sawyer W PTS 10 Los Angeles
10.06.85 Mike Hutchinson W RSC 9 Los Angeles
27.07.85 Shawn O'Sullivan L PTS 8 Calgary
20.08.85 Manning Galloway L PTS 10 Los Angeles
29.10.85 Kenny Lopez W PTS 10 Stockton
27.05.86 Felipe Canela L RSC 8 Irvine
04.09.86 Felipe Canela L PTS 10 San Jose
05.02.87 Francisco Armenta W RSC 2 Riverside
19.03.87 David Gutierrez DREW 10 Riverside
23.04.87 Davidson Andeh W RTD 1 Riverside
12.06.87 Russell Mitchell W PTS 12 Riverside
15.07.87 Derrick Kelly DREW 12 Riverside
16.10.87 Al Hamza Ufo W PTS 10 Atlantic City
03.02.88 Alex Ramos W PTS 12 Riverside
22.04.88 Russell Mitchell DREW 12 Paso Robles
Summary: 31 contests, won 22, drew 3, lost 6.

Aaron Lopez
San Antonio, USA
S. Bantamweight

03.11.81 Lalo Bonilla W RSC 3 San Antonio
22.11.81 Jesse Sierra W PTS 6 Corpus Christi
10.03.82 Felipe Morales W RSC 1 Laredo
22.04.82 Roger Trevino W RSC 3 Laredo
12.05.82 Enrique Flores W RSC 6 Alice
01.08.82 Adolfo Marquez W CO 1 San Antonio
20.10.82 Antonio Leal W PTS 8 San Antonio
01.12.82 Jose Salas W RSC 6 San Antonio
25.02.83 Miguel Flores W PTS 6 Corpus Christi
29.04.83 Carlos Flores W PTS 8 San Antonio
24.05.83 Pascual Aranda L PTS 8 San Antonio
24.08.83 Francisco Marquez W CO 1 San Antonio
30.11.83 Roberto Rodriguez W RSC 1 San Antonio
22.03.84 Nico Perez W RSC 8 San Antonio
24.05.84 Pascual Aranda W RSC 5 Houston
12.09.84 Hector Cortez W RSC 8 San Antonio
06.02.85 Jose Cazeres T DRAW 2 San Antonio
27.06.85 Armando Ugalde W PTS 10 San Antonio
04.02.86 Ricky Rogers W PTS 10 San Antonio
15.04.86 Carlos Flores W RSC 10 San Antonio
05.06.86 Kenny Allen W PTS 10 San Antonio
25.07.86 Mike Ayala L PTS 12 San Antonio
(NABF S. Bantamweight Title Challenge)
06.11.86 David Johnson W RSC 6 San Antonio
03.04.87 Daniel Zaragoza L PTS 12 San Antonio
(NABF S. Bantamweight Title Challenge)
28.08.87 Jose Sanabria DREW 10 Las Vegas
07.03.88 Irving Mitchell L PTS 10 Los Angeles
08.04.88 Jeff Franklin L PTS 12 Las Vegas
(Vacant USBA Featherweight Title)
Summary: 27 contests, won 20, drew 2, lost 5.

Hector Lopez
Los Angeles, USA. *Born* Mexico 01.02.67
Featherweight

01.01.85 Roberto Solis W PTS 6 Mexico City
05.03.85 Norman Moya W PTS 6 Houston
22.07.85 Moises Martinez W CO 3 Tijuana
07.08.85 Beto Gonzalez W RSC 1 Carson City
09.09.85 Ernesto Ramirez W CO 1 Tijuana
10.11.85 Joe Perez W PTS 8 Pomona
20.12.85 Felipe Olivar W CO 2 Los Angeles
25.02.86 Juan A. Lopez W PTS 10 Los Angeles
26.03.86 Frank Fazio W PTS 8 Las Vegas
13.06.86 Francisco Segura W PTS 10 Las Vegas
15.08.86 George Navarro L PTS 12 Atlantic City
09.10.86 Bruno Rabanales W PTS 10 Los Angeles
23.02.87 Refugio Rojas W PTS 10 Los Angeles
27.04.87 Bernard Taylor W RSC 9 Los Angeles
05.06.87 Leonardo Valdez W PTS 10 Los Angeles
01.10.87 George Navarro W TD 2 Los Angeles
Summary: 16 contests, won 15, lost 1.

Jose Mario Lopez
Mendoza, Argentine. *Born* 29.11.59
Former Argentinian Featherweight Champion

08.08.80 Victoriano Garcia W RTD 5 San Luis
03.10.80 Victoriano Garcia DREW 6 San Luis
19.12.80 Rodolfo Gonzalez W CO 4 San Juan
03.04.81 Jorge Castro DREW 6 Mendoza
15.05.81 Roberto Haidar DREW 8 Mendoza
02.10.81 Roberto Haidar W PTS 8 Lujan de Cuyo
30.10.81 Jose Heredia W RSC 2 Mendoza
02.04.82 Pascual Margara W RTD 5 Mendoza
23.04.82 David Gonzalez W RTD 8 Mendoza
20.08.82 Victoriano Garcia W PTS 10 Mendoza
13.10.82 Raul Cuevas W PTS 10 Mendoza
10.12.82 Luis H. Diaz W DIS 5 Mendoza
03.02.83 Alberto Rios W CO 2 Mendoza
10.03.83 Humberto Sanchez W PTS 10 Mendoza
22.04.83 Roberto Haidar W PTS 12 San Martin
08.07.83 Raul Perez W PTS 10 San Martin
12.08.83 Juan Herrera W CO 4 San Martin
24.08.83 Orlando Lucero W RSC 5 Buenos Aires
05.10.83 Carlos Laciar W PTS 10 Buenos Aires
02.11.83 Hugo Villarruel W PTS 10 Buenos Aires
09.12.83 Roberto Haidar W RSC 4 Mendoza
11.05.84 Julio Juarez W CO 1 Mendoza
06.07.84 Daniel Murua DREW 10 Mendoza
28.07.84 Adolfo Felice W PTS 10 Buenos Aires
16.08.84 Orlando Lucero W PTS 10 Cordoba
22.09.84 Carlos A. Velazquez W RSC 8 Buenos Aires
02.11.84 Ricardo Gil W RSC 8 Mendoza
07.12.84 Ramon Soria DREW 10 Mendoza
22.03.85 Hipolito Nunez DREW 10 San Juan
04.04.85 Esteban Bustus W RTD 8 Tucuman
04.05.85 Fernando Sosa L PTS 12 Buenos Aires
(Argentinian Featherweight Title Challenge)
05.07.85 Hipolito Nunez W PTS 10 Mendoza
14.08.85 Benjamin Sendin W CO 2 Buenos Aires
28.08.85 Armando Romero W RSC 8 Buenos Aires
21.09.85 Ramon Soria DREW 10 Buenos Aires
18.10.85 Luis Rodriguez W RTD 10 Rosario
13.12.85 Ramon Soria W PTS 10 Mendoza
04.04.86 Jose Gil W PTS 10 Mendoza
09.05.86 Hipolito Nunez DREW 10 San Juan
29.08.86 Hipolito Nunez DREW 10 Mendoza
10.10.86 Roberto de Fooz DREW 10 Mendoza
12.12.86 Antonio Sosa W PTS 10 San Martin
19.02.87 Osmar Avila W PTS 12 Mendoza
(Vacant Argentinian Featherweight Title)
03.07.87 Antonio Sosa W PTS 10 Rio Gallegos
25.07.87 Miguel Francia L PTS 12 Buenos Aires
(Argentinian Featherweight Title Defence)
04.12.87 Hugo Escudero W PTS 10 Mendoza
11.03.88 Herminio Camano W PTS 10 Mendoza
15.04.88 Ruben Traba W CO 5 Mendoza
Summary: 48 contests, won 36, drew 10, lost 2.

Lucio Lopez

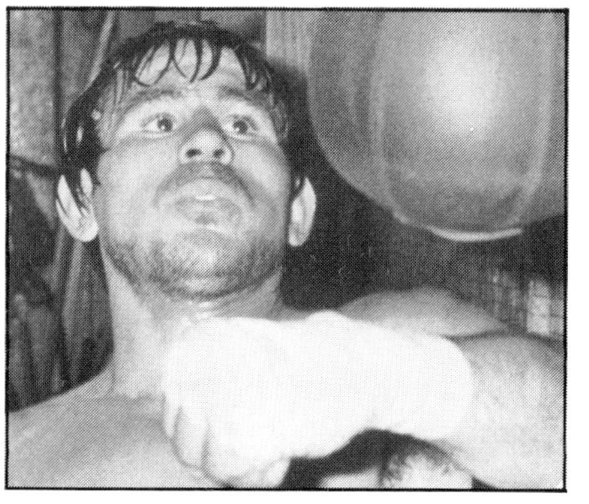

Lucio (Metralleta) Lopez
Mercedes, Argentine. *Born* 29.03.62
South American and Argentinan Bantamweight Champion

12.03.83 Julio Juarez W RSC 1 Buenos Aires
07.05.83 Raul Gomez W PTS 6 Buenos Aires
23.09.83 Christian Diaz W CO 2 Campana
15.10.83 Hipolito Caucota W PTS 8 Buenos Aires
09.12.83 Juan Scoles W CO 4 Santa Rosa
08.02.84 Domingo Alberto W RSC 3 Montevideo
23.03.84 Jose Narvaez W CO 3 Renanco
26.05.84 Jaime Loyola W CO 8 Buenos Aires
30.06.84 Cesar Villarruel W PTS 10 Buenos Aires
22.09.84 Luis Gerez W CO 8 Buenos Aires
11.01.85 Jose Gomez W CO 4 Mercedes
15.03.85 Jose Narvaez W CO 1 Corrientes
(Argentinan Bantamweight Title Challenge)
19.04.85 Luis Gerez W CO 2 Corrientes
11.05.85 Valdevino Monteiro W RTD 6 Mercedes
08.06.85 Gustavo Ballas W RTD 5 Buenos Aires
12.07.85 Jaime Miranda W RTD 6 Corrientes
20.09.85 Carlos Alves W CO 6 Corrientes
(Vacant South American Bantamweight Title)
15.11.85 Juan Ivalo W RTD 9 Mercedes
(Argentinian Bantamweight Title Defence)
13.12.85 Ruben Condori L PTS 10 Salta
21.03.86 Valdevino Monteiro W CO 1 Goya
24.05.86 Edgar Roman W PTS 10 Buenos Aires
06.09.86 Juan J. Estrada W PTS 10 Buenos Aires
04.10.86 Ruben Condori W PTS 10 Buenos Aires
08.11.86 Ruben Condori DREW 10 Corrientes
12.12.86 Juan Cortes W CO 7 Corrientes
(Argentinian Bantamweight Title Defence)
02.05.87 Raul Gomez W PTS 10 Puerto Madryn
21.08.87 Jorge Ramirez W RTD 7 Corrientes
19.09.87 Enrique Sanchez W PTS 10 Buenos Aires
18.12.87 Alejandro Montes W CO 6 Corrientes
30.04.88 Miguel Lora L PTS 12 Cartagena
(WBC Bantamweight Title Challenge)
Summary: 30 contests, won 27, drew 1, lost 2.

Tony Lopez
Sacramento, USA. *Born* 24.02.63
S. Featherweight

03.05.83 Juan Rodriguez W RSC 1 Sacramento
04.06.83 Ed Acosta W CO 1 Sacramento
28.06.83 Joe Cruz W CO 4 Sacramento
12.07.83 Gerald Issack W PTS 6 Sacramento
09.08.83 Leo Benitez W PTS 4 Sacramento
01.11.83 Juan Rivera W CO 1 Sacramento
15.11.83 Ruben Perales W RSC 1 Sacramento

29.11.83 Juan Torres W RSC 4 Sacramento
06.03.84 Memo Rojas W CO 2 Sacramento
03.04.84 Sam Espinosa W RSC 4 Sacramento
03.08.84 Tim Brooks W PTS 6 Reno
02.04.85 Mario Bautista W RSC 4 Sacramento
18.06.85 J. T. Walker W RSC 4 Sacramento
15.08.85 Baby de la Rosa W RSC 3 Sacramento
04.10.85 Roman Almaguer W RSC 3 Sacramento
18.12.85 Adam Garcia W PTS 10 Sacramento
03.03.86 Roberto Cantu W PTS 10 Sacramento
05.06.86 Arnel Arrozal W CO 2 Sacramento
20.07.86 Tim Brooks W PTS 10 Stateline
26.08.86 Cesar Zepeda W RSC 4 Stateline
27.09.86 Remington Garcia W RSC 4 Lake Tahoe
07.11.86 Roberto Cantu W RSC 3 Stateline
05.12.86 Heriberto Chavez W CO 2 Stateline
15.02.87 Tommy Cordova W PTS 10 Sacramento
21.05.87 Pedro Nolasco W PTS 10 Sacramento
01.07.87 Pedro Nolasco W RSC 8 Sacramento
01.09.87 Ramon Rico L DIS 7 Sacramento
25.09.87 Ramon Rico W CO 2 Sacramento
16.12.87 Gerardo Velasquez W RSC 3 Sacramento
25.03.88 Tony Pep W RSC 3 Sacramento
Summary: 30 contests, won 29, lost 1.

Miguel (Happy) Lora
Monteria, Colombia. *Born* 12.04.61
WBC Bantamweight Champion. Former Undefeated Fecarbox & Colombian S. Flyweight Champion. Former Undefeated Con. Am. Bantamweight Champion

27.07.79 Wilfredo Ruiz W PTS 6 Monteria
19.10.79 Alfredo Gomez W CO 1 Monteria
30.11.79 Tomas Maza W CO 1 Monteria
28.03.80 Justo Jorge W RSC 3 Monteria
12.06.80 Julio Soto Solano W PTS 12 Monteria
(Fecarbox S. Flyweight Title Challenge)
14.08.80 Orlando Tejedor W CO 1 Bogota
31.10.80 Juan Alvarez W PTS 10 Monteria
03.12.80 Arnoldo Sarmiento W RSC 3 Monteria
28.11.81 Carlos Arturo Osorio W PTS 10 Cerete
18.12.81 Luis Tapias W RSC 3 Monteria
26.02.82 Delimiro Cassiani W RSC 7 Monteria
30.07.82 Charles Maussa W RSC 7 Monteria
17.09.82 Miguel Perez W PTS 12 Monteria
(Colombian S. Flyweight Title Challenge)
12.05.83 Ruben Palacios W PTS 12 Cerete
(Con. Am. Bantamweight Title Challenge)
30.07.83 Jose Salazar W CO 3 Sincelejo
18.09.83 Pedro Romero W PTS 12 Cerete
(Con. Am. Bantamweight Title Defence)
17.12.83 Juan Diaz W RSC 5 Monteria
18.02.84 Edwin Rangel W PTS 10 Cartagena
03.07.84 Juan Torres W PTS 10 Miami
25.11.84 Jose Chacon W PTS 10 Monteria
10.05.85 Ramon Nery W CO 2 Miami
07.06.85 Diego Avila W RSC 8 Miami
09.08.85 Daniel Zaragoza W PTS 12 Miami
(WBC Bantamweight Title Challenge)
08.02.86 Wilfredo Vasquez W PTS 12 Miami
(WBC Bantamweight Title Defence)
23.08.86 Enrique Sanchez W RSC 6 Miami
(WBC Bantamweight Title Defence)
15.11.86 Albert Davila W PTS 12 Barranquilla
(WBC Bantamweight Title Defence)
25.07.87 Antonio Avelar W RSC 4 Miami
(WBC Bantamweight Title Defence)
27.11.87 Ray Minus W PTS 12 Miami
(WBC Bantamweight Title Defence)
30.04.88 Lucio Lopez W PTS 12 Cartagena
(WBC Bantamweight Title Defence)
Summary: 29 contests, won 29.

Javier Lucas
Tenexpa, Mexico. *Born* 30.11.60
Flyweight

22.12.79 Beto Colon W PTS 8 Acapulco
11.01.80 Rafael Guerra W RSC 2 Acapulco
01.02.80 Salvador Roque W RSC 3 Acapulco
21.03.80 Ben Velasquez W CO 1 Acapulco
23.05.80 Pedro Herrera W PTS 10 Acapulco
04.07.80 Mario Nava W CO 3 Acapulco
31.08.80 Jesus Becerra W CO 5 Acapulco
31.10.80 Leo Castellanos W PTS 10 Acapulco
27.02.81 Candido Tellez W RSC 8 Acapulco
24.04.81 Freddie Castillo L PTS 10 Acapulco
26.09.81 Freddie Castillo L PTS 10 Merida
29.01.82 Victor Diaz W CO 8 Acapulco
26.02.82 Jose Segovia W CO 1 Acapulco
23.04.82 Luis Aguilar W RSC 7 Acapulco
26.06.82 Tony Escobar W RSC 7 Mexico City
14.08.82 Gabriel Bernal L CO 5 Mexico City
23.10.82 Jorge M. Vera W CO 1 Mexico City
05.03.83 Rafael Alonso W PTS 10 Mexico City
15.04.83 Elfego Lopez W CO 4 Acapulco
02.06.83 Jimmy Fernandez W RSC 4 Mexico City
10.02.84 Adrian Cortez W RSC 2 Zihuatanejo
31.03.84 Arturo Mujica W RSC 4 Acapulco
01.06.84 Marco A. Benitez W PTS 10 Acapulco
12.10.84 Jose Gallegos W PTS 10 Acapulco
16.11.84 Enrique Aguilar W CO 2 Acapulco
22.06.85 Juan Herrera W RSC 10 Merida
31.01.86 Hilario Zapata L PTS 15 Panama City
(WBA Flyweight Title Challenge)
25.07.86 Martin Cardenas W CO 2 Tijuana
30.10.86 Azadin Anhar W CO 4 Torreon
19.12.86 Abner Arauza W CO 1 Acapulco
20.02.87 Orlando Canizales L RSC 9 San Jose
14.07.87 Artemio Ruiz W CO 2 Acapulco
19.09.87 Pedro Rabago W RSC 3 Obregon
28.11.87 Gonzalo Villalobros W PTS 10 Mexico City
25.03.88 Victor Alanis W RSC 6 Acapulco
Summary: 35 contests, won 30, lost 5.

Pretty Boy Lucas
Bulacan, Philippines. *Born* 20.12.65
Philippines M. Flyweight Champion

11.11.83 Alex de la Flor W PTS 4 Manila
18.02.84 Felipe Brazil W PTS 4 Malabon
31.03.84 Mohammad Raffi W CO 3 Malabon
27.04.84 Leonardo Saonoy W CO 1 Manila
27.07.84 Danny Duran W PTS 6 Manila
31.08.84 Felipe Brazil W PTS 6 Manila
08.03.85 Steve Ponan W RSC 7 Malabon
01.06.85 Lou Morabe W PTS 8 Malabon
27.07.85 Roberto Palarit W PTS 10 Malabon
30.08.85 Tito Abella W PTS 10 Novaliches
26.10.85 Ed Hemo W PTS 10 Manila
20.12.85 Rex Rapizo T DRAW 3 Manila
21.02.86 Robert Palarit W TD 8 Pasig
05.07.86 Jun Altarejos W PTS 10 Pasig
08.11.86 Jun Afable W PTS 12 Manila
(Philippines M. Flyweight Title Challenge)
06.03.87 Boy Selda W TD 4 Manila
03.07.87 Boy Selda W RSC 9 Malabon
28.10.87 Rizaldy Ocampo W RSC 6 Paranaque
(Philippines M. Flyweight Title Defence)
24.03.88 Samuth Sithnaruepol L RSC 11 Bangkok
(Vacant IBF M. Flyweight Title)
Summary: 19 contests, won 17, drew 1, lost 1.

Patrick Lumumba
Sweden. *Born* 27.07.59
Cruiserweight

17.12.83 Liam Coleman W RTD 1 Mariehamn
14.04.84 Hocine Tafer L RSC 4 Voiron
21.05.84 Marco Vitaglione W RSC 3 Helsinki
11.05.85 Winston Burnett W RSC 2 Vasa
24.11.85 Jose Seys W CO 3 Vasa
19.07.86 Walter Santemore W PTS 6 Wembley
05.09.86 Alfredo Evangelista W PTS 8 Madrid
01.08.87 James Broad L PTS 10 Las Vegas
16.10.87 Alfonso Ratliff W PTS 10 Atlantic City
09.04.88 Jeff Lampkin W PTS 8 Las Vegas
Summary: 10 contests, won 8, lost 2.

Dave (Boy) McAuley
Larne, Ireland. *Born* 15.06.61
Former Undefeated British Flyweight Champion

05.10.83 John Mwaimu DREW 6 Belfast
16.11.83 Dave Smith W CO 1 Belfast
25.01.84 Ian Colbeck W PTS 6 Belfast
27.02.84 Kenny Walsh DREW 6 Birmingham
17.09.84 Roy Williams W PTS 6 Brighton
13.10.84 John Mwaimu W PTS 6 Belfast
13.11.84 Dave George W RSC 6 Belfast
19.12.84 Graham Kid Clarke W RSC 4 Belfast
23.02.85 Johnny Mack W RSC 1 Belfast
08.06.85 Bobby McDermott W RSC 10 London
15.02.86 Kelvin Smart W DIS 6 Dublin
22.04.86 Charlie Brown W RSC 1 Belfast
20.10.86 Joe Kelly W CO 9 Glasgow
(Vacant British Flyweight Title)
25.04.87 Fidel Bassa L CO 13 Belfast
(WBA Flyweight Title Challenge)
03.12.87 Roy Thompson W PTS 10 Belfast
26.03.88 Fidel Bassa L PTS 12 Belfast
(WBA Flyweight Title Challenge)
Summary: 16 contests, won 12, drew 2, lost 2.

Mike (The Body Snatcher) McCallum
Jamaica. *Born* 07.12.56
Former Undefeated WBA L. Middleweight Champion

19.02.81 Rigoberto Lopez W RSC 4 Las Vegas
03.03.81 Rocky Fabrizio W RSC 1 Tampa
20.03.81 Ricky Sheppard W RSC 5 Tampa
02.04.81 Shelvy Wikerson W RSC 5 Tampa
24.04.81 Dan Chapman W RSC 4 New York
30.04.81 Charles Smith W RSC 5 Tampa
10.06.81 Freddy Creech W RSC 3 Tampa
19.07.81 Bruce Strauss W RSC 2 Youngstown
27.08.81 Turko Roque W RTD 3 Tampa
08.09.81 Ed Harris W CO 1 Tampa
08.10.81 Jimmy Heair W RSC 2 Tampa
22.01.82 Greg Young W RSC 5 New York
26.03.82 Gilberto Almonte W RSC 1 Kingston
30.04.82 Reggie Ford W CO 4 New York
11.06.82 Kevin Perry W PTS 10 New York
22.10.82 Carlos Betancourt W RSC 3 New York
13.11.82 Ayub Kalule W RSC 7 Atlantic City
26.04.83 Tony Suero W RSC 3 Atlantic City
31.08.83 Jose Vallejo W CO 5 Atlantic City
25.10.83 Manuel Jimenez W PTS 10 Atlantic City
10.03.84 Hasim Razzak W CO 1 Detroit
19.10.84 Sean Mannion W PTS 15 New York
(Vacant WBA L. Middleweight Title)
01.12.84 Luigi Minchillo W RSC 14 Milan
(WBA L. Middleweight Title Defence)
15.06.85 Marcos Martinez W RSC 2 Las Vegas
28.07.85 David Braxton W RSC 8 Miami
(WBA L. Middleweight Title Defence)
02.05.86 Jim Shavers W RSC 6 Atlantic City
23.08.86 Julian Jackson W RSC 2 Miami
(WBA L. Middleweight Title Defence)
15.09.86 Irwin Hines W RSC 3 Paris
25.10.86 Said Skouma W CO 9 Paris
(WBA L. Middleweight Title Defence)
21.03.87 Leroy Hester W CO 1 Kingston
19.04.87 Milton McCrory W RSC 10 Phoenix
(WBA L. Middleweight Title Defence)
18.07.87 Don Curry W CO 5 Las Vegas
(WBA L. Middleweight Title Defence)
01.03.88 Sumbu Kalambay L PTS 12 Pesaro
(WBA Middleweight Title Challenge)
Summary: 33 contests, won 32, lost 1.

Glenn McCrory
Annfield Plain, England. *Born* 23.09.64
British & Commonwealth Cruiserweight Champion

06.02.84 Barry Ellis W RSC 1 London
22.02.84 Denroy Bryan W PTS 6 London
21.03.84 Steve Abadom W PTS 6 London
30.04.84 Frank Robinson W PTS 6 London
09.05.84 Frank Robinson W RSC 4 London
13.06.84 Andrew Gerrard W PTS 6 Aberavon
06.09.84 Andrew Gerrard W PTS 8 Gateshead
27.10.84 Tony Velasco W PTS 8 Gateshead
24.11.84 Mike Perkins W PTS 8 Gateshead
19.01.85 Nate Robinson W RSC 2 Birmingham
20.02.85 Alex Williamson W PTS 8 London
27.03.85 Gypsy Carman W PTS 8 Gateshead
28.05.85 Alphonso Forbes W CO 1 London
03.09.85 John Westgarth L CO 4 Gateshead
10.12.85 Roy Skeldon W PTS 8 Gateshead
09.04.86 Rudi Pika L PTS 8 London
18.04.86 Anders Eklund L PTS 8 Randers
17.06.86 Dave Garside L RSC 7 Blackpool
07.10.86 Hughroy Currie L RSC 2 Oldham
25.11.86 Joe Adams W PTS 6 Louisville
08.01.87 Calvin Sherman W CO 1 Houston
05.02.87 Danny Lawford W PTS 8 Newcastle
18.02.87 Barry Ellis W PTS 8 London
31.03.87 Andy Straughn W RSC 10 Oldham
04.09.87 Chisanda Mutti W PTS 12 Gateshead
(Commonwealth Cruiserweight Title Challenge)
21.01.88 Tee Jay W PTS 12 London
(British Cruiserweight Title Challenge. Commonwealth Cruiserweight Title Defence)
22.04.88 Lou Gent W RTD 8 Gateshead
(British & Commonwealth Cruiserweight Title Defence)
Summary: 27 contests, won 22, lost 5.

Glenn McCrory celebrates after winning the British cruiserweight title from Tee Jay. Glenn successfully defended his Commonwealth belt in the same bout
John McDonald

Milton (The Iceman) McCrory
Detroit, USA. *Born* 07.02.62
NABF L. Middleweight Champion. Former WBC Welterweight Champion

10.09.80 Kevin Slaughter W CO 1 Detroit
20.09.80 Rod Kennebrew W CO 1 San Juan
16.10.80 Chuck Smith W CO 1 Toledo
23.10.80 Bill Hodges W RSC 1 Detroit
08.11.80 Raul Aguirre W CO 1 Detroit
22.11.80 James Dixon W CO 5 Cincinnati
02.12.80 Doc Bryant W RSC 1 Toledo
12.12.80 Alfonso Hayman W RSC 3 Detroit
29.01.81 Mao de la Rosa W CO 1 Detroit
19.02.81 Santiago Valdez W RSC 2 Detroit
09.04.81 Eddie Marcelle W RSC 2 Detroit
25.04.81 Alejos Rodriguez W RSC 4 Phoenix
27.05.81 Joey Robles W RSC 5 Phoenix
25.06.81 Steve Hearon W RSC 8 Houston
13.08.81 Rafael Rodriguez W RSC 7 Detroit
19.11.81 Arcadio Garcia W CO 3 Detroit
23.01.82 Randy Shields W RTD 8 Detroit
22.04.82 Pete Ranzany W PTS 10 Detroit
10.07.82 Roger Stafford W PTS 10 Phoenix
10.10.82 Victor Abraham W PTS 10 Detroit
19.03.83 Colin Jones DREW 12 Reno
(*Vacant WBC Welterweight Title*)
13.08.83 Colin Jones W PTS 12 Las Vegas
(*Vacant WBC Welterweight Title*)
14.01.84 Milton Guest W RSC 6 Detroit
(*WBC Welterweight Title Defence*)
15.04.84 Gilles Elbilia W RSC 6 Detroit
(*WBC Welterweight Title Defence*)
04.12.84 Lloyd Taylor W RSC 4 Atlantic City
09.03.85 Pedro Vilella W PTS 12 Paris
(*WBC Welterweight Title Defence*)
26.05.85 Luis Santana W RSC 2 Miami
14.07.85 Carlos Trujillo W RSC 3 Monte Carlo
(*WBC Welterweight Title Defence*)
06.12.85 Don Curry L CO 2 Las Vegas
(*WBC Welterweight Title Defence & WBA Welterweight Title Challenge*)
18.04.86 Keith Adams W PTS 10 Atlantic City
13.07.86 Doug de Witt W PTS 10 Las Vegas
26.11.86 Jorge Amparo W PTS 10 Las Vegas
07.03.87 Rafael Corona W RSC 1 Detroit
(*Vacant NABF L. Middleweight Title*)
19.04.87 Mike McCallum L RSC 10 Phoenix
(*WBA L. Middleweight Title Challenge*)
28.10.87 Herman Cavesuela W PTS 12 Las Vegas
(*NABF L. Middleweight Title Defence*)
19.11.87 Jerome Kelly W RSC 2 Windsor
10.04.88 Lupe Aquino L PTS 10 Atlantic City
Summary: 37 contests, won 33, drew 1, lost 3.

Steve McCrory
Detroit, USA. *Born* 13.04.64
Con. Am. S. Bantamweight Champion

19.10.84 Jeff Hanna W RSC 4 New York
14.11.84 Eddie Rangel W RSC 2 Detroit
04.12.84 Sonny Long W PTS 6 Atlantic City
29.01.85 Vidal Padilla W PTS 6 Phoenix
09.03.85 Louis Gomis DREW 6 Paris
18.04.85 Kenny Butts W PTS 8 Atlantic City
26.05.85 Kerry Allen W PTS 6 Miami

Steve McCrory
Peter Goldfield/USA

25.07.85 Donnie Parker W PTS 6 Birmingham
15.08.85 Luigi Camputaro W PTS 6 Atlantic City
17.11.85 Lee Cargle W PTS 8 Laughlin
03.12.85 Manuel Martinez W CO 1 Las Vegas
12.03.86 Ralph Gutierrez W PTS 10 Las Vegas
18.07.86 Jeff Fenech L RSC 14 Sydney
(*IBF Bantamweight Title Challenge*)
08.11.86 Jose Sanabria L RSC 5 Stateline
24.02.87 James Tolliver W RSC 5 Detroit
21.03.87 Chris Diaz W PTS 10 Detroit
28.04.87 Ramon Guillen W CO 2 Detroit
19.05.87 Jorge Rodriguez W PTS 10 Detroit
11.06.87 Mike Moreno W PTS 12 Detroit
(*Vacant Con. Am. S. Bantamweight Title*)
18.08.87 Jose Torres W RSC 2 Detroit
27.10.87 Jorge Rodriguez W PTS 10 Detroit
17.11.87 Tony Montoya W CO 7 Detroit
23.02.88 Omar Garcia W RSC 5 Detroit
30.03.88 Julio Blanco W RSC 5 Detroit
23.04.88 Idelfonso Bernal W RSC 2 Detroit
Summary: 25 contests, won 22, drew 1, lost 2.

Jim (Diamond) MacDonald
Nashville, USA. *Born* 27.08.58
L. Heavyweight

10.07.82 Bob Nicholson W CO 1 Phoenix
03.08.82 Chet Smith W CO 1 Phoenix
14.09.83 Mario Johnson W RSC 2 Nashville
29.10.83 Tony Jordan W CO 3 Fort Payne
29.12.83 Roy Saffold W CO 3 Nashville
27.02.84 Robert Thomas W CO 3 Muscle Shoals
07.03.84 Chester Peters W RSC 4 Nashville
19.04.84 David Franklin W RSC 5 Houston
24.04.84 Chris Wells W RSC 2 Nashville
24.05.84 Tim Eaton W PTS 8 Nashville
10.07.84 David Plowden W RSC 1 Nashville
30.08.84 Dennis Roberts W CO 2 Morristown
13.10.84 David Curry W RSC 4 Florence
17.02.85 Willie Edwards W CO 4 Houston
23.03.85 Johnny Williams W CO 3 Bristol
10.04.85 Cleveland Watkins W RSC 7 Atlantic City
06.06.85 Michael Spinks L RSC 8 Las Vegas
(*World L. Heavyweight Title Challenge*)
15.02.86 Al Rankin W PTS 10 Montreal
19.04.86 Grady Smith L PTS 10 Las Vegas
17.06.86 Arthel Lawhorne L RSC 5 Detroit
18.09.86 Clarence Osby W RSC 5 Atlantic City
26.11.86 Mike Costello W RSC 8 Atlantic City
21.02.87 Rusty Rosenberger W RSC 2 Atlantic City
03.05.87 Bobby Czyz L RSC 6 Atlantic City
(*IBF L. Heavyweight Title Challenge*)
21.01.88 Mike Sedillo L PTS 10 Sacramento
07.03.88 Sugar Boy Malingo L PTS 10 Orkney
Summary: 26 contests, won 20, lost 6.

Jim McDonnell
Stepney, England. *Born* 12.09.60
Former Undefeated EBU Featherweight Champion

22.03.83 Phil Duke W PTS 6 London
05.04.83 Willie Wilson W RSC 3 London
26.04.83 Ray Plant W RSC 3 London
04.10.83 Steve Pollard W RSC 5 London
06.12.83 Alec Irvine W PTS 8 London
23.01.84 Willie Wilson W CO 2 London
06.02.84 Gerry Beard W PTS 8 London
02.04.84 Gerry Beard W PTS 8 London
01.05.84 Keith Foreman W PTS 8 London
13.05.84 Rory Burke W PTS 8 Wembley
13.11.84 Steve Pollard W RSC 6 London
18.01.85 Pat Doherty W PTS 10 London
06.03.85 Haidar Nourredine W RSC 1 London
26.03.85 Clyde Ruan W PTS 10 Wembley
01.10.85 Jeff Roberts W PTS 8 Wembley
05.11.85 Jose Luis Vicho W CO 4 Wembley
(*Vacant EBU Featherweight Title*)
07.05.86 Ruben Palacios W RSC 7 London
19.07.86 Salvatore Bottiglieri W PTS 12 Wembley
(*EBU Featherweight Title Defence*)
04.11.86 Troy Davis W PTS 10 Wembley
24.03.87 Ricky Clements W RSC 5 Wembley
15.05.87 Samuel O'Near W RSC 1 Geneva
25.02.88 Rafael Gandarilla W PTS 10 London
29.03.88 Joel Segura W CO 7 Wembley
Summary: 23 contests, won 23.

James (Buddy) McGirt
New York, USA. *Born* 17.01.64
IBF L. Welterweight Champion. Former Undefeated Con. Am. L. Welterweight Champion

13.03.82 Lamont Haithcoach DREW 4 Bergen
22.05.82 Michael Palms W RSC 3 Atlantic City
21.09.82 Mike Evans W RSC 1 Bergen
30.09.82 Ray Rivera W CO 1 Totowa
30.12.82 Dave Bolden W CO 5 Bergen
16.02.83 Cesar Guzman W PTS 6 East Rutherford
21.04.83 Tom Dietz W RSC 3 Newark
26.05.83 Darnell Smith W RSC 1 Newark
06.09.83 Les Toney W RSC 1 Atlantic City
30.09.83 Larry Fleming W CO 3 New York
09.12.83 Richard Hernandez W RSC 7 New York
17.02.84 Felix Nance W RSC 2 New York
30.03.84 Jake Torrence W RSC 6 New York
25.05.84 Pete Padilla W RSC 10 New York
12.07.84 Manuel Toribio W CO 3 New York
15.12.84 Felix Nance W RSC 9 Uniondale
08.03.85 Michael Blunt W CO 1 Scranton
24.05.85 Allen Braswell W PTS 10 New York
11.07.85 Ralph Twinning W RSC 1 New York
29.08.85 Willie Rodriguez W RSC 7 New York
04.10.85 Jose Alejandro W RSC 7 New York
21.12.85 Sugar Boy Nando W RSC 5 Miami
(*Vacant Con. Am. L. Welterweight Title*)
21.02.86 Joey Ferrell W PTS 10 Atlantic City
10.03.86 Dave Odem W RSC 1 Uniondale
11.04.86 Kelly Koble W RSC 4 Los Angeles
20.05.86 Ricky Young W RSC 10 New York
23.06.86 Rudy Fuentes W RSC 8 New York
20.07.86 Frankie Warren L PTS 10 Corpus Christi
25.09.86 Saoul Mamby W PTS 10 New York
06.01.87 Joe Edens W RSC 1 Detroit
29.01.87 Eric Martin W PTS 10 New York
24.04.87 Vince Releford W RSC 2 Albany
(*Con. Am. L. Welterweight Title Defence*)
18.06.87 Sergio Aguirre W RSC 2 New York
06.08.87 Roger Brown W RSC 5 New York
01.10.87 Eduardo Lugo W RSC 3 New York
17.12.87 John Senegal W RSC 1 New York
14.02.88 Frankie Warren W RSC 12 Corpus Christi
(*Vacant IBF L. Welterweight Title*)
Summary: 37 contests, won 35, drew 1, lost 1.

Barry McGuigan (left) came back from nearly two years of inactivity with a resounding fourth round stoppage over Nicky Perez
John McDonald

Barry (The Clones Cyclone) McGuigan
Clones, Ireland. *Born* 28.02.61
Former WBA Featherweight Champion. Former Undefeated British & EBU Featherweight Champion

10.05.81 Selvin Bell W RSC 2 Dublin
20.06.81 Gary Lucas W RSC 4 Wembley
03.08.81 Peter Eubanks L PTS 8 Brighton
22.09.81 Jean-Marc Renard W PTS 8 Belfast
26.10.81 Terry Pizzaro W RSC 4 Belfast
08.12.81 Peter Eubanks W RSC 8 Belfast
27.01.82 Luis de la Sagra W PTS 8 Belfast
08.02.82 Ian Murray W RSC 3 London
23.02.82 Angel Oliver W RSC 3 Belfast
23.03.82 Angelo Licata W RTD 2 Belfast
22.04.82 Gary Lucas W CO 1 Enniskillen
14.06.82 Young Ali W CO 6 London
05.10.82 Jimmy Duncan W RTD 4 Belfast
09.11.82 Paul Huggins W RSC 5 Belfast
12.04.83 Vernon Penprase W RSC 2 Belfast
(Vacant British Featherweight Title)
22.05.83 Sammy Meck W RSC 6 Navan
09.07.83 Lavon McGowan W CO 1 Chicago
05.10.83 Ruben Herasme W CO 2 Belfast
16.11.83 Valerio Nati W CO 6 Belfast
(Vacant EBU Featherweight Title)
25.01.84 Charm Chiteule W RSC 10 Belfast
04.04.84 Jose Caba W RSC 7 Belfast
05.06.84 Esteban Eguia W CO 3 London
(EBU Featherweight Title Defence)
30.06.84 Paul de Vorce W RSC 5 Belfast
13.10.84 Felipe Orozco W CO 2 Belfast
19.12.84 Clyde Ruan W CO 4 Belfast
(British & EBU Featherweight Title Defence)
23.02.85 Juan Laporte W PTS 10 Belfast
26.03.85 Farid Gallouze W RTD 2 Wembley
(EBU Featherweight Title Defence)
08.06.85 Eusebio Pedroza W PTS 15 London
(WBA Featherweight Title Challenge)
28.09.85 Bernard Taylor W RTD 8 Belfast
(WBA Featherweight Title Defence)
15.02.86 Danilo Cabrera W RSC 14 Dublin
(WBA Featherweight Title Defence)
23.06.86 Steve Cruz L PTS 15 Las Vegas
(WBA Featherweight Title Defence)
20.04.88 Nicky Perez W RSC 4 London
Summary: 32 contests, won 30, lost 2.

Duke McKenzie
Croydon, England. *Born* 05.05.63
EBU Flyweight Champion & Former Undefeated British Flyweight Champion

23.11.82 Charlie Brown W RSC 1 Wembley
24.01.83 Andy King W RSC 2 London
27.02.83 Dave Pearson W RSC 1 Las Vegas
03.03.83 Gregorio Hernandez W RSC 3 Los Angeles
19.03.83 Lupe Sanchez W CO 2 Reno
18.10.83 Jerry Davis W RSC 2 Atlantic City
22.11.83 Alain Limarola W PTS 6 Wembley
15.01.84 David Capo W PTS 4 Atlantic City
23.05.84 Gary Roberts W CO 1 London
06.03.85 Julio Guerrero W PTS 8 London
05.06.85 Danny Flynn W RSC 4 London
(Vacant British Flyweight Title)
16.10.85 Orlando Maestre W PTS 8 London
19.02.86 Sonny Long W PTS 10 London
20.05.86 Charlie Magri W RTD 5 Wembley
(British Flyweight Title Defence & EBU Flyweight Title Challenge)
19.11.86 Lee Cargle W PTS 10 Atlantic City
17.12.86 Piero Pinna W PTS 12 Acqui Terme
(EBU Flyweight Title Defence)
24.03.87 Jose Diaz W PTS 8 Wembley
02.12.87 Juan Herrera W PTS 10 Wembley
09.03.88 Agapito Gomez W CO 2 Wembley
(EBU Flyweight Title Defence)
Summary: 19 contests, won 19.

Javier (Changuita) Marquez
Mexicali, Mexico. *Born* 24.08.62
Mexican Featherweight Champion

17.11.80 Arturo Manriquez W CO 1 Tijuana
27.12.80 Jesus Castro W CO 4 Tijuana
01.01.81 Miguel Ruiz W RSC 4 Mexicali
01.02.81 Baldo Gonzalez W CO 2 Mexicali
01.05.81 Antonio Escobar W CO 3 Mexicali
26.06.81 Juan Guzman W PTS 10 Mexicali
20.07.81 Juan Zarate W RSC 8 Tijuana
13.09.81 Daniel Zaragoza L RSC 8 Mexicali
20.11.81 Manuel Lopez W CO 5 Mexicali
01.01.82 Cisco Marquez W CO 4 Mexicali
30.05.82 Ray Rodriguez W PTS 10 Mexicali
30.08.82 Jose Luis Soto W CO 9 Tijuana
01.10.82 Rosendo Alonzo W CO 3 Mexicali
07.11.82 Diego Avila DREW 10 Mexicali
10.12.82 Leonardo Valdez L CO 9 Mexicali
28.04.83 Elias Rodriguez W RSC 1 Ensenada
18.07.83 Mauro Gutierrez W PTS 10 Tijuana
29.09.83 Rocky Alonzo T DRAW 8 Los Angeles
30.09.83 Julio Cesar W PTS 10 Chetumal
09.12.83 Martin Torres W RSC 5 Mexicali
01.01.84 Arturo Hernandez W PTS 10 Mexicali
18.02.84 Daniel Zaragoza L RSC 5 Mexicali
(Mexican Bantamweight Title Challenge)
28.04.84 Mario Nava W PTS 10 Tijuana
05.10.84 Pedro Galaviz W PTS 10 Mexicali
19.10.84 Martin Castro W RSC 7 Mexicali
01.12.84 Rosendo Alonzo W CO 1 Mexicali
16.03.85 Mauro Gutierrez W PTS 12 Mexicali
(Vacant Mexican Featherweight Title)
10.06.85 Lupe Pintor DREW 10 Mexicali
18.08.85 Ramon Rico W PTS 10 Salinas
01.11.85 Ramon Flores W RSC 6 Mexicali
(Mexican Featherweight Title Defence)
28.02.86 Pascualito Lopez W PTS 12 Torreon
(Mexican Featherweight Title Defence)
22.03.86 Martin Torres W PTS 10 Tijuana
19.04.86 Santos Moreno W PTS 12 Mexico City
(Mexican Featherweight Title Defence)
30.05.86 Martin Torres W RSC 5 Mexicali
(Mexican Featherweight Title Defence)
27.06.86 Hector Cortez W RSC 7 Mexicali
16.09.86 Manuel Juarez W PTS 12 Torreon
(Mexican Featherweight Title Defence)
06.12.86 Mauro Gutierrez L RSC 8 Tijuana
(Mexican Featherweight Title Defence)
22.05.87 Cenobio Nicolas W RSC 9 Mexicali
15.08.87 Bernard Taylor L TD 5 Reno
(NABF Featherweight Title Challenge)
30.10.87 Juan Meza W CO 8 Mexicali
01.01.88 Bruno Rabanales DREW 10 Mexicali
19.03.88 Rafael Morfin W PTS 12 Mexicali
(Mexican Featherweight Title Challenge)
Summary: 42 contests, won 33, drew 4, lost 5.

Terry Marsh
Basildon, England. *Born* 07.02.58
Former Undefeated IBF L. Welterweight Champion. Former Undefeated EBU & British L. Welterweight Champion

12.10.81 Andrew da Costa W PTS 6 London
28.10.81 Dave Sullivan W PTS 6 London
23.11.81 Kid Murray W PTS 6 London
08.12.81 Gary Brooks W PTS 6 Southend
19.02.82 Arthur Davis W PTS 6 London
09.03.82 Gerry McGrath W PTS 8 London
05.04.82 Lloyd Christie DREW 8 London
10.08.82 Dave Finigan W RSC 5 London
07.09.82 Robert Armstrong W PTS 8 London
11.10.82 Chris Sanigar W DIS 7 Bristol
19.02.83 Didier Kowalski W PTS 8 St Arnand
16.03.83 Andy Thomas W RSC 4 Cheltenham
26.04.83 Vernon Vanriel W PTS 10 London
09.11.83 Lee McKenzie W PTS 8 Southend
16.04.84 Tony Sinnott W PTS 12 Bradford
19.09.84 Clinton McKenzie W PTS 12 London
(British L. Welterweight Title Challenge)
05.12.84 Arthur Clarke W RSC 2 London
16.01.85 Peter Eubanks W RSC 7 London
28.05.85 Randy Mitchum W RSC 6 London
12.09.85 Lee McKenzie W PTS 10 Manchester
26.10.85 Alessandro Scapecchi W CO 6 Monte Carlo
(Vacant EBU L. Welterweight Title)
22.01.86 Tusikoleta Nkalankete W PTS 12 London
(EBU L. Welterweight Title Defence)
12.04.86 Francesco Prezisio W PTS 12 Isle of Man
(EBU L. Welterweight Title Defence)
28.05.86 Ricky Kaiser W CO 7 London
28.01.87 David Taylor W RSC 2 Croydon
04.03.87 Joe Manley W RSC 10 Basildon
(IBF L. Welterweight Title Challenge)
01.07.87 Akio Kameda W RTD 4 London
(IBF L. Welterweight Title Defence)
Summary: 27 contests, won 26, drew 1.

Terry Marsh (left) retired from the ring following the successful IBF light-welterweight title defence against the man from Japan, Akio Kameda
John McDonald

Mauro Martelli
Lausanne, Switzerland. *Born* 16.04.65
EBU Welterweight Champion

16.11.84 George Ssonko W PTS 6 Chavannes
26.12.84 Lifetu Basila W CO 3 Berne
26.01.85 Thierry Pierluigi W RSC 2 Chavannes
22.02.85 Bacha Ben Amar W PTS 6 Chavannes
26.03.85 Mohamed Zeroual W PTS 6 Geneva
30.04.85 Karim Ouattara W PTS 6 Geneva
07.06.85 Kid Bello W PTS 8 Lausanne
06.07.85 Idelfonso Martinez W RSC 4 Ascona
29.08.85 Mickey Lerwill W PTS 6 Geneva
18.10.85 Ngindola Engote W PTS 6 Lausanne
02.11.85 Patrick Grisot W PTS 6 Villeneuve
30.11.85 Domenico Ricci W PTS 6 Geneva
29.12.85 Robert Dormoy W RSC 6 Chavannes
09.03.86 Frankie Decaestecker W RTD 5 Chavannes
01.04.86 Rafael Fuentes W RTD 4 Geneva
26.04.86 Abdel Souihi W PTS 8 Berne
30.05.86 Joaquin Velasquez W PTS 6 Geneva
05.07.86 Cliff Gilpin W PTS 8 Ecubens
05.09.86 Franki Moro W PTS 8 Crissier
03.10.86 Rene Jacquot W PTS 10 Geneva
27.10.86 Yvon Segor W RSC 7 Geneva
26.11.86 Pietro Ciarla W CO 7 Martigny
28.12.86 Nazario Mariotti W RSC 8 Chavannes
29.01.87 Martin Camara W PTS 8 Crans Montana
28.02.87 John van Elteren W PTS 8 Lausanne
01.05.87 Kid Taylor W RSC 5 Bulle
15.05.87 Juan Rondon W PTS 8 Geneva
26.06.87 Alfonso Redondo W PTS 12 Geneva
(*EBU Welterweight Title Challenge*)
09.10.87 Erwin Heiber W PTS 12 Morges
(*EBU Welterweight Title Defence*)
27.12.87 Jean-Marie Touati W PTS 12 Martigny
(*EBU Welterweight Title Defence*)
04.03.88 Antoine Fernandez W PTS 12 Geneva
(*EBU Welterweight Title Defence*)
23.04.88 Steve Mitchell W PTS 8 Berck sur Mer
Summary: 32 contests, won 32.

Alberto (Hungaro) Martinez
Guadalajara, Mexico. *Born* 31.06.66
Former Mexican Bantamweight Champion

.07.81 Roman Escalante W PTS 10 Guadalajara
.08.81 Hilario Duran W PTS 10 Guadalajara
04.09.81 Gilberto Sosa DREW 10 Guadalajara
20.10.81 Gilberto Sosa L PTS 10 Guadalajara
10.07.82 Jorge de Alba W RSC 8 Guadalajara
28.08.82 Wilibaldo Salazar W PTS 10 Guadalajara
01.10.82 Juan Isidro W CO 5 Guadalajara
17.12.82 Rafael Alonso L PTS 10 Guadalajara
25.02.83 Victor Moreno W CO 2 Guadalajara
18.03.83 Chano Roman W RSC 1 La Paz
20.04.83 Hugo Rodriguez W RSC 7 Mexico City
25.05.83 Bernardo Ibarra L RSC 5 Mexico City
06.09.83 Juan Diaz W PTS 10 Hermosillo
.12.83 Enrique Aguilar W PTS 10 Hermosillo
03.03.84 Mario Chavez W RSC 10 Tijuana
29.05.84 Alex Mayorga L PTS 12 Tijuana
10.12.84 Juan J. Estrada W PTS 10 Tijuana
25.03.85 Raul Perez L PTS 10 Tijuana
17.05.85 Miguel Juarez W PTS 10 Acapulco
05.10.85 Gabriel Romero L PTS 10 Mexicali
01.01.86 Raul Lopez W CO 4 Torreon
25.01.86 Juan Lopez W RSC 6 Guadalajara
02.03.86 Miguel Cota W PTS 10 La Paz
05.05.86 David Reyes W CO 9 La Paz
07.11.86 Julio Blanco W PTS 10 Monterrey
03.04.87 Jorge Ramirez ND 12 Guadalajara
(*Mexican Bantamweight Title Challenge*)
29.05.87 Jorge Ramirez W RSC 10 Guadalajara
(*Mexican Bantamweight Title Challenge*)
31.07.87 Arturo Mendoza W RSC 8 Guadalajara
(*Mexican Bantamweight Title Defence*)
25.09.87 Rodolfo Ortega W RSC 5 Guadalajara
13.11.87 Miguel Juarez W PTS 10 Guadalajara
19.02.88 Fermin Morales L PTS 12 Juarez
(*Mexican Bantamweight Title Defence*)
Summary: 31 contests, won 22, drew 1, lost 7, nd 1.

Mario (Azabache) Martinez
Guadalajara, Mexico. *Born* 15.08.65
S. Featherweight

22.02.80 Juan Cejas W CO 1 Guadalajara
07.03.80 Guillermo Jimenez W RSC 6 Guadalajara
28.03.80 J. Carlos Rubio W CO 1 Guadalajara
06.06.80 Enrique Hernandez W CO 1 Guadalajara
22.06.80 J. Luis Villamar W PTS 10 Guadalajara
11.07.80 Arturo Hernandez W CO 7 Guadalajara
15.08.80 Javier Olmos W PTS 10 Guadalajara
12.09.80 Juan Cordero W PTS 10 Guadalajara
24.10.80 Chamaco Flores W RSC 3 Guadalajara
21.11.80 Arturo Hernandez W RSC 1 Guadalajara
05.12.80 Javier Muniz W PTS 10 Guadalajara
30.01.81 Alfredo Martinez W CO 3 Guadalajara
06.02.81 Tony Escobar W PTS 10 Guadalajara
27.03.81 Lobo Aguilar DREW 10 Vallarta
25.04.81 Felipe Hernandez W PTS 10 Mexico City
06.06.81 Rosendo Alonso L PTS 10 Guadalajara
04.09.81 Jorge Vera W CO 2 Guadalajara
13.11.81 Martin Garcia W RSC 8 Guadalajara
05.02.82 Ambrosio Luna W CO 1 Guadalajara
25.03.82 Artemio Ramirez W PTS 10 Guadalajara
30.04.82 Ubaldo Rivas W PTS 10 Guadalajara
06.08.82 Memo Mayorga W CO 10 Guadalajara
15.11.82 Arturo Hernandez DREW 10 Guadalajara
14.01.83 Gerardo Pena W PTS 10 Guadalajara
11.02.83 Gus Dominguez W PTS 10 Guadalajara
15.04.83 Mauro Gutierrez W PTS 10 Guadalajara
21.05.83 Boni Flores W RSC 6 Mexico City
09.07.83 Miguel Alvarez W PTS 10 Mexico City
02.09.83 Norberto Cabrera W PTS 10 Hermosillo
29.10.83 Justo Garcia W PTS 10 Guadalajara
16.12.83 Ad Zapata W RSC 1 Mazatlan
28.01.84 Rafael Gandarilla W RSC 7 Guadalajara
05.03.84 Kazuo Tanaka W CO 2 Tijuana
26.04.84 Ray Brooks W CO 2 Los Angeles
17.05.84 Roberto Castanon W RSC 6 Los Angeles
23.06.84 Rolando Navarrete W RSC 5 Los Angeles
13.09.84 Julio Cesar Chavez L RSC 8 Los Angeles
(*Vacant WBC S. Featherweight Title*)
17.01.85 Martin Morado W RSC 6 Los Angeles
07.03.85 Frank Newton W PTS 10 Los Angeles
02.05.85 Adrian Arreola W PTS 10 Los Angeles
06.07.85 Miguel Alvarez W RSC 6 Mexicali
15.08.85 Rod Sequenan W PTS 10 Los Angeles
07.11.85 Roger Mayweather L PTS 10 Los Angeles
30.01.86 Leonardo Valdez W RSC 10 Los Angeles
25.05.86 Ramon Marchena W RSC 7 Tijuana
03.07.86 Dana Roston W RSC 7 Los Angeles
12.09.86 Angel Garcia W RSC 6 Chicago
06.02.87 Jimmy Jackson W RSC 3 Los Angeles
09.07.87 Darrell Savoy W RSC 3 Los Angeles
21.08.87 Jorge Gomez W RSC 10 Tijuana
12.11.87 Jose Mosqueda W PTS 10 Los Angeles
29.02.88 Azumah Nelson L PTS 12 Los Angeles
(*Vacant WBC S. Featherweight Title*)
Summary: 52 contests, won 46, drew 2, lost 4.

Felix Marty
Santo Domingo, Dominican Republic
Dominican L. Flyweight & Flyweight Champion

12.08.83 Lucilo Nolasco DREW 4 La Romana
25.11.83 Vicente Arias DREW 4 Santo Domingo
19.12.83 Martin Lantigua W PTS 6 Santo Domingo
25.02.84 Negro Lopez W PTS 6 La Vega
19.08.84 Fello Ramos W PTS 8 Santiago
19.12.84 Jose Pena W PTS 4 Santo Domingo
23.02.85 Fernando Mateo DREW 10 Santo Domingo
31.08.85 Jose Pena W PTS 10 Santo Domingo
26.04.86 Fernando Mateo W PTS 6 Villa Altagracia
14.08.86 Jovanny Payano W CO 2 San Pedro
20.09.86 Julio Tejeda W CO 5 Santiago
27.10.86 Bernardo Diaz W PTS 12 Santo Domingo
(*Dominican L. Flyweight Title Challenge*)
27.07.87 Rafael Cabrera L PTS 12 Santiago
(*Dominican Flyweight Title Challenge*)
25.09.87 Rafael Cabrera W PTS 12 Santo Domingo
(*Dominican Flyweight Title Challenge*)
18.12.87 Fidel Bassa L PTS 12 Cartagena
(*WBA Flyweight Title Challenge*)
Summary: 15 contests, won 10, drew 3, lost 2.

Gary Mason
Wandsworth, England. *Born* Jamaica 15.12.62
Heavyweight

16.10.84 Al Malcolm W CO 1 London
14.12.84 Al Malcolm W RSC 2 Wembley
18.01.85 Frank Robinson W RSC 1 London
06.03.85 Luc Goosens W CO 1 London
05.11.85 Steve Gee W RSC 5 Wembley
04.12.85 Steve Gee W RSC 5 London
19.02.86 Denroy Bryan W CO 1 London
04.03.86 Charles Hostetter W RSC 1 Wembley
09.04.86 Louis Pergaud W RTD 4 London
24.04.86 Maurice Gomis W RSC 3 London
20.05.86 Ivy Brown W CO 2 Wembley
19.07.86 Mark Young W CO 5 Wembley
17.09.86 Lorenzo Boyd W CO 2 London
04.11.86 Donny Long W CO 1 Wembley
26.11.86 Oscar Holman W PTS 8 Wolverhampton
22.02.87 Rod Smith W RSC 1 Wembley
24.03.87 Richard Scott W RSC 1 Wembley
18.04.87 Woody Clark W RSC 2 London
26.05.87 Billy Joe Thomas W RSC 2 Wembley
30.08.87 Eddie Richardson W RSC 7 Marbella
25.09.87 Andre van den Oetelaar W CO 2 Southend
24.10.87 Andrew Gerrard W RSC 6 London
03.12.87 Sam Scaff W RSC 2 Southend
03.02.88 Alfonso Ratliff W RSC 6 Wembley
09.03.88 Rickey Parkey W RSC 1 Wembley
13.04.88 Manuel Clay Almedia W RSC 7 London
Summary: 26 contests, won 26.

Kenji Matsumura
Takasago, Japan. *Born* 15.02.60
OPBF Flyweight Champion

23.07.85 Shigenobu Nakasama W PTS 6 Takamatsu
29.10.85 Yukinari Oshiro W RSC 3 Osaka
23.01.86 Kentoku Nakama L PTS 10 Tokyo
22.03.86 Masaru Yoshimoto W RSC 9 Himeji
20.05.86 Francisco Montiel L PTS 10 Sendai
25.10.86 Hitoshi Taniuchi W RSC 9 Osaka
23.12.86 Putt Ohyuthanakorn W CO 2 Kakogawa
03.05.87 Tanomsak Singboebae W PTS 12 Kakogawa
(*OPBF Flyweight Title Challenge*)
14.09.87 Elysser Bautista W PTS 12 Himeji
(*OPBF Flyweight Title Defence*)
11.02.88 Cho-Woon Park W PTS 12 Himeji
(*OPBF Flyweight Title Defence*)
Summary: 10 contests, won 8, lost 2.

Miguel (Mask) Maturana
Quibdo, Colombia. *Born* 09.10.60
Bantamweight

02.04.82 Johnny Jackson W CO 2 Cartagena
19.06.82 William Ramos W CO 2 Cartagena
14.08.82 Pedro Barrera W RTD 9 Cartagena
30.10.82 Rene Merced W CO 4 Barranquilla
18.12.82 Ruben Palacios L RSC 10 Cartagena
(*Colombian Bantamweight Title Challenge*)
14.04.84 Francisco Alvarez W PTS 10 Cartagena
10.05.84 Antonio Nisperuza W PTS 8 Cartagena
06.06.84 Felipe Angulo W PTS 8 Sahagun
17.06.84 Pedro Barrera DREW 8 Monteria
28.07.84 Juan Polo Perez W CO 2 Cartagena
31.08.84 Valerio Zea W PTS 8 Cartagena
23.11.85 William Hernandez W CO 2 San Andres
27.12.85 Ezequiel Hernandez DREW 10 San Andres
15.02.86 Marciano Hernandez W CO 2 San Andres
04.04.86 Mario Agustino W CO 8 San Andres
18.04.86 Azael Moran L PTS 10 Panama City
14.12.86 Dorismel Zuniga W RSC 6 Turbo
23.01.87 Dorismel Zuniga W RSC 1 Cartagena
20.02.87 Efrain Betancourt W RSC 5 Cartagena
06.03.87 Orlando Hernandez W RSC 6 Cartagena
15.05.87 Kelvin Seabrooks L CO 5 Cartagena
(*Vacant IBF Bantamweight Title*)
06.11.87 Arcelio Diaz W PTS 10 Cartagena
01.12.87 Daniel Blanco W RSC 5 Cartagena
26.02.88 Luis Mendoza L RTD 4 Cartagena
Summary: 24 contests, won 18, drew 2, lost 4.

Roger (Black Mamba) Mayweather
Grand Rapids, USA. *Born* 24.04.61
WBC L. Welterweight Champion. Former Undefeated Con. Am. Lightweight Champion. Former WBA S. Featherweight Champion. Former Undefeated USBA S. Featherweight Champion

29.07.81 Andrew Ruiz W RSC 1 Las Vegas
05.08.81 Jaime Nava W PTS 8 Las Vegas
24.09.81 Javier Benitez W RSC 5 Las Vegas
21.10.81 Juan Hernandez W PTS 6 Las Vegas
07.11.81 Vinnie Hines W RSC 2 Las Vegas
14.11.81 Adrian Arreola W RSC 6 Las Vegas
24.01.82 Roberto Garcia W RSC 3 Las Vegas
03.04.82 Jimmy Blevins W PTS 10 Las Vegas
27.05.82 Kelvin Lampkin W PTS 10 Las Vegas
29.07.82 Carlton Sparrow W CO 4 Las Vegas
18.08.82 Arturo Leon W PTS 10 Las Vegas
29.09.82 Frankie Moultrie W RSC 9 Las Vegas

23.10.82 Ruben Munoz W PTS 12 Atlantic City
(USBA S. Featherweight Title Challenge)
17.11.82 Elmer Suttington W RSC 2 St Joseph
19.01.83 Sam Serrano W CO 8 San Juan
(WBA S. Featherweight Title Challenge)
20.04.83 Jorge Alvarado W RSC 8 San Jose
(WBA S. Featherweight Title Defence)
17.08.83 Benedicto Villablanca W CO 1 Las Vegas
(WBA S. Featherweight Title Defence)
26.02.84 Rocky Lockridge L CO 1 Beaumont
(WBA S. Featherweight Title Defence)
08.07.84 Tony Baltazar L PTS 10 Los Angeles
22.09.84 Efren Nieves W PTS 10 Grand Rapids
21.11.84 Martin Quiroz W RSC 3 Las Vegas
28.02.85 Billy White W RSC 5 Las Vegas
12.05.85 Kenny Baysmore W RSC 3 Tyler
(USBA S. Featherweight Title Challenge)
07.07.85 Julio Cesar Chavez L RSC 2 Las Vegas
(WBC S. Featherweight Title Challenge)
07.11.85 Mario Martinez W PTS 10 Los Angeles
15.01.86 Walter Sims W PTS 10 Las Vegas
12.03.86 Fred Pendleton L RSC 6 Las Vegas
03.07.86 Oscar Bejinez W RTD 8 Los Angeles
07.08.86 Sergio Zambrano W RTD 6 Los Angeles
28.11.86 Sammy Fuentes W RSC 9 Atlantic City
(Vacant Con. Am. Lightweight Title)
28.03.87 Pernell Whitaker L PTS 12 Norfolk
(Vacant NABF Lightweight Title)
14.05.87 Frankie Davis W RSC 4 Las Vegas
14.07.87 Mitchell Julien W RSC 3 Las Vegas
12.11.87 Rene Arredondo W RSC 6 Los Angeles
(WBC L. Welterweight Title Challenge)
05.01.88 Marvin Garris W RSC 7 Las Vegas
24.03.88 Mauricio Aceves W CO 3 Los Angeles
(WBC L. Welterweight Title Defence)
Summary: 36 contests, won 31, lost 5.

Raymond Medel
San Antonio, USA. *Born* 27.09.67
Former Undefeated USBA Flyweight Champion

11.12.84 Ruben Flores W CO 1 San Antonio
06.02.85 Leo Alvarado W PTS 4 San Antonio
26.02.85 Roland Gomez L PTS 4 Corpus Christi
09.04.85 Nelson Garcia W PTS 4 San Antonio
27.06.85 Juan Diaz W PTS 8 San Antonio
10.09.85 Polo Saucedo W RSC 5 San Antonio
25.09.85 John Vasquez W PTS 6 Corpus Christi
12.12.85 Gabriel Bernal L PTS 10 Houston
03.04.86 Mike Phelps L PTS 12 Beaumont
24.06.86 Armando Velasco W PTS 10 San Antonio
16.09.86 Azadin Anhar W PTS 10 San Antonio
08.02.87 Henry Brent W RSC 8 San Antonio
(USBA Flyweight Title Challenge)
01.05.87 Richard Abila W PTS 10 San Antonio
19.07.87 Obed Munoz W CO 5 San Antonio
10.11.87 Homero Aguilar W RSC 10 San Antonio
(USBA Flyweight Title Defence)
10.04.88 Pop Robinson W PTS 8 Atlantic City
Summary: 16 contests, won 13, lost 3.

John Meekins
New York, USA. *Born* 19.05.65
L. Welterweight

19.10.84 Carlos Ruiz W RSC 1 New York
14.11.84 Murray Frazier W CO 3 Atlantic City
27.12.84 Melvin Richardson W RSC 3 Atlantic City
14.02.85 John Rafuse W RSC 6 Atlantic City
07.03.85 Roger Brown W RSC 3 Atlantic City
02.05.85 Jose Alejandro W CO 3 Atlantic City
05.06.85 Ozzie O'Neal W RSC 7 Atlantic City
15.08.85 Sammy Young W RSC 3 Atlantic City
18.09.85 Joey Ferrell W PTS 10 Atlantic City
11.12.85 Martin Quiroz T DRAW 1 Atlantic City
24.01.86 Juan Santana W PTS 10 Atlantic City
21.03.86 Grant Walters W RTD 6 Atlantic City
01.08.86 Davey Montana W RSC 1 Atlantic City
05.09.86 Harold Brazier T DRAW 2 Atlantic City
(Vacant NABF L. Welterweight Title)
09.12.86 George Leach W RSC 5 Atlantic City
24.02.87 Harold Brazier L PTS 12 Atlantic City
(NABF L. Welterweight Title Challenge)
17.04.87 Sergio Aguirre W RSC 3 Atlantic City
23.06.87 Robert Guy W PTS 10 Atlantic City
18.09.87 Howard Stewart W CO 9 Atlantic City
15.01.88 Othal Dixon W RSC 2 Atlantic City
Summary: 20 contests, won 17, drew 2, lost 1.

Luis (Chicanero) Mendoza
San Onofre, Colombia. *Born* 1965
Former Undefeated Colombian Bantamweight & S. Bantamweight Champion

02.02.85 Luis Berrio W PTS 6 Cartagena
29.03.85 Onofre Valiente W CO 4 Cartagena
21.04.85 Valerio Zea W PTS 10 Cartagena
15.11.85 Darryl Pinckney W RSC 1 Miami
03.12.85 Kid Monzote W PTS 6 Miami
13.12.85 Jesse Williams L PTS 6 Miami
15.02.86 Tomas Maza W CO 4 San Andres
14.06.86 Ezequiel Hernandez W PTS 8 San Andres
05.07.86 Manuel Salgado W PTS 6 Cartagena
18.07.86 Alejandro Pastrana W CO 1 San Andres
12.09.86 Albeiro Arboleda W RSC 6 Cartagena
03.10.86 Miguel Ariza W CO 1 Cartagena
(Vacant Colombian Bantamweight Title)
31.10.86 Gustavo Zabala W RSC 9 Monteria
(Colombian Bantamweight Title Defence)
21.12.86 Ezequiel Hernandez W PTS 10 Cartagena
20.02.87 Alirio Macias W CO 2 Cartagena
13.03.87 Rafael Martinez W CO 1 Cartagena
03.04.87 Eduo Bermudez W CO 3 Cartagena
15.05.87 Moises Fuentes W PTS 10 Cartagena
(Colombian S. Bantamweight Title Challenge)
31.07.87 Gilberto Barcenas W CO 4 San Andres
04.09.87 Daniel Blanco W PTS 10 Cartagena
11.12.87 Enrique Sanchez W PTS 10 Cartagena
26.02.88 Miguel Maturana W RTD 4 Cartagena
Summary: 22 contests, won 21, lost 1.

Jean-Baptiste Mendy
France. *Born* 16.03.63
Lightweight

15.01.83 Gilles Beaurain W PTS 6 Guise
28.02.83 Yannick Blandin W PTS 6 Paris
07.03.83 Tiburce Mondelice W PTS 6 Paris
14.03.83 Lexter Boucaud W PTS 6 Paris
13.06.83 Norbert Alcade W RTD 2 Paris
06.08.83 Jean-Luc Sautreau DREW 6 Dijon
10.10.83 Abdel Chaboune W PTS 6 Paris
14.11.83 Lahcen Oumghar L RSC 3 Rotterdam
21.01.84 Nihat Er DREW 8 Montargis
02.03.84 Vicente Macias L PTS 8 Bayonne
25.03.84 David Mahmutovic W RSC 8 Titograd
13.04.84 Tony Vivarelli W PTS 6 Antibes
26.06.84 Dusan Radosavlievic W PTS 6 Belgrade
07.12.84 Vicente Macias W PTS 8 Bordeaux
29.03.85 Jesus Bezanilla W CO 1 Bordeaux
17.05.85 Sana Kabore W PTS 8 Dakar
01.06.85 Edgar Castro W PTS 8 Paris
03.02.86 Raphael Paoletti W PTS 8 Paris
14.03.86 Francisco Nunez W RSC 4 Bordeaux
05.04.86 Michel Siracusa W RTD 6 Bordeaux
23.05.86 Vicente Jorge W DIS 3 Bordeaux
07.06.86 I. Vako W RSC 6 Noumea
10.12.86 Mike Durvan W CO 3 Paris
05.02.87 Vicente Macias W CO 5 Bordeaux
28.02.87 Rafael Gandarilla W CO 7 Vincennes
12.05.87 Juan Salazar W CO 2 Le Mans
26.05.87 Aristide Acevedo W PTS 8 Villeurbanne
08.06.87 Arturo Hernandez W CO 5 Merignac
12.07.87 Sebastian Wilburn W CO 4 Merignac
08.10.87 Jose Mosqueda W PTS 8 Paris
06.11.87 Kevin Pritchard W CO 4 Antibes
19.12.87 Chris Silva W RTD 4 Paris
27.02.88 Angel Luis Garcia NC 2 San Juan
12.03.88 Angel Luis Garcia W CO 3 Levallios
Summary: 34 contests, won 29, drew 2, lost 2, nc 1.

Alberto Mercado
Puerto Rico. *Born* 02.01.61
Featherweight

27.10.80 Jose Latimer W CO 1 Trujillo
18.12.80 Osvaldo Morales W CO 1 Trujillo
15.01.81 Jose Martinez W RSC 2 San Juan
24.01.81 Elvin Gonzalez W CO 2 San Juan
10.04.81 Herman Ingram W PTS 6 New York
23.05.81 Javier Barajas W RSC 1 Las Vegas
25.06.81 Jose Figueroa W PTS 4 New York
06.08.81 Luis Burgos W CO 3 Cayey
16.10.81 David Capo W RSC 8 New York
29.10.81 Emilio Hernandez W RSC 2 San Juan
14.11.81 Ramon Berrera W RSC 5 Las Vegas
19.12.81 Lloyd Allen W PTS 10 Atlantic City
30.01.82 Jose Pozos W CO 5 Las Vegas
21.03.82 Sylvester Price W CO 3 Las Vegas
30.05.82 Juan Veloz W PTS 10 Las Vegas
26.06.82 Mike Rodriguez W RSC 3 Las Vegas
09.10.82 Charm Chiteule L PTS 10 Las Vegas
03.12.82 Tom Guillen W RSC 6 New Orleans
04.02.83 Juan Veloz DREW 10 New York
24.06.83 Felix Marquez W RSC 6 New York
07.08.83 Manuel Santos W RSC 6 San Juan
18.11.83 Edwin Salgado W RSC 4 San Juan
21.12.83 Refugio Rojas L PTS 12 Syracuse
(Vacant USBA Featherweight Title)
17.03.84 Osvaldo Acevedo W RSC 9 San Juan
20.06.84 Hector Sanchez W RSC 3 San Juan
03.11.84 Julio Guerrero W RSC 2 San Juan
02.02.85 Antonio Rivera L RSC 7 San Juan
29.06.85 Jesus Flores W RSC 10 Curacao
03.08.85 Luis Julio Perez W RSC 2 Cayey
20.11.85 Jose Mosqueda W RSC 6 Caguas
21.12.85 Edwart Chance W RSC 3 Caguas
03.05.86 Larry Highsmith W RSC 3 San Juan
07.06.86 Tommy Valoy L RSC 5 San Juan
12.09.86 Marcos Villasana L PTS 10 Chicago
16.03.87 Irving Mitchell W RSC 2 Los Angeles
27.04.87 Leonardo Valdez L PTS 10 Los Angeles
24.07.87 Leonardo Valdez L PTS 10 Las Vegas
09.10.87 Keith Stevenson L RSC 9 Las Vegas
14.01.88 Mario Gomez W RTD 3 Los Angeles
Summary: 39 contests, won 30, drew 1, lost 8.

Miguel Mercedes
La Romana, Dominican Republic. *Born* 14.05.60
Fecarbox Flyweight Champion

03.03.83 Alex Silva W CO 4 Los Angeles
12.07.84 Jose Diaz W CO 4 Los Angeles
13.09.84 Tony Flores W RSC 5 Los Angeles
17.11.84 Tony Escobar W PTS 10 Los Angeles
27.05.85 Yoshi Kurashita W RSC 5 Tokyo
05.12.85 Rae-Ki Ahn L PTS 10 Seoul
11.10.86 Armando Velasco W RSC 3 Mexico City
15.11.86 Alvaro Mercado W CO 2 Barranquilla
(Vacant Fecarbox Flyweight Title)
30.01.87 Carlos Diaz W CO 5 La Romana
18.06.87 Manuel Trujillo W CO 2 Los Angeles
12.11.87 Javier Diaz W PTS 10 Los Angeles
Summary: 11 contests, won 10, lost 1.

John Meekins (right) looks for an opening against Harold Brazier on 24 February 1987. Brazier retained his NABF light-welterweight title and broke Meekins' unbeaten streak
Peter Goldfield/USA

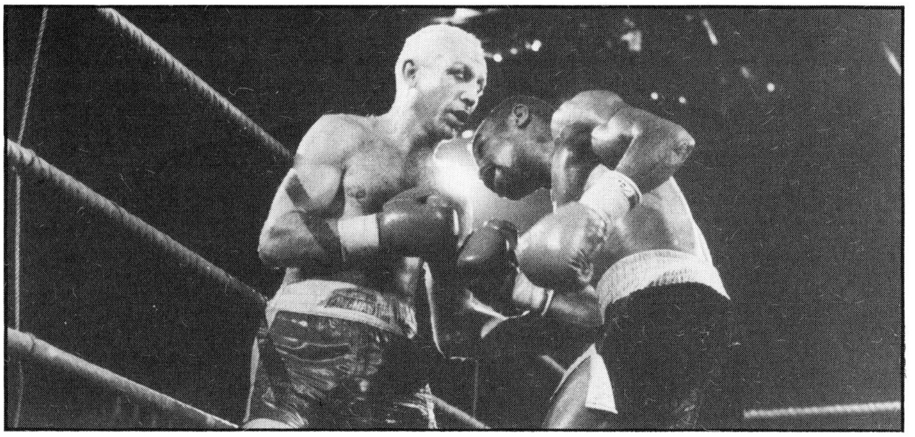

Barry Michael (left) lost his IBF super-featherweight title to Rocky Lockridge, when forced to retire with severe injuries John McDonald

Barry Michael
Melbourne, Australia. *Born* England 02.06.55
Former IBF S. Featherweight Champion. Former Undefeated Australian & Commonwealth Lightweight Champion

18.06.73 Mick McLean W PTS 3 Melbourne
25.06.73 Gary Leggett W PTS 3 Melbourne
23.07.73 Mick McLean W PTS 3 Melbourne
06.08.73 Neil Hankin W PTS 3 Melbourne
15.10.73 Dale Doherty W CO 2 Melbourne
22.10.73 Glenn Howard W PTS 3 Melbourne
19.11.73 Mick Maybury W CO 3 Melbourne
04.02.74 Des Pearce W PTS 4 Melbourne
18.02.74 Jimmy Brown L PTS 6 Melbourne
19.04.74 Dally Law DREW 6 Melbourne
07.03.75 Mick O'Brien W CO 4 Melbourne
11.04.75 Glenn Howard W PTS 6 Melbourne
28.04.75 Willie Leslie W PTS 6 Melbourne
02.06.75 Robbie Williams W CO 3 Melbourne
04.09.75 Glenn Howard W PTS 10 Melbourne
25.09.75 Keith Ball W PTS 10 Melbourne
20.11.75 Andy Broome W PTS 10 Melbourne
26.02.76 Dave Richards W PTS 10 Blacktown
23.04.76 Dave Richards W PTS 12 Melbourne
04.09.76 Nene Jun L PTS 10 Cebu City
26.11.76 Wong-So Suseno W PTS 10 Surabaya
22.12.76 Billy Moeller L PTS 15 Orange (*Commonwealth and Australian S. Featherweight Title Challenge*)
04.05.77 Joey Gibilisco W PTS 10 Melbourne
11.09.77 Juan J. Gimenez L PTS 10 Surabaya
29.09.77 Spurling Pharangeburn W PTS 10 Jakarta
16.10.77 Fred Ramashie W PTS 10 Surabaya
24.01.78 Don Marano W PTS 10 Melbourne
28.04.78 Jeff Malcolm L PTS 10 Melbourne
16.06.78 Kevin Franklin W RSC 3 Heidelberg
12.08.78 Billy Mulholland W PTS 15 Coonabarrabran (*Australian Lightweight Title Challenge*)
15.11.78 Billy Vivian W PTS 10 Merthyr
26.12.78 Lennox Blackmore L RSC 7 Georgetown
02.02.79 Blakeney Matthews W CO 8 Williamstown (*Australian Lightweight Title Defence*)
18.02.79 Lucky Gattelari W RTD 3 Moore Park (*Australian Lightweight Title Defence*)
05.07.79 Najib Daho L PTS 8 Aberavon
19.12.79 Jimmy Brown T DRAW 1 Williamstown (*Australian Lightweight Title Defence*)
19.04.80 Manny Ysrale W PTS 10 Footscray
17.09.80 Graham Bell W CO 6 Mount Pritchard (*Australian Lightweight Title Defence*)
17.12.80 Jimmy Brown W RSC 15 Melbourne (*Australian Lightweight Title Defence*)
07.01.81 Willie Tarika W PTS 12 Gosford (*Australian Lightweight Title Defence*)
08.02.81 Big Jim West W PTS 10 Sydney
06.05.81 Langton Tinago W PTS 15 Melbourne (*Commonwealth Lightweight Title Challenge*)
20.07.81 Dave McCabe W RSC 7 Melbourne (*Commonwealth Lightweight Title Defence*)
14.09.81 Al Carter W PTS 10 Melbourne
11.12.81 Willie Tarika W RSC 10 Melbourne (*Commonwealth & Australian Lightweight Title Defence*)
14.04.82 Augustin Rivera W PTS 10 Melbourne
22.07.82 Claude Noel L PTS 15 Melbourne (*Commonwealth Lightweight Title Defence*)
07.09.82 Mike Anderson W PTS 10 Honolulu
16.10.82 Nacho Jimenez W PTS 10 Honolulu
16.02.83 Frank Ropis W RSC 11 Melbourne
29.08.83 Tomas Chavez W PTS 10 Brisbane
26.02.84 Jerome Artis W PTS 10 Melbourne
14.04.84 Juhari DREW 12 Jakarta (*OPBF Lightweight Title Challenge*)
30.11.84 Juan Arroyo W RSC 8 Melbourne
22.02.85 Graeme Brooke W PTS 12 Melbourne (*Commonwealth Lightweight Title Challenge*)
12.07.85 Lester Ellis W PTS 15 Melbourne (*IBF S. Featherweight Title Challenge*)
18.10.85 Jin-Shik Choi W RSC 4 Darwin (*IBF S. Featherweight Title Defence*)
23.05.86 Mark Fernandez W RSC 4 Melbourne (*IBF S. Featherweight Title Defence*)
23.08.86 Najib Daho W PTS 12 Manchester (*IBF S. Featherweight Title Defence*)
09.08.87 Rocky Lockridge L RTD 8 Windsor (*IBF S. Featherweight Title Defence*)
Summary: 60 contests, won 48, drew 3, lost 9.

Tony (Mad Dog) Miller
Melbourne, Australia. *Born* England 20.09.64
Australian S. Featherweight Champion. Former Australian Featherweight Champion

27.06.84 Dean Colbung W RTD 6 Osborne Park
25.07.84 Carl Zappia W PTS 10 Belmont
28.08.84 Ron Smith W PTS 10 Morley
14.09.84 Phil Roberts W CO 8 Melbourne
19.09.84 Marty Feighan W PTS 8 Mount Pritchard
18.10.84 Jim Bowen W RSC 8 Melbourne
02.11.84 Rod Bowman W RSC 6 Melbourne
11.12.84 Ron Smith W RSC 10 Perth
20.02.85 Mark Cribb W RSC 10 Mount Pritchard
07.03.85 Dean Thomas W CO 2 Braybrook
24.03.85 Sam Gibilisco W PTS 12 Melbourne (*Australian S. Featherweight Title Challenge*)
26.04.85 Lulu Villaverde W PTS 10 Melbourne
09.06.85 Tiger Mann W RSC 4 Melbourne
12.07.85 Antonio Rivera DREW 10 Melbourne
13.09.85 Tony Pep W PTS 10 Melbourne
24.09.85 Roberto Nunez L RSC 4 Atlantic City
06.12.85 Carl Zappia W RSC 4 Perth (*Australian S. Featherweight Title Defence*)
23.02.86 Paul Ferreri W PTS 12 Preston (*Australian Featherweight Title Challenge*)
18.04.86 Marty Feighan W RSC 6 Canberra (*Australian Featherweight Title Defence*)
01.08.86 Rudy Cabiles W PTS 10 Melbourne
26.09.86 Craig Pevy W PTS 12 Perth (*Australian S. Featherweight Title Defence*)
09.10.86 Lester Ellis L PTS 10 Melbourne
03.04.87 Jeff Fenech L PTS 12 Melbourne (*Australian Featherweight Title Defence*)
24.09.87 Joe Hiyas W PTS 10 Perth
16.10.87 Armando Marin W PTS 8 Sydney
07.03.88 Nelson Rodriguez DREW 10 Sydney
Summary: 26 contests, won 21, drew 2, lost 3.

Ray Minus
Bahamas. *Born* 03.07.64
Commonwealth & Con. Am. Bantamweight Champion

18.06.82 Angel Torres W RSC 1 Nassau
19.11.82 Cornbread Williams L PTS 6 Freeport
25.02.83 Cornbread Williams W RSC 3 Nassau
30.04.83 Keith Cameron W RSC 2 Nassau
27.05.83 Sal Garcia DREW 6 Nassau
01.07.83 Terry Pizzaro W RSC 6 Nassau
02.09.83 Robert Mullins W RSC 8 Nassau
16.10.83 Osvaldo Acevedo W RTD 7 Nassau
23.12.83 Ron Garret W CO 2 Nassau
02.03.84 Edgar Acevedo W PTS 10 Nassau
31.03.84 Al Adger W CO 1 Nassau
18.05.84 Ray Garza W RSC 10 Freeport
29.06.84 Osvaldo Acevedo W PTS 10 Miami
28.07.84 Eddie Gonzales W CO 6 Nassau
28.09.84 Peter Harris W PTS 10 Nassau
30.11.84 Steve Guess W CO 1 Nassau
22.12.84 Juan Salazar W CO 8 Nassau
08.03.85 Kelvin Seabrooks W CO 3 Nassau
04.04.85 Keith Wallace W RSC 4 Digbeth
17.05.85 Alberto Cruz W CO 2 Nassau
12.07.85 Juan Castellanos W PTS 10 Nassau
09.08.85 Jose Mosqueda NC 4 Nassau
24.09.85 Sam David L CO 12 Atlantic City (*Vacant Con. Am. Bantamweight Title*)
27.09.86 Paul Ferreri W RTD 10 Nassau (*Vacant Commonwealth Bantamweight Title*)
06.03.87 Prudencio Cardona W PTS 10 Nassau
01.07.87 Sean Murphy W RSC 5 London (*Commonwealth Bantamweight Title Defence*)
27.11.87 Miguel Lora L PTS 12 Miami (*WBC Bantamweight Title Challenge*)
30.01.88 Enrique Sanchez W PTS 12 Nassau (*Vacant Con. Am. Bantamweight Title*)
30.04.88 Morgan Maphosa W CO 3 Nassau (*Vacant Commonwealth Bantamweight Title*)
Summary: 29 contests, won 24, drew 1, lost 3, nc 1.

Julio (Ardilla) Miranda
San Salvador, Argentine. *Born* 01.02.59
Argentinian S. Featherweight Champion

13.07.84 Juan Herrera W PTS 6 San Salvador
16.08.84 Juan Ervidia W PTS 10 San Salvador
07.09.84 Miguel Ledesma W PTS 6 San Salvador
05.10.84 Fausto Blanco W RTD 3 San Salvador
26.10.84 Miguel Ibarra W PTS 6 San Salvador
16.11.84 Anibal Sosa W PTS 8 San Salvador
14.12.84 Miguel Ibarra DREW 8 San Salvador
28.12.84 Luis A. Perez W PTS 10 La Cautiva
08.02.85 Reynaldo Cadena W PTS 10 San Salvador
08.03.85 Hipolito Caucota W PTS 10 San Salvador
03.04.85 Julio Ramirez W PTS 10 San Salvador
19.04.85 Carlos Ibarra W PTS 10 Tucuman
10.05.85 Carmelo Gonzalez W PTS 10 San Salvador
05.07.85 Jose Ayala W PTS 10 San Salvador
10.08.85 Ricardo Gil L TD 4 El Chamical
20.09.85 Reynaldo Cazon W PTS 10 Salta
18.10.85 Eduardo Galan W PTS 12 San Salvador
05.12.85 Esteban Bustos DREW 10 San Pedro
05.02.86 Mario Vizcaya W PTS 10 San Pedro
25.04.86 Jose Villarruel DREW 10 San Salvador
16.05.86 Donato Zamora W RTD 6 San Salvador
04.07.86 Fernando Fuentes W CO 3 San Salvador
08.08.86 Ricardo Gil DREW 10 Mendoza
29.08.86 Jorge Pompe W PTS 10 San Salvador
26.12.86 Julio Ramirez W PTS 10 San Salvador
18.02.87 Ruben Astorga W PTS 10 San Salvador
30.04.87 Faustino Barrios W PTS 12 San Salvador (*Argentinian S. Featherweight Title Challenge*)
12.06.87 Ricardo Gil W RSC 7 San Salvador
07.08.87 Jorge Pompe W PTS 10 Buenos Aires
02.10.87 Raul Gomez W PTS 10 San Salvador
04.12.87 Pedro Gutierrez W PTS 12 San Salvador (*Argentinian S. Featherweight Title Defence*)
18.03.88 Luis Rodriguez W PTS 10 Tucuman
Summary: 32 contests, won 27, drew 4, lost 1.

Mario (El Nia) Miranda
Barranquilla, Colombia. *Born* 15.05.60
Former Undefeated NABF S. Featherweight Champion. Former Undefeated Con. Am. & Colombian Featherweight Champion

27.05.79 Delimiro Cassiani W PTS 4 Barranquilla
28.06.79 Jose Jimenez W RSC 3 Barranquilla
27.07.79 Jose Salazar W PTS 6 Barranquilla
05.10.79 Jaime Espejo W PTS 6 Barranquilla
04.11.79 Pedro Vizcaino W RSC 7 Barranquilla
01.02.80 Misael Sanchez W RSC 4 Maicao
23.02.80 Jaime Ricardo W CO 4 Cartagena
29.03.80 Humberto Castillo W PTS 10 Cartagena
18.05.80 Francisco Castro W RSC 5 Barranquilla
27.06.80 Manuel Anaya W CO 3 Barranquilla
14.08.80 Raul Silva W PTS 10 Barranquilla
30.10.80 Armando Perez W RSC 11 Barranquilla
(*Colombian Featherweight Title Challenge*)
20.12.80 Juvencio Monserrat W CO 4 Barranquilla
07.03.81 Ruben Valdez W RSC 6 Cartagena
29.05.81 Memo Morales W PTS 12 Barranquilla
(*Vacant Con. Am. Featherweight Title*)
05.09.81 Jose Cervantes W CO 2 Cartagena
11.12.81 Juan Malavares W CO 1 Barranquilla
19.03.82 Rigoberto Riasco W RSC 3 Cartagena
19.06.82 Marcos Villasana W RSC 8 Cartagena
15.09.82 Juan Laporte L RTD 10 New York
(*Vacant WBC Featherweight Title*)
05.02.83 Francisco Fernandez W PTS 10 Panama City
28.10.83 Bernabe Montanez W PTS 10 Miami
14.11.83 Jorge Lujan L PTS 10 Panama City
02.12.83 Victor Fontanez W RSC 7 Miami
20.01.84 Rafael Escalera W PTS 10 Miami
18.02.84 Julio Llerena DREW 10 Cartagena
17.06.84 Bernabe Diaz W CO 10 Monteria
15.12.84 Terry Kemp W CO 4 Miami
05.05.85 Jose Mosqueda W PTS 10 Miami
20.07.85 Julio Llerena DREW 12 Cartagena
(*Vacant Con. Am. S. Featherweight Title*)
20.09.85 Pedro Barboza W RSC 4 Miami
19.12.85 Oscar Bejines L PTS 10 Los Angeles
07.02.86 Keith Jackson W PTS 10 Miami
04.03.86 James Lyons W RSC 2 Miami
04.04.86 Larry Highsmith W RSC 3 Miami
13.05.86 Carlos Albuerne W RSC 5 Bloomington
20.06.86 Jose Mosqueda W PTS 10 Hialeah
12.09.86 Geronimo Luquez W RSC 8 Miami
26.12.86 Adolfo Marte W CO 1 Key West
17.01.87 Dwight Pratchett W PTS 12 Miami
(*NABF S. Featherweight Title Challenge*)
16.05.87 Gustavo Martinez W CO 2 Miami
25.07.87 Raphe Sims W PTS 12 Miami
(*NABF S. Featherweight Title Defence*)
01.12.87 Felipe Angulo W PTS 10 Cartagena
Summary: 43 contests, won 38, drew 2, lost 3.

Brian Mitchell
South Africa. *Born* 30.08.61
WBA S. Featherweight Champion. Former Undefeated South African S. Featherweight Champion

15.08.81 Josef Monoane W PTS 4 Johannesburg
19.09.81 Bushy Mosoeu W PTS 4 Johannesburg
03.10.81 Tandi Mayisela W PTS 4 Johannesburg
31.10.81 Simon Zondo W RSC 4 Johannesburg
30.11.81 Moses Mthiyane W RSC 4 Durban
06.02.82 Phanuel Mosdane W RSC 2 Johannesburg
01.05.82 Jacob Morake L PTS 10 Kwa Thema
17.05.82 Joseph Tsotetsi W PTS 6 Johannesburg
26.06.82 Moses Sithebe W RSC 3 Orkney
30.07.82 Frank Khonkhobe DREW 6 Sebokeng
15.10.82 Frank Khonkhobe W PTS 10 Diepkloof
14.05.83 Jerome Gumede W PTS 8 Durban
09.04.83 Chris Whiteboy W RSC 9 Orkney
(*South African S. Featherweight Title Challenge*)
02.05.83 Bashew Sibaca W PTS 10 Durban
27.06.83 Graham Gcola W CO 2 Johannesburg
(*South African S. Featherweight Title Defence*)
06.08.83 Jacob Morake W PTS 12 Johannesburg
(*South African S. Featherweight Title Defence*)
21.11.83 Frank Khonkhobe W PTS 12 Johannesburg
(*South African S. Featherweight Title Defence*)
19.12.83 Blessing Ndlele W RSC 1 Durban
02.03.84 Jacob Morake W PTS 12 Springs
(*South African S. Featherweight Title Defence*)
31.03.84 Carlos Rodriguez W RSC 4 Johannesburg
16.04.84 Iland Matthews W PTS 6 Welkom
02.08.84 Nika Khumalo W CO 2 Cape Town
(*South African S. Featherweight Title Defence*)
01.12.84 Aladin Stevens W PTS 8 Sun City
11.02.85 Nyingi Mtya W RSC 3 Boksburg
30.03.85 Carlos Rodriguez W RSC 7 Sun City
27.04.85 Vicente Jorge W RSC 7 Johannesburg
27.07.85 Job Sisanga W PTS 8 Sun City
02.11.85 Jacob Morake W RSC 12 Sun City
(*South African S. Featherweight Title Defence*)
01.03.86 Julio Ruiz W CO 6 Sun City
14.06.86 Bushy Mosoeu W PTS 12 Sun City
(*South African S. Featherweight Title Defence*)
27.09.86 Alfredo Layne W RSC 10 Sun City
(*WBA S. Featherweight Title Challenge*)
27.03.87 Jose Rivera DREW 15 San Juan
(*WBA S. Featherweight Title Defence*)
16.05.87 Aurelio Benitez W RSC 2 Sun City
31.07.87 Francisco Fernandez W RSC 14 Panama City
(*WBA S. Featherweight Title Defence*)
03.10.87 Daniel Londas W PTS 15 Gravelines
(*WBA S. Featherweight Title Defence*)
19.12.87 Salvatore Curcetti W RTD 8 Capo D'Orlando
(*WBA S. Featherweight Title Defence*)
26.04.88 Jose Rivera W PTS 12 Madrid
(*WBA S. Featherweight Title Defence*)
Summary: 37 contests, won 34, drew 2, lost 1.

Tomas (Ton Molly) Molinares
Cartagena, Colombia. *Born* 06.04.65
Fecarbox Welterweight Champion. Former Undefeated Colombian Welterweight Champion

26.10.84 Arnobis Castro W PTS 6 Cartagena
01.03.85 Cristobal Torres W RSC 4 Barranquilla
29.03.85 Edison Benitez W RSC 5 Barranquilla
03.05.85 Mateo Valdez W PTS 8 Barranquilla
21.06.85 Simon Ramos W RSC 9 Cartagena
(*Colombian Welterweight Title Challenge*)
30.08.85 Jairo Segovia W CO 5 Barranquilla
27.09.85 Glen Savage W RTD 3 Barranquilla
18.10.85 Emiro Olivera W RSC 8 Cartagena
14.12.85 Ezequiel Sanchez W RTD 5 Barranquilla
31.01.86 Saul Julio W CO 5 Cartagena
14.03.86 Ruben Veliz W CO 2 Bogota
30.04.86 Carlos Trujillo W PTS 10 Barranquilla
17.10.86 Edgar Rodriguez W CO 4 Barranquilla
15.11.86 Sergio Sanchez W CO 3 Barranquilla
(*Vacant Fecarbox Welterweight Title*)
21.12.86 Jorge Manchego W RSC 6 Cartagena
13.02.87 Alberto Lindo W CO 4 Barranquilla
04.04.87 Max Cimarra W CO 3 San Andres
19.06.87 Eduardo Batista W RSC 6 Barranquilla
04.09.87 Simon Ramos W CO 2 Cartagena
24.10.87 Fernando Martinez W RSC 4 Miami
18.12.87 Eduardo Rodriguez W RTD 5 Cartagena
16.04.88 Emiro Olivera W CO 2 San Andres
30.04.88 Erik Perea W RSC 4 Cartagena
Summary: 23 contests, won 23.

John Montes
Los Angeles, USA. *Born* 19.07.61
L. Welterweight

18.10.79 Tim Martinez W RSC 2 Los Angeles
14.12.79 Willie Hall W PTS 5 San Bernardino
04.04.80 Eric Bonilla W PTS 6 San Bernardino
13.05.80 Eric Bonilla W PTS 6 San Bernardino
01.07.80 Gary Vinet W CO 3 San Bernardino
03.07.80 Juan Jiminez W CO 1 Los Angeles
28.08.80 Fidel Fraijo W RSC 6 Los Angeles
16.10.80 Fili Ramirez W PTS 10 Los Angeles
06.11.80 Jose Osuna W RSC 1 Los Angeles
13.12.80 Jerry Venzor W CO 1 El Paso
29.01.81 Carmelo Cruz W CO 2 Los Angeles
11.06.81 Pat Duran W CO 7 Los Angeles
18.07.81 Gustavo Rodriguez W CO 2 Beaumont
24.09.81 Jesus Salcedo W RTD 7 Los Angeles
15.10.81 Roberto Torres W RSC 2 Los Angeles
10.11.81 Arturo Leon W PTS 10 Los Angeles
19.11.81 Memo Arreola W RSC 4 Los Angeles
30.01.82 Rolando Avila W CO 4 Los Angeles
18.03.82 Leo Cruz W RSC 2 Los Angeles
08.04.82 Nacho Jiminez W RTD 2 Los Angeles
22.04.82 Eric Bonilla W RSC 4 Los Angeles
26.06.82 Manuel Abedoy W CO 2 Los Angeles
14.08.82 Hilmer Kenty L PTS 10 Albuquerque
12.02.83 Hector Camacho L CO 1 Anchorage
21.04.83 Dave Sanchez W RSC 2 Los Angeles
26.07.83 Joe Perez W PTS 10 Los Angeles
25.08.83 Sergio Medina W PTS 10 Los Angeles
12.07.84 Sergio Aguirre W RSC 3 Los Angeles
17.10.84 Julio Geraldo W CO 1 Reno
19.12.84 Chuck Peralta W RSC 2 Las Vegas
25.04.85 Tomas Chavez W RSC 4 Los Angeles
14.07.85 Cornelius Boza-Edwards L PTS 10 Tampa
09.03.86 Pernell Whitaker L PTS 10 Hampton
30.06.86 Ricky Lehman W CO 5 Irvine
24.09.86 Ford Jennings W RSC 1 Las Vegas
30.10.86 Martin Quiroz W CO 4 San Jose
12.01.87 Frankie Davis W PTS 10 Long Beach
29.06.87 Eric Martin W PTS 12 Irvine
16.09.87 Walter Sims W CO 2 Long Beach
Summary: 39 contests, won 35, lost 4.

Sung-Il Moon
South Korea
Bantamweight

08.03.87 Ric Bajelot W RSC 4 Seoul
17.05.87 Sakdising Singkungthon W CO 3 Pusan
16.08.87 Constancio Dangla W RSC 3 Mokpo
11.12.87 Tepratum Eakchatching W CO 2 Kwangju
21.02.88 Tony Pruitt W CO 3 Seoul
Summary: 5 contests, won 5.

Piero Morello
Villabate, Italy. *Born* 25.09.63
EBU S. Featherweight Champion. Former Undefeated Italian S. Featherweight Champion

27.02.85 Andrea Ricci W RSC 5 Lucca
16.05.85 Francis Aparicio W PTS 6 Pistoia
05.06.85 Najib Ben Brahim W RSC 3 Lucca
09.07.85 Abdoulaye Ba W RSC 2 Pistoia
27.09.85 Dzavid Mahmutovic W RSC 4 Lucca
26.10.85 Mwilambwe Tshikala W PTS 6 Monte Carlo
19.12.85 Jean-Luc Sautreau W PTS 6 Acona
29.01.86 Fernand Blanco L RSC 3 Catanzaro
26.06.86 Angelo Quintavalle W PTS 6 Giulianello
18.07.86 Faical Naifer W PTS 6 Pistoia
04.09.86 Fathi Kaabi W PTS 6 Silvi
11.10.86 Marco Cordeschi W PTS 6 Cefalu
17.12.86 Ley Umba Sengi W PTS 6 Acqui
14.02.87 Bruno de Montis W PTS 6 Lucca
06.05.87 Ivan Atencio W PTS 6 Lucca
02.08.87 Antonio Renzo W PTS 12 San Felice
(*Vacant Italian S. Featherweight Title*)
20.11.87 Jose A. Garcia W PTS 6 Margine
16.12.87 Julio Garcia W PTS 6 Villabate
17.02.88 Salvatore Curcetti W PTS 12 Brescia
(*EBU S. Featherweight Title Challenge*)
19.03.88 Faical Naifer W RSC 2 Latina
30.04.88 Donnie Parker W PTS 8 Montecatini
Summary: 21 contests, won 20, lost 1.

John (The Beast) Mugabi
England. *Born* Kampala, Uganda 04.03.60
L. Middleweight

05.12.80 Omar Karadenis W RSC 1 Cologne
13.02.81 Paolo Piras W RSC 2 Kiel
10.04.81 Mauro Hernandez W RTD 4 Kiel
11.05.81 Dennis Pryce W CO 1 London
30.05.81 Pedro Guerrero W RSC 2 Las Vegas
25.09.81 Ron Ford W CO 1 Cologne
31.10.81 John Mwamba W CO 1 Lusaka
16.11.81 Darwin Brewster W RSC 6 London
26.12.81 Sammy Floyd W CO 2 Gelsenkirchen
26.03.82 Curtis Taylor W CO 2 Kiel
02.05.82 Curtis Ramsey W RSC 1 Atlantic City
15.09.82 Steve Williams W RSC 4 New York
23.10.82 Doug Demmings W CO 5 Kiel
15.05.83 Roosevelt Green W RSC 1 Las Vegas
03.07.83 Gary Guiden W RSC 3 Tampa
05.08.83 Jeff Nelson W RSC 2 Tampa
16.09.83 Don Morgan W CO 1 Tampa
08.10.83 Eddie Gazo W RSC 4 Atlantic City
12.11.83 Curtis Parker W RSC 1 Tampa
19.02.84 James Green W RSC 10 Tampa
27.05.84 Wilbert Johnson W RSC 2 Maracaibo

05.08.84 Frank Fletcher W RSC 4 Tampa
25.09.84 Nino Gonzalez W CO 1 London
17.03.85 Earl Hargrove W RSC 1 Tampa
06.08.85 Brian Bradley W RSC 4 Atlantic City
10.03.86 Marvin Hagler L CO 11 Las Vegas
(World Middleweight Title Challenge)
05.12.86 Duane Thomas L RSC 3 Las Vegas
(Vacant WBC L. Middleweight Title)
22.01.88 Bryan Grant W RSC 2 Atlantic City
Summary: 28 contests, won 26, lost 2.

Takuya Muguruma
Osaka, Japan. *Born* 16.01.61
Former WBA Bantamweight Champion. Former Undefeated Japanese S. Bantamweight Champion

09.04.81 Kenji Miyagi W CO 2 Wakayama
28.05.81 Masamitsu Haruyama W PTS 4 Osaka
21.06.81 Wolf Yoshizaki W RSC 1 Wakayama
12.09.81 Tadashi Kouno W PTS 4 Osaka
07.12.81 Jun Yamaguchi W RSC 4 Kyoto
15.02.82 Mitsuru Sugitani W PTS 6 Osaka
19.06.82 Kenzu Takasugi W PTS 6 Iizuka
23.08.82 Sumihiro Suda W RSC 1 Kochi
01.10.82 Masayoshi Katayama W PTS 8 Tokyo
24.01.83 Kenzu Sugitani W RSC 6 Osaka
24.02.83 Masataka Katayama W RSC 2 Tsu
08.04.83 Fusao Imai W RSC 4 Tokyo
17.05.83 Kazumi Sato W CO 4 Kochi
08.09.83 Shojo Tabata W CO 1 Osaka
29.11.83 Hiroyuki Iwamoto W CO 4 Tokyo
(Japanese S. Bantamweight Title Challenge)
15.03.84 Kaoru Yoshioka W CO 3 Osaka
(Japanese S. Bantamweight Title Defence)
12.06.84 Kenji Kawamura W PTS 10 Tokyo
(Japanese S. Bantamweight Title Defence)
15.09.84 Masahide Ikehara W RSC 4 Osaka
(Japanese S. Bantamweight Title Defence)
04.12.84 Eiji Oyama DREW 10 Osaka
(Japanese S. Bantamweight Title Defence)
09.03.85 Yun-Kap Choi L PTS 12 Seoul
(Vacant OPBF S. Bantamweight Title)
24.06.85 Satoshi Koguchi W RSC 5 Osaka
(Japanese S. Bantamweight Title Defence)
29.10.85 Satoshi Okuma W RSC 2 Shiga
(Japanese S. Bantamweight Title Defence)
06.02.86 Kazuo Osamu W CO 5 Osaka
(Japanese S. Bantamweight Title Defence)
30.03.86 Sam-Yong Kim W CO 3 Itami Shi
21.08.86 Yun-Kap Choi W RSC 2 Osaka
03.12.86 Kyu-Chan Cho W RSC 2 Osaka
29.03.87 Azael Moran W CO 5 Moriguchi
(Vacant WBA Bantamweight Title)
24.05.87 Chan-Yung Park L RSC 11 Moriguchi
(WBA Bantamweight Title Defence)
09.09.87 Tom Ramos W CO 7 Osaka
17.01.88 Wilfredo Vasquez DREW 12 Osaka
(WBA Bantamweight Title Challenge)
Summary: 30 contests, won 26, drew 2, lost 2.

Benedicto Murillo
Colon, Panama
L. Flyweight

17.04.82 Martin Barcenas W PTS 4 Panama City
19.06.82 Adan White W PTS 4 Panama City
31.07.82 Victor Sierra W PTS 4 Colon
26.03.83 Ruben Aguirre W DIS 2 Colon
29.10.83 Wilbert Martinez W RSC 2 Colon
19.11.83 Julio Gudino W PTS 8 Panama City
17.12.83 Antonio Mitre W PTS 10 Colon
05.05.84 Jose de Jesus L RSC 7 Guaynabo
14.12.84 Leonardo Paredes W PTS 10 Colon
19.07.85 Virgilio Chifundo L PTS 12 Colon
(Latin American L. Flyweight Title Challenge)
27.09.85 Rodolfo Blanco DREW 10 Barranquilla
18.10.85 Agustin Garcia DREW 10 Cartagena
14.12.85 Virgilio Chifundo T DRAW 4 Panama City
31.01.86 Eduardo Tunon W PTS 10 Panama City
10.03.86 Virgilio Chifundo W PTS 10 Panama City
06.12.86 Carlos Orobio W CO 2 Panama City
26.02.87 Leonardo Paredes W PTS 10 Panama City
07.06.87 Myung-Woo Yuh L RSC 15 Pusan
(WBA L. Flyweight Title Challenge)
Summary: 18 contests, won 12, drew 3, lost 3.

Shunichi Nakajima
Nagasaki, Japan. *Born* 27.02.61
Japanese S. Flyweight Champion

12.06.84 Michihiro Saga W RSC 3 Tokyo
21.08.84 Kazuichi Murata W RSC 3 Tokyo
25.09.84 Masakatsu Toyooka W PTS 6 Tokyo
29.01.85 Shunji Tsuchiya W CO 2 Tokyo
22.04.85 Kazuki Higa W CO 4 Tokyo
29.06.85 Kwang-Joo Park W CO 3 Seoul
24.09.85 Tadashi Maruo L PTS 10 Tokyo
(Vacant Japanese S. Flyweight Title)
03.12.85 Hiroshi Yamamoto W PTS 10 Tokyo
15.03.86 Rae-Ki Ahn L PTS 10 Seoul
23.07.86 Yukito Tamakuma L PTS 6 Tokyo
21.10.86 Kazuo Katsuma W PTS 10 Tokyo
22.01.87 Hiroshi Yamamoto W PTS 10 Tokyo
26.05.87 Makoto Sawamura W RSC 5 Tokyo
25.06.87 Yasutaka Sakurai W PTS 6 Tokyo
29.08.87 Byong-Kwan Chung L PTS 12 Chungju
(OPBF S. Flyweight Title Challenge)
22.10.87 Masayuki Takahashi W CO 5 Tokyo
01.12.87 Shinji Ozawa W RSC 6 Tokyo
01.03.88 Koji Nishikawa W PTS 10 Tokyo
(Japanese S. Flyweight Title Challenge)
12.04.88 Jun Hoki W CO 8 Tokyo
Summary: 19 contests, won 15, lost 4.

Valerio Nati
Dovadola, Italy. *Born* 11.04.56
Former Undefeated EBU Featherweight Champion. Former EBU Bantamweight Champion. Former Undefeated Italian Bantamweight Champion

07.04.78 Domenico Palumbo W PTS 6 Faenza
19.05.78 Luigi Paravati W RSC 2 Forli
06.07.78 Antonio Franca W RTD 4 Lugo
19.07.78 Domenico Palumbo W RSC 3 Bellaria
21.10.78 Giulio Greco W CO 5 Pesaro
03.11.78 Salvatore Laconi W RSC 3 Forli
26.12.78 Nessim Zebellini W PTS 8 Bologna
13.04.79 Abdelkader Esmain W PTS 8 Forli
08.06.79 Luigi Tessarin W PTS 8 Ravenna
11.10.79 Helenio Ferreira DREW 8 Faenza
30.11.79 Giuseppe Fossati W PTS 12 Forli
(Italian Bantamweight Title Challenge)
15.03.80 Claudio Tanda W CO 1 Forli
24.04.80 Franco Buglione W RSC 3 Forli
31.05.80 Eloi da Silva W PTS 8 Sassari
06.08.80 Antonio Franca W RSC 5 Silvi
03.12.80 Juan Francisco Rodriguez W PTS 12 Forli
(Vacant EBU Bantamweight Title)
14.02.81 Dominique Cesari W PTS 8 Sassari
01.04.81 Vicente Rodriguez W RSC 5 Rome
(EBU Bantamweight Title Defence)
17.06.81 John Feeney W PTS 12 Cervia
(EBU Bantamweight Title Defence)
02.09.81 Jean-Jacques Souris W CO 2 Stintino
(EBU Bantamweight Title Defence)
20.11.81 Luis de la Sagra W PTS 12 Campobello
(EBU Bantamweight Title Defence)
27.01.82 Esteban Eguia W RSC 5 Castrocaro
(EBU Bantamweight Title Defence)
28.04.82 Giuseppe Fossati L PTS 12 Lignano
(EBU Bantamweight Title Defence)
10.11.82 Richard Saka DREW 8 Sassari
05.01.83 Mariano Garcia W RSC 1 Forio
24.02.83 Giuseppe Fossati DREW 12 Bologna
(EBU Bantamweight Title Challenge)
03.06.83 Richard Saka DREW 8 Porto Ferraio
05.08.83 Loris Stecca L PTS 12 Camaiore
(EBU Featherweight Title Challenge)
16.11.83 Barry McGuigan L CO 6 Belfast
(Vacant EBU Featherweight Title)
13.04.84 Vicente Fernandez W RSC 5 Milan
26.05.84 Orlando Maldonado W RSC 5 Guaynabo
02.07.84 Manuel Santos W PTS 8 Milan
06.10.84 Maurizio Lupino W PTS 8 Carrara
01.03.85 Ley Umba-Sengy W PTS 8 Forli
12.04.85 Julio Garcia W CO 1 Forli
08.06.85 Billy Hardy W RSC 4 Florence
09.07.85 Luis de la Sagra W CO 3 Forli
12.12.85 Ruben Palacios W PTS 10 Milan
26.12.85 Danny Lee W RSC 2 Modena
14.02.86 Steve Cleak W RSC 4 Milan
26.04.86 John Farrell W PTS 8 Lucca
20.06.86 Sonny Long W PTS 8 Paris
10.10.86 Chris Diaz W RSC 7 Cesena
13.03.87 Marc Armand W RSC 2 Forli
(Vacant EBU Featherweight Title)
22.05.87 Carlos Segura W CO 1 Jesi
24.07.87 Vincenzo Limatola W DIS 7 Silvi Mariani
(EBU Featherweight Title Defence)
21.11.87 Jose Hernandez W RSC 1 Trezzano
27.02.88 Ricky West W CO 2 San Juan
Summary: 48 contests, won 41, drew 4, lost 3.

George (Go Go) Navarro
New Jersey, USA. *Born* 11.05.65
Featherweight

17.05.83 Jim Woodhouse W PTS 4 Atlantic City
15.06.83 Angel Lopez L PTS 4 West Orange
09.08.83 Tony Coleman W RSC 1 Atlantic City
17.01.84 A. D. Wiggins W PTS 4 Atlantic City
01.03.84 Ewart Chance W RSC 1 Atlantic City
08.05.84 Doug Pettiford W PTS 6 Wilmington
04.09.84 Chester Richardson W PTS 6 Atlantic City
23.10.84 Derrick Wilkerson W RSC 3 Atlantic City
05.02.85 Mike Brown W PTS 6 Atlantic City
01.03.85 Mark Perea W RSC 6 Atlantic City
22.08.85 Tom Elston W RSC 5 Chicago
11.10.85 Benny Marquez W PTS 8 Chicago
21.03.86 Rene Resto W PTS 8 Atlantic City
20.06.86 Aristides Acevedo W PTS 10 Atlantic City
15.08.86 Hector Lopez W PTS 12 Atlantic City
16.03.87 Vince Christian W PTS 10 Los Angeles
30.06.87 Jaime Garza W PTS 10 Los Angeles
01.10.87 Hector Lopez L TD 2 Los Angeles
Summary: 18 contests, won 16, lost 2.

Jimmy Navarro
Peter Goldfield/USA

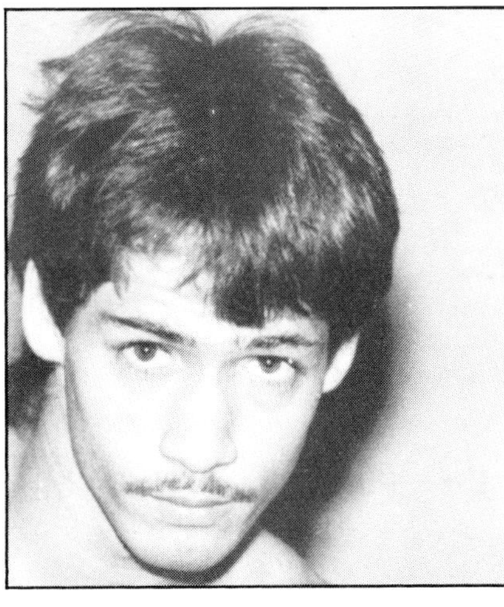

Jimmy Navarro
Miami, USA. *Born* 01.12.63
Bantamweight

10.11.84 Mauricio Guadamez W CO 2 Miami
15.12.84 Teo Centeno W RSC 3 Miami
02.02.85 Eddie Leanos W CO 1 Miami
12.02.85 Juan Molina W CO 1 Miami
29.03.85 Jorge Acosta W RSC 4 Miami
10.05.85 Dan Daniels W RSC 1 Miami
24.05.85 Melvin Miller W CO 3 Miami
28.06.85 Terry Pizzaro W RSC 6 Miami
24.08.85 Jorge Acosta W PTS 8 Miami
12.12.85 Teo Centeno W PTS 6 Miami
07.02.86 Ernesto Guerra W CO 3 Hialeah
04.03.86 Tony Pruitt W PTS 6 Atlantic City
18.04.86 Troy Fletcher W RSC 7 Atlantic City
20.06.86 Darryl Thigpen L RSC 4 Atlantic City
12.09.86 Tom Elston W PTS 8 Fort Lauderdale
24.10.86 Joe Paul W CO 1 Fort Lauderdale
14.11.86 Carlos Lopez W CO 6 Fort Lauderdale
30.01.87 Rolando Luna W RSC 4 Fort Lauderdale
20.03.87 Alberto Gonzalez W CO 1 Bridgetown
22.05.87 Temo Villanueva W RSC 2 Miami
18.09.87 David Gauvin W PTS 10 Atlantic City
04.12.87 Mando Trevino W RSC 1 Hialeah
Summary: 22 contests, won 21, lost 1.

Juan Nazario
Guaynabo, Puerto Rico. *Born* 27.09.63
Latin American Lightweight Champion

17.04.82 Edgar Cirino W PTS 4 San Juan
08.05.82 Roberto Ortiz W PTS 4 San Juan

24.07.82 Carlos Velez W PTS 4 San Juan
21.08.82 Rafael Pichardo W RSC 3 San Juan
15.09.82 Tom Tripp W CO 2 Aruba
02.10.82 Adrian Arreola L PTS 8 Las Vegas
04.03.83 Davey Lopez W CO 4 Curacao
01.05.83 Angel Lopez W PTS 6 San Juan
18.08.83 Sammy Fuentes W RSC 5 Trujillo
11.09.83 Jose Jimenez W CO 5 Port of Spain
03.02.84 Eduardo Prieto W RSC 9 Miami
17.03.84 Jose Vidal W RSC 9 San Juan
(Latin American Lightweight Title Challenge)
20.06.84 Carlos Albuerne W RSC 10 San Juan
14.09.84 Freddie Chumpitaz W PTS 10 Miami
19.12.84 Rosendo Ramirez W RSC 5 Las Vegas
28.06.85 Geronimo Luquez W PTS 10 Miami
23.08.86 Sammy Johnson W RSC 3 Miami
26.09.86 Jose Mosqueda W RTD 5 Miami
11.08.87 Edwin Rosario L CO 8 Chicago
(WBA Lightweight Title Defence)
Summary: 19 contests, won 17, lost 2.

Azumah Nelson

Accra, Ghana. *Born* 19.07.58
WBC S. Featherweight Champion. Former Undefeated WBC Featherweight Champion. Former Undefeated Ghanaian, ABU & Commonwealth Featherweight Champion

01.12.79 Billy Kwame W PTS 10 Accra
10.02.80 Henry Saddler W CO 9 Accra
(Ghanaian Featherweight Title Challenge)
17.04.80 Henry Optoki W CO 8 Accra
04.07.80 David Capo W PTS 10 Accra
11.09.80 Nii Nuer W CO 3 Accra
13.12.80 Joe Skipper W RSC 10 Accra
(ABU Featherweight Title Challenge)
24.02.81 Bossou Aziza W PTS 10 Lome
02.05.81 Don George W CO 5 Accra
18.08.81 Miguel Ruiz W RSC 3 Bakersfield
26.09.81 Brian Roberts W CO 5 Accra
(Vacant Commonwealth Featherweight Title)
04.12.81 Kabiru Akindele W CO 6 Freetown
(ABU & Commonwealth Featherweight Title Defence)
28.02.82 Charm Chiteule W RSC 10 Lusaka
(ABU & Commonwealth Featherweight Title Defence)
26.06.82 Mukaila Bukare W RSC 6 Accra
21.07.82 Salvador Sanchez L RSC 15 New York
(WBC Featherweight Title Challenge)
31.10.82 Irving Mitchell W RSC 5 McAfee
12.02.83 Ricky Wallace W PTS 10 Cleveland
17.08.83 Alvin Fowler W RSC 2 Las Vegas
23.09.83 Alberto Collazo W RSC 2 Richfield
02.11.83 Kabiru Akindele W CO 9 Lagos
(ABU & Commonwealth Featherweight Title Defence)
09.03.84 Hector Cortez W PTS 10 Las Vegas
08.12.84 Wilfredo Gomez W RSC 11 San Juan
(WBC Featherweight Title Challenge)
06.09.85 Juvenal Ordenes W CO 5 Miami
(WBC Featherweight Title Defence)
12.10.85 Pat Cowdell W CO 1 Birmingham
(WBC Featherweight Title Defence)
25.02.86 Marcos Villasana W PTS 12 Los Angeles
(WBC Featherweight Title Defence)
22.06.86 Danilo Cabrera W RSC 10 San Juan
(WBC Featherweight Title Defence)
07.03.87 Mauro Gutierrez W CO 6 Las Vegas
(WBC Featherweight Title Defence)
29.08.87 Marcos Villasana W PTS 12 Los Angeles
(WBC Featherweight Title Defence)
29.02.88 Mario Martinez W PTS 12 Los Angeles
(Vacant WBC S. Featherweight Title)
Summary: 28 contests, won 27, lost 1.

Daniel Netto

Coronel Pringles, Argentine. *Born* 16.02.61
Argentinian Cruiserweight Champion

12.11.83 Raul Paez W CO 2 Coronel Pringles
21.09.84 Alberto Ubelar W PTS 6 Parana
20.10.84 Raul Venturelli W PTS 6 Parana
14.12.84 Raul Venturelli W DIS 7 Coronel Pringles
06.09.85 Miguel Cea W CO 3 Trelew
31.01.86 Simon Ramirez W PTS 8 Mar del Plata
08.03.86 Hector Rohr W DIS 2 Coronel Pringles
10.05.86 Victor Robledo DREW 10 Coronel Pringles

Daniel Netto

07.09.86 Hector Rohr W CO 8 Coronel Pringles
(Argentinian Cruiserweight Title Challenge)
11.12.86 Jose Helguera W PTS 12 Tucuman
(Argentinian Cruiserweight Title Defence)
17.05.87 Anibal Perez W RSC 6 Coronel Pringles
19.07.87 Alberto Barragan W CO 5 Coronel Pringles
18.09.87 Jorge Dascola W PTS 12 Cordoba
(Argentinian Cruiserweight Title Defence)
Summary: 13 contests, won 12, drew 1.

Tusikoleta Nkalankete

France. *Born* Zaire 03.03.58
EBU L. Welterweight Champion. Former Undefeated French L. Welterweight Champion

26.03.79 Mauricio Fico W PTS 6 Paris
07.06.79 Jean-Marie Kante W PTS 6 Paris
15.06.79 Francis Bailleul W PTS 6 Conde
31.08.79 Isidoro Cabeza DREW 8 Madrid
16.02.80 Roberto Castanon L PTS 8 Leon
07.03.80 Jose Luis Pacheco L PTS 8 Palma
14.03.80 Andre Holyk W PTS 8 Lyons
13.06.80 Perico Fernandez W PTS 8 Palma
14.11.80 Jean Symos W RSC 8 Grivegne
02.02.81 Rene Martin W RSC 2 Paris
28.06.81 Payson Cholwe W PTS 10 Lusaka
21.09.81 Lloyd Hibbert L PTS 8 Wolverhampton
14.12.81 Joey Mack W PTS 8 Paris
14.08.82 Ramon Gomez-Fouz L PTS 8 Gijon
03.12.82 Carlos Foldes W DIS 7 Paris
(Vacant French L. Welterweight Title)
10.09.83 Rene Weller L PTS 8 Cologne
05.11.83 Didier Kowalski W RSC 7 Lille
(French L. Welterweight Title Defence)
02.03.84 Mohamed Lazmany DREW 12 Toulon
(French L. Welterweight Title Defence)
04.09.84 Patrizio Oliva L PTS 12 Acciaroli
(EBU L. Welterweight Title Challenge)
29.03.85 Antoine Vivarelli W RTD 9 Antibes
(French L. Welterweight Title Defence)
07.06.85 Philippe Arrendel W PTS 10 Cleon
(French L. Welterweight Title Defence)
14.03.86 Karim Rabbi W CO 3 Bordeaux
(French L. Welterweight Title Defence)
22.01.86 Terry Marsh L PTS 12 London
(EBU L. Welterweight Title Challenge)
15.05.86 Carlos Prieto DREW 8 Paris
03.08.86 Victor Acosta W RTD 4 Monte Carlo
06.02.87 Tony Laing W RSC 9 Antibes
(Vacant EBU L. Welterweight Title)
22.04.87 Alessandro Scapecchi W RSC 6 Catenia
(EBU L. Welterweight Title Defence)
03.10.87 Mohammed Kawoya W CO 3 Gravelines
(EBU L. Welterweight Title Defence)
Summary: 28 contests, won 18, drew 3, lost 7.

Orlin (Boscoe Bear) Norris

Lubbock, USA. *Born* 04.10.65
NABF Heavyweight Champion

16.06.86 Lionel Washington W RSC 3 Bakersfield
25.07.86 Levi Billups W RSC 1 San Diego
02.08.86 Olian Alexander L PTS 4 San Jose
18.09.86 Kenny Mitchell W PTS 4 San Diego
25.09.86 Ricky Reese W RSC 1 Irvine
28.10.86 Mike Bardwell W PTS 6 Reseda
21.11.86 David Smith W PTS 4 Reseda
05.02.87 Roger Troupe W RSC 2 Riverside
12.02.87 Rufus Hadley W PTS 10 Las Vegas
26.02.87 Mike Gans W CO 7 San Diego
20.03.87 Avery Rawls W PTS 10 Las Vegas
03.04.87 Eddie Richardson W CO 2 Las Vegas
27.05.87 Gary Lightbourne W PTS 10 Cleveland
13.08.87 Jean Barbie W CO 1 Los Angeles
04.09.87 Bill Thomas W RSC 3 Las Vegas
25.11.87 Larry Alexander W PTS 12 Las Vegas
(NABF Heavyweight Title Challenge)
23.02.88 Woody Clark W RSC 1 Reseda
19.03.88 Renaldo Snipes W PTS 12 Las Vegas
(NABF Heavyweight Title Defence)
Summary: 18 contests, won 17, lost 1.

Horace Notice

Birmingham, England. *Born* 07.08.57
British & Commonwealth Heavyweight Champion

24.10.83 Andrew Gerrard W PTS 6 London
30.11.83 Theo Josephs W CO 1 London
27.04.84 Andrew Gerrard W RSC 2 Wolverhampton
26.10.84 Paddy Finn W RSC 3 Wolverhampton
27.11.84 Winston Allen W PTS 6 Wembley
26.03.85 Bob Young W RSC 2 Wembley
03.10.85 Noel Quarless W CO 7 Liverpool
16.10.85 Anaclet Wamba W PTS 8 London
04.03.86 Curtis Jones W CO 2 Wembley
12.04.86 Hughroy Currie W RSC 6 Isle of Man
(British Heavyweight Title Challenge & Vacant Commonwealth Heavyweight Title)
07.05.86 Mike Jameson W PTS 10 London
04.03.87 Proud Kilimanjaro W RSC 8 Dudley
(Commonwealth Heavyweight Title Defence)
26.05.87 Dave Garside W RSC 5 Wembley
(British & Commonwealth Heavyweight Title Defence)
03.11.87 Paul Lister W CO 3 Sunderland
(British & Commonwealth Heavyweight Title Defence)
02.12.87 Dean Waters W RSC 4 Wembley
(Commonwealth Heavyweight Title Defence)
09.03.88 Hughroy Currie W RSC 10 London
(British & Commonwealth Heavyweight Title Defence)
Summary: 16 contests, won 16.

Michael Nunn

Iowa, USA. *Born* 14.04.63
NABF Middleweight Champion

20.12.84 John Borman W RSC 1 Las Vegas
08.02.85 Ismael Templos W RSC 4 Stateline
26.03.85 Robert Jackson W CO 1 Reseda
11.04.85 Carlos Campos W RSC 1 Las Vegas
21.05.85 I. W. Johnson W CO 1 Reseda
27.06.85 Larry Davis W RSC 2 Las Vegas
29.07.85 James Waire W RSC 3 Reseda
27.08.85 Marcos Geraldo W RSC 5 Reseda
25.09.85 Charles Campbell W PTS 8 Las Vegas
13.11.85 Jorge Amparo W PTS 8 Las Vegas
10.12.85 Billy Robertson W PTS 10 Los Angeles
28.01.86 Alvaro Granillo W RSC 2 Reseda
10.02.86 Charles Carter W RSC 3 Los Angeles
09.03.86 Carl Jones W PTS 10 Las Vegas
19.05.86 Felipe Vaca W RSC 4 Reseda
25.06.86 Randy Smith W PTS 10 Los Angeles
23.07.86 Charlie Boston W PTS 10 Las Vegas
19.09.86 Mike Tinley W PTS 10 Atlantic City
28.10.86 Orlando Paulding W CO 1 Reseda
21.11.86 Alex Ramos W PTS 12 Reseda
06.02.87 Willie Harris W RSC 6 Reseda
04.04.87 Charles Campbell W RSC 9 Las Vegas
24.04.87 Cecil Pettigrew W RSC 5 Davenport
02.07.87 Jose Duarte W RSC 2 Reseda
11.08.87 Frankie Owens W RSC 9 Las Vegas
11.09.87 Dale Jackson W PTS 10 Davenport
29.10.87 Darnell Knox W RSC 4 Las Vegas
(Vacant NABF Middleweight Title)
02.01.88 Kevin Watts W PTS 12 Reseda
(NABF Middleweight Title Defence)
19.03.88 Curtis Parker W CO 2 Las Vegas
(NABF Middleweight Title Defence)
Summary: 29 contests, won 29.

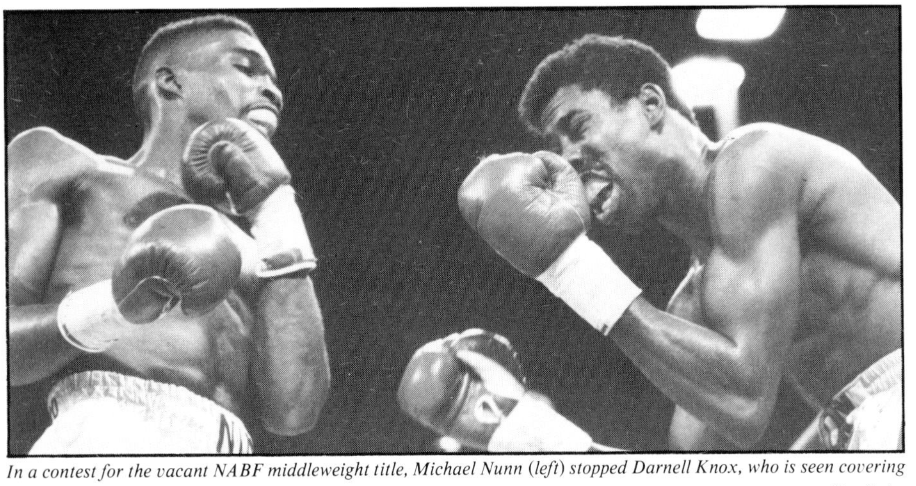

In a contest for the vacant NABF middleweight title, Michael Nunn (left) stopped Darnell Knox, who is seen covering up
Tom Casino

Charles (Young Dick Tiger) Nwokolo
Nigeria. *Born* 21.09.64
ABU Welterweight Champion

02.12.84 King Zoro W CO 4 Benin
03.03.85 Sammy Clay W CO 5 Lagos
26.04.85 Sunny Porne W CO 3 Lagos
02.06.85 Tooboy Breeks W CO 7 Benin
03.07.85 Collins Omozgaha W CO 5 Lagos
09.08.85 Tim Fantoma W CO 3 Benin
29.08.85 Sunny Bruce W CO 4 Kano
15.10.85 John Zu W CO 6 Lagos
30.10.85 Paul King W CO 7 Lagos
15.11.85 Amor Amissah W CO 8 Lagos
30.11.85 Yakina Taiwo W CO 11 Lagos
17.01.86 Adekunle Tytler W PTS 8 Lagos
02.05.86 Fighting Romanus W PTS 12 Lagos
(*Nigerian Welterweight Title Challenge*)
27.06.86 Judas Clottey W PTS 12 Lagos
(*ABU Welterweight Title Challenge*)
24.09.86 Rigoberto Lopez W PTS 10 Universal City
22.10.86 Jaime Montano W RSC 6 Los Angeles
14.11.86 Felipe Canela L PTS 12 Universal City
09.12.86 Dionsio Castillo W CO 2 Universal City
21.02.87 Antonio Espinal W CO 1 Lake Tahoe
27.04.87 Manning Galloway W PTS 12 Los Angeles
30.06.87 Bobby Joe Young W PTS 10 Los Angeles
17.07.87 Razor Addo Akwa W CO 9 Lagos
(*ABU Welterweight Title Defence*)
24.11.87 Diomedes Colome L PTS 10 Los Angeles
12.12.87 Rollin Williams L PTS 12 Phoenix
(*USBA Welterweight Title Challenge*)
20.04.88 Rigoberto Lopez W PTS 10 San Diego
Summary: 25 contests, won 22, lost 3.

Fully Obelmejias
San Jose, Venezuela. *Born* 01.01.53
Former Latin American L. Heavyweight Champion.
Former Undefeated Fecarbox Middleweight Champion

30.01.77 Franklyn Suzarra W RSC 1 Caracas
03.04.77 Franklyn Suzarra W RSC 2 Caracas
22.10.77 Jesus Garza W CO 9 Mexico City
18.11.77 Andre Beard W CO 2 San Diego
17.12.77 Rogelio Vera W RTD 2 Mexico City
04.02.78 Vicente Pinon W CO 2 Mexico City
28.02.78 Abel Cordova W PTS 10 Tuxtla
06.04.78 Rudy Robles W RSC 4 Tijuana
30.04.78 Rolando Martinez W RSC 1 Caracas
04.06.78 Jose Anglada W CO 1 Caracas
15.07.78 Sandy Torres W CO 4 Caracas
29.07.78 Willie Warren W RSC 8 Caracas
17.09.78 Johnny Heard W RSC 8 Caracas
12.11.78 Ken Blackwell W RSC 3 Caracas
17.12.78 Carlos Marks W RSC 9 Caracas
(*Fecarbox Middleweight Title Challenge*)
11.02.79 Angel Ortiz W CO 3 Caracas
01.04.79 Jaime Thomas W CO 4 Caracas
07.08.79 Luis Arias W CO 2 Caracas
(*Fecarbox Middleweight Title Defence*)
15.09.79 Sammy Floyd W RSC 10 Caracas
26.10.79 George Lee W RSC 3 Caracas
17.12.79 Ray Phillips W RSC 4 Caracas
03.03.80 Elisha Obed W RSC 3 Caracas
01.04.80 Abel Cordova W CO 2 Caracas
14.04.80 Walter Miranda W CO 1 Caracas
26.05.80 Lamont Lovelady W PTS 10 Caracas
30.06.80 Clifford Wills W RSC 3 Caracas
18.08.80 Felton Marshall W PTS 10 Caracas
10.09.80 Freddie Johnson W RSC 3 San Remo
31.10.80 Leroy Green W RSC 3 Rome
28.11.80 James Waire W RSC 3 Campione
17.01.81 Marvin Hagler L RSC 8 Boston
(*World Middleweight Title Challenge*)
04.05.81 Norberto Cabrera W CO 5 Caracas
30.05.81 Joe Gonsalvez W RSC 2 Caracas
31.08.81 Wayne Barker W RSC 2 Caracas
05.10.81 Eddie Gazo W CO 2 Caracas
07.11.81 Chong-Pal Park W RSC 8 Caracas
15.02.82 Johnny Wise W CO 2 Caracas
14.06.82 Reyes Escalera W CO 2 Barquisimeto
09.08.82 Willie Torres W RSC 8 Porlamar
30.10.82 Marvin Hagler L CO 5 San Remo
(*World Middleweight Title Challenge*)
22.10.83 Raymond Gonzalez W CO 4 St Vincent
14.12.83 Jeff Lampkin W PTS 8 Loano
25.02.84 Jerry Celestine W PTS 8 Paris
24.03.84 Henry Sims W CO 4 Chiavari
28.04.84 Arthel Lawhorne W PTS 8 Naples
14.07.84 Cesar Romero W PTS 8 Monte Carlo
22.09.84 Eric Winbush W PTS 8 Monte Carlo
15.12.84 Leon Taylor W CO 2 Catanzaro
21.07.85 Clarence Osby L PTS 8 Campione
30.05.86 Tomas Polo W PTS 12 Isla Margarita
(*Vacant Latin American L. Heavyweight Title*)
15.11.86 Leslie Stewart L RSC 4 Port of Spain
(*Latin American L. Heavyweight Title Defence*)
18.06.87 Chris Reid W RSC 10 New York
Summary: 52 contests, won 48, lost 4.

Ossie (Jaws) Ocasio
Puerto Rico. *Born* 12.08.55
Former WBA Cruiserweight Champion

20.02.76 Lorenzo Simons W RSC 3 San Juan
05.04.76 Rafael Guerrero W RSC 2 San Juan
25.04.76 Joe Renee W CO 1 San Juan
19.07.76 Ed Turner W PTS 8 San Juan
16.08.76 Aaron Solomon W RSC 2 San Juan
12.02.77 Ed Turner W CO 1 Bayamon
17.03.77 Gene Idolette W CO 1 San Juan
14.06.77 Clarence Norris W CO 2 Orlando
25.06.77 Frank Schram W RSC 4 Bayamon
12.07.77 Tommy Nickson W RSC 4 Orlando
08.04.78 Kevin Isaac W PTS 10 Bayamon
09.06.78 Jimmy Young W PTS 10 Las Vegas
28.01.79 Jimmy Young W PTS 10 San Juan
23.03.79 Larry Holmes L RSC 7 Las Vegas
20.11.79 Jack Sterling W CO 1 Miami
19.04.80 Michael Dokes DREW 10 San Juan
28.06.80 Michael Dokes L RSC 1 San Juan
23.10.80 Barry Funches W PTS 10 New York
17.03.81 John L. Gardner L CO 6 Wembley
13.02.82 Robbie Williams W PTS 15 Johannesburg
(*Vacant WBA Cruiserweight Title*)
15.12.82 Young Joe Louis W PTS 15 Chicago
(*WBA Cruiserweight Title Defence*)
20.05.83 Randy Stephens W PTS 15 Las Vegas
(*WBA Cruiserweight Title Defence*)
05.05.84 John Odhiambo W RSC 15 San Juan
(*WBA Cruiserweight Title Defence*)
01.12.84 Piet Crous L PTS 15 Sun City
(*WBA Cruiserweight Title Defence*)
23.03.86 Sixto Maldonado W PTS 10 Reno
15.05.87 Dwight Muhammad Qawi W PTS 10 Las Vegas
15.08.87 Evander Holyfield L RSC 11 St Tropez
(*WBA & IBF Cruiserweight Title Challenge*)
06.03.88 Pierre Coetzer W PTS 10 Captetown
Summary: 28 contests, won 22, drew 1, lost 5.

Hideyuki Ohashi
Yokohama, Japan. *Born* 08.03.65
Japanese L. Flyweight Champion

12.02.85 Masakatsu Aikata W RSC 1 Tokyo
07.05.85 Hideto Osanai W PTS 8 Tokyo
27.08.85 Tadashi Kuramochi W RSC 1 Tokyo
03.12.85 Masato Tanaka W CO 3 Tokyo
20.03.86 Bon-Jun Kim L PTS 10 Tokyo
23.06.86 Yoshiaki Nojima W PTS 10 Tokyo
(*Vacant Japanese L. Flyweight Title*)
14.12.86 Jung-Koo Chang L RSC 5 Inchon
(*WBC L. Flyweight Title Challenge*)
07.04.87 Masato Tanaka W CO 3 Tokyo
08.09.87 Yasutaka Sakurai W PTS 10 Tokyo
11.01.88 Tomohiro Kiyuna W PTS 10 Tokyo
(*Japanese L. Flyweight Title Challenge*)
Summary: 10 contests, won 8, lost 2.

Michael Olajide
Peter Goldfield/USA

Michael (The Silk) Olajide
Vancouver, Canada. *Born* Liverpool, England 08.12.63
Former Undefeated Con. Am. & Canadian Middleweight Champion

17.01.82 Johnny Gaines W CO 1 Victoria
07.02.82 Dale Dorset W RSC 3 Victoria
05.03.82 Don Oversby W CO 1 Victoria
17.06.82 Al Ford W PTS 8 Burnaby
24.03.83 Roosevelt Green W RSC 6 Vancouver
13.08.83 Tom Briscoe W CO 1 Kelowna
13.10.83 Joe Banks W CO 2 New Westminster
25.11.83 Stacy McSwain W PTS 8 Vancouver
12.03.84 Lancelot Innis W CO 4 New Westminster
10.05.84 Leonardo Bermudez W RSC 2 New Westminster
18.08.84 Rosendo Rubalcaba W PTS 10 Burnaby
10.04.85 Wayne Caplette W RSC 9 Vancouver
(*Vacant Canadian Middleweight Title*)
11.07.85 Reyes Escalera W RSC 5 Vancouver
10.08.85 Sakarai Ve W CO 9 Fiji
29.11.85 Elio Diaz W RSC 7 Vancouver
11.01.86 Curtis Parker W PTS 10 Atlantic City
10.04.86 James Green W PTS 10 Atlantic City
05.06.86 Randy Smith W PTS 10 Los Angeles
28.08.86 Knox Brown W RSC 9 New York
30.10.86 Ray Ray Gray W RSC 10 Atlantic City
08.01.87 Richard Burton W RSC 4 New York
(*Vacant Con. Am. Middleweight Title*)
01.02.87 Don Lee W RSC 9 Atlantic City
10.05.87 Troy Darrell W PTS 10 Atlantic City
10.10.87 Frank Tate L PTS 15 Las Vegas
(*Vacant IBF Middleweight Title*)
17.12.87 Frankie Owens W RSC 6 New York
04.02.88 Cecil Pettigrew W PTS 10 New York
06.03.88 Iran Barkley L RSC 5 New York
Summary: 27 contests, won 25, lost 2.

Patrizio Oliva

Naples, Italy. *Born* 28.01.59
Former WBA L. Welterweight Champion. Former Undefeated EBU & Italian L. Welterweight Champion

11.10.80 Nelson Gomez W PTS 6 Naples
25.10.80 Benedicto dos Santos W PTS 6 Pordenone
06.12.80 Eloi de Souza W RSC 6 Bologna
26.12.80 Mohamed El Kadoumi W PTS 6 Bologna
23.02.81 Georges Cotin W PTS 6 Rome
06.03.81 Mohatar II W RSC 4 Milan
20.03.81 Luigi Curcetti W PTS 8 Naples
04.04.81 Rosario di Tommaso W RSC 2 Compobasso
01.05.81 Rene Martin W RSC 4 Piacenza
16.05.81 Francesco Gallo W RSC 7 Padua
04.06.81 George Burton W PTS 6 New York
07.07.81 Charles Jurietti W RSC 4 Fornia
09.08.81 Patrizio Burini W RSC 1 Camaiore
04.11.81 Giuseppe Russi W CO 2 Ischia
(Italian L. Welterweight Title Challenge)
27.11.81 Rafael Gutierrez W RTD 5 Bologna
11.12.81 Mosimo Maeleke W PTS 8 Milan
27.12.81 Antonio Antino W RSC 3 Ischia
(Italian L. Welterweight Title Defence)
11.02.82 Bruno Simili W CO 8 Naples
(Italian L. Welterweight Title Defence)
06.03.82 Francesco Gallo W PTS 8 Giovinazzo
11.04.82 Giuseppe Martinese W PTS 12 Ischia
(Italian L. Welterweight Title Defence)
20.05.82 Sam Serunjogi W PTS 8 Vieste
29.05.82 Hugues Samo W PTS 8 Milan
08.08.82 Andre Holyk W RSC 4 Camerota
01.09.82 Luciano Navarra W PTS 12 Ischia
06.10.82 Dave McCabe W PTS 8 Gragnano
05.01.83 Robert Gambini W PTS 12 Ischia
(EBU L. Welterweight Title Challenge)
19.03.83 Francisco Leon W RTD 11 Naples
(EBU L. Welterweight Title Defence)
25.05.83 Jean-Marie Touati W RSC 6 Santo Margherita
(EBU L. Welterweight Title Defence)
31.07.83 Antonio Guinaldo W PTS 12 Rapallo
(EBU L. Welterweight Title Defence)
14.10.83 Juan J. Gimenez W PTS 12 Milan
(EBU L. Welterweight Title Defence)
21.12.83 Antony Murray W RSC 6 Naples
28.01.84 Jerome Artis W PTS 8 Marsala
22.02.84 Charles Allen W RSC 3 Gragnano
24.03.84 Kevin Austin W PTS 8 Chiavari
28.04.84 Ramon Gomez-Fouz W RSC 4 Naples
(EBU L. Welterweight Title Defence)
23.06.84 Ali Karim Muhammad W PTS 8 Campione
04.09.84 Tusikoleta Nkalankete W PTS 12 Acciaroli
(EBU L. Welterweight Title Defence)
15.12.84 Michel Giroud W RTD 7 Catanzaro
(EBU L. Welterweight Title Defence)
27.03.85 Alessandro Scapecchi W PTS 12 Nocera
(EBU L. Welterweight Title Defence)
21.07.85 Nick Parker W PTS 8 Campione
31.10.85 Steve Mitchell W PTS 8 Viterbo
08.12.85 Mark Lassien W PTS 10 Montreal
21.01.86 Ricky Kaiser W RSC 4 Naples
15.03.86 Ubaldo Sacco W PTS 15 Monte Carlo
(WBA L. Welterweight Title Challenge)
13.06.86 Ford Jennings W PTS 10 Praiano
30.07.86 Eric Martin W PTS 10 Capo D'Orlando
06.09.86 Brian Brunette W RSC 3 Naples
(WBA L. Welterweight Title Defence)
10.01.87 Rodolfo Gonzalez W PTS 15 Agrigento
(WBA L. Welterweight Title Defence)
04.07.87 Juan M. Coggi L CO 3 Ribera
(WBA L. Welterweight Title Defence)
Summary: 49 contests, won 48, lost 1.

Felipe Orozco

Barranquilla, Colombia. *Born* 16.06.59
S. Featherweight

12.06.80 Jose Zuniga W PTS 6 Monteria
01.08.80 Jaime Espejo W PTS 6 Barranquilla
12.09.80 Gabriel Pajaro W RSC 2 Barranquilla
30.10.80 Argemire Colon W RSC 2 Barranquilla
28.11.80 Pedro Perez W CO 3 Barranquilla
13.02.81 Julio Llerena W PTS 10 Barranquilla
27.03.81 Bernardino Rubio W PTS 10 Barranquilla
27.05.81 Leopoldo Frias W RTD 7 Barranquilla
26.06.81 Santiago Mendez W CO 2 Barranquilla
17.07.81 Carlos Bejerano W PTS 10 Barranquilla
23.10.81 Felix Rodriguez W PTS 10 Cartagena
08.01.82 Manuel Santos W RSC 2 Cartagena
14.05.82 Jacinto Fuentes W RSC 3 Barranquilla
06.08.82 Carlos Mendoza W RTD 7 Barranquilla
30.10.82 Juan Lopez W PTS 10 Barranquilla
25.02.83 Moro Cloney W CO 1 Miami
23.12.83 Bonifacio Flores W CO 7 Barranquilla
27.01.84 Francisco Fernandez W RSC 6 Barranquilla
26.05.84 Jaime Garza L CO 3 Miami
(WBC S. Bantamweight Title Challenge)
13.10.84 Barry McGuigan L CO 2 Belfast
29.03.85 Felipe Julio L RSC 4 Cartagena
14.03.86 Alvaro Bohorquez W PTS 12 Monteria
30.05.86 Luis Barrio W CO 4 Bogota
25.07.86 Rafael Silgado W CO 1 Barranquilla
22.10.86 Rocky Lockridge L PTS 10 Atlantic City
24.10.87 John Wesley W RSC 2 Miami
18.03.88 Jesse Williams W PTS 10 Miami
Summary: 27 contests, won 23, lost 4.

Emmanuel Otti

Kampala, Uganda. *Born* 04.04.60
Former Australian Middleweight Champion

07.12.81 Kostas Saxanidis L CO 3 Athens
04.04.82 Isnuf Okife W PTS 10 Izmis
02.06.82 Mache Oble W PTS 10 Cesje
16.06.82 Kostas Saxanidis L CO 5 Athens
22.07.82 Marcel Kralj W PTS 10 Nils
12.08.82 Latze Enzen W PTS 10 Zagreb
26.08.82 Kostas Saxanidis DREW 10 Athens
27.09.82 Kostas Saxanidis W PTS 10 Athens
12.10.82 Illiadis W PTS 10 Chios
28.10.82 Johnny Greco W PTS 10 Rhodes
28.03.83 Ricky Patterson W RSC 6 Brisbane
18.04.83 Sam Samuela W CO 2 Brisbane
06.06.83 Matareti Valu W PTS 10 Brisbane
25.07.83 Joe Kid W RSC 6 Brisbane
29.08.83 Marcos Geraldo L RSC 3 Brisbane
14.10.83 Matareti Valu W RSC 4 Surfers Paradise
28.11.83 Tom West W PTS 10 Brisbane
06.02.84 Kevin Wagstaff W RSC 2 Brisbane
19.03.84 Tom West W PTS 10 Brisbane
16.04.84 John Taupau W RSC 7 Brisbane
09.07.84 Richie Roberts W CO 3 Brisbane
(Australian Middleweight Title Challenge)
20.08.84 Brian Anderson L PTS 10 Brisbane
19.11.84 Peter Clay W RSC 9 Brisbane
20.02.85 Joe Nitiva L RSC 3 Mount Pritchard
26.08.85 Joe Nitiva DREW 10 Brisbane
21.09.85 Lou Cafaro L PTS 12 Perth
(Australian Middleweight Title Defence)
21.10.85 Lorina Niumataiwalu W PTS 10 Brisbane
17.03.86 Matareti Valu W PTS 10 Brisbane
13.06.86 Guy Waters L PTS 10 Gosford
07.07.86 Greg Pocock W CO 2 Brisbane
15.09.86 Young Stone W CO 3 Sydney
08.12.86 Mosese Villa W RSC 5 Brisbane
05.02.87 Jeff Harding L RTD 5 Sydney
25.05.87 Doug Sam L RSC 7 Brisbane
26.07.87 Chong-Pal Park L RSC 4 Kwangju
(IBF S. Middleweight Title Challenge)
Summary: 35 contests, won 23, drew 2, lost 10.

Fujio Ozaki

Japan. *Born* 07.10.61
Former Undefeated Japanese Lightweight & Welterweight Champion

19.05.80 Teruo Okuaki W RSC 1 Tokyo
01.07.80 Morio Watanabe W CO 1 Tokyo
30.09.80 Koji Kunisato W PTS 4 Tokyo
28.12.80 Yoshifumi Takeyama W PTS 6 Tokyo
01.03.81 Hidekazu Akai L RSC 3 Tokyo
18.07.81 Masanori Omori W PTS 6 Tokyo
10.10.81 Kazunori Taguchi W CO 1 Tokyo
23.11.81 Yoshihide Sawano W CO 6 Hachinohe
07.05.82 Kojiro Sasaki W RSC 8 Tokyo
06.08.82 Joken Narita W PTS 10 Tokyo
(Japanese Lightweight Title Challenge)
09.11.82 Hayao Shiba W CO 8 Tokyo
(Japanese Lightweight Title Defence)
22.02.83 Joken Narita W PTS 10 Tokyo
(Japanese Lightweight Title Defence)
03.06.83 Cheyenne Yamamoto L PTS 10 Tokyo
(Japanese Lightweight Title Defence)
02.09.83 Cheyenne Yamamoto W PTS 10 Tokyo
(Japanese Lightweight Title Challenge)
02.12.83 Hikaru Tomonari L CO 7 Tokyo
(Japanese Lightweight Title Defence)
19.03.84 Hiroaki Kato W CO 2 Kochi
05.04.84 Noboyuki Tabata W CO 4 Tokyo
02.08.84 Kozo Fukutani W CO 6 Tokyo
10.01.85 Yung-Bae Lee W RSC 8 Tokyo
06.06.85 Junya Kushikino W PTS 10 Tokyo
(Japanese Welterweight Title Challenge)
29.08.85 Junya Kushikino W RSC 8 Tokyo
(Japanese Welterweight Title Defence)
04.11.85 Nobutaka Kuwata W CO 8 Naha
(Japanese Welterweight Title Defence)
06.02.86 Noboyuki Tabata L PTS 10 Tokyo
(Japanese Welterweight Title Defence)
05.06.86 Noboyuki Tabata W CO 5 Tokyo
(Japanese Welterweight Title Challenge)
06.11.86 Akinori Yoshida W CO 4 Tokyo
(Japanese Welterweight Title Defence)
05.02.87 Hikaru Tomonari W RSC 4 Tokyo
(Japanese Welterweight Title Defence)
05.02.88 Marlon Starling L PTS 12 Atlantic City
(WBA Welterweight Title Challenge)
Summary: 27 contests, won 22, lost 5.

Jong-Jong Pacquing

Cagayan, Philippines
Former OPBF Lightweight Champion. Former Undefeated Philippines Lightweight Champion. Former Philippines S. Bantamweight Champion.

16.02.80 Eller Sinoyan W RSC 2 Cagayan
15.03.80 Romy Oborio W RSC 4 Cagayan
05.07.80 Carlos Aradora DREW 10 Butuan
16.08.80 Danny Canada W PTS 10 Cagayan
30.08.80 Erning Querobin W PTS 10 Cagayan
25.10.80 Siony Carupo W PTS 10 Cagayan
30.11.80 Rene Sedayon W PTS 10 Cagayan
27.12.80 Winnie Ampong W PTS 10 Cagayan
28.02.81 Baby Francisco W PTS 10 Cagayan
28.03.81 Divino Inocian W PTS 10 Cagayan
29.05.81 Divino Inocian L PTS 10 Cagayan
04.07.81 Rey Naduma W RSC 10 Cagayan
(Philippines S. Bantamweight Title Challenge)
24.08.81 Sandy Noora W PTS 10 Cagayan
26.09.81 Ronaldo Sumalis L PTS 10 Cagayan
31.10.81 Ric Diamale L PTS 12 Davao
(Philippines S. Bantamweight Title Defence)
28.11.81 Nerry Codilla W PTS 10 Cagayan
05.02.82 Melching Maquilan W PTS 10 Cagayan
17.04.82 Ronaldo Sumalis L PTS 10 Cagayan
28.05.82 Cesar Ligan W PTS 10 Cagayan
10.07.82 Nene Jun W RSC 5 Cebu
02.10.82 Nene Jun W RSC 7 Cagayan
31.10.82 Ric Dolotallas W PTS 10 Misamis
18.12.82 Roger Salas W PTS 10 Cagayan
05.02.83 Del Contado W RSC 8 Cagayan
05.03.83 Ric Dolotallas W PTS 10 Cagayan
16.04.83 Flash Villamer W PTS 12 Cagayan
(Philippines Lightweight Title Challenge)
30.07.83 Jun Escalera W RSC 5 Cagayan
30.09.83 Amy Pacana L PTS 12 Manila
(Philippines Lightweight Title Defence)
19.11.83 Bert Lozano W PTS 10 Cagayan
11.02.84 Amy Pacana W PTS 12 Cagayan
(Philippines Lightweight Title Challenge)
06.04.84 Rolando Aldemir W PTS 10 Cagayan
02.06.84 Johnny Sato L RSC 2 Cagayan
18.08.84 Kyu-Woon Choi L PTS 10 Pohang
23.09.84 Juhari W PTS 12 Jakarta
(Vacant OPBF Lightweight Title)
13.04.85 Dong-Koo Woo W RSC 4 Chinju
(OPBF Lightweight Title Defence)
17.02.85 Johannes Msiren W CO 12 Surabaya
(OPBF Lightweight Title Defence)
15.06.85 Carlos Parcia W RSC 6 Cagayan
07.07.85 Tsuyoshi Hamada L PTS 12 Tokyo
(OPBF Lightweight Title Defence)
26.08.85 Dale Artango L RSC 5 Brisbane
05.10.85 Fred Panerio W CO 5 Cagayan
01.03.86 Lito Pena W PTS 12 Cagayan
(Philippines Lightweight Title Challenge)
02.08.86 Amy Pacana W RSC 7 Cagayan
(Philippines Lightweight Title Defence)
31.01.87 Allan Alegria DREW 10 Cagayan
20.06.87 Jun Ramos W RSC 7 Tagum
23.11.87 Bong-Guk Kendy W RSC 4 Jakarta
08.02.88 Lito Pena W RSC 5 Cagayan
Summary: 46 contests, won 35, drew 2, lost 9.

Byung-Soo Park
South Korea. *Born* 15.11.64
OPBF Featherweight Champion. Former Undefeated South Korean Featherweight Champion

11.09.82 Soo-Keun Kim W RSC 4 Seoul
19.12.82 Choong-Guer Lee W RSC 4 Seoul
28.05.83 Choon-Sung Kim W PTS 4 Seoul
24.07.83 Young-Jim Kim W RSC 2 Seoul
17.09.83 Kyung-Woo Park W RSC 3 Seoul
11.12.83 Ik-Soo Bae W RSC 2 Seoul
13.12.83 Ki-Chul Bae W PTS 4 Seoul
15.12.83 Keuk-Yung Bang W PTS 4 Seoul
16.12.83 Jong-Hee You W PTS 4 Seoul
07.01.84 Hot-Ae Nam W RSC 3 Seoul
15.01.84 Yun-Kyu Kim W PTS 6 Seoul
01.03.84 Byung-Won You W PTS 6 Seoul
12.05.84 Marushiano Sekiyama W CO 1 Seoul
16.07.84 Akiyama Daro W RSC 3 Tokyo
18.10.84 Sung-Yun Kim L PTS 10 Seoul
27.04.85 Hyun-Il Kim W RSC 8 Seoul
07.09.85 Duangdee Tekiatphitak W CO 3 Seoul
09.11.85 Jae-Yong Hang DREW 10 Chonchun
25.01.86 Chan-Jung Chun W PTS 10 Daejon
(*South Korean Featherweight Title Challenge*)
15.03.86 Jae-Moon Yuh W PTS 10 Seoul
(*South Korean Featherweight Title Defence*)
15.06.86 Kwang-Hee Park W CO 1 Seoul
31.08.86 Won-Kyung Kim W PTS 10 Seoul
13.11.86 Chung-Ho Lee W RSC 5 Seoul
14.02.87 Hilbert Aragon W CO 3 Seoul
19.07.87 Woo-Chun Kim W CO 5 Pohang
(*South Korean Featherweight Title Defence*)
27.09.87 Jae-Yong Hwang W CO 2 Sangjoo
(*OPBF Featherweight Title Challenge*)
23.04.88 Lion Collins W RSC 1 Buju
(*OPBF Featherweight Title Defence*)
Summary: 27 contests, won 25, drew 1, lost 1.

Chan-Yung Park
South Korea. *Born* 10.06.63
Former WBA Bantamweight Champion

18.11.80 Chang-Sung Choi W CO 3 Seoul
20.11.80 Sang-Ho Choi W PTS 4 Seoul
23.11.80 Sang-Myun Choi W PTS 4 Seoul
29.11.80 Hyung-Shik An W PTS 4 Seoul
07.12.80 Kyung-Soo Lee L PTS 6 Seoul
18.01.81 In-Sop Bang W PTS 8 Seoul
02.04.81 Chan-Jung Chun DREW 8 Chunchon
03.06.81 Bong-Ho Lee W PTS 8 Taegu
13.08.81 Hyung-Shik An W PTS 8 Kwangju
03.01.82 Sam-Young Kim DREW 6 Seoul
24.03.82 Shoji Oguma L PTS 10 Tokyo
20.05.82 Yang-Il Shin W RSC 6 Seoul
01.08.82 Chung-Woo Chun W PTS 6 Seoul
03.10.82 Flash Jagdon W PTS 10 Seoul
31.10.82 Suvan Silpaya W PTS 10 Masan
13.01.83 Daonoi Sithsanae W CO 3 Seoul
10.04.83 Adan Uribe Perez W PTS 10 Seoul
17.06.83 Pablo Pepito W PTS 10 Seoul
03.08.83 Kaosai Galaxy L PTS 10 Bangkok
16.10.83 Sung-Moon Choi W PTS 10 Seoul
13.11.83 Neptali Alamag W PTS 10 Inchon
26.02.84 Sak Charsirirta W CO 3 Seoul
03.06.84 Rito Donayre W RSC 3 Seoul
08.07.84 Jorge Ramirez W PTS 10 Seoul
04.12.84 Ernie Cataluna W PTS 10 Seoul
31.03.85 Edgar Apatan W PTS 10 Seoul
25.08.85 Fel Malatag W CO 10 Seoul
02.02.86 Norio Hasegawa W CO 2 Seoul
19.10.86 Little Bangoyan W PTS 10 Seoul
24.05.87 Takuya Muguruma W RSC 11 Moriguchi
(*WBA Bantamweight Title Challenge*)
04.10.87 Wilfredo Vasquez L RSC 10 Seoul
(*WBA Bantamweight Title Defence*)
12.03.88 Masahatsu Sakuma W RSC 2 Seoul
Summary: 32 contests, won 26, drew 2, lost 4.

Chong-Pal Park
Chunranam-Do, South Korea. *Born* 11.08.60
WBA S. Middleweight Champion. Former Undefeated IBF S. Middleweight Champion. Former Undefeated OPBF & South Korean Middleweight Champion

26.11.77 Yong-Soo Chung W CO 1 Pusan
23.12.77 Kyung-Sik Kim W CO 2 Seoul
25.12.77 Seung-Hwan Kang W PTS 6 Seoul
25.03.78 Seung-Hwan Kang DREW 8 Seoul
14.06.78 Hung-Won Kang L RSC 1 Seoul
28.08.78 Kazuo Goshima W CO 1 Tokyo
17.12.78 Chang-Baek Choi W CO 3 Seoul
(*South Korean Middleweight Title Challenge*)
03.02.79 Tony Abarca W CO 2 Seoul
17.03.79 Alberto Cruz W CO 2 Taegu
22.04.79 Armando Boniquit W CO 3 Seoul
02.06.79 Michiro Horihata W CO 3 Seoul
22.08.79 Cassius Naito W CO 2 Pusan
(*Vacant OPBF Middleweight Title*)
27.01.80 Katsuo Esashi W CO 3 Seoul
(*OPBF Middleweight Title Defence*)
18.03.80 Kenji Shibata W CO 5 Seoul
(*OPBF Middleweight Title Defence*)
04.05.80 Rocky Joe W CO 8 Jakarta
(*OPBF Middleweight Title Defence*)
21.06.80 Fred Pastor W CO 4 Seoul
08.08.80 Peter Piamonte W RTD 4 Seoul
(*OPBF Middleweight Title Defence*)
24.09.80 Marcos Torkano W CO 5 Seoul
(*OPBF Middleweight Title Defence*)
03.11.80 Phil Davies W RSC 3 Seoul
(*OPBF Middleweight Title Defence*)
06.12.80 Joe Willisco W CO 3 Seoul
(*OPBF Middleweight Title Defence*)
05.04.81 Caesar Sasaki W CO 6 Seoul
(*OPBF Middleweight Title Defence*)
21.06.81 Kenji Shibata W CO 5 Seoul
(*OPBF Middleweight Title Defence*)
02.08.81 Sang-Ho Lee W CO 9 Seoul
09.09.81 Mana Pramchai W CO 11 Pusan
(*OPBF Middleweight Title Defence*)
07.11.81 Fully Obelmejias L RSC 8 Caracas
03.01.82 Mana Pramchai W CO 4 Seoul
(*OPBF Middleweight Title Defence*)
07.03.82 Richie Roberts W CO 8 Seoul
(*OPBF Middleweight Title Defence*)
18.04.82 Suwarno W RSC 4 Seoul
(*OPBF Middleweight Title Defence*)
18.07.82 Valence Haralan W CO 2 Seoul
(*OPBF Middleweight Title Defence*)
26.12.82 Naoto Suzuki W CO 4 Seoul
(*OPBF Middleweight Title Defence*)
10.04.83 Antonio Leyva W CO 4 Seoul
29.05.83 Kyung-Min Nah L CO 7 Seoul
(*OPBF Middleweight Title Defence*)
04.09.83 Kyung-Min Nah W RSC 4 Chunchon
(*OPBF Middleweight Title Challenge*)
06.11.83 Gary Hubble W CO 9 Seoul
04.12.83 Rosendo Ruvalcaba W CO 5 Seoul
05.02.84 Charles Carter W PTS 10 Seoul
17.06.84 Roosevelt Green W RSC 9 Seoul
22.07.84 Murray Sutherland W CO 11 Seoul
(*IBF S. Middleweight Title Challenge*)
07.10.84 Wally Carr W PTS 10 Seoul
02.01.85 Roy Gumbs W CO 2 Seoul
(*IBF S. Middleweight Title Defence*)
28.04.85 Chang-Hwan Noh W PTS 12 Pusan
30.06.85 Vinnie Curto W PTS 15 Seoul
(*IBF S. Middleweight Title Defence*)
02.01.86 Chang-Hwan Noh W CO 9 Seoul
11.04.86 Vinnie Curto W CO 15 Los Angeles
(*IBF S. Middleweight Title Defence*)
06.07.86 Lindell Holmes T DRAW 2 Chungju
(*IBF S. Middleweight Title Defence*)
14.09.86 Marvin Mack W PTS 15 Pusan
(*IBF S. Middleweight Title Defence*)
25.01.87 Doug Sam W RSC 15 Seoul
(*IBF S. Middleweight Title Defence*)
03.05.87 Lindell Holmes W PTS 15 Inchon
(*IBF S. Middleweight Title Defence*)
26.07.87 Emmanuel Otti W RSC 4 Kwangju
(*IBF S. Middleweight Title Defence*)
06.12.87 Jesus Gallardo W RSC 2 Seoul
(*Vacant WBA S. Middleweight Title*)
01.03.88 Polly Pasieron W CO 5 Chungju
(*WBA S. Middleweight Title Defence*)
Summary: 51 contests, won 46, drew 2, lost 3.

Cho-Woon Park
South Korea. *Born* 03.01.67
Former Undefeated OPBF L. Flyweight Champion. Former Undefeated South Korean L. Flyweight Champion

17.04.83 Hi-Suk Kim W RSC 3 Seoul
03.07.83 Eul-Chul Chung DREW 4 Seoul
26.07.83 Dae-Yung Kim W CO 4 Seoul
21.10.83 Jae-Nam Choi W PTS 4 Seoul
12.12.83 Sih-Yuk Chang W PTS 10 Seoul
14.12.83 Chang-Wha Shin W PTS 4 Seoul
16.12.83 Chung-Won Suh W PTS 4 Seoul
07.01.84 Sun-Yong Chung W PTS 4 Seoul
15.01.84 Jae-Chul Kim L PTS 6 Seoul
12.05.84 Chung-Bok Park W PTS 6 Inchon
23.06.84 Sung-Kyu Kim W PTS 6 Seoul
22.09.84 Chang-Yung Chang W PTS 8 Seoul
19.01.85 Dosa Kim W PTS 10 Suwon
(*Vacant South Korean L. Flyweight Title*)
06.04.85 Ul-Chul Chung W PTS 10 Taegu
(*South Korean L. Flyweight Title Defence*)
17.08.85 Dadoy Andujar W CO 7 Buchon
21.09.85 Chun Huh W PTS 10 Chochiwon
(*South Korean L. Flyweight Title Defence*)
11.01.86 Little Baguio DREW 12 Seoul
(*Vacant OPBF L. Flyweight Title*)
12.04.86 Little Baguio W PTS 12 Seoul
(*Vacant OPBF L. Flyweight Title*)
28.06.86 Junior Thompson W CO 3 Kunsan
(*OPBF L. Flyweight Title Defence*)
07.12.86 Jum-Hwan Choi L PTS 15 Pusan
(*Vacant IBF L. Flyweight Title*)
15.02.87 Rex Rapiso W RSC 12 Seoul
(*Vacant OPBF L. Flyweight Title*)
18.04.87 William Belan DREW 12 Seoul
(*OPBF L. Flyweight Title Defence*)
13.09.87 Ademar Amad W PTS 12 Jinju
(*OPBF L. Flyweight Title Defence*)
21.11.87 Joe Galagran W PTS 10 Eijoungbu
11.02.88 Kenji Matsumura L PTS 12 Himeji
(*OPBF Flyweight Title Challenge*)
Summary: 25 contests, won 19, drew 3, lost 3.

Rickey (The Hammer) Parkey
Morristown, USA. *Born* 07.11.56
Former IBF Cruiserweight Champion. Former Undefeated Con. Am. Cruiserweight Champion

24.10.81 Phil Clinard W RSC 2 Morristown
27.11.81 Miles Prince W RSC 5 Knoxville
30.01.82 James Smith L PTS 6 Knoxville
08.07.82 Tim Johnson W RSC 1 Knoxville
27.08.82 Frankie Hines W RSC 3 Knoxville
16.10.82 Maurice Moore W CO 4 Charlotte
08.01.83 Keith Allen W PTS 6 Pennington Gap
13.01.83 Bobby Jennings L PTS 8 Bristol
04.02.83 Keith Allen W RSC 4 Knoxville
12.03.83 Bob Morton W RTD 4 Raceland
26.05.83 Anthony Phillips W RSC 3 Knoxville
25.06.83 Phil Clinard W PTS 8 Pennington Gap
15.11.83 Stanley Ross W PTS 8 Atlantic City
11.01.84 Pat Cuillo W PTS 8 Atlantic City
20.05.84 Keith Wilson W CO 1 Hickory
11.09.84 Bernard Benton L PTS 12 Atlantic City
(*Vacant USBA Cruiserweight Title*)
30.10.84 Renaldo Snipes W PTS 10 Atlantic City
11.12.84 Broderick Mason W RSC 1 Atlantic City
23.04.85 Bobby Crabtree W RSC 1 Atlantic City
18.06.85 Mustafa Muhammad L PTS 10 Atlantic City
10.09.85 Michael Arms W PTS 12 Atlantic City
(*Vacant Con. Am. Cruiserweight Title*)
28.01.86 Carlos Hernandez W RSC 7 Atlantic City
25.10.86 Lee Roy Murphy W RSC 10 Marsala
(*IBF Cruiserweight Title Challenge*)
28.03.87 Chisanda Mutti W RSC 12 Camaiore
(*IBF Cruiserweight Title Defence*)
15.05.87 Evander Holyfield L RSC 3 Las Vegas
(*IBF Cruiserweight Title Defence*)
31.10.87 Johnny du Plooy L RSC 10 Sun City
09.03.88 Gary Mason L RSC 1 Wembley
Summary: 27 contests, won 20, lost 7.

Mike Parris
Guyana. *Born* 04.10.57
Guyanan Bantamweight Champion

28.11.82 Rey McBean W PTS 6 Georgetown
19.02.83 Rey McBean W PTS 6 Georgetown
03.04.83 Oswald Bowen W RSC 4 Georgetown
25.11.83 Anthony Andrews W PTS 12 Georgetown
(*Guyanan Bantamweight Title Challenge*)
24.02.84 Anthony Andrews L RSC 12 Georgetown
(*Guyanan Bantamweight Title Defence*)
02.06.85 Juan Bautista W PTS 10 Georgetown
27.08.85 Darius Ford W RSC 8 Georgetown
(*Vacant Guyanan Bantamweight Title*)
24.02.86 Darryl Pinkney W CO 7 Georgetown

10.12.85 Lucilo Nolasco W PTS 10 Los Angeles
04.02.86 Lupe Torres W PTS 10 La Paz
24.02.86 Ubaldo Gonzalez W CO 1 San Luis
13.03.86 Lucilo Nolasco W PTS 10 Tijuana
03.05.86 Rodolfo Ortega L PTS 10 Mexico City
16.06.86 Eliseo Olvera W RSC 2 Tijuana
18.07.86 Diego Avila W PTS 10 Tijuana
08.08.86 Miguel Pequeno W CO 3 Tijuana
30.08.86 Prudencio Cardona W PTS 10 Tijuana
10.11.86 Capri Lipkins W PTS 10 Tijuana
08.12.86 James Manning W PTS 10 Tijuana
27.01.87 Tony Escobar W RSC 10 Tijuana
20.03.87 Victor Moreno W CO 1 Mexicali
27.04.87 Calvin Williams W CO 1 Tijuana
06.07.87 Gaby Canizales W RSC 9 Tijuana
10.09.87 Edel Geronimo T DRAW 3 Los Angeles
12.10.87 Jorge Ramirez W PTS 10 Tijuana
07.12.87 Eduardo Torres W CO 1 Tijuana
01.02.88 Rodolfo Ortega W PTS 10 Tijuana
04.04.88 Martin Lopez W RSC 2 Tijuana
Summary: 41 contests, won 39, drew 1, lost 1.

Sakao Petchyindee

Sakad Petchyindee
Thailand. *Born* 20.04.58
Former OPBF Lightweight Champion. Former Undefeated Thai Lightweight Champion

10.11.77 Juan A. Lopez W PTS 10 Bangkok
.78 Hisami Mizuno W RSC 4 Bangkok
02.06.78 Wilfredo Gomez L RSC 3 Korat
(*WBC S. Bantamweight Title Challenge*)
06.09.84 Dowtorn Chuvatana W PTS 10 Bangkok
15.08.85 Sonsak Wantorn W CO 1 Bangkok
30.09.85 Singsamut Porchaivat W CO 1 Bangkok
28.12.85 Chausuriya Somtankuichab W CO 1 Bangkok
18.01.86 Payunsak Sissarmtaharn W CO 3 Bangkok
22.02.86 Boy Romero W CO 2 Kuwait
27.08.86 Pansaknoi Kiatkraison W CO 2 Bangkok
(*Vacant Thai Lightweight Title*)
28.10.86 Dale Artango W RSC 6 Bangkok
(*Vacant OPBF Lightweight Title*)
24.02.87 Juhari W PTS 12 Bangkok
(*OPBF Lightweight Title Defence*)
05.07.87 Bisenti Santoso W CO 1 Gresik
(*OPBF Lightweight Title Defence*)
28.02.88 Bong-Chun Park L PTS 12 Daejon
(*OPBF Lightweight Title Defence*)
Summary: 14 contests, won 12, lost 2.

Vince Pettway
Baltimore, USA. *Born* 09.11.65
Welterweight

27.02.84 Ali Muhammad W RSC 3 Atlantic City
18.04.84 Jo Jo Virgil W CO 2 Richmond
10.05.84 Vince Bailey W RSC 2 Baltimore
23.05.84 Reg Watkins W RSC 4 Pikesville
14.06.84 Ric Graves W CO 2 Richmond
29.08.84 Joey Soler W PTS 6 Atlantic City
06.09.84 Charles Robinson W RSC 2 Baltimore
16.10.84 James Keir W RSC 3 Baltimore
14.11.84 Tom Baker W DIS 8 Baltimore
08.04.85 Steve Mitchell W RSC 6 Atlantic City
20.06.85 Antoine Lark W RSC 2 Baltimore
21.08.85 Marvin Ladson W RSC 3 Baltimore
14.09.85 Keith Corbett W RSC 5 Atlantic City
07.11.85 Mike Hutchinson W RSC 3 Pikesville
03.12.85 Jose Alejandro W RSC 3 Atlantic City
07.02.86 Donald Gwynn W CO 1 Baltimore
22.03.86 Papo Figueroa W RSC 1 Atlantic City
15.04.86 George Leach L RSC 4 Baltimore
11.06.86 Leland Hart W RSC 7 Baltimore
28.08.86 Pete Seward W RSC 3 Mechanicsville
29.11.86 Marvin Ladson W RSC 2 Richmond
10.01.87 Jerome Artis W RSC 1 Richmond
21.03.87 Lopez McGee W RSC 1 Richmond
11.08.87 Miguel Narvaez W RSC 6 Chicago
06.01.88 Horace Shufford W PTS 10 Baltimore
04.03.88 Tim Knight W RSC 9 Richmond
09.04.88 Javier Suazo L CO 6 Las Vegas
Summary: 27 contests, won 25, lost 2.

Harold Petty
Peter Goldfield/USA

Harold Petty
Fort Worth, USA. *Born* 13.11.60
Former Undefeated Con. Am. S. Bantamweight Champion. Former NABF Bantamweight Champion

30.04.81 Eulilio Anquiano W RSC 1 Fort Worth
02.06.81 Tommy Wilson W PTS 4 Fort Worth
21.07.81 Sil Martinez W CO 6 Fort Worth
18.08.81 Ricky Cortez W RSC 3 Fort Worth
01.09.81 Mario Gomez W RSC 6 Laredo
07.10.81 Angel Lira W RSC 3 Beaumont
29.10.81 Alejandro Garcia W CO 3 Fort Worth
15.01.82 Norberto Castellano W PTS 8 Houston
28.01.82 Richard Sandoval L PTS 10 Las Vegas
03.04.82 Richard Sandoval L PTS 10 Las Vegas
13.05.82 Sergio Reyes W PTS 10 Fort Worth
10.06.82 Martin Hernandez W PTS 10 Las Vegas
29.07.82 Daniel Zaragoza W PTS 10 Las Vegas
09.09.82 Richard Avila W PTS 10 Fort Worth
21.10.82 Mario Chavez W PTS 12 Las Vegas
17.11.82 Fred Jackson W DIS 2 St Joseph
(*Vacant NABF Bantamweight Title*)
29.01.83 Jose Salas W RSC 3 Fort Worth
14.04.83 Sergio Castro W RSC 4 Las Vegas
17.05.83 Jose Cazares W RSC 6 Houston
17.06.83 Humberto Rodriguez W CO 4 Baton Rouge
08.08.83 Daniel Zaragoza W PTS 12 Houston
(*NABF Bantamweight Title Defence*)
22.09.83 James Manning W PTS 12 Portland
(*NABF Bantamweight Title Defence*)
08.10.83 Mario Chavez W PTS 10 Levelland
09.11.83 Hilario Zapata W RSC 10 Las Vegas
21.02.84 Jose Torres W PTS 10 Dallas
08.06.84 Osvaldo Acevedo L RSC 4 Miami
20.09.84 Greg Richardson L PTS 12 Las Vegas
(*NABF Bantamweight Title Defence*)
30.03.85 Arturo Tebaqui W RSC 6 Dallas
20.08.85 Kelvin Seabrooks W PTS 12 Atlantic City
(*Vacant Con. Am. S. Bantamweight Title*)
29.10.85 Nelson Ortiz W PTS 10 Atlantic City
12.06.86 Ramon Cruz W PTS 10 Atlantic City
26.09.86 Tony Talley W CO 3 Portland
23.03.87 Antonio Gonzalez W PTS 10 Tijuana
07.08.87 Jorge Urbina Diaz L PTS 10 San Jose
04.12.87 Marino Ramirez W PTS 10 Atlantic City
23.01.88 Sonny Long W PTS 10 St Louis
28.03.88 Carlos Romero L RSC 7 Los Angeles
Summary: 37 contests, won 31, lost 6.

Elly Pical
Saparua-Maluku, Indonesia. *Born* 24.03.60
IBF S. Flyweight Champion. Former Undefeated Indonesian & OPBF S. Flyweight Champion

10.12.82 Eddy Rafael W CO 5 Jakarta
19.12.82 Benny Nurianto W CO 6 Malang
06.02.83 Juwarno W CO 1 Malang
15.05.83 Moningko Palungan W CO 2 Malang
24.07.83 Edward Apay L PTS 10 Malang
18.08.83 Munadi W CO 2 Jakarta
11.09.83 Viboon Muangsurin W PTS 10 Jakarta
11.12.83 Wongso Indrajit W PTS 12 Surabaya
(*Indonesian S. Flyweight Title Challenge*)
30.03.84 Prayurasak Muangsurin W CO 1 Bangkok
19.05.84 Hi-Yun Chung W TD 4 Seoul
(*OPBF S. Flyweight Title Challenge*)
07.10.84 Matsuo Watanabe W RSC 6 Jakarta
(*OPBF S. Flyweight Title Defence*)
03.05.85 Joo-Do Chun W RSC 8 Jakarta
(*IBF S. Flyweight Title Challenge*)
25.08.85 Wayne Mulholland W RSC 3 Jakarta
(*IBF S. Flyweight Title Defence*)
15.02.86 Cesar Polanco L PTS 15 Jakarta
(*IBF S. Flyweight Title Defence*)
05.07.86 Cesar Polanco W CO 3 Jakarta
(*IBF S. Flyweight Title Challenge*)
03.12.86 Dong-Chun Lee W CO 10 Jakarta
(*IBF S. Flyweight Title Defence*)
28.02.87 Kaosai Galaxy L CO 14 Jakarta
(*WBA S. Flyweight Title Challenge*)
17.10.87 Tae-Il Chang W PTS 15 Jakarta
(*IBF S. Flyweight Title Challenge*)
20.02.88 Raul Diaz W PTS 15 Pontianak
(*IBF S. Flyweight Title Defence*)
Summary: 19 contests, won 16, lost 3.

Bernardo Pinango
Panama. *Born* Caracas, Venezuela 09.02.60
WBA S. Bantamweight Champion. Former Undefeated WBA Bantamweight Champion

01.08.81 Angel Torres DREW 6 Caracas
31.08.81 Angel Torres W RSC 1 Caracas
12.10.81 Nelson Rodriguez W RSC 1 Caracas
12.11.81 Angel Torres W PTS 6 Caracas
26.04.82 William Gonzalez W RSC 3 Caracas
12.07.82 Jimmy Chavez W RSC 7 Polamar
26.07.82 Jose Mosqueda ND 2 Cumana
04.10.82 Antonio Esparragoza DREW 10 Caracas
08.11.82 Tito Roque W RSC 5 Caracas
21.02.83 Arnel Arrozal W PTS 10 Valencia
07.03.83 Orlando Silva W CO 2 Caracas
11.04.83 Rene Aroy W RSC 5 Catia la Mar
02.05.83 Juan Resma W PTS 10 Caracas
08.08.83 Raul Gonzalez L PTS 10 Caracas
17.10.83 Raul Gonzalez W PTS 10 Caracas
06.02.84 Jose Sandoval W RSC 1 Caracas
27.02.84 Hector Vasquez W RSC 2 Caracas
19.03.84 Jesus Flores L PTS 10 Caracas
26.05.84 Milton Torres W PTS 10 Guaynabo
19.07.85 Jose Meneses W CO 5 Panama City
15.12.85 Jose Meneses W CO 5 Panama City
01.03.86 Benito Badilla W CO 8 Panama City
04.06.86 Gaby Canizales W PTS 15 East Rutherford
(*WBA Bantamweight Title Challenge*)
04.10.86 Ciro de Leva W RSC 10 Turin
(*WBA Bantamweight Title Defence*)
22.11.86 Simon Skosana W RSC 15 Johannesburg
(*WBA Bantamweight Title Defence*)
03.02.87 Frankie Duarte W PTS 15 Los Angeles
(*WBA Bantamweight Title Defence*)
03.10.87 Farid Benredjeb DREW 8 Gravelines
27.02.88 Juan Gervacio W PTS 12 San Juan
(*WBA S. Bantamweight Title Challenge*)
Summary: 28 contests, won 22, drew 3, lost 2, nd 1.

Rafael (Bomacional) Pineda
Colombia. *Born* 12.01.66
Lightweight

30.04.86 Jose Cassianis W RSC 5 Barranquilla
21.06.86 Jose Morelos W CO 2 San Onofre
25.07.86 Gustave Rodriguez W CO 2 Barranquilla
05.09.86 Santander Vargas W RSC 3 Barranquilla
17.10.86 Alfonso Chamorro W CO 2 Barranquilla
31.10.86 Moises Almanza W RSC 2 Monteria
21.12.86 Julio Llerena W RSC 10 Cartagena
13.02.87 Jesus Espitia W CO 1 Barranquilla
13.03.87 Arnovia Castro W RSC 4 Cartagena
04.04.87 Jose Cassianis W CO 2 San Andres
19.06.87 Fernando Sanchez W CO 1 Barranquilla
31.07.87 Andres Ramos W RSC 3 Barranquilla
04.09.87 Ildemar Paisan W PTS 10 Cartagena
23.10.87 Carlos Mendietta W CO 5 San Andres
18.12.87 Francisco Fernandez W RSC 5 Cartagena
02.04.88 Angel Beltre W CO 2 Atlantic City
Summary: 16 contests, won 16.

James (Little Warrior) Pipps
Galena Park, USA. *Born* 1961
Former Undefeated Con. Am. Bantamweight Champion

05.05.80 Corky Polando W CO 1 Phoenix
09.08.80 Ernest Woolridge W CO 2 Lake Charles
18.10.80 Lalo Anquino W CO 1 Lake Charles
24.02.81 Armando Laredo W RSC 3 Beaumont
12.05.81 Sil Martinez W PTS 6 Beaumont
17.07.81 Gilbert Favella W RSC 1 Beaumont
24.08.81 Miguel Flores W CO 2 Beaumont
28.08.81 Sil Martinez W CO 4 Beaumont
03.11.81 Alfredo Sandoval W CO 1 Beaumont
24.11.81 Rolando Avila W RSC 8 Beaumont
16.12.81 Antonio Sanchez W CO 1 Beaumont
28.01.82 Humberto Rodriguez W RSC 6 Orange
20.04.82 Gilbert Villacana W RSC 8 Orange
16.05.82 Fernando Martinez W RSC 6 Atlantic City
29.06.82 Martin Hernandez W RSC 4 Houston
01.08.82 Angel Lira W RSC 8 San Antonio
15.08.82 Enrique Castro W RSC 5 Atlantic City
25.09.82 Ricardo Varela W PTS 10 McAfee
19.10.82 Ramon Guillan W CO 4 Beaumont
13.11.82 Mario Chavez W PTS 10 Atlantic City
25.01.83 Victor Gamez W CO 1 Port Arthur
08.07.83 Leo Martinez W RSC 1 Beaumont
05.08.83 Angel Lira W RSC 6 Beaumont
12.11.83 Gaby Canizales L RSC 6 Beaumont
(*USBA Bantamweight Title Challenge*)
29.01.84 Pedro Gonzales W CO 1 Beaumont
26.02.84 Carlos Flores W PTS 10 Beaumont
15.01.85 Edgar Muniz W CO 4 Pasadena
09.05.85 James Manning W PTS 10 Houston
30.10.85 Carmelo Negron W PTS 10 Atlantic City
01.02.86 Norberto Castellano W CO 2 Beaumont
01.03.86 Rey Garza W CO 2 Beaumont
29.05.86 Pascual Aranda T DRAW 2 Houston
31.07.86 Jose Sanabria W PTS 10 Atlantic City
31.05.87 Mario Gonzalez W CO 6 Houston
31.07.87 Jesus Muniz W RSC 3 Corpus Christi
(*Vacant Con. Am. Bantamweight Title*)
08.10.87 Jose Gallegos W RSC 5 Houston
03.02.88 Oscar Chavarria W RSC 8 Houston
06.04.88 Jose Favila W CO 8 Houston
Summary: 38 contests, won 36, drew 1, lost 1.

Cesar (Patico) Polanco
Dominican Republic. *Born* 29.11.67
WBC International S. Flyweight Champion. Former IBF S. Flyweight Champion. Former Undefeated Con. Am. Flyweight Champion

25.05.83 Elpidio Jimenez W CO 1 Santiago
25.07.83 Sisia Noesi W PTS 4 Santiago
26.09.83 Rafael Ramos W PTS 6 Santiago
17.10.83 Vicente Arias W PTS 6 Santiago
16.11.83 Juan Maria Ortiz W RSC 1 Santiago
07.12.83 Rafael Ramos W RSC 3 Santiago
12.03.84 Bernardo Diaz W PTS 8 Santiago
13.09.84 Rafael Cabrera DREW 10 Santiago
20.10.84 Victor Espinal W CO 3 Santiago
31.01.85 David Reyes W RSC 4 Santiago
(*Vacant Con. Am. Flyweight Title*)
11.03.85 Isaias Rodriguez W DIS 2 Santiago
16.04.85 Elpidio de Paula W RSC 4 Santiago
16.11.85 Julio Gudino L PTS 10 Panama City
25.11.85 Fernando Mateo W CO 5 Santiago
15.02.86 Elly Pical W PTS 15 Jakarta
(*IBF S. Flyweight Title Challenge*)
05.07.86 Elly Pical L CO 3 Jakarta
(*IBF S. Flyweight Title Defence*)
29.04.87 Alfredo Gomez W CO 3 Curacao
16.08.87 Franco Cherchi W CO 6 Salerno
(*Vacant WBC International S. Flyweight Title*)
Summary: 18 contests, won 15, drew 1, lost 2.

James Pritchard
Louisville, USA. *Born* 27.04.61
Heavyweight

21.09.85 Vince Parker W CO 2 Las Vegas
17.01.86 Amanise Johnson W PTS 4 Atlanta
28.03.86 Allan Hudson W RSC 4 Las Vegas
25.04.86 John Morton W RSC 1 Louisville
24.06.86 Tim Miller W CO 2 Lexington
10.07.86 Louis Brooks W RSC 1 Houston
29.07.86 Melvin Epps W PTS 6 Lexington
28.08.86 Robert Evans W PTS 6 New York
03.10.86 Mike Johnson W CO 1 Louisville

James Pritchard
Peter Goldfield/USA

31.10.86 Warren Thompson W PTS 6 Atlantic City
25.11.86 Bobby Crabtree W RSC 2 Louisville
20.02.87 Mike Hunter DREW 6 Atlantic City
24.02.87 Larry Phelps W RSC 2 Lexington
17.03.87 Darrell Peppers W CO 2 Lexington
20.04.87 Kevin Cashmere W RSC 7 Lexington
28.07.87 Frankie Hines W RSC 2 Lexington
24.08.87 Mike Weaver L RSC 6 Louisville
05.01.88 Bruce Johnson W CO 5 Lexington
21.02.88 Mike Cohen W RSC 3 Frankfort
25.03.88 Steve Zouski W RSC 4 Chicago
28.04.88 Michael Dokes L RSC 7 New York
Summary: 21 contests, won 18, drew 1, lost 2.

Chris Pyatt
Leicester, England. *Born* 03.07.63
Former EBU L. Middleweight Champion & Former Undefeated British L. Middleweight Champion

01.03.83 Paul Murray W RTD 2 London
05.04.83 Billy Waith W RSC 8 London
28.04.83 Lee Hartshorn W RSC 3 Leicester
27.09.83 Darwin Brewster W PTS 8 Wembley
08.10.83 Tyrone Demby W RSC 2 Atlantic City
22.11.83 Tony Britton W RSC 4 Wembley
22.02.84 Judas Clottey W PTS 8 London
15.03.84 Pat Thomas W PTS 10 Leicester
09.05.84 Franki Moro W CO 4 Leicester
23.05.84 Alfonso Redondo W RSC 3 London
16.10.84 John Ridgman W RSC 1 London
16.11.84 Brian Anderson W PTS 12 Leicester
12.02.85 Helier Custos W RSC 5 London
05.06.85 Graeme Ahmed W RSC 3 London
01.07.85 Mosimo Maeleke W RSC 6 London
23.09.85 Sabiyala Diavilia L RSC 4 London
19.02.86 Prince Rodney W CO 9 London
(*British L. Middleweight Title Challenge*)
20.05.86 Thomas Smith W RSC 1 Wembley
17.09.86 John van Elteren W CO 1 London
(*Vacant EBU L. Middleweight Title*)
25.10.86 Renaldo Hernandez W RSC 3 Paris
28.01.87 Gianfranco Rosi L PTS 12 Perugia
(*EBU L. Middleweight Title Defence*)
18.04.87 Dennis Johnson W CO 2 London
26.05.87 Sammy Floyd W RSC 2 Wembley
28.10.87 Gilbert Josamu W PTS 8 Wembley
Summary: 24 contests, won 22, lost 2.

Dwight (Camden Buzzsaw) Muhammad Qawi
Baltimore, USA. *Born* 05.01.53
Former WBC L. Heavyweight Champion & Former WBA Cruiserweight Champion

19.04.78 Leonard Langley DREW 6 Washington
03.06.78 Lou Benson W PTS 6 Baltimore
02.11.78 Johnny Davis L PTS 6 New York
25.05.79 Lou Butler W PTS 6 Baltimore
03.07.79 Lou Butler W PTS 8 Atlantic City
26.09.79 Biff Cline W RSC 1 Baltimore
14.11.79 Johnny Wilburn W PTS 8 Baltimore
04.02.80 Theunis Kok W CO 10 Durban
29.03.80 Cornell Chavis W CO 1 Atlantic City
08.05.80 Leonard Langley W RSC 2 Atlantic City
05.06.80 Charlie Smith W RTD 4 Atlantic City
14.08.80 Rick Jester W RSC 3 Chicago
06.11.80 Tony Mesoraca W RTD 6 Atlantic City
08.01.81 Johnny Davis W PTS 10 Atlantic City
05.03.81 Al Bolden W PTS 10 Philadelphia
31.05.81 Mike Rossman W CO 7 Atlantic City
05.09.81 James Scott W PTS 10 Rahway
19.12.81 Matt Saad Muhammad W RSC 10 Atlantic City
(*WBC L. Heavyweight Title Challenge*)
21.03.82 Jerry Martin W RSC 6 Las Vegas
(*WBC L. Heavyweight Title Defence*)
07.08.82 Matt Saad Muhammad W RSC 6 Philadelphia
(*WBC L. Heavyweight Title Defence*)
20.11.82 Eddie Davis W RSC 11 Atlantic City
(*WBC L. Heavyweight Title Defence*)
18.03.83 Michael Spinks L PTS 15 Atlantic City
(*WBC L. Heavyweight Title Defence & WBA L. Heavyweight Title Challenge*)
17.09.83 Johnny Davis W PTS 10 Atlantic City
21.03.84 Vic Valentino W PTS 10 Atlantic City
12.12.84 Stanley Ross W PTS 10 Atlantic City
27.02.85 Michael Greer W PTS 10 Atlantic City
27.07.85 Piet Crous W CO 11 Sun City
(*WBA Cruiserweight Title Challenge*)
08.01.86 Ric Enis W CO 1 Atlantic City
23.03.86 Leon Spinks W RSC 6 Reno
(*WBA Cruiserweight Title Defence*)
12.07.86 Evander Holyfield L PTS 15 Atlanta
(*WBA Cruiserweight Title Defence*)
06.02.87 Sixto Maldonado W CO 4 Atlantic City
15.05.87 Ossie Ocasio L PTS 10 Las Vegas
15.08.87 Lee Roy Murphy W RSC 6 St Tropez
05.12.87 Evander Holyfield L CO 4 Atlantic City
(*IBF Cruiserweight Title Challenge*)
19.03.88 George Foreman L RSC 7 Las Vegas
Summary: 35 contests, won 28, drew 1, lost 6.

Jose (Pepo) Quinones
Puerto Rico. *Born* 13.09.61
Puerto Rican Middleweight Champion. Former Con. Am. Middleweight Champion

16.10.80 Jose Guerrero W CO 1 Los Angeles
20.11.80 Odell Hadley L PTS 4 Los Angeles
26.04.81 Aldo Polesel W RSC 2 Mantova
28.05.81 Jean-Philippe Truchelut W RSC 2 Milan
18.06.81 Paul Muyodi W RSC 1 Milan
28.10.81 Zack Bolden L PTS 4 Las Vegas
04.11.81 Warren Hardy W RSC 1 Las Vegas
14.11.81 Pedro Guerrero W CO 3 Las Vegas
21.11.81 Fred Hutchings L PTS 6 Las Vegas
22.05.82 Luis Palma W PTS 6 Las Vegas
29.05.82 Sumbu Kalambay L CO 2 Milan
21.10.82 Ron Ayers W PTS 6 Cleveland
19.01.83 Al Cook W CO 2 San Juan
16.03.83 Costello King W RSC 2 San Juan
01.05.83 Esteban Pizarro L RSC 4 San Juan
03.02.84 John Burney W PTS 6 Miami
14.03.84 Leroy Moore W RSC 1 Miami
04.04.84 Keith Adams DREW 8 Miami
04.05.84 Ed Flanning W CO 1 Miami
14.08.84 Elvis Parks DREW 8 Miami
30.03.85 Reyes Escalera W RSC 3 Santurce
26.04.85 Horacio Perez W RSC 4 New York
(*Vacant Con. Am. Middleweight Title*)
14.06.85 Arthur Holt W RSC 11 New York
(*Con. Am. Middleweight Title Defence*)
14.12.85 Esteban Pizarro L RSC 6 Catano
(*Con. Am. Middleweight Title Defence*)
01.03.86 Santos Solis W CO 4 Barceloneta
(*Vacant Puerto Rican Middleweight Title*)
29.08.86 Sean Mannion L PTS 10 Lowell
08.11.86 Victor Claudio L PTS 10 San Juan
20.02.87 Doug de Witt W RSC 3 Atlantic City
30.07.87 Gilberto Espinosa W PTS 10 San Juan
28.11.87 Errol Christie W RSC 4 Windsor
Summary: 30 contests, won 20, drew 2, lost 8.

Jorge (Schoolboy) Ramirez
Los Angeles, USA. *Born* 17.10.64
S. Bantamweight

13.11.82 Tony Montoya L PTS 4 Las Vegas
30.11.82 Tony Montoya L PTS 6 Las Vegas
20.01.83 Juan Rodriguez W PTS 6 Los Angeles
03.02.83 Adolfo Lopez L PTS 4 Los Angeles
19.04.83 Desi Newbill W PTS 6 El Cajon
02.05.83 Alfonso Velasquez DREW 6 El Cajon
02.06.83 Sam Espinosa W CO 1 Los Angeles
23.06.83 Juan Giron W CO 3 Los Angeles
15.07.83 Luis Hernandez W PTS 6 San Bernardino
26.08.83 Sam Espinosa DREW 8 Los Angeles
29.09.83 Vicente Juarez W RSC 2 Los Angeles
20.10.83 Ramon Almaguer DREW 8 Los Angeles

17.11.83 Adan Uribe W RSC 4 Los Angeles
01.12.83 Tony Escobar W RSC 9 Los Angeles
16.02.84 J. T. Walker W RSC 10 Los Angeles
12.04.84 Salvador Caballero W CO 2 Los Angeles
26.04.84 Hugo Partida W CO 2 Los Angeles
31.05.84 Pinky Rivera W CO 9 Los Angeles
17.11.84 Refugio Alvarado W RSC 4 Los Angeles
07.03.85 Ruben Solario W RSC 4 Los Angeles
20.05.85 Rocky Garcia L PTS 10 Los Angeles
03.07.85 Oscar Muniz W PTS 10 Los Angeles
26.09.85 Arturo Hernandez W CO 9 Tijuana
23.10.85 Oscar Bejinez L RSC 9 Tijuana
28.05.87 Ralph Gutierrez W PTS 8 Irvine
28.03.88 Jorge Urbina Diaz W RSC 5 Los Angeles
Summary: 26 contests, won 18, drew 3, lost 5

Jose Luis Ramirez

Huatabampo, Mexico. *Born* 02.12.58
WBC Lightweight Champion. Former Undefeated NABF & Mexican Lightweight Champion

25.03.73 Mario Amparan W RSC 6 Huatabampo
15.04.73 Noe Morales W CO 1 Huatabampo
29.04.73 Roberto Navarrete W CO 1 Huatabampo
15.05.73 Chuy Lopez W RSC 3 Huatabampo
12.07.73 Delfino Mendoza W CO 1 Huatabampo
01.08.73 Delfino Mendoza W PTS 6 Obregon
15.08.73 Lino Munoz W RSC 3 Obregon
30.08.73 Gustavo Guerrero W RSC 5 Huatabampo
20.09.73 Jesse Torres W RSC 1 Huatabampo
10.10.73 Indio Huicosa W PTS 6 Obregon
30.10.73 Chamaco Perez W RSC 5 Obregon
16.03.74 Mario Fontanel W RSC 3 Prieta
29.03.74 Indio Huicosa W RSC 2 Obregon
05.04.74 Gustavo Guerrero W PTS 8 Navojoa
07.05.74 Rudy Sanchez W RSC 2 Huatabampo
12.05.74 Jose Gonzalez W RSC 1 Obregon
17.05.74 Enrique Torres W RSC 3 Navojoa
14.06.74 Salomon Tapia W PTS 8 Navojoa
16.07.74 Pajaro Morales W RSC 5 Huatabampo
21.03.75 Pajaro Morales W RSC 2 Obregon
18.04.75 Jose Lizarraga W RSC 3 Guaymas
30.04.75 Sergio Enriquez L PTS 10 Obregon
21.05.75 Ernesto Castillo W RSC 2 Obregon
18.06.75 Nino Gonzalez W PTS 10 Obregon
15.08.75 Cono Lopez W RSC 3 Obregon
01.10.75 Lorenzo Maldonado W RSC 3 Obregon
13.02.76 Frankie Crawford W RSC 7 Obregon
17.05.76 Roy Esparza W RSC 4 Tijuana
07.06.76 Javier Rios W RSC 1 Culiacan
17.06.76 Nexae Macias W RSC 1 Obregon
06.08.76 Rolando Ramirez W RSC 5 Culiacan
13.09.76 Elio Hernandez W RSC 3 Tijuana
27.09.76 Jesus Delgado W RSC 3 Tijuana
05.11.76 Batoto Salazar W RSC 5 Guaymas
15.11.76 Jesus Lara W CO 4 Tijuana
11.02.77 Ramon Peraza W PTS 10 Los Mochis
12.04.77 Rolando Martinez W CO 1 La Paz
29.06.77 Carlos Ulloa W CO 1 Tijuana
07.07.77 Toluco Munoz W RSC 4 Los Mochis
01.08.77 Aurelio Muniz W PTS 10 Los Mochis
07.12.77 Camilo Ibarra W CO 7 Obregon
07.01.78 Joe Gallardo W CO 7 La Paz
03.02.78 Henry Jacobo W CO 5 Obregon
17.02.78 Indio Perez W CO 4 Obregon
28.04.78 Ruben Olivares L RSC 2 Obregon
23.06.78 Chito Felix W RSC 3 Huatabampo
07.07.78 Bobo Gonzalez W CO 2 Huatabampo
21.07.78 Salvador Torres W RSC 3 Obregon
01.09.78 Leonardo Bermudez W PTS 10 Obregon
20.10.78 David Bernal W CO 3 Tijuana
01.12.78 Cesar Savinon W CO 2 Obregon
02.02.79 Aurelio Muniz W RSC 9 Obregon
07.03.79 Julio Nava W CO 3 Hermosillo
06.04.79 Saul Montana W RSC 7 Guaymas
15.06.79 Beto Gutierrez W RSC 9 Obregon
(*Vacant Mexican Lightweight Title*)
08.07.79 Cachorro Estrella W CO 7 Huatabampo
27.07.79 Antonio Nava W PTS 10 Obregon
20.08.79 Ignacio Campos W RSC 6 Tijuana
28.09.79 Jose Luis Castillo W PTS 12 Obregon
(*Mexican Lightweight Title Defence*)
11.11.79 Joe Gallardo W CO 4 Huatabampo
26.11.79 Ignacio Campos W RSC 12 Tijuana
(*Mexican Lightweight Title Defence*)
19.12.79 Eric Bonilla W CO 4 Obregon
03.02.80 Jose Torres W CO 3 Mexicali
21.03.80 German Cuello W CO 8 Los Angeles
19.06.80 Rafael Nunez W CO 1 Tacoma
09.07.80 Jesus Lara W CO 7 Navojoa
10.08.80 Manuel Sanchez W RSC 6 Huatabampo
23.08.80 Dario de Jesus W CO 1 Los Angeles
11.10.80 Vicente Mijares W RSC 6 Mexico
(*Mexican Lightweight Title Defence*)
14.11.80 Alexis Arguello L PTS 10 Miami
07.02.81 Ernesto Garfias W RSC 7 Los Angeles
27.02.81 Abdul Bey W CO 3 Huatabampo
04.04.81 Celso Limon W CO 1 Hermosillo
10.05.81 Ezequiel Sanchez W PTS 10 Los Angeles
19.07.81 Ray Mancini L PTS 12 Warren
(*NABF Lightweight Title Challenge*)
31.08.81 Jose L. Soberanes W PTS 10 Navojoa
24.10.81 Benny Abarca W CO 6 Tuxtla
(*Mexican Lightweight Title Defence*)
19.03.82 Benny Abarca W CO 3 Culiacan
(*Mexican Lightweight Title Defence*)
08.05.82 Jorge Morales W PTS 10 San Jose
25.06.82 Ricardo Peralta W CO 6 San Jose
(*Mexican Lightweight Title Defence*)
27.08.82 Ernesto Herrera W CO 4 Obregon
10.09.82 Rigoberto Ruiz W CO 5 San Jose
01.10.82 Eleazar Delgado W CO 4 Tijuana
23.10.82 Ramon Avitia W RSC 6 Tijuana
(*Mexican Lightweight Title Defence*)
26.11.82 Frankie Moultrie W RSC 3 Houston
(*Vacant NABF Lightweight Title*)
27.02.83 Jesus Cebreros W CO 3 San Luis
01.05.83 Edwin Rosario L PTS 12 San Juan
(*Vacant WBC Lightweight Title*)
07.10.83 Joe Gallardo W CO 2 Guaymas
04.11.83 Manuel Sanchez W RSC 3 Naucalpan
01.01.84 Victor Kelly W RSC 3 Mazatlan
11.05.84 Hector Medina W CO 4 Mazatlan
02.06.84 Martin Quiroz W PTS 10 Oakland
03.11.84 Edwin Rosario W RSC 4 San Juan
(*WBC Lightweight Title Challenge*)
13.03.85 J. T. Walker W RSC 4 San Jose
06.06.85 Manny Hernandez W PTS 10 Las Vegas
10.08.85 Hector Camacho L PTS 12 Las Vegas
(*WBC Lightweight Title Defence*)
15.09.86 Nick Parker W RSC 6 Paris
25.10.86 Charlie Brown W PTS 10 Paris
10.12.86 John Senegal W RSC 2 Paris
27.03.87 Efrain Nieves W RSC 3 Cannes
16.04.87 Davis Taylor W PTS 10 Marseilles
12.05.87 Roger Brown W RSC 7 Le Mans
26.05.87 Steve Mitchell W CO 5 Villeurbanne
19.07.87 Terrence Alli W PTS 12 St Tropez
(*Vacant WBC Lightweight Title*)
10.10.87 Cornelius Boza-Edwards W CO 5 Paris
(*WBC Lightweight Title Defence*)
19.12.87 John Rafuse W RSC 4 Paris
12.03.88 Pernell Whitaker W PTS 12 Paris
(*WBC Lightweight Title Defence*)
Summary: 107 contests, won 101, lost 6.

Primo Ramos

Durango, Mexico. *Born* 09.06.60
NABF Lightweight Champion. Former Undefeated Mexican Lightweight Champion

05.06.81 Gary Stallworth W CO 1 Chicago
27.07.81 Wayne Ingram W CO 2 Chicago
21.08.81 Ramon Ochoa W RSC 5 Chicago
02.09.81 Nate Stewart W PTS 6 Chicago
03.11.81 Tony Travis W RSC 6 Chicago
28.11.81 Raul Bencomo W PTS 10 Chihuahua
11.03.82 Gary Brown W RSC 4 Chicago
15.09.82 Bobby Paggie W CO 1 Chicago
16.10.82 Robin Blake L PTS 10 Atlantic City
16.12.82 Terrence Alli L RSC 2 Atlantic City
11.03.83 Mando Cardoso W CO 6 Durango
08.04.83 Canon Hernandez W PTS 10 Durango
30.06.83 Othoniel Lopez W RSC 8 La Paz
15.07.83 Tony Soto W RSC 6 Durango
12.08.83 Tony Perez W RSC 5 Durango
02.09.83 Memin Barcenas W RSC 5 Durango
18.11.83 Ramiro Lozano W CO 8 Durango
08.12.83 Ted Hatfield W CO 3 Houston
30.12.83 Jose L. Castillo W RSC 5 Durango
07.01.84 Jose Rivera W PTS 10 Houston
02.02.84 Rafael Martinez W CO 2 Durango
25.02.84 Ezequiel Mosqueda L PTS 10 Houston
16.11.84 Melvin Paul L PTS 10 Houston
30.12.84 Gaspar Pool W PTS 10 Durango
05.03.85 Ezzard Charles W RSC 10 Houston
20.04.85 Juan Garcia W PTS 10 Durango
02.06.85 Charles Adams W CO 3 Durango
16.08.85 Martin Galvan W CO 6 Durango
18.10.85 Ricardo Peralta W PTS 10 Durango
20.03.86 Ricardo Peralta W PTS 12 Durango
(*Vacant Mexican Lightweight Title*)
06.06.86 Juan Escobar W CO 6 Durango
18.07.86 Jorge Gomez W CO 4 Durango
14.09.86 Herminio Delgado W RSC 10 Villahermosa
(*Vacant Mexican Lightweight Title*)
01.01.87 Rocky Balboa W PTS 12 Durango
(*Mexican Lightweight Title Defence*)
19.04.87 Meldrick Taylor L PTS 10 Phoenix
27.07.87 Vernon Buchanan W CO 3 Los Angeles
28.10.87 Frankie Randall W CO 2 Las Vegas
(*Vacant NABF Lightweight Title*)
16.04.88 Kearns Ibarra W RSC 1 Las Vegas
Summary: 38 contests, won 33, lost 5.

Frankie (The Surgeon) Randall

Morristown, USA. *Born* 25.09.61
Lightweight

04.02.83 Curtis Golston W CO 2 Knoxville
19.02.83 Marcell Wade W RSC 2 Las Vegas
12.03.83 Don Thorps W CO 1 Ashland
02.04.83 Frank Mackey W RSC 2 Lancaster
12.05.83 Charles Sweetenburg W CO 1 Bristol
26.05.83 Charles Sweetenburg W CO 2 Knoxville
25.06.83 Willie Taylor W DIS 4 Pennington Gap
16.09.83 Freddie Guzman W RSC 6 Tampa
21.10.83 Adolfo Marquez W CO 4 Monroe
12.11.83 Richard Lassiter W RSC 5 Tampa
02.12.83 Reese Smith W RSC 4 Tampa
01.02.84 Luis de Jesus W RSC 3 Tampa
15.03.84 Ezequiel Mosquera W PTS 8 Tampa
03.05.84 Jerome Artis W CO 2 Tampa
21.06.84 Jose Rentas W CO 2 Tampa
12.07.84 Steve Mitchell W CO 3 Tampa
30.08.84 Jose Gonzalez W RSC 6 Morristown
11.09.84 Eduardo Lugo W RSC 4 Tampa
17.10.84 Ezzard Charles Adams W PTS 10 Tampa
24.11.84 Shelton Nixon W RSC 2 Bristol
17.01.85 Rashid Aziz W RSC 2 Tampa
23.03.85 Fred Pendleton W RSC 5 Bristol
01.05.85 Davey Brown W PTS 10 Tampa
16.06.85 Edwin Rosario L PTS 10 London
05.10.85 Keith Jackson W CO 4 Morristown
12.12.85 Efrain Nieves W RSC 2 Tampa
30.05.86 Sammy Fuentes W RSC 2 Atlantic City
04.07.86 Fred Pendleton DREW 12 Atlantic City
(*Vacant USBA Lightweight Title*)
03.10.86 Aldemir Mosquera W RSC 3 Atlantic City
16.01.87 Al Martino W RSC 2 Atlantic City
25.03.87 Shelton le Blanc W RTD 5 Atlantic City
09.05.87 Joe Edens W RSC 3 Bristol
28.10.87 Primo Ramos L CO 2 Las Vegas
(*Vacant NABF Lightweight Title*)
19.03.88 Ricardo Cardenas W CO 1 Nashville
Summary: 34 contests, won 31, drew 1, lost 2.

Sam Reeson

Battersea, England. *Born* 05.01.63
EBU Cruiserweight Champion. Former Undefeated British Cruiserweight Champion

19.05.83 Calvin Earlington W PTS 6 London
17.10.83 Glenroy Taylor W PTS 6 London
08.11.83 Alex Romeo W PTS 6 London
28.11.83 Geoff Rymer W PTS 8 London
12.12.83 Eddie Cooper W PTS 6 Bedworth
03.02.84 John Joseph W PTS 8 Maidenhead
27.03.84 Gordon Stacey W PTS 8 London
17.04.84 Steve Lewin W PTS 8 London
18.09.84 Chris Lawson W PTS 8 London
03.10.84 Antonio Harris W PTS 8 Solihull
23.10.84 Michael Armstrong W CO 2 London
20.11.84 Paul Newman W PTS 8 London
24.01.85 Trevor Cattouse W RSC 6 London
26.02.85 Geoff Rymer W RSC 5 London
25.03.85 Theo Josephs W PTS 8 London
09.05.85 Liam Coleman W PTS 8 London
31.10.85 Stewart Lithgo W PTS 12 London
(*Vacant British Cruiserweight Title*)
09.12.85 Rubin Williams W PTS 10 London
10.01.86 Roy Smith W PTS 8 London
15.04.86 Roy Skeldon W PTS 8 London
29.05.86 Louis Pergaud L RSC 4 London
14.03.87 Roy Saffold W PTS 10 London
22.04.87 Manfred Jassman W PTS 12 London
(*Vacant EBU Cruiserweight Title*)
28.11.87 Luigi Ricci W CO 7 Windsor
(*EBU Cruiserweight Title Defence*)
Summary: 24 contests, won 23, lost 1.

Chris Reid

Chris (Shamrock Express) Reid
Brooklyn, USA. *Born* 14.03.63
L. Heavyweight

30.05.84 Glenn Johnson W RSC 1 Atlantic City
17.06.84 Ron Ayers W RSC 1 Tampa
30.06.84 Chris Coady W RSC 2 Belfast
26.09.84 Pedro Montero W RSC 1 Atlantic City
13.10.84 Paul Newman W RSC 3 Belfast
31.10.84 Ralph Smiley W PTS 6 Atlantic City
13.02.85 Miguel Rosa W RSC 1 Atlantic City
23.02.85 Cordwell Hylton W CO 3 Belfast
13.03.85 Fred Jordan W RSC 4 Atlantic City
24.04.85 Pop Nance T DRAW 2 Atlantic City
18.09.85 David Overton W CO 1 Atlantic City
28.09.85 Hugh Johnson W RSC 7 Belfast
26.11.85 Wesley Reid T DRAW 2 Atlantic City
05.02.86 Maurice Moore W RSC 1 Atlantic City
02.04.86 Darryl Spain W RSC 7 Totowa
14.08.86 Mark Frazie W RSC 7 New York
09.10.86 Marcos Geraldo W RTD 4 New York
08.01.87 Jerome Clouden W RSC 2 New York
09.04.87 Ian Mattis W RSC 6 New York
18.06.87 Fully Obelmejias L RSC 10 New York
12.11.87 Irwin Hines W RSC 4 New York
04.02.88 Doug Kaluza W CO 3 New York
17.03.88 Vince Hopper DREW 10 New York
Summary: 23 contests, won 19, drew 3, lost 1.

Vince Releford
Fort Worth, USA. *Born* 03.10.63
L. Welterweight

25.10.84 Keheven Johnson W PTS 4 Fort Worth
15.12.84 Vernon Larremore W CO 1 Fort Worth
09.02.85 Alex Medel W PTS 6 Midland
30.04.85 Gregorio Ibarra W CO 5 Fort Worth
27.06.85 Roberto Garcia W PTS 6 Las Vegas
11.09.85 Ricky Randall W CO 1 Houston
06.11.85 Bob Smith W RSC 1 Las Vegas
11.12.85 Mike Goudeau W CO 5 Houston
07.02.86 Stewart Baynes W PTS 8 Las Vegas
09.03.86 Paul Barton W RSC 7 Fort Worth
18.06.86 J. J. Watters DREW 10 Galveston
23.09.86 Ramon Cardenas W CO 2 Fort Worth
21.11.86 Sergio Valles W RSC 5 Fort Worth
26.12.86 Ricky Young W PTS 10 Atlantic City
24.04.87 James McGirt L RSC 2 Albany
(*Con. Am. L. Welterweight Title Challenge*)
19.01.88 Ronnie Shields W PTS 10 Fort Worth
Summary: 16 contests, won 14, drew 1, lost 1.

Jean-Marc Renard

Jean-Marc Renard
Huy, Belgium. *Born* 19.04.56
Former Undefeated EBU S. Featherweight Champion.
Former Undefeated Belgium Featherweight Champion

28.11.80 Marc Amand W PTS 6 Liege
16.01.81 Daniel Champagne W PTS 6 Liege
31.01.81 Claude Kessaci W PTS 6 Liege
28.02.81 Haidar Nourredine W PTS 6 Liege
17.04.81 Daniel Paysserand W RSC 1 Liege
16.05.81 Rafael Blanco W RSC 5 Liege
22.09.81 Barry McGuigan L PTS 8 Belfast
10.12.81 Steve Sammy Sims L PTS 8 Newport
26.02.82 Angelo Licata W PTS 10 Brustem
(*Belgian Featherweight Title Challenge*)
23.03.82 Richie Foster W RSC 5 Belfast
15.05.82 Andre Blanco W PTS 8 Zele
23.06.82 Haidar Nourredine W PTS 8 Bressoux
25.12.82 Dominique Cesari W RTD 4 Izegem
14.01.83 Andre Blanco W PTS 8 Zele
04.02.83 Sammy Meck W PTS 8 Grivegnee
18.03.83 Jose Luis Vicho W PTS 8 Brustem
06.05.83 Mohamed Maalem W RTD 2 Grivegnee
24.09.83 John Sharkey W PTS 8 Oostrobeke
01.11.83 Don George W CO 4 Izegem
25.12.83 Farid Gallouze W RSC 3 Izegem
22.01.84 Steve Pollard W PTS 8 Izegem
12.04.84 Alfredo Raininger W PTS 12 Casavatore
(*EBU S. Featherweight Title Challenge*)
07.07.84 Pat Cowdell L PTS 12 Birmingham
(*EBU S. Featherweight Title Defence*)
01.11.84 Moussa Sangare W PTS 8 Izegem
25.01.85 Sammy Meck W DIS 7 Charleroi
15.02.85 Kamel Djadda W RSC 6 Huy
22.03.85 Mohamed Maalem W RTD 2 Brustem
24.06.85 Jose Maillot W RTD 4 Liege
02.08.85 Vicente Fernandez W RTD 5 Rochefort
19.10.85 Vicente Macias W RSC 4 Middlekerke
29.01.86 Marco Gallo W RSC 8 Catanzaro
(*Vacant EBU S. Featherweight Title*)
18.04.86 Fernando Rodriguez W CO 8 Brustem
(*EBU S. Featherweight Title Defence*)
30.08.86 Pat Doherty W RSC 5 Middlekerke
31.10.86 Najib Daho W RTD 5 Kortrijk
(*EBU S. Featherweight Title Defence*)
20.12.86 Daniel Londas DREW 12 St Ouen
(*EBU S. Featherweight Title Defence*)
11.03.87 Antonio Renzo W RSC 8 Cosenza
(*EBU S. Featherweight Title Defence*)
06.06.87 Jeff Roberts W RSC 2 Chaudfontaine
01.11.87 John Farrell W RTD 7 Izegem
05.12.87 Jose Garcia W RSC 6 Natoye
25.12.87 Paul Huggins W RTD 8 Izegem
10.04.88 Kevin Pritchard W RSC 3 Grivegnee
Summary: 41 contests, won 37, drew 1, lost 3.

Vince Releford (left), hands held low, on his way to a points victory over Ricky Young, 26 December 1986
Peter Goldfield/USA

Jose (Nino) Ribalta
Miami, USA. *Born* Cuba 31.03.63
Heavyweight

20.01.82 J. C. Richardson W RSC 2 Fort Lauderdale
05.02.82 Doug Fowler W CO 2 Miami
21.05.82 Ken Davis W PTS 6 Miami
18.06.82 Ken Ring W CO 3 Hialeah
09.07.82 Gabriel Sainz W CO 2 Hialeah
20.07.82 Curtis Gaskins W RSC 2 Fort Lauderdale
03.09.82 Al Leticky W CO 1 Hialeah
21.10.82 John L. Johnson W CO 1 Hialeah
06.11.82 Nate Robinson W RSC 5 Fort Lauderdale
14.01.83 Miles Prince W RSC 2 Hialeah
18.02.83 Ricardo Richardson L RSC 7 Hialeah
29.04.83 Ron Harry W RSC 6 Hialeah
03.06.83 Tom Prater W PTS 8 Hialeah
01.09.83 Robert Evans W PTS 8 Atlantic City
28.10.83 Ishaq Hussein W RSC 6 Atlantic City
15.12.83 Juan Figueroa W DIS 7 Atlantic City
08.03.84 Jim Jones W PTS 8 Miami
26.07.84 Nate Robinson W RSC 2 Miami
18.10.84 Cecil Coffee DREW 10 Atlantic City
29.04.85 James Smith L PTS 10 Buffalo
23.07.85 Ernie Barr W PTS 10 Miami
11.09.85 Marvis Frazier L PTS 10 Atlantic City
04.03.86 Al Houck W RSC 3 Miami
04.04.86 Jeff Feeney W RSC 1 Miami
13.05.86 David Jaco W CO 5 Bloomington
20.06.86 Ricky Keller W CO 1 Miami
17.08.86 Mike Tyson L RSC 10 Atlantic City
26.09.86 Johnny Williams W RSC 2 Miami
17.01.87 Leon Spinks W RSC 1 Miami
16.05.87 Mark Young W PTS 10 Miami
12.09.87 Steve Zouski W PTS 10 Miami
Summary: 31 contests, won 26, drew 1, lost 4.

Greg (The Flea) Richardson
Youngstown, USA. *Born* 1958
Former Undefeated USBA S. Bantamweight Champion.
Former Undefeated NABF Bantamweight Champion

26.02.82 Al Dunlap W CO 1 Niles
17.03.82 Henry Lee W CO 1 Niles
08.05.82 Brett Livingston W PTS 4 Davison
23.08.82 Clarence Miller W RSC 2 Atlantic City
29.09.82 James Tolliver W PTS 4 Bookfield
14.10.82 Francis Childs L PTS 6 Conshohocken
24.04.83 Francis Childs W PTS 8 Atlantic City
27.07.83 Baby Kid Chocolate W PTS 8 Philadelphia
27.09.83 Felix Marquez W PTS 8 Atlantic City
15.11.83 Sonny Long W PTS 8 Atlantic City
17.01.84 Diego Rosario W PTS 8 Atlantic City
03.04.84 John Norman W RSC 4 Atlantic City
17.04.84 Romy Navarrete W PTS 10 Honolulu
26.05.84 Edgar Acevedo W PTS 10 Miami
31.07.84 Roy Muniz W RSC 8 Atlantic City
20.09.84 Harold Petty W PTS 12 Las Vegas
(*NABF Bantamweight Title Challenge*)
13.11.84 Alfonso Lopez W PTS 10 Atlantic City

Greg Richardson
Peter Goldfield/USA

25.01.85 James Manning W PTS 12 Portland
(*NABF Bantamweight Title Defence*)
04.06.85 Oscar Muniz W PTS 12 Atlantic City
(*USBA S. Bantamweight Title Challenge*)
01.10.85 James Tolliver W PTS 12 Atlantic City
14.08.86 Ron Cisneros W PTS 10 Lynnwood
26.11.86 Robert Shannon W PTS 12 Tacoma
(*USBA S. Bantamweight Title Defence*)
05.06.87 Darryl Thigpen W PTS 12 Los Angeles
(*USBA S. Bantamweight Title Defence*)
10.07.87 Jeff Fenech L RTD 5 Sydney
(*WBC S. Bantamweight Title Challenge*)
20.11.87 Jesse Benavides L PTS 12 Atlantic City
(*Vacant USBA S. Bantamweight Title*)
Summary: 25 contests, won 22, lost 3.

Antonio (Tonito) Rivera
Puerto Rico. *Born* 05.12.63
Former IBF Featherweight Champion. Former Puerto Rican S. Bantamweight Champion

26.02.81 Humberto Maldonado W RSC 1 Trujillo
06.03.81 Angel Torres W PTS 4 San Juan
26.03.81 Luis Ramos W RSC 3 Bayamon
22.05.81 Herminio Adorno L PTS 6 San Juan
09.07.81 Herminio Adorno W RSC 1 Trujillo
08.08.81 Elvin Gonzalez L PTS 6 San Juan
24.10.81 Ismael Espinosa W RSC 2 Trujillo
09.01.82 Ramon Canales W CO 3 San Juan
20.05.82 Frankie Granados W RSC 1 San Juan
16.07.82 Antonio Rodriguez W CO 2 Santo Domingo
31.07.82 Elvin Gonzalez W RSC 6 San Juan
09.10.82 Enrique Sanchez L PTS 10 Santo Domingo
12.02.83 Orlando Perez W PTS 12 Canovanas
(*Vacant Puerto Rican S. Bantamweight Title*)
16.04.83 Memo Armengot W CO 2 Trujillo
07.05.83 Feliciano Perez W RSC 5 Guaynabo
14.12.83 Manuel Santos W RSC 8 San Juan
26.07.84 Vince Christian W RSC 5 New York
01.09.84 Juan Veloz L RSC 11 Carolina
(*Puerto Rican S. Bantamweight Title Defence*)
02.02.85 Alberto Mercado W RSC 7 San Juan
12.07.85 Tony Miller DREW 10 Melbourne
05.10.85 Irving Mitchell W RSC 5 Guaynabo
30.08.86 Ki-Yung Chung W RTD 10 Osan
(*IBF Featherweight Title Challenge*)
23.01.88 Calvin Grove L RSC 4 Gamaches
(*IBF Featherweight Title Defence*)
Summary: 23 contests, won 17, drew 1, lost 5.

Jose Rivera
Bayamon, Puerto Rico. *Born* 1963
S. Featherweight

14.08.80 Bernabe Montanez DREW 4 San Juan
17.10.80 Monserrat Teron L PTS 4 Trujillo Alto
05.06.82 Enrique Maxwell W CO 1 San Juan
21.03.83 Miguel Santana DREW 6 Bayamon
17.08.83 Nelson Rodriguez W RSC 3 Trujillo Alto
03.09.83 Jose Ortiz W RSC 6 Trujillo Alto
17.03.84 Alberto Batista W CO 2 Hato Rey
23.06.84 Victor Aponte W PTS 6 San Juan
08.12.84 Jose Rosa W RSC 2 San Juan
08.02.85 Chris Anderson W CO 2 San Juan
24.05.85 Rey Estades W PTS 10 San Juan
04.10.85 Luis Rivera W CO 1 San Juan
06.12.85 Edgar Castro W RSC 2 San Juan
27.03.87 Brian Mitchell DREW 15 San Juan
(*WBA S. Featherweight Title Challenge*)
21.11.87 Ramiro Lozano W RSC 2 Las Vegas
26.04.88 Brian Mitchell L PTS 12 Madrid
(*WBA S. Featherweight Title Challenge*)
Summary: 16 contests, won 11, drew 3, lost 2.

Roberto Rivera
Puerto Rico
Fecarbox, Con. Am. & Puerto Rican Featherweight Champion

28.04.82 Ramon Peluyera W PTS 4 San Juan
12.06.82 Rene Merced W PTS 4 San Juan
31.07.82 Carlos Hernandez W PTS 4 San Juan
18.09.82 Rene Merced W PTS 6 San Juan
16.10.82 Pedro Arroyo L RSC 1 San Juan
27.12.82 Manuel Batista L PTS 8 Santo Domingo
09.04.83 Nelson Rodriguez W RSC 4 San Juan
10.12.83 Juvenal Ordenes L PTS 10 Miami
10.08.84 Melciades Pena W PTS 10 Curacao
08.12.84 Carlos Mateo W PTS 8 Hato Rey
26.01.85 Juan Torres W RSC 10 Hato Rey
(*Puerto Rican Featherweight Title Challenge*)
19.05.86 Alvaro Narvaez W PTS 12 San Juan
(*Fecarbox Featherweight Title Challenge*)
10.01.87 Atilano Quinones L CO 10 San Juan
21.03.87 Alberto Reyes W PTS 12 San Juan
(*Fecarbox Featherweight Title Defence & Vacant Con. Am. Featherweight Title*)
28.05.87 Atilano Quinones W CO 5 San Juan
(*Fecarbox & Con. Am. Featherweight Title Defence*)
24.03.88 Francisco Alvarez W RSC 10 San Juan
(*Fecarbox Featherweight Title Defence*)
Summary: 16 contests, won 12, lost 4.

Graciano Rocchigiani
Rheinhausen, West Germany. *Born* 29.12.63
IBF S. Middleweight Champion. West German L. Heavyweight Champion. Former Undefeated West German Middleweight Champion

10.09.83 Esperno Postl W RSC 2 Cologne
07.10.83 Marnix Heytens W RSC 1 Frankfurt
05.11.83 Jan Lefeber W PTS 4 Mannheim
14.01.84 Chaed Ringo W RSC 2 Dusseldorf
10.02.84 Mauro da Cruz W PTS 6 Frankfurt
24.02.84 Mick Morris W PTS 4 Hamburg
27.04.84 Franz Dorfer W RTD 2 Berlin
15.09.84 Butangi Nzolameso W PTS 6 Dortmund
05.10.84 Tony Britton W PTS 8 Frankfurt
01.12.84 Philippe Seys W PTS 8 Dusseldorf
09.03.85 T. P. Jenkins W RSC 6 Dusseldorf
26.04.85 Steve Johnson W PTS 10 Frankfurt
31.08.85 Moussa Mukandjo W PTS 10 Berlin
08.11.85 Rudiger Bitterling W RSC 3 Dusseldorf
(*Vacant West German Middleweight Title*)
29.11.85 Antoine Alcantara W CO 2 Frankfurt
01.03.86 James Cook W PTS 8 Cologne
12.05.86 Ian Lazarus W CO 8 Mannheim
03.10.86 Manfred Jassman W PTS 10 Berlin
(*West German L. Heavyweight Title Challenge*)
13.09.87 Ahmed Laghiali W RSC 2 Bad Homburg
03.10.87 Tommy Taylor W PTS 8 Stukenbrock
17.10.87 Lahcen Hamdi W RSC 3 Gifhorn
30.10.87 John Held W PTS 8 Bad Homburg
05.12.87 Mustafa Hamsho W CO 1 Dusseldorf
12.03.88 Vince Boulware W RSC 8 Dusseldorf
(*Vacant IBF S. Middleweight Title*)
Summary: 24 contests, won 24.

Ralf Rocchigiani
Rheinhausen, West Germany. *Born* 12.03.63
Former Undefeated West German Cruiserweight Champion

05.11.83 Hans Gimborn W CO 1 Mannheim
02.12.83 Horst Schulze W RSC 1 Stuttgart
14.01.84 Eddy Vandenhouwele W PTS 4 Dusseldorf
06.02.84 Alan Ash W PTS 6 Hamburg
24.02.84 Helmut Ulka W PTS 6 Hamburg
09.03.84 Francesco Campi W RSC 3 Frankfurt
13.04.84 Mike McCoy W PTS 6 Hagen
28.04.84 Liam Coleman DREW 6 Hamburg
08.06.84 Mladen Grubesic W PTS 6 Kassel
22.06.84 Brahim Ferisovic W RSC 3 Munich
15.09.84 Juan A. Barrera W PTS 6 Dortmund
05.10.84 Trevor Cattouse W CO 3 Frankfurt
20.10.84 Paul Muyodi DREW 6 Salzufen
01.12.84 Manfred Jassman L PTS 10 Dusseldorf
(*West German L. Heavyweight Title Challenge*)
10.05.85 Manfred Jassman DREW 10 Berlin
(*West German L. Heavyweight Title Challenge*)
21.08.85 Josef Kossmann W CO 2 Hamburg
(*Vacant West German Cruiserweight Title*)
31.08.85 Jose Seys W PTS 8 Berlin
29.11.85 Tom Collins W PTS 8 Frankfurt
20.12.85 Ibelo Moano W PTS 8 Russelsheim
01.03.86 Mikan Popovic W DIS 7 Cologne
12.05.86 Mladen Grubesic W RSC 2 Mannheim
03.10.86 Alex Blanchard L PTS 12 Berlin
(*EBU L. Heavyweight Title Challenge*)
27.02.87 Alex Zeh DREW 10 Hamburg
25.09.87 Manfred Jassman W PTS 10 Berlin
(*West German Cruiserweight Title Challenge*)
30.10.87 Tommy Taylor W PTS 8 Bad Homburg
05.12.87 Chisanda Mutti W PTS 10 Dusseldorf
23.01.88 Alex Zeh W CO 9 Hamburg
(*West German Cruiserweight Title Defence*)
19.02.88 Agamil Yilderim DREW 8 Berlin
26.04.88 Marvin Camel W PTS 10 Cologne
Summary: 29 contests, won 22, drew 5, lost 2.

Jose Adilson (Maguila) Rodrigues
Sao Paulo, Brazil. *Born* 12.06.58
Former Undefeated Con. Am. Heavyweight Champion. South American & Brazilian Heavyweight Champion

04.02.83 Jose Tavares W RTD 3 Sao Paulo
19.03.83 Alaerte Vaz W CO 2 Sao Paulo
14.05.83 Francisco Dias W CO 2 Sao Paulo
02.07.83 Waldemar Paulino W CO 1 Sao Paulo
(*Brazilian Heavyweight Title Challenge*)
15.08.83 Eduardo Olivera W CO 2 Sao Paulo
12.09.83 Marcos Tosto W CO 1 Sao Paulo
05.02.84 Domingo D'Elia W RSC 8 Sao Paulo
08.04.84 Antonio Musladino W CO 6 Sao Paulo
13.05.84 Mike White W PTS 10 Sao Paulo
29.07.84 Louis Pergaud W RTD 9 Sao Paulo
09.09.84 Juan Figueroa W CO 1 Sao Paulo
(*South American Heavyweight Title Challenge*)
28.10.84 Georg Butzbach W RSC 1 Sao Paulo
16.12.84 Louis Pergaud W RSC 9 Sao Paulo
10.02.85 Walter Santemore W RTD 5 Sao Paulo
31.03.85 Daniel Falconi L CO 3 Sao Paulo
09.06.85 Nate Robinson W CO 1 Sao Paulo
04.08.85 Peter Mulindwa W CO 2 Sao Paulo
06.10.85 Albert Syben W RTD 6 Sao Paulo
17.11.85 Andre van den Oetelaar L CO 5 Sao Paulo
02.03.86 Vedat Akova W RSC 3 Sao Paulo
18.05.86 Daniel Falconi W CO 7 Sao Paulo
(*South American Heavyweight Title Defence*)
27.07.86 Andre van den Oetelaar W CO 3 Sao Paulo
05.10.86 Melvin Epps W PTS 10 Sao Paulo
21.12.86 Rick Sekorski W PTS 12 Sao Paulo
(*Vacant Con. Am. Heavyweight Title*)
15.03.87 Felipe Rodriguez W CO 7 Sao Paulo
31.05.87 Lorenzo Boyd W CO 2 Curitiba
21.06.87 Mike Jameson W PTS 10 Sao Paulo
09.08.87 James Smith W PTS 10 Sao Paulo
11.10.87 Reggie Gross W PTS 10 Araraquara
20.12.87 Alfredo Evangelista W PTS 10 Rio de Janeiro
14.03.88 Jorge Cambiaso W CO 7 Buenos Aires
(*S. American Heavyweight Title Defence*)
Summary: 31 contests, won 29, lost 2.

Mauricio Rodriguez
Miami, USA. *Born* 1958
Con. Am. Welterweight Champion

02.04.81 James Averitt W RSC 3 Tampa
16.04.81 Mitch Thomas W PTS 4 Tampa
10.06.81 Jerome Cox W PTS 4 Tampa
18.07.81 Willie Jenkins W CO 1 Tampa
10.09.81 Roosevelt Moss W RSC 3 Tampa
24.09.81 Rondell Stevenson W RSC 4 Tampa
27.10.81 Manny Vega W CO 1 Tampa

11.11.81 Gene Taylor W PTS 6 Tampa
10.12.81 Ron Smith W PTS 8 Tampa
06.01.82 Paul Gentry W RSC 6 Tampa
11.02.82 Dexter Smith W PTS 8 Tampa
25.02.82 Carlos Santana W PTS 10 Tampa
02.05.82 Carlos Santana L PTS 10 Tampa
18.06.82 Dexter Smith W PTS 10 Hialeah
24.10.82 Anthony Bryant W PTS 6 Tampa
08.12.82 Dario de Jesus W PTS 8 Miami
04.03.83 Randy Mitchum W PTS 8 Tampa
08.07.83 Robert Lee W PTS 8 Tampa
26.08.83 Martin Rojas W PTS 10 Miami
18.11.83 Joe Hawkins W CO 6 Tampa
08.12.83 Adolfo Medel L PTS 8 Miami
01.11.85 William Goodman W PTS 4 Fort Lauderdale
13.12.85 John Stewart W PTS 6 Miami
04.03.86 Clinton Mack W PTS 6 Miami
25.04.86 Lorenzo Guzman W PTS 10 Hialeah
23.05.86 Dario de Jesus W CO 3 Miami
27.06.86 Cornelius Drane W RSC 8 Miami
26.09.86 Martin Rojas W PTS 10 Miami
21.11.86 Aldemar Mosquera W PTS 10 Hialeah
28.02.87 Eduardo Brinoles W PTS 10 Miami
12.09.87 Orlando Orozco W PTS 12 Miami
(Vacant Con. Am. Welterweight Title)
15.01.88 Danny Vargas W PTS 10 Miami
11.03.88 Fernando Martinez W RSC 8 Hialeah
Summary: 33 contests, won 31, lost 2.

Jesus (Sugar Baby) Rojas

Barranquilla, Colombia. *Born* 01.02.62
Former WBC S. Flyweight Champion. Former Undefeated Con. Am. & Latin American Flyweight Champion

13.02.81 Wilfredo Ruiz W PTS 6 Barranquilla
26.06.81 William Velazquez W PTS 6 Barranquilla
17.07.81 Alfredo Gomez W PTS 6 Barranquilla
18.09.81 Virgilio Palomo W PTS 10 Bogota
30.10.81 Francisco Quiroz W PTS 10 Barranquilla
15.01.82 Rafael Julio W PTS 10 Cartagena
14.05.82 Bernardo Gonzalez W RSC 4 Barranquilla
06.08.82 Rodolfo Flores W PTS 10 Barranquilla
02.10.82 Ramon Perez W RSC 8 Miami
30.10.82 Jose Badilla W CO 4 Miami
19.11.82 Gabriel Sepulveda W RTD 10 Miami
(Vacant Latin American Flyweight Title)
18.12.82 Alfonso Lopez W PTS 10 Cartagena
11.03.83 Joe Jackson W RSC 2 Miami
08.04.83 Enrique Guadamez W CO 3 Miami
29.04.83 Juan Ortiz W CO 3 Miami
10.06.83 Steve Whetstone W RSC 8 Miami
29.07.83 Alfonso Lopez W PTS 12 Miami
(Con. Am. Flyweight Title Challenge)
26.11.83 Norgi Castro W RSC 8 Miami
27.01.84 Nestor Obregon W RSC 9 Barranquilla
13.03.84 Rudy Crawford W RSC 6 Miami
18.04.84 Felipe Mojica W RSC 8 Miami
28.09.84 Jose Garcia W RSC 4 Miami
12.02.85 Nelson Garcia W CO 3 Miami
24.05.85 Lee Cargle W RSC 7 Miami
20.07.85 Juan Polo Perez DREW 10 Cartagena
26.04.86 Armando Acuna W CO 2 Miami
30.05.86 Juan Pagan W RSC 1 Miami
11.07.86 Rafael Orono W PTS 10 Miami
15.11.86 Jessie Williams W PTS 10 Barranquilla
08.08.87 Santos Laciar W PTS 12 Miami
(WBC S. Flyweight Title Challenge)
24.10.87 Gustavo Ballas W RSC 4 Miami
(WBC S. Flyweight Title Defence)
08.04.88 Gilberto Roman L PTS 12 Miami
(WBC S. Flyweight Title Defence)
Summary: 32 contests, won 30, drew 1, lost 1.

Juan Domingo (Martillo) Roldan

Freyre, Argentine. *Born* 06.03.57
Former Undefeated Argentinian and South American Middleweight Champion

08.12.78 Jorge Servin W RSC 1 San Francisco
26.01.79 Juan Huascarriaga W CO 1 Las Varillas
09.02.79 Luis A. Gutierrez W CO 1 San Francisco
23.03.79 Irineo Cabrera W CO 1 Rafaela
06.04.79 Luis Carcacha W RTD 3 San Francisco
20.04.79 Oscar Lopez W CO 4 Sunchales
11.05.79 Hugo Obregon W PTS 10 Cordoba
24.05.79 Natalio Ibarra W PTS 10 Brinkmann
08.06.79 Hugo Obregon W RSC 11 San Francisco
29.06.79 Oscar Perez W CO 2 Rafaela
20.07.79 Alberto Almiron W RTD 5 Cordoba
10.08.79 Ramon Perez W PTS 12 San Francisco
24.08.79 Alberto Cardozo W RSC 3 Morteros
07.09.79 Natalio Ibarra W RTD 4 Freyre
21.09.79 Juan C. Bogado L RTD 8 Cordoba
22.12.79 Alfredo Cruz W RSC 8 Buenos Aires
18.01.80 Roberto Ortiz W CO 2 San Francisco
08.02.80 Juan Bogado W PTS 10 San Francisco
22.02.80 Marcos Perez W CO 6 Morteros
15.03.80 Alfredo Cruz W CO 7 Buenos Aires
11.04.80 Ramon Perez W RSC 8 San Francisco
16.05.80 Ricardo Ortiz W PTS 10 San Francisco
06.06.80 Jorge Salgado W RSC 7 San Francisco
27.06.80 Aldo Carmona W CO 3 Salta
08.07.80 Rogelio Zarza W PTS 10 San Francisco
22.08.80 Roberto Marziali W CO 1 Las Varillas
04.10.80 Ricardo Ortiz W PTS 10 San Francisco
07.11.80 Ramon Perez W PTS 12 Cordoba
21.11.80 Enrique Coronel W RTD 7 Salta
05.12.80 Jose Duran W RTD 6 San Francisco
19.12.80 Carlos Peralta DREW 12 Cordoba
16.01.81 Marcos Perez W PTS 10 Villa Carlos
13.02.81 Manuel Navarro W TD 6 Mar del Plata
13.03.81 Jacinto Fernandez W PTS 12 San Francisco
(Argentinian Middleweight Title Challenge)
13.06.81 Jose Maria Flores W CO 3 Buenos Aires
26.06.81 Rogelio Zarza W PTS 10 Jujuy
10.07.81 Jose Vega W CO 1 San Francisco
24.07.81 Ric Molina W RTD 5 Tucuman
11.09.81 Julio C. Arancibia W RSC 2 Tucuman
10.10.81 Jacinto Fernandez DREW 10 Buenos Aires
22.01.82 Juan Peralta W PTS 10 Monteros
12.02.82 Carlos Flores W CO 2 Pergamino
(Vacant South American Middleweight Title)
06.03.82 Ray Phillips W CO 1 Buenos Aires
16.04.82 Marcos Perez W CO 1 Corrientes
11.05.82 Ricardo Arce L DIS 3 Buenos Aires
11.07.82 Ricardo Arce W CO 2 Buenos Aires
13.08.82 Rogelio Zarza W RTD 6 Corrientes
11.09.82 Jacinto Fernandez W CO 2 Buenos Aires
08.10.82 Carlos Peralta W PTS 10 San Francisco
30.10.82 Reggie Ford W CO 1 San Remo
10.12.82 Jose Vega W CO 2 Cordoba
14.01.83 Carlos Peralta ND 3 El Trebol
11.02.83 Wilbur Henderson W RSC 8 Worcester
27.05.83 Teddy Mann W PTS 10 Providence
06.08.83 Roberto Ruiz W CO 8 Buenos Aires
16.09.83 Eduardo Contreras W PTS 10 San Francisco
10.11.83 Frank Fletcher W CO 6 Las Vegas
30.03.84 Marvin Hagler L RSC 10 Las Vegas
(World Middleweight Title Challenge)
14.07.84 Andre Mongalema W PTS 10 Monte Carlo
14.02.86 Carlos Fernandez W CO 2 Ceres
29.03.86 Angel Caro W CO 6 Villa Angela
10.05.86 Jorge Salgado W PTS 10 Buenos Aires
10.06.86 Eduardo Contreras W PTS 10 Cordoba
01.08.86 Darryl Penn W CO 3 San Francisco
29.08.86 Miguel Maldonado W CO 2 Rosario
13.09.86 Juan C. Gimenez W PTS 10 Buenos Aires
18.10.86 J. B. Williamson W PTS 10 Buenos Aires
13.12.86 Carlos Herrera W RSC 2 Buenos Aires
06.02.87 Tomas Polo W CO 4 Rosario
06.04.87 James Kinchen W RSC 9 Las Vegas
15.05.87 Clarismundo Silva W CO 2 Comodoro
29.10.87 Thomas Hearns L CO 4 Las Vegas
(Vacant WBC Middleweight Title)
Summary: 72 contests, won 65, drew 2, lost 4, nd 1.

Adrian Roman

Cordoba, Argentine. *Born* 17.05.60
Argentinian Flyweight Champion

21.07.78 Manuel Saucedo W CO 2 Cordoba
01.09.78 Francisco Barrios W PTS 6 Cordoba
29.09.78 Raul Cuevas W DIS 3 Cordoba
27.10.78 Jose Lopez W PTS 8 Cordoba
19.01.79 Raul Cuevas W RSC 2 Salta
02.03.79 Ramon Baez W CO 2 Cordoba
06.04.79 Luis Gomez W CO 9 Cordoba
02.06.79 Jose Ibiris W PTS 10 Cordoba
05.07.79 Jose Ibiris W PTS 10 Cordoba
14.09.79 Jose Ibiris W PTS 10 Tucuman
05.10.79 Luis Gomez W PTS 10 Tucuman
19.10.79 Ruben Condori W TD 7 Cordoba
14.03.80 Jose Izquierdo W PTS 10 Cordoba
19.04.80 Ruben Condori DREW 10 Buenos Aires
06.06.80 Santos Laciar L CO 3 Cordoba
22.08.80 Carlos Sosa W CO 12 Cordoba
15.11.80 Jose Ibiris W RSC 10 Buenos Aires
04.04.81 Miguel Lazarte DREW 10 Buenos Aires
05.06.81 Domingo Aragon W PTS 12 Presedencia
31.07.81 Rodolfo Rodriguez W PTS 10 Cordoba
18.09.81 Federico Condori W CO 2 Salta
09.10.81 Ruben Condori L PTS 12 Salta
(Vacant Argentinian Flyweight Title)
19.02.82 Ruben Condori W PTS 10 Cordoba
19.03.82 Ramon Rodriguez W RTD 10 Cordoba
10.09.82 Ruben Condori W RSC 7 Salta
(Argentinian Flyweight Title Challenge)
15.10.82 Rodolfo Rodriguez W RTD 7 Cordoba
12.11.82 Jose Gomez W RTD 8 Cordoba
11.12.82 Gustavo Ballas L PTS 10 Buenos Aires
04.03.83 Mario de Marco W PTS 10 Cordoba
06.04.83 Alberto Pacheco W CO 3 Buenos Aires
(Argentinian Flyweight Title Defence)
03.06.83 Juan Ivalo W DIS 10 Cordoba
25.11.83 Juan C. Cortes DREW 10 Cordoba
31.12.83 Ruben Condori L PTS 12 Salta
(South American Flyweight Title Challenge)
16.03.84 Ruben Condori W PTS 12 Cordoba
(Argentinian Flyweight Title Defence)
14.04.84 Hector Patri W PTS 10 Cordoba
08.06.84 Ramon Albers L PTS 10 Concordia
10.08.84 Juan C. Cortez DREW 10 Cordoba
14.09.84 Ramon Albers L PTS 12 Concordia
(Argentinian Flyweight Title Defence)
16.11.84 Jaime Miranda W RSC 6 Cordoba
22.01.85 Jose Narvaez DREW 10 La Rioja
08.03.85 Ruben Condori L PTS 10 Salta
10.05.85 Ramon Albers W PTS 10 Sunchales
06.07.85 Alberto Pacheco W CO 9 Dolores
(Argentinian Flyweight Title Challenge)
04.10.85 Ramon Albers W PTS 12 Concordia
(Argentinian Flyweight Title Defence)
18.04.86 Jose Cufre W CO 3 Cordoba
(Argentinian Flyweight Title Defence)
11.07.86 Gustavo Ballas DREW 10 Cordoba
30.08.86 Gilberto Sosa W CO 5 Cordoba
10.10.86 Ramon Albers W PTS 12 Cordoba
(Argentinian Flyweight Title Defence)
04.04.87 Victor Fuentealba W PTS 10 Trelew
08.08.87 Juan Garcia W RSC 1 Miami
16.10.87 Daniel Lagos W RTD 8 Rawson
(Argentinian Flyweight Title Defence)
30.01.88 Domingo Aragon W CO 2 Monte Hermoso
08.04.88 Jose Badilla W CO 9 Cordoba
Summary: 53 contests, won 40, drew 6, lost 7.

Gilberto Roman

Mexicali, Mexico. *Born* 29.11.61
WBC S. Flyweight Champion

29.08.81 Gilberto Morales W CO 7 Villahermosa
13.09.81 Leonardo Valdez W RSC 8 Mexicali
30.10.81 Leo Castellano W CO 1 Acapulco
09.12.81 Juan Montalvo W CO 1 Mexico City
16.01.82 Juan Zarate W RSC 2 Mexico City
19.02.82 Gil Villacana W RSC 7 Mexicali
19.03.82 Huracan Hernandez W RSC 7 Acapulco
02.04.82 Alejo Garcia W PTS 10 Mexico City
28.05.82 Ciro Cayetano W CO 8 Acapulco
12.06.82 Heriberto Saavedra W PTS 10 Mexico City
03.07.82 Diego Avila L DIS 7 Mexico City
21.08.82 Bobby Ruiz W RSC 6 Mexico City
22.09.82 Fidel Martinez W CO 4 Mexico City
16.10.82 Carlos de la Paz W RSC 5 Mexico City
29.11.82 Ramon Nogueda W CO 4 Tijuana
15.12.82 Lupe Acosta W CO 6 Tijuana
01.02.83 Tony Escobar W RSC 10 Tijuana
14.02.83 Baldo Gonzalez W CO 2 Tijuana
06.03.83 Jimmy Fernandez W RSC 7 Mexicali
15.04.83 Jose Sosa W RSC 3 Mexicali
19.05.83 Jose Torres W PTS 10 Los Angeles
20.06.83 Armando Loredo W PTS 10 Houston
08.07.83 Pedro Rojas W CO 2 Poza Rica
15.09.83 Ron Cisneros W RSC 7 Los Angeles
03.11.83 George Garcia W RSC 9 Los Angeles
02.12.83 Freddie Santos W CO 4 Los Angeles
13.01.84 Rodolfo Martinez W RSC 8 Mexicali
15.03.84 Paul Ferreri W PTS 10 Los Angeles
31.03.84 Manuel Aguilar W CO 6 Mexicali
17.06.84 Berlin Olivetti W RSC 2 Watson Ville
01.10.84 Bernardo Ibarra W PTS 10 Tijuana
30.10.84 Wayne Lyman W CO 2 Culver City
01.12.84 Diego Avila W RSC 8 Mexicali
01.01.85 Antonio Avelar L DIS 5 Mexicali
28.01.85 Jorge Ramirez L PTS 10 Tijuana
30.03.85 Antonio Avelar W RSC 7 Mexicali

04.05.85 Oscar Bolivar W RSC 6 Aruba
07.06.85 Mario Gomez W PTS 10 Nuevo Laredo
06.07.85 Freddy Santos W RSC 5 Mexicali
23.08.85 Armando Morales W CO 5 Carmen
20.09.85 Arnulfo Luna W CO 4 Campeche
20.11.85 Fidel Martinez W CO 2 Acapulco
29.11.85 Arturo Castillo W PTS 10 Aguascalientes
30.03.86 Jiro Watanabe W PTS 12 Osaka
(*WBC S. Flyweight Title Challenge*)
15.05.86 Edgar Monserrat W PTS 12 Paris
(*WBC S. Flyweight Title Defence*)
18.07.86 Ruben Condori W PTS 12 Salta
(*WBC S. Flyweight Title Defence*)
30.08.86 Santos Laciar DREW 12 Cordoba
(*WBC S. Flyweight Title Defence*)
15.12.86 Kongtoranee Payakarun W PTS 12 Bangkok
(*WBC S. Flyweight Title Defence*)
31.01.87 Antoine Montero W RSC 9 Montpelier
(*WBC S. Flyweight Title Defence*)
19.03.87 Frank Cedeno W PTS 12 Mexicali
(*WBC S. Flyweight Title Defence*)
16.05.87 Santos Laciar L RSC 11 Reims
(*WBC S. Flyweight Title Defence*)
30.10.87 Jorge Ramirez W RSC 4 Mexicali
08.04.88 Jesus Rojas W PTS 12 Miami
(*WBC S. Flyweight Title Challenge*)
Summary: 53 contests, won 48, drew 1, lost 4.

Maurizio Ronzoni
Gorla Minore, Italy. *Born* 11.03.59
Former Undefeated Italian L. Welterweight Champion

09.11.84 Charles Ssali W PTS 6 Carbonia
26.01.85 Kamel Touati W PTS 6 Gallarate
08.03.85 Giuseppe Mercuri W RSC 2 Novara
20.04.85 Abdel Souhihi W RSC 5 Lumezzane
21.06.85 Benito Murillo W PTS 6 Lumezzane
21.07.85 Jose Castillo W RSC 3 Campione
26.10.85 Francesco Gallo W PTS 6 Monte Carlo
19.12.85 Julien Segly W PTS 6 Ancona
01.03.86 Raffaele Paoletti W PTS 8 Lumezzane
18.10.86 Stanko Suhadolnik W PTS 6 Lodrignano
21.11.86 Alessandro Scapecchi W PTS 12 Campione
(*Italian L. Welterweight Title Challenge*)
11.04.87 Rebai Hamda W RSC 5 Bologna
29.01.88 Bruno Simili W RSC 3 Rimini
10.04.88 Tahar Ayari W CO 3 Iglesias
Summary: 14 contests, won 14.

Edwin (Chapo) Rosario
Santurce, Puerto Rico. *Born* 15.03.63
Former WBA Lightweight Champion and Former WBC Lightweight Champion

03.03.79 Jorge Ortega W CO 2 Santo Domingo
03.03.79 Juan Caro W CO 1 Santo Domingo
27.03.79 Enrique Maldonado W CO 3 Santo Domingo
12.05.79 Julio Miranda W CO 4 Santo Domingo
20.07.79 Jose Villegas W CO 5 San Diego
01.08.79 James Sowell W CO 2 Los Angeles
22.09.79 Ramon Cruz W RSC 2 San Juan
18.02.80 Leopoldo Frias W CO 2 Puerto Rico
10.03.80 Pascual Polanco W RSC 4 San Juan
07.07.80 Jose Luis Lara W RSC 2 Bloomington
22.08.80 Javier Flores W RSC 9 Las Vegas
10.04.81 Tony Trys W RSC 4 New York
23.05.81 Jose Resendez W RSC 6 Las Vegas
25.06.81 Refugio Rojas W RSC 2 New York
18.07.81 Rodrigo Aguirre W CO 8 Tampa
16.09.81 James Martinez W PTS 10 Las Vegas
14.11.81 Roberto Garcia W CO 2 Las Vegas
10.12.81 Ernesto Herrera W CO 3 Tampa
30.01.82 Ezzard Charles Adams W CO 3 Las Vegas
21.03.82 Dennis Quimayousie W RSC 1 Las Vegas
22.05.82 Edwin Viruet W RSC 3 Las Vegas
01.05.83 Jose Luis Ramirez W PTS 12 San Juan
(*Vacant WBC Lightweight Title*)
17.03.84 Robert Elizondo W RSC 1 San Juan
(*WBC Lightweight Title Defence*)
23.06.84 Howard Davis W PTS 12 San Juan
(*WBC Lightweight Title Defence*)
03.11.84 Jose Luis Ramirez L RSC 4 San Juan
(*WBC Lightweight Title Defence*)
13.03.85 Eduardo Valdez W RSC 3 Atlantic City
15.04.85 Alberto Ramos W RSC 2 New York
16.06.85 Frankie Randall W PTS 10 London
27.12.85 Roque Montoya W RSC 7 Latham
13.06.86 Hector Camacho L PTS 12 New York
(*WBC Lightweight Title Challenge*)
26.09.86 Livingstone Bramble W CO 2 Miami
(*WBA Lightweight Title Challenge*)
07.03.87 Roger Brown W CO 2 Las Vegas
11.08.87 Juan Nazario W CO 8 Chicago
(*WBA Lightweight Title Defence*)
21.11.87 Julio Cesar Chavez L RSC 11 Las Vegas
(*WBA Lightweight Title Defence*)
Summary: 34 contests, won 31, lost 3.

Gianfranco Rosi
Assisi, Italy. *Born* 05.08.57
WBC L. Middleweight Champion. Former Undefeated EBU L. Middleweight Champion. Former EBU Welterweight Champion. Former Undefeated Italian Welterweight Champion

10.09.79 Francesco Sanna W PTS 6 Perugia
19.10.79 Scipione Colaianni W RSC 2 Perugia
24.11.79 Maurice Renaud W PTS 6 Marsciano
29.12.79 Zdravko Jovicic W RSC 1 Perugia
08.03.80 Patrick Babouran W PTS 6 Spoleto
31.05.80 Nelson Gomez L RSC 7 Spoleto
27.08.80 Jose Ribeiro W DIS 2 Senigallia
14.09.80 Mauro da Cruz W PTS 8 Ellera
29.11.80 Ernesto Ros W PTS 8 Spoleto
17.12.80 Fili Zaccheo W RSC 1 Senigallia
07.03.81 Francesco Gallo W PTS 8 Perugia
10.04.81 Claudio Pereira W PTS 8 Perugia
22.05.81 Piero Spadaccini W PTS 8 Pattoli
12.07.81 Claudio Pereira W PTS 8 Assis
12.09.81 Antonio Torsello W RSC 2 Perugia
13.11.81 Bechir Jelassi W PTS 8 Rome

Edwin Rosario (right) on the attack, but he failed to take Hector Camacho's WBC lightweight title on 13 June 1986
Tom Casino

Gianfranco Rosi

04.12.81 Oscar Aparicio W PTS 8 Perugia
16.04.82 Giuseppe di Padova W RTD 7 Perugia
(*Italian Welterweight Title Challenge*)
12.06.82 Mosimo Maeleke W PTS 8 Todi
17.07.82 Mosimo Maeleke W PTS 8 Assisi
15.08.82 Antonio Torsello W RSC 2 Alberobello
(*Italian Welterweight Title Defence*)
16.09.82 Antonio Antino W PTS 8 Perugia
15.10.82 Everaldo Costa W RSC 7 Perugia
(*Italian Welterweight Title Defence*)
11.02.83 Mosimo Maeleke W PTS 8 Perugia
22.04.83 Pierangelo Pira W RTD 5 Perugia
(*Italian Welterweight Title Defence*)
01.07.83 Luciano Navarra W PTS 8 Vibo
30.09.83 Francesco Gallo W RSC 8 Modena
(*Italian Welterweight Title Defence*)
12.11.83 Mike Essett W DIS 4 Perugia
03.03.84 Manuel de Jesus W PTS 8 Riva del Garda
31.03.84 John McClean W CO 7 Spoleto
18.05.84 Yvon Segor W PTS 10 Cannes
07.07.84 Perico Fernandez W PTS 12 Perugia
(*Vacant EBU Welterweight Title*)
17.11.84 Martin Rojas W PTS 10 Riva del Garda
05.01.85 Lloyd Honeyghan L CO 3 Perugia
(*EBU Welterweight Title Defence*)
15.06.85 Inino Bolamba W PTS 8 Spoleto
11.10.85 Domenico Ricci W RTD 3 Perugia
23.11.85 Gaetano Caso W CO 8 Viterbo
(*Italian Welterweight Title Challenge*)
28.12.85 Wo Lomani Wo W PTS 10 Terni
15.05.86 Jean-Marie Touatti W PTS 10 Le Cannet
20.06.86 Joaquin Velasquez W PTS 8 Rio Secco
28.01.87 Chris Pyatt W PTS 12 Perugia
(*EBU L. Middleweight Title Challenge*)
06.05.87 Emilo Sole W RSC 2 Lucca
(*EBU L. Middleweight Title Defence*)
27.05.87 Marc Ruocco W DIS 5 Cannes
(*EBU L. Middleweight Title Defence*)
02.10.87 Lupe Aquino W PTS 12 Perugia
(*WBC L. Middleweight Title Challenge*)
03.01.88 Duane Thomas W RSC 7 Genoa
(*WBC L. Middleweight Title Defence*)
Summary: 45 contests, won 43, lost 2.

Angelo Rottoli
Presezzo, Italy. *Born* 14.12.58
Cruiserweight. Former Undefeated Italian Heavyweight Champion

04.12.81 Damien Marignan DREW 6 Bergamo
26.12.81 Jose Centa W CO 3 Cremona
06.02.82 Fred Voltine W PTS 6 Boldone
13.03.82 N'Folly Coly W RSC 1 Bergamo
02.04.82 Jose Centa W RSC 3 Bergamo
17.04.82 Damien Marignan W RSC 1 Bergamo
09.07.82 Leo Centorrino W DIS 5 Pineto
30.07.82 Primo Ruberti W RSC 4 Ballabio
14.10.82 Avenamar Peralta W RSC 2 Marano
10.12.82 George Ajio W CO 2 Ferrara
24.03.83 Guido Trane W PTS 8 Bergamo
13.05.83 Peter Mulindwa W PTS 8 Boario
22.09.83 Antxon Iraeta W RSC 4 Roseto
04.11.83 Daniele Laghi W RSC 8 Bergamo
(*Italian Heavyweight Title Challenge*)
30.03.84 Guido Trane W PTS 12 Bergamo
(*Italian Heavyweight Title Defence*)
18.08.84 Rinaldo Pelizzari W CO 11 Gargnano
(*Italian Heavyweight Title Defence*)

21.12.84 Guido Trane DREW 12 Bergamo
(Italian Heavyweight Title Defence)
07.04.85 Juan Quintana W PTS 8 Atlantic City
21.06.85 Guido Trane W PTS 12 Verceia
(Italian Heavyweight Title Defence)
19.10.85 Henry Sims W PTS 8 Monaco
21.12.85 Richard Lainhart W RSC 1 Pesaro
19.04.86 Narciso Maldonado W PTS 8 San Remo
02.07.86 Pop Nance W DIS 3 Agnone
18.10.86 Steve Mormino W PTS 10 Sella
20.12.86 Bobby Joe Thomas W PTS 10 Lecce
21.02.87 Carlos de Leon L RTD 4 Bergamo
(WBC Cruiserweight Title Challenge)
21.06.87 Danny Lawford W PTS 8 Perugia
04.07.87 Mickey Pryor W RSC 1 Ribera
31.10.87 Keith Vining W RSC 6 Bergamo
13.02.88 Mbuyamba Kalongo W RSC 6 Azzano
Summary: 30 contests, won 27, drew 2, lost 1.

Donovan Ruddock
Peter Goldfield/USA

Donovan (Razor) Ruddock
Toronto, Canada. *Born* Jamaica, 21.12.63
Heavyweight

20.03.82 Wes Rowe W RSC 4 Toronto
24.04.82 Garland Tipton W CO 2 Toronto
01.06.82 Arthur Hall W PTS 4 Atlantic City
13.08.82 Al Williams W RSC 1 Welland
08.04.83 Bill Hollis W PTS 6 Toronto
26.04.83 Phil Brown DREW 6 Montreal
25.09.83 Conroy Nelson W PTS 10 Toronto
28.02.84 Cedric Parsons W RSC 7 Dartmouth
31.07.84 Ricardo Peterson W PTS 8 Halifax
20.10.84 Oscar Holman W PTS 8 Dartmouth
30.04.85 David Jaco L RSC 7 Dartmouth
25.02.86 Carlton Jones W CO 1 Toronto
28.05.86 John Westgarth W CO 7 London
08.07.86 Al Houck W RSC 1 Halifax
23.08.86 Mike Weaver W PTS 10 Fayetville
16.05.87 Robert Evans W RSC 5 Easton
15.06.87 Carlos Hernandez W DIS 7 Atlantic City
29.08.87 Juan Quintana W RSC 2 Easton
24.11.87 Eddie Richardson W RSC 4 Halifax
26.04.88 Larry Alexander W RSC 2 Camden
Summary: 20 contests, won 18, drew 1, lost 1.

Dave Russell
Ferntree Gully, Australia. *Born* 16.06.60
OPBF & Australian Cruiserweight Champion

26.10.83 Leo Moore W DIS 4 Laverton
04.12.83 Mandingo W CO 8 Melbourne
04.07.84 Daniel Saylor W PTS 8 Melbourne
26.07.84 Sam N'Gata DREW 8 Melbourne
24.09.84 Frank Robinson W PTS 6 London
01.10.84 Lee White W PTS 6 London
22.10.84 John Westgarth DREW 8 South Shields
16.11.84 Mandingo W CO 3 Melbourne
15.02.85 Steve Aczel W RTD 5 Melbourne
(OPBF & Australian Heavyweight Title Challenge)
26.04.85 Wally Carr W PTS 10 Melbourne
13.09.85 Daniel Saylor W CO 2 Melbourne
05.10.85 Bernie Kavanagh W RSC 4 Melbourne
16.12.85 Aisea Nama W CO 1 Melbourne
15.03.86 Dean Waters L CO 10 Swan Hill
(OPBF & Australian Heavyweight Title Defence)
09.05.86 Chisanda Mutti L CO 11 Melbourne
(Commonwealth Cruiserweight Title Challenge)
30.04.87 Kevin Wagstaff W CO 2 Melbourne
(OPBF & Australian Cruiserweight Title Challenge)
13.11.87 Lavell Stanley W RSC 3 Ferntree Gully
29.01.88 Kevin Cashmere W PTS 10 Croydon
Summary: 18 contests, won 14, drew 2, lost 2.

Wilibaldo (Willy) Salazar
Totolan, Mexico. *Born* 1965
NABF L. Flyweight Champion & Mexican Flyweight Champion

14.03.80 Enrique Hernandez W PTS 4 Guadalajara
09.05.80 Manuel Sanchez W CO 2 Guadalajara
18.07.80 Idelfonso Bernal L RSC 4 Guadalajara
22.08.80 Julio Martinez W PTS 8 Guadalajara
12.09.80 Jorge de Alba W RSC 5 Guadalajara
17.10.80 Idelfonso Bernal W PTS 8 Guadalajara
05.12.80 Carlos Carmona W RSC 3 Guadalajara
20.02.81 Ricardo Antonio W RSC 6 Guadalajara
03.04.81 Arturo del Villar W RSC 1 Guadalajara
29.05.81 Agustin Soberanes W RSC 1 Guadalajara
03.07.81 Artemio Ruiz L CO 5 Guadalajara
07.08.81 Enrique Torres L CO 6 Culiacan
12.02.82 Baldomero Santos L PTS 10 Guadalajara
27.05.82 Angel Ortega W RSC 5 Guadalajara
26.06.82 Joel Vazquez W CO 2 Guadalajara
28.08.82 Alberto Martinez L PTS 10 Guadalajara
22.10.82 Miguel Espinoza W RSC 4 Guadalajara
22.02.83 Fidel Martinez L CO 6 Mexico City
01.04.83 Rodolfo Flores L RSC 7 Mexico City
03.06.83 Jesus Portillo DREW 10 Guadalajara
29.10.83 Arturo Tovar W RTD 7 Guadalajara
09.12.83 Rafael Guerra L RSC 2 Guadalajara
07.12.84 Carlos Gomez W PTS 10 Guadalajara
15.02.85 Adolfo Anguiano W PTS 10 Guadalajara
21.04.85 Santiago Mendez L RSC 5 Merida
12.08.85 Javier Guerrero L PTS 10 Mexico City
10.10.85 Anastacios Rosas W RSC 10 Tepic
01.11.85 Rafael Alonso W PTS 10 Guadalajara
16.12.85 Agustin Cardenas W RSC 5 Guadalajara
07.03.86 Antonio Escobar L RSC 9 Guadalajara
05.04.86 Babe Luis W PTS 10 Guadalajara
30.05.86 Abner Arauza W CO 1 Guadalajara
13.06.86 Adolfo Anguiano W PTS 12 Guadalajara
29.08.86 Valente Flores W CO 1 Guadalajara
24.10.86 Gilberto Sosa W CO 2 Guadalajara
27.12.86 Memo Flores W RSC 8 Mexico City
30.01.87 Sergio Garcia W PTS 10 Monterrey
14.03.87 Isidro Perez W RSC 5 Mexico City
24.06.87 Jose Manuel Diaz W PTS 12 Los Angeles
(Vacant NABF L. Flyweight Title)
21.08.87 Gilberto Sosa W CO 1 Guadalajara
(Mexican Flyweight Title Challenge)
09.10.87 Rafael Morales W RSC 9 Guadalajara
(Mexican Flyweight Title Defence)
04.12.87 Julio Cardona W RTD 5 Tucson
(NABF L. Flyweight Title Defence)
07.02.88 Myung-Woo Yuh L PTS 12 Seoul
(WBA L. Flyweight Title Challenge)
Summary: 43 contests, won 30, drew 1, lost 12.

Jose Sanabria
Venezuela. *Born* 16.12.63
Bantamweight

30.03.84 Wilfredo Navas W PTS 4 Chivacoa
13.04.84 Ali Camacho L PTS 4 Barquisimeto
25.05.84 Alfonso Rendon W PTS 4 Chivacoa
16.06.84 Felix Benitez DREW 6 Maracay
13.07.84 Felix Benitez W RSC 2 Carupano
16.08.84 Ali Camacho W PTS 6 Maracay
03.09.84 Jose Villegas W RSC 3 San Fèlipe
01.03.85 Edgar Alcala W PTS 6 Guigue
08.06.85 Luis Aparicio W RSC 2 Caracas
02.09.85 Felix Guzman W PTS 10 Catia
21.12.85 Rogelio Chacin W CO 1 Machiquez
31.07.86 James Pipps L PTS 10 Atlantic City
08.11.86 Steve McCrory W RSC 5 Stateline
23.01.87 Hurley Snead W PTS 10 Atlantic City
05.07.87 Robert Shannon W PTS 10 Las Vegas
28.08.87 Aaron Lopez DREW 10 Las Vegas
27.12.87 Seung-Hoon Lee L PTS 15 Pohang
(IBF S. Bantamweight Title Challenge)
Summary: 17 contests, won 12, drew 2, lost 3.

Helio Santana
Brazil. *Born* 05.11.62
Welterweight

12.01.85 Jesie Maciel W RTD 4 Rio
24.01.85 Ismael dos Santos W CO 3 Rio
24.03.85 Roberto Silva W RTD 2 Sao Paulo
27.04.85 Julio Sanchez W PTS 10 Rio
18.08.85 Claudio Pereira W CO 5 Sao Paulo
29.09.85 Eladio Gomez W CO 5 Sao Paulo
29.11.85 Anibal Pantaleon W CO 6 Sao Paulo
18.05.86 Ubaldo Figueredo W CO 1 Sao Paulo
27.07.86 Jose Bezerra W PTS 8 Sao Paulo
24.08.86 Alberto Avalos W RTD 4 Campo Grande
05.10.86 Jorge Paredes W CO 2 Sao Paulo
21.12.86 Juan Cruces W PTS 10 Sao Paulo
15.03.87 Ricardo Barrios W RSC 8 Sao Paulo
09.08.87 Ramon Suarez W CO 1 Sao Paulo
15.11.87 Mario Matthysse W PTS 10 Sao Paulo
16.01.88 Enrique Bordon W CO 2 Sao Paulo
06.04.88 Hector Vilte W PTS 10 Sao Paulo
11.04.88 Antonio Juarez W PTS 10 Sao Paulo
Summary: 18 contests, won 18.

Luis (Chi Chi) Santana
Dominican Republic. *Born* 19.11.58
NABF Welterweight Champion

03.12.81 Ernesto Herrera W CO 4 Los Angeles
04.05.82 Don Estridge W RSC 2 Las Vegas
23.05.82 Mike Ruelas DREW 4 Las Vegas
19.06.82 Jose Cardenas W CO 2 Las Vegas
01.07.82 Charles Williams W RSC 1 Las Vegas
07.07.82 Charles Lacour W CO 6 Los Angeles
19.08.82 Willie Paul W RSC 1 Las Vegas
02.09.82 John Herbert W CO 6 Los Angeles
23.09.82 Chuck Peralta W PTS 6 Las Vegas
21.10.82 Randy Holmes W RSC 1 Las Vegas
13.11.82 Chuck Peralta W RSC 4 Las Vegas
25.11.82 Harry Truman W RSC 3 Las Vegas
19.02.83 David Marsala W RSC 1 Las Vegas
10.03.83 Joe Moliere W RSC 7 Las Vegas
31.03.83 Doug James W RSC 3 Los Angeles
21.04.83 Manny Valenzuela W CO 1 Las Vegas
10.05.83 Brian Matthews L PTS 8 Phoenix
30.06.83 Miguel Mayon W PTS 8 Las Vegas
25.10.83 Agapito Ramirez W PTS 6 Las Vegas
10.11.83 Jesus Gonzalez W CO 2 Las Vegas
05.03.84 Brian Matthews W PTS 10 Phoenix
30.03.84 Art Geronimo W RSC 4 Las Vegas
12.04.84 Reggie Miller L PTS 10 Las Vegas
12.07.84 Felipe Canela W PTS 10 Las Vegas
27.09.84 Dennis Horne W RSC 4 Las Vegas
28.11.84 Glen Corbus W CO 2 Las Vegas
10.01.85 Noe Ramirez W RSC 2 Stateline
12.02.85 Gary Baca W RSC 6 Phoenix
16.04.85 Darrell Chambers W RSC 3 Las Vegas
26.05.85 Milton McCrory L RSC 2 Miami
17.02.86 Nat Dryer L PTS 10 Phoenix
25.06.86 Manning Galloway W TD 8 Los Angeles
05.08.86 Tomas Perez W PTS 10 Las Vegas
04.09.86 Kenny Lopez W RSC 4 Oakland
07.11.86 Allen Braswell W RSC 9 Stateline
(Vacant NABF Welterweight Title)
05.03.87 Tommy Ayers L RSC 4 Las Vegas
(NABF Welterweight Title Defence)
21.06.87 Darrin Van Horn L PTS 10 Lexington
27.07.87 Ali Salaam W CO 9 Los Angeles
03.11.87 Derrick Kelly L PTS 10 Los Angeles
03.01.88 Shawn O'Sullivan W RSC 11 Las Vegas
(Vacant NABF Welterweight Title)
12.02.88 Rod Starks W RSC 2 Las Vegas
12.03.88 Royan Hammond L PTS 10 Las Vegas
Summary: 42 contests, won 33, drew 1, lost 8.

Miguel (El Zorro) Santana
Puerto Rico. *Born* 09.02.65
Former Undefeated Puerto Rican Lightweight Champion

31.07.82 Ramon Canales W RSC 2 San Juan
11.12.82 Carlos Hernandez W PTS 4 Cidra
21.03.83 Jose Rivera DREW 6 Bayamon
30.06.83 Victor Aponte W PTS 6 Trujillo
16.10.83 Jose L. Rivas W PTS 6 Rio Piedras
27.10.83 Alfredo de Leon W RSC 1 Trujillo
26.05.84 Charles Baez W RSC 4 San Juan
13.07.84 Jose Rivas W RSC 2 Trujillo
01.09.84 Javier Fragoso W CO 6 Carolina
(Puerto Rican Lightweight Title Challenge)

11.10.84 Victor Aponte W PTS 10 Aguadilla
09.03.85 Wilfredo Lanza W RSC 1 San Juan
(Puerto Rican Lightweight Title Defence)
20.04.85 Angel L. Garcia W RSC 6 Catano
(Puerto Rican Lightweight Title Defence)
29.10.85 Antonio Rodriguez W PTS 8 Curacao
03.12.85 Orlando Romero W RSC 4 Miami
13.12.85 Miguel Aguado W CO 5 Miami
02.04.86 Wesley Shuler W RSC 5 Syracuse
02.05.86 Mike Gamble W PTS 8 Atlantic City
18.07.86 Rodney Moore W PTS 10 Atlantic City
27.09.86 Terrence Alli L PTS 12 Atlantic City
(Vacant USBA Lightweight Title)
19.12.86 Felix Gonzalez W RSC 6 Atlantic City
25.03.87 Tim Burgess DREW 10 Atlantic City
23.06.87 Anthony Fletcher W PTS 10 Atlantic City
25.07.87 Pernell Whitaker L RSC 6 Norfolk
(Vacant USBA Lightweight Title)
23.12.87 Terrence Alli L PTS 10 Atlantic City
11.04.88 Greg Haugen L TD 11 Tacoma
(IBF Lightweight Title Challenge)
Summary: 25 contests, won 19, drew 2, lost 4.

Kelvin (The Stinger) Seabrooks
Charlotte, USA. *Born* 10.03.63
IBF Bantamweight Champion & Former Undefeated USBA Bantamweight Champion

09.10.81 Peanut Hughes W CO 1 High Point
08.12.81 Rondell Stevenson W RSC 2 Charleston
14.01.82 Vince Christian L PTS 4 Atlantic City
09.03.82 Francis Childs L PTS 4 Chadds Ford
13.05.82 Mike Jeter W CO 1 Anderson
15.06.82 Jerome Coffee L PTS 8 Nashville
17.07.82 Kenny Mitchell L PTS 8 Atlantic City
20.08.82 Terry Pizzaro W PTS 8 Orlando
16.10.82 Donald Alston W RSC 3 Charlotte
16.12.82 Gary Benton W CO 1 Charlotte
15.02.83 Terry Pizzaro W RSC 3 Atlantic City
01.03.83 Rocky Garrett W RSC 2 Charleston
22.03.83 Ewart Chance W RSC 3 Atlantic City
10.05.83 Wilfred Padron W PTS 10 Charleston
21.06.83 Carmelo Negron L RSC 7 Atlantic City
13.12.83 Alfonso Mitchell W RSC 2 Atlantic City
24.01.84 Dave Grayton W PTS 8 Atlantic City
06.03.84 Myron Taylor L PTS 10 Atlantic City
03.04.84 Juan Veloz L PTS 10 Atlantic City
24.05.84 Lane Killian W RSC 5 Nashville
25.08.84 Gaby Canizales L PTS 12 Laredo
(USBA Bantamweight Title Challenge)
14.11.84 Chester Richardson W PTS 8 Baltimore
05.12.84 Pat Cowdell L RSC 5 London
04.02.85 Calvin Grove L PTS 10 Atlantic City
08.03.85 Ray Minus W CO 3 Nassau
19.03.85 Lane Killian W RSC 5 Atlantic City
02.05.85 Tommy Cordova L PTS 10 Atlantic City
05.08.85 Reed Hall W RSC 2 Atlantic City
20.08.85 Harold Petty L PTS 12 Atlantic City
(Vacant Con. Am. Bantamweight Title)
02.12.85 Rodney Bowman W RSC 3 Sydney
10.12.85 Vernon Buchanan L RSC 6 Atlantic City
10.03.86 Fred Jackson W CO 2 Sydney
15.08.86 Tony Reyes W CO 1 Charlotte
01.03.87 Louis Curtis W PTS 12 Alexandria
(Vacant USBA Bantamweight Title)
15.05.87 Miguel Maturana W CO 5 Cartagena
(Vacant IBF Bantamweight Title)
04.07.87 Thierry Jacob NC 9 Calais
(IBF Bantamweight Title Defence)
18.11.87 Ernie Cataluna W RSC 4 San Cataldo
(IBF Bantamweight Title Defence)
06.02.88 Fernando Beltran W RSC 2 Paris
(IBF Bantamweight Title Defence)
Summary: 38 contests, won 24, lost 13, nc 1.

Mike Sedillo
Chino, USA. *Born* 22.12.59
L. Heavyweight

21.03.83 Mike de Luca W RSC 3 Los Angeles
05.04.83 Ron Richardson W PTS 4 El Cajon
23.04.83 Dick Harrell W RSC 1 Los Angeles
06.05.83 Ron Richardson W PTS 6 Chino
25.07.83 Dick Harrell W PTS 6 Los Angeles
29.08.83 Ken Ringo W CO 1 Los Angeles
30.09.83 Lamont Shumate W CO 2 Los Angeles
14.11.83 Darrell Hackett W PTS 10 Los Angeles
30.01.84 James Salerno W PTS 10 Los Angeles
23.04.84 Glen Smith W CO 10 Los Angeles
09.01.85 Grover Robinson L PTS 12 Los Angeles
31.03.85 Tom Covington W PTS 6 Laughlin
01.05.85 Ricky Locke W RSC 2 Bakersfield
20.05.85 Ray Mitchell W PTS 6 Los Angeles
09.07.85 John Antic W RSC 4 Bakersfield
25.09.85 Ian Mattis W RSC 7 Las Vegas
06.11.85 Fred Guzman L PTS 10 Las Vegas
15.05.86 Ron Daniels W RSC 8 San Diego
10.07.86 Virgil Hill L PTS 8 Los Angeles
30.10.86 Glenn Kennedy L PTS 12 Irvine
26.03.87 Arthur Weathers W CO 2 San Jose
16.04.87 Jerry Okorodudu W RSC 8 San Rafaela
17.07.87 Terry Walker W RSC 3 San Jose
02.10.87 Randy Smith W PTS 10 Pleasanton
21.01.88 Jim MacDonald W PTS 10 Sacramento
29.04.88 Tony Willis L PTS 12 Houston
(NABF L. Heavyweight Title Challenge)
Summary: 26 contests, won 21, lost 5.

Robert Shannon
Edmonds, USA. *Born* 11.11.62
Bantamweight

14.09.84 Carlos Rodriguez W RSC 1 Everett
11.12.84 Allen Hutchinson W CO 2 Seattle
09.02.85 Henry Wilson W CO 3 Vallejo
22.03.85 Nabor Saucedo W CO 6 Vallejo
24.06.85 Ralph Gutierrez W PTS 6 Irvine
06.08.85 Lucilo Nolasco W PTS 8 Everett
01.10.85 Ralph Gutierrez W PTS 8 Everett
30.10.85 Don Porter W PTS 6 Las Vegas
04.12.85 Pedro Gonzalez W CO 2 Everett
14.01.86 Lawrie Miera W PTS 6 Reno
05.02.86 Sonny Long W PTS 8 Everett
25.02.86 Danny Garcia DREW 6 Las Vegas
19.03.86 Kerry Allen DREW 8 Tampa
21.04.86 Sevarino Garcia W PTS 8 Lynnwood
14.08.86 Kerry Allen W RSC 7 Lynnwood
26.11.86 Greg Richardson L PTS 12 Tacoma
(USBA S. Bantamweight Title Challenge)
26.03.87 Arnel Arrozal W PTS 8 Portland
05.07.87 Jose Sanabria L PTS 10 Las Vegas
08.02.88 Azael Moran W CO 2 Los Angeles
Summary: 19 contests, won 15, drew 2, lost 2.

Jesse Shelby
Fort Worth, USA. *Born* 1960
Cruiserweight

16.04.83 Will Brigham W CO 4 Lubbock
26.04.83 Rick Myers W RSC 5 Fort Worth
16.05.83 Marcus Dorsey W CO 2 Houston
30.06.83 Eric Enslin W CO 3 Las Vegas
25.08.83 Jimmy Bills W RSC 3 Las Vegas
17.09.83 Tom Covington W RSC 2 Las Vegas
08.10.83 Milton Jarrells W RSC 1 Levelland
20.01.84 Jim Montgomery W PTS 8 Las Vegas
29.03.84 Reg Walker L PTS 6 Las Vegas
11.10.84 Milton Jarrells W RSC 8 Houston
02.04.85 Paul Madison W RSC 1 Fort Worth
12.05.85 Everett Martin L PTS 6 Tyler
10.09.85 Arthur Weathers T DRAW 1 Fort Worth
21.09.85 Tom Trimm W RSC 9 Conroe
02.02.86 Tony Oville W RSC 2 Lake Charles
06.04.86 Evander Holyfield L RSC 3 Corpus Christi
26.06.86 Chuck McDowell W RSC 1 Fort Worth
26.09.86 Lorenzo Canady W PTS 10 Portland
18.11.86 J. B. Williamson W RSC 8 Los Angeles
22.01.87 Jeff Lampkin L PTS 10 Los Angeles
19.03.87 Sherman Griffin L RSC 11 Houston
05.05.87 Tony Wilson W RSC 2 Leeds
18.08.87 Tim Bullock W CO 4 Detroit
27.10.87 Arthel Lawhorne W RSC 5 Detroit
07.03.88 Doug Sam W PTS 10 Sydney
Summary: 25 contests, won 19, drew 1, lost 5.

Ronnie Shields
Port Arthur, USA. *Born* 06.06.58
Former Undefeated NABF L. Welterweight Champion

19.08.80 Ramiro Hernandez W CO 1 Beaumont
16.09.80 Frank Lawson W RSC 3 Beaumont
11.11.80 Jerry Reyes W CO 4 Houston
07.02.81 Faustino Pena W PTS 10 Houston
02.04.81 Faustino Pena W CO 7 Fort Worth
23.04.81 Jose Hernandez W RSC 2 Fort Worth
02.05.81 Guillermo Miranda L RTD 6 Mexico City
17.07.81 Ed Modicue W RSC 7 Beaumont
01.08.81 Carlos Villacana W CO 2 Houston
06.10.81 Archie Crews W CO 1 Houston
12.12.81 Larry Bonds W PTS 10 Houston
02.03.82 Oscar Saucedo W RSC 3 Houston
27.03.82 Floyd Pearson W RSC 3 Atlantic City
08.05.82 Monroe Brooks W PTS 10 Dallas
18.08.82 Eddie Campbell W RSC 4 San Juan
02.10.82 Pete Podgorski W RSC 1 Atlantic City
17.11.82 Bruce Curry L PTS 12 St Joseph
(Vacant NABF L. Welterweight Title)
19.03.83 Jimmy Blevins W PTS 10 Reno
28.05.83 Fili Ramirez W CO 3 Las Vegas
19.10.83 Chuck Peralta W RSC 6 Las Vegas
17.11.83 Saoul Mamby W PTS 12 Cleveland
(Vacant NABF L. Welterweight Title)
26.02.84 Martin Rojas W RSC 8 Beaumont
15.07.84 Bill Costello L PTS 12 Kingston
(WBC L. Welterweight Title Challenge)
18.01.85 Eduardo Valdez W RSC 4 Houston
20.02.85 Randy Mitchum W RSC 4 Beaumont
25.03.85 Joe Manley W PTS 12 New York
(NABF L. Welterweight Title Defence)
27.08.85 James Martinez W RSC 5 Houston
22.01.86 Sergio Aguirre W RSC 4 Houston
11.05.86 Frankie Warren L PTS 12 Corpus Christi
(Vacant USBA L. Welterweight Title)
02.12.86 Tsuyoshi Hamada L PTS 12 Tokyo
(WBC L. Welterweight Title Challenge)
22.06.87 Cassius Clay Horne DREW 10 Phoenix
09.10.87 Rodolfo Gonzalez W PTS 10 Los Angeles
19.01.88 Vince Releford L PTS 10 Fort Worth
Summary: 33 contests, won 26, drew 1, lost 6.

Tony Sibson
Leicester, England. *Born* 09.04.58
Former Undefeated British, Commonwealth & EBU Middleweight Champion

09.04.76 Charlie Richardson W RSC 2 Birmingham
06.05.76 John Breen W PTS 6 Birmingham
26.05.76 Liam White W PTS 6 Wolverhampton
14.07.76 Jimmy Pickard W PTS 6 Wolverhampton
10.09.76 Bonny McKenzie W RSC 7 Digbeth
22.10.76 Clive Davidson W PTS 8 Digbeth
03.11.76 Neville Estaban W PTS 8 Caister
30.11.76 John Breen W RSC 5 Dudley
14.12.76 Tim McHugh W RSC 4 West Bromwich
11.01.77 Tony Burnett W PTS 8 Wolverhampton
19.01.77 Roy Gumbs W PTS 8 Solihull
10.02.77 Arthur Winfield W RSC 2 Coventry
25.02.77 Tashy Jones W CO 1 Digbeth
24.03.77 Bonny McKenzie W RSC 7 Leicester
07.04.77 Steve Walker W PTS 8 Dudley
21.04.77 Tony Burnett W PTS 8 Liverpool
27.04.77 Sonny Kamunga W PTS 8 Leicester
18.10.77 Pat Thomas DREW 8 Wolverhampton
08.11.77 Wayne Bennett W PTS 8 West Bromwich
30.11.77 Oscar Angus W RTD 6 Wolverhampton
23.01.78 John Smith W CO 5 Wolverhampton
06.03.78 Errol McKenzie W CO 2 Wolverhampton
31.03.78 Mac Nicholson W RSC 7 Liverpool
04.04.78 Steve Walker W RSC 5 Wolverhampton
25.04.78 Mac Nicholson W RSC 1 London
23.05.78 Lottie Mwale L CO 1 Leicester
29.06.78 Danny McLoughlin W CO 3 Wolverhampton
18.07.78 Bonny McKenzie W PTS 8 Wakefield
12.09.78 Keith Bussey W RSC 8 Wembley
24.10.78 Eddie Smith L PTS 8 London
07.11.78 Gerard Nosley W RSC 7 Wembley
05.03.79 Eddie Smith W PTS 10 Wolverhampton
10.04.79 Frankie Lucas W RSC 5 London
(Vacant British Middleweight Title)
15.05.79 Al Clay W CO 7 Wembley
26.06.79 Jacques Chinon W RSC 8 Leicester
09.10.79 Willie Classen W CO 2 London
06.11.79 Kevin Finnegan L PTS 15 London
(British Middleweight Title Defence)
29.11.79 Robert Powell W RSC 1 Liverpool
22.01.80 James Waire W PTS 10 London
04.03.80 Chisanda Mutti W PTS 15 Wembley
(Vacant Commonwealth Middleweight Title)
03.06.80 Marciano Bernardi W PTS 10 London
27.09.80 Bob Coolidge W CO 7 Wembley
08.12.80 Matteo Salvemini W CO 7 London
(EBU Middleweight Title Challenge)
27.01.81 Norberto Cabrera W PTS 10 London
17.03.81 Andre Mongalema W PTS 10 Wembley
14.05.81 Andoni Amana W PTS 12 Bilbao
(EBU Middleweight Title Defence)
15.09.81 Alan Minter W CO 3 Wembley
(EBU Middleweight Title Defence)

24.11.81 Nicola Cirelli W CO 10 Wembley
(EBU Middleweight Title Defence)
21.02.82 Dwight Davison W PTS 12 Birmingham
04.05.82 Jacques Chinon W RSC 10 Wembley
(EBU Middleweight Title Defence)
14.09.82 Antonio Garrido W RTD 8 Wembley
11.02.83 Marvin Hagler L RSC 6 Worcester
(World Middleweight Title Challenge)
08.10.83 John Collins W RSC 2 Atlantic City
22.11.83 Manuel Jiminez W RSC 8 Wembley
15.01.84 Don Lee L RSC 8 Atlantic City
25.02.84 Louis Acaries W PTS 12 Paris
(EBU Middleweight Title Challenge)
27.11.84 Mark Kaylor W PTS 12 Wembley
(British & Commonwealth Middleweight Title Challenge. EBU Middleweight Title Defence)
22.01.86 Juan Elizondo W CO 2 London
19.03.86 Abdul Amoru Sanda W PTS 12 London
(Commonwealth Middleweight Title Defence)
16.04.86 Luis Rivera W PTS 10 London
10.09.86 Dennis Andries L RSC 9 London
(WBC & British L. Heavyweight Title Challenge)
16.09.87 Brian Anderson W RSC 7 London
(Commonwealth Middleweight Title Defence & British Middleweight Title Challenge)
07.02.88 Frank Tate L CO 10 Stafford
(IBF Middleweight Title Challenge)
Summary: 63 contests, won 55, drew 1, lost 7.

John Sichula
Zambia. *Born* 29.07.58
Commonwealth S. Featherweight Champion. Former Undefeated ABU S. Featherweight Champion

28.02.82 Valentine Kangwa W PTS 6 Lusaka
.05.82 Lezza Poko W CO 4 Ndola
04.07.82 Kabiru Akindele W PTS 8 Lagos
02.09.82 David Malo W RSC 3 Ndola
28.11.82 Ray Akway W CO 4 Lusaka
30.01.83 Steve Sting W RSC 4 Lusaka
02.03.83 Valentine Kangwa W RSC 4 Lusaka
.05.83 Prince Harold W CO 2 Lusaka
03.09.83 Safiu Okebadan W RSC 8 Lusaka
(Vacant ABU S. Featherweight Title)
04.11.83 Haste Sankisa W RSC 6 Lusaka
.12.83 Bossou Aziza W RSC 6 Lusaka
04.02.84 Langton Tinago W CO 5 Harare
(Commonwealth S. Featherweight Title Challenge)
13.04.84 Johnny Rubin DREW 6 Hagen
27.04.84 Hugo Carrizo W PTS 8 Berlin
08.06.84 Haidar Nourredine W RTD 3 Baunatal
22.06.84 Antonio Franca W RSC 3 Munich
25.08.84 Frank Realihno W CO 2 Lusaka
05.10.84 Robert Mullins W RSC 4 Frankfurt
16.11.84 Lester Ellis L PTS 12 Melbourne
(Commonwealth S. Featherweight Title Defence)
05.05.85 Modest Napunyi W PTS 6 Lusaka
08.06.85 Haste Sankisa W CO 3 Lusaka
(Vacant Commonwealth S. Featherweight Title & ABU S. Featherweight Title Defence)
16.12.85 Lester Ellis W RSC 4 Melbourne
26.10.86 Sam Akromah L PTS 12 Accra
(Commonwealth & ABU S. Featherweight Title Defence)
29.08.87 Sam Akromah W PTS 12 Lusaka
(Commonwealth & ABU S. Featherweight Title Challenge)
27.11.87 Arturo Hernandez W RSC 4 Russelsheim
26.04.88 Joel Segura W CO 5 Cologne
Summary: 26 contests, won 23, drew 1, lost 2.

(Rockin') Robbie Sims
Brockton, USA. *Born* 05.11.59
Former Undefeated USBA Middleweight Champion

17.05.80 Troy Vaughn W RSC 4 Las Vegas
18.08.80 Dave Dean W CO 1 Boston
02.10.80 Danny Heath W RSC 1 Boston
25.11.80 Roberto Thomas W RSC 4 Boston
17.01.81 Bill Harrington W RSC 2 Boston
12.02.81 Len Villers W RSC 5 Boston
06.03.81 Jamal Arbubakrr W PTS 8 Worcester
12.04.81 James Green W PTS 8 Atlantic City
13.06.81 Don Dimazio W RSC 2 Boston
06.08.81 Jesus Castro W RSC 3 Atlantic City
16.09.81 Odell Leonard W RTD 6 Boston
23.12.81 Johnny Heard W PTS 10 Providence
17.01.82 Bobby Czyz L PTS 10 Atlantic City
30.04.82 Fred Reed W RSC 5 Yarmouth
10.07.82 Jose Green W CO 4 Warwick
20.08.82 Bruce Thompson W CO 1 Plymouth
16.10.82 Clint Jackson L PTS 10 Atlantic City
04.02.83 Murray Sutherland DREW 10 Worcester
23.03.83 Tony Chiaverini W RSC 5 Worcester
03.08.83 Mike Tinley L PTS 10 Atlantic City
01.09.83 Ted Mann W PTS 10 Atlantic City
25.10.83 Charlie Hecker W CO 2 Portland
06.01.84 Iran Barkley W RSC 6 Atlantic City
29.03.84 Curtis Ramsey W PTS 10 Las Vegas
10.05.84 Danny Long W PTS 12 Brockton
26.07.84 Mike Baker W RSC 5 Miami
01.11.84 Mike Tinley L PTS 10 Atlantic City
30.05.85 Stacey McSwain W CO 4 Portland
30.08.85 Doug de Witt W PTS 10 Atlantic City
06.12.85 Mario Tineo W RSC 4 Las Vegas
09.03.86 John Collins W RSC 1 Las Vegas
(USBA Middleweight Title Challenge)
23.06.86 Roberto Duran W PTS 10 Las Vegas
12.02.87 Tim Williams DREW 10 Las Vegas
10.04.87 Lee Sanders W RSC 5 Las Vegas
18.03.88 Ralph Smiley W RSC 9 Boston
Summary: 35 contests, won 29, drew 2, lost 4.

Michael Simwelu
Lusaka, Zambia. *Born* 27.04.63
ABU Heavyweight Champion

27.12.84 Charles Chileshe W CO 3 Lusaka
27.02.85 Foster Katiba W CO 1 Lusaka
05.05.85 James Chabinga W RSC 1 Lusaka
01.06.85 Big John Hugo W CO 1 Lusaka
08.07.85 Captain Marvel W RSC 1 Lusaka
01.03.86 Barry Ellis W RTD 4 Cologne
18.03.86 George Aijo W RSC 6 Russelsheim
12.05.86 Ivan Matekovic W CO 2 Hamburg
03.10.86 Ian Priest W RSC 2 Berlin
10.10.86 Dan Murphy W CO 1 Russelsheim
16.11.86 Chris Jacobs W PTS 8 Friedrichsdorf
01.12.86 Carl Gaffney W RSC 7 Arnhem
27.02.87 Bobby Crabtree W RSC 5 Hamburg
03.04.87 Louis Pergaud DREW 8 Dusseldorf
29.08.87 Proud Kilimanjaro W RSC 7 Bulawayo
(ABU Heavyweight Title Challenge)
16.11.87 Andre van den Oetelaar W CO 3 Arnhem
05.03.88 Lorenzo Boyd W CO 3 Karlsruhe
12.03.88 David Jaco L CO 1 Dusseldorf
Summary: 18 contests, won 16, drew 1, lost 1.

Tanomsak Singboebae
Thailand. *Born* 15.04.65
Former OPBF Flyweight Champion. Former Undefeated Thai Flyweight Champion

10.06.85 Kamonded Singrungrote W PTS 6 Bangkok
10.09.85 Viboon Kiatsorlos W PTS 6 Bangkok
02.10.85 Utichai Siskempetch W RSC 5 Bangkok
01.11.85 Narong Na Bamrung W PTS 6 Bangkok
05.12.85 Pisit Singrungrote W PTS 6 Bangkok
02.01.86 Wiraded Sor Wateanan W PTS 6 Bangkok
11.02.86 Somded Kiatsonyut W RSC 2 Bangkok
06.03.86 Nongbird Napataya W PTS 10 Bangkok
(Thai Flyweight Title Challenge)
12.05.86 Narkalart Kiatsontaya W RSC 5 Bangkok
04.09.86 Prateep Sor Sawadwalee W CO 2 Bangkok
15.10.86 Anburi Sanusi W RSC 4 Bangkok
(Vacant OPBF Flyweight Title)
03.12.86 Narkalart Kiatsontaya W CO 4 Bangkok
12.01.87 Sakchai Kiatsontaya W RSC 2 Bangkok
01.03.87 Soon-Jung Kang W PTS 12 Bangkok
(OPBF Flyweight Title Defence)
03.05.87 Kenji Matsumura L PTS 12 Kakogawa
(OPBF Flyweight Title Defence)
09.07.87 Panchai Kiatsontaya W CO 1 Bangkok
13.08.87 Daonoi Sissaen W CO 3 Bangkok
20.09.87 Louie Gonzalez W CO 2 Bangkok
14.12.87 Frank Cedeno W PTS 10 Bangkok
21.02.88 Nakrob Sorpayathai W CO 3 Bangkok
Summary: 20 contests, won 19, lost 1.

Samuth Sithnaruepol
Chonburi, Thailand. *Born* 17.05.59
IBF M. Flyweight Champion. Former Undefeated OPBF & Thai M. Flyweight Champion

08.05.82 Sirisak Sakcharlat W CO 2 Bangkok
20.06.82 Sentien Sithkempetch W PTS 6 Bangkok
13.08.82 Pomprai Siripong W CO 4 Bangkok
29.08.82 Prayursak Muangsurin L RSC 4 Bangkok
24.10.82 Sarmprang Tienhirang W PTS 6 Bangkok
21.11.82 Pudpard Boonthavee L RSC 4 Bangkok
09.03.83 Vunjai Sorsanti W CO 2 Bangkok
06.06.83 Narong Pornthavee W PTS 6 Bangkok
25.08.83 Samart Sakadam L RSC 5 Bangkok
14.10.83 Kairung Sithphayak W PTS 6 Bangkok
18.12.83 Dangsak Kiatsonthaya W PTS 6 Bangkok
02.01.84 Nakaraja Kiatsonthaya L PTS 6 Bangkok
11.02.84 Oh-Kong Son L CO 5 Seoul
15.02.84 Sangnarong Sithseemok W CO 2 Bangkok
18.03.84 Nopachai Sakporcharen W CO 2 Bangkok
10.04.84 Thongtep Petchsriraja W CO 2 Bangkok
07.07.84 Narong Nabumrung L RSC 3 Bangkok
16.09.84 Chaiya Singchachvan L PTS 6 Bangkok
25.10.84 Thongthorng Chorsuenanarn W RSC 3 Bangkok
14.11.84 Kongkrung Kiatkliangkai L PTS 8 Bangkok
10.01.85 Putt Ohyuthanakorn W PTS 6 Bangkok
14.02.85 Thavat Kiatpongchinda L PTS 8 Bangkok
02.05.85 Pormongkol Sithkodom W PTS 6 Bangkok
29.06.85 Narong Nabumrung W RSC 4 Bangkok
27.07.85 Kwanjai Sorpengpis L PTS 6 Bangkok
28.08.85 Kongkrung Kiatkliangkai W PTS 6 Bangkok
31.10.85 Kwanjai Sorpengpis W PTS 6 Bangkok
26.12.85 Putt Ohyuthanakorn W PTS 10 Bangkok
(Thai M. Flyweight Title Challenge)
19.01.86 Nopachai Sakdipohcharern W CO 2 Bangkok
18.02.86 Thavat Kiatpongchinda W PTS 6 Bangkok
19.03.86 Daonoi Sithprakan W RSC 2 Bangkok
28.04.86 Kenji Ono W PTS 12 Bangkok
(Vacant OPBF M. Flyweight Title)
25.12.86 Kwanjai Sorpengpis L PTS 6 Bangkok
19.02.87 Norikazu Kawana W CO 5 Bangkok
(OPBF M. Flyweight Title Defence)
29.03.87 Kaopongnoi Thaveerat W CO 2 Bangkok
12.04.87 Thanjai Kiatthavatchai W RSC 3 Bangkok
01.06.87 John Arief DREW 12 Surabaya
(OPBF M. Flyweight Title Defence)
29.10.87 Thongthep Petchsriraja W RSC 4 Bangkok
26.11.87 Pornmonkon Chorwaikun W PTS 8 Bangkok
31.12.87 Densor Tranikul W RSC 7 Bangkok
(OPBF M. Flyweight Title Defence)
24.03.88 Pretty Boy Lucas W RSC 11 Bangkok
(Vacant IBF M. Flyweight Title)
Summary: 41 contests, won 29, drew 1, lost 11.

Simon Skosana
Springs, South Africa. *Born* 29.12.57
South African Bantamweight Champion

04.05.79 Victor Tladi W PTS 4 Springs
03.08.79 Ben Thusi L RSC 1 Springs
30.03.80 Lucas Nkoana W PTS 4 Springs
01.08.80 James Sibeko W PTS 4 Springs
31.10.80 Richard Modise W PTS 6 Springs
06.02.81 Edison Ramagole L CO 5 Kwa Thema
30.10.81 Joshua Mahlangu W PTS 4 Diepkloof
05.11.82 Edison Ramagole W CO 7 Sebokeng
26.11.82 Paul Tshela W CO 2 Springs
28.01.83 Fransie Badenhorst W PTS 6 Diepkloof
15.04.83 Gift Xalura W CO 4 Springs
05.08.83 Israel Papane W CO 1 Springs
19.08.83 Joseph Ngubane W PTS 8 Soweto
30.09.83 Paulus Tshehla W RSC 6 Natalspruit
28.10.83 Jack Mathys W RSC 2 Springs
03.02.84 Phindile Gaika W PTS 12 Springs
(South African Bantamweight Title Challenge)
10.03.84 Roy Somer W RSC 7 Diepkloof
25.05.84 Olvin Mthembu W PTS 8 Springs
10.08.84 Jose de la Cruz Lopez W CO 7 Springs
12.10.84 Richard Smith W RSC 7 Johannesburg
(South African Bantamweight Title Defence)
21.09.85 Edgar Roman W PTS 10 Johannesburg
09.11.85 Jeff Hanna W PTS 10 Johannesburg
03.04.86 Fransie Badenhorst W PTS 12 Durban
(South African Bantamweight Title Defence)

07.06.86 Phindile Gaika W RSC 7 Springs
(South African Bantamweight Title Defence)
06.09.86 Julio Soto Solano W PTS 10 Durban
22.11.86 Bernardo Pinango L RSC 15 Johannesburg
(WBA Bantamweight Title Challenge)
24.05.87 Jesus Bastardo W PTS 10 Johannesburg
28.06.87 Fransie Badenhorst W PTS 12 Springs
(South African Bantamweight Title Defence)
15.02.88 Tony Pruitt W CO 7 Durban
28.03.88 Fundile Shushwana W RSC 11 Johannesburg
Summary: 30 contests, won 27, lost 3.

Said Skouma
France. *Born* Casablanca 28.08.58
Former Undefeated EBU & French L. Middleweight Champion

06.11.81 Mustapha Yazidi W PTS 6 Tarbes
18.12.81 Mohamed Ghaby W RSC 2 Fumel
15.01.82 Gerard Doizy W RTD 3 Tarbes
12.03.82 Jean-Pierre Moreau W RTD 3 Tarbes
23.04.82 Abdel Ben Ameur W CO 1 Clermont
07.05.82 Wo Lomani Wo W RSC 4 Fumel
28.10.82 Uwe Wissenbach W CO 1 Paris
20.12.82 Dennis Pryce W CO 6 Fumel
04.02.83 Esperno Postl W RSC 5 St Etienne
24.02.83 Lloyd Christie L PTS 8 Paris
19.05.83 Fred Coranson W RTD 8 Paris
01.07.83 Jean-Louis Coquin W PTS 8 Paris
26.11.83 Richard Rodriguez W PTS 12 Nimes
(Vacant French L. Middleweight Title)
25.05.84 Jimmy Cable L RSC 11 Toulouse
(Vacant EBU L. Middleweight Title)
26.10.84 Philippe Monin W RTD 8 Echirolles
07.12.84 Helier Custos W PTS 8 Bordeaux
25.01.85 Yvon Segor W CO 7 Pointe a Pitre
22.03.85 Germain le Maitre W RTD 5 Tarbes
(French L. Middleweight Title Challenge)
18.10.85 Luigi Marini W RSC 4 Antibes
30.11.85 Enrico Scacchia W CO 6 Geneva
(Vacant EBU L. Middleweight Title)
10.04.86 Angelo Liquori W RTD 8 Antibes
(EBU L. Middleweight Title Defence)
23.05.86 Alfonso Redondo W RSC 4 Bordeaux
(EBU L. Middleweight Title Defence)
24.08.86 Kenny Butler W RSC 2 Juan les Pins
25.10.86 Mike McCallum L CO 9 Paris
(WBA L. Middleweight Title Challenge)
06.02.87 Judas Clottey L DIS 5 Antibes
28.02.87 Tomas Garcia W RSC 4 Vincennes
27.03.87 Buster Drayton L RTD 10 Cannes
(IBF L. Middleweight Title Challenge)
23.06.87 Knox Brown W CO 6 Cannes
06.11.87 Hugo Marinangelli W DIS 7 Antibes
03.03.88 Jake Torrance W RTD 5 Casablanca
Summary: 30 contests, won 25, lost 5.

Hurley Snead
Detroit, USA. *Born* 29.08.59
Former Undefeated USBA Bantamweight Champion

09.07.81 James Tolliver W CO 6 Detroit
22.08.81 Thomas Elton W RSC 2 Traverse City
17.11.81 Lupe Sanchez W CO 1 Phoenix
17.12.81 Jose Coronado W PTS 6 Phoenix
28.01.82 Jose Coronado W PTS 6 Phoenix
18.02.82 Juan Veloz L PTS 6 Phoenix
16.03.82 Miguel Flores W CO 4 Phoenix
20.04.82 Phil Welther W RSC 1 Phoenix
29.04.82 Brian Johnson W RSC 1 Atlantic City
20.05.82 Danny Young W RSC 2 Phoenix
10.07.82 Jesse Hernandez W CO 1 Phoenix
03.08.82 Rudy Perez T DRAW 1 Phoenix
04.09.82 Victor Arguello W CO 1 Detroit
10.10.82 Sergio Castro W PTS 10 Detroit
19.03.83 Humberto Rodriguez W PTS 8 Reno
12.06.83 Armando Ugalde W PTS 10 Phoenix
23.09.83 James Tolliver W RSC 3 Richfield
14.01.84 Jose Torres W PTS 10 Detroit
11.03.84 Javier Gonzalez W CO 1 Detroit
15.04.84 Manuel Cedeno W PTS 10 Detroit
28.06.84 Norberto Castellano W PTS 10 Detroit
14.11.84 Alfredo Rangel W RSC 2 Detroit
30.01.85 Javier Barajas W RSC 11 Phoenix
18.04.85 Tony Coleman W RSC 4 Detroit
06.06.85 Osvaldo Acevedo W RSC 5 Detroit
(Vacant USBA Bantamweight Title)
22.08.85 Ernesto Guevara W CO 1 Detroit
12.09.85 Fred Jackson NC 12 Detroit
(USBA Bantamweight Title Defence)
06.12.85 Jose Torres W RSC 4 Las Vegas
10.02.86 Ron Cisneros W PTS 10 Laughlin
26.03.86 Hector Cortez W PTS 10 Las Vegas
15.08.86 Pedro Rodriguez W RSC 5 Detroit
20.11.86 Kenny Butts W RSC 6 Detroit
23.01.87 Jose Sanabria L PTS 10 Atlantic City
27.10.87 Jorge Samona W RSC 4 Detroit
28.01.88 Julio Blanco W PTS 10 Detroit
23.02.88 Mario Lozano W RSC 6 Detroit
30.03.88 Carlos Flores W PTS 10 Detroit
Summary: 37 contests, won 33, drew 1, lost 2, nc 1.

Renaldo (Mr Reindeer) Snipes
Houston, USA. *Born* 15.08.56
Former Undefeated Con. Am. Heavyweight Champion

18.11.78 Carl Halliburton W RSC 1 Chicago
10.12.78 Hal Emerson W PTS 4 White Plains
14.02.79 Sam Miller W CO 3 White Plains
04.03.79 Ron Hope W PTS 4 White Plains
11.04.79 Dave Smith W CO 4 White Plains
23.05.79 Barry Funches W CO 3 White Plains
20.06.79 Charles Cox W PTS 6 White Plains
08.07.79 Eugene Green W PTS 6 New York
10.10.79 Mike Tarasewich W PTS 8 White Plains
05.12.79 Tyrone Harlee W RSC 4 White Plains
16.04.80 Dave Johnson W PTS 8 White Plains
14.05.80 James Reid W CO 3 White Plains
11.06.80 Johnny Warr W PTS 8 White Plains
09.08.80 Robert Coley W CO 1 Atlantic City
17.09.80 Larry Alexander W RSC 2 White Plains
18.10.80 Rodell Dupree W RSC 3 Atlantic City
25.11.80 Malik Dozier W RSC 5 Boston
17.12.80 Dwain Bonds W RSC 8 White Plains
22.01.81 Leroy Boone W PTS 10 White Plains
08.03.81 Jumbo Cummings W PTS 10 Atlantic City
17.05.81 Mustafa Muhammad W PTS 10 Atlantic City
09.08.81 Gerrie Coetzee W PTS 10 Tarrytown
06.11.81 Larry Holmes L RSC 11 Pittsburgh
(WBC Heavyweight Title Challenge)
21.03.82 Scott Frank DREW 10 Atlantic City
05.06.82 Tim Witherspoon L PTS 10 Las Vegas
02.10.82 Trevor Berbick W PTS 10 Atlantic City
20.05.83 Greg Page L PTS 12 Las Vegas
(USBA Heavyweight Title Challenge)
23.09.83 Alfredo Evangelista L PTS 10 Richfield
30.10.84 Rickey Parkey L PTS 10 Atlantic City
10.07.86 Bobby Crabtree W RSC 5 New York
24.07.86 Dennis Fikes W RSC 2 New York
17.08.86 Donnie Long W PTS 10 Atlantic City
12.12.86 Tyrell Biggs L PTS 10 New York
09.04.87 Melvin Epps W RSC 5 New York
04.06.87 Richard Scott W PTS 10 New York
23.07.87 Terry Anderson W CO 10 New York
(Vacant Con. Am. Heavyweight Title)
19.03.88 Orlin Norris L PTS 12 Las Vegas
(NABF Heavyweight Title Challenge)
Summary: 37 contests, won 29, drew 1, lost 7.

Michael (Jinx) Spinks
St Louis, USA. *Born* 13.07.56
Former Undefeated IBF Heavyweight Champion.
Former Undefeated World L. Heavyweight Champion

17.04.77 Eddie Benson W CO 1 Las Vegas
07.05.77 Luis Rodriguez W PTS 6 St Louis
01.06.77 Joe Bordon W CO 2 Montreal
23.08.77 Jasper Brisbane W RSC 1 Philadelphia
13.09.77 Ray Elson W CO 1 Los Angeles
22.10.77 Gary Summerhays W PTS 10 Las Vegas
15.02.78 Tom Bethea W PTS 8 Las Vegas
15.12.78 Eddie Phillips W CO 4 White Plains
24.11.79 Mark Hans W RSC 1 Bloomington
01.02.80 Johnny Wilburn W PTS 8 Louisville
24.02.80 Ramon Ronquillo W RTD 7 Atlantic City
06.05.80 Murray Sutherland W PTS 10 Kiamesha
02.08.80 Dave Conteh W RSC 8 Baton Rouge
18.10.80 Yaqui Lopez W RSC 7 Atlantic City
24.01.81 Willie Taylor W RSC 8 Philadelphia
28.03.81 Marvin Johnson W CO 4 Atlantic City
18.07.81 Mustafa Muhammad W PTS 15 Las Vegas
(WBA L. Heavyweight Title Challenge)
07.11.81 Vonzell Johnson W RSC 7 Atlantic City
(WBA L. Heavyweight Title Defence)
13.02.82 Mustapha Wasajja W RSC 6 Atlantic City
(WBA L. Heavyweight Title Defence)
11.04.82 Murray Sutherland W RSC 8 Atlantic City
(WBA L. Heavyweight Title Defence)
12.06.82 Jerry Celestine W RSC 8 Atlantic City
(WBA L. Heavyweight Title Defence)
18.09.82 Johnny Davis W RSC 9 Atlantic City
(WBA L. Heavyweight Title Defence)
18.03.83 Dwight Muhammad Qawi W PTS 15 Atlantic City
(WBA L. Heavyweight Title Defence & WBC L. Heavyweight Title Challenge)
25.11.83 Oscar Rivadaneyra W RSC 10 Vancouver
(World L. Heavyweight Title Defence)
25.02.84 Eddie Davis W PTS 12 Atlantic City
(WBA & WBC L. Heavyweight Title Defence. Vacant IBF L. Heavyweight Title)
23.02.85 David Sears W RSC 3 Atlantic City
(World L. Heavyweight Title Defence)
06.06.85 Jim MacDonald W RSC 8 Las Vegas
(World L. Heavyweight Title Defence)

Renaldo Snipes watches as a prostrate Terry Anderson is counted out in the tenth round of their Continental American heavyweight title battle
Tom Casino

21.09.85 Larry Holmes W PTS 15 Las Vegas *(IBF Heavyweight Title Challenge)*
19.04.86 Larry Holmes W PTS 15 Las Vegas *(IBF Heavyweight Title Defence)*
06.09.86 Steffen Tangstad W RSC 4 Las Vegas *(IBF Heavyweight Title Defence)*
15.06.87 Gerry Cooney W RSC 5 Atlantic City
Summary: 31 contests, won 31.

Marlon Starling
Peter Goldfield/USA

Marlon (Magic Man) Starling
Hartford, USA. *Born* 29.08.58
WBA Welterweight Champion. Former USBA & NABF Welterweight Champion

27.07.79 Tim la Valley W RSC 3 Hartford
07.09.79 Hubert Jackson W PTS 4 Hartford
27.09.79 Jerry North W PTS 4 Hartford
17.10.79 Hector Ortiz W PTS 6 Hartford
05.11.79 John Saxton W RSC 4 Hartford
09.01.80 Charlie Newell W CO 7 Hartford
28.02.80 Frank Minigan W RSC 4 Hartford
08.04.80 Feliciano Cintron W RSC 6 Hartford
23.05.80 Eddie Campbell W PTS 8 Hartford
20.06.80 Benji Goldstone W RSC 5 Hartford
03.11.80 Dave Bolden W RSC 3 Hartford
25.11.80 Curtis Taylor W PTS 10 Hartford
16.01.81 Ruby Ortiz W PTS 10 Hartford
09.02.81 Bruce Strauss W CO 2 Hartford
10.04.81 Floyd Mayweather W PTS 10 Hartford
24.04.81 Miguel Hernandez W RSC 8 New York
29.05.81 Johnny Cooper W RSC 1 Hartford
25.06.81 Juan Hidalgo W RSC 5 New York
28.08.81 Jackie Morrell W RSC 2 New York
29.01.82 Danny Paul W PTS 10 Hartford
22.03.82 Jose Santana W CO 1 Hartford
23.04.82 Ricky Camaro W RSC 3 New Haven
05.06.82 Babs McCarthy W CO 9 Hartford
17.07.82 Kevin Morgan W RSC 1 New York *(USBA Welterweight Title Challenge)*
10.09.82 Mao de la Rosa W PTS 10 Hartford
23.10.82 Don Curry L PTS 12 Atlantic City *(USBA Welterweight Title Defence & NABF Welterweight Title Challenge)*
07.01.83 Manuel Madera W RSC 3 Hartford
05.02.83 Jose Baret W CO 4 Atlantic City
23.04.83 Kevin Howard W PTS 12 Hartford *(Vacant NABF and USBA Welterweight Titles)*
24.07.83 Tommy Ayers W PTS 12 Atlantic City *(NABF and USBA Welterweight Title Defence)*
10.11.83 Sammy Rookard W RSC 5 Hartford
26.11.83 Bob Graddy W CO 3 Hartford
04.02.84 Don Curry L PTS 15 Atlantic City *(WBA Welterweight Title Challenge & Vacant IBF Welterweight Title)*
17.04.84 Lupe Aquino W PTS 12 Atlantic City *(NABF and USBA Welterweight Title Defence)*
15.06.84 Pedro Vilella L PTS 12 New York *(NABF Welterweight Title Defence)*
26.04.85 Floyd Mayweather W PTS 12 Atlantic City *(USBA Welterweight Title Defence)*
07.08.85 Reggie Miller W PTS 10 Atlantic City
22.11.85 Simon Brown W PTS 12 Atlantic City *(USBA Welterweight Title Defence)*
24.01.86 Leo Davis W RSC 2 Hartford
07.04.86 Ralph Twinning W RTD 6 Chicago
18.05.86 Johnny Bumphus L TD 6 Providence *(USBA Welterweight Title Defence)*
19.09.86 Dexter Smith W RSC 5 Hartford
30.10.86 Roberto Mendez W RSC 4 Hartford
18.02.87 Pedro Vilella W PTS 10 Hartford
05.06.87 Norberto Bueno W CO 3 Hartford
22.08.87 Mark Breland W CO 11 Columbia *(WBA Welterweight Title Challenge)*
05.02.88 Fujio Ozaki W PTS 12 Atlantic City *(WBA Welterweight Title Defence)*
16.04.88 Mark Breland DREW 12 Las Vegas *(WBA Welterweight Title Defence)*
Summary: 48 contests, won 43, drew 1, lost 4.

Loris Stecca
San Arcangelo, Italy. *Born* 30.03.60
Former WBA S. Bantamweight Champion. Former Undefeated EBU & Italian Featherweight Champion

18.10.80 Angelo Quintavalle W RSC 3 Rimini
14.11.80 Ignazio Fara W RSC 4 Pesaro
03.12.80 Pietro Donati W CO 1 Forli
26.12.80 David Mahmutovic W RSC 1 Bologna
24.01.81 Antonio Franca W CO 4 Padova
07.02.81 Michael Morvan W CO 2 Rimini
20.02.81 Andrea Ricci W DIS 4 Faenza
20.03.81 David Mahmutovic W RSC 3 Ancona
17.04.81 Koichi Oshi W RSC 4 Rimini
29.04.81 Martin Antich W RSC 2 Gatteo
14.05.81 Angel Oliver W PTS 8 Milan
11.06.81 Melquiades da Silva W PTS 8 Milan
24.07.81 Luis de la Sagra W RSC 4 Rimini
09.08.81 Melquiades da Silva W RSC 7 Camaiore
29.08.81 Juan Francisco Rodriguez W RSC 4 Via Reggio
15.10.81 Hector Molina W PTS 8 Milan
13.11.81 Marco Gallo W PTS 12 Rimini *(Italian Featherweight Title Challenge)*

Loris Stecca

26.12.81 Manuel Carrasco W RSC 2 Rimini
09.02.82 Baltazar Arroyo W DIS 2 Las Vegas
18.02.82 Cucu Talamantes W CO 3 Los Angeles
20.03.82 Mariano Rodriguez W RSC 3 Rimini
12.05.82 Pasquale Mazza W RSC 4 L'Aquila *(Italian Featherweight Title Defence)*
06.07.82 Alain Lefol W RSC 4 Rimini
04.08.82 Isidoro Cabeza W RSC 5 Rimini
26.08.82 Phil Watford W RSC 5 Los Angeles
02.09.82 Javier Barajas W PTS 10 Los Angeles
09.10.82 Sammy Meck DREW 8 Rimini
02.12.82 Salvatore Melluzzo W RSC 6 Foggia *(Italian Featherweight Title Defence)*
28.01.83 Jose Luis Vicho W PTS 8 Morciano
07.04.83 Steve Sammy Sims W RSC 5 Sassari *(Vacant EBU Featherweight Title)*
15.06.83 Robert Mullins W PTS 8 Bologna
05.08.83 Valerio Nati W PTS 12 Camaiore *(EBU Featherweight Title Defence)*
13.01.84 Jeff Hanna W RSC 5 Riva del Garda
22.02.84 Leonardo Cruz W RSC 12 Milan *(WBA S. Bantamweight Title Challenge)*
13.04.84 Victor Bultron W RSC 5 Milan
26.05.84 Victor Callejas L RSC 8 Guaynabo *(WBA S. Bantamweight Title Defence)*
16.02.85 Tony Cisneros W RSC 3 Reno
16.03.85 Pat Doherty W RSC 5 Rimini
04.05.85 Mike Huckabee W RSC 3 Feltre
08.06.85 Lane Killian W RSC 5 Castelar
27.07.85 Cleo Garcia W RSC 5 Carrara
08.11.85 Victor Callejas L RTD 6 Rimini *(WBA S. Bantamweight Title Challenge)*
04.07.86 Ron Cisneros W PTS 8 Porlezza
03.08.86 Ernesto Guevara W CO 2 Monte Carlo
22.09.86 Ley Umba Sengy W PTS 8 Siracusa
14.11.86 Kirk Stengle W RSC 3 San Giuseppe
19.12.86 Sonny Long W PTS 8 Ancona
13.08.87 Francisco Arreola DREW 8 Forli
11.04.87 Mark Brannon W RSC 6 Bologna
15.05.87 Jose Gonzalez W PTS 8 Geneva
11.07.87 Anthony Williams W CO 6 Corsico
16.08.87 Ricky West W PTS 8 Salerno
28.11.87 Cesar Almonte W DIS 4 Oristano
29.01.88 Jose Gallegos W PTS 8 Rimini
10.04.88 Miguel Pequeno W RSC 4 Iglesias
Summary: 55 contests, won 51, drew 2, lost 2.

Maurizio Stecca
San Arcangelo, Italy. *Born* 19.03.63
Featherweight

01.12.84 Francis Aparicio W RSC 3 Milan
26.12.84 Julio Garcia W PTS 6 Modena
05.01.85 Jean-Paul Guillard W CO 2 Perugia
27.01.85 Haidar Nourredine W PTS 6 Riva del Garda
16.02.85 Kid Castillo W PTS 6 Reno
15.03.85 Vicente Fernandez W PTS 6 Rimini
04.05.85 Dave Murden W PTS 6 Feltre
08.06.85 Don Doster W RSC 2 Castellar
06.07.85 Haidar Nourredine W RSC 6 Ancona
28.09.85 Don Bryant W CO 2 Sassari
12.10.85 Tom Elston W PTS 8 Cesena
13.12.85 John Feeney W PTS 8 Cesena
07.03.86 Jose Luis Vicho W RSC 3 Rimini
02.04.86 Ricky West W PTS 8 Totowa
09.05.86 John Maloney W RTD 1 Sassari
30.05.86 Farid Benredjeb W PTS 8 Abano Terme
03.08.86 Ley Umba Sengi W PTS 8 Roccaraso
19.09.86 Jeff Hanna W PTS 8 Lerici
10.10.86 Felix Cortez W RSC 6 Cesena
28.11.86 Arturo Hernandez W PTS 10 Abano Terme
08.01.87 Cleo Garcia W PTS 8 New York
14.02.87 Juan Muriel W PTS 8 Lucca
27.03.87 Sonny Long W PTS 8 Cagliari
22.04.87 Luis Rodriguez W PTS 8 Catania
12.06.87 Francisco Arreola W PTS 10 Bula
16.08.87 Jose Hernandez W RSC 2 Salerno
09.10.87 Silford Ashby W CO 2 Aosta
28.11.87 Manuel Rodriguez W RSC 7 Oristano
11.12.87 Julian Solis W DIS 6 Livorno
12.03.88 Angel Hernandez W PTS 8 Lerici
22.04.88 Fidel Martinez W RSC 5 Milan
Summary: 31 contests, won 31.

Leslie Stewart
Trinidad. *Born* 1961
Former WBA L. Heavyweight Champion. Former Undefeated Commonwealth, Latin American & Con Am. L. Heavyweight Champion

24.01.82 Michael Hospedales W RSC 4 Port of Spain
30.04.82 Ashton Antoine W PTS 8 Marabella
14.05.82 Easy Boy Michael W RSC 2 Port of Spain
30.07.82 Gil Rosario W RSC 9 Port of Spain
30.10.82 Ricardo Richardson W RSC 4 Port of Spain
25.02.83 Zima Baman W RSC 4 Port of Spain
12.05.83 Leon McDonald W RSC 1 Port of Spain
11.09.83 Carlos Flores W RSC 4 Port of Spain *(Latin American L. Heavyweight Title Challenge)*
11.11.83 Willie Taylor W PTS 10 Port of Spain
16.12.83 Tom Collins W PTS 10 Port of Spain
16.03.84 Larry Lane W PTS 10 Port of Spain
28.09.84 Elvis Parks W RSC 9 Miami
10.11.84 James Salerno W PTS 10 Miami
01.03.85 Mark Frazie W CO 8 Port of Spain *(Vacant Con. Am. L. Heavyweight Title)*

05.09.85 Sid Outlaw W RSC 6 Atlantic City
05.11.85 Dave Barrows W RSC 2 Atlantic City
07.02.86 Cecil Pettigrew W RSC 9 Atlantic City
16.05.86 Ernie Jackson W CO 2 Atlantic City
12.08.86 Horacio Perez W RSC 2 Atlantic City
25.11.86 Harry Daniels W CO 2 Atlantic City
05.03.87 Bastante Blanco W RTD 6 Atlantic City
01.06.87 Darryl Spain W RSC 5 Philadelphia
25.08.87 Stacy McSwain DREW 10 Atlantic City
06.11.87 Doug de Witt L PTS 13 Atlantic City
(Vacant USBA Middleweight Title)
12.02.88 Tyrone Frazier W PTS 10 Atlantic City
Summary: 20 contests, won 18, drew 1, lost 1.

Christophe Tiozzo
St Denis, France. *Born* 01.06.63
EBU Middleweight Champion

29.10.85 Karl Barwise W PTS 8 Paris
08.12.85 Vint Hammock W RSC 3 Montreal
03.02.86 Danny Vandal W CO 2 Paris
15.03.86 Jim Shavers W PTS 8 Monte Carlo
15.05.86 Mike Peoples W PTS 8 New York
09.10.86 Wesley Reed W RSC 4 New York
25.10.86 T. P. Jenkins W RTD 4 St Nazaire
07.11.86 Jose Rosemain W RTD 5 Paris
13.12.86 Andre Mongalema W PTS 8 Paris
29.01.87 Troy Watson W PTS 8 New York
27.04.87 Derrick Drane W CO 4 Paris
16.06.87 Jimmy Cable W CO 5 St Nazaire
09.07.87 John Moore W RSC 7 New York
17.09.87 Tim Knight W RSC 4 New York
09.11.87 Jeff Llanas W CO 4 Villeurbanne
21.12.87 Carlos Tite W CO 3 Paris
04.02.88 Charles Campbell W PTS 10 New York
11.03.88 Lester Yarbrough W CO 7 Montbrisson
18.04.88 Pierre Joly W PTS 12 Paris
(EBU Middleweight Title Challenge)
Summary: 19 contests, won 19.

German Torres
Celaya, Mexico. *Born* 1958
Former Undefeated Japanese & Mexican L. Flyweight Champion

27.08.75 Miguel Landin W RSC 5 Mexico City
10.09.75 Fabian Garcia W RSC 2 Mexico City
27.12.75 Amado Ursua L RSC 3 Mexico City
18.02.76 Pedro Hernandez W RSC 3 Mexico City
25.03.76 Chuy Vascasio W RSC 6 Mexico City
23.04.76 Pedro Galaviz L RSC 7 Guadalajara
01.01.77 Antonio Morales W RSC 4 Gomez Palacio
19.02.77 Rocky Mijares L RSC 8 Gomez Palacio
28.07.77 Joel Gatica W CO 2 Tlapehuala
04.10.77 Cecilio Ostos W CO 4 Matamoros
30.11.77 Lupe Madera W PTS 8 Santiago
28.04.78 Carlos Cantu W PTS 10 Nuevo Laredo
10.07.78 Esteban Guzman W CO 3 Ciudad Victoria
30.09.78 Cecilio Ostos W RSC 6 Matamoros
23.12.78 Pajarito Frias W RSC 3 Celaya
28.03.79 Leo Santos W CO 4 Mexico City
16.05.79 Pedro Moreno W RSC 5 Mexico City
27.06.79 Alejandro Flores W RSC 7 Mexico City
04.08.79 Candido Tellez W PTS 10 Mexico City
14.09.79 Ganchito Guzman W CO 2 Celaya
05.10.79 Cecilio Cabrera W CO 3 Reynosa
24.11.79 Jose Zavala W RSC 7 Mexico City
(Vacant Mexican L. Flyweight Title)
29.12.79 Arturo Tebaqui W CO 3 Hermosillo
26.01.80 Mario Gatica W RSC 2 Mexico City
07.03.80 Jose Zavala W PTS 10 Los Mochis
19.04.80 Tomas Cuellar W CO 3 Mexico City
10.05.80 Armando Perez W RSC 5 Mexico City
22.05.80 Mark Pacheco W RSC 9 Los Angeles
26.07.80 Amado Ursua W RSC 6 Mexico City
(Mexican L. Flyweight Title Defence)
09.10.80 Lupe Madera W TD 11 Mexico City
(Mexican L. Flyweight Title Defence)
19.12.80 Victor Salcedo W RSC 6 Las Vegas
24.01.81 Jorge Vera DREW 10 Mexico City
28.03.81 Luis Garcia W CO 3 Mexico City
(Mexican L. Flyweight Title Defence)
15.08.81 Hilario Zapata L PTS 15 Panama City
(WBC L. Flyweight Title Challenge)
31.10.81 Amado Ursua L PTS 12 Campeche
(Mexican L. Flyweight Title Defence)
23.01.82 Joey Olivo W PTS 10 Mexico City
27.03.82 Francisco Montiel W RSC 6 Mexico City
(Vacant Mexican L. Flyweight Title)
07.06.82 Katsumi Sato W CO 6 Tokyo
06.09.82 Katsumi Taniguchi W CO 3 Tokyo
10.10.82 Yuko Kazaki W CO 6 Tokyo
30.10.82 Chong-Kwan Chung W CO 9 Seoul
13.12.82 Takahashi Nakayama W RSC 6 Tokyo
05.02.83 Chano Muniz W CO 5 Tamaulipas
21.03.83 Soon-Jung Kang W PTS 10 Tokyo
02.06.83 Manabu Irie W CO 4 Okinawa
10.09.83 Jung-Koo Chang L PTS 12 Daejon
(WBC L. Flyweight Title Challenge)
12.12.83 Masaharu Inami W RSC 3 Tokyo
(Japanese L. Flyweight Title Challenge)
28.01.84 Bernardo Ibarra W PTS 10 Mexico City
15.03.84 Eleoncio Mercedes W RSC 9 Los Angeles
12.04.84 Alfonso Lopez W RSC 6 Los Angeles
14.05.84 Mitsuo Watanabe W CO 4 Tokyo
09.07.84 Bi-Won Chung W PTS 10 Seoul
22.09.84 Dong-Yong Hwan L PTS 10 Seoul
01.01.85 Luis Hernandez W CO 3 Mexico City
22.02.85 Javier Gonzalez W CO 4 Cuernavaca
27.04.85 Jung-Koo Chang L PTS 12 Pusan
(WBC L. Flyweight Title Challenge)
06.06.85 Yoshiyuki Uchikoshi W RSC 6 Tokyo
18.08.85 Jorge Cano L PTS 10 Mexico City
01.01.86 Leon Diaz W RSC 4 Torreon
13.04.86 Jung-Koo Chang L PTS 12 Kwangju
(WBC L. Flyweight Title Challenge)
07.03.87 Santiago Mendez W PTS 10 Mexico City
01.05.87 Artemio Ruiz W PTS 10 Acapulco
20.06.87 Emilio Santos W CO 2 Mexico City
15.08.87 Rodolfo Alvarado T DRAW 7 Mexico City
14.11.87 Francisco Montiel T DRAW 8 Obregon
Summary: 65 contests, won 52, drew 3, lost 10.

Tyrone Trice
Milwaukee, USA. *Born* 24.10.63
Welterweight

26.05.83 Rodney Moore W PTS 4 Atlantic City
04.06.83 Fred Tice W RSC 1 Traverse City
12.06.83 Willie Maxwell W CO 1 Phoenix
10.07.83 Manuel Torivio W CO 2 Atlantic City
24.08.83 Dave Odem W PTS 6 Waterford
30.09.83 Leslie Toney W RSC 2 Milwaukee
27.10.83 Victor Gordon W RSC 4 Atlantic City
03.02.84 Nate Stewart W RSC 2 Chicago
11.02.84 Kean McGill W RSC 2 Detroit
15.04.84 Bobby Graddy W RSC 6 Detroit
03.05.84 Teddy Hatfield W RSC 2 Detroit
31.05.84 Pedro Gallardo W RSC 6 Detroit
28.06.84 Fred Pendelton L RSC 1 Detroit
15.08.84 Tyrone Moore W PTS 10 Las Vegas
24.10.84 Anthony Bryant W CO 3 Detroit
06.04.85 Kenny Willis W RSC 3 Atlantic City
22.08.85 Jesus de la Cruz W RSC 1 Detroit
12.09.85 Tyrone Moore W PTS 10 Detroit
21.10.85 Jose Gonzalez W CO 5 Detroit
21.11.85 Dave Odem W RTD 6 Detroit
23.01.86 Mike Bradley W RTD 3 Detroit
28.02.86 Steve Mitchell W RSC 6 Laughlin
22.03.86 Jesse Flores W RSC 4 Reno
24.04.86 Ray Jones W RSC 2 Detroit
10.06.86 Curtis Summitt W RSC 1 Detroit
24.10.86 Dennis Johnson W RSC 7 Detroit
06.08.87 Steve Little W PTS 10 New York
10.10.87 Walter Cowans W RSC 2 Sandusky
20.11.87 Mike English W RSC 1 Detroit
23.04.88 Simon Brown L RSC 14 Berck sur Mer
(Vacant IBF Welterweight Title)
Summary: 30 contests, won 28, lost 2.

Tony (T.N.T.) Tubbs
Cincinnati, USA. *Born* 15.02.58
Former WBA Heavyweight Champion

14.06.80 Bruce Scott W CO 1 Cincinnati
02.08.80 Jerry Hunter W CO 4 Cincinnati
07.11.80 Ron Draper W PTS 6 San Antonio
14.11.80 John L. Johnson W RSC 1 Miami
22.11.80 Larry Simms W RTD 3 Cincinnati
29.11.80 Mike Creel W RTD 3 Los Angeles
21.08.81 Dennis Wimbley W RSC 2 Elizabeth
04.10.81 Jeff Sims W CO 1 Newport
21.11.81 Jesse Brown W CO 1 Erlanger
19.12.81 Don Halpin W PTS 8 Pittsburgh
11.04.82 Baker Tinsley W RSC 3 Atlantic City
12.06.82 Claman Parker W RSC 1 Atlantic City
07.08.82 Clarence Hill W PTS 10 Albuquerque
18.09.82 Steve Zouski W RSC 5 Atlantic City
25.02.83 Larry Givens W RSC 7 Cincinnati
10.04.83 Jimmy Young W PTS 10 Pittsburgh
09.09.83 Gordie Racette W PTS 10 Las Vegas
18.03.84 Tom Trimm W RSC 2 Santa Monica
09.11.84 Jerry Williams W RSC 7 Las Vegas
16.01.85 Tim Miller W RSC 2 Las Vegas
15.03.85 James Smith W PTS 10 Las Vegas
29.04.85 Greg Page W PTS 15 Buffalo
(WBA Heavyweight Title Challenge)
17.01.86 Tim Witherspoon L PTS 15 Atlanta
(WBA Heavyweight Title Defence)
20.04.87 Mike Jameson W PTS 10 Santa Monica
30.05.87 Jerry Halstead W PTS 10 Las Vegas
29.09.87 Eddie Gonzalez W RTD 3 Anaheim
21.03.88 Mike Tyson L RSC 2 Tokyo
(World Heavyweight Title Challenge)
Summary: 27 contests, won 25, lost 2.

Tony Tucker
Grand Rapids, USA. *Born* 27.12.58
Former IBF Heavyweight Champion & Former Undefeated USBA Heavyweight Champion

01.11.80 Chuck Gardner W CO 3 Lake Tahoe
02.12.80 Jesse Clark W CO 1 Toledo

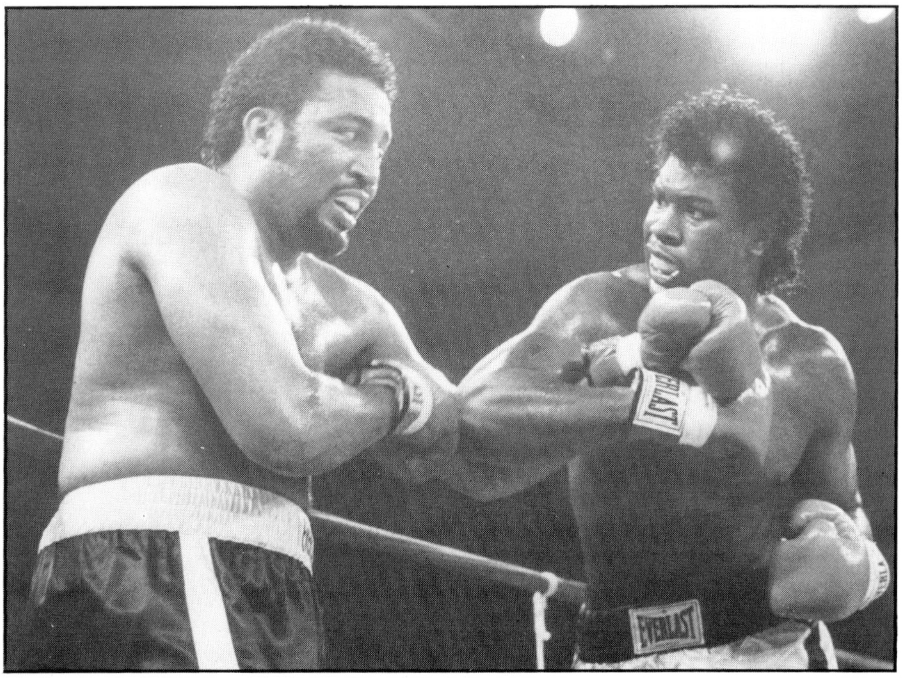

Prior to winning the IBF heavyweight title, Tony Tucker (right) beat James Broad on points for the USBA title, 26 September 1986
IBF/Bill Baron

11.12.80 Max Smith W CO 5 Chicago
16.01.81 Victor Rodriguez W RSC 2 San Antonio
29.01.81 Willie Kents W CO 1 Detroit
22.02.81 Robert Evans W RSC 6 Atlantic City
09.04.81 Al Jones W CO 1 Detroit
30.04.81 Chip Tyler W RSC 7 Las Vegas
22.08.81 Jerry Hunter W RSC 1 Traverse City
16.09.81 Harvey Steichen W RSC 3 Las Vegas
17.10.81 Frank Farmer W CO 1 Traverse City
18.05.82 Grady Daniels W RSC 5 Atlantic City
05.06.82 Charles Atlas W RSC 1 Rochester
15.06.82 James Dixon W PTS 8 Atlantic City
30.06.82 Lupe Guerra W RSC 2 Syracuse
08.07.82 Richard Cade W RSC 6 Atlantic City
13.08.82 Danny Sutton NC 3 Nashville
07.11.83 James Holley W RSC 1 Chicago
01.12.83 Linwood Jones W CO 5 Chicago
20.12.83 James Dixon W RSC 6 Chicago
24.02.84 Larry Givens W CO 4 Chicago
15.03.84 Sam Jeter W CO 1 Chicago
19.04.84 Walter Santemore W RSC 1 Detroit
09.05.84 Dave Johnson W RSC 2 Chicago
15.06.84 Eddie Lopez W RSC 9 Las Vegas
22.09.84 Jimmy Young W PTS 10 Grand Rapids
24.10.84 O. T. Davis W CO 1 Detroit
02.11.84 Danny Sutton W PTS 10 Chicago
28.06.85 Bobby Crabtree W RSC 4 Hammond
19.10.85 David Jaco W RSC 3 Monte Carlo
27.02.86 Eddie Richardson W PTS 10 Chicago
10.07.86 Eddie Richardson W CO 4 Houston
07.08.86 Otis Bates W CO 2 Houston
26.09.86 James Broad W PTS 12 Atlantic City *(Vacant USBA Heavyweight Title)*
30.05.87 James Douglas W RSC 10 Las Vegas *(Vacant IBF Heavyweight Title)*
01.08.87 Mike Tyson L PTS 12 Las Vegas *(IBF Heavyweight Title Defence. WBA & WBC Heavyweight Title Challenge)*
Summary: 36 contests, won 34, lost 1, nc 1.

(Iron) Mike Tyson
New York, USA. *Born* 30.06.66
World Heavyweight Champion

06.03.85 Hector Mercedes W CO 1 Albany
10.04.85 Trent Singleton W RSC 1 Albany
23.05.85 Don Halpin W RSC 4 Albany
20.06.85 Rick Spain W CO 1 Atlantic City
11.07.85 John Anderson W RTD 2 Atlantic City
19.07.85 Larry Sims W CO 3 Poughkeepsie
15.08.85 Lorenzo Canady W RSC 1 Atlantic City
05.09.85 Michael Johnson W CO 1 Atlantic City
09.10.85 Donnie Long W RSC 1 Atlantic City
25.10.85 Robert Colay W CO 1 Atlantic City
01.11.85 Sterling Benjamin W RSC 1 Latham
13.11.85 Eddie Richardson W CO 1 Houston
22.11.85 Conroy Nelson W RSC 2 Latham
06.12.85 Sam Scaff W RSC 1 New York
27.12.85 Mark Young W CO 1 Latham
10.01.86 David Jaco W RSC 1 Albany
24.01.86 Mike Jameson W RSC 5 Atlantic City
16.02.86 Jesse Ferguson W RSC 6 Troy
10.03.86 Steve Zouski W CO 3 Nassau
03.05.86 James Tillis W PTS 10 Glens Falls
20.05.86 Mitch Green W PTS 10 New York
13.06.86 Reggie Gross W RSC 1 New York
28.06.86 Bill Hosea W CO 1 Troy
11.07.86 Lorenzo Boyd W CO 2 Swan Lake
26.07.86 Marvis Frazier W CO 1 Glens Falls
17.08.86 Jose Ribalta W RSC 10 Atlantic City
06.09.86 Alfonso Ratliff W RSC 2 Las Vegas
22.11.86 Trevor Berbick W RSC 2 Las Vegas *(WBC Heavyweight Title Challenge)*
07.03.87 James Smith W PTS 12 Las Vegas *(WBC Heavyweight Title Defence & WBA Heavyweight Title Challenge)*
30.05.87 Pinklon Thomas W RSC 6 Las Vegas *(WBA & WBC Heavyweight Title Defence)*
01.08.87 Tony Tucker W PTS 12 Las Vegas *(WBA & WBC Heavyweight Title Defence. IBF Heavyweight Title Challenge)*
16.10.87 Tyrell Biggs W RSC 7 Atlantic City *(World Heavyweight Title Defence)*
22.01.88 Larry Holmes W RSC 4 Atlantic City *(WBA & WBC Heavyweight Title Defence)*
21.03.88 Tony Tubbs W RSC 2 Tokyo *(World Heavyweight Title Defence)*
Summary: 34 contests, won 34.

Yoshiyuki Uchida
Japan. *Born* 18.05.59
Former Undefeated Japanese S. Flyweight Champion

07.02.81 Hiroyasu Kato L PTS 4 Tokyo
05.04.81 Masanori Kasuya W CO 1 Tokyo
09.06.81 Hiroshi Kiazato W RSC 1 Tokyo
17.09.81 Masayuki Nakamura W CO 3 Tokyo
05.10.81 Muneo Taira W RSC 3 Tokyo
16.11.81 Hiroyasu Kato W CO 1 Tokyo
20.12.81 Norio Ichikawa W RSC 6 Tokyo
15.02.82 Hideo Sakamoto W RSC 6 Osaka
20.06.82 Yasuhiro Kinoshita W RSC 2 Kashima
17.07.82 Masaki Sono W RSC 2 Tokyo
05.10.82 Masaki Sono W CO 2 Shiki
17.01.83 Shinji Takagi W CO 3 Tokyo
16.04.83 Yasuo Azato DREW 10 Nagasaki
12.07.83 Ryuji Ichinomiya W CO 1 Kamifukuoka
18.10.83 Isao Kimura W RSC 3 Osaka
23.02.84 Gonzaburo Nobu W CO 6 Tokyo
27.04.84 Fumito Hasegawa W CO 4 Tokyo
15.06.84 Heishin Tokuchi W PTS 8 Osaka
25.02.85 Tsutomu Kawakami W PTS 10 Tokyo
27.08.85 Koji Kobayashi W CO 7 Tokyo
24.03.86 Jo Shiranui W CO 5 Tokyo
22.05.86 Koji Nishikawa L PTS 10 Tokyo *(Japanese Flyweight Title Challenge)*
23.02.87 Hiroaki Kanaya W RSC 8 Tokyo
21.09.87 Yon Inazuma W RSC 5 Tokyo *(Vacant Japanese S. Flyweight Title)*
Summary: 24 contests, won 21, drew 1, lost 2.

Cardenio Ulloa
Puerto Vargas, Chile. *Born* 30.10.56
Latin American Bantamweight Champion. Former Undefeated Con. Am. Bantamweight Champion

23.05.80 Nelson Bustamante W PTS 6 Santiago
09.07.80 Ramon Blanco W CO 5 Santiago
23.07.80 Juan Catanan W CO 1 Santiago
16.08.80 Ramon Blanco W CO 2 Braunau
15.10.80 Jose Carmona W RSC 2 Santiago
29.10.80 Juan Aravena W CO 3 Santiago
26.11.80 Tito Herbert W RSC 1 Santiago
31.01.81 Arturo Neira W PTS 8 El Salvador
06.03.81 Jorge Santis W CO 1 Santiago
03.04.81 Cristobal Ramos W CO 2 Santiago
11.04.81 Guillen Acevedo W RSC 5 El Salvador
22.05.81 Esteban Bustos DREW 8 Santiago
14.10.81 Agustin Ceballos W CO 4 Santiago
18.11.81 Hector Martinez W RSC 2 Santiago
07.12.81 Agustin Ceballos W CO 4 Santiago
26.02.82 Alfredo Herrera W CO 2 Santiago *(Vacant Con. Am. Bantamweight Title)*
20.03.82 Roberto Condori W PTS 10 Santiago
31.05.82 Juan Rios W PTS 8 Santiago
14.08.82 Humberto Torres W CO 2 Puerto Montt
15.10.82 Jorge Fernandez W RTD 6 Talcahuano
27.11.82 Bernabe Mendez W CO 1 Melipilla
25.03.83 Raul Cuevas W RSC 3 Santiago
21.05.83 Cristobal Ramos W CO 5 Loncoche
17.09.83 Jorge Sepulveda W CO 8 Lebu
11.12.83 Jose Ortiz W CO 1 Miami
20.01.84 Hector Martinez W RSC 7 Miami
24.02.84 Julio Osorio W CO 5 Miami
03.04.84 Jose Lopez W CO 6 Miami
31.07.84 Edgar Muniz W RSC 1 Miami
15.12.84 Richard Sandoval L RSC 8 Miami *(WBA Bantamweight Title Challenge)*
29.03.85 Diego Avila L PTS 10 Miami
24.05.85 Jorge Franco W RTD 4 Puerto Montt
03.07.85 Armando Romero W PTS 10 Santiago
01.12.85 Benito Badilla L CO 5 Santiago *(Latin American Bantamweight Title Challenge)*
28.02.86 Juan Garcia W RSC 2 San Felipe
21.03.86 Esteban Bustos W PTS 10 Antofagasta
30.04.86 Benito Badilla W CO 5 Antofagasta *(Latin American Bantamweight Title Challenge)*
28.05.86 Jose Cabrera W RTD 4 Talca
03.06.86 Javier Brown W CO 3 Santiago
08.08.86 Jose Narvaez W RSC 3 Santiago
13.09.86 Luis Gerez W CO 1 Santiago
29.11.86 Ramon Rodriguez W CO 2 Santiago
08.11.86 Raul Gutierrez W CO 2 Santiago
19.12.86 Roberto Haidar W RSC 3 Santiago
16.01.87 Jorge Monardez W RTD 5 Santiago *(Latin American Bantamweight Title Defence)*
06.02.87 Eloy Alca W PTS 10 Santiago
27.03.87 Raul Ojeda W PTS 10 Temuco
19.05.87 Ezequiel Hernandez W TD 3 Santiago
24.06.87 Jose Chacon W PTS 10 Santiago
25.07.87 Gliserio Velazco W RSC 4 Santiago
30.10.87 Jose Salazar W CO 2 Santiago
11.12.87 Jose Chacon W PTS 12 Santiago *(Latin American Bantamweight Title Defence)*
06.02.88 Edwin Ampuero W PTS 10 Copiapo
02.04.88 Carlos Solis W CO 1 Castro
Summary: 54 contests, won 50, drew 1, lost 3.

Tarmo Uusivirta
Finland. *Born* 05.02.57
L. Heavyweight

25.06.82 Mick Morris W PTS 6 Hankoo
01.10.82 Deano Wallace W CO 2 Helsinki
09.04.83 Andre Mongalema W RSC 5 Blendecques
18.09.83 Maurice Bufi W RTD 5 Jyvaskyla
05.11.83 Dick Katende L PTS 8 Mannheim
17.12.83 Martin McEwan W CO 2 Mariehamn
18.02.84 Juan M. Holgado W CO 3 Copenhagen
11.05.84 Arthur Holt L PTS 8 New York
21.05.84 Jose Seys L CO 5 Helsinki
27.10.84 Esperno Postl W RSC 4 Mariehamn
09.03.85 Willie Wright W PTS 8 Copenhagen
11.05.85 Paul Tchoue W PTS 8 Vasa
24.11.85 Philippe Seys W CO 2 Vasa
26.03.86 Alex Blanchard DREW 10 Amsterdam
09.11.86 Jimmy Cable W PTS 10 Vasa
21.11.86 Joe Cooper W RSC 2 Copenhagen
26.12.86 Enrico Scacchia DREW 10 Berne
26.10.87 James Cook W PTS 10 Jyvaskyla
15.01.88 Mboyanga Kalombo W PTS 4 Skive
07.02.88 Tony Burke W RTD 8 Laukka
Summary: 20 contests, won 15, drew 2, lost 3.

Jorge Vaca
Guadalajara, Mexico. *Born* 14.12.59
Former WBC Welterweight Champion. Former Undefeated Mexican Welterweight Champion

10.02.78 Luis Piceno W CO 2 Guadalajara
15.03.78 Alfonso Rodriguez W CO 3 Guadalajara
28.04.78 Juan Ramirez W CO 4 Guadalajara
19.05.78 Tony Castillo W CO 2 Guadalajara
16.06.78 Rodolfo Valero L CO 3 Monterrey
01.09.78 Nemesio Ontiveros W RSC 4 Guadalajara
06.10.78 Alejo Agosto W RSC 5 Guadalajara
16.03.79 Alberto Lopez W PTS 10 Guadalajara
15.11.79 Rodolfo Valero L CO 5 Guadalajara
22.08.80 Jesse Blanco W CO 4 Guadalajara
10.10.80 Juan Elizondo L CO 2 Guadalajara
14.11.80 Ranulfo Cardona W RSC 3 Guadalajara
16.01.81 Nicolas Herrera W CO 3 Guadalajara
27.02.81 Juan Elizondo W RSC 7 Guadalajara
28.08.81 Leo Bermudez W CO 4 Guadalajara
09.10.81 Juan Ochoa W RSC 1 Guadalajara
06.11.81 Ramon Beltran W CO 1 Guadalajara
04.12.81 Jose Soberanes W RSC 4 Guadalajara
28.05.82 Jose Alvarez W CO 5 Guadalajara
03.09.82 Jose Soberanes W CO 2 Guadalajara
26.02.83 Sergio Sanchez W RSC 3 Mexico City
09.06.83 Tomas Perez L CO 8 Los Angeles
02.09.83 Lalo Dominguez W RSC 6 Los Angeles
13.01.84 Rocky Granillo DREW 10 Mexicali
28.03.84 Gil Canchola W RSC 2 Tijuana *(Mexican Welterweight Title Challenge)*
29.05.84 Gerardo Derbez W RSC 2 Tijuana *(Mexican Welterweight Title Defence)*
12.07.84 Alfonso Long W PTS 10 Los Angeles
11.09.84 Herman Montes L CO 2 Tijuana
26.10.84 Alberto Lopez W RSC 9 Guadalajara *(Mexican Welterweight Title Defence)*
11.01.85 Ray Morales W CO 1 Juarez *(Mexican Welterweight Title Defence)*
22.03.85 Gerardo Derbez W RSC 9 Juarez *(Mexican Welterweight Title Defence)*
02.05.85 Herman Montes W RSC 3 Los Angeles
15.08.85 Tommy Richardson W PTS 10 Los Angeles
29.11.85 Gerardo Derbez W RSC 6 Guadalajara *(Mexican Welterweight Title Defence)*
10.01.86 Sergio Medina W PTS 12 Guadalajara *(Mexican Welterweight Title Defence)*
25.03.86 Juan Escobar W CO 3 Tijuana
20.06.86 Sergio Medina W RSC 10 Guadalajara *(Mexican Welterweight Title Defence)*
08.09.86 Ruben Villaman W CO 6 Tijuana *(Mexican Welterweight Title Defence)*

01.12.86 Roman Nunez W RSC 3 Tijuana
(Mexican Welterweight Title Defence)
19.12.86 Pipino Cuevas W CO 2 Guadalajara
21.02.87 Miguel Dominguez W RSC 6 Guadalajara
(Mexican Welterweight Title Defence)
27.03.87 David Franklin W CO 2 Guadalajara
25.04.87 Ruben Villaman W RSC 5 Mexico City
(Mexican Welterweight Title Defence)
26.06.87 Juan Villa W RSC 2 Guadalajara
(Mexican Welterweight Title Defence)
21.08.87 Saoul Mamby W PTS 10 Tijuana
28.10.87 Lloyd Honeyghan W TD 8 Wembley
(WBC Welterweight Title Challenge)
29.03.88 Lloyd Honeyghan L CO 3 Wembley
(WBC Welterweight Title Defence)
Summary: 47 contests, won 40, drew 1, lost 6.

Tommy (Canonero) Valoy

Dominican Republic. *Born* 11.01.64
Former Undefeated Dominican & Latin American S. Bantamweight Champion. Former Undefeated Con. Am. S. Bantamweight Champion

12.04.82 Isaias Rodriguez W CO 1 Santo Domingo
28.06.82 Eugenio Paulino W CO 2 Santo Domingo
12.08.82 Maximo Villanueva W CO 1 Santo Domingo
15.09.82 Reinaldo Ramirez W CO 2 Santo Domingo
02.12.82 Pascual Polanco W CO 4 Santo Domingo
25.02.83 Carlos Romero L CO 10 Santo Domingo
04.05.83 Jose Salazar W CO 1 Santo Domingo
26.08.83 Antonio Rodriguez W CO 5 Santo Domingo
(Dominican S. Bantamweight Title Challenge)
03.10.83 Jose Rivera W CO 2 Santo Domingo
06.02.84 Juan Medina W RSC 2 Santo Domingo
30.03.84 Jeff Roberts W RSC 1 Curacao
29.06.84 Papo Melendez W CO 1 Curacao
31.08.84 Ruben Palacios W CO 1 Curacao
(Con. Am. S. Bantamweight Title Challenge)
19.12.84 Orlando Perez W CO 1 Santo Domingo
06.04.85 Edwin Salgado W RSC 2 Santurce
28.07.85 Humberto Mejias W RSC 1 Miami
21.10.85 Marcelo Beckford W RSC 2 Miami
(Vacant Latin American S. Bantamweight Title)
19.12.85 Hector Martinez W PTS 10 Santo Domingo
28.03.86 Jose Salazar W CO 4 Curacao
07.06.86 Alberto Mercado W RSC 5 San Juan
16.01.87 Louie Espinosa L RSC 4 Phoenix
(Vacant WBA S. Bantamweight Title)
30.07.87 Javier Ruiz W PTS 10 San Juan
28.09.87 Rafael de Jesus W CO 3 Santo Domingo
27.02.88 Prudencio Cardona W RSC 9 San Juan
Summary: 24 contests, won 22, lost 2.

Darrin Van Horn

Kentucky, USA. *Born* 07.09.68
L. Middleweight

02.09.84 Leon Kerlinger W CO 2 New Orleans
13.11.84 Reuben Moran W RSC 2 Lafayette
20.11.84 Willie Rimmer W PTS 6 Jefferson
04.12.84 Rodney Jones W RSC 2 St Bernard
18.12.84 Jaime Hobbs W RSC 1 Morgan City
16.01.85 Mike French W CO 1 Lafayette
08.02.85 David Seville W CO 2 Lafayette
21.02.85 James Mitchell W RSC 5 Morgan City
04.03.85 Jesse Hopskins W CO 1 Metairie
07.03.85 Derrick Earvin W PTS 4 Gadsdon
20.03.85 James Sanders W CO 4 Lafayette
18.04.85 Ron Paige W CO 1 Monroe
07.05.85 Wesley Morton W PTS 6 New Orleans
10.06.85 Alonzo Stringfellow W RSC 1 Metairie
26.06.85 Reg Dixon W PTS 6 Lafayette
08.08.85 Robert Manous W RSC 3 Metairie
06.09.85 Earl White W RSC 6 Gretna
17.09.85 Pablo Valdez W CO 4 Metairie
02.10.85 Javier Muniz W RSC 4 Houma
22.10.85 Reg Dixon W PTS 6 Metairie
21.01.86 Ed Montague W PTS 8 Metairie
06.03.86 Norberto Sabater W RSC 2 Metairie
15.04.86 David Ramsey W CO 4 Lafayette
24.06.86 Donald Gwinn W RSC 5 Lexington
01.07.86 Keheven Johnson W RSC 8 New Orleans
09.09.86 Sammy Floyd W PTS 10 Lexington
13.01.87 Danny Thomas W PTS 10 Lexington
24.02.87 James Moore W RSC 6 Lexington
20.04.87 Elio Diaz W PTS 10 Lexington
21.06.87 Luis Santana W PTS 10 Lexington
25.08.87 Greg Taylor W PTS 8 Lexington
17.09.87 Norberto Bueno W CO 3 New York
17.10.87 Juan Villa W PTS 10 Atlantic City
05.12.87 Joe Summers W PTS 10 Atlantic City
21.02.88 John Munduga W RSC 7 Frankfurt
Summary: 35 contests, won 35.

Wilfredo Vasquez

Bayamon, Puerto Rico. *Born* 02.08.61
WBA Bantamweight Champion. Former Undefeated Puerto Rican Bantamweight Champion

29.01.81 William Ramos L PTS 4 Trujillo
26.02.81 Felix Cortez W CO 2 San Juan
26.03.81 Roberto Mercedes W RSC 3 Bayamon
30.04.81 Eusebio Espinal DREW 6 Trujillo
17.06.81 Rey Roque W CO 2 Miami
08.08.81 Herminio Adorno W PTS 6 Trujillo
29.08.81 Pedro Alindato W CO 6 Trujillo
03.03.82 Orlando Perez W RSC 7 San Juan
21.03.82 Rudy Perez W PTS 6 Las Vegas
30.05.82 Ion Traian W RSC 2 Las Vegas
26.06.82 Jose Martinez W CO 2 Las Vegas
06.08.82 Sonny Long W PTS 10 New York
19.10.82 Rudy Perez W RSC 2 Las Vegas
04.02.83 Eugenio Paulino W RSC 5 New York
01.05.83 Andres Torres W CO 8 Puerto Rico
22.07.83 Robert Mullins W CO 3 New York
31.10.83 Ramon Cruz W CO 1 Atlantic City
25.11.83 Pedro Rodriguez W RSC 3 Las Vegas
17.03.84 Juan Torres W RSC 4 San Juan
(Vacant Puerto Rican Bantamweight Title)
23.06.84 Julio Guerrero T DRAW 2 San Juan
19.09.84 Javier Barajas W PTS 10 Las Vegas
03.11.84 Norgie Castro W RSC 2 San Juan
13.03.85 Jeff Whaley W RSC 3 Atlantic City

Darrin Van Horn (right) blasts into Joe Summers, who surprisingly went the distance
Peter Goldfield/USA

09.08.85 Osvaldo Acevedo W RSC 5 Miami
08.02.86 Miguel Lora L PTS 12 Miami
(*WBC Bantamweight Title Challenge*)
24.05.86 Jose Cervantes W CO 3 San Juan
31.05.86 Antonio Avelar L RSC 8 Miami
04.10.86 Jesus Muniz W CO 8 San Juan
14.03.87 Juan Carazo W CO 1 San Juan
11.04.87 Lee Cargle W RSC 5 San Juan
04.10.87 Chan-Yung Park W RSC 10 Seoul
(*WBA Bantamweight Title Challenge*)
17.01.88 Takuya Muguruma DREW 12 Osaka
(*WBA Bantamweight Title Defence*)
Summary: 32 contests, won 26, drew 3, lost 3.

Manuel Vilchez
Cabnimas, Venezuela. *Born* 23.04.64
Former Undefeated Latin American S. Bantamweight Champion. Former Venezuelan S. Bantamweight Champion

20.04.85 Geomar Figueroa W RSC 3 Margarita
11.05.85 Felix Benitez W PTS 4 Caracas
08.06.85 Luis Blanco W PTS 4 Caracas
29.06.85 Jose Sierra W RSC 3 Curacao
15.07.85 Wilfredo Navas W RSC 3 Maracaibo
24.08.85 Rogelio Chacin W RSC 3 Maracaibo
02.11.85 Edixon Hernandez W RSC 4 Maracaibo
23.11.85 Rogelio Chacin W RSC 1 Guayamo
15.02.86 Ali Camacho W PTS 10 Ojeda
19.05.86 Juan Torres W RSC 11 San Juan
(*Vacant Latin American S. Bantamweight Title*)
04.10.86 Eduo Bermudez W RSC 3 Ojeda
29.11.86 Juan Medina W RSC 2 Maracaibo
21.03.87 Felix Guzman W CO 3 Maracay
(*Vacant Venezuelan S. Bantamweight Title*)
23.05.87 Francisco Arroyo W DIS 7 Turmero
(*Latin American S. Bantamweight Title Defence*)
15.07.87 Louie Espinosa L RSC 15 Phoenix
(*WBA S. Bantamweight Title Challenge*)
21.11.87 Alfonso Rendon L PTS 12 Turmero
(*Venezuelan S. Bantamweight Title Defence*)
Summary: 16 contests, won 14, lost 2.

Marcos Villasana
Acapulco, Mexico. *Born* 18.06.60
Former Undefeated Mexican Featherweight Champion

.78 Lucerito Montor W CO 2 Acapulco
.78 Gato Clemente W CO 2 Acapulco
.78 Chato Noqueda W CO 2 Acapulco
.78 Jose Jimenez W CO 3 Acapulco
.78 Victor Banos W CO 1 Acapulco
11.01.78 Roberto Hernandez W CO 3 Acapulco
20.01.78 Flavio Renteria W CO 1 Acapulco
10.02.78 Javier Jimenez W CO 4 Acapulco
21.04.78 David Perez W CO 1 Acapulco
.05.78 Victor Banos DREW 10 Acapulco
.06.78 Pedro Garcia W CO 6 Acapulco
29.07.78 Arturo Cabrera W CO 3 Acapulco
13.09.78 Ricardo Perez W CO 9 Acapulco
.79 Roberto Martinez W CO 4 Acapulco
.79 Renato Campos W CO 4 Acapulco
23.03.79 Pedro Martinez W RSC 4 Apatzingan
09.06.79 Alfonso Ramirez W PTS 10 Mexico City
14.07.79 Artemio Ramirez L RSC 7 Mexico City
27.10.79 Ambrosio Luna L PTS 10 Mexico City
30.11.79 Ramiro Garcia W PTS 10 Acapulco
25.01.80 Augustin Macias W PTS 10 Acapulco
29.02.80 Jorge Morales W CO 4 Apatzingan
28.03.80 Francisco Parra W CO 8 Acapulco
.05.80 Balam Torres W RSC 4 Acapulco
05.07.80 Pablo Ramirez W RSC 1 Mexico City
24.09.80 Juan Jimenez W CO 2 Mexico City
15.10.80 Carlos Ibarra W RSC 9 Mexico City
03.12.80 Javier Barcenas W RSC 8 Mexico City
31.01.81 Artemio Ramirez W RSC 1 Mexico City
04.04.81 Federico Carreno W RSC 5 Mexico City
27.06.81 Cenobio Nicolas W CO 4 Mexico City
15.08.81 Miguel Alvarez W PTS 10 Mexico City
18.12.81 Justo Garcia W PTS 12 Acapulco
(*Mexican Featherweight Title Challenge*)
19.03.82 Juan Paredes W RSC 8 Acapulco
(*Mexican Featherweight Title Defence*)
19.06.82 Mario Miranda L RSC 8 Cartagena
28.08.82 Norberto Cabrera W CO 2 Mexico City
(*Mexican Featherweight Title Defence*)
13.11.82 Reyes Gonzalez W CO 2 Mexico City
(*Mexican Featherweight Title Defence*)
26.02.83 Gerald Hayes W PTS 10 San Antonio
06.05.83 Santos Moreno W RSC 6 Juarez
(*Mexican Featherweight Title Defence*)
11.07.83 Justo Garcia W RSC 5 Houston
(*Mexican Featherweight Title Defence*)
09.12.83 Maximo Ballesteros W CO 4 Los Angeles
15.03.84 Joaquin Acuna W RSC 6 Los Angeles
(*Mexican Featherweight Title Defence*)
31.03.84 Ruben Herasme W RSC 4 San Juan
17.05.84 Tyrone Downes W RSC 4 Los Angeles
06.07.84 Rosendo Ramirez W RSC 1 Houston
13.09.84 Idabeth Rojas W RSC 9 Los Angeles
17.11.84 Antonio de la Paz W RSC 9 Los Angeles
(*Mexican Featherweight Title Defence*)
02.05.85 Hector Cortes W RSC 7 Los Angeles
06.07.85 Leonardo Valdez L PTS 10 Mexicali
26.09.85 Ricardo Varela W CO 3 Los Angeles
25.02.86 Azumah Nelson L PTS 12 Los Angeles
(*WBC Featherweight Title Challenge*)
03.07.86 Aristides Acevedo T DRAW 1 Los Angeles
12.09.86 Alberto Mercado W PTS 10 Chicago
05.02.87 Angel Hernandez W CO 4 Los Angeles
29.08.87 Azumah Nelson L PTS 12 Los Angeles
(*WBC Featherweight Title Challenge*)
24.03.88 Jaime Garza W CO 5 Los Angeles
Summary: 56 contests, won 48, drew 2, lost 6.

Nicky Walker
Carson City, USA. *Born* 1962
S. Middleweight

13.05.82 Paddy Wilson W PTS 4 Carson City
27.05.82 Angelo Marchetti W RSC 2 Las Vegas

Frankie Warren (right), the favourite, came unstuck against James McGirt in their contest for the vacant IBF light-welterweight title Tom Casino

03.07.82 Kurt Berry W CO 2 Gardnerville
31.07.82 Lester Jackson W CO 1 Lake Tahoe
09.09.82 Tim Felty W RSC 1 Stateline
30.09.82 Billy Brigham W CO 6 Carson City
29.10.82 Danny Coyne W CO 3 Carson City
20.11.82 Hudson Jackson W PTS 6 Everett
22.12.82 Sam Turner W CO 1 Stateline
20.01.83 Ingolf Heitman W CO 2 Santa Rosa
10.02.83 Noe Ramirez L RSC 4 Tonopah
31.03.83 Bob Thomas W CO 3 Carson City
06.04.83 Malachi Malone W CO 2 Stockton
13.04.83 Elden Cress W RSC 4 Reno
30.04.83 Paddy Wilson W RSC 3 Sparks
03.07.83 Jim Cook W RSC 1 Gardnerville
24.08.83 Doug Holliman W PTS 8 Reno
24.09.83 Johnny Nava DREW 10 Stateline
30.10.83 Noe Ramirez W PTS 10 Carson City
09.02.84 Burgess Scruggs W RSC 5 Tonopah
14.04.84 Jim Shavers W PTS 10 Carson City
20.04.84 Billy Robinson W CO 2 Klamath Falls
12.05.84 Charles Carter L PTS 10 Lake Tahoe
01.09.84 I. W. Johnson W PTS 10 Reno
30.10.84 Ken Johnson W CO 3 Carson City
10.01.85 Doug Holliman W PTS 10 Stateline
23.02.85 Danny Blake DREW 10 Carson City
25.01.86 Tom Covington W PTS 10 Carson City
01.03.86 Tony Golden W PTS 10 Carson City
23.03.86 James Williams W CO 4 Reno
25.04.86 Dwayne Muniz W RSC 5 Stateline
11.07.86 James Williams W PTS 10 Lake Tahoe
17.10.86 Danny Blake W PTS 10 Watsonville
07.02.87 I. W. Johnson W RSC 8 Reno
09.04.87 Rubin Williams W RSC 5 Tonopah
26.04.87 James Waire W PTS 10 Reno
04.09.87 Charles Carter W RSC 5 Reno
30.01.88 Jeff McCall W RSC 5 Carson City
Summary: 38 contests, won 34, drew 2, lost 2.

Frankie (Panchito) Warren
Corpus Christi, USA. *Born* 1959
USBA L. Welterweight Champion

09.10.82 Jack Alvarez W PTS 4 Las Vegas
26.01.83 Ismael Aguilar W RSC 2 Alice
16.06.83 Rodney Sanchez W CO 2 Corpus Christi
08.07.83 Lopez McGee W RSC 3 Corpus Christi
12.08.83 Danny Favella W PTS 6 Corpus Christi
05.10.83 Honorio Valle W RSC 3 Corpus Christi
07.12.83 Frank Govea W RSC 5 Corpus Christi
29.12.83 Enrique Flores W RSC 3 Harlingen
21.03.84 Garland Wright W RSC 6 Atlantic City
20.05.84 Ford Jennings W PTS 8 Corpus Christi
26.09.84 Oscar Caston W RSC 4 Atlantic City
16.11.84 Willie Rodriguez W PTS 10 Corpus Christi
26.12.84 Dave Odem W CO 7 Atlantic City
30.03.85 Dwayne Prim W RSC 8 Dallas
24.04.85 Ricky Kaiser W RSC 3 Atlantic City
10.07.85 Tomas Chavez W RSC 2 Corpus Christi
25.10.85 Michael Bradley W CO 8 Anchorage
19.01.86 Robert Elizondo W RSC 7 Corpus Christi
06.04.86 Sammy Fuentes W PTS 10 Corpus Christi
11.05.86 Ronnie Shields W PTS 12 Corpus Christi
(*Vacant USBA L. Welterweight Title*)
20.07.86 James McGirt W PTS 10 Corpus Christi
19.11.86 Ozzie O'Neal W RSC 5 Atlantic City
(*USBA L. Welterweight Title Defence*)
15.02.87 Gene Hatcher W PTS 10 Sacramento
31.07.87 Efren Nieves W RTD 4 Corpus Christi
07.01.88 Bryan Davenport W CO 1 Houston
14.02.88 James McGirt L RSC 12 Corpus Christi
(*Vacant IBF L. Welterweight Title*)
Summary: 26 contests, won 25, lost 1.

Troy Waters
Sydney, Australia. *Born* London, England 23.04.65
Commonwealth & Australian L. Middleweight Champion

17.10.84 John Piggott W CO 6 Woy Woy
22.02.85 Sean Gray W CO 3 Gosford
26.04.85 Tony Naidu W PTS 6 Sydney
19.07.85 Graeme Locker W PTS 8 Sydney
22.11.85 Tony Campbell W CO 3 Gosford
15.03.86 In-Chull Baek L PTS 12 Seoul
(*OPBF L. Middleweight Title Challenge*)
25.11.86 Paul Toweel W PTS 12 Cardiff
(*Vacant Australian L. Middleweight Title*)
08.05.87 Dwain Lockman W RSC 7 Sydney
15.08.87 Lloyd Hibbert W RSC 4 Hobart
(*Commonwealth L. Middleweight Title Challenge*)
06.11.87 Benito Fernandez W RSC 10 Hobart
Summary: 10 contests, won 9, lost 1.

Michael Watson
Islington, England. *Born* 15.03.65
Middleweight

16.10.84 Winston Wray W RSC 4 London
26.02.85 John Elliott W RSC 8 London
14.04.85 Dennis Sheehan W RSC 3 London
05.06.85 Gary Tomlinson W RSC 4 London
05.11.85 Martin McEwan W RSC 6 Wembley
19.02.86 Karl Barwise W RSC 3 London
07.05.86 Carlton Warren W PTS 6 London
20.05.86 James Cook L PTS 8 Wembley
19.07.86 Simon Collins W CO 1 Wembley
04.11.86 Alan Baptiste W PTS 8 Wembley
19.01.87 Ian Chantler W RTD 4 London
22.02.87 Ralph Smiley W PTS 8 Wembley
19.03.87 Cliff Gilpin W PTS 8 London
05.10.87 Franki Moro W RSC 4 London
28.10.87 Sam Houston W RSC 2 Wembley
03.02.88 Don Lee W RSC 5 Wembley
09.03.88 Kenny Styles W RSC 9 Wembley
13.04.88 Joe McKnight W RSC 4 London
Summary: 18 contests, won 17, lost 1.

Kevin Watts
Peter Goldfield/USA

Kevin (Killer) Watts
Pineville, USA. *Born* 09.09.61
Middleweight

08.11.83 David Barrow W RSC 4 Atlantic City
17.01.84 Gene Dixon W CO 1 Atlantic City
08.02.84 Russell Hart W RSC 1 Atlantic City
25.02.84 Keith Todd L RSC 4 Atlantic City
05.06.84 Ali Bilal Bey W RSC 4 Atlantic City
07.08.84 Neil Jackson W PTS 4 Atlantic City
11.09.84 Larry Davis W PTS 6 Atlantic City
23.10.84 Osley Silas W PTS 4 Atlantic City
20.11.84 Jerome Johnson W PTS 8 Atlantic City
15.01.85 Ed Barnes W RSC 4 Atlantic City
15.05.85 William Perry W RSC 5 Atlantic City
19.06.85 Ali Bilal Bey W RSC 5 Atlantic City
22.10.85 Ralph Smiley W RSC 3 Atlantic City
12.11.85 Dwight Walker W PTS 10 Atlantic City
11.02.86 James Green W PTS 10 Atlantic City
15.07.86 Joe McKnight W RSC 6 Atlantic City
02.10.86 Jorge Amparo L PTS 10 Atlantic City
27.12.86 Frank Tate L PTS 10 Atlantic City
26.02.87 Steve Darnell W PTS 10 Atlantic City
10.10.87 Eddie Hall W PTS 8 Las Vegas
20.11.87 Tyrone Frazier DREW 10 Atlantic City
02.01.88 Michael Nunn L PTS 12 Reseda
(*NABF Middleweight Title Challenge*)
Summary: 22 contests, won 17, drew 1, lost 4.

Mike (Black Hercules) Weaver
Gatesville, USA. *Born* 14.06.52
Former WBA Heavyweight Champion. Former Undefeated USBA Heavyweight Champion

14.09.72 Howard Smith L RSC 3 Los Angeles
31.10.72 Howard Smith L PTS 5 Bakersfield
02.02.73 Carlos Lopez W PTS 5 San Bernardino
28.02.73 Billy Ryan L RSC 2 Fresno
10.09.73 Lynch Martin W CO 1 Los Angeles
11.10.73 Tony Pulu W RSC 4 Los Angeles
09.11.73 Bob Swoopes W RSC 1 San Diego
12.12.73 Larry Frazier L RSC 2 San Francisco
21.02.74 Ellis McKinley W PTS 6 Los Angeles
22.03.74 Rod Bobick L PTS 10 Los Angeles
31.05.74 Orville Qualls W CO 2 San Diego
26.07.74 Duane Bobick L RSC 7 San Diego
24.08.74 Mani Vaca W PTS 10 Honolulu
27.06.75 Tony Doyle W RSC 9 San Diego
14.07.76 Jodie Ballard W PTS 10 Las Vegas
04.11.76 Fonomanu Sekona W CO 6 San Carlos
17.01.77 Dwain Bonds W RSC 8 Las Vegas
01.04.77 Bill Sharkey W PTS 10 New York
13.09.77 Dave Martinez W CO 1 Anchorage
15.11.77 Pedro Lovell W PTS 10 Anaheim
24.01.78 Stan Ward L PTS 12 Sacramento
19.08.78 Leroy Jones L PTS 12 Los Angeles
(*NABF Heavyweight Title Challenge*)
17.09.78 Mike Creel W RSC 2 Reno
22.10.78 Bernardo Mercado W RSC 5 Reno
05.12.78 Abdul Khan W RSC 2 Reno
18.01.79 Stan Ward W RSC 9 Las Vegas
02.03.79 Oliver Phillips W CO 4 Las Vegas
22.06.79 Larry Holmes L RSC 12 New York
(*WBC Heavyweight Title Challenge*)
24.09.79 Harry Terrell W RSC 4 Los Angeles
24.11.79 Scott Ledoux W PTS 12 Bloomington
(*Vacant USBA Heavyweight Title*)
31.03.80 John Tate W CO 15 Knoxville
(*WBA Heavyweight Title Challenge*)
25.10.80 Gerrie Coetzee W CO 13 Sun City
(*WBA Heavyweight Title Defence*)
03.10.81 James Tillis W PTS 15 Rosemont
(*WBA Heavyweight Title Defence*)
10.12.82 Michael Dokes L RSC 1 Las Vegas
(*WBA Heavyweight Title Defence*)
20.05.83 Michael Dokes DREW 15 Las Vegas
(*WBA Heavyweight Title Challenge*)
30.09.83 Stan Ward W RSC 9 Los Angeles
31.08.84 Billy Joe Thomas W CO 7 Las Vegas
09.11.84 Tony Anthony W DIS 1 Las Vegas
15.06.85 Pinklon Thomas L CO 8 Las Vegas
(*WBC Heavyweight Title Challenge*)
16.02.86 Carl Williams W RSC 2 Troy
05.04.86 James Smith L RSC 1 Latham
23.08.86 Donovan Ruddock L PTS 10 Fayetville
24.08.87 James Pritchard W RSC 6 Louisville
28.11.87 Johnny du Plooy W RTD 6 Johannesburg
30.04.88 Johnny du Plooy L CO 2 Sun City
Summary: 45 contests, won 30, drew 1, lost 14.

Rene Weller
Pforzheim, West Germany. *Born* 21.11.53
EBU & West German Lightweight Champion

06.06.81 Potito Dimuro W PTS 6 Cologne
16.08.81 Ken Foreman W CO 2 Hamburg
25.09.81 Dieter Schantz W CO 4 Cologne
(*Vacant West German Lightweight Title*)
22.10.81 Jackie Turner W RSC 3 Frankfurt
06.11.81 Hector Molina W CO 1 Kiel
26.12.81 Rafael Valdez W CO 3 Gelsenkirchen
15.01.82 Isidoro Cabeza W PTS 6 Hamburg
23.01.82 Bruno Demontis W RSC 7 Berlin
25.02.82 Peter Eubanks W PTS 8 Munich
30.04.82 Rodolfo Sanchez W PTS 10 Cologne
12.06.82 Floyd Pearson W CO 3 Mannheim
26.06.82 Charles Lacour W PTS 8 Las Vegas
24.09.82 Potito Dimuro W RSC 7 Frankfurt
23.10.82 Eddie Murray W CO 2 Berlin
13.11.82 Isidoro Cabeza W PTS 8 Mannheim
04.12.82 Willie Booth W PTS 10 Cologne
26.02.83 Santiago Alvarez W RTD 6 Mannheim
04.03.83 Charlie Nash W RSC 4 Cologne
29.06.83 Lucio Cusma DREW 12 Brolo
(*EBU Lightweight Title Challenge*)
10.09.83 Tusikoleta Nkalankete W PTS 8 Cologne
07.10.83 James Ortega W RSC 1 Frankfurt
05.11.83 Laurent Grimbert W RSC 5 Mannheim
02.12.83 Hugo Carrizo W RSC 5 Stuttgart

09.03.84 Lucio Cusma W PTS 12 Frankfurt
(EBU Lightweight Title Challenge)
13.04.84 Jose Antonio Garcia W RSC 9 Hagen
(EBU Lightweight Title Defence)
27.04.84 Jurgen Himmler W RTD 4 Berlin
26.05.84 Daniel Londas W PTS 12 Dusseldorf
(EBU Lightweight Title Defence)
05.10.84 George Feeney W PTS 12 Frankfurt
(EBU Lightweight Title Defence)
20.10.84 Oscar Kipcoeck W RSC 4 Salzhuflen
30.03.85 Vicente Jorge W PTS 8 Dortmund
26.04.85 Frederic Geoffroy W CO 11 Frankfurt
(EBU Lightweight Title Defence)
01.06.85 Kiziki Tiwizana W PTS 8 Mannheim
07.09.85 Raffaele Paoletti W RSC 7 Aachen
10.01.86 Gert Bo Jacobsen L RSC 8 Randers
(EBU Lightweight Title Defence)
01.03.86 Moussa Sangare W PTS 8 Cologne
18.03.86 Mike Durvan W PTS 8 Russelsheim
12.05.86 Konny Mittermeier W PTS 10 Hamburg
(West German Lightweight Title Defence)
27.06.86 Georg Vlachos W PTS 8 Grevenmacher
10.10..86 Faical Naifer W PTS 8 Russelsheim
02.05.87 Konny Mittermeier W CO 9 Hamburg
(West German Lightweight Title Defence)
03.06.87 Fernando Blanco W PTS 8 Bad Homburg
15.08.87 Tony Bawa W PTS 8 Bad Homburg
14.09.87 Manfred Findenig W PTS 8 Bad Hamburg
27.11.87 Gary Gamble W PTS 8 Russelsheim
16.01.88 George Vlachos W CO 2 Lubeck
(West German Lightweight Title Defence)
04.03.88 Jose Maillot W PTS 12 Karlsruhe
(Vacant EBU Lightweight Title)
09.04.88 Jose Hernando W PTS 8 Hamburg
Summary: 47 contests, won 45, drew 1, lost 1.

Pernell (Sweet Pea) Whitaker
Norfolk, USA. *Born* 02.01.64
Former Undefeated NABF & USBA Lightweight Champion

15.11.84 Farrain Comeaux W RSC 2 New York
20.01.85 Daviel Avery W RSC 4 Atlantic City
13.03.85 Mike Golden W CO 4 Norfolk
20.04.85 Nick Parker W PTS 6 Corpus Christi
20.07.85 John Senegal W RSC 2 Norfolk
30.08.85 Teddy Hatfield W RSC 3 Atlanta
12.11.85 Jesus de la Cruz W CO 1 Houston
09.03.86 John Montes W PTS 10 Hampton
16.08.86 Rafael Williams W PTS 10 Atlantic City
09.10.86 Rafael Gandarilla W PTS 10 New York
19.12.86 Alfredo Layne W PTS 10 Norfolk
28.03.87 Roger Mayweather W PTS 12 Norfolk
(Vacant NABF Lightweight Title)
28.06.87 Jim Flores W CO 1 Houston
25.07.87 Miguel Santana W RSC 6 Norfolk
(Vacant USBA Lightweight Title)
19.12.87 Davey Montana W RSC 4 Paris
12.03.88 Jose Luis Ramirez L PTS 12 Paris
(WBC Lightweight Title Challenge)
Summary: 16 contests, won 15, lost 1.

Carl (The Truth) Williams
New York, USA. *Born* 11.11.59
USBA Heavyweight Champion

22.01.82 Greg Stephany W PTS 4 New York
31.03.82 Dwight Triplett W RSC 1 New York
30.04.82 Lou Alexander W RSC 2 New York
28.05.82 Dan Townsend W RSC 1 New York
11.06.82 Barry Funches W RSC 6 New York
20.08.82 Dave Starkey W RSC 3 New York
22.10.82 Michael Greer W RSC 3 New York
08.12.82 Leroy Boone W PTS 8 New York
18.02.83 Richard Cade W RSC 1 New York
24.04.83 Robert Hill W RSC 3 Atlantic City
30.06.83 David Jaco W RTD 1 Atlantic City
16.08.83 Woody Clark W PTS 10 Atlantic City
09.09.83 Percell Davis W RSC 4 Las Vegas
07.03.84 Lou Benson W RSC 2 White Plains
09.08.84 Terry Mims W CO 3 New York
23.10.84 James Tillis W PTS 10 Atlantic City
20.05.85 Larry Holmes L PTS 15 Reno
(IBF Heavyweight Title Challenge)
31.08.85 Jesse Ferguson W RSC 10 Atlantic City
16.02.86 Mike Weaver L RSC 2 Troy
21.06.87 Bert Cooper W RTD 7 Atlantic City
(Vacant USBA Heavyweight Title)

Carl Williams
Peter Goldfield/USA

17.10.87 Mike Gans W RSC 7 Atlantic City
27.01.88 Rodney Frazier W RSC 1 San Diego
(USBA Heavyweight Title Defence)
Summary: 22 contests, won 20, lost 2.

Charles (Prince) Williams
Cleveland, USA. *Born* 1962
IBF L. Heavyweight Champion. Former Undefeated USBA L. Heavyweight Champion

27.06.78 Henry Bunch L PTS 4 Washington
07.02.79 Mike Hardin DREW 4 Richfield
21.03.79 Willis Crawford W PTS 4 Richfield
27.04.79 Willis Crawford W RSC 3 Dayton
19.05.79 Gus Turner W PTS 4 Findley
20.09.79 Sam Bryant W RSC 1 Richfield
30.04.80 Sylvester Wilder W RSC 1 Struthers
06.05.80 Tim Johnson W CO 1 Canton
17.05.80 Mike Hardin DREW 6 Dayton
13.04.81 Rocky Templeton W RSC 2 Akron
28.05.81 Marc Ball W CO 2 Akron
29.10.81 Jeff Lampkin L RSC 6 Warren
12.12.81 Al Bolden W RSC 4 Monroe
15.12.82 Kemper Morton W PTS 4 Galion
01.03.83 Reggie Gross L RSC 1 Baltimore
24.06.83 Anthony Witherspoon W PTS 8 Warwick

Charles Williams
Peter Goldfield/USA

23.09.84 Clarence Osby W RSC 1 Grand Rapids
08.11.84 Marvin Johnson L PTS 10 Indianapolis
02.03.85 Marcus Jackson W PTS 6 Atlantic City
03.06.85 Pop Nance W RSC 1 Atlantic City
05.08.85 Arthur Hall W CO 1 Atlantic City
03.10.85 Mike Fisher W RSC 5 Atlantic City
03.12.85 Jeff Lampkin W PTS 10 Atlantic City
18.04.86 Arthel Lawhorne W RSC 3 Atlantic City
19.08.86 Eric Winbush W PTS 10 Philadelphia
20.09.86 James Salerno W PTS 12 Indianapolis
(Vacant USBA L. Heavyweight Title)
14.07.87 Joe Dolphin W RSC 2 Philadelphia
(USBA L. Heavyweight Title Defence)
29.10.87 Bobby Czyz W RTD 9 Las Vegas
(IBF L. Heavyweight Title Challenge)
18.04.88 James Shavers W RTD 4 Paris
Summary: 29 contests, won 23, drew 2, lost 4.

Mike Williams
Houston, USA. *Born* 16.06.63
Heavyweight

13.09.84 Walter Morris W RSC 3 Houston
08.03.85 Hanif Islam W PTS 4 White Plains
18.03.85 James Boyd W CO 3 Houston
23.08.85 Ron Turner W PTS 4 Atlantic City
12.02.86 Carl Dorsey W RSC 3 Houston
02.05.86 John Barbier W RSC 3 Conroe
05.07.86 Terry Armstrong W PTS 6 Conroe
17.10.86 Tommy Taylor W RSC 5 Las Vegas
14.12.86 Bob Obey W RSC 4 Houston
08.01.87 James Tillis W RSC 8 Houston
12.02.87 Billy Joe Thomas W CO 7 New York
09.04.87 Ken Elliott W RSC 3 Houston
22.05.87 Rufus Hadley W PTS 10 Houston
14.10.87 Tim Witherspoon L PTS 10 Atlantic City
07.01.88 Leon Dixon W RSC 2 Houston
03.02.88 Art Terry W PTS 10 Houston
Summary: 16 contests, won 15, lost 1.

Rollin Williams
Peter Goldfield/USA

Rollin Williams
Phoenix, USA. *Born* 29.06.66
USBA Welterweight Champion

22.07.84 Fausto Medina W PTS 8 Albuquerque
09.08.84 Juan Gaxiola W RSC 1 Las Vegas
27.08.84 Larry Yazzie W CO 3 Tucson
27.09.84 Curtis Baker W PTS 6 Las Vegas
21.11.84 Peter Cunningham W PTS 6 Las Vegas
15.01.85 Eddie Walker W PTS 8 Phoenix
26.02.85 Ricardo Lomeli W CO 5 Phoenix
06.06.85 Rigoberto Lopez L CO 7 San Diego
03.08.85 Javier Suazo L PTS 8 Phoenix
25.09.85 Pat Jefferson L PTS 10 Tucson
26.10.85 Lee Mascarenas W CO 1 Farmington
01.11.85 Rick Lehman W PTS 12 Tucson
14.01.86 Laurie Mann L PTS 10 Reno
25.01.86 Pedro Rocha W RTD 6 Nogales
25.02.86 Rodolfo Gonzalez L PTS 4 Los Angeles

17.03.86 Danny Paul W PTS 8 Phoenix
25.04.86 Greg Tutt W RSC 2 Stateline
23.05.86 Reggie Miller W PTS 8 Las Vegas
11.07.86 Javier Suazo T DRAW 9 Las Vegas
02.01.87 Steve Little W PTS 8 Atlantic City
07.02.87 Lorenzo Guzman W RSC 2 Las Vegas
30.06.87 Tommy Ayers W PTS 12 Atlantic City
(*Vacant USBA Welterweight Title*)
18.09.87 Rigoberto Lopez W DIS 3 Phoenix
12.12.87 Charles Nwokolo W PTS 12 Phoenix
(*USBA Welterweight Title Defence*)
Summary: 24 contests, won 18, drew 1, lost 5.

Tony Willis
Peter Goldfield/USA

Tony Willis
Maywood, USA. *Born* 04.10.61
NABF L. Heavyweight Champion. Former Undefeated USBA L. Heavyweight Champion

23.10.84 Jerry Harris W CO 3 Highlands
14.12.84 Mike Hildreth W RSC 3 River Grove
31.01.85 Vernon Bridges W PTS 6 Detroit
16.02.85 Tom Lins W RSC 1 Dixon
25.02.85 James McNeal W CO 1 Chicago
12.04.85 Tim Johnson W PTS 6 Chicago
17.07.85 Phil Brown W RSC 1 Akron
08.08.85 James Wilder W RSC 5 Chicago
22.03.86 Larry Burrell W RSC 4 Chicago
25.07.86 Marcos Geraldo W RSC 10 Chicago
09.04.87 Everett Martin W RSC 7 Houston
26.06.87 Willie Edwards W RSC 4 Atlantic City
(*NABF L. Heavyweight Title Challenge*)
13.08.87 Louis Coleman W PTS 10 Houston
24.11.87 Ramzi Hassan W RSC 12 Los Angeles
(*Vacant USBA L. Heavyweight Title*)
29.04.88 Mike Sedillo W PTS 12 Houston
(*NABF L. Heavyweight Title Defence*)
Summary: 15 contests, won 15.

Frank Winterstein
France. *Born* 10.07.59
Former Undefeated French Middleweight Champion

19.01.80 Joachim Oliveira W RSC 2 Argenteuil
25.01.80 Christian D'Helft W PTS 6 Corbeil
08.03.80 Maurice Renaud W PTS 6 Epinay
05.04.80 Santo Jaconelli W RSC 5 Massy
18.04.80 Cyrille Barbe W RSC 2 St Genevieve
26.04.80 Jean-Philippe Truchelut W RTD 3 Noisy
03.05.80 Eugene Dovin W RSC 1 Paris
06.06.80 Santo Jaconelli W RTD 2 Massy
13.06.80 Jean-Luc Lamy W RSC 6 Coubertin
06.10.80 Bader Ouakhai W RSC 3 Paris
27.10.80 Dragan Tadic W RSC 2 Paris
14.11.80 Felix N'Coumba W CO 2 Paris
27.11.80 Walengua N'Kongo W RTD 1 Paris
08.12.80 Lieti Mandoze W RTD 2 Paris
16.01.81 Mick Morris W CO 2 Paris
29.01.81 Fefe Mobana W RTD 3 Paris
16.02.81 Earl Edwards W PTS 6 Paris
13.03.81 Maurice Renaud W PTS 6 Villeurbanne
04.04.81 Eugene Dovin W RSC 3 St Etienne
10.04.81 Serge Sinelnikov W PTS 6 Villaneuve
15.05.81 Mike Burton W CO 5 Paris
22.05.81 Justin M'Foudi W RSC 2 Nimes
26.09.81 Branko Barakovic W CO 3 Paris
20.11.81 Jose Luis Duran W RSC 5 Nice
26.11.81 Bob Patterson W CO 3 Paris
19.02.82 Fred Coranson W RTD 5 Nice
07.10.82 Sonny Kamunga W CO 3 Paris
04.11.82 Horace McKenzie W CO 3 Bezons
25.11.82 Joel Bonnetaz DREW 8 Marseilles
25.03.83 Louis Acaries L CO 4 Paris
(*EBU Middleweight Title Challenge*)
01.07.83 Joel Bonnetaz W RSC 3 Paris
(*French Middleweight Title Challenge*)
27.11.83 Jacques Chinon W PTS 12 Nimes
(*French Middleweight Title Defence*)
12.11.84 Cliff Gilpin W PTS 10 Paris
04.03.85 Sammy Brennan W RSC 7 St Ouen
29.03.85 Lahcen M'Hamdi W RSC 2 Bordeaux
06.05.85 Doug James W CO 3 Grenoble
14.01.86 Luigi Marini W CO 2 Paris
08.02.86 Tony Britton W RSC 7 Lille
21.02.86 Willie Wright W PTS 8 St Ouen
17.03.86 Bruce Jackson W PTS 8 Paris
28.04.86 Brian Anderson W RSC 8 Paris
13.10.86 Ron Malek W CO 3 Paris
17.11.86 Eddie Smith W RSC 2 Paris
20.12.86 Tony Davenport W RSC 2 St Ouen
18.04.87 Tony Burke W CO 3 Nimes
16.11.87 Sean Mannion W PTS 8 St Ouen
Summary: 46 contests, won 44, drew 1, lost 1.

Anthony Witherspoon
Philadelphia, USA. *Born* 1956
Cruiserweight

17.06.81 Brian Morrison W CO 1 Philadelphia
30.07.81 Larry Jefferson W RSC 1 Philadelphia
02.09.81 Jim Brown W CO 2 Philadelphia
26.09.81 James van Keuren W RSC 1 Atlantic City
19.12.81 Bernard McLean W RSC 1 Atlantic City
12.06.82 Ed Smith W RSC 2 Atlantic City
24.03.83 Randy Coleman W RTD 2 Newark
24.06.83 Charles Williams L PTS 8 Warwick
10.09.83 Jerry Martin L PTS 10 Atlantic City
11.01.84 Jeff Lampkin W PTS 10 Atlantic City
11.04.84 Reggie Gross W RSC 7 Baltimore
20.09.84 Tim Broady L CO 2 Atlantic City
12.12.84 Charles Price W CO 1 Pikesville
23.02.85 Mike Lee W PTS 8 Atlantic City
06.05.85 Tony Nelson W PTS 10 Atlantic City
05.08.85 James Salerno W PTS 10 Atlantic City
03.10.85 Willie Edwards L PTS 12 Atlantic City
(*NABF L. Heavyweight Title Challenge*)
20.02.87 Al Shoffner W RSC 7 Philadelphia
27.03.87 Robert Obey W RSC 3 Cannes
15.05.87 Ricardo Spain W PTS 8 Las Vegas
24.10.87 Alek Penarski W RSC 1 London
Summary: 21 contests, won 17, lost 4.

(Terrible) Tim Witherspoon
Philadelphia, USA. *Born* 27.12.57
Former WBC & WBA Heavyweight Champion. Former Undefeated NABF Heavyweight Champion

30.10.79 Joey Adams W RSC 1 Upper Darby
26.04.80 Robert Ritchie W CO 1 Lynchburg
09.05.80 Robert Evans W PTS 6 Commack
20.07.80 Charles Cox W RSC 5 McAfee
24.10.80 Oliver Wright W RSC 2 Philadelphia
11.12.80 James Reid W RTD 6 Philadelphia
24.01.81 Ed Bednarik W CO 1 Philadelphia
07.02.81 Marvin Stinson W PTS 10 Atlantic City
11.04.81 Dave Johnson W PTS 8 Kiamesha Lake
17.06.81 Bobby Jordan W RSC 4 Philadelphia
30.07.81 Jerry Williams W RTD 7 Philadelphia
07.11.81 Curtis Gaskins W RSC 2 Atlantic City
05.12.81 Alfonso Ratliff W RSC 7 Atlantic City
20.03.82 Luis Acosta W CO 2 Atlantic City
05.06.82 Renaldo Snipes W PTS 10 Las Vegas
20.05.83 Larry Holmes L PTS 12 Las Vegas
(*WBC Heavyweight Title Challenge*)
16.07.83 Floyd Cummings W PTS 10 Las Vegas
23.09.83 James Tillis W RSC 1 Richfield
(*Vacant NABF Heavyweight Title*)
09.03.84 Greg Page W PTS 12 Las Vegas
(*Vacant WBC Heavyweight Title*)
31.08.84 Pinklon Thomas L PTS 12 Las Vegas
(*WBC Heavyweight Title Defence*)
25.03.85 Mark Wills W RSC 9 Los Angeles
29.04.85 James Broad W CO 2 Buffalo
(*NABF Heavyweight Title Challenge*)
15.06.85 James Smith W PTS 12 Las Vegas
(*NABF Heavyweight Title Defence*)
06.09.85 Larry Beilfus W RSC 1 Miami
12.10.85 Sam Scaff W RSC 4 Birmingham
17.01.86 Tony Tubbs W PTS 15 Atlanta
(*WBA Heavyweight Title Challenge*)
19.07.86 Frank Bruno W RSC 11 Wembley
(*WBA Heavyweight Title Defence*)
12.12.86 James Smith L RSC 1 New York
(*WBA Heavyweight Title Defence*)
04.08.87 Mark Wills W RSC 1 Atlantic City
14.10.87 Mike Williams W PTS 10 Atlantic City
17.02.88 Mauricio Villegas W RSC 9 London
Summary: 31 contests, won 28, lost 3.

Bobby Joe Young
Peter Goldfield/USA

Bobby Joe Young
Stuebenville, USA. *Born* 04.03.59
Welterweight

29.08.80 Pedro Vilella L PTS 4 New York
09.09.80 Bob Buscombe W RTD 1 Warren
10.10.80 Alf Doubouchet W RSC 2 New York
28.10.80 Efren Sifuentes W RSC 1 Warren
09.12.80 Tony Taylor W RSC 2 Warren
17.12.80 Eddie Campbell W CO 3 Steubenville
07.01.81 Danny Chapman W RSC 4 New York
28.02.81 Papo Figueroa W CO 3 Atlantic City
12.03.81 Willie Thomas W RSC 2 New York
08.05.81 Greg Harper W CO 4 Fairmont
31.05.81 Curtis Taylor W RSC 1 Atlantic City
30.06.81 Mike Herron W PTS 8 Philadelphia
25.07.81 Leotis Burgess W RSC 5 Atlantic City
06.11.81 Mike Blunt W RSC 2 Pittsburgh
10.12.81 Babs McCarthy W RSC 5 Atlantic City
28.02.82 Don Morgan W RSC 7 Atlantic City
27.03.82 Kevin Howard L PTS 10 Philadelphia
09.07.82 Pedro Acosta W RSC 2 Bridgeport
19.07.82 Pete Seward W RSC 1 Atlantic City
22.09.82 Raul Hernandez W RSC 3 Atlantic City
23.10.82 Mark Harris W PTS 10 Lancaster
03.03.83 Jose Vallejo W PTS 10 Ambridge
10.04.83 Nino la Rocca L RSC 8 San Remo
10.07.83 Darrell Chambers W RSC 9 Atlantic City
23.09.83 Jeff Malcolm L PTS 10 Cleveland
03.03.84 Sam Lantion W RSC 6 Hamilton
06.04.84 Eduardo Romero W CO 2 New York
08.11.84 Dennis Fain W RSC 8 Steubenville
12.01.85 Darryl Anthony L RSC 9 Atlantic City
17.04.85 Larry McCall W RSC 8 Steubenville
31.05.85 Donald Gwynne W CO 2 Wheeling
23.07.85 Gary Roemhild W PTS 10 Atlantic City
08.10.85 Ken Shannon W PTS 10 Atlantic City
22.05.86 Felipe Montellano W PTS 10 Atlantic City
16.09.86 Matt Farrago DREW 10 Syracuse
03.05.87 David Noel W TD 8 Atlantic City

30.06.87 Charles Nwokolo L PTS 10 Los Angeles
08.08.87 Aaron Pryor W CO 7 Sunrise
Summary: 38 contests, won 31, drew 1, lost 6.

Myung-Woo Yuh
South Korea. *Born* 10.01.64
WBA L. Flyweight Champion. Former Undefeated OPBF L. Flyweight Champion

28.03.82 Byung-Boum Choi W PTS 4 Chinju
28.04.82 Joo-Young Lee W PTS 4 Seoul
16.05.82 Chang-Yung Chang W PTS 4 Seoul
21.05.82 Joo-Ho Kwon W PTS 4 Seoul
23.05.82 Youn-Ri Moon W PTS 4 Seoul
25.05.82 Ki-Soo Kim W PTS 4 Seoul
05.06.82 Nam-Sok Yun W PTS 4 Seoul
31.07.82 Hyo-Young Park W PTS 6 Seoul
30.10.82 Ki-Chang Kim W PTS 8 Taegu
05.12.82 Ki-Yung Kim W PTS 8 Chinju
23.01.83 Kyung-Shik Park W PTS 10 Daejon
05.03.83 Rae-Ki Ahn W PTS 8 Seoul
04.12.83 Ha-Shik Lim W PTS 8 Seoul
15.04.84 Little Baguio W CO 2 Seoul
27.05.84 Bi-Won Chung W PTS 10 Seoul
02.12.84 Edwin Inocencio W CO 3 Seoul
(*Vacant OPBF L. Flyweight Title*)
24.02.85 Tagabus Jaya W CO 3 Seoul
(*OPBF L. Flyweight Title Defence*)
08.09.85 Oh-Kong Son W RSC 7 Seoul
08.12.85 Joey Olivo W PTS 15 Seoul
(*WBA L. Flyweight Title Challenge*)
09.03.86 Jose de Jesus W PTS 15 Suwon
(*WBA L. Flyweight Title Defence*)
14.06.86 Tomohiro Kiyuna W RSC 12 Inchon
(*WBA L. Flyweight Title Defence*)
30.11.86 Mario de Marco W PTS 15 Seoul
(*WBA L. Flyweight Title Defence*)
01.03.87 Eduardo Tunon W RSC 1 Seoul
(*WBA L. Flyweight Title Defence*)
07.06.87 Benedicto Murillo W RSC 15 Pusan
(*WBA L. Flyweight Title Defence*)
20.09.87 Rodolfo Blanco W CO 8 Inchon
(*WBA L. Flyweight Title Defence*)
07.02.88 Wilibaldo Salazar W PTS 12 Seoul
(*WBA L. Flyweight Title Defence*)
Summary: 26 contests, won 26.

Hilario Zapata
Panama City, Panama. *Born* 19.08.58
Former WBC L. Flyweight Champion. Former WBA Flyweight Champion

28.10.77 Victor Lopez W RSC 3 Colon
26.11.77 Cesar Becerra W RSC 3 Panama City
04.03.78 Humberto Mayorga W PTS 4 Panama City
15.04.78 Alfredo Thomas W RSC 3 Panama City
02.06.78 Juan Guzman W RSC 10 Panama City
19.08.78 Yong-Hwang Kim W PTS 10 Seoul
28.10.78 Alfonso Lopez L PTS 12 Panama City
(*Vacant Latin American L. Flyweight Title*)
14.01.79 Ramon Perez W RSC 9 San Juan
07.04.79 Nestor Obregon W PTS 10 Panama City
23.06.79 Freddie Castillo W PTS 12 Panama City
06.10.79 Jose Ricardo W RSC 7 Colon
24.03.80 Shigeo Nakajima W PTS 15 Tokyo
(*WBC L. Flyweight Title Challenge*)
07.06.80 Chi-Bok Kim W PTS 15 Seoul
(*WBC L. Flyweight Title Defence*)
04.08.80 Hector Melendez W PTS 15 Caracas
(*WBC L. Flyweight Title Defence*)
17.09.80 Shigeo Nakajima W RSC 11 Gifu
(*WBC L. Flyweight Title Defence*)
01.12.80 Reynaldo Becerra W PTS 15 Caracas
(*WBC L. Flyweight Title Defence*)
08.02.81 Joey Olivo W RSC 13 Panama City
(*WBC L. Flyweight Title Defence*)
24.04.81 Rudy Crawford W PTS 15 San Francisco
(*WBC L. Flyweight Title Defence*)
15.08.81 German Torres W PTS 15 Panama City
(*WBC L. Flyweight Title Defence*)
06.11.81 Sor Vorasingh W RSC 10 Korat
(*WBC L. Flyweight Title Defence*)
06.02.82 Amado Ursua L CO 2 Panama City
(*WBC L. Flyweight Title Defence*)
20.07.82 Tadashi Tomori W PTS 15 Kanazawa
(*WBC L. Flyweight Title Challenge*)
18.09.82 Jung-Koo Chang W PTS 15 Chonju
(*WBC L. Flyweight Title Defence*)
30.11.82 Tadashi Tomori W RSC 8 Tokyo
(*WBC L. Flyweight Title Defence*)
26.03.83 Jung-Koo Chang L RSC 3 Daejon
(*WBC L. Flyweight Title Defence*)
09.11.83 Harold Petty L RSC 10 Las Vegas
23.06.84 Juan Polo Perez W PTS 10 Atlapa
14.07.84 Ramon Nery W PTS 10 Panama City
01.09.84 Alex Miranda W RSC 9 Panama City
10.10.84 Alberto Castro W PTS 10 Isla Margarita
08.12.84 Santos Laciar L PTS 15 Buenos Aires
(*WBA Flyweight Title Challenge*)
28.12.84 Rafael Cabrera W PTS 10 Panama City
02.02.85 Ramon Espinal W RSC 1 Panama City
30.03.85 Alonzo Gonzales W PTS 10 Panama City
05.10.85 Alonzo Gonzales W PTS 15 Panama City
(*Vacant WBA Flyweight Title*)
31.01.86 Javier Lucas W PTS 15 Panama City
(*WBA Flyweight Title Defence*)
07.04.86 Shuichi Hozumi W PTS 15 Nirasaki
(*WBA Flyweight Title Defence*)
05.07.86 Dodie Penalosa W PTS 15 Manila
(*WBA Flyweight Title Defence*)
13.09.86 Alberto Castro W PTS 15 Panama City
(*WBA Flyweight Title Defence*)
06.12.86 Claudemir Dias W PTS 15 Salvador
(*WBA Flyweight Title Defence*)
13.02.87 Fidel Bassa L PTS 15 Barranquilla
(*WBA Flyweight Title Defence*)
15.08.87 Fidel Bassa DREW 15 Panama City
(*WBA Flyweight Title Challenge*)
Summary: 42 contests, won 35, drew 1, lost 6.

Daniel Zaragoza
Mexico City, Mexico. *Born* 11.12.57
WBC S. Bantamweight Champion. Former Undefeated NABF S. Bantamweight Champion. Former WBC Bantamweight Champion. Former Undefeated Mexican Bantamweight Champion

17.10.80 Ernesto Gutierrez W CO 4 Poza Rica
18.12.80 Porfiro Urrutia W RSC 3 Tampico
21.02.81 Joel Segura W CO 3 Meridan
29.03.81 Jesus Maravilla W CO 2 Villahermosa
15.05.81 Jose Zapata W PTS 10 Villahermosa
27.06.81 Roque Guillen W RSC 3 Tuxtla
22.07.81 Alonzo Gonzales W PTS 10 Los Angeles
28.08.81 Rayito Gonzalez W CO 4 Campeche
13.09.81 Javier Marquez W RSC 8 Mexicali
30.10.81 Julio Avendano W CO 5 Acapulco
20.11.81 Mario Chavez W PTS 10 Mexicali
12.02.82 Miguel Juarez W PTS 10 Acapulco
05.03.82 Francisco Mayo W RSC 5 Acapulco
23.04.82 Ramon Concha W RSC 2 Acapulco
29.07.82 Harold Petty L PTS 10 Las Vegas
04.09.82 Jorge Ramirez W PTS 12 Mexico City
(*Mexican Bantamweight Title Challenge*)
29.11.82 Jesus Lopez W PTS 12 Tijuana
(*Mexican Bantamweight Title Defence*)
29.01.83 Lorenzo Ramirez W PTS 10 Los Angeles
18.03.83 Rigoberto Estrada W PTS 12 Juarez
(*Mexican Bantamweight Title Defence*)
27.05.83 Jesus Lopez W PTS 12 Juarez
(*Mexican Bantamweight Title Defence*)
08.08.83 Harold Petty L PTS 12 Houston
(*NABF Bantamweight Title Challenge*)
26.09.83 Martin Torres W RSC 5 Tijuana
(*Mexican Bantamweight Title Defence*)
30.10.83 Rodolfo Martinez W RSC 11 Guadalajara
(*Mexican Bantamweight Title Defence*)
16.12.83 Rigoberto Estrada W PTS 12 Juarez
(*Mexican Bantamweight Title Defence*)
18.02.84 Javier Marquez W RSC 5 Mexicali
(*Mexican Bantamweight Title Defence*)
17.03.84 Patrick Young W CO 4 Mexicali
21.05.84 Mario Gomez W RSC 3 Tijuana
(*Mexican Bantamweight Title Defence*)
21.09.84 Jorge Ramirez W DIS 11 Juarez
(*Mexican Bantamweight Title Defence*)
30.11.84 Jorge Ramirez W PTS 12 La Paz
(*Mexican Bantamweight Title Defence*)
04.05.85 Fred Jackson W DIS 7 Aruba
(*Vacant WBC Bantamweight Title*)
09.08.85 Miguel Lora L PTS 12 Miami
(*WBC Bantamweight Title Defence*)
11.04.86 Jeff Fenech L PTS 10 Sydney
04.07.86 Antonio Gonzalez W PTS 10 Tijuana
29.08.86 Raul Negrete W TD 7 Tijuana
06.12.86 Mike Ayala W CO 7 San Antonio
(*NABF S. Bantamweight Title Challenge*)
03.04.87 Aaron Lopez W PTS 12 San Antonio
(*NABF S. Bantamweight Title Defence*)
28.06.87 Ramiro Adames W RSC 5 Houston
31.07.87 Darryl Thigpen W PTS 12 San Antonio
(*NABF S. Bantamweight Title Defence*)
17.12.87 Noe Gonzalez W RSC 7 Naucalpan
29.02.88 Carlos Zarate W RSC 10 Los Angeles
(*Vacant WBC S. Bantamweight Title*)
Summary: 40 contests, won 36, lost 4.

Carlos Zarate
Mexico City, Mexico. *Born* 23.05.51
Former WBC Bantamweight Champion

02.02.70 Luis Castaneda W CO 3 Cuernavaca
02.03.70 Jose Pavon W CO 1 Cuernavaca
18.12.70 Alfredo Perez W CO 2 Acapulco
28.01.72 Emiliano Mayoral W RSC 3 Acapulco
07.02.72 Jose Gonzalez W CO 2 Tampico
19.03.72 Jose Morales W RSC 2 Mexico City
19.08.72 Jesus Escobedo W CO 2 Monterrey
08.09.72 Chato Patino W CO 2 Ciudad Madero
31.10.72 Armando Carrasco W CO 2 Villahermosa
03.12.72 Chilango Perez W RSC 2 La Paz
06.02.73 Chilango Perez W CO 2 La Paz
02.06.73 Chilango Perez W CO 2 La Paz
12.07.73 Sugar Pino W CO 2 Cuernavaca
21.08.73 Al Torres W RSC 5 Tijuana
02.10.73 Caguamo Castaneda W RSC 9 Tijuana
12.12.73 Sixto Perez W CO 2 Tijuana
30.01.74 Victor Ramirez W PTS 10 Mexico City
22.02.74 Carlos Armenta W CO 1 Matamoros
09.04.74 Alfonso Ibarra W CO 2 Tijuana
03.05.74 Chamaco Limon W CO 3 Monterrey
25.05.74 Juan Ordonez W CO 3 Mexico City
03.08.74 Magallo Lozada W RSC 5 Mexico City
27.10.74 Francisco Cruz W RSC 2 Mexicali
23.11.74 James Martinez W RSC 7 Los Angeles
04.02.75 Alberto Cabanig W RSC 4 Ciudad Victoria
14.03.75 Joe Guevara W RSC 4 Los Angeles
20.06.75 Orlando Amores W CO 3 Los Angeles
16.08.75 Jose Sanchez W RSC 3 Mexico City
20.09.75 Benicio Sosa W RSC 4 Los Angeles
11.10.75 Jorge Torres W RSC 9 Guadalajara
07.12.75 Nestor Jimenez W CO 2 Mexicali
27.03.76 Cesar Deciga W RSC 4 Monterrey
08.05.76 Rodolfo Martinez W CO 9 Los Angeles
(*WBC Bantamweight Title Challenge*)
26.06.76 Felix Llanos W CO 2 Mexicali
02.08.76 Tony Paredes W RSC 2 Chihuahua
28.08.76 Paul Ferreri W RSC 12 Los Angeles
(*WBC Bantamweight Title Defence*)
13.11.76 Waruinge Nakayama W CO 4 Culiacan
(*WBC Bantamweight Title Defence*)
05.02.77 Fernando Cabanela W RSC 3 Mexico City
(*WBC Bantamweight Title Defence*)
23.04.77 Alfonso Zamora W RSC 4 Los Angeles
29.10.77 Danilo Batista W RSC 6 Los Angeles
(*WBC Bantamweight Title Defence*)
02.12.77 Juan Francisco Rodriguez W RSC 5 Madrid
(*WBC Bantamweight Title Defence*)
25.02.78 Albert Davila W RSC 8 Los Angeles
(*WBC Bantamweight Title Defence*)
22.04.78 Andres Hernandez W RSC 13 San Juan
(*WBC Bantamweight Title Defence*)
09.06.78 Emilio Hernandez W CO 4 Las Vegas
(*WBC Bantamweight Title Defence*)
30.09.78 Rudy Gonzalez W CO 4 Matamoros
28.10.78 Wilfredo Gomez L RSC 5 San Juan
(*WBC S. Bantamweight Title Challenge*)
10.03.79 Mensah Kpalongo W CO 3 Los Angeles
(*WBC Bantamweight Title Defence*)
01.05.79 Celso Chaires W RSC 5 Houston
02.06.79 Lupe Pintor L PTS 15 Las Vegas
(*WBC Bantamweight Title Defence*)
25.02.86 Adam Garcia W PTS 4 Los Angeles
12.04.86 Jose Luis Mora W CO 3 Zacapu
01.05.86 Hector Napoles W CO 2 Torreon
23.05.86 Jesus Muniz W PTS 10 Chicago
19.07.86 Alejandro Garcia W CO 2 Juarez
13.09.86 Gerardo Esparza W CO 5 Zapopan
21.11.86 Eddie Rodriguez W RSC 3 San Jose
13.12.86 Alex Galvan W RSC 7 Fresno
20.02.87 Francis Childs W RSC 4 San Jose
05.05.87 John Boyd W RSC 5 Los Angeles
19.06.87 Tony Montoya W RSC 3 San Jose
15.08.87 Richard Savage W TD 4 Mexico City
16.10.87 Jeff Fenech L TD 4 Sydney
(*WBC S. Bantamweight Title Challenge*)
29.02.88 Daniel Zaragoza L RSC 10 Los Angeles
(*Vacant WBC S. Bantamweight Title*)
Summary: 63 contests, won 59, lost 4.

The Hall of Fame

Twelve of the all-time greats as seen through the eyes of Ron Olver, a leading boxing historian.

JAMES J. CORBETT

JAMES J. CORBETT gave a new image to the sport, changing it from the bare-knuckle era to boxing with gloves under the Marquess of Queensberry Rules, and projecting science and ringcraft rather than brute force. Inevitably he became known as "Gentleman Jim".

He was born on 1 September, 1866, in San Francisco, California, of Irish parents, where his father kept a livery stable. His first fight was at St Ignatius College with the school bully, who was older and much bigger and as a result both boys were expelled.

Jim didn't fare much better at Sacred Heart College where he had a difference of opinion with a teacher who hit him on the hand with a wooden pole. He didn't wait to be hit again and after being chased by other teachers, butted one in the stomach, which resulted in yet another expulsion.

On leaving school he got a job at the Nevada Bank as a messenger boy where he stayed for six years, until 1886, and finished up as assistant receiving teller.

James J. liked boxing, and took part in several sessions with his friends in his father's stable, but he much preferred baseball. Indeed, he was being groomed for the big time when he had an accident, splitting his hand between the little and third fingers, which finished his baseball ambitions.

It was then that he thought more seriously about taking up boxing. A friend, Lew Harding, took him around the clubs, some of them extremely rough, where he boxed without any kind of tuition, and did reasonably well.

However, when he joined the Olympic Club, his limitations were exposed, and it wasn't until instructor Walter Watson was imported from England that he made good progress. His parents were not too happy at first, as they had wanted him to become a priest.

When Jack Dempsey, "The Nonpareil", visited the club, Jim sparred with the champion and acquitted himself well, which gave him the encouragement to pursue a career in boxing.

He had several meetings with tough Joe Choynski, the first in his father's stable, when he knocked Joe out in about a minute. The return was in a quarry, with the same result, and later for good measure Jim knocked out Joe's older brother.

The third fight was in the loft of a barn, and the sheriff stopped that one in round six. The fourth was on a barge, where Jim knocked out Joe in round 27 and after that they became firm friends. Their last meeting was Corbett's first official bout as a professional.

There was a shock when he was matched with the famous Jake Kilrain in 1890. It was a six-rounder; Jim won easily on points and earned 3,500 dollars. The following year there was an even bigger shock when he agreed to meet the Negro Peter Jackson, whom everybody else was avoiding.

Both wore five-ounce gloves, but without bandages and Jim was conceding quite a slice of weight with Jackson scaling over fourteen stones. Also there was a considerable amount of betting on the fight. After four hours both were tired and still game, but during round 60 the referee Hiram Cook left the ring for half a minute and was seen to be talking to a group of people, who it was alleged had bet on Jackson.

In round 61, he suddenly stopped the action, and said "No Contest. All bets off."

There was consternation. Jim protested, but to no avail and on the way to the dressing-room Jackson fell down exhausted, to be carried off by his seconds. Jim said he knew then that he had been "robbed".

The original arrangement was 8,500 dollars to the winner, 1,500 to the loser, with 5,000 each for a draw. But when our hero went for his money he was given only 2,500. However, his fans ran a testimonial at the Grand Opera House, San Francisco, to make up for the loss.

Champion John L. Sullivan also agreed to spar with him, but insisted they wear evening dress, and the four-rounds exhibition fell flat.

Jim was also doing a bit of acting, touring the country in plays under impresario William J. Brady, who then became his fight manager, with his old friend Billy Delaney as trainer. Sullivan now issued a public challenge to Frank Slavin, Charlie Mitchell and Corbett for a purse of 25,000 dollars, with an outside bet of 10,000 dollars, winner take all. But he wanted 10,000 dollars from the opponent as security.

Not easy, but after finding sponsors, the money was deposited and the fight was staged at the Olympic Club, New Orleans, in September 1892. The first world title fight with five-ounce gloves under the Marquess of Queensberry Rules with Bat Masterton as referee. Jim kayoed John L. in the 21st round and the following month started a nation-wide tour in the play, *Gentleman Jack*. It was a fine performance, for the new champion had been conceding nearly three stones.

In 1894 he successfully defended against Charlie Mitchell with a three-rounds victory, and later that year went into the record books by boxing two 2-minute rounds with Peter Courtney at Orange, New Jersey for Kinetoscope, claimed to be the first motion picture of a fight.

A title fight was arranged with Bob Fitzsimmons for October 1895, but called off owing to adverse legislation. Jim was so fed up that he announced his retirement from the ring, and "presented" the title to Peter Maher. Fitz then proceeded to knock out Maher in one round, but no one took much notice, and Corbett was still considered to be the champion. At last, in March 1897, Jim defended against Fitz, who kayoed him with a body blow in round fourteen, the famous solar-plexus punch. Corbett looked to be well ahead when the unexpected end came.

He had just one fight in 1898, when he was disqualified against Tom Sharkey. His chief second, Con McVey jumped into the ring when the sailor got a little rough and the referee seemed to be doing nothing about it.

To all intents and purposes Jim then retired, opening a café on Broadway. Yet he couldn't get boxing out of his mind. In May 1900 he made a comeback against Jim Jeffries, who had taken the title from Fitzsimmons. Scheduled for 25 rounds, he seemed to be comfortably ahead after 22, but in the 23rd session he bounded back off the ropes straight into Jeffries' left hand, and was knocked cold.

Even then he wasn't satisfied and the following August he stopped Kid McCoy in round nine, before having another crack at Jeffries' title in August 1903. This time the 27-year-old Corbett was knocked out in round ten, and this time he retired for good.

He will for ever be remembered for introducing skill into a sport which had formerly been notable for the survival of the fittest. Both in and out of the ring he deserved his nickname "Gentleman Jim". He died on 18 February, 1933, at Bayside, Long Island, New York, and was elected to Boxing's Hall of Fame in 1954.

Historical action depicts James J. Corbett (right), the defending heavyweight champion, warding off Bob "Ruby Robert" Fitzsimmons in March, 1897. This was the battle in which Corbett lost his title in the fourteenth round, the victim of the famous "solar plexus" punch

JOE FRAZIER

When the American Federal Grand Jury indicted undefeated world heavyweight champion Muhammad Ali for draft evasion in May 1967, the World Boxing Association immediately stripped him of his title and suspended him from boxing at any venue under their jurisdiction. The New York State Athletic Commission quickly followed suit.

The WBA arranged an elimination competition to find a successor to Ali, naming eight contenders, including Joe Frazier. However, Joe's manager, Yank Durham, withdrew him, stating that Joe deserved a straight crack at the vacant crown.

The NYSAC then came up with their solution — a title fight between Joe and "Buster" Mathis — which Yank was quite happy to go along with. In March 1968 Frazier stopped Mathis to win the New York version, and the following month Jimmy Ellis beat Jerry Quarry to annex the WBA crown.

Ali was still recognised in some quarters, so there were now three fighters who claimed the world title. Frazier successfully defended the New York crown against Manuel Ramos, Oscar Bonavena, Dave Zyglewicz and Jerry Quarry, whilst Ellis successfully defended his WBA title against Floyd Patterson.

In February 1970 Frazier and Ellis were matched for the undisputed world title, Joe winning in five rounds. That same month Ali called a press conference to announce his retirement from the ring, having been inactive for three years, only to change his mind and start a comeback the following October. He stopped Jerry Quarry and Oscar Bonavena, and in March 1971 was matched with Frazier for the title. Joe won a unanimous points verdict, and also had the satisfaction of putting Ali on the canvas.

There was no longer any doubt. Joe Frazier was undisputed heavyweight champion of the world.

Joseph William Frazier, later to be nicknamed "Smokin' Joe", was born on 12 January, 1944, at Beaufort, South Carolina, youngest of thirteen children to Rubin and Dolly Frazier, four of whom died.

His father owned a 500-acre farm, and all the children worked on the farm as soon as they were old enough. The year before Joe was born Rubin lost his left arm following a gun accident, so from then on Joe acted as his father's left arm, doing everything on that side that his father couldn't manage.

From the age of seven Joe drove his father's pickup truck and loved motors. Two years later he started taking an interest in boxing, built his own little gym in a shed and spent hours punching an improvised heavy bag.

The Fraziers were a religious family, and when Joe started boxing seriously he read extracts from the Bible before every fight. At Robert Small High School he reached the ninth grade, only to be expelled for fighting with a boy who called his mother names. He then took a job in construction.

In September 1959, still under the age of 16, he married his childhood sweetheart, Florence Smith. There were to be five children. Joe wanted to succeed, moved to New York for a year, then to Philadelphia, where he got a job in a slaughterhouse at 105 dollars a week.

When he was 18 Joe visited the Police Athletic League gym in Philadelphia, where Duke Dugent was the instructor. It was there that Yancey Durham took a look at him, deciding that Joe was too fat (he weighed over 17 stones), his legs were short, and altogether he didn't look the part. But Yank noted one important factor — Joe could certainly punch.

Duke Dugent turned the flab into muscle, formulated exercises to put right Joe's awkwardness, and to give him balance and strengthen his neck muscles, which got him down to less than fifteen stones. In 1963 and 1964 Joe won the Middle Atlantic Golden Gloves title, and took part in the Olympic Trials, stopping six opponents before being outpointed by "Buster" Mathis in the final. Joe believed he had won.

A disappointed Frazier thought about quitting boxing altogether; then came the break that was to alter his whole career. He was selected as a travelling reserve with the Olympic team, and just before they were due to leave for Japan Joe boxed an exhibition with "Buster", who broke a finger on his right hand with a punch that landed on Joe's head.

There was no alternative at this late stage. Joe was to take "Buster's" place in the Olympic team. It is now history that he became the first American to win the Olympic heavyweight title. And he boxed in the final with a broken thumb on his left hand.

Joe arrived home, unable to work or fight. There was no money coming in, Christmas was close by, and his children would expect presents. Then the public responded. Appeals were made on the radio and in newspapers. Gifts were sent, in money and in kind, ensuring the Fraziers were comfortable over the holiday period, and he was given a job as a janitor in the local Baptist Church.

It was a year before the thumb healed properly and in August 1965 he opened his pro career with a one-round win over Woody Goss. Joe was being guided by Yank Durham, and the following year he was backed by a group called Cloverlay Inc., 40 local businessmen. His future was now assured.

He stopped top men like Eddie Machen, George Chuvalo, and Doug Jones, also outpointing Oscar Bonavena, prior to beating Mathis for the New York title, which I have already described, and going on to beat Ellis and Ali.

Joe then defended his title against Terry Daniels and Ron Stander before losing the crown to George Foreman in January 1973. He was down six times, and the fight was stopped in round two. Beaten, yes. Finished, no. Six months later he came to Britain to outpoint Joe Bugner, and in January 1974 he was outpointed by Ali for the NABF title.

There followed quick wins over Jerry Quarry and Jimmy Ellis before the "rubber" fight with Ali, who had regained the world title by stopping Foreman. Joe was stopped in the fourteenth round in October 1975, but still he wouldn't stop trying, and his one fight in 1976 ended in a five-round defeat by George Foreman. Joe didn't box again until December 1981, when he boxed a ten-round draw with Floyd Cummings.

Joe's career spanned 16 years, yet he had just 37 contests. Only two men beat him, Muhammid Ali and George Foreman, and no less than thirteen of these were title fights of one kind or another.

In 1971 and 1975 he received the Edward J. Neil Memorial Award, and in 1980 was elected to Boxing's Hall of Fame.

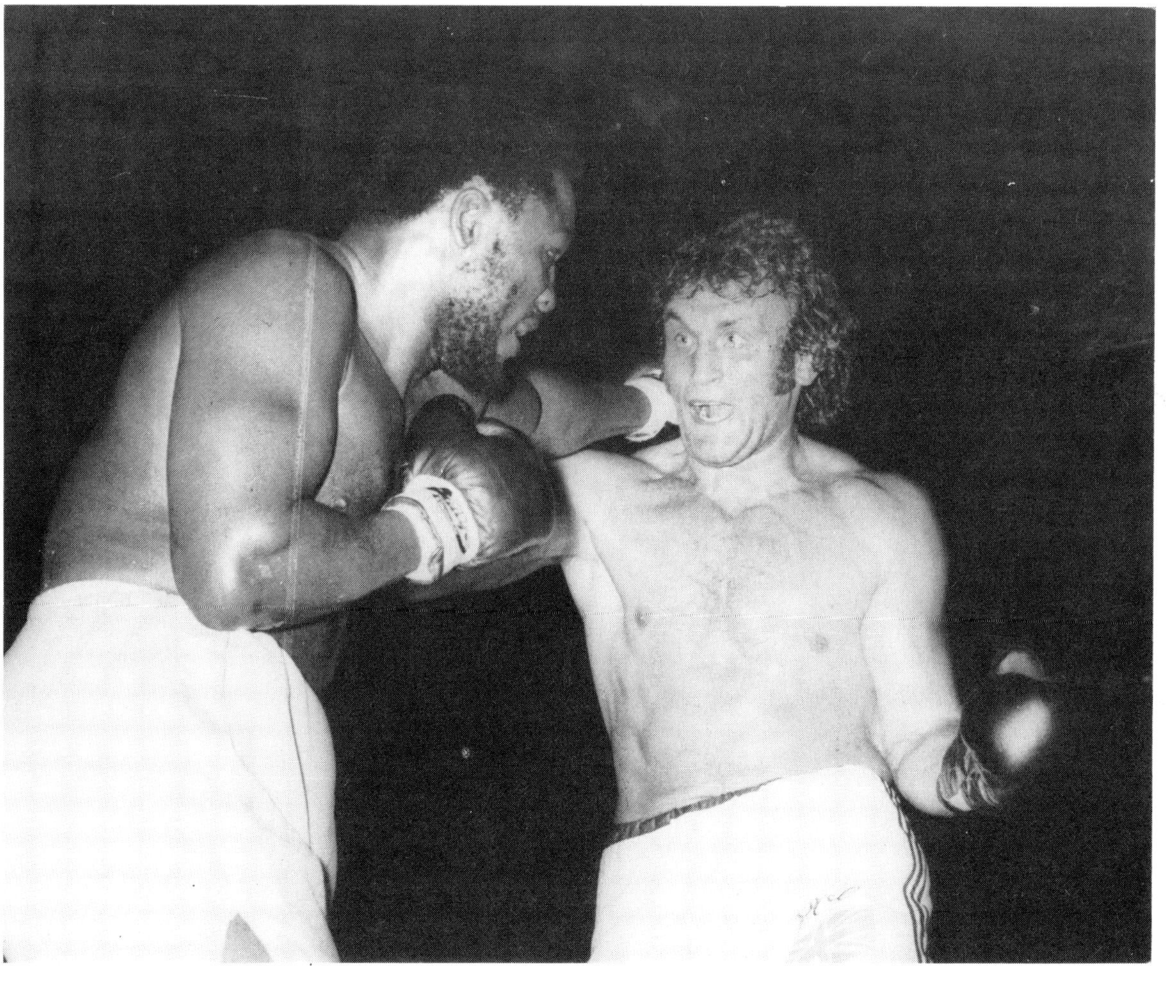

Following his losing heavyweight title contest against George Foreman, Joe (left) next fought in England, where he beat a young Joe Bugner over twelve rounds

ROCKY GRAZIANO

ROCKY GRAZIANO was the self-confessed "bad boy" of boxing. He came from a violent background on New York's East Side, was in and out of reform school and prison, deserted from the Army, yet overcame all the odds to become world middleweight champion.

He was born Rocco Barbella on 1 January, 1922, and as he was being delivered in the back room, his father Nick and friends were shooting dice in the front. Nick and Rocco's mother Ida were both born in New York, but their parents had been born in Italy.

Nick was a professional fighter, and a good-class welterweight, making his debut at the age of 18. He and Ida were married in 1916, and he had around 70 contests before calling it a day.

When Rocky was born he was the Barbella's fifth child, but only he and brother Joe survived. Nick drove a horse-drawn hearse for the local undertaker, but money was scarce. In the summer Rocky dug up clams; in the winter the family lived on macaroni. Nick had not always been employed, and there was a lot of hunger.

The young Rocky and his mother collected driftwood for the stove, their only means of heating the house, also coal from the railway tracks. Their "home" had cracks in the walls and more than its fair share of rats.

He hated school and authority. He frequently played truant, and often took heavy beatings from his father as punishment. Jimmy Capa, a friend of his father, fixed him up with a set of boxing gloves, but things didn't work out. His father had a dream of elder brother Joe becoming a world champion, and Rocky was often an unwilling sparring-partner.

Joe used to knock him around in front of friends, and Nick encouraged him to do so. Rocky was running wild now, mixing with gangs, and after a beating by Joe he used to take it out on the other kids.

He played truant once too often, and was put on probation. His probation officer was named Callahan, and they immediately struck up a rapport. He used to take Rocky to different places, and the lad realised there was another world outside gangs and street-fighting.

Meanwhile there were family problems. Mother was drinking heavily, and had a nervous breakdown. Rocky started stealing and sleeping rough, and eventually was sent to live with his grandmother. For the first time he seemed happy, but the old habits died hard, and while stealing a kid's scooter, he collided with a car and fractured his leg.

He was eleven years old when he was sent to live in the Catholic Protectory, but that didn't work out either. A few years later, and Rocky got his revenge for the beatings inflicted on him by brother Joe, when he waited for him to come home from work, and knocked him out. He said he had to get it out of his system.

His friend Terry Young, a future welterweight star, encouraged him to join the local Boys' Club, where he met Cus D'Amato, who entered him for the Metropolitan AAU championships and he won the welterweight title.

For this Rocky received a gold medal, which he sold for six dollars. From then on he boxed often, selling the medals and also obtaining fifteen dollars for watches. Soon he was "earning" 60 dollars per week. Easy money, but he still couldn't keep out of trouble, with charges like assault and robbery. He was in and out of prison, then in 1940 Eddie Coco fixed him up with a few pro fights at 35 dollars a time. He boxed under the name of "Robert Barber," and all went well until he was booked for violation of parole and sent to Reform School.

He was released in October 1941, inducted into the Army in January 1942, put on a charge after an altercation with a corporal, knocked out the captain who was the presiding officer, and then deserted.

Terry Young took him to Stillman's Gym, where he met Irving Cohen, who became his manager. He was returned to the Army, but deserted again, and in March 1942 had his first official pro fight, knocking out Curtis Hightower. Not wishing to box under his own name, he chose the surname of one of his friends, "Graziano". He was again caught, and sent to a Detention Barracks, then finally given a discharge.

In June 1943, he continued his fight career, won most of his bouts, many by stoppages, and in September 1946 met champion Tony Zale for the world title. Tony took all Rocky had to offer, and knocked him out in round six. There was a return nearly twelve months later, and it also ended in round six, but this time it was Zale who was stopped. Unbelievable as it may have seemed, Rocky Graziano was champion of the world.

Another twelve months passed, and Rocky's first defence was a "rubber" match against Zale, who won by a knockout in round three. It was their last meeting. Three all-action bouts which produced a total of over a million dollars at the gate. Tony's share was nearly 280,000 dollars.

Graziano continued fighting for another four years, and had another 21 bouts, in which he was undefeated. Then in April 1952 he met "Sugar" Ray Robinson for the latter's world middleweight title. Rocky was 32, and although Ray was older by two years he was in fine form after successfully regaining his title from Randy Turpin and defending it against Carl "Bobo" Olson. He was knocked out in round three.

Five months later he was outpointed by Chuck Davey, and retired to become an entertainer, in theatres, clubs and especially on TV, with great success. His autobiography was entitled *Somebody Up There Likes Me*, and a film was made with the same title, starring Paul Newman.

Rocky Graziano was elected to Boxing's Hall of Fame in 1971.

Great action from the second meeting between Tony Janiro and Rocky Graziano in October 1950. With fifteen thousand fans screaming themselves hoarse, Rocky (right) punched out a thrilling points victory where science was not the order of the day

LEN HARVEY

THE FIRST boxer of note I ever saw on a licensed show was Len Harvey. My father took me to watch a promotion at Plymouth, where I was born, and on that occasion Len stopped Welshman Glen Moody in six rounds. I couldn't help but admire his skills, and that, of course, is what boxing is all about — the "Noble Art Of Self Defence", the art of hitting your opponent, feinting him into leaving openings, but at the same time doing your best to prevent him hitting you back, by ducking, weaving, blocking, parrying, side-stepping, in fact all the scientific methods which Len employed so successfully.

Len became my idol, and later my friend. He became a "regular" at the annual dinners of the Boxing Writers' Club, and we had many interesting conversations. His widow Florence, affectionately known as "Blossom", lives just a short bus ride from me in North London and we often exchange letters and 'phone calls. She is without doubt the most knowledgeable lady on the sport of boxing I have ever met. Today her memory is as clear as it ever was.

Harvey was born in Cornwall on 11 July, 1907. His father Ted and mother Ada Jane were Cornish, and there were three other children, Ted, Wilfred and Winifred. Len's father was a farm labourer who emigrated to Canada to try and get a better job, and by 1914 was all set to bring the family over. Then came World War I which brought Ted back and the family moved to Devonport, Plymouth, where he got a job as a blacksmith in the local dockyard.

Ted Harvey was a fight fan, and later became a top trainer at the Devonport and Devonia Boxing Club. All three sons joined the club, and they all attended the professional shows at the Cosmopolitan Gymnasium, known as "the Cosmo". This was where Len made his pro debut at the age of twelve, and up to the end of 1922 had lost only two out of 20 bouts, all of which were in Plymouth.

On leaving school Len went to work in a garage, and in January 1923 came his first "away" contest, when he went to London's famous National Sporting Club to outpoint Young Bill Lewis in his first ten-rounder. Later that year he outpointed Kid Socks in his first fifteen (two-minute) rounder, and just carried on winning. He started as a flyweight, worked his way through the divisions, and in April 1926 was selected to meet Harry Mason for the latter's British welterweight crown.

At this stage of his career he had taken part in 61 recorded bouts, losing only three, the last defeat being against Johnny Sullivan, a verdict which was hotly disputed. This was Len's first 20-rounder, and he was still only 18 years old.

Len's father had now contracted him for seven years with the famous Dan Sullivan, matchmaker for the Blackfriars "Ring". The young Harvey boxed there regularly between 1924 and 1928, and on the odd occasion after that. The result of the Mason fight was a draw, although many thought Len had won the contest.

In January 1928 he and Florence were married. She was the sister of Dick Laws, who boxed as "Bert" Laws, and they set up home in Islington, London.

Len eventually won the British middleweight title by knocking out Alex Ireland in May 1929 and successfully defended it against Jack Hood in October on points. He drew in a rematch with Jack in December, thus keeping his title. In 1930 there was a further successful defence against Steve McCall, and after outpointing a top American Dave Shade at the Albert Hall, it was decided that he should try his luck in the United States. Florence went with him along with the trainer, Archie Watson.

His first opponent was Vince Dundee, who was down twice, but still got the verdict. There was a return, with the same result, and again Len was "robbed". His last fight in the States was against Ben Jeby where he was beaten on points after going in the ring, weak from the effects of influenza.

By now the Harveys had a young son, Leonard Terence, which seemed to give Len added inspiration. He successfully defended his British title against Jock McAvoy, then outpointed Len Johnson in a bout not recognised by the

Board of Control because of Johnson's colour.

In July 1932 he was matched with Marcel Thil for the world title, losing on points. By now Harvey had severed his connection with Dan Sullivan, and hired Charlie Rose and Wally May as his mentors. This was followed by a hard fought British title bout with durable Jack Casey, which he won on points but he later lost the crown to Jock McAvoy in April 1933. In this contest he was handicapped by an injured right hand, sustained against Casey, but had his eyes set on moving up a weight, maybe two weights, and wanted to get this one out of the way.

Having drawn with Eddie Phillips in a non-title fight, Len felt confident when they met for the light-heavyweight title in June 1933, and won on points. And he set up a record by boxing for British titles at three different weights in the shortest time when he outpointed Jack Petersen for the heavyweight crown in November 1933, just over seven months from the day he lost his middleweight title.

After annexing the Empire heavyweight title by beating Larry Gains in 1934, he lost both the British and Empire titles to Jack Petersen later that year, retiring in round twelve after boxing seven rounds with a closed left eye. He was out of the ring for nearly six months, coming back to draw with German heavyweight Walter Neusel.

Harvey then relinquished the light-heavyweight title, and lost a bid for the heavyweight crown to Jack Petersen on points in 1936. Following the opening of Harringay Arena, Sydney Hulls established himself at the new venue which left Wembley, with Arthur Elvin in charge, short of a matchmaker. He chose Len Harvey, who in turn chose himself as top of the bill for their next promotion. His opponent — none other than the world light-heavyweight champion John Henry Lewis, who would be putting his title at stake.

The bout took place in November 1936. It was an excellent contest, and in spite of a strong finish by the Cornishman the verdict went against him. Some thought Len deserved to win, but all agreed that considering he boxed with an injured right hand from round three he had never given a more spirited performance, and he received a great ovation.

This was by no means the end. In 1938 he annexed the British light-heavyweight title by outpointing Jock McAvoy, and won the vacant heavyweight title against Eddie Phillips. The following year he added the vacant Empire heavyweight crown to his laurels by stopping Larry Gains, before outpointing Jock McAvoy in a fight billed as for the "vacant world light-heavyweight title", which included Len's British and Empire crowns.

With the coming of World War II, he joined the Royal Air Force. So did a youngster called Freddie Mills. These two met for Len's three titles in June 1942. Len went down in round two, then was sent through the ropes, which were very slack. On the way he banged his head, and by the time he had got back into the ring he had been counted out. The following November he announced his retirement, still holding the British and Empire heavyweight titles.

After the war the Harveys took a pub at Erith, only to suffer the biggest tragedy of their lives when their son Terry died suddenly. A week later Len was in hospital, having contracted pneumonia. For a time his life was in danger, and even though he recovered his health he was never the same afterwards.

They later took various pubs, ending up at the Star & Garter in Islington and on Len becoming a Senior Citizen they went to live at Penn Road, Holloway, where Florence still resides. Len continued to attend functions, was associated with the London Ex-Boxers' Association, and was the first holder of the Joe Bromley Ring Award for Outstanding Services to Boxing, presented by the Boxing Writers' Club in 1967.

He died on 28 November, 1976, arguably the most popular boxer Britain has ever produced, a gentleman inside and outside the ring, and an example to anyone taking up the sport which was his life.

Len (left) regained his British light-heavyweight title when he outpointed Jock "The Rochdale Thunderbolt" McAvoy over fifteen rounds in April 1938. The pair met four times in all, with Len victorious on three occasions

JIMMY McLARNIN

As a professional fighter Jimmy McLarnin boxed in every division from flyweight to welterweight, and it took him ten years of hard slogging before he won the world welterweight title. His three fights with Barney Ross are legendary, and all went the full fifteen rounds.

There was an early tragedy in Jimmy's career which had nothing to do with him, but obviously had had some effect. The world flyweight champion Pancho Villa had won the title from Welshman Jimmy Wilde, in 1923, and in July 1925, met the 18-year-old McLarnin in a non-title fight. It was only the latter's fourth ten-rounder, but he beat Pancho on points.

Ten days later Pancho was dead. Apparently he had gone into the ring with infected gums after having a wisdom tooth pulled out. Blood poisoning followed, which caused his death. Jimmy did the right thing: just carried on with his career, and concentrated on training and improving his game.

Although some record-books differ as to his place of birth, the official registration states that Jimmy was born at Hillsborough, twelve miles from Belfast, on 19 December, 1907. He was only two years old when the family emigrated to Canada, where his father's sister lived.

Jimmy had eleven brothers and sisters, and as a kid sold newspapers in the streets. Other kids had the same idea, and often there were fights if one boy wanted to take over someone else's pitch.

He was just ten years old when he had his first paid fight, the purse being one dollar. Jimmy was fortunate to meet Pop Foster, a man who was to have a great influence on his career. Pop knew the lad's father, and they erected a gym to teach him the basic skills.

Jimmy's first official bout was in 1923, and he went on to win a series of four-rounders before moving to California. There he boxed principally at Oakland and Vernon, and among his victims was the former Olympic champion Fidel La Barba. His first defeat came against Bud Taylor, who would go on to win the world bantamweight crown, and his next outing was against the unfortunate Pancho Villa. He then stopped Jackie Fields in two.

After stopping Louis Kid Kaplan and Sid Terris (one round), Jimmy met Sammy Mandell for the world lightweight title, but was outpointed. He was guaranteed 50,000 dollars, and did well in his first fifteen-rounder. That was 1928, and he subsequently outpointed Mandell twice in ten-rounders. During 1930, he stopped lightweight champion Al Singer in three rounds, and by now he had developed into a welterweight, with the nickname "Baby Face".

One of the greatest fighters, who at that time had never been given a title shot, was Billy Petrolle, "The Fargo Express". He and Jimmy met on three occasions during the early thirties. Billy easily won the first on points, but Jimmy won the other two, then had a rest for twelve months.

Pop Foster was guiding him most astutely, but unfortunately picked the wrong opponent for Jimmy's return to the ring in August 1932. The choice was former welter champion Lou Brouillard, a southpaw, who beat him on points.

Former champion Benny Leonard, who at this stage was attempting a comeback at the age of 36, was defeated inside six rounds and following a stoppage of Sammy Fuller Jimmy was matched with Young Corbett III for the world welterweight title. Corbett was another southpaw, but hardly had a chance to take his stance before Jimmy knocked him out in the opening round to win the title.

That was Jimmy's only fight in 1933, and his next three contests were all with Barney Ross, spread over a period of twelve months. He took a year off after the Corbett victory and Ross was his first defence. Jimmy always said it was a mistake not to fight more often, but he was plagued with hand injuries.

He and Pop had decided that if he beat Ross he would retire from the ring. Instead Barney won on points and took the title. So Jimmy wanted to get his revenge, and did so in their return, a points win giving him back the title.

Their first fight had brought him 60,000 dollars, the second even more.

Their third battle, in May 1935, was one which Jimmy always contended he had won comfortably. Many others agreed with him, but it was Barney who got the verdict. The referee was Jack Dempsey, although the decision was made by the three judges, who voted unanimously for Ross.

Three fights in 1936 completed Jimmy's career, and he went out with a flourish. The first two were against lightweight champion Tony Canzoneri, who won the first, with Jimmy getting revenge in the return. In between Tony had lost his title to Lou Ambers, who was to be Jimmy's last opponent. That night McLarnin boxed brilliantly to outpoint the champ and go out in a blaze of glory. He was still only 29 years old, but was happy to retire at the top.

The family later returned to live on the Pacific coast, where Jimmy opened a machine shop in Los Angeles. Business was understandably brisk during the war years, so much so that after hostilities had ceased he was able to sell out with a large profit. He then operated a tool-and-die business, followed by a travel agency in Hollywood, and in 1970 launched his own company, McLarnin Sales, to represent the interests of major firms.

Jimmy now turned to golf for a hobby, taking part in celebrity tournaments like the Bing Crosby Classic, and by now he was living in a luxury home at Glendale, California, with wife Lillian, son Jimmy, and their three daughters.

He was elected to Boxing's Hall of Fame in 1956.

Jimmy (left) seen destroying the comeback of the former lightweight champion Benny Leonard in October 1932. Two fights later McLarnin won the welterweight title with a first round kayo over Young Corbett III

FREDDIE MILLS

FREDDIE MILLS was undoubtedly one of Britain's most popular fighters, a lovable character who knew only one way to box — to keep coming forward, throwing punches from both hands, hoping to wear down the opposition. Most times it worked, otherwise he would never have become world light-heavyweight champion.

I knew him long before then, in the pre-war days when he was working on Sam McKeowen's boxing booth in Devon. We lost touch until after hostilities had ceased, by which time he had won the world title. I saw him beat Gus Lesnevich, to avenge a previous world title defeat, and I was there when he lost the title to Joey Maxim, although he fought a courageous battle.

Freddie was born in Bournemouth on 26 June, 1919 where he had one brother and a sister. At the age of ten he was put on two years probation for stealing a pair of skates from an empty house and was also fined £1.

He was also given a severe talking-to, and often said that this had the effect on making him see right from wrong, and he made up his mind never to go wrong again. Almost immediately he joined a youth club, where he started boxing.

His brother Charlie was a fighter, and when Freddie got a set of boxing gloves for his birthday he knew that he was hooked. Also, from the age of fourteen he worked as a milkman with Percy Cook, brother of former Welsh champion Gordon Cook.

Percy acted as his coach, and Freddie won a Novices Competition at the local Ice Rink run by Jack Turner, stopping three opponents, and winning a silver rose bowl, which his mother proudly kept on view in the Mills household.

Jack Turner was manager, booth proprietor and general factotum, and arranged a contest for the Mills boy at Weymouth, which he drew. Following that result, Freddie and Jack signed a five-years contract.

The young fighter had all sorts of jobs, selling newspapers, milkman, grocer's assistant, gardener, garage hand, and digging worms to sell to fishermen before he became a full-time pro, and left home to travel with the booths. It was here that he met Welshman Gypsy Daniels, the man who knocked out Max Schmeling. Freddie and Gypsy had loads of "fights" on the booths, and it was the latter who gave him his cauliflower ear.

His pro debut came in 1936, and he was unbeaten in 17 bouts before being knocked out by George Davis. There was a return, and Freddie lost on points but his knuckles were giving him trouble, so he paid a visit to that famous bone manipulator Eddie Mallett, who put matters right.

Mills then showed his punching power by knocking out Dave McCleave (twice), Charlie Parkin, Moe Moss, Elfryn Morris, Yorkie Bentley, Billy Fuller, Seaman Long — all clean knockouts.

In January 1940 he joined the Royal Air Force as a PT Instructor, and the following August hitch-hiked to Liverpool, where he outpointed the great Jock McAvoy. For this fight he received £50, but said he would have boxed Jock for nothing. His official manager was Bob Turner, brother of Jack, and when Bob announced his intention of joining the RAF in 1941, Ted Broadribb took over as Freddie's manager.

The following year things started to happen for him. First he defeated McAvoy in one round in a final eliminator for the British title, and in June beat the holder, Len Harvey, when the latter was knocked out of the ring and couldn't get back in time. The Empire title was also at stake.

In 1944 Freddie tackled Jack London for the vacant British and Empire heavyweight titles, but was outpointed. He was never heavy enough to compete against the top men in this division, and on these occasions courage alone was not enough. Nevertheless he thought he had done enough to get the verdict over London, but referee C. B. Thomas thought otherwise.

Mills then had a spell in India, giving exhibitions to the troops, and when it was all over he was matched by promoter Jack Solomons to fight Lesnevich for the world title in 1946. Nat Seller became his trainer, but a fortnight before the contest Freddie's father died and although he wanted postponement his mother persuaded him to honour his contract.

In round two he was down, and said he remembered nothing after that. After being down three more times, he walked to the wrong corner at the end of the round. The bout was stopped in round ten when he went down again, but Lesnevich was cut by the left eye and his nose was broken, although still champion.

That same year he unsuccessfully tackled heavyweights Bruce Woodcock and Joe Baksi, the latter stopping him in six. But he came back in 1947 to win the European light-heavyweight title, and in April 1948 beat Ken Shaw in one round in a final eliminator for the British heavyweight title.

Three months later came the return with Lesnevich, and this time there could be no doubt as to who was the better man. In fact in round eight he floored the champion, and many thought Gus had failed to beat the count. Freddie was well worth his points verdict.

In November 1948 he went to South Africa to knock out Johnny Ralph in a final eliminator for the Empire heavyweight title which followed his marriage to manager Broadribb's daughter Chrissie. In June 1949 he was knocked out in round fourteen by Bruce Woodcock for the British, European and Empire heavyweight titles, and had just one more fight, losing his world title in 1950, when he was knocked out by Maxim in round ten.

A tenacious, pugnacious looking Freddie Mills (left), hammers away at Len Harvey during their contest at the Tottenham Hotspur football ground in June 1942. Harvey was just not strong enough and Freddie knocked his man out of the ring in the second round for a memorable victory, which also earned him the British and Commonwealth light-heavyweight titles

Mills went out like a champion. He lost three teeth, didn't remember much of what went on after that, but never stopped fighting back. He never knew when he was beaten, and sometimes had too much courage for his own good.

Ted Broadribb then asked him to retire, although he took a lot of persuading, but it turned out to be the start of a whole new career for him.

He turned to managing, then promoting, but was put out of business because of the crippling entertainment tax on boxing imposed by the government. He later became a radio and TV personality, in programmes like *Six Five Special,* and also acted in several films. He was also an author and boxing columnist for a Sunday newspaper.

We became great friends, and he often rang me for information on foreign boxers who had been engaged to appear on British shows. One example: he rang me to ask "Who's this Ben Buker The Second who's coming over here to meet Peter Waterman, Ron?" I replied "He's a Spanish welterweight, Freddie." There was a pause, then he commented "Do you know, I've never even heard of Ben Buker The First."

Freddie had a marvellous sense of humour, loved children, loved playing Santa Claus at children's parties, and has been likened to a big, huggable bear. In spite of his many successes, his size in hats never got bigger. In short, he had a heart of gold.

By now he had acquired a Chinese restaurant in London's Charing Cross Road, which in 1963 was transformed into a club named the Freddie Mills Nite Spot. He had his own act in the cabaret, and everything seemed to be going well even though there were rumours about financial difficulties, but aren't there always?

In January 1965 at the Annual Dinner of the Boxing Writers' Club, to which I had been elected in the '50s, I had as one of my regular guests, the famous American band leader Roy Fox, whom Freddie knew. They chatted away happily and arranged to take their families to the London Zoo. Freddie seemed in great spirits.

It came as a great personal shock, therefore, when on 25 July, 1965, came the news that he had been found shot to death in the front seat of his car. The coroner's verdict was suicide, which in spite of the evidence, I still find difficult to believe.

FLOYD PATTERSON

In September 1955 Rocky Marciano knocked out Archie Moore in defence of his world heavyweight title, and subsequently announced his retirement from the ring. Just over a year later Archie was matched with Floyd Patterson for the vacant crown and Floyd knocked out "The Old Mongoose" in five rounds to become not only the new champion, but the youngest fighter ever to win the world heavyweight title. He was 21 years old.

It was quite an achievement for a lad who came up the hard way, who had been so unsure of himself, shy, with an inferiority complex that took a lot of curing.

Floyd was born at Waco, California, on 4 January, 1935. The family moved to Brooklyn when he was one year old, and kept moving from place to place, always looking for more space. He had two elder brothers, Frank and Billy, and there were another eight children to follow.

His father Thomas was a labourer, working on construction, and also as a longshoreman and truck helper. He worked hard for his large family, and often took a secondary job, which meant he was well nigh exhausted when he arrived home.

The young Patterson had all sorts of hang-ups and used to walk the streets a lot. He kept his head down, tried to avoid people, played truant, hid in the cellar, stole things, and ended up in juvenile court. Here it was decided that he would benefit from an education at the Wiltwyck School for Boys, which was for the emotionally disturbed, at Esopus, New York. He was just eleven years old.

This move proved to be the making of Floyd. There was no punishment, no use of the cane, in fact, every pupil was given his chance to get on the right road. He learned to read and write, to conduct himself properly, and he even boxed a little in the gym, although he wasn't keen on it.

When he left there at twelve years of age, his outlook was altogether different. He had three bouts at Wiltwyck, winning them all, and things improved a lot in his next school, the Cyprus W. Field School, where he made up his mind that he wanted to earn a living out of boxing.

His brothers were both boxers. Billy served in the Army in Korea, but sustained a detached retina, which cut short his pro career. Frank was a New York Golden Gloves champion, and on the way kayoed Ralph Tiger Jones, who as a pro beat the legendary "Sugar" Ray Robinson. Unfortunately, Frank didn't make the grade as a pro.

Both brothers used to train at the Carlton YMCA gym, and Floyd used to tag along. Later they trained at the Gramercy Park gym, near his school, and soon he worked out there too.

The owner of the gym was Cus D'Amato, who lived there, with Frank Lavelle as his trainer. They supplied the gear, on the understanding that if anyone turned pro Cus would automatically become his manager.

Brother Frank also shared in Floyd's training, and didn't pull his punches. There were times when the latter felt like packing it in, but Cus persuaded him that this was normal practice for most youngsters starting out.

By 1950 he had improved so much that he was entered for the New York *Daily News* Golden Gloves tournament in the 10st. 7lb. sub-novice division. He won a couple of bouts, got complacent, and lost the next one, saying afterwards that it taught him a lesson.

When he left school he got a job as a delivery boy at 17 dollars a week, and in 1952 went to Helsinki with the American Olympic team, winning the Gold Medal in the middleweight division. Altogether he had 45 amateur bouts, winning 40.

Cus decided he was now ready for the professional ranks. His début came in September 1952, and there were thirteen straight wins before he was outpointed by the former world light-heavyweight champion Joey Maxim, for a purse of 5,000 dollars. The verdict was disputed.

The purse for his début was 300 dollars, a fortune, as he was working for the Gramercy Park Hotel for 44 dollars per week. His next purse was over 1,000 dollars, so he bought himself a Cadillac, which was the first of many.

In 1953 the New York Boxing Writers voted him "Rookie Of The Year," and Floyd was delighted to receive his presentation from the great Joe Louis at the Hotel Astor.

He won every fight from then until losing his title to Ingemar Johansson in 1959. Having beaten Moore for the vacant crown, he successfully defended against Tommy Jackson, Pete Rademacher, Roy Harris and Brian London. Then he was caught by the right hand that became known as "Ingo's Bingo" and was down seven times before the referee intervened.

In 1956 Floyd had married his childhood sweetheart Sandra, a fine partnership, and it was she who consoled him after his defeat, advising him to retire. But his pride had been hurt. He was inactive for twelve months, then came a return with Johansson. The former champion had learned a lot from their first fight, kept away from that right hand, and knocked his man out. The title was his again.

There just had to be a third fight, and it took place in March 1961. Floyd again knocked out Ingo, and successfully defended against Tom McNeeley before losing his crown to Sonny Liston in 1962. He lost again to Liston in 1963, both fights ending in the first round.

There were thoughts of retirement, but he decided to carry on, and in November 1965 met the new champion, Muhammad Ali, only to be stopped in round twelve. Patterson came to London in 1966, and kayoed Henry Cooper in four, and in 1968 was outpointed by Jimmy Ellis for the WBA heavyweight title.

He didn't box in 1969, but started again in 1970, and won nine straight fights before meeting Muhammad Ali again, this time for the NABF title. After being stopped in seven, this time he decided to stay retired.

It had been a fine career, with only eight defeats in 64 bouts, spread over 20 years, and it was estimated that he earned nearly eight million dollars. He still makes personal appearances, and both he and brother Ray are members of the Swedish Ex-Boxers' Associaton. Ray married and settled there.

I met Floyd on several occasions when he was over here to fight Henry Cooper, and he came across as a shy, modest man who really appreciated the opportunities that had been given him, not only in the ring, but in life.

Records of course are made to be beaten, but fans will always remember those who established them. You can't beat being a "first". Floyd was the first Olympic champion to win the world heavyweight title, the youngest man to win the world heavyweight title, and the first man to regain the world heavyweight title.

He was awarded the Edward J. Neil Trophy in 1956 and 1960, and was elected to Boxing's Hall of Fame in 1976.

Floyd (right) became the then youngest man in ring history to win the world heavyweight title when he beat Archie Moore on a fifth round kayo in November 1956. "Ancient Archie" is seen crumbling under a blistering salvo of punches which spelt out the finish

WILLIE PEP

In 1973 former world featherweight champion Willie Pep and his friend Robert Sacchi wrote a book entitled *Friday's Heroes,* and when they came to Britain to launch the book I was privileged to meet them. I still possess the copy they autographed, which featured not only Willie's biography, but the stories of some of the great American ringmen we were fortunate to see in action on our TV screens several years ago in *Fight Of The Week.*

The Pep record was fantastic. As an amateur he had 62 bouts, losing only three. As a professional he won his first 62 fights, annexing the world title in his 56th. Later came another long winning run of 73 contests, with a career total of 241 bouts, losing just eleven.

He was born Guglielmo Papaleo in Middletown, Connecticut, on 19 September, 1922, of Italian extraction. His father, from Syracuse in Sicily, was a construction worker, and couldn't read or write in English.

As a youngster, Willie grew up in a tough neighbourhood, used to shine shoes, and often got into fights with other kids, who were invariably bigger. So he went to the local gym, but looked so frail that he was thrown out. He went back, this time with his headgear, and was allowed to stay.

In 1937 he started his amateur career, and got eight dollars a fight, which he gave to his mother, although his father often gave him a small amount back. One night he had two fights, for which he received 50 dollars. He wanted to buy a sports coat and slacks, so he kept ten dollars and gave mother the other 40.

She wanted to know where he'd got the extra money, thinking he may have stolen it. So he had to tell his father he got it from boxing. Whereupon Mr. Papaleo told him he could fight twice a week for that kind of money (father was earning fifteen dollars per week at the time).

Also, his father made sure he did his roadwork and that he went to bed early. Willie boxed out of Norwich, Conn., sometimes at a place called the Du-Well Athletic Club. He eventually became State flyweight champion, and one night was matched with a tall featherweight from out of town, who outpointed him.

Only afterwards did he find out that his opponent was "Sugar" Ray Robinson, a Golden Gloves champion, who apparently wasn't allowed to box for cash in New York, so used to go to any state who would pay for his services. That was in 1938, and Willie got eight dollars, of which Buster, his "manager", took seven.

In 1939 he won the State bantamweight title, before turning pro in July 1940, getting rid of Buster, and taking Lou Viscusi as manager, with Bill Gore as trainer. They proved to be a great team, and the winning run continued through 1941 and 1942, averaging over 20 bouts per year.

He twice beat Joey Archibald, who had just lost his world featherweight title to Chalky Wright, and in November 1942 Willie outpointed Wright to annex the world title. He thus became the youngest boxer to win a world title for 40 years, and broke the record receipts for a featherweight bout indoors.

At the end of 1942 Sammy Angott announced his retirement as world lightweight champion, but in March 1943 decided to make a comeback, and outpointed Pep in his first bout. It was the end of a great run, but Willie came back to defend his world title successfully against Sal Bartolo in June.

He had a peculiar war service. He wanted to join the Army, but was persuaded to join the Navy. But because of a perforated eardrum he was employed as water boy for the Navy football team and after a short time he was discharged.

Then the Army came after him, and he got a cushy job as a military policeman at a hospital, in which there was a jail that housed Army personnel who had committed various "crimes", such as going absent without leave.

He was honourably discharged in 1944, and immediately got on with his boxing career. In July 1944 he got a lot of satisfaction when outpointing Manuel Ortiz, as the Ortiz camp had put out the story that he was Manuel's sparmate a few years earlier, which was perfectly true.

The following September he again outpointed Chalky Wright, after which Bill Corum of the New York *Journal-American* dubbed him "Will o' the Wisp", a name which stuck with him. He then made further successful defences against Phil Terranova and Sal Bartolo.

In January 1947 Willie was involved in a 'plane crash. The 'plane, containing 21 passengers, overshot Newark Airport and ended up in the woods at Middleville, New Jersey. There was snow, and visibility was bad. Five were killed, but the fighter survived at the cost of a broken leg and two broken vertebrae in his back.

The casts came off five months later, and he defied doctors' advice, going back into the ring immediately. After half a dozen bouts he again successfully defended his title, against Jock Leslie. Earlier he had sued for 250,000 dollars after the 'plane crash, but when the insurance company learned of his title defence they refused to pay.

The highlights of his career were undoubtedly his four world title fights with Sandy Saddler. Their first meeting was in October 1948. No-one thought Sandy would cause Pep much trouble. However, the latter was caught cold, and he lost his title after being stopped in four rounds.

The return came in February 1949. It was one of the greatest bouts ever seen, and Willie won on points. Contest number three in September 1950, was a rough, tough scrap, and when Pep injured a shoulder in round eight, he was unable to continue.

Their last meeting, in September 1951, was without doubt the dirtiest fight I have ever seen. I watched it on film, and was surprised the referee didn't throw them both out. There was tripping, wrestling, and numerous other fouls. On one occasion the referee got tangled with the boxers and he, too, went down. Saddler won in the ninth when Willie's left eye was closed and he couldn't continue.

The former champion continued to box, and his last attempt to try and regain his old crown came in September 1958, when at the age of 36 he tackled world champion Hogan Kid Bassey in a non-title ten-rounder. Although doing well, in round nine he was floored twice, and the bout was stopped.

He immediately retired, only to return six years later, when he won nine bouts in a row, but lost the tenth on points to Calvin Woodward in March 1966. This time enough was enough.

Willie Pep was one of the most brilliant boxers of all time, and was elected to Boxing's Hall of Fame in 1963.

Willie (right), a masterful boxer, met another craftsman in the Frenchman Ray Famechon, when he defended his world featherweight title in March 1950. The bout went the full fifteen rounds, but Pep was just too clever for his rival, winning handsomely

BARNEY ROSS

The story of Barney Ross is one of the saddest in boxing history. Retiring in 1938 after winning world titles at three different weights, he joined the United States Marines, being awarded a citation for bravery at Guadalcanal, but had to be injected with so much morphine to ease the pain from his wounds that he became "hooked". Then had to go through the additional agony to try and cure the addiction, which he eventually did.

Barney came through several other traumatic situations in his youth, but had the will-power to overcome them, and to become a world champion respected by all.

He was born in New York on 23 December, 1909, real name Barnet David Rosofsky. His father Isidore was born in Russia, where he married Sarah, and when the Jews were being persecuted they saved up for two years in order to raise enough money to go to America, arriving in 1903.

Barney had four brothers, Ben, Morrie, Sammy and Georgie, and one sister, Ida. Four other children had died in infancy. When Barney was two the family moved to Chicago, where his parents ran a small grocery store.

He was much below average height for his age, and the other kids used to make fun of him. There were gang fights between the Italians, the Poles, the Irish and the Jews, and although Barney tried to avoid them, there were times when he couldn't help getting involved. He was nearly blinded by a rock, and suffered permanent injury to his left arm from a crowbar.

There was a lot of petty thieving, in which he became involved. His one worry was that his father would find out, and when he did he got the biggest hiding of his life.

Tragedy struck early. He was coming up to his fourteenth birthday, and was on his way to the store one morning when a friend told him that something had happened. When he arrived his father was on the floor, having been shot when two youths came to rob the store and panicked. His father was unconscious for over a day, recovered briefly, then died.

His mother had a miscarriage, and was admitted to hospital, also suffering from shock. She was away for some time and Barney was very bitter, forsook his religious beliefs, got involved in illegal dice games, being picked up by the police once or twice. He went from job to job, eventually going to Al Capone, yes, *the* Al Capone, the gangster, who used him as an errand boy, delivering messages.

His mother thought he was working at a cinema, but he was earning a lot of money. Eventually Al advised him to try and get a legitimate job, and he found work with Sears Roebuck, the large department store.

One of those who came out of the ghetto where he lived was Jackie Fields, who went on to win the world welterweight title. Barney used to watch him in the gym, and was persuaded to visit Kid Howard's local gym where he could train for a fight as amateurs got medals, which they used to sell for cash. However, Howard turned him away, saying he was too frail. Young Rosofsky pleaded for a chance, so Howard put him in to spar with Dave Shade, who became a top middleweight and fought Len Harvey. Barney was told if he could knock the cigar out of Dave's mouth he would be given a fight. He did so.

He became a fine amateur, winning the Golden Gloves in Chicago, and going on to beat the New York featherweight Al Santora in the Inter-City match. The same year, 1929, he turned pro, merely to get more money to look after the family. He progressed quickly, beating former featherweight champion Battling Battalino in 1932, and Billy Petrolle in March 1933. The following June he outpointed Tony Canzoneri to annex the world lightweight and junior welterweight titles, and three months later successfully defended in a return against Canzoneri.

His managers were Sam Pian and Art Winch, and Al Capone became one of his greatest fans, often buying loads of tickets, and offering some to Barney for his friends. The ring-name of "Barney Ross" came in his amateur days when the newspapers were reporting his contests and he didn't want his mother to find out that he had been boxing, for the fear of upsetting her.

He was a soft touch and on becoming the champion he found he was making a lot of new "friends", to whom he gave substantial hand-outs, as well as helping his old friends from the ghetto.

He became a gambler, on horse-racing, fights, two flys crawling up a wall — anything. He was introduced to horse-racing by entertainer Al Jolson, and got "hooked". He bet big and he lost big.

Barney successfully defended his junior welterweight crown against Sammy Fuller, Pete Nebo, Frankie Klick (a draw), but he needed a big pay-day to make good his gambling losses.

So a match was arranged with world welterweight champion Jimmy McLarnin. Manager Pian was against it. His fighter would be giving away around ten pounds, but Barney was adamant. If he won he would hold three world titles at the same time and in May 1934 he outpointed McLarnin to make that a reality.

Unfortunately Barney's junior welter crown was not universally recognised, and Henry Armstrong later gained world-wide recognition as the first man to hold three world titles simultaneously.

In September 1934 he lost his welterweight championship to Jimmy McLarnin, although the verdict was hotly disputed. But he then successfully defended his junior title against Frankie Klick and Henry Woods before again meeting McLarnin in May 1935. This time there could be no doubting that Barney had won.

He gave up his junior crown, also his lightweight title, and made successful defences of his welterweight championship against Izzy Janazzo and Ceferino Garcia before losing it to Henry Armstrong in May 1938. Barney took a beating. His corner wanted to stop it, but each time he refused. He could hardly stand or lift his gloves at the end, but he went out like a champion.

Ross resisted all offers to continue boxing, some of them very large. He had a part in the play *Golden Boy*, he ran a cocktail lounge, then came the news that the Japs had bombed Pearl Harbour. Now nearly 33, Barney enlisted in the Marines. In November 1942 he was wounded at Guadalcanal in the Solomon Islands, when under constant attack from the Japs. It was reported that he had killed 22 of the enemy, was made a corporal on the spot and later given the Silver Star Medal and a Presidential Citation. While in hospital he was promoted to sergeant.

He was suffering badly from malaria, chills, high fever, body shaking. Part of the treatment was the injection of morphine, and Barney got hooked on the drug. Eventually he decided to risk even more pain by being admitted to the government hospital in Lexington for treatment. It was like a nightmare, but in 1947 he was cured.

After that he devoted his time to helping and advising other addicts, also talking about the problem to police, judges, social workers — anyone. He settled down to a normal life with his wife Cathy. And his mother was still alive, although blind, living comfortably in the Jewish Orthodox Home for the Aged in Chicago.

Barney was awarded the Edward J. Neil Trophy in 1942, and was elected to the Boxing Hall of Fame in 1956. He died on 17 January, 1967, from cancer after a long illness.

Looking for his third world title belt at different weights, Barney (right) feints for an opening against the defending welterweight champion, Jimmy McLarnin, in New York, May 1934. At the end of fifteen hard rounds, Ross became the new champion by a split-decision, thus holding the lightweight, light-welterweight and welterweight titles at the same time

JOHN L. SULLIVAN

JOHN L. SULLIVAN will go down in history as the last of the bare-knuckle champions, and the first to box for the world heavyweight title under modern rules with five-ounce gloves.

He was born in October 1858, at Roxbury, Boston, and the "L" stood for Lawrence. His father Michael came from Tralee, County Kerry, Ireland, and his mother from Athlone. They had emigrated to the United States when they were young, ambitious, and wanted to make a better living for the family.

It would appear that John L. had an interest in the sport from an early age, for when he was fifteen years old he played truant from Boston College to attend the funeral of bare-knuckle fighter John Camel Heenan.

John's father wanted him to be a Roman Catholic priest, but the lad showed little aptitude and preferred to play baseball. When he was 16 he got a job as a plumber's labourer, only to give it up after an altercation with the foreman, during which he planted a lethal punch on the man's jaw.

When he was 18 he was already a heavyweight, and a year later began his fighting career, almost by accident. Tom Scannell was the local champion and was having a benefit performance at the Dudley Street Opera House where John was also taking part, doing a strong-man act. This proved popular with the audience, but not so with Scannell, who hated not being in the limelight.

Thus Tom challenged anyone in the audience to a contest, and said he would knock them out in three rounds. John accepted, and quickly knocked out the fighter. Sullivan was a tinsmith at the time, but very much wanted to continue to fight, so he used to visit the local pubs and challenge anyone. This was the start of his public boast: "I can lick any man in the house!"

In 1881 he had his first important fight, against John Flood, which took place on a barge in New York. The purses were 750 dollars for the winner, 250 to the loser. Flood lasted only eight rounds, and not for nothing was John dubbed "The Boston Strong Boy."

The following year he met Paddy Ryan for the world heavyweight title. Ryan was American champion, it was a bare-knuckle fight, and the ring was in front of the Barnes Hotel, Mississippi City for a purse of 5,000 dollars, winner take all. John stopped his man in the ninth; and believe it or not, this was only Ryan's second fight as he had won the American title in his first.

Two important happenings in 1883; John L. was married to Annie Bates, but separated after only a month or two and as both were Roman Catholics, there was no divorce. And in May of that year, he suffered his first knockdown at the hands of England's Charlie Mitchell. They met at Madison Square Garden for the gate, which was 16,000 dollars, and although floored himself in round one, the champion put Charlie on the canvas several times before the police stopped the fight in the fourth on the grounds that the bout was illegal because of Sullivan's alleged prize-ring methods.

Mitchell again challenged the champion, and the contest, over four rounds with gloves, was scheduled for June 1884 at Madison Square Garden. The story goes that when John L. got into the ring he was drunk. He was taken back to the dressing-room, and Mitchell sportingly said that he was sorry John was ill, and he would be happy to box him when he was better.

Sullivan learned his lesson, and didn't drink again for a long while. However, he continued to win his fights, and in 1885 beat old rival Paddy Ryan in 50 seconds, the time it took the police to stop the fight.

All sorts of things happened in 1887. He broke his left arm against Patsy Cardiff, but the result was a draw and he was challenged by Jake Kilrain, who posted 1,000 dollars. The champion ignored this, and sailed for England. By now he had changed his manager, from Pat Sheedy to Ed Holske, and before he left he was presented with the championship belt, worth 10,000 dollars, at the Boston Theatre.

Once in England, arrangements were made for John L. to meet Mitchell again, £500 a side, and the bout took place in 1888 at Chantilly, France, bare-knuckle, under London Prize Ring rules. It lasted 39 rounds and over three hours, at Baron Rothschild's park, in heavy rain. And it was attended by just 41 spectators.

Reports of the fight state that Mitchell was down fifteen times but with both men exhausted and the fact that it was getting dark the referee, B. J. Angle of England, called it a draw.

The champion didn't fight again for 16 months, returning in July 1889 to defend his title against Jake Kilrain for 10,000 dollars a side. There was now a large question-mark over his condition as he had been very ill, allegedly from too much alcohol, and although he was reported to be fit again, no one knew quite what to expect.

The fight took place at Richburg, Mississippi, lasting two hours 16 min., with Kilrain being floored and carried to his corner in round 75. Both men were arrested, later appearing before the State Court, and were sentenced to twelve months' imprisonment. The appeal dragged on for a year, and the sentence was eventually reduced to a 1,000 dollar fine.

Perhaps it was as well that something like this happened, for this was the last of the bare-knuckle championships. Sullivan then started a theatrical career, moving around America with the play *Honest Hearts and Willing Hands*. He then toured Australia in 1891, returning home the following year to defend his title against James J. Corbett.

This was the first world heavyweight title fight under the Marquess of Queensberry Rules, with five-ounce gloves, and it took place at the Olympic Club, New Orleans, for a purse of 25,000 dollars plus a sidestake of 20,000. When Sullivan started training for this fight he weighed over 16 stones, but got down to just over fifteen on fight day, with Corbett scaling twelve stones ten pounds. The story of the battle is well known. Suffice it to say that John L. was no match for James J. and was knocked out in round 21.

The effect was amazing. He continued touring with his play, and wherever he went met with warmness and appreciation, but sadly, the drink problem remained. There were to be two more fights, a no-decision bout with Tom Sharkey in 1896, and a two-rounds win over Jack McCormick in 1905 at Grand Rapids, which no-one took very seriously.

John L. continued to make personal appearances, and had a vaudeville act. He lived for some time at the Vanderbilt Hotel, New York, but in 1902 he went bankrupt. To his credit he shook off the drink problem, and earned enough money from his vaudeville act so that he was able to meet his creditors and settle all of his debts. After that there were periods of drink, followed by periods of abstinence.

One day he realised the futility of his way of life, gave up alcohol completely, and earned a living mainly by telling people about the dangers of drink, using himself as an example.

In 1908 — a little late, one might think — John divorced his wife and married Kate Harkins. Sadly, she died in 1917. John was shattered, and he passed away at Abingdon, Massachusetts, on 2 February, 1918, to be buried in Calvary Cemetery, Boston.

John L. Sullivan does not appear in the list of world heavyweight champions under the Marquess of Queensberry Rules, but no-one can deny his influence on the sport.

The beginning of heavyweight boxing with gloves saw the last of the bare knuckle champions, John L. Sullivan (right) deposed as the world champion by a young James J. Corbett. Corbett, boxing in a scientific fashion, bewildered John L. to record a 21st round knockout at New Orleans in September 1892

GENE TUNNEY

GENE TUNNEY remains the only world heavyweight champion who retired still holding the title — and stayed retired. He earned fame as the only man to beat Jack Dempsey twice, both times over the unusual title distance of ten rounds.

He was born James Joseph Tunney in New York on 25 May, 1898, of Irish parentage. On his tenth birthday his father gave him a set of boxing gloves, and Gene put them to immediate use. He invited a few friends over, who were only too willing to have a go, and at the end of the day they all retired to bed with swellings and bruises, tired but happy. It sure was a wonderful birthday.

Gene learned the basic moves of boxing from cartoons drawn by Bob Edgren, columnist of the New York *Evening World*. However, at school he excelled at swimming, handball, basketball, sprinting and the long jump.

At the age of fifteen he got a job with the Ocean Steamship Company — wages five dollars a week and after a year he was promoted to mail clerk with a raise of six dollars. He was anxious to do well, and took courses in mathematics and English.

Twelve months later he started sparring with his friend Willie Ward, who had turned professional. They both joined the Villagers' Athletic Club in Greenwich Village, and later he became acquainted with Willie Green, who was ten years older, and had been a pro for some time.

Volunteers were required to spar with Willie. None were too keen, but Gene said he was willing to box three "threes". He was hit harder than he had ever been hit before, but went the distance, and vowed never again to spar with a pro.

However, Willie asked him again. Gene didn't want to lose face, and agreed. Another painful process, but he was gaining in confidence, and when invited to spar publicly with Willie at the Knight of Columbus Council Hall he had no hesitation in agreeing. All went well; they gave several public exhibitions after that, and eventually Willie got fed up with trying unsuccessfully to knock him out. They stopped sparring, and Gene became Willie's pupil.

Apart from the day job, he became athletics instructor and general organiser at Public School 41. Billy Jacobs, matchmaker at the Sharkey Athletic Club, wanted him to turn pro, but he wasn't keen. After all, he had regular employment, and was now a rate clerk.

Eventually Willie Green and publican Eddie O'Brien persuaded him that it would be a good move. In July 1915 he made his début against seasoned pro Bobby Dawson, stopping him in seven rounds for a purse of 18 dollars.

He had a few more winning fights, but injured his left elbow playing basketball, in March 1917. The arm was put in plaster, but after it had been removed the arm was only half the size of the right. America had now entered World War I, and Gene volunteered for the Marines, only to be rejected because of the arm injury.

Exercise was advised, and he became a Life Guard at Keansburg, New Jersey, quitting the Ocean Steamship Company. When sparring on the beach he was hit on the elbow, and although the arm had made progress the trouble started again. So he went back home with no job, no money, and a partly-paralysed elbow.

Then he had a stroke of luck. A friend put him in touch with a German physician named Dr Frederick de Kraft, who diagnosed traumatic neuritis. After six months treatment he was completely cured. Strength came back to normal, but the left arm remained shorter than the right throughout his career.

In June 1918 he was accepted for the Marines, and twelve months later won the American Expeditionary Force light-heavyweight title in France by outpointing Ted Jamison, after coming through around 20 qualifying bouts. He also beat Bob Martin, AEF heavyweight champion, although conceding nearly two stones.

Right then Tunney decided to make professional boxing his career. He won a succession of bouts in 1920–21,. and in January 1922 outpointed the veteran Battling Levinsky to annex the American light-heavyweight title.

The following May he defended his crown against Harry Greb. His troubles started during training. He damaged both hands, an eye injury re-opened, and there were pains from his elbow. During the fight he fractured his nose in round one, his left eye was badly cut, and in round three his right eye went.

Inevitably he lost the verdict, the only defeat in his entire career, but he did well to last the distance and duly received 22,500 dollars. The return was in February 1923 when he won a disputed verdict and the "rubber" match came in December. Gene took the verdict, this time more conclusively.

Tunney was now in fine form, and in July 1924 floored the legendary Frenchman Georges Carpentier four times before stopping him in the final round. He later met Greb in two "no-decision" fights, and after the last one Harry said he didn't want to box him any more. But he became Gene's greatest fan, and Tunney always had the greatest respect for him.

After the Carpentier fight Gene said he could no longer make the light-heavyweight limit comfortably, and would concentrate on the heavyweight crown. In June 1925 he beat Tom Gibbons, a leading contender, and in November defeated tough Johnny Risko. This paved the way for a shot at Jack Dempsey's crown, which came in September 1926.

He had studied Dempsey for several years, watching films of his fights, and was confident of exploiting the champion's weaknesses. And that is exactly what happened when they met at Philadelphia, with Gene gaining a comfortable verdict.

Neither boxed a serious bout until the return one year later, in Chicago. Tunney was floored in round seven, referee Dave Barry refused to start the count until Dempsey had gone to a neutral corner, and some allege that the champion was down for fourteen seconds.

Gene said he was in full possession of his faculties from the official count of "two" and rose at the official "nine". It was the first time he had ever been on the canvas, but he recovered in fine style. Later in that round, as Dempsey came in, Gene caught him with a right under the heart and years later Dempsey said it was the hardest punch he had ever received. "I thought I was going to die," he added.

Jack was floored briefly in round eight, was on the receiving end for the last two rounds, and Tunney got the verdict. The champion didn't box again until July 1928, when he stopped Tom Heeney in the eleventh. That was his last fight.

He then married heiress Polly Lauder in Rome in October 1928, and became an executive of several companies, including the Denham Tyre Co., the Stamford Construction Co., and the Morris Plan. He was given a commission as an officer in the Marine Reserve Corps, was a captain in the Navy during World War II, and was placed in charge of their physical training programme.

He was known as "The Fighting Marine", and his purses in title fights were 200,000 dollars for the first fight with Dempsey; 990,445 from live gate in their second bout; and a guaranteed 525,000 dollars against Heeney.

He was elected to the Boxing Hall of Fame in 1955, and received the James J. Walker Memorial Award in 1941.

Gene died in Greenwich, Connecticut, on 7 November, 1978 at the age of 80.

Jack Dempsey is floored by Gene in their return meeting in September 1927, which became known as "the battle of the long count". Tunney was on the floor for around fourteen seconds in the seventh round, but had recovered sufficiently to put his rival down before winning on points over ten rounds

RANDY TURPIN

There have been many world title fights in which a British boxer has been the underdog, but none more significant than the contest for the middleweight championship at London's Exhibition Hall, Earl's Court, on 10 July, 1951, when Britain's Randolph Turpin took on the legendary "Sugar" Ray Robinson. And beat him!

Freddie Mills had lost his world light-heavyweight crown, Terry Allen had lost his world flyweight title, and Britain badly needed a boost at that time. Then along came young Randolph, with a punch calculated to stop anyone, and with just two defeats in nearly five years as a pro. His ten previous bouts had all been won inside the scheduled distance.

But was this enough to defeat a man who was regarded as the best pound-for-pound fighter of all time?

On the Letters Page of *Boxing News* dated 4 July, 1951, appeared the following from Mr. T. F. G. Jones of Uttoxeter, which commenced: "May I take this opportunity of deploring the matching of our middleweight champion Randolph Turpin with "Sugar" Ray Robinson . . . at the moment he is little more than a novice and has never been called upon to travel the full distance of fifteen rounds.

"Randy is altogether too young and inexperienced to fight this superman . . . why should we pin our hopes on a possible knock-out victory (for this is the only way he can hope to win), when in a year's time he should be a much improved fighter?"

I'm quite sure this was the view of many others at that time. The *Boxing News* editorial view was merely "The world champion must be regarded as favourite", with a lot of "ifs" about whether Randy could land his pet punches. But most boxing writers predicted a Robinson victory.

When Turpin won it was to alter his whole life, which had started from humble beginnings. He was born in Leamington Spa on 7 June, 1928 where his mother Beatrice, a local lady had married Lionel from British Guiana when he settled in the Midlands after coming back from World War I.

There were five children: Dick, Joan, Jackie, Kathy and Randy, but when the latter was still an infant his father died as the result of being gassed during the war. Later, when he was only three, Randy nearly died from double pneumonia.

In 1931 Beatrice married Ernest Manley, which made things easier for the family. The youngest Turpin went to West Gate Council School, and soon became a fine athlete. Once when swimming, a sport at which he excelled, he was kept underwater by reeds for so long that he damaged an ear drum and was partially deaf for the rest of his life.

Randy became a member of the Leamington Boys' Club, and was helped considerably by John "Gerry" Gibbs, a police inspector, who ran the boxing at the club.

Amateur honours came thick and fast. 1943 — British 8 st. champion Junior 'A' Class. 1944 — British 9 st. 7 lb. champion Junior 'B' Class. 1945 — British 10 st. 7 lb. champion Junior 'B' Class, and the ABA welterweight champion, the unprecedented feat of winning Junior and Senior titles the same season.

During World War II when Dick was in the Army, Jackie in the Merchant Navy, and Joan and Kathy in the WRAF, Randy worked for a local building firm. But in 1945 Randy joined the Navy as assistant cook. He won the Navy title in 1946, also the ISBA title, and the ABA crown, before punching for pay.

Brother Dick had turned pro in 1937, with George Middleton as his manager and Jackie and Randy followed suit in 1946.

He went through the top middleweights like a knife through butter with most of his wins coming inside schedule. Only two men beat him, Albert Finch and Jean Stock, and in 1950 he knocked out Finch to win the British title. The following year he kayoed Luc van Dam in one round to annex the European crown, then came two fights with "Sugar" Ray Robinson.

The first he won on points, in one of the biggest upsets in fistic history. There was a civic welcome. Never had Leamington known anything like this. But there had been a return clause in the contracts, so just two months later Randy was in the New York Polo Grounds, with Robinson in the other corner, determined to get his revenge on the "Leamington Licker," as everyone now called him.

At the end of round nine it seemed that Robinson was tiring, and early in round ten "Sugar Ray's" left eye was cut. As Randy came forward to follow up his advantage he was caught with a right hand and went to the canvas. He was up at "nine"; Robinson punched away, Randy defended, covered up, waiting for the bell, which was imminent.

But referee Ruby Goldstein decided that the British boy was taking too much punishment, and stopped the fight. There were protests from the British camp, but to no avail. Randy had lost his world title. So was the referee right?

Here are the facts. The referee had them level on points at the end of round nine and there were just eight seconds to go before the end of round ten. Only a few days before the fight an American boxer named George Flores who had been knocked out at Madison Square Garden, died in hospital. Could this have had anything to do with referee Goldstein's judgement? It's all water under the bridge now, of course.

Home again, Turpin's successes continued. In 1952 he stopped Don Cockell to win the British and Empire light-heavyweight titles and won the Empire middleweight crown by defeating George Angelo on points. He also remarried, having been divorced from Mary Stack. His new bride was Gwen Price, the daughter of a Welsh farmer.

In 1953 Randy beat Charles Humez for the European title, and followed it by losing on points to Carl "Bobo" Olson for the vacant world middleweight title. This wasn't the old Turpin. But he was as game as they come, and did well to survive until the final bell.

There were only two bouts in 1954, and in the second he was stopped by Tiberio Mitri in one round, thus losing his European title. In 1955 he successfully defended his British and Empire light-heavyweight titles by knocking out Alex Buxton, and he again stopped Alex the following year in defence of his British crown. In 1957 he outpointed Arthur Howard to keep his British title, which he never lost in the ring and his final bout came in 1958 when he was knocked out by Yolande Pompey.

His career over, Randy started work in manager George Middleton's scrapyard, and his retirement was announced officially at the "Last Night at Harringay" show, when many champions appeared as a tribute to this great arena, which was now closing down.

Randy was cheered to the echo when his turn came to step into the ring, but when he stepped out of it he knew that this was the end. What would his future hold?

It is alleged that he earned £300,000 in the ring, but somehow most of this had disappeared. The Inland Revenue wanted their cut, which was substantial. His hotel in Wales, the Great Orme, had turned into a failure, so he opened a transport café in Leamington. He himself did the cooking.

The debts were still piling up, so Randy took up professional wrestling. Then, in 1962, his stepfather Ernie died. It was just one more setback, which was followed by a receiving order for over £17,000. In 1964 a compulsory purchase order was served on his transport café, which was to be used for a car park.

On 17 May, 1966, Randy committed suicide, in the bedroom above the café, a tragic end for such a great champion.

In one of the great post-war fistic upsets, Randy (left) gave the legendary "Sugar" Ray Robinson a boxing lesson over fifteen memorable rounds in July 1951. Robinson had come to London expecting an easy defence, but went home shorn of his world middleweight title

World Championship Boxing, 1890–1988

The following records attempt to set out by weight division every champion and championship bout contested under Queensberry Rules since the beginning of gloves (2 oz minimum).

Boxing grew up in Great Britain, and quickly spread to the USA, but it was not until the champions of these two countries came together in the latter part of the last century that it developed on an international scale. Organisations then came into existence solely for the purpose of controlling professional boxing. The National Sporting Club of Britain was formed in 1891, later to be amalgamated into the British Boxing Board of Control during 1929. By the early part of the century the sport had also begun to boom among the French, who in 1911 were instrumental in setting up the International Boxing Union to look after the interests of boxing in Europe. Following World War II the body became known as the European Boxing Union. In America many states had allowed boxing to take place, but in 1920 the New York State Athletic Commission was legally constituted under the Walker Law to govern the sport. Also at the same time several of the independent states of America became affiliated to form the National Boxing Association, which by 1962 was re-named the World Boxing Association. In an effort to create a balance of power, Britain supported the setting up of the World Boxing Council, formed in 1963, which brought together New York and its satellite states, with the BBBC, the Commonwealth and the EBU. Recently the International Boxing Federation, an offshoot of the WBA, has sprung into prominence on the world boxing stage.

Over the years many new weight divisions have been formed and original classes have been restructured. For example the bantamweight division limit, which in 1890 stood at 112 lbs, was gradually increased until it reached an internationally accepted 118 lbs in 1909. Similarly other weight limits rose, e.g. featherweight: 1890 (118 lbs) – 1909 (126 lbs); welterweight: 1892 (142 lbs) – 1909 (147 lbs); middleweight: 1891 (154 lbs) – 1909 (160 lbs).

The following data does not include "No Decision" bouts, champions awarded titles without a contest, or claimants with no realistic backing. Note that the champions in bold are accorded universal recognition.

Championship Status Code:
AUSTR = Australia; CALIF = California; EBU = European Boxing Union; FR = France; GB = Great Britain; IBF = International Boxing Federation; IBU = International Boxing Union; LOUIS = Louisiana; MARY = Maryland; MASS = Massachusetts; NBA = National Boxing Association; NY = New York; PEN = Pennsylvania; USA = United States; WBA = World Boxing Association; WBC = World Boxing Council.

Current World Bodies: weight classifications

lbs	WBA	WBC	IBF
108	Junior-Flyweight	Light-Flyweight	Junior-Flyweight
112	Flyweight	Flyweight	Flyweight
115	Junior-Bantamweight	Super-Flyweight	Junior-Bantamweight
118	Bantamweight	Bantamweight	Bantamweight
122	Junior-Featherweight	Super-Bantamweight	Junior-Featherweight
126	Featherweight	Featherweight	Featherweight
130	Junior-Lightweight	Super-Featherweight	Junior-Lightweight
135	Lightweight	Lightweight	Lightweight
140	Junior-Welterweight	Super-Lightweight	Junior-Welterweight
147	Welterweight	Welterweight	Welterweight
154	Junior-Middleweight	Super-Welterweight	Junior-Middleweight
160	Middleweight	Middleweight	Middleweight
168	—	—	Super-Middleweight
175	Light-Heavyweight	Light-Heavyweight	Light-Heavyweight
190	Junior-Heavyweight	—	Cruiserweight
195	—	Cruiserweight	—
+	Heavyweight	Heavyweight	Heavyweight

* Undefeated champions (does not include title holders who were stripped or lost recognition)

Mini–Flyweight (105 lbs)

Title Holders

	Birthplace	Tenure	Status
Kyung-Yung Lee*	S Korea	1987 – 1988	IBF
Hiroki Ioka	Japan	1987 –	WBC
Luis Gamez	Venezuela	1988 –	WBA
Samuth Sithnaruepol	Thailand	1988 –	IBF

Title Bouts

14.06.87 Kyung-Yung Lee W CO 2 Masaharu Kawakami, Bujok, S Korea (IBF)
18.10.87 Hiroki Ioka W PTS 12 Mai Thornburifarm, Osaka, Japan (WBC)
10.01.88 Luis Gamez W PTS 12 Bung-Jung Kim, Pusan, S Korea (WBA)
31.01.88 Hiroki Ioka W RSC 12 Kyung-Yung Lee, Osaka, Japan (WBC)
24.03.88 Samuth Sithnaruepol W RSC 11 Pretty Boy Lucas, Bangkok (IBF)
24.04.88 Luis Gamez W RSC 3 Kenji Yokozawa, Tokyo, Japan (WBA)

Light-Flyweight (108 lbs)

Title Holders

	Birthplace	Tenure	Status
Franco Udella	Italy	1975	WBC
Jaime Rios	Panama	1975 – 1976	WBA
Luis Estaba	Venezuela	1975 – 1978	WBC
Juan Guzman	Dom Republic	1976	WBA
Yoko Gushiken	Japan	1976 – 1981	WBA
Freddie Castillo	Mexico	1978	WBC
Sor Vorasingh	Thailand	1978	WBC
Sung-Jun Kim	S Korea	1978 – 1980	WBC
Shigeo Nakajima	Japan	1980	WBC
Hilario Zapata	Panama	1980 – 1982	WBC
Pedro Flores	Mexico	1981	WBA
Hwan-Jin Kim	S Korea	1981	WBA
Katsuo Tokashiki	Japan	1981 – 1983	WBA
Amado Ursua	Mexico	1982	WBC
Tadashi Tomori	Japan	1982	WBC
Hilario Zapata	Panama	1982 – 1983	WBC
Jung-Koo Chang	S Korea	1983 –	WBC
Lupe Madera	Mexico	1983 – 1984	WBA
Dodie Penalosa	Philippines	1983 – 1986	IBF
Francisco Quiroz	Dom Republic	1984 – 1985	WBA
Joey Olivo	USA	1985	WBA
Myung-Woo Yuh	S Korea	1985 –	WBA
Jum-Hwan Choi	S Korea	1987 –	IBF

Title Bouts

04.04.75 Franco Udella W DIS 12 Valentin Martinez, Milan, Italy (WBC)
Franco Udella forfeited WBC recognition (failure to defend against Rafael Lovera)
23.08.75 Jaime Rios W PTS 15 Rigoberto Marcano, Panama C, Panama (WBA)
13.09.75 Luis Estaba W CO 4 Rafael Lovera, Caracas, Venezuela (WBC)
17.12.75 Luis Estaba W RSC 10 Takenobu Shimabakuro, Okinawa, Japan (WBC)
03.01.76 Jaime Rios W PTS 15 Kazunori Tenryu, Kagoshima, Japan (WBA)
14.02.76 Luis Estaba W PTS 15 Leo Palacios, Caracas, Venezuela (WBC)
02.05.76 Luis Estaba W PTS 15 Juan Alvarez, Caracas, Venezuela (WBC)
01.07.76 Juan Guzman W PTS 15 Jaime Rios, St Domingo, Dom Republic (WBA)
17.07.76 Luis Estaba W CO 3 Franco Udella, Maracay, Venezuela (WBC)
26.09.76 Luis Estaba W RTD 10 Rodolfo Rodriguez, Caracas, Venezuela (WBC)
10.10.76 Yoko Gushiken W CO 7 Juan Guzman, Kofu, Japan (WBA)
21.11.76 Luis Estaba W RSC 10 Valentin Martinez, Caracas, Venezuela (WBC)
30.01.77 Yoko Gushiken W PTS 15 Jaime Rios, Tokyo, Japan (WBA)
15.05.77 Luis Estaba W PTS 15 Rafael Pedroza, Caracas, Venezuela (WBC)
22.05.77 Yoko Gushiken W PTS 15 Rigoberto Marcano, Sapporo, Japan (WBA)
17.07.77 Luis Estaba W PTS 15 Ricardo Estupinan, Cruz, Venezuela (WBC)
21.08.77 Luis Estaba W RSC 11 Juan Alvarez, Cruz, Venezuela (WBC)
18.09.77 Luis Estaba W CO 15 Orlando Hernandez, Caracas, Venezuela (WBC)
09.10.77 Yoko Gushiken W RSC 4 Montsayarm Mahachai, Oita, Japan (WBA)
30.10.77 Luis Estaba W PTS 15 Sor Vorasingh, Caracas, Venezuela (WBC)
29.01.78 Yoko Gushiken W RSC 14 Aniceto Vargas, Nagoya, Japan (WBA)
19.02.78 Freddie Castillo W RSC 14 Luis Estaba, Caracas, Venezuela (WBC)
06.05.78 Sor Vorasingh W PTS 15 Freddie Castillo, Bangkok, Thailand (WBC)
07.05.78 Yoko Gushiken W RSC 13 Jaime Rios, Hiroshima, Japan (WBA)
29.07.78 Sor Vorasingh W RTD 5 Luis Estaba, Caracas, Venezuela (WBC)
30.09.78 Sung-Jun Kim W CO 3 Sor Vorasingh, Seoul, S Korea (WBC)
15.10.78 Yoko Gushiken W CO 5 Sang-Il Chung, Tokyo, Japan (WBA)

07.01.79 Yoko Gushiken W CO 7 Rigoberto Marcano, Kawasaki, Japan (WBA)
31.03.79 Sung-Jun Kim DREW 15 Hector Melendez, Seoul, S Korea (WBC)
08.04.79 Yoko Gushiken W RSC 7 Alfonso Lopez, Tokyo, Japan (WBA)
28.07.79 Sung-Jun Kim W PTS 15 Stony Carupo, Seoul, S Korea (WBC)
29.07.79 Yoko Gushiken W PTS 15 Rafael Pedroza, Kitakyushi, Japan (WBA)
21.10.79 Sung-Jun Kim W PTS 15 Hector Melendez, Seoul, S Korea (WBC)
28.10.79 Yoko Gushiken W RSC 7 Tito Abella, Tokyo, Japan (WBA)
03.01.80 Shigeo Nakajima W PTS 15 Sung-Jun Kim, Tokyo, Japan (WBC)
27.01.80 Yoko Gushiken W PTS 15 Yong-Hyun Kim, Osaka, Japan (WBA)
24.03.80 Hilario Zapata W PTS 15 Shigeo Nakajima, Tokyo, Japan (WBC)
01.06.80 Yoko Gushiken W RSC 8 Martin Vargas, Kochi C, Japan (WBA)
07.06.80 Hilario Zapata W PTS 15 Chi-Bok Kim, Seoul, S Korea (WBC)
04.08.80 Hilario Zapata W PTS 15 Hector Melendez, Caracas, Venezuela (WBC)
17.09.80 Hilario Zapata W RSC 11 Shigeo Nakajima, Gifu, Japan (WBC)
12.10.80 Yoko Gushiken W PTS 15 Pedro Flores, Kanazawa, Japan (WBA)
01.12.80 Hilario Zapata W PTS 15 Reynaldo Becerra, Caracas, Venezuela (WBC)
08.02.81 Hilario Zapata W RSC 13 Joey Oliva, Panama C, Panama (WBC)
08.03.81 Pedro Flores W RTD 12 Yoko Gushiken, Gushikawa, Japan (WBA)
24.04.81 Hilario Zapata W PTS 15 Rudy Crawford, San Francisco, USA (WBC)
19.07.81 Hwan-Jin Kim W RSC 13 Pedro Flores, Taegu, S Korea (WBA)
15.08.81 Hilario Zapata W PTS 15 German Torres, Panama C, Panama (WBC)
11.10.81 Hwan-Jin Kim W PTS 15 Alfonso Lopez, Daejon, S Korea (WBA)
06.11.81 Hilario Zapata W RSC 10 Sor Vorasingh, Korat, Thailand (WBC)
16.12.81 Katsuo Tokashiki W PTS 15 Hwan-Jin Kim, Sendai, Japan (WBA)
06.02.82 Amado Ursua W CO 2 Hilario Zapata, Panama C, Panama (WBC)
04.04.82 Katsuo Tokashiki W PTS 15 Lupe Madera, Sendai, Japan (WBA)
13.04.82 Tadashi Tomori W PTS 15 Amado Ursua, Tokyo, Japan (WBC)
07.07.82 Katsuo Tokashiki W CO 8 Masahara Inami, Tokyo, Japan (WBA)
20.07.82 Hilario Zapata W PTS 15 Tadashi Tomori, Kanazawa, Japan (WBC)
18.09.82 Hilario Zapata W PTS 15 Jung-Koo Chang, Chonju, S Korea (WBC)
10.10.82 Katsuo Tokashiki W PTS 15 Sung-Nam Kim, Tokyo, Japan (WBA)
30.11.82 Hilario Zapata W RSC 8 Tadashi Tomori, Tokyo, Japan (WBC)
09.01.83 Katsuo Tokashiki W PTS 15 Hwan-Jin Kim, Kyoto, Japan (WBA)
26.03.83 Jung-Koo Chang W RSC 3 Hilario Zapata, Daejon, S Korea (WBC)
10.04.83 Katsuo Tokashiki DREW 15 Lupe Madera, Tokyo, Japan (WBA)
11.06.83 Jung-Koo Chang W RSC 2 Masaharu Iha, Taegu, S Korea (WBC)
10.07.83 Lupe Madera W RSC 4 Katsuo Tokashiki, Tokyo, Japan (WBA)
10.09.83 Jung-Koo Chang W PTS 12 German Torres, Daejon, S Korea (WBC)
23.10.83 Lupe Madera W PTS 12 Katsuo Tokashiki, Sapporo, Japan (WBA)
10.12.83 Dodie Penalosa W RSC 11 Satoshi Shingaki, Osaka, Japan (IBF)
31.03.84 Jung-Koo Chang W PTS 12 Sot Chitalada, Pusan, S Korea (WBC)
13.05.84 Dodie Penalosa W RSC 9 Jae-Hong Kim, Seoul, S Korea (IBF)
19.05.84 Francisco Quiroz W CO 9 Lupe Madera, Maracaibo, Venezuela (WBA)
18.08.84 Jung-Koo Chang W RSC 9 Katsuo Tokashiki, Pohang, S Korea (WBC)
18.08.84 Francisco Quiroz W CO 2 Victor Sierra, Panama C, Panama (WBA)
16.11.84 Dodie Penalosa W PTS 15 Jum-Hwan Choi, Manila, Philippines (IBF)
15.12.84 Jung-Koo Chang W PTS 12 Tadashi Kuramochi, Pusan, S Korea (WBC)
29.03.85 Joey Olivo W PTS 15 Francisco Quiroz, Miami, USA (WBA)
27.04.85 Jung-Koo Chang W PTS 12 German Torres, Ulsan, S Korea (WBC)
28.07.85 Joey Olivo W PTS 15 Moon-Jin Choi, Seoul, S Korea (WBA)
03.08.85 Jung-Koo Chang W PTS 15 Francisco Montiel, Seoul, S Korea (WBC)
12.10.85 Dodie Penalosa W CO 3 Yani Hagler, Jakarta, Indonesia (IBF)
Dodie Penalosa forfeited title (challenged Hilario Zapata for the WBA flyweight title)
10.11.85 Jung-Koo Chang W PTS 12 Jorge Cano, Daejon, S Korea (WBC)
08.12.85 Myung-Woo Yuh W PTS 15 Joey Olivo, Seoul, S Korea (WBA)
09.03.86 Myung-Woo Yuh W PTS 15 Jose de Jesus, Suwon, S Korea (WBA)
13.04.86 Jung-Koo Chang W PTS 12 German Torres, Kwangju, S Korea (WBC)
14.06.86 Myung-Woo Yuh W RSC 12 Tomohiro Kiyuna, Inchon, S Korea (WBA)
13.09.86 Jung-Koo Chang W PTS 12 Francisco Montiel, Seoul, S Korea (WBC)
30.11.86 Myung-Woo Yuh W PTS 15 Mario de Marco, Seoul, S Korea (WBA)
07.12.86 Jum-Hwan Choi W PTS 15 Cho-Woon Park, Pusan, S Korea (IBF)
14.12.86 Jung-Koo Chang W RSC 5 Hideyuki Ohashi, Inchon, S Korea (WBC)
01.03.87 Myung-Woo Yuh W RSC 1 Eduardo Tunon, Seoul, S Korea (WBA)
29.03.87 Jum-Hwan Choi W PTS 15 Tacy Macalos, Seoul, S Korea (IBF)
19.04.87 Jung-Koo Chang W RSC 6 Efren Pinto, Seoul, S Korea (WBC)
07.06.87 Myung-Woo Yuh W RSC 15 Benedicto Murillo, Pusan, S Korea (WBA)
28.06.87 Jung-Koo Chang W RSC 10 Agustin Garcia, Seoul, S Korea (WBC)
05.07.87 Jum-Hwan Choi W RSC 4 Toshihiko Matsuta, Seoul, S Korea (IBF)
09.08.87 Jum-Hwan Choi W RSC 3 Azadin Anhar, Jakarta, Indonesia (IBF)
20.09.87 Myung-Woo Yuh W CO 8 Rodolfo Blanco, Inchon, S Korea (WBA)
13.12.87 Jung-Koo Chang W PTS 12 Isidro Perez, Seoul, S Korea (WBC)
07.02.88 Myung-Woo Yuh W PTS 12 Wilibaldo Salazar, Seoul, S Korea (WBA)

Flyweight (112 lbs)

Title Holders

	Birthplace	Tenure	Status
Sid Smith	England	1913	GB/IBU
Bill Ladbury	England	1913 – 1914	GB/IBU
Percy Jones	Wales	1914	GB/IBU
Tancy Lee	Scotland	1915	GB/IBU
Joe Symonds	England	1915 – 1916	GB/IBU
Jimmy Wilde	Wales	1916	GB/IBU
Jimmy Wilde	Wales	1916 – 1923	
Pancho Villa *	Philippines	1923 – 1925	
Fidel la Barba	USA	1925 – 1927	USA
Fidel la Barba *	USA	1927	
Frenchy Belanger	Canada	1927 – 1928	NBA
Izzy Schwartz	USA	1927 – 1929	NY
Newsboy Brown	Russia	1928	CALIF
Frankie Genaro	USA	1928 – 1929	NBA
Johnny Hill	Scotland	1928 – 1929	GB/CALIF
Emile Pladner	France	1929	NBA/IBU
Frankie Genaro	USA	1929 – 1931	NBA/IBU
Willie la Morte	USA	1929 – 1930	NY
Midget Wolgast	USA	1930 – 1935	NY
Young Perez	Tunisia	1931 – 1932	NBA/IBU
Jackie Brown	England	1932 – 1935	NBA/IBU
Benny Lynch	Scotland	1935 – 1937	NBA
Small Montana	Philippines	1935 – 1937	NY/CALIF
Valentin Angelmann	France	1936 – 1937	IBU
Benny Lynch	Scotland	1937	
Peter Kane	England	1938 – 1943	
Jackie Paterson	Scotland	1943 – 1947	
Rinty Monaghan	Ireland	1947 – 1948	NBA
Rinty Monaghan *	Ireland	1948 – 1950	
Terry Allen	England	1950	
Dado Marino	Hawaii	1950 – 1952	
Yoshio Shirai	Japan	1952 – 1954	
Pascual Perez	Argentine	1954 – 1960	
Pone Kingpetch	Thailand	1960 – 1962	
Fighting Harada	Japan	1962 – 1963	
Pone Kingpetch	Thailand	1963	
Hiroyuki Ebihara	Japan	1963 – 1964	
Pone Kingpetch	Thailand	1964 – 1965	
Salvatore Burruni	Italy	1965	
Salvatore Burruni	Italy	1965 – 1966	WBC
Horacio Accavallo *	Argentine	1966 – 1968	WBA
Walter McGowan	Scotland	1966	WBC
Chartchai Chionoi	Thailand	1966 – 1969	WBC
Efren Torres	Mexico	1969 – 1970	WBC
Hiroyuki Ebihara	Japan	1969	WBA
Bernabe Villacampo	Philippines	1969 – 1970	WBA
Chartchai Chionoi	Thailand	1970	WBC
Berkrerk Chartvanchai	Thailand	1970	WBA
Masao Ohba *	Japan	1970 – 1973	WBA
Erbito Salavarria	Philippines	1970 – 1971	WBC
Betulio Gonzalez	Venezuela	1972	WBC
Venice Borkorsor *	Thailand	1972 – 1973	WBC
Chartchai Chionoi	Thailand	1973 – 1974	WBA
Betulio Gonzalez	Venezuela	1973 – 1974	WBC
Shoji Oguma	Japan	1974 – 1975	WBC
Susumu Hanagata	Japan	1974 – 1975	WBA
Miguel Canto	Mexico	1975 – 1979	WBC
Erbito Salavarria	Philippines	1975 – 1976	WBA
Alfonso Lopez	Panama	1976	WBA
Guty Espadas	Mexico	1976 – 1978	WBA
Betulio Gonzalez	Venezuela	1978 – 1979	WBA
Chan-Hee Park	Korea	1979 – 1980	WBC
Luis Ibarra	Panama	1979 – 1980	WBA
Tae-Shik Kim	S Korea	1980	WBA
Shoji Oguma	Japan	1980 – 1981	WBC
Peter Mathebula	S Africa	1980 – 1981	WBA
Santos Laciar	Argentine	1981	WBA
Antonio Avelar	Mexico	1981 – 1982	WBC
Luis Ibarra	Panama	1981	WBA
Juan Herrera	Mexico	1981 – 1982	WBA
Prudencio Cardona	Colombia	1982	WBC
Santos Laciar *	Argentine	1982 – 1985	WBA
Freddie Castillo	Mexico	1982	WBC
Eleoncio Mercedes	Dom Republic	1982 – 1983	WBC
Charlie Magri	Tunisia	1983	WBC
Frank Cedeno	Philippines	1983 – 1984	WBC
Soon-Chun Kwon	S Korea	1983 – 1985	IBF
Koji Kobayashi	Japan	1984	WBC
Gabriel Bernal	Mexico	1984	WBC
Sot Chitalada	Thailand	1984 –	WBC
Hilario Zapata	Panama	1985 – 1987	WBA
Chong-Kwan Chung	S Korea	1985 – 1986	IBF
Bi-Won Chung	S Korea	1986	IBF
Hi-Sup Shin	S Korea	1986 – 1987	IBF
Fidel Bassa	Colombia	1987 –	WBA
Dodie Penalosa	Philippines	1987	IBF
Chang-Ho Choi	S Korea	1987 – 1988	IBF
Rolando Bohol	Philippines	1988 –	IBF

Title Bouts

11.04.13 Sid Smith W PTS 20 Eugene Criqui, Paris, France (GB/IBU)
02.06.13 Bill Ladbury W RSC 11 Sid Smith, London, England (GB/IBU)
26.01.14 Percy Jones W PTS 20 Bill Ladbury, London, England (GB/IBU)
26.03.14 Percy Jones W PTS 20 Eugene Criqui, Liverpool, England (GB/IBU)
Percy Jones forfeited GB/IBU recognition (overweight for defence against Joe Symonds)
25.01.15 Tancy Lee W RSC 17 Jimmy Wilde, London, England (GB/IBU)
18.10.15 Joe Symonds W RSC 16 Tancy Lee, London, England (GB/IBU)
14.02.16 Jimmy Wilde W RSC 12 Joe Symonds, London, England (GB/IBU)
24.04.16 Jimmy Wilde W RTD 11 Johnny Rosner, Liverpool, England (GB/IBU)
26.06.16 Jimmy Wilde W RSC 11 Tancy Lee, London, England (GB/IBU)

31.07.16 Jimmy Wilde W CO 10 Johnny Hughes, London, England (GB/IBU)
18.12.16 Jimmy Wilde W CO 11 Young Zulu Kid, London, England
12.03.17 Jimmy Wilde W RTD 4 George Clark, London, England
18.06.23 Pancho Villa W CO 7 Jimmy Wilde, New York C, USA
13.10.23 Pancho Villa W PTS 15 Benny Schwartz, Baltimore, USA
08.02.24 Pancho Villa W PTS 15 Georgie Marks, New York C, USA
30.05.24 Pancho Villa W PTS 15 Frankie Ash, New York C, USA
01.05.25 Pancho Villa W PTS 15 Clever Sencio, Manila, Philippines
Pancho Villa left title vacant (died from blood poisoning)
22.08.25 Fidel la Barba W PTS 10 Frankie Genaro, Los Angeles, USA (USA)
08.07.26 Fidel la Barba W PTS 10 Georgie Rivers, Los Angeles, USA (USA)
21.01.27 Fidel la Barba W PTS 12 Elky Clark, New York C, USA
Fidel la Barba relinquished title (entered university)
28.11.27 Frenchy Belanger W PTS 10 Frankie Genaro, Toronto, Canada (NBA)
16.12.27 Izzy Schwartz W PTS 15 Newsboy Brown, New York C, USA (NY)
19.12.27 Frenchy Belanger W PTS 12 Ernie Jarvis, Toronto, Canada (NBA)
03.01.28 Newsboy Brown W PTS 10 Johnny McCoy, Los Angeles, USA (CALIF)
06.02.28 Frankie Genaro W PTS 10 Frenchy Belanger, Toronto, Canada (NBA)
09.04.28 Izzy Schwartz W PTS 15 Routier Parra, New York C, USA (NY)
20.07.28 Izzy Schwartz W DIS 4 Frisco Grande, New York C, USA (NY)
03.08.28 Izzy Schwartz W CO 4 Little Jeff Smith, New York C, USA (NY)
29.08.28 Johnny Hill W PTS 15 Newsboy Brown, London, England (GB/CALIF)
Johnny Hill ceased to be recognised by the GB-Californian authorities (this followed a defeat by Emile Pladner in a non-title bout, February, 1929)
02.03.29 Emile Pladner W CO 1 Frankie Genaro, Paris, France (NBA/IBU)
12.03.29 Izzy Schwartz W PTS 12 Frenchy Belanger, Toronto, Canada (NY)
18.04.29 Frankie Genaro W DIS 5 Emile Pladner, Paris, France (NBA/IBU)
22.08.29 Willie la Morte W PTS 15 Izzy Schwartz, Newark, USA (NY)
17.10.29 Frankie Genaro W PTS 15 Ernie Jarvis, London, England (NBA/IBU)
21.11.29 Willie la Morte W CO 7 Frisco Grande, Paterson, USA (NY)
Willie la Morte forfeited NY recognition (failure to meet Midget Wolgast)
18.01.30 Frankie Genaro W RTD 12 Yvon Trevidic, Paris, France (NBA/IBU)
21.03.30 Midget Wolgast W PTS 15 Black Bill, New York C, USA (NY)
16.05.30 Midget Wolgast W CO 6 Willie la Morte, New York C, USA (NY)
10.06.30 Frankie Genaro W PTS 10 Frenchy Belanger, Toronto, Canada (NBA/IBU)
06.08.30 Frankie Genaro W PTS 10 Willie la Morte, Newark, USA (NBA/IBU)
26.12.30 Frankie Genaro DREW 15 Midget Wolgast, New York C, USA
25.03.31 Frankie Genaro DREW 15 Victor Ferrand, Madrid, Spain (NBA/IBU)
13.07.31 Midget Wolgast W PTS 15 Ruby Bradley, New York C, USA (NY)
30.07.31 Frankie Genaro W CO 6 Jackie Harmon, Waterbury, USA (NBA/IBU)
03.10.31 Frankie Genaro W PTS 15 Valentin Angelmann, Paris, France (NBA/IBU)
27.10.31 Young Perez W CO 2 Frankie Genaro, Paris, France (NBA/IBU)
31.10.32 Jackie Brown W RSC 13 Young Perez, Manchester, England (NBA/IBU)
12.06.33 Jackie Brown W PTS 15 Valentin Angelmann, London, England (NBA/IBU)
11.12.33 Jackie Brown W PTS 15 Ginger Foran, Manchester, England (NBA/IBU)
18.06.34 Jackie Brown DREW 15 Valentin Angelmann, Manchester, England (NBA/IBU)
Jackie Brown forfeited IBU recognition (failure to defend against Valentin Angelmann)
09.09.35 Benny Lynch W RTD 2 Jackie Brown, Manchester, England (NBA)
16.09.35 Small Montana W PTS 10 Midget Wolgast, Oakland, USA (NY/CALIF)
06.01.36 Valentin Angelmann W RTD 5 Kid David, Paris, France (IBU)
16.09.36 Benny Lynch W CO 8 Pat Palmer, Glasgow, Scotland (NBA)
12.12.36 Valentin Angelmann W PTS 15 Ernst Weiss, Pairs, France (IBU)
Valentin Angelmann ceased to be recognised by the IBU (increasing weight)
19.01.37 Benny Lynch W PTS 15 Small Montana, Wembley, England
13.10.37 Benny Lynch W CO 13 Peter Kane, Glasgow, Scotland
Benny Lynch forfeited title (overweight for scheduled defence against Jackie Jurich)
22.09.38 Peter Kane W PTS 15 Jackie Jurich, Liverpool, England
19.06.43 Jackie Paterson W CO 1 Peter Kane, Glasgow, Scotland
10.07.46 Jackie Paterson W PTS 15 Joe Curran, Glasgow, Scotland
Jackie Paterson forfeited title (overweight for scheduled defence against Dado Marino)
20.10.47 Rinty Monaghan W PTS 15 Dado Marino, London, England (NBA)
23.03.48 Rinty Monaghan W CO 7 Jackie Paterson, Belfast, Ireland
05.04.49 Rinty Monaghan W PTS 15 Maurice Sandeyron, Belfast, Ireland
30.09.49 Rinty Monaghan DREW 15 Terry Allen, Belfast, Ireland
Rinty Monaghan relinquished title (retired)
25.04.50 Terry Allen W PTS 15 Honore Pratesi, London, England
01.08.50 Dado Marino W PTS 15 Terry Allen, Honolulu, Hawaii
01.11.51 Dado Marino W PTS 15 Terry Allen, Honolulu, Hawaii
19.05.52 Yoshio Shirai W PTS 15 Dado Marino, Tokyo, Japan
15.11.52 Yoshio Shirai W PTS 15 Dado Marino, Tokyo, Japan
18.05.53 Yoshio Shirai W PTS 15 Tanny Campo, Tokyo, Japan
27.10.53 Yoshio Shirai W PTS 15 Terry Allen, Tokyo, Japan
23.05.54 Yoshio Shirai W PTS 15 Leo Espinosa, Tokyo, Japan
26.11.54 Pascual Perez W PTS 15 Yoshio Shirai, Tokyo, Japan
30.05.55 Pascual Perez W CO 5 Yoshio Shirai, Tokyo, Japan
11.01.56 Pascual Perez W PTS 15 Leo Espinosa, Bs Aires, Argentine
30.06.56 Pascual Perez W RTD 11 Oscar Suarez, Montevideo, Uruguay
03.08.56 Pascual Perez W RSC 5 Ricardo Valdez, Tandil, Argentine
30.03.57 Pascual Perez W CO 1 Dai Dower, Bs Aires, Argentine
07.12.57 Pascual Perez W CO 3 Young Martin, Bs Aires, Argentine
19.04.58 Pascual Perez W PTS 15 Ramon Arias, Caracas, Venezuela
15.12.58 Pascual Perez W PTS 15 Dommy Ursua, Manila, Philippines
10.08.59 Pascual Perez W PTS 15 Kenji Yonekura, Tokyo, Japan
05.11.59 Pascual Perez W CO 13 Sadao Yaoita, Osaka, Japan
16.04.60 Pone Kingpetch W PTS 15 Pascual Perez, Bangkok, Thailand
22.09.60 Pone Kingpetch W RSC 8 Pascual Perez, Los Angeles, USA
27.06.61 Pone Kingpetch W PTS 15 Mitsunori Seki, Tokyo, Japan
30.05.62 Pone Kingpetch W PTS 15 Kyo Noguchi, Tokyo, Japan
10.10.62 Fighting Harada W CO 11 Pone Kingpetch, Tokyo, Japan
12.01.63 Pone Kingpetch W PTS 15 Fighting Harada, Tokyo, Japan
18.09.63 Hiroyuki Ebihara W CO 1 Pone Kingpetch, Tokyo, Japan
23.01.64 Pone Kingpetch W PTS 15 Hiroyuki Ebihara, Bangkok, Thailand
23.04.65 Salvatore Burruni W PTS 15 Pone Kingpetch, Rome, Italy
Salvatore Burruni forfeited WBA recognition (failure to defend against Horacio Accavallo)
02.12.65 Salvatore Burruni W CO 13 Rocky Gattellari, Sydney, Australia (WBC)
01.03.66 Horacio Accavallo W PTS 15 Katsuyoshi Takayama, Tokyo, Japan (WBA)
14.06.66 Walter McGowan W PTS 15 Salvatore Burruni, Wembley, England (WBC)
15.07.66 Horacio Accavallo W PTS 15 Hiroyuki Ebihara, Bs Aires, Argentine (WBA)
10.12.66 Horacio Accavallo W PTS 15 Efren Torres, Bs Aires, Argentine (WBA)
30.12.66 Chartchai Chionoi W RSC 9 Walter McGowan, Bangkok, Thailand (WBC)
26.07.67 Chartchai Chionoi W CO 3 Puntip Keosuriya, Bangkok, Thailand (WBC)
13.08.67 Horacio Accavallo W PTS 15 Hiroyuki Ebihara, Bs Aires, Argentine (WBA)
Horacio Accavallo relinquished WBA version of title (retired)
19.09.67 Chartchai Chionoi W RSC 7 Walter McGowan, Wembley, England (WBC)
28.01.68 Chartchai Chionoi W RSC 13 Efren Torres, Mexico C, Mexico (WBC)
10.11.68 Chartchai Chionoi W PTS 15 Bernabe Villacampo, Bangkok, Thailand (WBC)
23.02.69 Efren Torres W RSC 8 Chartchai Chionoi, Mexico C, Mexico (WBC)
30.03.69 Hiroyuki Ebihara W PTS 15 Jose Severino, Sapporo, Japan (WBA)
19.10.69 Bernabe Villacampo W PTS 15 Hiroyuki Ebihara, Tokyo, Japan (WBA)
28.11.69 Efren Torres W PTS 15 Susumu Hanagata, Guadalajara, Mexico (WBC)
20.03.70 Chartchai Chionoi W PTS 15 Efren Torres, Bangkok, Thailand (WBC)
06.04.70 Berkrerk Chartvanchai W PTS 15 Bernabe Villacampo, Bangkok (WBA)
21.10.70 Masao Ohba W RSC 13 Berkrerk Chartvanchai, Tokyo, Japan (WBA)
07.12.70 Erbito Salavarria W RSC 2 Chartchai Chionoi, Bangkok, Thailand (WBC)
01.04.71 Masao Ohba W PTS 15 Betulio Gonzalez, Tokyo, Japan (WBA)
30.04.71 Erbito Salavarria W PTS 15 Susumu Hanagata, Manila, Philippines (WBC)
23.10.71 Masao Ohba W PTS 15 Fernando Cabanela, Tokyo, Japan (WBA)
20.11.71 Erbito Salavarria DREW 15 Betulio Gonzalez, Caracus, Venezuela (WBC)
Erbito Salavarria forfeited WBC recognition (allegedly used an illegal stimulant)
04.03.72 Masao Ohba W PTS 15 Susumu Hanagata, Tokyo, Japan (WBA)
03.06.72 Betulio Gonzalez W CO 4 Socrates Batoto, Caracus, Venezuela (WBC)
20.06.72 Masao Ohba W CO 5 Orlando Amores, Tokyo, Japan (WBA)
29.09.72 Venice Borkorsor W RTD 10 Betulio Gonzalez, Bangkok, Thailand (WBC)
02.01.73 Masao Ohba W RSC 12 Chartchai Chionoi, Tokyo, Japan (WBA)
Masao Ohba left WBA version of title vacant (died in a road accident)
09.02.73 Venice Borkorsor W PTS 15 Erbito Salavarria, Bangkok, Thailand (WBC)
Venice Borkorsor relinquished WBC version of title (moved up to bantamweight)
17.05.73 Chartchai Chionoi W RSC 4 Fritz Chervet, Bangkok, Thailand (WBA)
04.08.73 Betulio Gonzalez W PTS 15 Miguel Canto, Caracas, Venezuela (WBC)
27.10.73 Chartchai Chionoi W PTS 15 Susumu Hanagata, Bangkok, Thailand (WBA)
17.11.73 Betulio Gonzalez W RSC 11 Alberto Morales, Caracas, Venezuela (WBC)
27.04.74 Chartchai Chionoi W PTS 15 Fritz Chervet, Zurich, Switzerland (WBA)
20.07.74 Betulio Gonzalez W RSC 10 Franco Udella, Sabbiadoro, Italy (WBC)
01.10.74 Shoji Oguma W PTS 15 Betulio Gonzalez, Tokyo, Japan (WBC)
18.10.74 Susumu Hanagata W RSC 6 Chartchai Chionoi, Yokohama, Japan (WBA)
08.01.75 Miguel Canto W PTS 15 Shoji Oguma, Sendai, Japan (WBC)
01.04.75 Erbito Salavarria W PTS 15 Susumu Hanagata, Toyama, Japan (WBA)
24.05.75 Miguel Canto W PTS 15 Betulio Gonzalez, Monterrey, Mexico (WBC)
23.08.75 Miguel Canto W RSC 11 Jiro Takada, Merida, Mexico (WBC)
07.10.75 Erbito Salavarria W PTS 15 Susumu Hanagata, Yokohama, Japan (WBA)
13.12.75 Miguel Canto W PTS 15 Ignacio Espinal, Merida, Mexico (WBC)
27.02.76 Alfonso Lopez W RSC 15 Erbito Salavarria, Manila, Philippines (WBA)
21.04.76 Alfonso Lopez W PTS 15 Shoji Oguma, Tokyo, Japan (WBA)
15.05.76 Miguel Canto W PTS 15 Susumu Hanagata, Merida, Mexico (WBC)
02.10.76 Guty Espadas W RSC 13 Alfonso Lopez, Los Angeles, USA (WBA)
03.10.76 Miguel Canto W PTS 15 Betulio Gonzalez, Caracas, Venezuela (WBC)
19.11.76 Miguel Canto W PTS 15 Orlando Javierta, Los Angeles, USA (WBC)
01.01.77 Guty Espadas W RTD 7 Jiro Takada, Tokyo, Japan (WBA)
24.04.77 Miguel Canto W PTS 15 Reyes Arnal, Caracas, Venezuela (WBC)
30.04.77 Guty Espadas W RSC 13 Alfonso Lopez, Merida, Mexico (WBA)
15.06.77 Miguel Canto W PTS 15 Kimio Furesawa, Tokyo, Japan (WBC)
17.09.77 Miguel Canto W PTS 15 Martin Vargas, Merida, Mexico (WBC)
19.11.77 Guty Espadas W CO 8 Alex Santana, Los Angeles, USA (WBA)
30.11.77 Miguel Canto W PTS 15 Martin Vargas, Santiago, Chile (WBC)
02.01.78 Guty Espadas W RSC 7 Kimio Furesawa, Tokyo, Japan (WBA)
04.01.78 Miguel Canto W PTS 15 Shoji Oguma, Tokyo, Japan (WBC)
18.04.78 Miguel Canto W PTS 15 Shoji Oguma, Tokyo, Japan (WBC)
13.08.78 Betulio Gonzalez W PTS 15 Guty Espadas, Maracay, Venezuela (WBA)
04.11.78 Betulio Gonzalez W RSC 12 Martin Vargas, Maracay, Venezuela (WBA)
20.11.78 Miguel Canto W PTS 15 Tacomron Vibonchai, Houston, USA (WBC)
29.01.79 Betulio Gonzalez DREW 15 Shoji Oguma, Hamamatsu, Japan (WBA)
10.02.79 Miguel Canto W PTS 15 Antonio Avelar, Merida, Mexico (WBC)
18.03.79 Chan-He Park W PTS 15 Miguel Canto, Pusan, S Korea (WBC)
19.05.79 Chan-He Park W PTS 15 Tsutomo Igarashi, Seoul, S Korea (WBC)
06.07.79 Betulio Gonzalez W CO 12 Shoji Oguma, Utsunomiya, Japan (WBA)
09.09.79 Chan-He Park DREW 15 Miguel Canto, Seoul, S Korea (WBC)
16.11.79 Luis Ibarra W PTS 15 Betulio Gonzalez, Maracay, Venezuela (WBA)
16.12.79 Chan-He Park W CO 2 Guty Espadas, Pusan, S Korea (WBC)
09.02.80 Chan-He Park W PTS 15 Arnel Arrozal, Seoul, S Korea (WBC)
16.02.80 Tae-Shik Kim W CO 2 Luis Ibarra, Seoul, S Korea (WBA)
13.04.80 Chan-He Park W PTS 15 Alberto Morales, Taegu, S Korea (WBC)
18.05.80 Shoji Oguma W CO 9 Chan-He Park, Seoul, S Korea (WBC)
29.06.80 Tae-Shik Kim W PTS 15 Arnel Arrozal, Seoul, S Korea (WBA)

28.07.80 Shoji Oguma W PTS 15 Sung-Jun Kim, Tokyo, Japan (WBC)
18.10.80 Shoji Oguma W PTS 15 Chan-He Park, Sendai, Japan (WBC)
13.12.80 Peter Mathebula W PTS 15 Tae-Shik Kim, Los Angeles, USA (WBA)
03.02.81 Shoji Oguma W PTS 15 Chan-He Park, Tokyo, Japan (WBC)
28.03.81 Santos Laciar W RSC 7 Peter Mathebula, Orlando, Soweto (WBA)
12.05.81 Antonio Avelar W CO 7 Shoji Oguma, Mito C, Japan (WBC)
06.06.81 Luis Ibarra W PTS 15 Santos Laciar, Bs Aires, Argentine (WBA)
30.08.81 Antonio Avelar W CO 2 Tae-Shik Kim, Seoul, S Korea (WBC)
26.09.81 Juan Herrera W CO 11 Luis Ibarra, Merida, Mexico (WBA)
26.12.81 Juan Herrera W RSC 7 Betulio Gonzalez, Merida, Mexico (WBA)
20.03.82 Prudencio Cardona W CO 1 Antonio Avelar, Tampico, Mexico (WBC)
01.05.82 Santos Laciar W RSC 13 Juan Herrera, Merida, Mexico (WBA)
24.07.82 Freddie Castillo W PTS 15 Prudencio Cardona, Merida, Mexico (WBC)
14.08.82 Santos Laciar W PTS 15 Betulio Gonzalez, Maracaibo, Venezuela (WBA)
05.11.82 Santos Laciar W RSC 13 Steve Muchoki, Copenhagen, Denmark (WBA)
06.11.82 Eleoncio Mercedes W PTS 15 Freddie Castillo, Los Angeles, USA (WBC)
04.03.83 Santos Laciar W CO 9 Ramon Neri, Cordoba, Argentine (WBA)
15.03.83 Charlie Magri W RSC 7 Eleoncio Mercedes, Wembley, England (WBC)
05.05.83 Santos Laciar W RSC 2 Shuichi Hozumi, Shizuoka, Japan (WBA)
17.07.83 Santos Laciar W CO 1 Hi-Sup Shin, Cheju, S Korea (WBA)
27.09.83 Frank Cedeno W RSC 6 Charlie Magri, Wembley, England (WBC)
24.12.83 Soon-Chun Kwon W CO 5 Rene Busayong, Seoul, S Korea (IBF)
18.01.84 Koji Kobayashi W RSC 2 Frank Cedeno, Tokyo, Japan (WBC)
28.01.84 Santos Laciar W PTS 15 Juan Herrera, Marsala, Italy (WBA)
25.02.84 Soon-Chun Kwon W CO 12 Roger Castillo, Seoul, S Korea (IBF)
09.04.84 Gabriel Bernal W CO 2 Koji Kobayashi, Tokyo, Japan (WBC)
19.05.84 Soon-Chun Kwon W PTS 15 Ian Clyde, Daejon, S Korea (IBF)
01.06.84 Gabriel Bernal W RSC 11 Antoine Montero, Nimes, France (WBC)
07.09.84 Soon-Chun Kwon NC 12 Joaquin Caraballo, Chungju, S Korea (IBF)
15.09.84 Santos Laciar W CO 10 Prudencio Cardona, Cordoba, Argentine (WBA)
08.10.84 Sot Chitalada W PTS 12 Gabriel Bernal, Bangkok, Thailand (WBC)
08.12.84 Santos Laciar W PTS 15 Hilario Zapata, Bs Aires, Argentine (WBA)
25.01.85 Soon-Chun Kwon DREW 15 Chong-Kwan Chung, Daejon, S Korea (IBF)
20.02.85 Sot Chitalada W RTD 4 Charlie Magri, London, England (WBC)
14.04.85 Soon-Chun Kwon W CO 3 Shinobu Kawashima, Pohang, S Korea (IBF)
06.05.85 Santos Laciar W PTS 15 Antoine Montero, Grenoble, France (WBA)
Santos Laciar relinquished WBA version of title (moved up to super-flyweight)
22.06.85 Sot Chitalada DREW 12 Gabriel Bernal, Bangkok, Thailand (WBC)
17.07.85 Soon-Chun Kwon DREW 15 Chong-Kwan Chung, Masan, S Korea (IBF)
05.10.85 Hilario Zapata W PTS 15 Alonzo Gonzales, Panama C, Panama (WBA)
20.12.85 Chong-Kwan Chung W RSC 4 Soon-Chun Kwon, Taegu, S Korea (IBF)
31.01.86 Hilario Zapata W PTS 15 Javier Lucas, Panama C, Panama (WBA)
22.02.86 Sot Chitalada W PTS 12 Freddie Castillo, Kuwait (WBC)
07.04.86 Hilario Zapata W PTS 15 Suichi Hozumi, Nirasaki, Japan (WBA)
27.04.86 Bi-Won Chung W PTS 15 Chong-Kwan Chung, Pusan, S Korea (IBF)
05.07.86 Hilario Zapata W PTS 15 Dodie Penalosa, Manila, Philippines (WBA)
02.08.86 Hi-Sup Shin W RSC 15 Bi-Won Chung, Inchon, S Korea (IBF)
13.09.86 Hilario Zapata W PTS 15 Alberto Castro, Panama C, Panama (WBA)
22.11.86 Hi-Sup Shin W RSC 13 Henry Brent, Chunchon, S Korea (IBF)
06.12.86 Hilario Zapata W PTS 15 Claudemir Dias, Salvador, Brazil (WBA)
10.12.86 Sot Chitalada W PTS 12 Gabriel Bernal, Bangkok, Thailand (WBC)
13.02.87 Fidel Bassa W PTS 15 Hilario Zapata, Barranquilla, Colombia (WBA)
22.02.87 Dodie Penalosa W CO 5 Hi-Sup Shin, Inchon, S Korea (IBF)
25.04.87 Fidel Bassa W CO 13 Dave McAuley, Belfast, Ireland (WBA)
15.08.87 Fidel Bassa DREW 15 Hilario Zapata, Panama C, Panama (WBA)
05.09.87 Chang-Ho Choi W CO 11 Dodie Penalosa, Manila, Philippines (IBF)
05.09.87 Sot Chitalada W CO 4 Rae-Ki Ahn, Bangkok, Thailand (WBC)
18.12.87 Fidel Bassa W PTS 12 Felix Marty, Cartagena, Colombia (WBA)
16.01.88 Rolando Bohol W PTS 15 Chang-Ho Choi, Manila, Philippines (IBF)
31.01.88 Sot Chitalada W RSC 7 Hideaki Kamishiro, Osaka, Japan (WBC)
26.03.88 Fidel Bassa W PTS 12 Dave McAuley, Belfast, Ireland (WBA)

Super-Flyweight (115 lbs)

Title Holders

	Birthplace	Tenure	Status
Rafael Orono	Venezuela	1980 – 1981	WBC
Chul-Ho Kim	S Korea	1981 – 1982	WBC
Gustavo Ballas	Argentine	1981	WBA
Rafael Pedroza	Panama	1981 – 1982	WBA
Jiro Watanabe	Japan	1982 – 1984	WBA
Rafael Orono	Venezuela	1982 – 1983	WBC
Payao Poontarat	Thailand	1983 – 1984	WBC
Joo-Do Chun	S Korea	1983 – 1985	IBF
Jiro Watanabe	Japan	1984 – 1986	WBC
Elly Pical	Indonesia	1985 – 1986	IBF
Kaosai Galaxy	Thailand	1984 –	WBA
Cesar Polanco	Dom Republic	1986	IBF
Gilberto Roman	Mexico	1986 – 1987	WBC
Elly Pical	Indonesia	1986 – 1987	IBF
Santos Laciar	Argentine	1987	WBC
Tae-Il Chang	S Korea	1987	IBF
Jesus Rojas	Colombia	1987 – 1988	WBC
Elly Pical	Indonesia	1987 –	IBF
Gilberto Roman	Mexico	1988 –	WBC

Title Bouts

02.02.80 Rafael Orono W PTS 15 Seung-Hoon Lee, Caracas, Venezuela (WBC)
14.04.80 Rafael Orono W PTS 15 Ramon Soria, Caracas, Venezuela (WBC)
28.07.80 Rafael Orono DREW 15 Willie Jensen, Caracas, Venezuela (WBC)
15.09.80 Rafael Orono W RSC 3 Jovito Rengifo, Barquisimeto, Venezuela (WBC)
24.01.81 Chul-Ho Kim W CO 9 Rafael Orono, San Christobal, Venezuela (WBC)
22.04.81 Chul-Ho Kim W PTS 15 Jiro Watanabe, Seoul, S Korea (WBC)
29.07.81 Chul-Ho Kim W CO 13 Willie Jensen, Pusan, S Korea (WBC)
12.09.81 Gustavo Ballas W RSC 8 Sok-Chul Baek, Bs Aires, Argentine (WBA)
18.11.81 Chul-Ho Kim W RSC 9 Jackal Maruyama, Pusan, S Korea (WBC)
05.12.81 Rafael Pedroza W PTS 15 Gustavo Ballas, Panama C, Panama (WBA)
10.02.82 Chul-Ho Kim W CO 8 Koki Ishii, Taegu, S Korea (WBC)
08.04.82 Jiro Watanabe W PTS 15 Rafael Pedroza, Osaka, Japan (WBA)
04.07.82 Chul-Ho Kim DREW 15 Raul Valdez, Daejon, S Korea (WBC)
29.07.82 Jiro Watanabe W RSC 9 Gustavo Ballas, Osaka, Japan (WBA)
11.11.82 Jiro Watanabe W RTD 12 Shoji Oguma, Hamamatsu, Japan (WBA)
28.11.82 Rafael Orono W CO 6 Chul-Ho Kim, Seoul, S Korea (WBC)
31.01.83 Rafael Orono W CO 4 Pedro Romero, Caracas, Venezuela (WBC)
24.02.83 Jiro Watanabe W CO 8 Luis Ibanez, Tsu C, Japan (WBA)
09.05.83 Rafael Orono W PTS 12 Raul Valdez, Caracas, Venezuela (WBC)
23.06.83 Jiro Watanabe W PTS 15 Roberto Ramirez, Sendai, Japan (WBA)
06.10.83 Jiro Watanabe W RTD 11 Soon-Chun Kwon, Osaka, Japan (WBA)
29.10.83 Rafael Orono W RSC 5 Orlando Maldonado, Caracas, Venezuela (WBC)
27.11.83 Payao Poontarat W PTS 12 Rafael Orono, Pattaya, Thailand (WBC)
10.12.83 Joo-Do Chun W CO 5 Ken Kasugai, Osaka, Japan (IBF)
28.01.84 Joo-Do Chun W CO 12 Prayoonsak Muangsurin, Seoul, S Korea (IBF)
15.03.84 Jiro Watanabe W RSC 15 Celso Chavez, Osaka, Japan (WBA)
Jiro Watanabe forfeited WBA recognition (failure to defend against Kaosai Galaxy)
17.03.84 Joo-Do Chun W CO 1 Diego de Villa, Kwangju, S Korea (IBF)
28.03.84 Payao Poontarat W RSC 10 Guty Espadas, Bangkok, Thailand (WBC)
26.05.84 Joo-Do Chun W RSC 6 Felix Marques, Wonju, S Korea (IBF)
05.07.84 Jiro Watanabe W PTS 12 Payao Poontarat, Osaka, Japan (WBC)
20.07.84 Joo-Do Chun W CO 7 William Develos, Pusan, S Korea (IBF)
21.11.84 Kaosai Galaxy W CO 6 Eusebio Espinal, Bangkok, Thailand (WBA)
29.11.84 Jiro Watanabe W RSC 11 Payao Poontarat, Kumamoto, Japan (WBC)
06.01.85 Joo-Do Chun W CO 15 Kwang-Gu Park, Ulsan, S Korea (IBF)
06.03.85 Kaosai Galaxy W CO 7 Dong-Chun Lee, Bangkok, Thailand (WBA)
03.05.85 Elly Pical W RSC 8 Joo-Do Chun, Jakarta, Indonesia (IBF)
09.05.85 Jiro Watanabe W PTS 12 Julio Solano, Tokyo, Japan (WBC)
17.07.85 Kaosai Galaxy W RSC 5 Rafael Orono, Bangkok, Thailand (WBA)
25.08.85 Elly Pical W RSC 3 Wayne Mulholland, Jakarta, Indonesia (IBF)
17.09.85 Jiro Watanabe W RSC 7 Katsuo Katsuma, Osaka, Japan (WBC)
13.12.85 Jiro Watanabe W CO 5 Yun-Sok Hwang, Taegu, S Korea (WBC)
23.12.85 Kaosai Galaxy W RSC 2 Edgar Monserrat, Bangkok, Thailand (WBA)
15.02.86 Cesar Polanco W PTS 15 Elly Pical, Jakarta, Indonesia (IBF)
30.03.86 Gilberto Roman W PTS 12 Jiro Watanabe, Osaka, Japan (WBC)
15.05.86 Gilberto Roman W PTS 12 Edgar Monserrat, Paris, France (WBC)
05.07.86 Elly Pical W CO 3 Cesar Polanco, Jakarta, Indonesia (IBF)
18.07.86 Gilberto Roman W PTS 12 Ruben Condori, Salta, Argentine (WBC)
30.08.86 Gilberto Roman DREW 12 Santos Laciar, Cordoba, Argentine (WBC)
01.11.86 Kaosai Galaxy W CO 5 Israel Contreras, Curacao, DWI (WBA)
03.12.86 Elly Pical W CO 10 Dong-Chun Lee, Jakarta, Indonesia (IBF)
Elly Pical forfeited title (challenged for the WBA S. flyweight title)
15.12.86 Gilberto Roman W PTS 12 Kongtoranee Payakarun, Bangkok, Thai. (WBC)
31.01.87 Gilberto Roman W RSC 9 Antoine Montero, Montpelier, France (WBC)
28.02.87 Kaosai Galaxy W CO 14 Elly Pical, Jakarta, Indonesia (WBA)
19.03.87 Gilberto Roman W PTS 12 Frank Cedeno, Mexicali, Mexico (WBC)
16.05.87 Santos Laciar W RSC 11 Gilberto Roman, Reims, France (WBC)
17.05.87 Tae-Il-Chang W PTS 15 Soon-Chun Kwon, Pusan, S Korea (IBF)
08.08.87 Jesus Rojas W PTS 12 Santos Laciar, Miami, USA (WBC)
12.10.87 Kaosai Galaxy W RSC 3 Byong-Kwan Chung, Bangkok, Thailand (WBA)
17.10.87 Elly Pical W PTS 15 Tae-Il Chang, Jakarta, Indonesia (IBF)
24.10.87 Jesus Rojas W RSC 4 Gustavo Ballas, Miami, USA (WBC)
26.01.88 Kaosai Galaxy W PTS 12 Kongtoranee Payakarun, Bangkok (WBA)
20.02.88 Elly Pical W PTS 15 Raul Diaz, Pontianak, Indonesia (IBF)
08.04.88 Gilberto Roman W PTS 12 Jesus Rojas, Miami, USA (WBC)

Bantamweight (118 lbs)

Title Holders

	Birthplace	Tenure	Status
Billy Plimmer	England	1892 – 1895	
Pedlar Palmer	England	1895 – 1899	
Terry McGovern *	USA	1899 – 1900	
Harry Forbes	USA	1901 – 1903	
Frankie Neil	USA	1903 – 1904	
Joe Bowker *	England	1904 – 1905	
Jimmy Walsh *	USA	1905 – 1907	
Owen Moran	England	1907	GB
Johnny Coulon	Canada	1908 – 1914	USA
Digger Stanley	England	1910 – 1912	GB/IBU
Charles Ledoux	France	1912 – 1913	GB/IBU
Eddie Campi	USA	1913 – 1914	GB/IBU
Kid Williams	Denmark	1914	GB/IBU
Kid Williams	Denmark	1914 – 1917	
Pete Herman	USA	1917 – 1920	
Joe Lynch	USA	1920 – 1921	
Pete Herman	USA	1921	
Johnny Buff	USA	1921 – 1922	
Joe Lynch	USA	1922 – 1923	

Abe Goldstein	USA	1923 – 1924	NY
Abe Goldstein	USA	1924	
Eddie Martin	USA	1924 – 1925	
Charlie Rosenberg	USA	1925 – 1927	
Teddy Baldock	England	1927	GB
Bud Taylor *	USA	1927 – 1928	NBA
Willie Smith	S Africa	1927 – 1929	GB
Bushy Graham *	Italy	1928 – 1929	NY
Al Brown	Panama	1929 – 1931	NY/IBU
Pete Sanstol	Norway	1931	NBA
Al Brown	Panama	1931 – 1934	
Sixto Escobar	Puerto Rico	1934 – 1935	NBA
Al Brown	Panama	1934 – 1935	NY/IBU
Baltazar Sangchilli	Spain	1935 – 1936	NY/IBU
Lou Salica	USA	1935	NBA
Sixto Escobar	Puerto Rico	1935 – 1936	NBA
Tony Marino	USA	1936	NY/IBU
Sixto Escobar	Puerto Rico	1936 – 1937	
Harry Jeffra	USA	1937 – 1938	
Sixto Escobar *	Puerto Rico	1938 – 1939	
Lou Salica	USA	1940 – 1942	
Manuel Ortiz	USA	1942 – 1947	
Harold Dade	USA	1947	
Manuel Ortiz	USA	1947 – 1950	
Vic Toweel	S Africa	1950 – 1952	
Jimmy Carruthers *	Australia	1952 – 1954	
Robert Cohen	Algeria	1954 – 1956	NY/EBU
Raton Macias	Mexico	1955 – 1957	NBA
Mario D'Agata	Italy	1956 – 1957	NY/EBU
Alphonse Halimi	Algeria	1957	NY/EBU
Alphonse Halimi	Algeria	1957 – 1959	
Joe Becerra *	Mexico	1959 – 1960	
Alphonse Halimi	Algeria	1960 – 1961	EBU
Eder Jofre	Brazil	1960 – 1962	NBA
Johnny Caldwell	Ireland	1961 – 1962	EBU
Eder Jofre	Brazil	1962 – 1965	
Fighting Harada	Japan	1965 – 1968	
Lionel Rose	Australia	1968 – 1969	
Ruben Olivares	Mexico	1969 – 1970	
Chucho Castillo	Mexico	1970 – 1971	
Ruben Olivares	Mexico	1971 – 1972	
Rafael Herrera	Mexico	1972	
Enrique Pinder	Panama	1972	
Enrique Pinder	Panama	1972 – 1973	WBC
Romeo Anaya	Mexico	1973	WBA
Rafael Herrera	Mexico	1973 – 1974	WBC
Arnold Taylor	S Africa	1973 – 1974	WBA
Soo-Hwan Hong	S Korea	1974 – 1975	WBA
Rodolfo Martinez	Mexico	1974 – 1976	WBC
Alfonso Zamora	Mexico	1975 – 1977	WBA
Carlos Zarate	Mexico	1976 – 1979	WBC
Jorge Lujan	Panama	1977 – 1980	WBA
Lupe Pintor	Mexico	1979 – 1983	WBC
Julian Solis	Puerto Rico	1980	WBA
Jeff Chandler	USA	1980 – 1984	WBA
Albert Davila *	USA	1983 – 1985	WBC
Richard Sandoval	USA	1984 – 1986	WBA
Satoshi Shingaki	Japan	1984 – 1985	IBF
Jeff Fenech *	Australia	1985 – 1987	IBF
Daniel Zaragoza	Mexico	1985	WBC
Miguel Lora	Colombia	1985 –	WBC
Gaby Canizales	USA	1986	WBA
Bernardo Pinango *	Venezuela	1986 – 1987	WBA
Takuya Muguruma	Japan	1987	WBA
Kelvin Seabrooks	USA	1987 –	IBF
Chan-Yung Park	S Korea	1987	WBA
Wilfredo Vasquez	Puerto Rico	1987 –	WBA

Title Bouts

09.05.92 Billy Plimmer W PTS 10 Tommy Kelly, New York C, USA
28.12.92 Billy Plimmer W 8 Joe McGrath, New York C, USA
24.09.94 Billy Plimmer DREW 25 Johnny Murphy, New Orleans, USA
26.11.94 Billy Plimmer W CO 3 Charley Kelly, New York C, USA
28.05.95 Billy Plimmer W CO 7 George Corfield, London, England
25.11.95 Pedlar Palmer W DIS 14 Billy Plimmer, London, England
18.10.97 Pedlar Palmer W PTS 20 Dave Sullivan, London, England
12.12.98 Pedlar Palmer W RSC 17 Billy Plimmer, London, England
17.04.99 Pedlar Palmer W RSC 3 Billy Rotchford, London, England
22.09.99 Terry McGovern W CO 1 Pedlar Palmer, Tuckahoe, USA
22.12.99 Terry McGovern W CO 2 Harry Forbes, New York C, USA
Terry McGovern relinquished title (moved up to featherweight)
11.11.01 Harry Forbes W CO 2 Dan Dougherty, St Louis, USA
23.01.02 Harry Forbes W CO 4 Dan Dougherty, St Louis, USA
27.02.02 Harry Forbes W PTS 15 Tommy Feltz, St Louis, USA
01.05.02 Harry Forbes DREW 20 Johnny Reagan, St Louis, USA
23.12.02 Harry Forbes W RSC 7 Frankie Neil, Oakland, USA
27.02.03 Harry Forbes W PTS 10 Andrew Tokell, Detroit, USA
13.08.03 Frankie Neil W CO 2 Harry Forbes, San Francisco, USA
04.09.03 Frankie Neil W CO 15 Billy de Coursey, Los Angeles, USA
16.10.03 Frankie Neil DREW 20 Johnny Reagan, Los Angeles, USA
17.06.04 Frankie Neil W CO 3 Harry Forbes, Chicago, USA
17.10.04 Joe Bowker W PTS 20 Frankie Neil, London, England
29.05.05 Joe Bowker W PTS 20 Pinky Evans, London, England
Joe Bowker relinquished title (moved up to featherweight)
20.10.05 Jimmy Walsh W PTS 15 Digger Stanley, Chelsea, Mass, USA
Jimmy Walsh relinquished title (moved up to featherweight)
22.04.07 Owen Moran W PTS 20 Al Delmont, London, England (GB)
Owen Moran ceased to be recognised by GB (unable to make the weight he campaigned as a featherweight)
08.01.08 Johnny Coulon W PTS 10 Kid Murphy, Peoria, USA (USA)
29.01.08 Johnny Coulon W PTS 10 Kid Murphy, Peoria, USA (USA)
10.02.08 Johnny Coulon W CO 9 Cooney Kelly, Peoria, USA (USA)
11.02.09 Johnny Coulon W RTD 5 Kid Murphy, New York C, USA (USA)
30.01.10 Johnny Coulon W CO 9 Earl Denning, New Orleans, USA (USA)
19.02.10 Johnny Coulon W PTS 10 Jim Kendrick, New Orleans, USA (USA)
06.03.10 Johnny Coulon W CO 19 Jim Kendrick, New Orleans, USA (USA)
17.10.10 Digger Stanley W CO 8 Joe Bowker, London, England (GB)
05.12.10 Digger Stanley W PTS 20 Johnny Condon, London, England (GB)
19.12.10 Johnny Coulon NC 3 Earl Denning, Memphis, USA (USA)
26.02.11 Johnny Coulon W PTS 20 Frankie Conley, New Orleans, USA (USA)
14.09.11 Digger Stanley W PTS 20 Ike Bradley, Liverpool, England (GB)
03.02.12 Johnny Coulon W PTS 20 Frankie Conley, Los Angeles, USA (USA)
18.02.12 Johnny Coulon W PTS 20 Frankie Burns, New Orleans, USA (USA)
22.04.12 Digger Stanley W PTS 20 Charles Ledoux, London, England (GB/IBU)
23.06.12 Charles Ledoux W CO 7 Digger Stanley, Dieppe, France (GB/IBU)
24.06.13 Eddie Campi W PTS 20 Charles Ledoux, Los Angeles, USA (GB/IBU)
31.01.14 Kid Williams W CO 12 Eddie Campi, Los Angeles, USA (GB/IBU)
09.06.14 Kid Williams W CO 3 Johnny Coulon, Los Angeles, USA
28.09.14 Kid Williams W CO 4 Kid Herman, Philadelphia, USA
06.12.15 Kid Williams DREW 20 Frankie Burns, New Orleans, USA
07.02.16 Kid Williams DREW 20 Pete Herman, New Orleans, USA
09.01.17 Pete Herman W PTS 20 Kid Williams, New Orleans, USA
05.11.17 Pete Herman W PTS 20 Frankie Burns, New Orleans, USA
22.12.20 Joe Lynch W PTS 15 Pete Herman, New York C, USA
25.07.21 Pete Herman W PTS 15 Joe Lynch, New York C, USA
23.09.21 Johnny Buff W PTS 15 Pete Herman, New York C, USA
10.11.21 Johnny Buff W PTS 15 Jackie Sharkey, New York C, USA
10.07.22 Joe Lynch W RTD 14 Johnny Buff, New York C, USA
22.12.22 Joe Lynch W PTS 15 Midget Smith, New York C, USA
Joe Lynch forfeited NY recognition (withdrew from a scheduled defence against Joe Burman)
10.10.23 Abe Goldstein W PTS 12 Joe Burman, New York C, USA (NY)
21.03.24 Abe Goldstein W PTS 15 Joe Lynch, New York C, USA
16.07.24 Abe Goldstein W PTS 15 Charles Ledoux, New York C, USA
08.09.24 Abe Goldstein W PTS 15 Tommy Ryan, New York C, USA
19.12.24 Eddie Martin W PTS 15 Abe Goldstein, New York C, USA
20.03.25 Charlie Rosenberg W PTS 15 Eddie Martin, New York C, USA
23.07.25 Charlie Rosenberg W CO 4 Eddie Shea, New York C, USA
02.03.26 Charlie Rosenberg W PTS 10 George Butch, St Louis, USA
Charlie Rosenberg forfeited title (overweight for defence against Bushy Graham)
26.03.27 Bud Taylor DREW 10 Tony Canzoneri, Chicago, USA (NBA)
05.05.27 Teddy Baldock W PTS 15 Archie Bell, London, England (GB)
24.06.27 Bud Taylor W PTS 10 Tony Canzoneri, Chicago, USA (NBA)
Bud Taylor relinquished NBA version of title (weight making difficulties)
06.10.27 Willie Smith W PTS 15 Teddy Baldock, London, England (GB)
Willie Smith ceased to be recognised in GB (made no effort to defend)
23.05.28 Bushy Graham W PTS 15 Izzy Schwartz, New York C, USA (NY)
Bushy Graham relinquished NY version of title (weight making difficulties)
18.06.29 Al Brown W PTS 15 Vidal Gregorio, New York C, USA (NY)
28.08.29 Al Brown W PTS 10 Knud Larsen, Copenhagen, Denmark (NY/IBU)
08.02.30 Al Brown W DIS 4 Johnny Erickson, New York C, USA (NY/IBU)
04.10.30 Al Brown W PTS 15 Eugene Huat, Paris, France (NY/IBU)
11.02.31 Al Brown W PTS 10 Nick Bensa, Paris, France (NY/IBU)
20.05.31 Pete Sanstol W PTS 10 Archie Bell, Montreal, Canada (NBA)
25.08.31 Al Brown W PTS 15 Pete Sanstol, Montreal, Canada
27.10.31 Al Brown W PTS 15 Eugene Huat, Montreal, Canada
10.07.32 Al Brown W PTS 15 Kid Francis, Marseilles, France
19.09.32 Al Brown W CO 1 Emile Pladner, Toronto, Canada
18.03.33 Al Brown W PTS 12 Dom Bernasconi, Milan, Italy
03.07.33 Al Brown W PTS 15 Johnny King, Manchester, England
19.02.34 Al Brown W PTS 15 Young Perez, Paris, France
Al Brown forfeited NBA recognition (failure to defend against Baby Casanova)
26.06.34 Sixto Escobar W CO 9 Baby Casanova, Montreal, Canada (NBA)
08.08.34 Sixto Escobar W PTS 15 Eugene Huat, Montreal, Canada (NBA)
01.11.34 Al Brown W CO 10 Young Perez, Tunis, Tunisia (NY/IBU)
01.06.35 Baltazar Sangchilli W PTS 15 Al Brown, Valencia, Spain (NY/IBU)
26.08.35 Lou Salica W PTS 15 Sixto Escobar, New York C, USA (NBA)
15.11.35 Sixto Escobar W PTS 15 Lou Salica, New York C, USA (NBA)
29.06.36 Tony Marino W CO 14 Baltazar Sangchilli, New York C, USA (NY/IBU)
31.08.36 Sixto Escobar W RSC 13 Tony Marino, New York C, USA
13.10.36 Sixto Escobar W CO 1 Carlos Quintana, New York C, USA
21.02.37 Sixto Escobar W PTS 15 Lou Salica, San Juan, Puerto Rico
23.09.37 Harry Jeffra W PTS 15 Sixto Escobar, New York C, USA
20.02.38 Sixto Escobar W PTS 15 Harry Jeffra, San Juan, Puerto Rico
02.04.39 Sixto Escobar W PTS 15 Kayo Morgan, San Juan, Puerto Rico
Sixto Escobar relinquished title (weight making difficulties)
04.03.40 Lou Salica DREW 15 George Pace, Toronto, Canada (NBA)
24.09.40 Lou Salica W PTS 15 George Pace, New York C, USA

13.01.41 Lou Salica W PTS 15 Tommy Forte, Philadelphia, USA
25.04.41 Lou Salica W PTS 15 Lou Transparenti, Baltimore, USA
16.06.41 Lou Salica W PTS 15 Tommy Forte, Philadelphia, USA
07.08.42 Manuel Ortiz W PTS 12 Lou Salica, Los Angeles, USA
01.01.43 Manuel Ortiz W PTS 10 Kenny Lindsay, Portland, USA
27.01.43 Manuel Ortiz W RSC 10 George Freitas, Oakland, USA
10.03.43 Manuel Ortiz W RSC 11 Lou Salica, Oakland, USA
28.04.43 Manuel Ortiz W CO 6 Lupe Cordoza, Fort Worth, USA
26.05.43 Manuel Ortiz W PTS 15 Joe Robleto, Los Angeles, USA
12.07.43 Manuel Ortiz W CO 7 Joe Robleto, Seattle, USA
01.10.43 Manuel Ortiz W CO 4 Leonardo Lopez, Los Angeles, USA
23.11.43 Manuel Ortiz W PTS 15 Benny Goldberg, Los Angeles, USA
14.03.44 Manuel Ortiz W PTS 15 Ernesto Aguilar, Los Angeles, USA
04.04.44 Manuel Ortiz W PTS 15 Tony Olivera, Los Angeles, USA
12.09.44 Manuel Ortiz W CO 4 Luis Castillo, Los Angeles, USA
14.11.44 Manuel Ortiz W RSC 9 Luis Castillo, Los Angeles, USA
25.02.46 Manuel Ortiz W CO 13 Luis Castillo, San Francisco, USA
26.05.46 Manuel Ortiz W CO 5 Kenny Lindsay, Los Angeles, USA
10.06.46 Manuel Ortiz W CO 11 Jackie Jurich, San Francisco, USA
06.01.47 Harold Dade W PTS 15 Manuel Ortiz, San Francisco, USA
11.03.47 Manuel Ortiz W PTS 15 Harold Dade, Los Angeles, USA
30.05.47 Manuel Ortiz W PTS 15 Kui Kong Young, Honolulu, Hawaii
20.12.47 Manuel Ortiz W PTS 15 Tirso del Rosario, Manila, Philippines
04.07.48 Manuel Ortiz W RSC 8 Memo Valero, Mexicali, Mexico
01.03.49 Manuel Ortiz W PTS 15 Dado Marino, Honolulu, Hawaii
31.05.50 Vic Toweel W PTS 15 Manuel Ortiz, Johannesburg, S Africa
02.12.50 Vic Toweel W RTD 10 Danny O'Sullivan, Johannesburg, S Africa
17.11.51 Vic Toweel W PTS 15 Luis Romero, Johannesburg, S Africa
26.01.52 Vic Toweel W PTS 15 Peter Keenan, Johannesburg, S Africa
15.11.52 Jimmy Carruthers W CO 1 Vic Toweel, Johannesburg, S Africa
21.03.53 Jimmy Carruthers W CO 10 Vic Toweel, Johannesburg, S Africa
13.11.53 Jimmy Carruthers W PTS 15 Pappy Gault, Sydney, Australia
02.05.54 Jimmy Carruthers W PTS 12 Chamrern Songkitrat, Bangkok, Thailand
Jimmy Carruthers relinquished title (retired)
19.09.54 Robert Cohen W PTS 15 Chamrern Songkitrat, Bangkok, Thailand (NY/EBU)
09.03.55 Raton Macias W RSC 11 Chamrern Songkitrat, San Francisco, USA (NBA)
03.09.55 Robert Cohen DREW 15 Willie Toweel, Johannesburg, S Africa (NY/EBU)
25.03.56 Raton Macias W CO 10 Leo Espinosa, Mexico C, Mexico (NBA)
29.06.56 Mario D'Agata W RTD 6 Robert Cohen, Rome, Italy (NY/EBU)
01.04.57 Alphonse Halimi W PTS 15 Mario D'Agata, Paris, France (NY/EBU)
15.06.57 Raton Macias W RSC 11 Dommy Ursua, San Francisco, USA (NBA)
06.11.57 Alphonse Halimi W PTS 15 Raton Macias, Los Angeles, USA
08.07.59 Joe Becerra W CO 8 Alphonse Halimi, Los Angeles, USA
04.02.60 Joe Becerra W CO 9 Alphonse Halimi, Los Angeles, USA
23.05.60 Joe Becerra W PTS 15 Kenji Yonekura, Tokyo, Japan
Joe Becerra relinquished title (retired)
25.10.60 Alphonse Halimi W PTS 15 Freddie Gilroy, Wembley, England (EBU)
18.11.60 Eder Jofre W CO 6 Eloy Sanchez, Los Angeles, USA (NBA)
25.03.61 Eder Jofre W RTD 9 Piero Rollo, Rio de Janeiro, Brazil (NBA)
30.05.61 Johnny Caldwell W PTS 15 Alphonse Halimi, Wembley, England (EBU)
19.08.61 Eder Jofre W RSC 7 Ramon Arias, Caracas, Venezuela (NBA)
31.10.61 Johnny Caldwell W PTS 15 Alphonse Halimi, Wembley, England (EBU)
18.01.62 Eder Jofre W RTD 10 Johnny Caldwell, Sao Paulo, Brazil
04.05.62 Eder Jofre W RSC 10 Herman Marquez, San Francisco, USA
11.09.62 Eder Jofre W CO 6 Joe Medel, Sao Paulo, Brazil
04.04.63 Eder Jofre W CO 3 Katsutoshi Aoki, Tokyo, Japan
18.05.63 Eder Jofre W RTD 11 Johnny Jamito, Quezon C, Philippines
27.11.64 Eder Jofre W CO 7 Bernardo Caraballo, Bogota, Colombia
17.05.65 Fighting Harada W PTS 15 Eder Jofre, Nagoya, Japan
30.11.65 Fighting Harada W PTS 15 Alan Rudkin, Tokyo, Japan
01.06.66 Fighting Harada W PTS 15 Eder Jofre, Tokyo, Japan
03.01.67 Fighting Harada W PTS 15 Joe Medel, Nagoya, Japan
04.07.67 Fighting Harada W PTS 15 Bernardo Caraballo, Tokyo, Japan
26.02.68 Lionel Rose W PTS 15 Fighting Harada, Tokyo, Japan
02.07.68 Lionel Rose W PTS 15 Takao Sakurai, Tokyo, Japan
06.12.68 Lionel Rose W PTS 15 Chucho Castillo, Los Angeles, USA
08.03.69 Lionel Rose W PTS 15 Alan Rudkin, Melbourne, Australia
22.08.69 Ruben Olivares W CO 5 Lionel Rose, Los Angeles, USA
12.12.69 Ruben Olivares W RSC 2 Alan Rudkin, Los Angeles, USA
18.04.70 Ruben Olivares W PTS 15 Chuchu Castillo, Los Angeles, USA
16.10.70 Chuchu Castillo W RSC 14 Ruben Olivares, Los Angeles, USA
03.04.71 Ruben Olivares W PTS 15 Chucho Castillo, Los Angeles, USA
25.10.71 Ruben Olivares W RSC 14 Katsutoshi Kanazawa, Nagoya, Japan
14.12.71 Ruben Olivares W RSC 11 Jesus Pimental, Los Angeles, USA
19.03.72 Rafael Herrera W CO 8 Ruben Olivares, Mexico C, Mexico
30.07.72 Enrique Pinder W PTS 15 Rafael Herrera, Panama C, Panama
Enrique Pinder forfeited WBC recognition (failure to defend against the stipulated challenger)
20.01.73 Romeo Anaya W CO 3 Enrique Pinder, Panama C, Panama (WBA)
15.04.73 Rafael Herrera W RSC 12 Rodolfo Martinez, Monterrey, Mexico (WBC)
28.04.73 Romeo Anaya W PTS 15 Rogelio Lara, Los Angeles, USA (WBA)
18.08.73 Romeo Anaya W CO 3 Enrique Pinder, Los Angeles, USA (WBA)
13.10.73 Rafael Herrera W PTS 15 Venice Borkorsor, Los Angeles, USA (WBC)
03.11.73 Arnold Taylor W CO 14 Romeo Anaya, Johannesburg, S Africa (WBA)
25.05.74 Rafael Herrera W CO 6 Romeo Anaya, Mexico C, Mexico (WBC)
03.07.74 Soo-Hwan Hong W PTS 15 Arnold Taylor, Durban, S Africa (WBA)
07.12.74 Rodolfo Martinez W RSC 4 Rafael Herrera, Merida, Mexico (WBC)
28.12.74 Soo-Hwan Hong W PTS 15 Fernando Canabela, Seoul, S Korea (WBA)
14.03.75 Alfonso Zamora W CO 4 Soo-Hwan Hong, Los Angeles, USA (WBA)
31.05.75 Rodolfo Martinez W RSC 7 Nestor Jiminez, Bogota, Colombia (WBC)
30.08.75 Alfonso Zamora W CO 4 Thanomjit Sukhothai, Los Angeles, USA (WBA)
08.10.75 Rodolfo Martinez W PTS 15 Hisami Numata, Sendai, Japan (WBC)
06.12.75 Alfonso Zamora W CO 2 Socrates Batoto, Mexico C, Mexico (WBA)
30.01.76 Rodolfo Martinez W PTS 15 Venice Borkorsor, Bangkok, Thailand (WBC)
03.04.76 Alfonso Zamora W CO 2 Eusebio Pedroza, Mexicali, Mexico (WBA)
08.05.76 Carlos Zarate W CO 9 Rodolfo Martinez, Los Angeles, USA (WBC)
10.07.76 Alfonso Zamora W CO 3 Gilberto Illueca, Juarez, Mexico (WBA)
28.08.76 Carlos Zarate W RSC 12 Paul Ferreri, Los Angeles, USA (WBC)
16.10.76 Alfonso Zamora W RSC 12 Soo-Hwan Hong, Inchon, S Korea (WBA)
13.11.76 Carlos Zarate W CO 4 Waruinge Nakayama, Culiacan, Mexico (WBC)
05.02.77 Carlos Zarate W RSC 3 Fernando Cabanela, Mexico C, Mexico (WBC)
29.10.77 Carlos Zarate W RSC 6 Danilio Batista, Los Angeles, USA (WBC)
19.11.77 Jorge Lujan W CO 10 Alfonso Zamora, Los Angeles, USA (WBA)
02.12.77 Carlos Zarate W RSC 5 Juan Francisco Rodriguez, Madrid, Spain (WBC)
25.02.78 Carlos Zarate W RSC 8 Albert Davila, Los Angeles, USA (WBC)
18.03.78 Jorge Lujan W RTD 11 Roberto Rubaldino, San Antonio, USA (WBA)
22.04.78 Carlos Zarate W RSC 13 Andres Hernandez, San Juan, Puerto Rico (WBC)
09.06.78 Carlos Zarate W CO 4 Emilio Hernandez, Las Vegas, USA (WBC)
15.09.78 Jorge Lujan W PTS 15 Albert Davila, New Orleans, USA (WBA)
10.03.79 Carlos Zarate W CO 3 Mensah Kpalongo, Los Angeles, USA (WBC)
08.04.79 Jorge Lujan W RSC 15 Cleo Garcia, Las Vegas, USA (WBA)
02.06.79 Lupe Pintor W PTS 15 Carlos Zarate, Las Vegas, USA (WBC)
06.10.79 Jorge Lujan W CO 15 Roberto Rubaldino, McAllen, USA (WBA)
09.02.80 Lupe Pintor W RSC 12 Alberto Sandoval, Los Angeles, USA (WBC)
02.04.80 Jorge Lujan W RSC 9 Shuichi Isogami, Tokyo, Japan (WBA)
11.06.80 Lupe Pintor DREW 15 Eijiro Murata, Tokyo, Japan (WBC)
29.08.80 Julian Solis W PTS 15 Jorge Lujan, Miami, USA (WBA)
19.09.80 Lupe Pintor W CO 12 Johnny Owen, Los Angeles, USA (WBC)
14.11.80 Jeff Chandler W RSC 14 Julian Solis, Miami, USA (WBA)
19.12.80 Lupe Pintor W PTS 15 Albert Davila, Las Vegas, USA (WBC)
31.01.81 Jeff Chandler W PTS 15 Jorge Lujan, Philadelphia, USA (WBA)
22.02.81 Lupe Pintor W PTS 15 Jose Uziga, Houston, USA (WBC)
05.04.81 Jeff Chandler DREW 15 Eijiro Murata, Tokyo, Japan (WBA)
25.07.81 Jeff Chandler W CO 7 Julian Solis, Atlantic C, USA (WBA)
26.07.81 Lupe Pintor W RSC 8 Jovito Rengifo, Las Vegas, USA (WBC)
22.09.81 Lupe Pintor W CO 15 Hurricane Teru, Nagoya, Japan (WBC)
10.12.81 Jeff Chandler W RSC 13 Eijiro Murata, Atlantic C, USA (WBA)
27.03.82 Jeff Chandler W RSC 6 Johnny Carter, Philadelphia, USA (WBA)
03.06.82 Lupe Pintor W RSC 11 Seung-Hoon Lee, Los Angeles, USA (WBC)
Lupe Pintor forfeited WBC recognition (unable to defend due to a motorcycle accident)
27.10.82 Jeff Chandler W RSC 9 Miguel Iriarle, Atlantic C, USA (WBA)
13.03.83 Jeff Chandler W PTS 15 Gaby Canizales, Atlantic C, USA (WBA)
01.09.83 Albert Davila W CO 12 Kiko Bejines, Los Angeles, USA (WBC)
11.09.83 Jeff Chandler W RSC 10 Eijiro Murata, Tokyo, Japan (WBA)
17.12.83 Jeff Chandler W RSC 7 Oscar Muniz, Atlantic C, USA (WBA)
07.04.84 Richard Sandoval W RSC 15 Jeff Chandler, Atlantic C, USA (WBA)
16.04.84 Satoshi Shingaki W RSC 8 Elmer Magallano, Kashiwara, Japan (IBF)
26.05.84 Albert Davila W RSC 11 Enrique Sanchez, Miami, USA (WBC)
Albert Davila relinquished WBC version of title (back injury)
04.08.84 Satoshi Shingaki W PTS 15 Joves de la Puz, Naha C, Japan (IBF)
22.09.84 Richard Sandoval W PTS 15 Edgar Roman, Monte Carlo (WBA)
15.12.84 Richard Sandoval W RSC 8 Cardenio Ulloa, Miami, USA (WBA)
26.04.85 Jeff Fenech W RSC 9 Satoshi Shingaki, Sydney, Australia (IBF)
04.05.85 Daniel Zaragoza W DIS 7 Fred Jackson, Aruba, DWI (WBC)
09.08.85 Miguel Lora W PTS 12 Daniel Zaragoza, Miami, USA (WBC)
23.08.85 Jeff Fenech W CO 3 Satoshi Shingaki, Sydney, Australia (IBF)
02.12.85 Jeff Fenech W PTS 15 Jerome Coffee, Sydney, Australia (IBF)
08.02.86 Miguel Lora W PTS 12 Wilfredo Vasquez, Miami, USA (WBC)
10.03.86 Gaby Canizales W RSC 7 Richard Sandoval, Las Vegas, USA (WBA)
04.06.86 Bernardo Pinango W PTS 15 Gaby Canizales, E Rutherford, USA (WBA)
18.07.86 Jeff Fenech W RSC 14 Steve McCrory, Sydney, Australia (IBF)
Jeff Fenech relinquished title (challenged for the WBC S. bantamweight title)
23.08.86 Miguel Lora W RSC 6 Enrique Sanchez, Miami, USA (WBC)
04.10.86 Bernardo Pinango W RSC 10 Ciro de Leva, Turin, Italy (WBA)
15.11.86 Miguel Lora W PTS 12 Albert Davila, Barranquilla, Colombia (WBC)
22.11.86 Bernardo Pinango W RSC 15 Simon Skosana, Johannesburg, S Africa (WBA)
03.02.87 Bernardo Pinango W PTS 15 Frankie Duarte, Los Angeles, USA (WBA)
Bernardo Pinango relinquished title (retired)
29.03.87 Takuya Muguruma W CO 5 Azael Moran, Moriguchi, Japan (WBA)
15.05.87 Kelvin Seabrooks W CO 5 Miguel Maturana, Cartagena, Columbia (IBF)
24.05.87 Chan-Yung Park W RSC 11 Takuya Muguruma, Moriguchi, Japan (WBA)
04.07.87 Kelvin Seabrooks NC 9 Thierry Jacob, Calais, France (IBF)
25.07.87 Miguel Lora W RSC 4 Antonio Avelar, Miami, USA (WBC)
04.10.87 Wilfredo Vasquez W RSC 10 Chan-Yung Park, Seoul, S Korea (WBA)
18.11.87 Kelvin Seabrooks W RSC 4 Ernie Cataluna, San Cataldo, Italy (IBF)
27.11.87 Miguel Lora W PTS 12 Ray Minus, Miami, USA (WBC)
17.01.88 Wilfredo Vasquez DREW 12 Takuya Muguruma, Osaka, Japan (WBA)
06.02.88 Kelvin Seabrooks W RSC 2 Fernando Beltran, Paris, France (IBF)
30.04.88 Miguel Lora W PTS 12 Lucio Lopez, Cartagena, Colombia (WBC)

Super-Bantamweight (122 lbs)

Title Holders

	Birthplace	Tenure	Status
Jack Kid Wolfe	USA	1922 – 1923	NY
Rigoberto Riasco	Panama	1976	WBC
Royal Kobayashi	Japan	1976	WBC
Dong-Kyun Yum	S Korea	1976 – 1977	WBC

Wilfredo Gomez *	Puerto Rico	1977 – 1983	WBC
Soo-Hwan Hong	S Korea	1977 – 1978	WBA
Ricardo Cardona	Colombia	1978 – 1980	WBA
Leo Randolph	USA	1980	WBA
Sergio Palma	Argentine	1980 – 1982	WBA
Leonardo Cruz	Dom Republic	1982 – 1984	WBA
Jaime Garza	USA	1983 – 1984	WBC
Bobby Berna	Philippines	1983 – 1984	IBF
Loris Stecca	Italy	1984	WBA
Seung-In Suh	S Korea	1984 – 1985	IBF
Victor Callejas	Puerto Rico	1984 – 1986	WBA
Juan Meza	Mexico	1984 – 1985	WBC
Ji-Won Kim *	S Korea	1985 – 1986	IBF
Lupe Pintor	Mexico	1985 – 1986	WBC
Samart Payakarun	Thailand	1986 – 1987	WBC
Louie Espinosa	USA	1987	WBA
Seung-Hoon Lee *	S Korea	1987 – 1988	IBF
Jeff Fenech *	Australia	1987 – 1988	WBC
Juan Gervacio	Dom Republic	1987 – 1988	WBA
Bernardo Pinango	Venezuela	1988 –	WBA
Daniel Zaragoza	Mexico	1988 –	WBC

Title Bouts

21.09.22 Jack Kid Wolfe W PTS 15 Joe Lynch, New York C, USA (NY)
Jack Kid Wolfe ceased to be recognised by NY (overweight for defence against Carl Duane – title fell into disuse)
03.04.76 Rigoberto Riasco W RTD 8 Waruinge Nakayama, Panama C, Panama (WBC)
12.06.76 Rigoberto Riasco W CO 10 Livio Nolasco, Panama C, Panama (WBC)
01.08.76 Rigoberto Riasco W PTS 15 Dong-Kyun Yum, Pusan, S Korea (WBC)
10.10.76 Royal Kobayashi W RSC 8 Rigoberto Riasco, Tokyo, Japan (WBC)
24.11.76 Dong-Kyun Yum W PTS 15 Royal Kobayashi, Seoul, S Korea (WBC)
13.02.77 Dong-Kyun Yum W PTS 15 Jose Cervantes, Seoul, S Korea (WBC)
21.05.77 Wilfredo Gomez W CO 12 Dong-Kyun Yum, San Juan, Puerto Rico (WBC)
11.07.77 Wilfredo Gomez W CO 5 Raol Tirado, San Juan, Puerto Rico (WBC)
26.11.77 Soo-Hwan Hong W CO 3 Hector Carrasquilla, Panama C, Panama (WBA)
19.01.78 Wilfredo Gomez W CO 3 Royal Kobayashi, Kitakyushu, Japan (WBC)
01.02.78 Soo-Hwan Hong W PTS 15 Yu Kasahara, Tokyo, Japan (WBA)
08.04.78 Wilfredo Gomez W RSC 7 Juan Antonio Lopez, Bayamon, Puerto Rico (WBC)
06.05.78 Ricardo Cardona W RSC 12 Soo-Hwan Hong, Seoul, S Korea (WBA)
02.06.78 Wilfredo Gomez W RSC 3 Sakad Petchyindee, Korat, Thailand (WBC)
02.09.78 Ricardo Cardona W PTS 15 Ruben Valdez, Cartagena, Colombia (WBA)
09.09.78 Wilfredo Gomez W RSC 13 Leonardo Cruz, San Juan, Puerto Rico (WBC)
28.10.78 Wilfredo Gomez W RSC 5 Carlos Zarate, San Juan, Puerto Rico (WBC)
12.11.78 Ricardo Cardona W PTS 15 Soon-Hyun Chung, Seoul, S Korea (WBA)
09.03.79 Wilfredo Gomez W RSC 5 Nestor Jimenez, New York C, USA (WBC)
16.06.79 Wilfredo Gomez W RSC 5 Jesus Hernandez, San Juan, Puerto Rico (WBC)
23.06.79 Ricardo Cardona W PTS 15 Soon-Hyun Chung, Seoul, S Korea (WBA)
06.09.79 Ricardo Cardona W PTS 15 Yukio Segawa, Hachinhoe, Japan (WBA)
28.09.79 Wilfredo Gomez W RSC 10 Carlos Mendoza, Las Vegas, USA (WBC)
26.10.79 Wilfredo Gomez W RSC 5 Nicky Perez, New York C, USA (WBC)
15.12.79 Ricardo Cardona W PTS 15 Sergio Palma, Barranquilla, Colombia (WBA)
03.02.80 Wilfredo Gomez W RTD 6 Ruben Valdez, Las Vegas, USA (WBC)
04.05.80 Leo Randolph W RSC 15 Ricardo Cardona, Seattle, USA (WBA)
09.08.80 Sergio Palma W CO 6 Leo Randolph, Washington, USA (WBA)
22.08.80 Wilfredo Gomez W RSC 5 Derrick Holmes, Las Vegas, USA (WBC)
08.11.80 Sergio Palma W RSC 9 Ulisses Morales, Bs Aires, Argentine (WBA)
13.12.80 Wilfredo Gomez W CO 3 Jose Cervantes, Miami, USA (WBC)
04.04.81 Sergio Palma W PTS 15 Leonardo Cruz, Bs Aires, Argentine (WBA)
15.08.81 Sergio Palma W RSC 12 Ricardo Cardona, Bs Aires, Argentine (WBA)
03.10.81 Sergio Palma W PTS 15 Vichit Muangroi-et, Bs Aires, Argentine (WBA)
15.01.82 Sergio Palma W PTS 15 Jorge Lujan, Cordoba, Argentine (WBA)
27.03.82 Wilfredo Gomez W RSC 6 Juan Meza, Atlantic C, USA (WBC)
11.06.82 Wilfredo Gomez W CO 10 Juan Antonio Lopez, Las Vegas, USA (WBC)
12.06.82 Leonardo Cruz W PTS 15 Sergio Palma, Miami, USA (WBA)
18.08.82 Wilfredo Gomez W RTD 7 Roberto Rubaldino, San Juan, Puerto Rico (WBC)
13.11.82 Leonardo Cruz W CO 8 Benito Badilla, San Juan, Puerto Rico (WBA)
03.12.82 Wilfredo Gomez W RSC 14 Lupe Pintor, New Orleans, USA (WBC)
Wilfredo Gomez relinquished WBC version of title (moved up to featherweight)
16.03.83 Leonardo Cruz W PTS 15 Soon-Hyun Chung, San Juan, Puerto Rico (WBA)
15.06.83 Jaime Garza W RSC 2 Bobby Berna, Los Angeles, USA (WBC)
26.08.83 Leonardo Cruz W PTS 15 Cleo Garcia, St Domingo, Dom Republic (WBA)
04.12.83 Bobby Berna W RTD 11 Seung-In Suh, Seoul, S Korea (IBF)
22.02.84 Loris Stecca W RSC 12 Leonardo Cruz, Milan, Italy (WBA)
15.04.84 Seung-In Suh W CO 10 Bobby Berna, Seoul, S Korea (IBF)
26.05.84 Jaime Garza W CO 3 Felipe Orozco, Miami, USA (WBC)
26.05.84 Victor Callejas W RSC 8 Loris Stecca, Guaynabo, Puerto Rico (WBA)
08.07.84 Seung-In Suh W CO 4 Cleo Garcia, Seoul, S Korea (IBF)
03.11.84 Juan Meza W CO 1 Jaime Garza, Kingston NY, USA (WBC)
03.01.85 Ji-Won Kim W CO 10 Seung-In Suh, Seoul, S Korea (IBF)
02.02.85 Victor Callejas W PTS 15 Seung-Hoon Lee, San Juan, Puerto Rico (WBA)
30.03.85 Ji-Won Kim W PTS 15 Ruben Palacios, Suwon, S Korea (IBF)
19.04.85 Juan Meza W RSC 6 Mike Ayala, Los Angeles, USA (WBC)
28.06.85 Ji-Won Kim W CO 4 Bobby Berna, Pusan, S Korea (IBF)
18.08.85 Lupe Pintor W PTS 12 Juan Meza, Mexico C, Mexico (WBC)
09.10.85 Ji-Won Kim W CO 1 Seung-In Suh, Seoul, S Korea (IBF)
08.11.85 Victor Callejas W RTD 6 Loris Stecca, Rimini, Italy (WBA)
Victor Callejas forfeited WBA recognition (failure to defend against Louie Espinosa)
18.01.86 Samart Payakarun W CO 5 Lupe Pintor, Bangkok, Thailand (WBC)
01.06.86 Ji-Won Kim W CO 2 Rudy Casicas, Inchon, S Korea (IBF)
Ji-Won Kim relinquished title (retired)
10.12.86 Samart Payakarun W CO 12 Juan Meza, Bangkok, Thailand (WBC)
16.01.87 Louie Espinosa W RSC 4 Tommy Valoy, Phoenix, USA (WBA)
18.01.87 Seung-Hoon Lee W CO 9 Prayoonsak Muangsurin, Pohang, S Korea (IBF)
05.04.87 Seung-Hoon Lee W CO 10 Jorge Urbina Diaz, Seoul, S Korea (IBF)
08.05.87 Jeff Fenech W RSC 4 Samart Payakarun, Sydney, Australia (WBC)
10.07.87 Jeff Fenech W RTD 5 Greg Richardson, Sydney, Australia (WBC)
15.07.87 Louie Espinosa W RSC 15 Manuel Vilchez, Phoenix, USA (WBA)
19.07.87 Seung-Hoon Lee W CO 5 Lion Collins, Seoul, S Korea (IBF)
15.08.87 Louie Espinosa W CO 9 Mike Ayala, San Antonio, USA (WBA)
16.10.87 Jeff Fenech W TD 4 Carlos Zarate, Sydney, Australia (WBC)
Jeff Fenech relinquished WBC version of title (weight making difficulties)
28.11.87 Juan Gervacio W PTS 12 Louie Espinosa, San Juan, Puerto Rico (WBA)
27.12.87 Seung-Hoon Lee W PTS 15 Jose Sanabria, Pohang, S Korea (IBF)
Seung-Hoon Lee relinquished IBF version of title (aiming to challenge for either the WBA/WBC titles)
27.02.88 Bernardo Pinango W PTS 12 Juan Gervacio, San Juan, Puerto Rico (WBA)
29.02.88 Daniel Zaragoza W RSC 10 Carlos Zarate, Los Angeles, USA (WBC)

Featherweight (126 lbs)

Title Holders

	Birthplace	Tenure	Status
George Dixon	Canada	1890 – 1897	
Solly Smith	USA	1897 – 1898	USA
Ben Jordan	England	1898 – 1899	GB
Dave Sullivan	Ireland	1898	USA
George Dixon	Canada	1898 – 1899	USA
George Dixon	Canada	1899 – 1900	
Terry McGovern	USA	1900 – 1901	
Young Corbett II	USA	1901 – 1903	
Abe Attell	USA	1903 – 1904	
Tommy Sullivan	USA	1904 – 1905	
Abe Attell	USA	1906 – 1912	
Abe Attell	USA	1912	USA
Jim Driscoll	Wales	1912 – 1913	GB/IBU
Johnny Kilbane	USA	1912 – 1913	USA
Johnny Kilbane	USA	1913 – 1923	
Johnny Dundee	Italy	1922 – 1923	NY
Eugene Criqui	France	1923	
Johnny Dundee *	Italy	1923 – 1924	
Kid Kaplan *	Russia	1925 – 1926	
Honeyboy Finnegan	USA	1926 – 1927	MASS
Benny Bass	Russia	1927 – 1928	NBA
Tony Canzoneri	USA	1927 – 1928	NY
Tony Canzoneri	USA	1928	
Andre Routis	France	1928 – 1929	
Bat Battalino	USA	1929 – 1932	
Tommy Paul	USA	1932 – 1933	NBA
Kid Chocolate	Cuba	1932 – 1933	NY
Freddie Miller	USA	1933 – 1936	NBA
Baby Arizmendi	Mexico	1934 – 1935	NY
Baby Arizmendi	Mexico	1935 – 1936	CALIF
Mike Belloise	USA	1936	NY
Petey Sarron	USA	1936 – 1937	NBA
Henry Armstrong	USA	1936 – 1937	CALIF
Henry Armstrong *	USA	1937 – 1938	NBA/NY
Maurice Holtzer	France	1937 – 1938	IBU
Leo Rodak	USA	1938 – 1939	NBA
Joey Archibald	USA	1938 – 1939	NY
Joey Archibald	USA	1939 – 1940	
Joey Archibald	USA	1940	NY
Jimmy Perrin	USA	1940	LOUIS
Petey Scalzo	USA	1940 – 1941	NBA
Harry Jeffra	USA	1940 – 1941	NY
Joey Archibald	USA	1941	NY
Richie Lemos	USA	1941	NBA
Chalky Wright	Mexico	1941 – 1942	NY
Harry Jeffra	USA	1941 – 1942	MARY
Jackie Wilson	USA	1941 – 1943	NBA
Willie Pep	USA	1942 – 1946	NY
Jackie Callura	Canada	1943	NBA
Phil Terranova	USA	1943 – 1944	NBA
Sal Bartolo	USA	1944 – 1946	NBA
Willie Pep	USA	1946 – 1948	
Sandy Saddler	USA	1948 – 1949	
Willie Pep	USA	1949 – 1950	
Sandy Saddler *	USA	1950 – 1957	
Hogan Kid Bassey	Nigeria	1957 – 1959	
Davey Moore	USA	1959 – 1963	
Sugar Ramos	Cuba	1963 – 1964	
Vicente Saldivar *	Mexico	1964 – 1967	
Raul Rojas	USA	1967 – 1968	WBA
Howard Winstone	Wales	1968	WBC
Jose Legra	Cuba	1968 – 1969	WBC
Shozo Saijyo	Japan	1968 – 1971	WBA
Johnny Famechon	France	1969 – 1970	WBC

Vicente Saldivar	Mexico	1970	WBC
Kuniaki Shibata	Japan	1970 – 1972	WBC
Antonio Gomez	Venezuela	1971 – 1972	WBA
Clemente Sanchez	Mexico	1972	WBC
Ernesto Marcel *	Panama	1972 – 1974	WBA
Jose Legra	Cuba	1972 – 1973	WBC
Eder Jofre	Brazil	1973 – 1974	WBC
Ruben Olivares	Mexico	1974	WBA
Bobby Chacon	USA	1974 – 1975	WBC
Alexis Arguello *	Nicaragua	1974 – 1977	WBA
Ruben Olivares	Mexico	1975	WBC
David Kotey	Ghana	1975 – 1976	WBC
Danny Lopez	USA	1976 – 1980	WBC
Rafael Ortega	Panama	1977	WBA
Cecilio Lastra	Spain	1977 – 1978	WBA
Eusebio Pedroza	Panama	1978 – 1985	WBA
Salvador Sanchez *	Mexico	1980 – 1982	WBC
Juan Laporte	Puerto Rico	1982 – 1984	WBC
Min-Keun Chung	S Korea	1984 – 1985	IBF
Wilfredo Gomez	Puerto Rico	1984	WBC
Azumah Nelson *	Ghana	1984 – 1988	WBC
Barry McGuigan	Ireland	1985 – 1986	WBA
Ki-Yung Chung	S Korea	1985 – 1986	IBF
Steve Cruz	USA	1986 – 1987	WBA
Antonio Rivera	Puerto Rico	1986 – 1988	IBF
Antonio Esparragoza	Venezuela	1987 –	WBA
Calvin Grove	USA	1988 –	IBF
Jeff Fenech	Australia	1988 –	WBC

Title Bouts

27.06.90 George Dixon W RTD 18 Nunc Wallace, London, England
23.10.90 George Dixon W RSC 40 Johnny Murphy, Prodivence, USA
31.03.91 George Dixon W RSC 22 Cal McCarthy, Troy, USA
28.07.91 George Dixon W CO 5 Abe Willis, San Francisco, USA
27.06.92 George Dixon W CO 14 Fred Johnson, New York C, USA
06.09.92 George Dixon W CO 8 Jack Skelly, New Orleans, USA
07.08.93 George Dixon W CO 3 Eddie Pierce, New York C, USA
25.09.93 George Dixon W CO 7 Solly Smith, New York C, USA
27.08.95 George Dixon W PTS 25 Johnny Griffin, Boston, USA
05.12.95 George Dixon DREW 10 Frank Erne, New York C, USA
17.03.96 George Dixon W 8 Jerry Marshall, Boston, USA
16.06.96 George Dixon DREW 20 Martin Flaherty, Boston, USA
25.09.96 George Dixon DREW 20 Tommy White, New York C, USA
22.01.97 George Dixon W CO 6 Billy Murphy, New York C, USA
15.02.97 George Dixon DREW 20 Jack Downey, New York C, USA
26.04.97 George Dixon W PTS 20 Johnny Griffin, New York C, USA
23.07.97 George Dixon DREW 20 Dal Hawkins, San Francisco, USA
04.10.97 Solly Smith W PTS 20 George Dixon, San Francisco, USA (USA)
01.07.98 Ben Jordan W PTS 25 George Dixon, New York C, USA (GB)
07.07.98 Solly Smith W DIS 7 Billy O'Donnell, Buffalo, USA (USA)
01.08.98 Solly Smith DREW 25 Tommy White, New York C, USA (USA)
26.09.98 Dave Sullivan W RTD 5 Solly Smith, New York C, USA (USA)
11.11.98 George Dixon W DIS 10 Dave Sullivan, New York C, USA (USA)
29.11.98 George Dixon W PTS 25 Oscar Gardner, New York C, USA (USA)
17.01.99 George Dixon W CO 10 Young Pluto, New York C, USA (USA)
15.05.99 George Dixon W PTS 20 Kid Broad, Buffalo, USA (USA)
29.05.99 Ben Jordan W CO 9 Harry Greenfield, London, England (GB)
Ben Jordan ceased to be recognised by GB (this followed a defeat by Eddie Santry in October, 1899)
02.06.99 George Dixon W PTS 25 Joe Bernstein, New York C, USA (USA)
11.07.99 George Dixon W PTS 20 Tommy White, Denver, USA (USA)
11.08.99 George Dixon DREW 20 Eddie Santry, New York C, USA (USA)
02.11.99 George Dixon W PTS 25 Will Curley, New York C, USA
21.11.99 George Dixon W PTS 25 Eddie Lenny, New York C, USA
09.01.00 Terry McGovern W RSC 9 George Dixon, New York C, USA
01.02.00 Terry McGovern W CO 5 Eddie Santry, Chicago, USA
09.03.00 Terry McGovern W CO 3 Oscar Gardner, New York C, USA
12.06.00 Terry McGovern W CO 3 Tommy White, New York C, USA
02.11.00 Terry McGovern W CO 7 Joe Bernstein, Louisville, USA
30.04.01 Terry McGovern W CO 4 Oscar Gardner, San Francisco, USA
29.05.01 Terry McGovern W CO 5 Aurelio Herrera, San Francisco, USA
28.11.01 Young Corbett W CO 2 Terry McGovern, Hartford, USA
16.10.02 Young Corbett II W RTD 8 Joe Bernstein, Baltimore, USA
14.01.03 Young Corbett II W 18 Austin Rice, Hot Springs, USA
26.02.03 Young Corbett II DREW 20 Eddie Hanlon, San Francisco, USA
31.03.03 Young Corbett II W CO 11 Terry McGovern, San Francisco, USA
Young Corbett II lost general recognition (weight making difficulties)
03.09.03 Abe Attell W PTS 20 Johnny Reagan, St Louis, USA
01.02.04 Abe Attell W RSC 5 Harry Forbes, St Louis, USA
23.06.04 Abe Attell W PTS 20 Johnny Reagan, St Louis, USA
13.10.04 Tommy Sullivan W CO 5 Abe Attell, St Louis, USA
Tommy Sullivan forfeited title (inactivity)
22.02.06 Abe Attell W PTS 15 Jimmy Walsh, Chelsea, Mass, USA
15.03.06 Abe Attell W DIS 3 Tony Moran, Baltimore, USA
11.05.06 Abe Attell DREW 20 Kid Herman, Los Angeles, USA
04.07.06 Abe Attell W PTS 20 Frankie Neil, Los Angeles, USA
30.10.06 Abe Attell W PTS 20 Harry Baker, Los Angeles, USA
16.11.06 Abe Attell W PTS 15 Billy de Coursey, San Diego, USA
07.12.06 Abe Attell W CO 8 Jimmy Walsh, Los Angeles, USA
18.01.07 Abe Attell W CO 8 Harry Baker, Los Angeles, USA
24.05.07 Abe Attell W PTS 20 Kid Solomon, Los Angeles, USA
29.10.07 Abe Attell W CO 4 Freddie Weeks, Los Angeles, USA
01.01.08 Abe Attell DREW 25 Owen Moran, San Francisco, USA
31.01.08 Abe Attell W RTD 13 Frankie Neil, San Francisco, USA
28.02.08 Abe Attell W CO 7 Eddie Kelly, San Francisco, USA
30.04.08 Abe Attell W CO 4 Tommy Sullivan, San Francisco, USA
07.09.08 Abe Attell DREW 23 Owen Moran, San Francisco, USA
14.01.09 Abe Attell W CO 10 Freddie Weeks, Goldfield, USA
04.02.09 Abe Attell W CO 7 Eddie Kelly, New Orleans, USA
26.03.09 Abe Attell W CO 8 Frankie White, Dayton, USA
28.02.10 Abe Attell W CO 6 Harry Forbes, New York C, USA
22.08.10 Abe Attell W CO 3 Eddie Marino, Calgary, Canda
05.09.10 Abe Attell W CO 17 Billy Lauder, Calgary, Canada
24.10.10 Abe Attell W PTS 10 Johnny Kilbane, Kansas City, USA
13.11.10 Abe Attell DREW 15 Frankie Conley, New Orleans, USA
Abe Attell forfeited GB/IBU recognition (failure to defend against Driscoll)
22.02.12 Johnny Kilbane W PTS 20 Abe Attell, Los Angeles, USA (USA)
21.05.12 Johnny Kilbane DREW 12 Jimmy Walsh, Boston, USA (USA)
03.06.12 Jim Driscoll W CO 12 Jean Poesy, London, England (GB/IBU)
14.10.12 Johnny Kilbane W PTS 12 Eddie O'Keefe, Cleveland, USA (USA)
03.12.12 Johnny Kilbane W RSC 8 Monte Attell, Cleveland, USA (USA)
27.01.13 Jim Driscoll DREW 20 Owen Moran, London, England (GB/IBU)
Jim Driscoll ceased to be recognised by the IBU/GB (he relinquished the European featherweight title in July 1913)
29.04.13 Johnny Kilbane DREW 20 Johnny Dundee, Los Angeles, USA (USA)
16.09.13 Johnny Kilbane W PTS 12 Jimmy Walsh, Boston, USA
04.09.16 Johnny Kilbane W CO 3 K. O. Chaney, Cedar Point, USA
26.03.17 Johnny Kilbane DREW 12 Eddie Wallace, Bridgeport, USA
21.04.20 Johnny Kilbane W CO 7 Alvie Miller, Lorain, USA
17.08.21 Johnny Kilbane W CO 7 Danny Frush, Cleveland, USA
15.08.22 Johnny Dundee W CO 9 Danny Frush, New York C, USA (NY)
02.06.23 Eugene Criqui W CO 6 Johnny Kilbane, New York C, USA
26.07.23 Johnny Dundee W PTS 15 Eugene Criqui, New York C, USA
Johnny Dundee relinquished title (moved up to super-featherweight)
02.01.25 Kid Kaplan W RTD 9 Danny Kramer, New York C, USA
27.08.25 Kid Kaplan DREW 15 Babe Herman, Waterbury, USA
18.12.25 Kid Kaplan W PTS 15 Babe Herman, New York C, USA
28.06.26 Kid Kaplan W CO 10 Bobby Garcia, Hartford, USA
Kid Kaplan relinquished title (weight making difficulties)
15.11.26 Honeyboy Finnegan W PTS 10 Chick Suggs, Boston, USA (MASS)
Honeyboy Finnegan ceased to be recognised by Massachusetts (unable to make the weight any longer)
12.09.27 Benny Bass W PTS 10 Red Chapman, Philadelphia, USA (NBA)
24.10.27 Tony Canzoneri W PTS 15 Johnny Dundee, New York C, USA (NY)
10.02.28 Tony Canzoneri W PTS 15 Benny Bass, New York C, USA
28.09.28 Andre Routis W PTS 15 Tony Canzoneri, New York C, USA
27.05.29 Andre Routis W RSC 3 Buster Brown, Baltimore, USA
23.09.29 Bat Battalino W PTS 15 Andre Routis, Hartford, USA
15.07.30 Bat Battalino W CO 5 Ignacio Fernandez, Hartford, USA
12.12.30 Bat Battalino W PTS 15 Kid Chocolate, New York C, USA
22.05.31 Bat Battalino W PTS 15 Fidel la Barba, New York C, USA
01.07.31 Bat Battalino W PTS 10 Bobby Brady, Jersey C, USA
23.07.31 Bat Battalino W PTS 10 Freddie Miller, Cincinnati, USA
04.11.31 Bat Battalino W PTS 10 Earl Maestro, Chicago, USA
Bat Battalino forfeited title (overweight for a defence against Freddie Miller)
26.05.32 Tommy Paul W PTS 10 Johnny Pena, Detroit, USA (NBA)
13.10.32 Kid Chocolate W CO 12 Lew Feldman, New York C, USA (NY)
09.12.32 Kid Chocolate W PTS 15 Fidel la Barba, New York C, USA (NY)
13.01.33 Freddie Miller W PTS 10 Tommy Paul, Chicago, USA (NBA)
28.02.33 Freddie Miller W PTS 10 Baby Arizmendi, Los Angeles, USA (NBA)
21.03.33 Freddie Miller W PTS 10 Speedy Dado, Los Angeles, USA (NBA)
19.05.33 Kid Chocolate W PTS 15 Seaman Tommy Watson, New York C, USA (NY)
Kid Chocolate forfeited NY recognition (failure to defend against Frankie Klick)
01.01.34 Freddie Miller W PTS 10 Jackie Sharkey, Cincinnati, USA (NBA)
30.08.34 Baby Arizmendi W PTS 15 Mike Belloise, New York C, USA (NY)
Baby Arizmendi forfeited NY recognition (He contested the Californian version without NY authority)
21.09.34 Freddie Miller W PTS 15 Nel Tarleton, Liverpool, England (NBA)
01.01.35 Baby Arizmendi W PTS 12 Henry Armstrong, Mexico C, Mexico (CALIF)
17.02.35 Freddie Miller W CO 1 Jose Girones, Barcelona, Spain (NBA)
12.06.35 Freddie Miller W PTS 15 Nel Tarleton, Liverpool, England (NBA)
22.10.35 Freddie Miller W PTS 15 Vernon Cormier, Boston, USA (NBA)
18.02.36 Freddie Miller W PTS 12 Johnny Pena, Seattle, USA (NBA)
02.03.36 Freddie Miller W PTS 15 Petey Sarron, Miami, USA (NBA)
11.05.36 Petey Sarron W PTS 15 Freddie Miller, Washington, USA (NBA)
22.07.36 Petey Sarron W PTS 15 Baby Manuel, Dallas, USA (NBA)
04.08.36 Henry Armstrong W PTS 10 Baby Arizmendi, Los Angeles, USA (CALIF)
03.09.36 Mike Belloise W CO 9 Dave Crowley, New York C, USA (NY)
Mike Belloise ceased to be recognised by NY (this followed the defeat by Henry Armstrong for the Californian title claim)
27.10.36 Henry Armstrong W PTS 10 Mike Belloise, Los Angeles, USA (CALIF)
04.09.37 Petey Sarron W PTS 12 Freddie Miller, Johannesburg, S Africa (NBA)
05.10.37 Maurice Holtzer W PTS 15 Phil Dolhem, Algiers, Algeria (IBU)
29.10.37 Henry Armstrong W CO 6 Petey Sarron, New York C, USA (NY/NBA)
Henry Armstrong relinquished NY/NBA version of title (he began to campaign in a higher weight division)

19.02.38 Maurice Holtzer DREW 15 Maurice Dubois, Geneva, Switzerland (IBU)
Maurice Holtzer ceased to be recognised by the IBU (he relinquished the EBU featherweight title in July, 1938)
17.06.38 Leo Rodak W PTS 15 Jackie Wilson, Baltimore, USA (NBA)
17.10.38 Joey Archibald W PTS 15 Mike Belloise, New York C, USA (NY)
24.10.38 Leo Rodak W PTS 15 Freddie Miller, Washington, USA (NBA)
18.04.39 Joey Archibald W PTS 15 Leo Rodak, Providence, USA
Joey Archibald forfeited NBA recognition (refused to defend against Petey Scalzo)
28.09.39 Joey Archibald W PTS 15 Harry Jeffra, Washington, USA (NY)
08.05.40 Jimmy Perrin W PTS 15 Bobby Ruffin, New Orleans, USA (LOUIS)
Jimmy Perrin ceased to be recognised by Louisiana (this followed a defeat by Petey Scalzo in a non-title bout, August, 1940)
15.05.40 Petey Scalzo W CO 6 Frankie Covelli, Washington, USA (NBA)
20.05.40 Harry Jeffra W PTS 15 Joey Archibald, Baltimore, USA (NY)
10.07.40 Petey Scalzo W RSC 15 Bobby Poison Ivy, Hartford, USA (NBA)
29.07.40 Harry Jeffra W PTS 15 Spider Armstrong, Baltimore, USA (NY)
12.05.41 Joey Archibald W PTS 15 Harry Jeffra, Washington, USA (NY)
19.05.41 Petey Scalzo W PTS 15 Phil Zwick, Milwaukee, USA (NBA)
01.07.41 Richie Lemos W CO 5 Petey Scalzo, Los Angeles, USA (NBA)
11.09.41 Chalky Wright W CO 11 Joey Archibald, Washington, USA (NY)
15.09.41 Harry Jeffra W PTS 12 Lou Transparenti, Baltimore, USA (MARY)
18.11.41 Jackie Wilson W PTS 12 Richie Lemos, Los Angeles, USA (NBA)
16.12.41 Jackie Wilson W PTS 12 Richie Lemos, Los Angeles, USA (NBA)
19.06.42 Chalky Wright W RSC 10 Harry Jeffra, Baltimore, USA (NY)
25.09.42 Chalky Wright W PTS 15 Lulu Constantino, New York C, USA (NY)
20.11.42 Willie Pep W PTS 15 Chalky Wright, New York C, USA (NY)
18.01.43 Jackie Callura W PTS 15 Jackie Wilson, Providence, USA (NBA)
18.03.43 Jackie Callura W PTS 15 Jackie Wilson, Boston, USA (NBA)
08.06.43 Willie Pep W PTS 15 Sal Bartolo, Boston, USA (NY)
16.08.43 Phil Terranova W CO 8 Jackie Callura, New Orleans, USA (NBA)
27.12.43 Phil Terranova W RSC 6 Jackie Callura, New Orleans, USA (NBA)
10.03.44 Sal Bartolo W PTS 15 Phil Terranova, Boston, USA (NBA)
05.05.44 Sal Bartolo W PTS 15 Phil Terranova, Boston, USA (NBA)
29.09.44 Willie Pep W PTS 15 Chalky Wright, New York C, USA (NY)
15.12.44 Sal Bartolo W PTS 15 Willie Roache, Boston, USA (NBA)
19.02.45 Willie Pep W PTS 15 Phil Terranova, New York C, USA (NY)
03.05.46 Sal Bartolo W CO 6 Spider Armstrong, Boston, USA (NBA)
07.06.46 Willie Pep W CO 12 Sal Bartolo, New York C, USA
22.08.47 Willie Pep W CO 12 Jock Leslie, Flint, USA
24.02.48 Willie Pep W RSC 10 Humberto Sierra, Miami, USA
29.10.48 Sandy Saddler W CO 4 Willie Pep, New York C, USA
11.02.49 Willie Pep W PTS 15 Sandy Saddler, New York C, USA
20.09.49 Willie Pep W RSC 7 Eddie Compo, Waterbury, USA
16.01.50 Willie Pep W CO 5 Charley Riley, St Louis, USA
17.03.50 Willie Pep W PTS 15 Ray Famechon, New York C, USA
08.09.50 Sandy Saddler W RTD 8 Willie Pep, New York C, USA
26.09.51 Sandy Saddler W RTD 9 Willie Pep, New York C, USA
25.02.55 Sandy Saddler W PTS 15 Teddy Davis, New York C, USA
18.01.56 Sandy Saddler W RSC 13 Flash Elorde, San Francisco, USA
Sandy Saddler relinquished title (retired)
24.06.57 Hogan Kid Bassey W RSC 10 Cherif Hamia, Paris, France
01.04.58 Hogan Kid Bassey W CO 3 Ricardo Moreno, Los Angeles, USA
18.03.59 Davey Moore W RTD 13 Hogan Kid Bassey, Los Angeles, USA
19.08.59 Davey Moore W RTD 10 Hogan Kid Bassey, Los Angeles, USA
29.08.60 Davey Moore W PTS 15 Kazuo Takayama, Tokyo, Japan
08.04.61 Davey Moore W CO 1 Danny Valdez, Los Angeles, USA
13.11.61 Davey Moore W PTS 15 Kazuo Takayama, Tokyo, Japan
17.08.62 Davey Moore W RSC 2 Olli Maki, Helsinki, Finland
21.03.63 Sugar Ramos W RTD 10 Davey Moore, Los Angeles, USA
13.07.63 Sugar Ramos W PTS 15 Rafiu King, Mexico C, Mexico
28.02.64 Sugar Ramos W RTD 6 Mitsunori Seki, Tokyo, Japan
09.05.64 Sugar Ramos W PTS 15 Floyd Robertson, Accra, Ghana
26.09.64 Vicente Saldivar W RTD 11 Sugar Ramos, Mexico C, Mexico
06.12.64 Vicente Saldivar W RSC 11 Delfino Rosales, Guanajuato, Mexico
07.05.65 Vicente Saldivar W RSC 15 Raul Rojas, Los Angeles, USA
07.09.65 Vicente Saldivar W PTS 15 Howard Winstone, London, England
12.02.66 Vicente Saldivar W CO 2 Floyd Robertson, Mexico C, Mexico
07.08.66 Vicente Saldivar W PTS 15 Mitsunori Seki, Mexico C, Mexico
29.01.67 Vicente Saldivar W RSC 7 Mitsunori Seki, Mexico C, Mexico
15.06.67 Vicente Saldivar W PTS 15 Howard Winstone, Cardiff, Wales
14.10.67 Vicente Saldivar W RTD 12 Howard Winstone, Mexico C, Mexico
Vicente Saldivar relinquished title (retired)
14.12.67 Raul Rojas W PTS 15 Antonio Herrera, Los Angeles, USA (WBA)
23.01.68 Howard Winstone W RSC 9 Mitsunori Seki, London, England (WBC)
28.03.68 Raul Rojas W PTS 15 Enrique Higgins, Los Angeles, USA (WBA)
24.07.68 Jose Legra W RSC 5 Howard Winstone, Porthcawl, Wales (WBC)
28.09.68 Shozo Saijyo W PTS 15 Raul Rojas, Los Angeles, USA (WBA)
21.01.69 Johnny Famechon W PTS 15 Jose Legra, London, England (WBC)
09.02.69 Shozo Saijyo W PTS 15 Pedro Gomez, Tokyo, Japan (WBA)
28.07.69 Johnny Famechon W PTS 15 Fighting Harada, Sydney, Australia (WBC)
07.09.69 Shozo Saijyo W CO 2 Jose Pimental, Sapporo, Japan (WBA)
06.01.70 Johnny Famechon W CO 14 Fighting Harada, Tokyo, Japan (WBC)
08.02.70 Shozo Saijyo W PTS 15 Godfrey Stevens, Tokyo, Japan (WBA)
09.05.70 Vicente Saldivar W PTS 15 Johnny Famechon, Rome, Italy (WBC)
05.07.70 Shozo Saijyo W PTS 15 Frankie Crawford, Sendai, Japan (WBA)
11.12.70 Kuniaki Shibata W RSC 12 Vicente Saldivar, Tijuana, Mexico (WBC)
28.02.71 Shozo Saijyo W PTS 15 Frankie Crawford, Utsonomuja, Japan (WBA)
03.06.71 Kuniaki Shibata W CO 1 Raul Cruz, Tokyo, Japan (WBC)
02.09.71 Antonio Gomez W RSC 5 Shozo Saijyo, Tokyo, Japan (WBA)
11.11.71 Kuniaki Shibata DREW 15 Ernesto Marcel, Matsuyama, Japan (WBC)
06.02.72 Antonio Gomez W CO 7 Raul Martinez, Maracay, Venezuela (WBA)
19.05.72 Clemente Sanchez W CO 3 Kuniaki Shibata, Tokyo, Japan (WBC)
19.08.72 Ernesto Marcel W PTS 15 Antonio Gomez, Maracay, Venezuela (WBA)
03.12.72 Ernesto Marcel W RSC 6 Enrique Garcia, Panama C, Panama (WBA)
16.12.72 Jose Legra W RSC 10 Clemente Sanchez, Monterrey, Mexico (WBC)
05.05.73 Eder Jofre W PTS 15 Jose Legra, Brasilia, Brazil (WBC)
14.07.73 Ernesto Marcel W RTD 11 Antonio Gomez, Panama C, Panama (WBA)
08.09.73 Ernesto Marcel W CO 9 Spider Nemoto, Panama C, Panama (WBA)
21.10.73 Eder Jofre W CO 4 Vicente Saldivar, Salvador, Brazil (WBC)
Eder Jofre forfeited WBC recognition (failure to defend against Alfredo Marcano)
16.02.74 Ernesto Marcel W PTS 15 Alexis Arguello, Panama C, Panama (WBA)
Ernesto Marcel relinquished WBA version of title (retired)
09.07.74 Ruben Olivares W RSC 7 Zensuke Utagawa, Los Angeles, USA (WBA)
07.09.74 Bobby Chacon W RSC 9 Alfredo Marcano, Los Angeles, USA (WBC)
23.11.74 Alexis Arguello W CO 13 Ruben Olivares, Los Angeles, USA (WBA)
01.03.75 Bobby Chacon W CO 2 Jesus Estrada, Los Angeles, USA (WBC)
15.03.75 Alexis Arguello W RSC 8 Leonel Hernandez, Caracas, Venezuela (WBA)
31.05.75 Alexis Arguello W RSC 2 Rigoberto Riasco, Managua, Nicaragua (WBA)
20.06.75 Ruben Olivares W RSC 2 Bobby Chacon, Los Angeles, USA (WBC)
20.09.75 David Kotey W PTS 15 Ruben Olivares, Los Angeles, USA (WBC)
12.10.75 Alexis Arguello W CO 5 Royal Kobayashi, Tokyo, Japan (WBA)
06.03.76 David Kotey W RSC 12 Flipper Uehara, Accra, Ghana (WBC)
19.06.76 Alexis Arguello W CO 3 Salvatore Torres, Los Angeles, USA (WBA)
Alexis Arguello relinquished WBA version of title (moved up to super featherweight)
16.07.76 David Kotey W RSC 3 Shig Fukuyama, Tokyo, Japan (WBC)
05.11.76 Danny Lopez W PTS 15 David Kotey, Accra, Ghana (WBC)
15.01.77 Rafael Ortega W PTS 15 Francisco Coronado, Panama C, Panama (WBA)
29.05.77 Rafael Ortega W PTS 15 Flipper Uehara, Okinawa, Japan (WBA)
13.09.77 Danny Lopez W RSC 7 Jose Torres, Los Angeles, USA (WBC)
17.12.77 Cecilio Lastra W PTS 15 Rafael Ortega, Torrelavega, Spain (WBA)
15.02.78 Danny Lopez W RSC 6 David Kotey, Las Vegas, USA (WBC)
15.04.78 Eusebio Pedroza W CO 13 Cecilio Lastra, Panama C, Panama (WBA)
23.04.78 Danny Lopez W RSC 6 Jose de Paula, Los Angeles, USA (WBC)
02.07.78 Eusebio Pedroza W RSC 12 Ernesto Herrera, Panama C, Panama (WBA)
15.09.78 Danny Lopez W CO 2 Juan Malvarez, New Orleans, USA (WBC)
21.10.78 Danny Lopez W DIS 4 Fel Clemente, Pesaro, Italy (WBC)
27.11.78 Eusebio Pedroza W PTS 15 Enrique Solis, San Juan, Puerto Rico (WBA)
09.01.79 Eusebio Pedroza W RTD 13 Royal Kobayashi, Tokyo, Japan (WBA)
10.03.79 Danny Lopez W CO 2 Danny Castanon, Salt Lake C, USA (WBC)
08.04.79 Eusebio Pedroza W RSC 11 Hector Carrasquilla, Panama C, Panama (WBA)
17.06.79 Danny Lopez W CO 15 Mike Ayala, San Antonio, USA (WBC)
21.07.79 Eusebio Pedroza W RSC 12 Ruben Olivares, Houston, USA (WBA)
25.09.79 Danny Lopez W RSC 3 Jose Caba, Los Angeles, USA (WBC)
17.11.79 Eusebio Pedroza W RSC 11 Johnny Aba, Port Moresby, P N Guinea (WBA)
22.01.80 Eusebio Pedroza W PTS 15 Spider Nemoto, Tokyo, Japan (WBA)
02.02.80 Salvador Sanchez W RSC 13 Danny Lopez, Phoenix, USA (WBC)
29.03.80 Eusebio Pedroza W CO 9 Juan Malvarez, Panama C, Panama (WBA)
12.04.80 Salvador Sanchez W PTS 15 Ruben Castillo, Tucson, USA (WBC)
21.06.80 Salvador Sanchez W RSC 14 Danny Lopez, Las Vegas, USA (WBC)
20.07.80 Eusebio Pedroza W CO 9 Sa-Wang Kim, Seoul, S Korea (WBA)
13.09.80 Salvador Sanchez W PTS 15 Pat Ford, San Antonio, USA (WBC)
04.10.80 Eusebio Pedroza W PTS 15 Rocky Lockridge, McAfee, USA (WBA)
13.12.80 Salvador Sanchez W PTS 15 Juan Laporte, El Paso, USA (WBC)
14.02.81 Eusebio Pedroza W CO 13 Pat Ford, Panama C, Panama (WBA)
22.03.81 Salvador Sanchez W RSC 10 Roberto Castanon, Las Vegas (WBC)
01.08.81 Eusebio Pedroza W CO 7 Carlos Pinango, Caracas, Venezuela (WBA)
21.08.81 Salvador Sanchez W RSC 8 Wilfredo Gomez, Las Vegas, USA (WBC)
05.12.81 Eusebio Pedroza W CO 5 Bashew Sibaca, Panama C, Panama (WBA)
12.12.81 Salvador Sanchez W PTS 15 Pat Cowdell, Houston, USA (WBC)
24.01.82 Eusebio Pedroza W PTS 15 Juan Laporte, Atlantic C, USA (WBA)
08.05.82 Salvador Sanchez W PTS 15 Rocky Garcia, Dallas, USA (WBC)
21.07.82 Salvador Sanchez W RSC 15 Azumah Nelson, New York C, USA (WBC)
Salvador Sanchez left WBC version of title vacant (killed in a road crash)
15.09.82 Juan Laporte W RTD 10 Mario Miranda, New York C, USA (WBC)
16.10.82 Eusebio Pedroza DREW 15 Bernard Taylor, Charlotte, USA (WBA)
20.02.83 Juan Laporte W PTS 12 Ruben Castillo, San Juan, Puerto Rico (WBC)
24.04.83 Eusebio Pedroza W PTS 15 Rocky Lockridge, Liguma, Italy (WBA)
25.06.83 Juan Laporte W PTS 12 Johnny de la Rosa, San Juan, Puerto Rico (WBC)
22.10.83 Eusebio Pedroza W PTS 15 Jose Caba, San Remo, Italy (WBA)
04.03.84 Min-Keun Oh W CO 2 Joko Arter, Seoul, S Korea (IBF)
31.03.84 Wilfredo Gomez W PTS 12 Juan Laporte, San Juan, Puerto Rico (WBC)
27.05.84 Eusebio Pedroza W PTS 15 Angel Mayor, Maracaibo, Venezuela (WBA)
10.06.84 Min-Keun Oh W PTS 15 Kelvin Lampkin, Seoul, S Korea (IBF)
08.12.84 Azumah Nelson W RSC 11 Wilfredo Gomez, San Juan, Puerto Rico (WBC)
02.02.85 Eusebio Pedroza W PTS 15 Jorge Lujan, Panama C, Panama (WBA)
07.04.85 Min-Keun Oh W PTS 15 Irving Mitchell, Pusan, S Korea (IBF)
08.06.85 Barry McGuigan W PTS 15 Eusebio Pedroza, London, England (WBA)
06.09.85 Azumah Nelson W CO 5 Juvenal Ordenes, Miami, USA (WBC)
28.09.85 Barry McGuigan W RTD 8 Bernard Taylor, Belfast, Ireland (WBA)
12.10.85 Azumah Nelson W CO 1 Pat Cowdell, Birmingham, England (WBC)
29.11.85 Ki-Yung Chung W RSC 15 Min-Keun Oh, Chonju, S Korea (IBF)
15.02.86 Barry McGuigan W RSC 14 Danilo Cabrera, Dublin, Ireland (WBA)
16.02.86 Ki-Yung Chung W RTD 6 Tyrone Jackson, Ulsan, S Korea (IBF)
25.02.86 Azumah Nelson W PTS 12 Marcos Villasana, Los Angeles, USA (WBC)
18.05.86 Ki-Yung Chung W PTS 15 Richard Savage, Taegu, S Korea (IBF)
22.06.86 Azumah Nelson W RSC 10 Danilo Cabrera, San Juan, Puerto Rico (WBC)
23.06.86 Steve Cruz W PTS 15 Barry McGuigan, Las Vegas, USA (WBA)

30.08.86 Antonio Rivera W RTD 10 Ki-Yung Chung, Osan, S Korea (IBF)
06.03.87 Antonio Esparragoza W RSC 12 Steve Cruz, Fort Worth, USA (WBA)
07.03.87 Azumah Nelson W CO 6 Mauro Gutierrez, Las Vegas, USA (WBC)
26.07.87 Antonio Esparragoza W CO 10 Pascual Aranda, Houston, USA (WBA)
29.08.87 Azumah Nelson W PTS 12 Marcos Villasana, Los Angeles, USA (WBC)
Azumah Nelson relinquished WBC version of title (weight making difficulties)
23.01.88 Calvin Grove W RSC 4 Antonio Rivera, Gamaches, France (IBF)
07.03.88 Jeff Fenech W RSC 10 Victor Callejas, Sydney, Australia (WBC)

Super-Featherweight (130 lbs)

Title Holders

	Birthplace	Tenure	Status
Johnny Dundee	Italy	1921 – 1923	NY
Jack Bernstein	USA	1923	NBA/NY
Johnny Dundee	Italy	1923 – 1924	NBA/NY
Kid Sullivan	USA	1924 – 1925	NBA/NY
Mike Ballerino	USA	1925	NBA/NY
Tod Morgan	USA	1925 – 1929	NBA/NY
Benny Bass	USA	1929	NBA/NY
Benny Bass	Russia	1929 – 1931	NBA
Kid Chocolate	Cuba	1931 – 1933	NBA
Frankie Klick	USA	1933 – 1934	NBA
Sandy Saddler	USA	1949 – 1950	OHIO
Harold Gomes	USA	1959 – 1960	NBA
Flash Elorde	Philippines	1960 – 1965	NBA
Flash Elorde	Philippines	1965 – 1967	
Yoshiaki Numata	Japan	1967	
Hiroshi Kobayashi	Japan	1967 – 1969	
Hiroshi Kobayashi	Japan	1969 – 1971	WBA
Rene Barrientos	Philippines	1969 – 1970	WBC
Yoshiaki Numata	Japan	1970 – 1971	WBC
Alfredo Marcano	Venezuela	1971 – 1972	WBA
Ricardo Arredondo	Mexico	1971 – 1974	WBC
Ben Villaflor	Philippines	1972 – 1973	WBA
Kuniaki Shibata	Japan	1973	WBA
Ben Villaflor	Philippines	1973 – 1976	WBA
Kuniaki Shibata	Japan	1974 – 1975	WBC
Alfredo Escalera	Puerto Rico	1975 – 1978	WBC
Sam Serrano	Puerto Rico	1976 – 1980	WBA
Alexis Arguello *	Nicaragua	1978 – 1980	WBC
Yasutsune Uehara	Japan	1980 – 1981	WBA
Rafael Limon	Mexico	1980 – 1981	WBC
Cornelius Boza-Edwards	Uganda	1981	WBC
Sam Serrano	Puerto Rico	1981 – 1983	WBA
Rolando Navarrete	Philippines	1981 – 1982	WBC
Rafael Limon	Mexico	1982	WBC
Bobby Chacon	USA	1982 – 1983	WBC
Roger Mayweather	USA	1983 – 1984	WBA
Hector Camacho *	Puerto Rico	1983 – 1984	WBC
Rocky Lockridge	USA	1984 – 1985	WBA
Hwan-Kil Yuh	S Korea	1984 – 1985	IBF
Julio Cesar Chavez *	Mexico	1984 – 1987	WBC
Lester Ellis	Australia	1985	IBF
Wilfredo Gomez	Puerto Rico	1985 – 1986	WBA
Barry Michael	Australia	1985 – 1987	IBF
Alfredo Layne	Panama	1986	WBA
Brian Mitchell	S Africa	1986 –	WBA
Rocky Lockridge	USA	1987 –	IBF
Azumah Nelson	Ghana	1988 –	WBC

Title Bouts

18.11.21 Johnny Dundee W DIS 5 K. O. Chaney, New York C, USA (NY)
06.07.22 Johnny Dundee W PTS 15 Jackie Sharkey, New York C, USA (NY)
28.08.22 Johnny Dundee W PTS 15 Pepper Martin, New York C, USA (NY)
02.02.23 Johnny Dundee W PTS 15 Elino Flores, New York C, USA (NY)
30.05.23 Jack Bernstein W PTS 15 Johnny Dundee, New York C, USA (NY/NBA)
25.06.23 Jack Bernstein W CO 5 Freddie Jacks, Philadelphia, USA (NY/NBA)
17.12.23 Johnny Dundee W PTS 15 Jack Bernstein, New York C, USA (NY/NBA)
20.06.24 Kid Sullivan W PTS 10 Johnny Dundee, New York C, USA (NY/NBA)
18.08.24 Kid Sullivan W PTS 15 Pepper Martin, New York C, USA (NY/NBA)
15.10.24 Kid Sullivan W CO 5 Mike Ballerino, New York C, USA (NY/NBA)
01.04.25 Mike Ballerino W PTS 10 Kid Sullivan, Philadelphia, USA (NY/NBA)
06.07.25 Mike Ballerino W PTS 15 Pepper Martin, New York C, USA (NY/NBA)
02.12.25 Tod Morgan W RTD 10 Mike Ballerino, Los Angeles, USA (NY/NBA)
03.06.26 Tod Morgan W RTD 6 Kid Sullivan, New York C, USA (NY/NBA)
30.09.26 Tod Morgan W PTS 15 Joe Glick, New York C, USA (NY/NBA)
19.10.26 Tod Morgan W PTS 10 Johnny Dundee, San Francisco, USA (NY/NBA)
19.11.26 Tod Morgan W PTS 15 Carl Duane, New York C, USA (NY/NBA)
28.05.27 Tod Morgan W PTS 12 Vic Foley, Vancouver, Canada (NY/NBA)
16.12.27 Tod Morgan W DIS 14 Joe Glick, New York C, USA (NY/NBA)
24.05.28 Tod Morgan W PTS 15 Eddie Martin, New York C, USA (NY/NBA)
18.07.28 Tod Morgan W PTS 15 Eddie Martin, New York C, USA (NY/NBA)
03.12.28 Tod Morgan DREW 10 Santiago Zorilla, San Francisco, USA (NY/NBA)
05.04.29 Tod Morgan W PTS 10 Santiago Zorilla, Los Angeles, USA (NY/NBA)
20.05.29 Tod Morgan W PTS 10 Baby Sal Sorio, Los Angeles, USA (NY/NBA)
20.12.29 Benny Bass W CO 2 Tod Morgan, New York C, USA (NY/NBA)
Benny Boss ceased to be recognised by NY (NY abolished weight division)
03.02.30 Benny Bass W RSC 4 Davey Abad, St Louis, USA (NBA)
05.01.31 Benny Bass W PTS 10 Lew Massey, Philadelphia, USA (NBA)
15.07.31 Kid Chocolate W RSC 7 Benny Bass, Philadelphia, USA (NBA)
10.04.32 Kid Chocolate W PTS 15 Davey Abad, Havana, Cuba (NBA)
04.08.32 Kid Chocolate W PTS 10 Eddie Shea, Chicago, USA (NBA)
01.05.33 Kid Chocolate W PTS 10 Johnny Farr, Philadelphia, USA (NBA)
04.12.33 Kid Chocolate W PTS 10 Frankie Wallace, Cleveland, USA (NBA)
25.12.33 Frankie Klick W RSC 7 Kid Chocolate, Philadelphia, USA (NBA)
Frankie Klick ceased to be recognised by the NBA (title fell into disuse)
06.12.49 Sandy Saddler W PTS 10 Orlando Zulueta, Cleveland, USA (OHIO)
18.04.50 Sandy Saddler W RSC 9 Lauro Salas, Cleveland, USA (OHIO)
Sandy Saddler ceased to be recognised by Ohio (failure to defend after regaining the featherweight title)
20.07.59 Harold Gomes W PTS 15 Paul Jorgensen, Providence, USA (NBA)
16.03.60 Flash Elorde W CO 7 Harold Gomes, Quezon C, Philippines (NBA)
17.08.60 Flash Elorde W CO 1 Harold Gomes, San Francisco, USA (NBA)
19.03.61 Flash Elorde W PTS 15 Joey Lopes, Manila, Philippines (NBA)
16.12.61 Flash Elorde W RSC 1 Sergio Caprari, Manila, Philippines (NBA)
23.06.62 Flash Elorde W PTS 15 Auburn Copeland, Manila, Philippines (NBA)
16.02.63 Flash Elorde W PTS 15 Johnny Bizzarro, Manila, Philippines (WBA)
16.11.63 Flash Elorde W DIS 11 Love Allotey, Quezon C, Philippines (WBA)
27.07.64 Flash Elorde W RSC 12 Teruo Kosaka, Tokyo, Japan (WBA)
05.06.65 Flash Elorde W CO 15 Teruo Kosaka, Quezon C, Philippines
04.12.65 Flash Elorde W PTS 15 Kang-Il Suh, Quezon C, Philippines
22.10.66 Flash Elorde W PTS 15 Vicente Derado, Quezon C, Philippines
15.06.67 Yoshiaki Numata W PTS 15 Flash Elorde, Tokyo, Japan
14.12.67 Hiroshi Kobayashi W CO 12 Yoshiaki Numata, Tokyo, Japan
30.03.68 Hiroshi Kobayashi DREW 15 Rene Barrientos, Tokyo, Japan
06.10.68 Hiroshi Kobayashi W PTS 15 Jaime Valladeres, Tokyo, Japan
Hiroshi Kobayashi forfeited WBC recognition (failure to defend against Rene Barrientos)
15.02.69 Rene Barrientos W PTS 15 Ruben Navarro, Quezon C, Philippines (WBC)
06.04.69 Hiroshi Kobayashi W PTS 15 Antonio Amaya, Tokyo, Japan (WBA)
09.11.69 Hiroshi Kobayashi W PTS 15 Carlos Canete, Tokyo, Japan (WBA)
05.04.70 Yoshiaki Numata W PTS 15 Rene Barrientos, Tokyo, Japan (WBC)
23.08.70 Hiroshi Kobayashi W PTS 15 Antonio Amaya, Tokyo, Japan (WBA)
27.09.70 Yoshiaki Numata W CO 5 Raul Rojas, Tokyo, Japan (WBC)
03.01.71 Yoshiaki Numata W PTS 15 Rene Barrientos, Shizuaka, Japan (WBC)
03.03.71 Hiroshi Kobayashi W PTS 15 Ricardo Arredondo, Tokyo, Japan (WBA)
30.05.71 Yoshiaki Numata W PTS 15 Lionel Rose, Hiroshima, Japan (WBC)
29.07.71 Alfredo Marcano W RTD 10 Hiroshi Kobayashi, Aomori, Japan (WBA)
10.10.71 Ricardo Arredondo W CO 10 Yoshiaki Numata, Sendai, Japan (WBC)
07.11.71 Alfredo Marcano W RSC 4 Kenji Iwata, Caracas, Venezuela (WBA)
29.01.72 Ricardo Arredondo W PTS 15 Jose Marin, San Jose, Costa Rica (WBC)
22.04.72 Ricardo Arredondo W CO 5 William Martinez, Mexico C, Mexico (WBC)
25.04.72 Ben Villaflor W PTS 15 Alfredo Marcano, Honolulu, Hawaii (WBA)
05.09.72 Ben Villaflor DREW 15 Victor Echegaray, Honolulu, Hawaii (WBA)
15.09.72 Ricardo Arredondo W CO 12 Susumu Okabe, Tokyo, Japan (WBC)
06.03.73 Ricardo Arredondo W PTS 15 Apollo Yoshio, Fukuoka C, Japan (WBC)
12.03.73 Kuniaki Shibata W PTS 15 Ben Villaflor, Honolulu, Hawaii (WBA)
19.06.73 Kuniaki Shibata W PTS 15 Victor Echegaray, Tokyo, Japan (WBA)
01.09.73 Ricardo Arredondo W RSC 6 Morito Kashiwaba, Tokyo, Japan (WBC)
18.10.73 Ben Villaflor W CO 1 Kuniaki Shibata, Honolulu, Hawaii (WBA)
28.02.74 Kuniaki Shibata W PTS 15 Ricardo Arredondo, Tokyo, Japan (WBC)
14.03.74 Ben Villaflor DREW 15 Apollo Yoshio, Toyama, Japan (WBA)
27.06.74 Kuniaki Shibata W PTS 15 Antonio Amaya, Tokyo, Japan (WBC)
03.08.74 Kuniaki Shibata W RSC 15 Ramiro Bolanos, Tokyo, Japan (WBC)
24.08.74 Ben Villaflor W RSC 2 Yasutsune Uehara, Honolulu, Hawaii (WBA)
13.03.75 Ben Villaflor W PTS 15 Hyun-Chi Kim, Quezon C, Philippines (WBA)
27.03.75 Kuniaki Shibata W PTS 15 Ould Makloufi, Fukuoka C, Japan (WBC)
05.07.75 Alfredo Escalera W CO 2 Kuniaki Shibata, Kasamatsu, Japan (WBC)
20.09.75 Alfredo Escalera DREW 15 Leonel Hernandez, Caracas, Venezuela (WBC)
12.12.75 Alfredo Escalera W RSC 9 Sven-Erik Paulsen, Oslo, Norway (WBC)
12.01.76 Ben Villaflor W RSC 13 Morito Kashiwaba, Tokyo, Japan (WBA)
20.02.76 Alfredo Escalera W RSC 13 Jose Fernandez, San Juan, Puerto Rico (WBC)
01.04.76 Alfredo Escalera W RSC 6 Buzzsaw Yamabe, Nara, Japan (WBC)
13.04.76 Ben Villaflor DREW 15 Sam Serrano, Honolulu, Hawaii (WBA)
01.07.76 Alfredo Escalera W PTS 15 Buzzsaw Yamabe, Nara, Japan (WBC)
18.09.76 Alfredo Escalera W RTD 12 Ray Lunny, San Juan, Puerto Rico (WBC)
16.10.76 Sam Serrano W PTS 15 Ben Villaflor, San Juan, Puerto Rico (WBA)
30.11.76 Alfredo Escalera W PTS 15 Tyrone Everett, Philadelphia, USA (WBC)
15.01.77 Sam Serrano W RSC 11 Alberto Herrera, Guayaquil, Ecuador (WBA)
17.03.77 Alfredo Escalera W RSC 6 Ronnie McGarvey, San Juan, Puerto Rico (WBC)
16.05.77 Alfredo Escalera W CO 8 Carlos Becerril, Landover, USA (WBC)
26.06.77 Sam Serrano W PTS 15 Leonel Hernandez, Cruz, Venezuela (WBA)
27.08.77 Sam Serrano W PTS 15 Apollo Yoshio, San Juan, Puerto Rico (WBA)
10.09.77 Alfredo Escalera W PTS 15 Sigfredo Rodriguez, San Juan, Puerto Rico (WBC)
19.11.77 Sam Serrano W RSC 10 Tae-Ho Kim, San Juan, Puerto Rico (WBA)
28.01.78 Alexis Arguello W RSC 13 Alfredo Escalera, Bayamon, Puerto Rico (WBC)
18.02.78 Sam Serrano W PTS 15 Mario Martinez, San Juan, Puerto Rico (WBA)
29.04.78 Alexis Arguello W RSC 5 Rey Tam, Los Angeles, USA (WBC)
03.06.78 Alexis Arguello W CO 1 Diego Alcala, San Juan, Puerto Rico (WBC)
08.07.78 Sam Serrano W RSC 9 Oh-Young Ho, San Juan, Puerto Rico (WBA)
10.11.78 Alexis Arguello W PTS 15 Arturo Leon, Las Vegas, USA (WBC)
29.11.78 Sam Serrano W PTS 15 Takas Maruki, Nagoya, Japan (WBA)
04.02.79 Alexis Arguello W CO 13 Alfredo Escalera, Rimini, Italy (WBC)
18.02.79 Sam Serrano W PTS 15 Julio Valdez, San Juan, Puerto Rico (WBA)
14.04.79 Sam Serrano W RSC 8 Nkosana Mgxaji, Capetown, S Africa (WBA)
08.07.79 Alexis Arguello W RSC 11 Rafael Limon, New York C, USA (WBC)
16.11.79 Alexis Arguello W RTD 7 Bobby Chacon, Los Angeles, USA (WBC)

20.01.80 Alexis Arguello W RSC 11 Ruben Castillo, Tucson, USA (WBC)
03.04.80 Sam Serrano W RSC 13 Battle Hawk Kazama, Nara, Japan (WBA)
27.04.80 Alexis Arguello W RSC 4 Rolando Navarrete, San Juan, Puerto Rico (WBC)
Alexis Arguello relinquished WBC version of title (moved up to lightweight)
02.08.80 Yasutsune Uehara W CO 6 Sam Serrano, Detroit, USA (WBA)
20.11.80 Yasutsune Uehara W PTS 15 Leonel Hernandez, Tokyo, Japan (WBA)
11.12.80 Rafael Limon W RSC 15 Ildefonso Bethelmy, Los Angeles, USA (WBC)
08.03.81 Cornelius Boza-Edwards W PTS 15 Rafael Limon, Stockton, USA (WBC)
09.04.81 Sam Serrano W PTS 15 Yasutsune Uehara, Wakayama, Japan (WBA)
30.05.81 Cornelius Boza-Edwards W RTD 13 Bobby Chacon, Las Vegas, USA (WBC)
29.06.81 Sam Serrano W PTS 15 Leonel Hernandez, Caracas, Venezuela (WBA)
29.08.81 Rolando Navarrete W CO 5 Cornelius Boza-Edwards, Reggio, Italy (WBC)
10.12.81 Sam Serrano W RSC 12 Hikaru Tomonari, San Juan, Puerto Rico (WBA)
16.01.82 Rolando Navarrete W CO 11 Chung-Il Choi, Manila, Philippines (WBC)
29.05.82 Rafael Limon W CO 12 Rolando Navarrete, Las Vegas, USA (WBC)
05.06.82 Sam Serrano NC 11 Benedicto Villablanca, Santiago, Chile (WBA)
18.09.82 Rafael Limon W RSC 7 Chung-Il Choi, Los Angeles, USA (WBC)
11.12.82 Bobby Chacon W PTS 15 Rafael Limon, Sacramento, USA (WBC)
19.01.83 Roger Mayweather W CO 8 Sam Serrano, San Juan, Puerto Rico (WBA)
20.04.83 Roger Mayweather W RSC 8 Jorge Alvarado, San Jose, USA (WBA)
15.05.83 Bobby Chacon W PTS 12 Cornelius Boza-Edwards, Las Vegas, USA (WBC)
Bobby Chacon forfeited WBC recognition (contractual dispute)
07.08.83 Hector Camacho W RSC 5 Rafael Limon, San Juan, Puerto Rico (WBC)
17.08.83 Roger Mayweather W CO 1 Benedicto Villablanca, Las Vegas, USA (WBA)
18.11.83 Hector Camacho W CO 5 Rafael Solis, San Juan, Puerto Rico (WBC)
Hector Camacho relinquished WBC version of title (moved up to lightweight)
26.02.84 Rocky Lockridge W CO 1 Roger Mayweather, Beaumont, USA (WBA)
22.04.84 Hwan-Kil Yuh W PTS 15 Rod Sequenan, Seoul, S Korea (IBF)
12.06.84 Rocky Lockridge W RSC 11 Taej-In Moon, Anchorage, Alaska (WBA)
13.09.84 Julio Cesar Chavez W RSC 8 Mario Martinez, Los Angeles, USA (WBC)
16.09.84 Hwan-Kil Yuh W CO 6 Sak Galexi, Pohang, S Korea (IBF)
27.01.85 Rocky Lockridge W RSC 6 Kamel Bou Ali, Riva del Garda, Italy (WBA)
15.02.85 Lester Ellis W PTS 15 Hwan-Kil Yuh, Melbourne, Australia (IBF)
19.04.85 Julio Cesar Chavez W RSC 6 Ruben Castillo, Los Angeles, USA (WBC)
26.04.85 Lester Ellis W CO 13 Rod Sequenan, Melbourne, Australia (IBF)
19.05.85 Wilfredo Gomez W PTS 15 Rocky Lockridge, San Juan, Puerto Rico (WBA)
07.07.85 Julio Cesar Chavez W RSC 2 Roger Mayweather, Las Vegas, USA (WBC)
12.07.85 Barry Michael W PTS 15 Lester Ellis, Melbourne, Australia (IBF)
22.09.85 Julio Cesar Chavez W PTS 12 Dwight Pratchett, Las Vegas, USA (WBC)
18.10.85 Barry Michael W RSC 4 Jin-Shik Choi, Darwin, Australia (IBF)
15.05.86 Julio Cesar Chavez W RSC 5 Faustino Barrios, Paris, France (WBC)
23.05.86 Barry Michael W RSC 4 Mark Fernandez, Melbourne, Australia (IBF)
24.05.86 Alfredo Layne W RSC 9 Wilfredo Gomez, San Juan, Puerto Rico (WBA)
13.06.86 Julio Cesar Chavez W RSC 7 Refugio Rojas, New York C, USA (WBC)
03.08.86 Julio Cesar Chavez W PTS 12 Rocky Lockridge, Monte Carlo (WBC)
23.08.86 Barry Michael W PTS 12 Najib Daho, Manchester, England (IBF)
27.09.86 Brian Mitchell W RSC 10 Alfredo Layne, Sun C, S Africa (WBA)
12.12.86 Julio Cesar Chavez W PTS 12 Juan Laporte, New York C, USA (WBC)
27.03.87 Brian Mitchell DREW 15 Jose Rivera, San Juan, Puerto Rico (WBA)
18.04.87 Julio Cesar Chavez W RSC 3 Francisco Tomas Cruz, Nimes, France (WBC)
31.07.87 Brian Mitchell W RSC 14 Francisco Fernandez, Panama C (WBA)
09.08.87 Rocky Lockridge W RTD 8 Barry Michael, Windsor, England (IBF)
21.08.87 Julio Cesar Chavez W PTS 12 Danilo Cabrera, Tijuana, Mexico (WBC)
Julio Cesar Chavez relinquished WBC version of title (won WBA lightweight title)
03.10.87 Brian Mitchell W PTS 15 Daniel Londas, Gravelines, France (WBA)
25.10.87 Rocky Lockridge W RSC 10 Johnny de la Rosa, Tucson, USA (IBF)
19.12.87 Brian Mitchell W RTD 8 Salvatore Curcetti, Capo D'Orlando, Italy (WBA)
29.02.88 Azumah Nelson W PTS 12 Mario Martinez, Los Angeles, USA (WBC)
02.04.88 Rocky Lockridge W PTS 15 Harold Knight, Atlantic C, USA (IBF)
26.04.88 Brian Mitchell W PTS 12 Jose Rivera, Madrid, Spain (WBA)

Lightweight (135 lbs)

Title Holders

	Birthplace	Tenure	Status
George Lavigne	USA	1896 – 1899	
Frank Erne	Switzerland	1899 – 1902	
Joe Gans	USA	1902 – 1904	
Jimmy Britt	USA	1904 – 1905	
Battling Nelson	Denmark	1905 – 1906	
Joe Gans	USA	1906 – 1908	
Battling Nelson	Denmark	1908 – 1910	
Ad Wolgast	USA	1910 – 1912	
Willie Ritchie	USA	1912 – 1914	
Freddie Welsh	Wales	1914 – 1917	
Benny Leonard *	USA	1917 – 1925	
Jimmy Goodrich	USA	1925	NY
Rocky Kansas	USA	1925 – 1926	
Sammy Mandell	USA	1926 – 1930	
Al Singer	USA	1930	
Tony Canzoneri	USA	1930 – 1933	
Barney Ross *	USA	1933 – 1935	
Tony Canzoneri	USA	1935 – 1936	
Lou Ambers	USA	1936 – 1938	
Henry Armstrong	USA	1938 – 1939	
Lou Ambers	USA	1939 – 1940	
Sammy Angott	USA	1940 – 1941	NBA
Lew Jenkins	USA	1940 – 1941	NY
Sammy Angott *	USA	1941 – 1942	
Beau Jack	USA	1942 – 1943	NY
Slugger White	USA	1943	MARY
Bob Montgomery	USA	1943	NY
Sammy Angott	USA	1943 – 1944	NBA
Beau Jack	USA	1943 – 1944	NY
Bob Montgomery	USA	1944 – 1947	NY
Juan Zurita	Mexico	1944 – 1945	NBA
Ike Williams	USA	1945 – 1947	NBA
Ike Williams	USA	1947 – 1951	
Jimmy Carter	USA	1951 – 1952	
Lauro Salas	Mexico	1952	
Jimmy Carter	USA	1952 – 1954	
Paddy de Marco	USA	1954	
Jimmy Carter	USA	1954 – 1955	
Wallace Bud Smith	USA	1955 – 1956	
Joe Brown	USA	1956 – 1962	
Carlos Ortiz	Puerto Rico	1962 – 1965	
Ismael Laguna	Panama	1965	
Carlos Ortiz	Puerto Rico	1965 – 1968	
Carlos Teo Cruz	Dom Republic	1968 – 1969	
Mando Ramos	USA	1969 – 1970	
Ismael Laguna	Panama	1970	
Ken Buchanan	Scotland	1970 – 1971	
Ken Buchanan	Scotland	1971 – 1972	WBA
Pedro Carrasco	Spain	1971 – 1972	WBC
Mando Ramos	USA	1972	WBC
Roberto Duran	Panama	1972 – 1978	WBA
Chango Carmona	Mexico	1972	WBC
Rodolfo Gonzalez	Mexico	1972 – 1974	WBC
Guts Ishimatsu	Japan	1974 – 1976	WBC
Esteban de Jesus	Puerto Rico	1976 – 1978	WBC
Roberto Duran *	Panama	1978 – 1979	
Jim Watt	Scotland	1979 – 1981	WBC
Ernesto Espana	Venezuela	1979 – 1980	WBA
Hilmer Kenty	USA	1980 – 1981	WBA
Sean O'Grady	USA	1981	WBA
Alexis Arguello *	Nicaragua	1981 – 1983	WBC
Claude Noel	Trinidad	1981	WBA
Arturo Frias	USA	1981 – 1982	WBA
Ray Mancini	USA	1982 – 1984	WBA
Edwin Rosario	Puerto Rico	1983 – 1984	WBC
Charlie Brown	USA	1984	IBF
Harry Arroyo	USA	1984 – 1985	IBF
Livingstone Bramble	USA	1984 – 1986	WBA
Jose Luis Ramirez	Mexico	1984 – 1985	WBC
Jimmy Paul	USA	1985 – 1986	IBF
Hector Camacho *	Puerto Rico	1985 – 1987	WBC
Edwin Rosario	Puerto Rico	1986 – 1987	WBA
Greg Haugen	USA	1986 – 1987	IBF
Vinny Pazienza	USA	1987 – 1988	IBF
Jose Luis Ramirez	Mexico	1987 –	WBC
Julio Cesar Chavez	Mexico	1987 –	WBA
Greg Haugen	USA	1988 –	IBF

Title Bouts

01.06.96 George Lavigne W CO 17 Dick Burge, London, England
27.10.96 George Lavigne W CO 24 Jack Everhardt, New York C, USA
08.02.97 George Lavigne W PTS 25 Kid McPartland, New York C, USA
28.04.97 George Lavigne W 11 Eddie Connolly, New York C, USA
29.10.97 George Lavigne W RTD 12 Joe Walcott, San Francisco, USA
17.03.98 George Lavigne DREW 20 Jack Daly, Cleveland, USA
28.09.98 George Lavigne DREW 20 Frank Erne, New York C, USA
25.11.98 George Lavigne W PTS 20 Tom Tracy, San Francisco, USA
03.07.99 Frank Erne W PTS 20 George Lavigne, Buffalo, USA
04.12.99 Frank Erne DREW 25 Jack O'Brien, New York C, USA
23.03.00 Frank Erne W RTD 12 Joe Gans, New York C, USA
12.05.02 Joe Gans W CO 1 Frank Erne, Fort Erie, Canada
27.06.02 Joe Gans W CO 3 George McFadden, San Francisco, USA
24.07.02 Joe Gans W CO 15 Rufe Turner, Oakland, USA
17.09.02 Joe Gans W CO 5 Gus Gardner, Baltimore, USA
13.10.02 Joe Gans W CO 5 Kid McPartland, Fort Erie, Canada
01.01.03 Joe Gans W DIS 11 Gus Gardner, New Britain, USA
11.03.03 Joe Gans W RTD 11 Steve Crosby, Hot Springs, USA
29.05.03 Joe Gans W CO 10 Willie Fitzgerald, San Francisco, USA
04.07.03 Joe Gans W CO 5 Buddy King, Butte, USA
12.01.04 Joe Gans W PTS 10 Willie Fitzgerald, Detroit, USA
31.10.04 Joe Gans W DIS 5 Jimmy Britt, San Francisco, USA
Joe Gans lost general recognition (refused to make the weight)
20.12.04 Jimmy Britt W PTS 20 Battling Nelson, San Francisco, USA
05.05.05 Jimmy Britt W PTS 20 Jabez White, San Francisco, USA
21.07.05 Jimmy Britt W PTS 20 Kid Sullivan, San Francisco, USA
09.09.05 Battling Nelson W CO 18 Jimmy Britt, San Francisco, USA
03.09.06 Joe Gans W DIS 42 Battling Nelson, Goldfield, USA
01.01.07 Joe Gans W CO 8 Kid Herman, Tonopah, USA
09.09.07 Joe Gans W RTD 6 Jimmy Britt, San Francisco, USA

27.09.07 Joe Gans W PTS 20 George Memsic, Los Angeles, USA
01.04.08 Joe Gans W CO 3 Spike Robson, Philadelphia, USA
14.05.08 Joe Gans W RSC 11 Rudy Unholz, San Francisco, USA
04.07.08 Battling Nelson W CO 17 Joe Gans, San Francisco, USA
09.09.08 Battling Nelson W CO 21 Joe Gans, San Francisco, USA
29.05.09 Battling Nelson W CO 23 Dick Hyland, San Francisco, USA
22.06.09 Battling Nelson W CO 5 Jack Clifford, Oklahoma C, USA
22.02.10 Ad Wolgast W RSC 40 Battling Nelson, Richmond, USA
17.03.11 Ad Wolgast W RSC 9 George Memsic, Los Angeles, USA
31.03.11 Ad Wolgast W RTD 5 Antonio la Grave, San Francisco, USA
26.04.11 Ad Wolgast W RSC 2 One-Round Hogan, New York C, USA
27.05.11 Ad Wolgast W RTD 17 Frankie Burns, San Francisco, USA
04.07.11 Ad Wolgast W CO 13 Owen Moran, San Francisco, USA
04.07.12 Ad Wolgast W CO 13 Joe Rivers, Los Angeles, USA
28.11.12 Willie Ritchie W DIS 16 Ad Wolgast, San Francisco, USA
04.07.13 Willie Ritchie W CO 11 Joe Rivers, San Francisco, USA
17.04.14 Willie Ritchie W PTS 20 Tommy Murphy, San Francisco, USA
07.07.14 Freddie Welsh W PTS 20 Willie Ritchie, London, England
04.07.16 Freddie Welsh W DIS 11 Ad Wolgast, Denver, USA
04.09.16 Freddie Welsh W PTS 20 Charley White, Colorado Springs, USA
28.05.17 Benny Leonard W RSC 9 Freddie Welsh, New York C, USA
25.07.17 Benny Leonard W CO 3 Johnny Kilbane, Philadelphia, USA
05.07.20 Benny Leonard W CO 9 Charley White, Benton Harbor, USA
26.11.20 Benny Leonard W RSC 14 Joe Welling, New York C, USA
14.01.21 Benny Leonard W RSC 6 Richie Mitchell, New York C, USA
10.02.22 Benny Leonard W PTS 15 Rocky Kansas, New York C, USA
04.07.22 Benny Leonard W RSC 8 Rocky Kansas, Michigan C, USA
23.07.23 Benny Leonard W PTS 15 Lew Tendler, New York C, USA
Benny Leonard relinquished title (retired)
13.07.25 Jimmy Goodrich W RSC 2 Stanislaus Loayza, New York C, USA (NY)
07.12.25 Rocky Kansas W PTS 15 Jimmy Goodrich, Buffalo, USA
03.07.26 Sammy Mandell W PTS 10 Rocky Kansas, Chicago, USA
21.05.28 Sammy Mandell W PTS 15 Jimmy McLarnin, New York C, USA
02.08.29 Sammy Mandell W PTS 10 Tony Canzoneri, Chicago, USA
17.07.30 Al Singer W CO 1 Sammy Mandell, New York C, USA
14.11.30 Tony Canzoneri W CO 1 Al Singer, New York C, USA
24.04.31 Tony Canzoneri W CO 3 Jackie Kid Berg, Chicago, USA
10.09.31 Tony Canzoneri W PTS 15 Jackie Kid Berg, New York C, USA
20.11.31 Tony Canzoneri W PTS 15 Kid Chocolate, New York C, USA
04.11.32 Tony Canzoneri W PTS 15 Billy Petrolle, New York C, USA
23.06.33 Barney Ross W PTS 10 Tony Canzoneri, Chicago, USA
12.09.33 Barney Ross W PTS 15 Tony Canzoneri, New York C, USA
Barney Ross relinquished title (moved up to welterweight)
10.05.35 Tony Canzoneri W PTS 15 Lou Ambers, New York C, USA
04.10.35 Tony Canzoneri W PTS 15 Al Roth, New York C, USA
03.09.36 Lou Ambers W PTS 15 Tony Canzoneri, New York C, USA
07.05.37 Lou Ambers W PTS 15 Tony Canzoneri, New York C, USA
23.09.37 Lou Ambers W PTS 15 Pedro Montanez, New York C, USA
17.08.38 Henry Armstrong W PTS 15 Lou Ambers, New York C, USA
22.08.39 Lou Ambers W PTS 15 Henry Armstrong, New York C, USA
Lou Ambers forfeited NBA recognition (failure to defend against Davey Day)
03.05.40 Sammy Angott W PTS 15 Davey Day, Louisville, USA (NBA)
10.05.40 Lew Jenkins W RSC 3 Lou Ambers, New York C, USA (NY)
22.11.40 Lew Jenkins W RSC 2 Pete Lello, New York C, USA (NY)
02.05.41 Sammy Angott W PTS 12 Dave Castilloux, Louisville, USA (NBA)
19.12.41 Sammy Angott W PTS 15 Lew Jenkins, New York C, USA
15.05.42 Sammy Angott W PTS 15 Allie Stolz, New York C, USA
Sammy Angott relinquished title (retired)
18.12.42 Beau Jack W CO 3 Tippy Larkin, New York C, USA (NY)
04.01.43 Slugger White W PTS 15 Willie Joyce, Baltimore, USA (MARY)
21.05.43 Bob Montgomery W PTS 15 Beau Jack, New York C, USA (NY)
27.10.43 Sammy Angott W PTS 15 Slugger White, Los Angeles, USA (NBA)
19.11.43 Beau Jack W PTS 15 Bob Montgomery, New York C, USA (NY)
03.03.44 Bob Montgomery W PTS 15 Beau Jack, New York C, USA (NY)
08.03.44 Juan Zurita W PTS 15 Sammy Angott, Los Angeles, USA (NBA)
18.04.45 Ike Williams W CO 2 Juan Zurita, Mexico C, Mexico (NBA)
30.04.46 Ike Williams W RSC 8 Enrique Bolanos, Los Angeles, USA (NBA)
28.06.46 Bob Montgomery W CO 13 Allie Stolz, New York C, USA (NY)
04.09.46 Ike Williams W CO 9 Ronnie James, Cardiff, Wales (NBA)
26.11.46 Bob Montgomery W CO 8 Wesley Mouzon, Philadelphia, USA (NY)
04.08.47 Ike Williams W CO 6 Bob Montgomery, Philadelphia, USA
25.05.48 Ike Williams W PTS 15 Enrique Bolanos, Los Angeles, USA
12.07.48 Ike Williams W RSC 6 Beau Jack, Philadelphia, USA
23.09.48 Ike Williams W CO 10 Jesse Flores, New York C, USA
21.07.49 Ike Williams W RSC 4 Enrique Bolanos, Los Angeles, USA
05.12.49 Ike Williams W PTS 15 Freddie Dawson, Philadelphia, USA
25.05.51 Jimmy Carter W RSC 14 Ike Williams, New York C, USA
14.11.51 Jimmy Carter W PTS 15 Art Aragon, Los Angeles, USA
01.04.52 Jimmy Carter W PTS 15 Lauro Salas, Los Angeles, USA
14.05.52 Lauro Salas W PTS 15 Jimmy Carter, Los Angeles, USA
15.10.52 Jimmy Carter W PTS 15 Lauro Salas, Chicago, USA
24.04.53 Jimmy Carter W RSC 4 Tommy Collins, Boston, USA
12.06.53 Jimmy Carter W RSC 13 George Araujo, New York C, USA
11.11.53 Jimmy Carter W CO 5 Armand Savoie, Montreal, Canada
05.03.54 Paddy de Marco W PTS 15 Jimmy Carter, New York C, USA
17.11.54 Jimmy Carter W RSC 15 Paddy de Marco, San Francisco, USA
29.06.55 Wallace Bud Smith W PTS 15 Jimmy Carter, Boston, USA
19.10.55 Wallace Bud Smith W PTS 15 Jimmy Carter, Cincinnati,USA
24.08.56 Joe Brown W PTS 15 Wallace Bud Smith, New Orleans, USA
13.02.57 Joe Brown W RSC 10 Wallace Bud Smith, Miami, USA
19.06.57 Joe Brown W RSC 15 Orlando Zulueta, Denver, USA
04.12.57 Joe Brown W RSC 11 Joey Lopes, Chicago, USA
07.05.58 Joe Brown W RSC 8 Ralph Dupas, Houston, USA
23.07.58 Joe Brown W PTS 15 Kenny Lane, Houston, USA
11.02.59 Joe Brown W PTS 15 Johnny Busso, Houston, USA
03.06.59 Joe Brown W RTD 8 Paolo Rossi, Washington, USA
02.12.59 Joe Brown W RTD 5 Dave Charnley, Houston, USA
28.10.60 Joe Brown W PTS 15 Cisco Andrade, Los Angeles, USA
18.04.61 Joe Brown W PTS 15 Dave Charnley, London, England
28.10.61 Joe Brown W PTS 15 Bert Somodio, Quezon C, Philippines
21.04.62 Carlos Ortiz W PTS 15 Joe Brown, Las Vegas, USA
03.12.62 Carlos Ortiz W CO 5 Teruo Kosaka, Tokyo, Japan
07.04.63 Carlos Ortiz W RSC 13 Doug Vaillant, San Juan, Puerto Rico
15.02.64 Carlos Ortiz W RSC 14 Flash Elorde, Manila, Philippines
11.04.64 Carlos Ortiz W PTS 15 Kenny Lane, San Juan, Puerto Rico
10.04.65 Ismael Laguna W PTS 15 Carlos Ortiz, Panama C, Panama
13.11.65 Carlos Ortiz W PTS 15 Ismael Laguna, San Juan, Puerto Rico
20.06.66 Carlos Ortiz W RSC 12 Johnny Bizzarro, Pittsburgh, USA
22.10.66 Carlos Ortiz W RSC 5 Sugar Ramos, Mexico C, Mexico
28.11.66 Carlos Ortiz W CO 14 Flash Elorde, New York C, USA
01.07.67 Carlos Ortiz W RSC 4 Sugar Ramos, San Juan, Puerto Rico
16.08.67 Carlos Ortiz W PTS 15 Ismael Laguna, New York C, USA
29.06.68 Carlos Teo Cruz W PTS 15 Carlos Ortiz, St Domingo, Puerto Rico
28.09.68 Carlos Teo Cruz W PTS 15 Mando Ramos, Los Angeles, USA
18.02.69 Mando Ramos W RSC 11 Carlos Teo Cruz, Los Angeles, USA
04.10.69 Mando Ramos W RSC 6 Yoshiaki Numata, Los Angeles, USA
03.03.70 Ismael Laguna W RTD 9 Mando Ramos, Los Angeles, USA
07.06.70 Ismael Laguna W RSC 13 Guts Ishimatsu, Panama C, Panama
26.09.70 Ken Buchanan W PTS 15 Ismael Laguna, San Juan, Puerto Rico
12.02.71 Ken Buchanan W PTS 15 Ruben Navarro, Los Angeles, USA
Ken Buchanan forfeited WBC recognition (failure to defend against Pedro Carrasco)
13.09.71 Ken Buchanan W PTS 15 Ismael Laguna, New York C, USA (WBA)
05.11.71 Pedro Carrasco W DIS 11 Mando Ramos, Madrid, Spain (WBC)
18.02.72 Mando Ramos W PTS 15 Pedro Carrasco, Los Angeles, USA (WBC)
26.06.72 Roberto Duran W RSC 13 Ken Buchanan, New York C, USA (WBA)
28.06.72 Mando Ramos W PTS 15 Pedro Carrasco, Madrid, Spain (WBC)
15.09.72 Chango Carmona W RSC 8 Mando Ramos, Los Angeles, USA (WBC)
10.11.72 Rodolfo Gonzalez W RTD 12 Chango Carmona, Los Angeles, USA (WBC)
20.01.73 Roberto Duran W CO 5 Jimmy Robertson, Panama C, Panama (WBA)
17.03.73 Rodolfo Gonzalez W RSC 9 Ruben Navarro, Los Angeles, USA (WBC)
02.06.73 Roberto Duran W RSC 8 Hector Thompson, Panama C, Panama (WBA)
08.09.73 Roberto Duran W RSC 10 Guts Ishimatsu, Panama C, Panama (WBA)
27.10.73 Rodolfo Gonzalez W RTD 10 Antonio Puddu, Los Angeles, USA (WBC)
16.03.74 Roberto Duran W RSC 11 Esteban de Jesus, Panama C, Panama (WBA)
11.04.74 Guts Ishimatsu W CO 8 Rodolfo Gonzalez, Tokyo, Japan (WBC)
13.09.74 Guts Ishimatsu DREW 15 Tury Pineda, Nagoya, Japan (WBC)
28.11.74 Guts Ishimatsu W CO 12 Rodolfo Gonzalez, Osaka, Japan (WBC)
21.12.74 Roberto Duran W RSC 1 Masataka Takayama, San Jose, Costa Rica (WBA)
27.02.75 Guts Ishimatsu W PTS 15 Ken Buchanan, Tokyo, Japan (WBC)
02.03.75 Roberto Duran W CO 14 Ray Lampkin, Panama C, Panama (WBA)
05.06.75 Guts Ishimatsu W PTS 15 Tury Pineda, Osaka, Japan (WBC)
04.12.75 Guts Ishimatsu W CO 14 Alvaro Rojas, Tokyo, Japan (WBC)
14.12.75 Roberto Duran W CO 15 Leoncio Ortiz, San Juan, Puerto Rico (WBA)
08.05.76 Esteban de Jesus W PTS 15 Guts Ishimatsu, Bayamon, Puerto Rico (WBC)
22.05.76 Roberto Duran W CO 14 Lou Bizzarro, Erie, USA (WBA)
10.09.76 Esteban de Jesus W CO 7 Hector Medina, Bayamon, Puerto Rico (WBC)
15.10.76 Roberto Duran W CO 1 Alvaro Rojas, Los Angeles, USA (WBA)
29.01.77 Roberto Duran W CO 13 Vilomar Fernandez, Miami, USA (WBA)
12.02.77 Esteban de Jesus W RSC 6 Buzzsaw Yamabe, Bayamon, Puerto Rico (WBC)
25.06.77 Esteban de Jesus W CO 11 Vicente Mijares, Bayamon, Puerto Rico (WBC)
17.09.77 Roberto Duran W PTS 15 Edwin Viruet, Philadelphia, USA (WBA)
21.01.78 Roberto Duran W CO 12 Esteban de Jesus, Las Vegas, USA
Roberto Duran relinquished title (moved up to welterweight)
17.04.79 Jim Watt W RSC 12 Alfredo Pitalua, Glasgow, Scotland (WBC)
16.06.79 Ernesto Espana W CO 13 Claude Noel, San Juan, Puerto Rico (WBA)
04.08.79 Ernesto Espana W RSC 9 Johnny Lira, Chicago, USA (WBA)
03.11.79 Jim Watt W RSC 9 Roberto Vasquez, Glasgow, Scotland (WBC)
02.03.80 Hilmer Kenty W RSC 9 Ernesto Espana, Detroit, USA (WBA)
14.03.80 Jim Watt W RSC 4 Charlie Nash, Glasgow, Scotland (WBC)
07.06.80 Jim Watt W PTS 15 Howard Davis, Glasgow, Scotland (WBC)
02.08.80 Hilmer Kenty W RSC 9 Yong-Ho Oh, Detroit, USA (WBA)
20.09.80 Hilmer Kenty W RSC 4 Ernesto Espano, San Juan, Puerto Rico (WBA)
01.11.80 Jim Watt W RSC 12 Sean O'Grady, Glasgow, Scotland (WBC)
08.11.80 Hilmer Kenty W PTS 15 Vilomar Fernandez, Detroit, USA (WBA)
12.04.81 Sean O'Grady W PTS 15 Hilmer Kenty, Atlantic C, USA (WBA)
Sean O'Grady forfeited WBA recognition (contractual dispute)
20.06.81 Alexis Arguello W PTS 15 Jim Watt, Wembley, England (WBC)
12.09.81 Claude Noel W PTS 15 Gato Gonzalez, Atlantic C, USA (WBA)
03.10.81 Alexis Arguello W RSC 14 Ray Mancini, Atlantic C, USA (WBC)
21.11.81 Alexis Arguello W CO 7 Robert Elizondo, Las Vegas, USA (WBC)
05.12.81 Arturo Frias W CO 8 Claude Noel, Las Vegas, USA (WBA)
30.01.82 Arturo Frias W TD 9 Ernesto Espana, Atlantic C, USA (WBA)
13.02.82 Alexis Arguello W RSC 6 Bubba Busceme, Beaumont, USA (WBC)
08.05.82 Ray Mancini W RSC 1 Arturo Frias, Las Vegas, USA (WBA)
22.05.82 Alexis Arguello W CO 5 Andy Ganigan, Las Vegas, USA (WBC)
Alexis Arguello relinquished WBC version of title (moved up to light-welterweight)
24.07.82 Ray Mancini W RSC 6 Ernesto Espana, Warren, USA (WBA)
13.11.82 Ray Mancini W RSC 14 Deuk-Koo Kim, Las Vegas, USA (WBA)

01.05.83 Edwin Rosario W PTS 12 Jose Luis Ramirez, San Juan, Puerto Rico (WBC)
15.09.83 Ray Mancini W CO 9 Orlando Romero, New York C, USA (WBA)
14.01.84 Ray Mancini W RSC 3 Bobby Chacon, Reno, USA (WBA)
30.01.84 Charlie Choo Choo Brown W PTS 15 Melvin Paul, Atlantic C, USA (IBF)
17.03.84 Edwin Rosario W RSC 1 Robert Elizondo, San Juan, Puerto Rico (WBC)
15.04.84 Harry Arroyo W RSC 14 Charlie Choo Choo Brown, Atlantic C, USA (IBF)
01.06.84 Livingstone Bramble W RSC 14 Ray Mancini, Buffalo, USA (WBA)
23.06.84 Edwin Rosario W PTS 12 Howard Davis, San Juan, Puerto Rico (WBC)
01.09.84 Harry Arroyo W RSC 8 Charlie W.L. Brown, Youngstown, USA (IBF)
03.11.84 Jose Luis Ramirez W RSC 4 Edwin Rosario, San Juan, Puerto Rico (WBC)
12.01.85 Harry Arroyo W RSC 11 Terrence Ali, Atlantic C, USA (IBF)
16.02.85 Livingstone Bramble W PTS 15 Ray Mancini, Reno, USA (WBA)
06.04.85 Jimmy Paul W PTS 15 Harry Arroyo, Atlantic C, USA (IBF)
30.06.85 Jimmy Paul W RSC 14 Robin Blake, Las Vegas, USA (IBF)
10.08.85 Hector Camacho W PTS 12 Jose Luis Ramirez, Las Vegas, USA (WBC)
16.02.86 Livingstone Bramble W RSC 13 Tyrone Crawley, Reno, USA (WBA)
04.06.86 Jimmy Paul W PTS 15 Irleis Perez, E Rutherford, USA (IBF)
13.06.86 Hector Camacho W PTS 12 Edwin Rosario, New York C, USA (WBC)
15.08.86 Jimmy Paul W PTS 15 Darryl Tyson, Detroit, USA (IBF)
26.09.86 Hector Camacho W PTS 12 Cornelius Boza-Edwards, Miami, USA (WBC)
Hector Camacho relinquished WBC version of title (moved up to light-welterweight)
26.09.86 Edwin Rosario W CO 2 Livingstone Bramble, Miami, USA (WBA)
05.12.86 Greg Haugen W PTS 15 Jimmy Paul, Las Vegas, USA (IBF)
07.06.87 Vinny Pazienza W PTS 15 Greg Haugen, Providence, USA (IBF)
19.07.87 Jose Luis Ramirez W PTS 12 Terrence Alli, St Tropez, France (WBC)
11.08.87 Edwin Rosario W CO 8 Juan Nazario, Chicago, USA (WBA)
10.10.87 Jose Luis Ramirez W CO 5 Cornelius Boza-Edwards, Paris, France (WBC)
21.11.87 Julio Cesar Chavez W RSC 11 Edwin Rosario, Las Vegas, USA (WBA)
06.02.88 Greg Haugen W PTS 15 Vinny Pazienza, Atlantic C, USA (IBF)
12.03.88 Jose Luis Ramirez W PTS 12 Pernell Whitaker, Paris, France (WBC)
11.04.88 Greg Haugen W TD 11 Miguel Santana, Tacoma, USA (IBF)
16.04.88 Julio Cesar Chavez W RSC 6 Rodolfo Aguilar, Las Vegas, USA (WBA)

Light-Welterweight (140 lbs)

Title Holders

	Birthplace	Tenure	Status
Mushy Callahan	USA	1926 – 1929	NBA/NY
Mushy Callahan	USA	1929 – 1930	NBA
Jackie Kid Berg	England	1930 – 1931	NBA
Tony Canzoneri	USA	1931 – 1932	NBA
Johnny Jadick	USA	1932 – 1933	NBA
Battling Shaw	Mexico	1933	NBA
Tony Canzoneri	USA	1933	NBA
Barney Ross *	USA	1933 – 1935	NBA
Tippy Larkin	USA	1946 – 1947	MASS/NY
Carlos Ortiz	Puerto Rico	1959 – 1960	NBA
Duilio Loi	Italy	1960 – 1962	NBA
Eddie Perkins	USA	1962	NBA
Duilio Loi *	Italy	1962 – 1963	NBA
Roberto Cruz	Philippines	1963	WBA
Eddie Perkins	USA	1963 – 1965	WBA
Eddie Perkins	USA	1965	
Carlos Hernandez	Venezuela	1965 – 1966	
Sandro Lopopolo	Italy	1966 – 1967	
Paul Fujii	Hawaii	1967 – 1968	
Paul Fujii	Hawaii	1968	WBA
Nicolino Loche	Argentine	1968 – 1972	WBA
Pedro Adigue	Philippines	1968 – 1970	WBC
Bruno Arcari *	Italy	1970 – 1974	WBC
Alfonso Frazer	Panama	1972	WBA
Antonio Cervantes	Colombia	1972 – 1976	WBA
Perico Fernandez	Spain	1974 – 1975	WBC
Saensak Muangsurin	Thailand	1975 – 1976	WBC
Wilfred Benitez	USA	1976 – 1977	WBA
Miguel Velasquez	Spain	1976	WBC
Saensak Muangsurin	Thailand	1976 – 1978	WBC
Antonio Cervantes	Colombia	1977 – 1980	WBA
Wilfred Benitez	USA	1977	NY
Sang-Hyun Kim	S Korea	1978 – 1980	WBC
Saoul Mamby	USA	1980 – 1982	WBC
Aaron Pryor *	USA	1980 – 1983	WBA
Leroy Haley	USA	1982 – 1983	WBC
Bruce Curry	USA	1983 – 1984	WBC
Johnny Bumphus	USA	1984	WBA
Bill Costello	USA	1984 – 1985	WBC
Gene Hatcher	USA	1984 – 1985	WBA
Aaron Pryor	USA	1984 – 1986	IBF
Ubaldo Sacco	Argentine	1985 – 1986	WBA
Lonnie Smith	USA	1985 – 1986	WBC
Patrizio Oliva	Italy	1986 – 1987	WBA
Gary Hinton	USA	1986	IBF
Rene Arredondo	Mexico	1986	WBC
Tsuyoshi Hamada	Japan	1986 – 1987	WBC
Joe Manley	USA	1986 – 1987	IBF
Terry Marsh *	England	1987	IBF
Juan M. Coggi	Argentine	1987 –	WBA
Rene Arredondo	Mexico	1987 –	WBC
Roger Mayweather	USA	1987 –	WBC
James McGirt	USA	1988 –	IBF

Title Bouts

21.09.26 Mushy Callahan W PTS 10 Pinkey Mitchell, Los Angeles, USA (NY/NBA)
14.03.27 Mushy Callahan W CO 2 Andy Divodi, New York C, USA (NY/NBA)
31.05.27 Mushy Callahan W PTS 10 Spug Myers, Chicago, USA (NY/NBA)
28.05.29 Mushy Callahan W CO 3 Fred Mahan, Los Angeles, USA (NY/NBA)
Mushy Callahan ceased to be recognised by NY (NY abolished weight division)
18.02.30 Jackie Kid Berg W RTD 10 Mushy Callahan, London, England (NBA)
29.05.30 Jackie Kid Berg W RSC 4 Al Delmont, Newark, USA (NBA)
03.09.30 Jackie Kid Berg W PTS 10 Buster Brown, Newark, USA (NBA)
23.01.31 Jackie Kid Berg W PTS 10 Goldie Hess, Chicago, USA (NBA)
10.04.31 Jackie Kid Berg W PTS 10 Billy Wallace, Detroit, USA (NBA)
24.04.31 Tony Canzoneri W CO 3 Jackie Kid Berg, Chicago, USA (NBA)
13.07.31 Tony Canzoneri W PTS 10 Cecil Payne, Los Angeles, USA (NBA)
29.10.31 Tony Canzoneri W PTS 10 Phillie Griffin, Newark, USA (NBA)
18.01.32 Johnny Jadick W PTS 10 Tony Canzoneri, Philadelphia, USA (NBA)
18.07.32 Johnny Jadick W PTS 10 Tony Canzoneri, Philadelphia, USA (NBA)
20.02.33 Battling Shaw W PTS 10 Johnny Jadick, New Orleans, USA (NBA)
21.05.33 Tony Canzoneri W PTS 10 Battling Shaw, New Orleans, USA (NBA)
23.06.33 Barney Ross W PTS 10 Tony Canzoneri, Chicago, USA (NBA)
26.07.33 Barney Ross W RSC 6 Johnny Farr, Kansas C, USA (NBA)
17.11.33 Barney Ross W PTS 10 Sammy Fuller, Chicago, USA (NBA)
07.02.34 Barney Ross W PTS 12 Pete Nebo, New Orleans, USA (NBA)
05.03.34 Barney Ross DREW 10 Frankie Klick, San Francisco, USA (NBA)
27.03.34 Barney Ross W PTS 10 Bobby Pacho, Los Angeles, USA (NBA)
10.12.34 Barney Ross W PTS 12 Bobby Pacho, Cleveland, USA (NBA)
28.01.35 Barney Ross W PTS 10 Frankie Klick, Miami, USA (NBA)
09.04.35 Barney Ross W PTS 12 Harry Woods, Seattle, USA (NBA)
Barney Ross relinquished NBA version of title (he decided to concentrate on the welterweight division – title fell into disuse)
29.04.46 Tippy Larkin W PTS 12 Willie Joyce, Boston, USA (MASS)
13.09.46 Tippy Larkin W PTS 12 Willie Joyce, New York C, USA (MASS/NY)
Tippy Larkin ceased to be recognised by NY and Massachusetts (this followed a defeat by Ike Williams in a non-title bout, June, 1947)
12.06.59 Carlos Ortiz W RTD 2 Kenny Lane, New York C, USA (NBA)
04.02.60 Carlos Ortiz W CO 10 Battling Torres, Los Angeles, USA (NBA)
15.06.60 Carlos Ortiz W PTS 15 Duilio Loi, San Francisco, USA (NBA)
01.09.60 Duilio Loi W PTS 15 Carlos Ortiz, Milan, Italy (NBA)
10.05.61 Duilio Loi W PTS 15 Carlos Ortiz, Milan, Italy (NBA)
21.10.61 Duilio Loi DREW 15 Eddie Perkins, Milan, Italy (NBA)
14.09.62 Eddie Perkins W PTS 15 Duilio Loi, Milan, Italy (NBA)
15.12.62 Duilio Loi W PTS 15 Eddie Perkins, Milan, Italy (NBA)
Duilio Loi relinquished NBA version of title (retired)
21.03.63 Roberto Cruz W CO 1 Battling Torres, Los Angeles, USA (WBA)
15.06.63 Eddie Perkins W PTS 15 Roberto Cruz, Manila, Philippines (WBA)
04.01.64 Eddie Perkins W RSC 13 Yoshinori Takahashi, Tokyo, Japan (WBA)
18.04.64 Eddie Perkins W PTS 15 Bunny Grant, Kingston, Jamaica (WBA)
18.01.65 Carlos Hernandez W PTS 15 Eddie Perkins, Caracas, Venezuela
15.05.65 Carlos Hernandez W RSC 4 Mario Rossito, Maracaibo, Venezuela
10.07.65 Carlos Hernandez W CO 3 Percy Hayles, Kingston, Jamaica
30.04.66 Sandro Lopopolo W PTS 15 Carlos Hernandez, Rome, Italy
21.10.66 Sandro Lopopolo W RSC 7 Vicente Rivas, Rome, Italy
30.04.67 Paul Fujii W RTD 2 Sandro Lopopolo, Tokyo, Japan
16.11.67 Paul Fujii W CO 4 Willi Quatuor, Tokyo, Japan
Paul Fujii forfeited WBC recognition (failure to defend against Pedro Adigue)
12.12.68 Nicolino Loche W RTD 9 Paul Fujii, Tokyo, Japan (WBA)
14.12.68 Pedro Adigue W PTS 15 Adolph Pruitt, Quezon C, Philippines (WBC)
03.05.69 Nicolino Loche W PTS 15 Carlos Hernandez, Bs Aires, Argentine (WBA)
11.10.69 Nicolino Loche W PTS 15 Joao Henrique, Bs Aires, Argentine (WBA)
01.02.70 Bruno Arcari W PTS 15 Pedro Adigue, Rome, Italy (WBC)
16.05.70 Nicolino Loche W PTS 15 Adolph Pruitt, Bs Aires, Argentine (WBA)
10.07.70 Bruno Arcari W DIS 6 Rene Roque, Lignano, Italy (WBC)
30.10.70 Bruno Arcari W CO 3 Raymundo Dias, Genoa, Italy (WBC)
06.03.71 Bruno Arcari W PTS 15 Joao Henrique, Rome, Italy (WBC)
03.04.71 Nicolino Loche W PTS 15 Domingo Barrera, Bs Aires, Argentine (WBA)
26.06.71 Bruno Arcari W RSC 9 Enrique Jana, Palermo, Italy (WBC)
10.10.71 Bruno Arcari W CO 10 Domingo Corpas, Genoa, Italy (WBC)
11.12.71 Nicolino Loche W PTS 15 Antonio Cervantes, Bs Aires, Argentine (WBA)
10.03.72 Alfonso Frazer W PTS 15 Nicolino Loche, Panama C, Panama (WBA)
10.06.72 Bruno Arcari W CO 12 Joao Henrique, Genoa, Italy (WBC)
17.06.72 Alfonso Frazer W RTD 4 Al Ford, Panama C, Panama (WBA)
28.10.72 Antonio Cervantes W CO 10 Alfonso Frazer, Panama C, Panama (WBA)
02.12.72 Bruno Arcari W PTS 15 Costa Azevedo, Turin, Italy (WBC)
16.02.73 Antonio Cervantes W PTS 15 Josua Marquez, San Juan, Puerto Rico (WBA)
17.03.73 Antonio Cervantes W RTD 9 Nicolino Loche, Maracay, Venezuela (WBA)
19.05.73 Antonio Cervantes W RSC 5 Alfonso Frazer, Panama C, Panama (WBA)
08.09.73 Antonio Cervantes W RSC 5 Carlos Giminez, Bogota, Columbia (WBA)
04.12.73 Antonio Cervantes W PTS 15 Lion Furuyama, Panama C, Panama (WBA)
16.02.74 Bruno Arcari W DIS 8 Tony Ortiz, Turin, Italy (WBC)
Bruno Arcari relinquished WBC version of title (weight making difficulties)
02.03.74 Antonio Cervantes W CO 6 Chang-Kil Lee, Cartagena, Colombia (WBA)
27.07.74 Antonio Cervantes W CO 2 Victor Ortiz, Cartagena, Colombia (WBA)
21.09.74 Perico Fernandez W PTS 15 Lion Furuyama, Rome, Italy (WBC)
26.10.74 Antonio Cervantes W CO 8 Shinchi Kadoto, Tokyo, Japan (WBA)
19.04.75 Perico Fernandez W CO 9 Joao Henrique, Barcelona, Spain (WBC)
17.05.75 Antonio Cervantes W PTS 15 Esteban de Jesus, Panama C, Panama (WBA)
15.07.75 Saensak Muangsurin W RTD 8 Perico Fernandez, Bangkok, Thailand (WBC)
15.11.75 Antonio Cervantes W RTD 7 Hector Thompson, Panama C, Panama (WBA)
25.01.76 Saensak Muangsurin W PTS 15 Lion Furuyama, Tokyo, Japan (WBC)

06.03.76 Wilfred Benitez W PTS 15 Antonio Cervantes, San Juan, Puerto Rico (WBA)
31.05.76 Wilfred Benitez W PTS 15 Emiliano Villa, San Juan, Puerto Rico (WBA)
30.06.76 Miguel Velasquez W DIS 4 Saensak Muangsurin, Madrid, Spain (WBC)
16.10.76 Wilfred Benitez W RSC 3 Tony Petronelli, San Juan, Puerto Rico (WBA)
Wilfred Benitez forfeited WBA recognition (failure to defend against Antonio Cervantes)
29.10.76 Saensak Muangsurin W RSC 2 Miguel Velasquez, Segovia, Spain (WBC)
15.01.77 Saensak Muangsurin W RSC 15 Monroe Brooks, Chiang, Thailand (WBC)
02.04.77 Saensak Muangsurin W CO 6 Guts Ishimatsu, Tokyo, Japan (WBC)
17.06.77 Saensak Muangsurin W PTS 15 Perico Fernandez, Madrid, Spain (WBC)
25.06.77 Antonio Cervantes W RSC 5 Carlos Giminez, Maracaibo, Venezuela (WBA)
03.08.77 Wilfred Benitez W RSC 15 Guerrero Chavez, New York C, USA (NY)
Wilfred Benitez ceased to be recognised by NY (moved up to welterweight)
20.08.77 Saensak Muangsurin W RSC 6 Mike Everett, Roi-Et, Thailand (WBC)
22.10.77 Saensak Muangsurin W PTS 15 Saoul Mamby, Korat, Thailand (WBC)
05.11.77 Antonio Cervantes W PTS 15 Adriano Marrero, Maracay, Venezuela (WBA)
29.12.77 Saensak Muangsurin W RTD 13 Jo Kimpuani, Chanthabun, Thailand (WBC)
08.04.78 Saensak Muangsurin W CO 13 Francisco Moreno, Hat Yai, Thailand (WBC)
28.04.78 Antonio Cervantes W CO 6 Tonga Kiatvayupakdi, Udon, Thailand (WBA)
26.08.78 Antonio Cervantes W RSC 9 Norman Sekgapane, Bothswana (WBA)
30.12.78 Sang-Hyun Kim W CO 13 Saensak Muangsurin, Seoul, S Korea (WBC)
18.01.79 Antonio Cervantes W PTS 15 Miguel Montilla, New York C, USA (WBA)
03.06.79 Sang-Hyun Kim W PTS 15 Fitzroy Guisseppi, Seoul, S Korea (WBC)
25.08.79 Antonio Cervantes W PTS 15 Kwang-Min Kim, Seoul, S Korea (WBA)
04.10.79 Sang-Hyun Kim W CO 11 Masahiro Yokai, Tokyo, Japan (WBC)
23.02.80 Saoul Mamby W CO 14 Sang-Hyun Kim, Seoul, S Korea (WBC)
29.03.80 Antonio Cervantes W RSC 7 Miguel Montilla, Cartagena, Colombia (WBA)
07.07.80 Saoul Mamby W RSC 13 Esteban de Jesus, Bloomington, USA (WBC)
02.08.80 Aaron Pryor W CO 4 Antonio Cervantes, Cincinnati, USA (WBA)
02.10.80 Saoul Mamby W PTS 15 Maurice Watkins, Las Vegas, USA (WBC)
22.11.80 Aaron Pryor W RSC 6 Gaetan Hart, Cincinnati, USA (WBA)
12.06.81 Saoul Mamby W PTS 15 Jo Kimpuani, Detroit, USA (WBC)
27.06.81 Aaron Pryor W RSC 2 Lennox Blackmore, Las Vegas, USA (WBA)
29.08.81 Saoul Mamby W PTS 15 Thomas Americo, Jakarta, Indonesia (WBC)
14.11.81 Aaron Pryor W RSC 7 Dujuan Johnson, Cleveland, USA (WBA)
20.12.81 Saoul Mamby W PTS 15 Obisia Nwankpa, Lagos, Nigeria (WBC)
21.03.82 Aaron Pryor W RSC 12 Miguel Montilla, Atlantic C, USA (WBA)
26.06.82 Leroy Haley W PTS 15 Saoul Mamby, Cleveland, USA (WBC)
04.07.82 Aaron Pryor W RSC 6 Akio Kameda, Cincinnati, USA (WBA)
20.10.82 Leroy Haley W PTS 15 Juan Giminez, Cleveland, USA (WBC)
12.11.82 Aaron Pryor W RSC 14 Alexis Arguello, Miami, USA (WBA)
13.02.83 Leroy Haley W PTS 12 Saoul Mamby, Cleveland, USA (WBC)
02.04.83 Aaron Pryor W RSC 3 Sang-Hyun Kim, Atlantic C, USA (WBA)
18.05.83 Bruce Curry W PTS 12 Leroy Haley, Las Vegas, USA (WBC)
07.07.83 Bruce Curry W RSC 7 Hidekazu Akai, Osaka, Japan (WBC)
09.09.83 Aaron Pryor W CO 10 Alexis Arguello, Las Vegas, USA (WBA)
Aaron Pryor relinquished WBA version of title (retired)
19.10.83 Bruce Curry W PTS 12 Leroy Haley, Las Vegas, USA (WBC)
22.01.84 Johnny Bumphus W PTS 15 Lorenzo Garcia, Atlantic C, USA (WBA)
29.01.84 Bill Costello W RSC 10 Bruce Curry, Beaumont, USA (WBC)
01.06.84 Gene Hatcher W RSC 11 Johnny Bumphus, Buffalo, USA (WBA)
22.06.84 Aaron Pryor W PTS 15 Nicky Furlano, Toronto, Canada (IBF)
15.07.84 Bill Costello W PTS 12 Ronnie Shields, Kingston NY, USA (WBC)
03.11.84 Bill Costello W PTS 12 Saoul Mamby, Kingston NY, USA (WBC)
15.12.84 Gene Hatcher W PTS 15 Ubaldo Sacco, Fort Worth, USA (WBA)
16.02.85 Bill Costello W PTS 12 Leroy Haley, Kingston NY, USA (WBC)
02.03.85 Aaron Pryor W PTS 15 Gary Hinton, Atlantic C, USA (IBF)
Aaron Pryor forfeited title (inactive)
21.07.85 Ubaldo Sacco W RSC 9 Gene Hatcher, Campione, Italy (WBA)
21.08.85 Lonnie Smith W RSC 8 Bill Costello, New York C, USA (WBC)
15.03.86 Patrizio Oliva W PTS 15 Ubaldo Sacco, Monte Carlo (WBA)
26.04.86 Gary Hinton W PTS 15 Antonio Reyes Cruz, Lucca, Italy (IBF)
05.05.86 Rene Arredondo W RSC 5 Lonnie Smith, Los Angeles, USA (WBC)
24.07.86 Tsuyoshi Hamada W CO 1 Rene Arredondo, Tokyo, Japan (WBC)
06.09.86 Patrizio Oliva W RSC 3 Brian Brunette, Naples, Italy (WBA)
30.10.86 Joe Manley W CO 10 Gary Hinton, Hartford, USA (IBF)
02.12.86 Tsuyoshi Hamada W PTS 12 Ronnie Shields, Tokyo, Japan (WBC)
10.01.87 Patrizio Oliva W PTS 15 Rodolfo Gonzalez, Agrigento, Italy (WBA)
04.03.87 Terry Marsh W RSC 10 Joe Manley, Basildon, England (IBF)
01.07.87 Terry Marsh W RTD 6 Akio Kameda, London, England (IBF)
Terry Marsh relinquished IBF version of title (retired)
04.07.87 Juan M. Coggi W CO 3 Patrizio Oliva, Ribera, Italy (WBA)
22.07.87 Rene Arredondo W RSC 6 Tsuyoshi Hamada, Tokyo, Japan (WBC)
12.11.87 Roger Mayweather W RSC 6 Rene Arredondo, Los Angeles, USA (WBC)
14.02.88 James McGirt W RSC 12 Frankie Warren, Corpus Christi, USA (IBF)
24.03.88 Roger Mayweather W CO 3 Mauricio Aceves, Los Angeles, USA (WBC)

Welterweight (147 lbs)

Title Holders

	Birthplace	Tenure	Status
Mysterious Billy Smith	USA	1892 – 1894	
Tommy Ryan *	USA	1894 – 1898	
Mysterious Billy Smith	USA	1898 – 1900	
Rube Ferns	USA	1900	
Matty Matthews	USA	1900 – 1901	
Rube Ferns	USA	1901	
Joe Walcott	Barbados	1901 – 1904	
Dixie Kid	USA	1904 – 1905	
Honey Mellody	USA	1906 – 1907	
Mike Twin Sullivan *	USA	1907 – 1908	
Jimmy Gardner	USA	1908 – 1910	USA
Harry Lewis	USA	1910 – 1912	GB/FR
Jimmy Clabby	USA	1910 – 1912	USA/AUSTR
Waldemar Holberg	Denmark	1914	AUSTR
Tom McCormick	Ireland	1914	AUSTR
Matt Wells	England	1914 – 1915	AUSTR
Mike Glover	USA	1915	USA
Jack Britton	USA	1915	USA
Ted Kid Lewis	England	1915 – 1916	
Jack Britton	USA	1916 – 1917	
Ted Kid Lewis	England	1917 – 1919	
Jack Britton	USA	1919 – 1922	
Mickey Walker	USA	1922 – 1926	
Pete Latzo	USA	1926 – 1927	
Joe Dundee	Italy	1927 – 1929	
Jackie Fields	USA	1929	NBA
Jackie Fields	USA	1929 – 1930	
Young Jack Thompson	USA	1930	
Tommy Freeman	USA	1930 – 1931	
Young Jack Thompson	USA	1931	
Lou Brouillard	Canada	1931 – 1932	
Jackie Fields	USA	1932 – 1933	
Young Corbett III	Italy	1933	
Jimmy McLarnin	Ireland	1933 – 1934	
Barney Ross	USA	1934	
Jimmy McLarnin	Ireland	1934 – 1935	
Barney Ross	USA	1935 – 1938	
Henry Armstrong	USA	1938 – 1940	
Fritzie Zivic	USA	1940 – 1941	
Red Cochrane	USA	1941 – 1946	
Marty Servo *	USA	1946	
Sugar Ray Robinson *	USA	1946 – 1951	
Johnny Bratton	USA	1951	NBA
Kid Gavilan	Cuba	1951 – 1952	NBA/NY
Kid Gavilan	Cuba	1952 – 1954	
Carmen Basilio	USA	1953	NY
Johnny Saxton	USA	1954 – 1955	
Tony de Marco	USA	1955	
Carmen Basilio	USA	1955 – 1956	
Johnny Saxton	USA	1956	
Carmen Basilio *	USA	1956 – 1957	
Virgil Akins	USA	1958	
Don Jordan	Dom Republic	1958 – 1960	
Benny Kid Paret	Cuba	1960 – 1961	
Emile Griffith	Virgin Islands	1961	
Benny Kid Paret	Cuba	1961 – 1962	
Emile Griffith	Virgin Islands	1962 – 1963	
Luis Rodriguez	Cuba	1963	
Emile Griffith *	Virgin Islands	1963 – 1966	
Curtis Cokes	USA	1966 – 1967	WBA
Charley Shipes	USA	1966 – 1967	CALIF
Curtis Cokes	USA	1967 – 1969	
Jose Napoles	Cuba	1969 – 1970	
Billy Backus	USA	1970 – 1971	
Jose Napoles *	Cuba	1971 – 1975	
Hedgemon Lewis	USA	1972 – 1974	NY
Jose Napoles	Cuba	1975	WBC
Angel Espada	Puerto Rico	1975 – 1976	WBA
John H. Stracey	England	1975 – 1976	WBC
Carlos Palomino	Mexico	1976 – 1979	WBC
Pipino Cuevas	Mexico	1976 – 1980	WBA
Wilfred Benitez	USA	1979	WBC
Sugar Ray Leonard	USA	1979 – 1980	WBC
Roberto Duran	Panama	1980	WBC
Thomas Hearns	USA	1980 – 1981	WBA
Sugar Ray Leonard	USA	1980 – 1981	WBC
Sugar Ray Leonard *	USA	1981 – 1982	
Don Curry	USA	1983 – 1984	WBA
Don Curry	USA	1984 – 1985	WBA/IBF
Milton McCrory	USA	1983 – 1985	WBC
Don Curry	USA	1985 – 1986	
Lloyd Honeyghan	Jamaica	1986	
Lloyd Honeyghan	Jamaica	1986 – 1987	WBC/IBF
Mark Breland	USA	1987	WBA
Marlon Starling	USA	1987 –	WBA
Jorge Vaca	Mexico	1987 – 1988	WBC
Lloyd Honeyghan	Jamaica	1988 –	WBC
Simon Brown	Jamaica	1988 –	IBF

Title Bouts

14.12.92 Mysterious Billy Smith W CO 14 Danny Needham, San Francisco, USA
17.04.93 Mysterious Billy Smith W CO 2 Tom Williams, New York C, USA
26.07.94 Tommy Ryan W PTS 20 Mysterious Billy Smith, Minneapolis, USA
18.01.95 Tommy Ryan W 3 Nonpareil Jack Dempsey, New York C, USA
27.05.95 Tommy Ryan NC 18 Mysterious Billy Smith, New York C, USA
25.11.96 Tommy Ryan W DIS 9 Mysterious Billy Smith, New York C, USA
23.12.96 Tommy Ryan W CO 4 Bill Payne, Syracuse, USA
24.02.97 Tommy Ryan W CO 9 Tom Tracy, Syracuse, USA
Tommy Ryan relinquished title (moved up to middleweight)

04.04.98 Mysterious Billy Smith DREW 25 Joe Walcott, Bridgeport, USA
29.07.98 Mysterious Billy Smith W PTS 25 George Green, New York C, USA
25.08.98 Mysterious Billy Smith W PTS 25 Matty Matthews, New York C, USA
05.09.98 Mysterious Billy Smith DREW 25 Andy Walsh, New York C, USA
03.10.98 Mysterious Billy Smith W CO 20 Jim Judge, Scranton, USA
07.10.98 Mysterious Billy Smith W PTS 25 Charley McKeever, New York C, USA
06.12.98 Mysterious Billy Smith W PTS 20 Joe Walcott, New York C, USA
24.01.99 Mysterious Billy Smith W CO 14 Billy Edwards, New York C, USA
10.03.99 Mysterious Billy Smith W RSC 14 George Lavigne, San Francisco, USA
29.06.99 Mysterious Billy Smith DREW 20 Charley McKeever, New York C, USA
04.08.99 Mysterious Billy Smith DREW 25 Andy Walsh, New York C, USA
08.11.99 Mysterious Billy Smith W PTS 20 Charley McKeever, New York C, USA
15.01.00 Rube Ferns W DIS 21 Mysterious Billy Smith, Buffalo, USA
13.08.00 Rube Ferns W RTD 15 Eddie Connolly, Buffalo, USA
01.09.00 Rube Ferns W PTS 15 Matty Matthews, Detroit, USA
16.10.00 Matty Matthews W PTS 15 Rube Ferns, Detroit, USA
29.04.01 Matty Matthews W PTS 20 Tom Couhig, Louisville, USA
24.05.01 Rube Ferns W CO 10 Matty Matthews, Toronto, Canada
23.09.01 Rube Ferns W CO 9 Frank Erne, Fort Erie, Canada
18.12.01 Joe Walcott W RSC 5 Rube Ferns, Fort Erie, Canada
23.06.02 Joe Walcott W PTS 15 Tommy West, London, England
02.04.03 Joe Walcott DREW 20 Billy Woods, Los Angeles, USA
29.04.04 Dixie Kid W DIS 20 Joe Walcott, San Francisco, USA
12.05.04 Dixie Kid DREW 20 Joe Walcott, San Francisco, USA
Dixie Kid lost general recognition (failure to defend the title within a reasonable period)
30.09.04 Joe Walcott DREW 20 Joe Gans, San Francisco, USA
16.10.06 Honey Mellody W PTS 15 Joe Walcott, Chelsea Mass, USA
29.11.06 Honey Mellody W RSC 12 Joe Walcott, Chelsea, Mass, USA
23.04.07 Mike Twin Sullivan W PTS 20 Honey Mellody, Los Angeles, USA
01.11.07 Mike Twin Sullivan W PTS 20 Frank Field, Goldfield, USA
27.11.07 Mike Twin Sullivan W CO 13 Kid Farmer, Los Angeles, USA
23.04.08 Mike Twin Sullivan W PTS 25 Jimmy Gardner, Los Angeles, USA
Mike Twin Sullivan relinquished title (eye injury)
07.11.08 Jimmy Gardner W PTS 15 Jimmy Clabby, New Orleans, USA (USA)
26.11.08 Jimmy Gardner DREW 20 Jimmy Clabby, New Orleans, USA (USA)
Jimmy Gardner ceased to be recognised in the USA (unable to make the weight)
19.02.10 Harry Lewis DREW 25 Willie Lewis, Paris, France (FR)
23.04.10 Harry Lewis DREW 25 Willie Lewis, Paris, France (FR)
04.05.10 Harry Lewis W CO 3 Peter Brown, Paris, France (FR)
27.06.10 Harry Lewis W RTD 7 Young Joseph, London, England (GB/FR)
05.09.10 Jimmy Clabby W CO 13 Guy Buckles, Sheridan, USA (USA)
02.11.10 Jimmy Clabby W RSC 7 Bob Bryant, Sydney, Australia (USA/AUSTR)
26.12.10 Jimmy Clabby W CO 1 Gus Devitt, Brisbane, Australia (USA/AUSTR)
Jimmy Clabby ceased to be recognised by Australia/USA (he grew into a fully fledged middleweight before being able to consolidate his claim)
25.01.11 Harry Lewis W CO 4 Johnny Summers, London, England (GB/FR)
Harry Lewis ceased to be recognised in GB and France (this followed two losing contests against Johnny Mathieson in 1912)
01.01.14 Waldemar Holberg W PTS 20 Ray Bronson, Melbourne, Australia (AUSTR)
24.01.14 Tom McCormick W DIS 6 Waldemar Holberg, Melbourne, Australia (AUSTR)
14.02.14 Tom McCormick W CO 1 Johnny Summers, Sydney, Australia (AUSTR)
21.03.14 Matt Wells W PTS 20 Tom McCormick, Sydney, Australia (AUSTR)
01.06.15 Mike Glover W PTS 12 Matt Wells, Boston, USA (USA)
22.06.15 Jack Britton W PTS 12 Mike Glover, Boston, USA (USA)
31.08.15 Ted Kid Lewis W PTS 12 Jack Britton, Boston, USA
27.09.15 Ted Kid Lewis W PTS 12 Jack Britton, Boston, USA
26.10.15 Ted Kid Lewis W PTS 12 Joe Mandot, Boston, USA
02.11.15 Ted Kid Lewis W PTS 12 Milburn Saylor, Boston, USA
23.11.15 Ted Kid Lewis W CO 1 Jimmy Duffy, Boston, USA
01.03.16 Ted Kid Lewis W PTS 20 Harry Stone, New Orleans, USA
24.04.16 Jack Britton W PTS 20 Ted Kid Lewis, New Orleans, USA
06.06.16 Jack Britton W PTS 12 Mike O'Dowd, Boston, USA
17.10.16 Jack Britton W PTS 12 Ted Kid Lewis, Boston, USA
14.11.16 Jack Britton DREW 12 Ted Kid Lewis, Boston, USA
21.11.16 Jack Britton W PTS 12 Charley White, Boston, USA
25.06.17 Ted Kid Lewis W PTS 20 Jack Britton, Dayton, USA
13.11.17 Ted Kid Lewis W RSC 4 Johnny McCarthy, San Francisco, USA
17.05.18 Ted Kid Lewis W PTS 20 Johnny Tillman, Denver, USA
17.03.19 Jack Britton W CO 9 Ted Kid Lewis, Canton, USA
01.12.19 Jack Britton W CO 11 Billy Ryan, Canton, USA
31.05.20 Jack Britton W PTS 15 Johnny Griffiths, Akron, USA
23.08.20 Jack Britton DREW 12 Lou Bogash, Bridgeport, USA
06.09.20 Jack Britton W PTS 10 Ray Bronson, Cedar Point, USA
07.02.21 Jack Britton W PTS 15 Ted Kid Lewis, New York C, USA
03.06.21 Jack Britton DREW 10 Dave Shade, Portland, USA
10.06.21 Jack Britton DREW 10 Frank Barrieau, Portland, USA
17.02.22 Jack Britton DREW 15 Dave Shade, New York C, USA
26.06.22 Jack Britton W DIS 13 Benny Leonard, New York C, USA
01.11.22 Mickey Walker W PTS 15 Jack Britton, New York C, USA
08.10.23 Mickey Walker NC 9 Jimmy Jones, Newark, USA
02.06.24 Mickey Walker W PTS 10 Lew Tendler, Philadelphia, USA
01.10.24 Mickey Walker W CO 6 Bobby Barrett, Philadelphia, USA
21.09.25 Mickey Walker W PTS 15 Deve Shade, New York C, USA
20.05.26 Pete Latzo W PTS 10 Mickey Walker, Scranton, USA
29.06.26 Pete Latzo W CO 5 Willie Harmon, Newark, USA
09.07.26 Pete Latzo W DIS 4 George Levine, New York C, USA
03.06.27 Joe Dundee W PTS 15 Pete Latzo, New York C, USA
07.07.28 Joe Dundee W CO 8 Hilario Martinez, Philadelphia, USA
25.03.29 Jackie Fields W PTS 10 Young Jack Thompson, Chicago, USA (NBA)
25.07.29 Jackie Fields W DIS 2 Joe Dundee, Detroit, USA
09.05.30 Young Jack Thompson W PTS 15 Jackie Fields, Detroit, USA
05.09.30 Tommy Freeman W PTS 15 Young Jack Thompson, Cleveland, USA
09.01.31 Tommy Freeman W PTS 10 Pete August, Hot Springs, USA
26.01.31 Tommy Freeman W PTS 10 Eddie Murdoch, Oklahoma C, USA
05.02.31 Tommy Freeman W CO 5 Duke Trammel, Memphis, USA
09.02.31 Tommy Freeman W CO 5 Al Kid Kober, New Orleans, USA
01.03.31 Tommy Freeman W PTS 10 Alfredo Gaona, Mexico C, Mexico
14.04.31 Young Jack Thompson W RTD 12 Tommy Freeman, Cleveland, USA
23.10.31 Lou Brouillard W PTS 15 Young Jack Thompson, Boston, USA
28.01.32 Jackie Fields W PTS 10 Lou Brouillard, Chicago, USA
22.02.33 Young Corbett III W PTS 10 Jackie Fields, San Francisco, USA
29.05.33 Jimmy McLarnin W CO 1 Young Corbett III, Los Angeles, USA
28.05.34 Barney Ross W PTS 15 Jimmy McLarnin, New York C, USA
17.09.34 Jimmy McLarnin W PTS 15 Barney Ross, New York C, USA
28.05.35 Barney Ross W PTS 15 Jimmy McLarnin, New York C, USA
27.11.36 Barney Ross W PTS 15 Izzy Jannazzo, New York C, USA
23.09.37 Barney Ross W PTS 15 Ceferino Garcia, New York C, USA
31.05.38 Henry Armstrong W PTS 15 Barney Ross, New York C, USA
25.11.38 Henry Armstrong W PTS 15 Ceferino Garcia, New York C, USA
05.12.38 Henry Armstrong W RSC 3 Al Manfredo, Cleveland, USA
10.01.39 Henry Armstrong W PTS 10 Baby Arizmendi, Los Angeles, USA
04.03.39 Henry Armstrong W RSC 4 Bobby Pacho, Havana, Cuba
16.03.39 Henry Armstrong W CO 1 Lew Feldman, St Louis, USA
31.03.39 Henry Armstrong W CO 12 Davey Day, New York C, USA
25.05.39 Henry Armstrong W PTS 15 Ernie Roderick, London, England
09.10.39 Henry Armstrong W RSC 4 Al Manfredo, Des Moines, USA
13.10.39 Henry Armstrong W CO 2 Howard Scott, Minneapolis, USA
20.10.39 Henry Armstrong W CO 3 Richie Fontaine, Seattle, USA
24.10.39 Henry Armstrong W PTS 10 Jimmy Garrison, Los Angeles, USA
30.10.39 Henry Armstrong W RSC 4 Bobby Pacho, Denver, USA
11.12.39 Henry Armstrong W CO 7 Jimmy Garrison, Cleveland, USA
04.01.40 Henry Armstrong W CO 5 Joe Ghnouly, St Louis, USA
24.01.40 Henry Armstrong W RSC 9 Pedro Montanez, New York C, USA
26.04.40 Henry Armstrong W RSC 7 Paul Junior, Boston, USA
24.05.40 Henry Armstrong W RSC 5 Ralph Zanelli, Boston, USA
21.06.40 Henry Armstrong W RSC 3 Paul Junior, Portland, USA
23.09.40 Henry Armstrong W CO 4 Phil Furr, Washington, USA
04.10.40 Fritzie Zivic W PTS 15 Henry Armstrong, New York C, USA
17.01.41 Fritzie Zivic W RSC 12 Henry Armstrong, New York C, USA
29.07.41 Red Cochrane W PTS 15 Fritzie Zivic, Newark, USA
01.02.46 Marty Servo W CO 4 Red Cochrane, New York C, USA
Marty Servo relinquished title (retired)
20.12.46 Sugar Ray Robinson W PTS 15 Tommy Bell, New York C, USA
24.06.47 Sugar Ray Robinson W RSC 8 Jimmy Doyle, Cleveland, USA
19.12.47 Sugar Ray Robinson W RSC 6 Chuck Taylor, Detroit, USA
28.06.48 Sugar Ray Robinson W PTS 15 Bernard Docusen, Chicago, USA
11.07.49 Sugar Ray Robinson W PTS 15 Kid Gavilan, Philadelphia, USA
09.08.50 Sugar Ray Robinson W PTS 15 Charlie Fusari, Jersey C, USA
Sugar Ray Robinson relinquished title (moved up to middleweight)
14.03.51 Johnny Bratton W PTS 15 Charlie Fusari, Chicago, USA (NBA)
18.05.51 Kid Gavilan W PTS 15 Johnny Bratton, New York C, USA (NBA/NY)
29.08.51 Kid Gavilan W PTS 15 Billy Graham, New York C, USA (NBA/NY)
04.02.52 Kid Gavilan W PTS 15 Bobby Dykes, Miami, USA (NBA/NY)
07.07.52 Kid Gavilan W RSC 11 Gil Turner, Philadelphia, USA
05.10.52 Kid Gavilan W PTS 15 Billy Graham, Havana, Cuba
11.02.53 Kid Gavilan W RTD 9 Chuck Davey, Chicago, USA
06.06.53 Carmen Basilio W PTS 12 Billy Graham, Syracuse, USA (NY)
25.07.53 Carmen Basilio DREW 12 Billy Graham, Syracuse, USA (NY)
18.09.53 Kid Gavilan W PTS 15 Carmen Basilio, Syracuse, USA
13.11.53 Kid Gavilan W PTS 15 Johnny Bratton, Chicago, USA
20.10.54 Johnny Saxton W PTS 15 Kid Gavilan, Philadelphia, USA
01.04.55 Tony de Marco W RSC 14 Johnny Saxton, Boston, USA
10.06.55 Carmen Basilio W RSC 12 Tony de Marco, Syracuse, USA
30.11.55 Carmen Basilio W RSC 12 Tony de Marco, Boston, USA
14.03.56 Johnny Saxton W PTS 15 Carmen Basilio, Chicago, USA
12.09.56 Carmen Basilio W RSC 9 Johnny Saxton, Syracuse, USA
22.02.57 Carmen Basilio W CO 2 Johnny Saxton, Cleveland, USA
Carmen Basilio relinquished title (moved up to middleweight)
05.06.58 Virgil Akins W RSC 4 Vince Martinez, St Louis, USA
05.12.58 Don Jordan W PTS 15 Virgil Akins, Los Angeles, USA
24.04.59 Don Jordan W PTS 15 Virgil Akins, St Louis, USA
10.07.59 Don Jordan W PTS 15 Denny Moyer, Portland, USA
27.05.60 Benny Kid Paret W PTS 15 Don Jordan, Las Vegas, USA
10.12.60 Benny Kid Paret W PTS 15 Federico Thompson, New York C, USA
01.04.61 Emile Griffith W CO 13 Benny Kid Paret, Miami, USA
03.06.61 Emile Griffith W RSC 12 Gaspar Ortega, Los Angeles, USA
30.09.61 Benny Kid Paret W PTS 15 Emile Griffith, New York C, USA
24.03.62 Emile Griffith W RSC 12 Benny Kid Paret, New York C, USA
13.07.62 Emile Griffith W PTS 15 Ralph Dupas, Las Vegas, USA
08.12.62 Emile Griffith W RTD 9 Jorge Fernandez, Las Vegas, USA
21.03.63 Luis Rodriguez W PTS 15 Emile Griffith, Los Angeles, USA
08.06.63 Emile Griffith W PTS 15 Luis Rodriguez, New York C, USA
12.06.64 Emile Griffith W PTS 15 Luis Rodriguez, Las Vegas, USA
22.09.64 Emile Griffith W PTS 15 Brian Curvis, Wembley, England
30.03.65 Emile Griffith W PTS 15 Jose Stable, New York C, USA
10.12.65 Emile Griffith W PTS 15 Manuel Gonzalez, New York C, USA
Emile Griffith relinquished title (moved up to middleweight)

24.08.66 Curtis Cokes W PTS 15 Manuel Gonzalez, New Orleans, USA (WBA)
28.11.66 Curtis Cokes W PTS 15 Jean Josselin, Dallas, USA (WBA)
07.12.66 Charlie Shipes W RSC 10 Percy Manning, Hayward, USA (CALIF)
19.05.67 Curtis Cokes W RSC 10 Francois Pavilla, Dallas, USA (WBA)
02.10.67 Curtis Cokes W RSC 8 Charlie Shipes, Oakland, USA
16.04.68 Curtis Cokes W RSC 5 Willie Ludick, Dallas, USA
21.10.68 Curtis Cokes W PTS 15 Ramon la Cruz, New Orleans, USA
18.04.69 Jose Napoles W RSC 13 Curtis Cokes, Los Angeles, USA
29.06.69 Jose Napoles W RTD 10 Curtis Cokes, Mexico C, Mexico
17.10.69 Jose Napoles W PTS 15 Emile Griffith, Los Angeles, USA
15.02.70 Jose Napoles W RSC 15 Ernie Lopez, Los Angeles, USA
03.12.70 Billy Backus W RSC 4 Jose Napoles, Syracuse, USA
04.06.71 Jose Napoles W RSC 8 Billy Backus, Los Angeles, USA
14.12.71 Jose Napoles W PTS 15 Hedgemon Lewis, Los Angeles, USA
28.03.72 Jose Napoles W CO 7 Ralph Charles, Wembley, England
10.06.72 Jose Napoles W RSC 2 Adolph Pruitt, Monterrey, Mexico
16.06.72 Hedgemon Lewis W PTS 15 Billy Backus, Syracuse, USA (NY)
08.12.72 Hedgemon Lewis W PTS 15 Billy Backus, Syracuse, USA (NY)
28.02.73 Jose Napoles W CO 7 Ernie Lopez, Los Angeles, USA
23.06.73 Jose Napoles W PTS 15 Roger Menetrey, Grenoble, France
22.09.73 Jose Napoles W PTS 15 Clyde Gray, Toronto, Canada
03.08.74 Jose Napoles W RSC 9 Hedgemon Lewis, Mexico C, Mexico
14.12.74 Jose Napoles W CO 3 Horacio Saldano, Mexico C, Mexico
30.03.75 Jose Napoles W TD 12 Armando Muniz, Acapulco, Mexico
Jose Napoles relinquished WBA version of title (the WBC defence requirement clashed with that of the WBA)
28.06.75 Angel Espada W PTS 15 Clyde Gray, San Juan, Puerto Rico (WBA)
12.07.75 Jose Napoles W PTS 15 Armando Muniz, Mexico C, Mexico (WBC)
11.10.75 Angel Espada W PTS 15 Johnny Gant, San Juan, Puerto Rico (WBA)
06.12.75 John H. Stracey W RSC 6 Jose Napoles, Mexico C, Mexico (WBC)
20.03.76 John H. Stracey W RSC 10 Hedgemon Lewis, Wembley, England (WBC)
27.04.76 Angel Espada W RSC 8 Alfonso Hayman, San Juan, Puerto Rico (WBA)
22.06.76 Carlos Palomino W RSC 12 John H. Stracey, Wembley, England (WBC)
17.07.76 Pipino Cuevas W RSC 2 Angel Espada, Mexicali, Mexico (WBA)
27.10.76 Pipino Cuevas W CO 6 Shoji Tsujimoto, Kanazawa, Japan (WBA)
22.01.77 Carlos Palomino W RSC 15 Armando Muniz, Los Angeles, USA (WBC)
12.03.77 Pipino Cuevas W CO 2 Miguel Campanino, Mexico C, Mexico (WBA)
14.06.77 Carlos Palmonio W CO 11 Dave Boy Green, Wembley, England (WBC)
06.08.77 Pipino Cuevas W CO 2 Clyde Gray, Los Angeles, USA (WBA)
13.09.77 Carlos Palomino W PTS 15 Everaldo Azevedo, Los Angeles, USA (WBC)
19.11.77 Pipino Cuevas W RSC 11 Angel Espada, San Juan, Puerto Rico (WBA)
10.12.77 Carlos Palomino W CO 13 Jose Palacios, Los Angeles, USA (WBC)
11.02.78 Carlos Palomino W CO 7 Ryu Sorimachi, Las Vegas, USA (WBC)
04.03.78 Pipino Cuevas W RSC 9 Harold Weston, Los Angeles, USA (WBA)
18.03.78 Carlos Palomino W RSC 9 Mimoun Mohatar, Las Vegas, USA (WBC)
20.05.78 Pipino Cuevas W RSC 1 Billy Backus, Los Angeles, USA (WBA)
27.05.78 Carlos Palomino W PTS 15 Armando Muniz, Los Angeles, USA (WBC)
09.09.78 Pipino Cuevas W RSC 2 Pete Ranzany, Sacramento, USA (WBA)
14.01.79 Wilfred Benitez W PTS 15 Carlos Palomino, San Juan, Puerto Rico (WBC)
29.01.79 Pipino Cuevas W RSC 2 Scott Clark, Los Angeles, USA (WBA)
25.03.79 Wilfred Benitez W PTS 15 Harold Weston, San Juan, Puerto Rico (WBC)
30.07.79 Pipino Cuevas W PTS 15 Randy Shields, Chicago, USA (WBA)
30.11.79 Sugar Ray Leonard W RSC 15 Wilfred Benitez, Las Vegas, USA (WBC)
08.12.79 Pipino Cuevas W RSC 10 Angel Espada, Los Angeles, USA (WBA)
31.03.80 Sugar Ray Leonard W CO 4 Dave Boy Green, Landover, USA (WBC)
06.04.80 Pipino Cuevas W CO 5 Harold Volbrecht, Houston, USA (WBA)
20.06.80 Roberto Duran W PTS 15 Sugar Ray Leonard, Montreal, Canada (WBC)
02.08.80 Thomas Hearns W RSC 2 Pipino Cuevas, Detroit, USA (WBA)
25.11.80 Sugar Ray Leonard W RTD 8 Roberto Duran, New Orleans, USA (WBC)
06.12.80 Thomas Hearns W CO 6 Luis Primera, Detroit, USA (WBA)
28.03.81 Sugar Ray Leonard W RSC 10 Larry Bonds, Syracuse, USA (WBC)
25.04.81 Thomas Hearns W RSC 12 Randy Shields, Phoenix, USA (WBA)
25.06.81 Thomas Hearns W RSC 4 Pablo Baez, Houston, USA (WBA)
16.09.81 Sugar Ray Leonard W RSC 14 Thomas Hearns, Las Vegas, USA
15.02.82 Sugar Ray Leonard W RSC 3 Bruce Finch, Reno, USA
Sugar Ray Leonard relinquished title (retired)
13.02.83 Don Curry W PTS 15 Jun-Sok Hwang, Fort Worth, USA (WBA)
19.03.83 Milton McCrory DREW 12 Colin Jones, Reno, USA (WBC)
13.08.83 Milton McCrory W PTS 12 Colin Jones, Las Vegas, USA (WBC)
03.09.83 Don Curry W RSC 1 Roger Stafford, Marsala, Italy (WBA)
14.01.84 Milton McCrory W RSC 6 Milton Guest, Detroit, USA (WBC)
04.02.84 Don Curry W PTS 15 Marlon Starling, Atlantic C, USA (WBA/IBF)
15.04.84 Milton McCrory W RSC 6 Gilles Ebilia, Detroit, USA (WBC)
21.04.84 Don Curry W RTD 7 Elio Diaz, Fort Worth, USA (WBA/IBF)
22.09.84 Don Curry W RSC 6 Nino la Rocca, Monte Carlo (WBA/IBF)
19.01.85 Don Curry W RSC 4 Colin Jones, Birmingham, England (WBA/IBF)
09.03.85 Milton McCrory W PTS 12 Pedro Vilella, Paris, France (WBC)
14.07.85 Milton McCrory W RSC 3 Carlos Trujillo, Monte Carlo (WBC)
06.12.85 Don Curry W CO 2 Milton McCrory, Las Vegas, USA (WBA/WBC)
09.03.86 Don Curry W CO 2 Eduardo Rodriguez, Fort Worth, USA (WBA)
27.09.86 Lloyd Honeyghan W RTD 6 Don Curry, Atlantic C, USA
Lloyd Honeyghan relinquished WBA version of title (wanted to avoid a meeting with the WBA's leading contender Harold Volbrecht on the grounds of apartheid)
06.02.87 Mark Breland W CO 7 Harold Volbrecht, Atlantic C, USA (WBA)
22.02.87 Lloyd Honeyghan W RSC 2 Johnny Bumphus, Wembley, England (IBF)
18.04.87 Lloyd Honeyghan W PTS 12 Maurice Blocker, London, England (WBC)
22.08.87 Marlon Starling W CO 11 Mark Breland, Columbia, USA (WBA)
30.08.87 Lloyd Honeyghan W RSC 1 Gene Hatcher, Marbella, Spain (WBC)
28.10.87 Jorge Vaca W TD 8 Lloyd Honeyghan, Wembley, England (WBC)
Lloyd Honeyghan forfeited IBF recognition (title vacated following Vaca defeat)
05.02.88 Marlon Starling W PTS 12 Fujio Ozaki, Atlantic C, USA (WBA)
29.03.88 Lloyd Honeyghan W CO 3 Jorge Vaca, Wembley, England (WBC)
16.04.88 Marlon Starling DREW 12 Mark Breland, Las Vegas, USA (WBA)
23.04.88 Simon Brown W RSC 14 Tyrone Trice, Berck sur Mer, France (IBF)

Light-Middleweight (154 lbs)

Title Holders

	Birthplace	Tenure	Status
Denny Moyer	USA	1962 – 1963	WBA
Ralph Dupas	USA	1963	WBA
Sandro Mazzinghi	Italy	1963 – 1965	WBA
Nino Benvenuti	Italy	1965 – 1966	WBA
Ki-Soo Kim	S Korea	1966 – 1968	WBA
Sandro Mazzinghi	Italy	1968 – 1969	WBA
Freddie Little	USA	1969 – 1970	
Carmelo Bossi	Italy	1970 – 1971	
Koichi Wajima	Japan	1971 – 1974	
Oscar Albarado	USA	1974 – 1975	
Koichi Wajima	Japan	1975	
Koichi Wajima	Japan	1975	WBA
Miguel de Oliveira	Brazil	1975	WBC
Jae-Do Yuh	S Korea	1975 – 1976	WBA
Elisha Obed	Bahamas	1975 – 1976	WBC
Koichi Wajima	Japan	1976	WBA
Jose Duran	Spain	1976	WBA
Eckhard Dagge	W Germany	1976 – 1977	WBC
Miguel Castellini	Argentine	1976 – 1977	WBA
Eddie Gazo	Nicaragua	1977 – 1978	WBA
Rocky Mattioli	Italy	1977 – 1979	WBC
Masashi Kudo	Japan	1978 – 1979	WBA
Maurice Hope	Antigua	1979 – 1981	WBC
Ayub Kalule	Uganda	1979 – 1981	WBA
Wilfred Benitez	USA	1981 – 1982	WBC
Sugar Ray Leonard *	USA	1981	WBA
Tadashi Mihara	Japan	1981 – 1982	WBA
Davey Moore	USA	1982 – 1983	WBA
Thomas Hearns *	USA	1982 – 1986	WBC
Roberto Duran *	Panama	1983 – 1984	WBA
Mark Medal	USA	1984	IBF
Mike McCallum *	Jamaica	1984 – 1987	WBA
Carlos Santos	Puerto Rico	1984 – 1986	IBF
Buster Drayton	USA	1986 – 1987	IBF
Duane Thomas	USA	1986 – 1987	WBC
Matthew Hilton	Canada	1987 –	IBF
Lupe Aquino	Mexico	1987	WBC
Gianfranco Rosi	Italy	1987 –	WBC
Julian Jackson	Virgin Islands	1987 –	WBA

Title Bouts

20.10.62 Denny Moyer W PTS 15 Joey Giambra, Portland, USA (WBA)
19.02.63 Denny Moyer W PTS 15 Stan Harrington, Honolulu, Hawaii (WBA)
29.04.63 Ralph Dupas W PTS 15 Denny Moyer, New Orleans, USA (WBA)
17.06.63 Ralph Dupas W PTS 15 Denny Moyer, Baltimore, USA (WBA)
07.09.63 Sandro Mazzinghi W CO 9 Ralph Dupas, Milan, Italy (WBA)
02.12.63 Sandro Mazzinghi W RSC 13 Ralph Dupas, Sydney, Australia (WBA)
03.10.64 Sandro Mazzinghi W RSC 12 Tony Montano, Genoa, Italy (WBA)
11.12.64 Sandro Mazzinghi W PTS 15 Fortunato Manca, Rome, Italy (WBA)
18.06.65 Nino Benvenuti W CO 6 Sandro Mazzinghi, Milan, Italy (WBA)
17.12.65 Nino Benvenuti W PTS 15 Sandro Mazzinghi, Rome, Italy (WBA)
25.06.66 Ki-Soo Kim W PTS 15 Nino Benvenuti, Seoul, S Korea (WBA)
17.12.66 Ki-Soo Kim W PTS 15 Stan Harrington, Seoul, S Korea (WBA)
03.10.67 Ki-Soo Kim W PTS 15 Freddie Little, Seoul, S Korea (WBA)
25.05.68 Sandro Mazzinghi W PTS 15 Ki-Soo Kim, Milan, Italy (WBA)
25.10.68 Sandro Mazzinghi NC 9 Freddie Little, Rome, Italy (WBA)
Sandro Mazzinghi forfeited WBA recognition (failure to defend against Freddie Little)
17.03.69 Freddie Little W PTS 15 Stan Hayward, Las Vegas, USA
09.09.69 Freddie Little W CO 2 Hisao Minami, Osaka, Japan
20.03.70 Freddie Little W PTS 15 Gerhard Piaskowy, Berlin, W Germany
09.07.70 Carmelo Bossi W PTS 15 Freddie Little, Monza, Italy
29.04.71 Carmelo Bossi DREW 15 Jose Hernandez, Madrid, Spain
31.10.71 Koichi Wajima W PTS 15 Carmelo Bossi, Tokyo, Japan
07.05.72 Koichi Wajima W CO 1 Domenico Tiberia, Tokyo, Japan
03.10.72 Koichi Wajima W CO 3 Matt Donovan, Tokyo, Japan
09.01.73 Koichi Wajima DREW 15 Miguel de Oliviera, Tokyo, Japan
19.04.73 Koichi Wajima W PTS 15 Ryu Sorimachi, Osaka, Japan
14.08.73 Koichi Wajima W RTD 12 Silvani Bertini, Sappora, Japan
05.02.74 Koichi Wajima W PTS 15 Miguel de Oliviera, Tokyo, Japan
03.06.74 Oscar Albarado W CO 15 Koichi Wajima, Tokyo, Japan
08.10.74 Oscar Albarado W RSC 7 Ryu Sorimachi, Tokyo, Japan
21.01.75 Koichi Wajima W PTS 15 Oscar Albarado, Tokyo, Japan
Koichi Wajima forfeited WBC recognition (failure to defend against Miguel de Oliviera)
07.05.75 Miguel de Oliviera W PTS 15 Jose Duran, Monte Carlo (WBC)
07.06.75 Jae-Do Yuh W RSC 7 Koichi Wajima, Kitakyushi, Japan (WBA)

11.11.75 Jae-Do Yuh W RSC 6 Masahiro Misako, Shizuoka, Japan (WBA)
13.11.75 Elisha Obed W RTD 10 Miguel de Oliviera, Paris, France (WBC)
17.02.76 Koichi Wajima W CO 15 Jae-Do Yuh, Tokyo, Japan (WBA)
28.02.76 Elisha Obed W CO 2 Tony Gardner, Nassau, Bahamas (WBC)
25.04.76 Elisha Obed W PTS 15 Sea Robinson, Abidjan, Ivory Coast (WBC)
18.05.76 Jose Duran W CO 14 Koichi Wajima, Tokyo, Japan (WBA)
18.06.76 Eckhard Dagge W RTD 10 Elisha Obed, Berlin, W Germany (WBC)
18.09.76 Eckhard Dagge W PTS 15 Emile Griffith, Berlin, W Germany (WBC)
08.10.76 Miguel Castellini W PTS 15 Jose Duran, Madrid, Spain (WBA)
05.03.77 Eddie Gazo W PTS 15 Miguel Castellini, Managua, Nicaragua (WBA)
15.03.77 Eckhard Dagge DREW 15 Maurice Hope, Berlin, W Germany (WBC)
07.06.77 Eddie Gazo W RSC 11 Koichi Wajima, Tokyo, Japan (WBA)
06.08.77 Rocky Mattioli W CO 5 Eckhard Dagge, Berlin, W Germany (WBC)
13.09.77 Eddie Gazo W PTS 15 Kenji Shibata, Tokyo, Japan (WBA)
18.12.77 Eddie Gazo W PTS 15 Chae-Keun Lim, Inchon, S Korea (WBA)
11.03.78 Rocky Mattioli W CO 7 Elisha Obed, Melbourne, Australia (WBC)
14.05.78 Rocky Mattioli W RSC 5 Jose Duran, Pescara, Italy (WBA)
09.08.78 Masashi Kudo W PTS 15 Eddie Gazo, Akita, Japan (WBA)
13.12.78 Masashi Kudo W PTS 15 Ho-In Joo, Osaka, Japan (WBA)
04.03.79 Maurice Hope W RTD 8 Rocky Mattioli, San Remo, Italy (WBC)
13.03.79 Masashi Kudo W PTS 15 Manuel Gonzalez, Tokyo, Japan (WBA)
20.06.79 Masashi Kudo W RSC 12 Manuel Gonzalez, Yokkaichi, Japan (WBA)
25.09.79 Maurice Hope W RSC 7 Mike Baker, Wembley, England (WBC)
24.10.79 Ayub Kalule W PTS 15 Masashi Kudo, Akita, Japan (WBA)
06.12.79 Ayub Kalule W PTS 15 Steve Gregory, Copenhagen, Denmark (WBA)
17.04.80 Ayub Kalule W RTD 11 Emiliano Villa, Copenhagen, Denmark (WBA)
12.06.80 Ayub Kalule W PTS 15 Marijan Benes, Randers, Denmark (WBA)
12.07.80 Maurice Hope W RSC 11 Rocky Mattioli, Wembley, England (WBC)
06.09.80 Ayub Kalule W PTS 15 Bushy Bester, Aarhus, Denmark (WBA)
26.11.80 Maurice Hope W PTS 15 Carlos Herrera, Wembley, England (WBC)
24.05.81 Wilfred Benitez W CO 12 Maurice Hope, Las Vegas, USA (WBC)
25.06.81 Sugar Ray Leonard W RSC 9 Ayub Kalule, Houston, USA (WBA)
Sugar Ray Leonard relinquished WBA version of title (he decided to concentrate on the welterweight division)
07.11.81 Tadashi Mihara W PTS 15 Rocky Fratto, Rochester, USA (WBA)
14.11.81 Wilfred Benitez W PTS 15 Carlos Santos, Las Vegas, USA (WBC)
30.01.82 Wilfred Benitez W PTS 15 Roberto Duran, Las Vegas, USA (WBC)
02.02.82 Davey Moore W RSC 6 Tadashi Mihara, Tokyo, Japan (WBA)
26.04.82 Davey Moore W CO 5 Charlie Weir, Johannesburg, S Africa (WBA)
17.07.82 Davey Moore W RSC 10 Ayub Kalule, Atlantic C, USA (WBA)
03.12.82 Thomas Hearns W PTS 15 Wilfred Benitez, New Orleans, USA (WBC)
29.01.83 Davey Moore W CO 4 Gary Guiden, Atlantic C, USA (WBA)
16.06.83 Roberto Duran W RSC 8 Davey Moore, New York C, USA (WBA)
Roberto Duran relinquished WBA version of title (retired)
11.02.84 Thomas Hearns W PTS 12 Luigi Minchillo, Detroit, USA (WBC)
11.03.84 Mark Medal W RSC 5 Earl Hargrove, Atlantic C, USA (IBF)
15.06.84 Thomas Hearns W CO 2 Roberto Duran, Las Vegas, USA (WBC)
15.09.84 Thomas Hearns W RSC 3 Fred Hutchings, Saginaw, USA (WBC)
19.10.84 Mike McCallum W PTS 15 Sean Mannion, New York C, USA (WBA)
02.11.84 Carlos Santos W PTS 15 Mark Medal, New York C, USA (IBF)
01.12.84 Mike McCallum W RSC 14 Luigi Minchillo, Milan, Italy (WBA)
01.06.85 Carlos Santos W PTS 15 Louis Acaries, Paris, France (IBF)
Carlos Santos forfeited title (failure to defend against Davey Moore)
28.07.85 Mike McCallum W RSC 8 David Braxton, Miami, USA (WBA)
04.06.86 Buster Drayton W PTS 15 Carlos Santos, E Rutherford, USA (IBF)
23.06.86 Thomas Hearns W RSC 8 Mark Medel, Las Vegas, USA (WBC)
Thomas Hearns relinquished WBC version of title (moved up to middleweight)
23.08.86 Mike McCallum W RSC 2 Julian Jackson, Miami, USA (WBA)
24.08.86 Buster Drayton W RSC 10 Davey Moore, Juan les Pins, France (IBF)
25.10.86 Mike McCallum W CO 9 Said Skouma, Paris, France (WBA)
05.12.86 Duane Thomas W RSC 3 John Mugabi, Las Vegas, USA (WBC)
27.03.87 Buster Drayton W RTD 10 Said Skouma, Cannes, France (IBF)
19.04.87 Mike McCallum W RSC 10 Milton McCrory, Phoenix, USA (WBA)
27.06.87 Matthew Hilton W PTS 15 Buster Drayton, Montreal, Canada (IBF)
12.07.87 Lupe Aquino W PTS 12 Duane Thomas, Bordeaux, France (WBC)
18.07.87 Mike McCallum W CO 5 Don Curry, Las Vegas, USA (WBA)
Mike McCallum relinquished WBA version of title (moved up to challenge for WBA middleweight title)
02.10.87 Gianfranco Rosi W PTS 12 Lupe Aquino, Perugia, Italy (WBC)
16.10.87 Matthew Hilton W RTD 2 Jack Callahan, Atlantic C, USA (IBF)
21.11.87 Julian Jackson W RSC 3 In-Chul Baek, Las Vegas, USA (WBA)
03.01.88 Gianfranco Rosi W RSC 7 Duane Thomas, Genoa, Italy (WBC)

Middleweight (160 lbs)

Title Holders

	Birthplace	Tenure	Status
Bob Fitzsimmons *	England	1891 – 1897	
Kid McCoy	USA	1897 – 1898	
Tommy Ryan *	USA	1898 – 1907	
Stanley Ketchel	USA	1907 – 1908	
Billy Papke	USA	1908	
Stanley Ketchel *	USA	1908 – 1910	
Billy Papke	USA	1911 – 1912	GB
Frank Mantell	USA	1912 – 1913	USA
Billy Papke	USA	1912 – 1913	IBU
Frank Klaus	USA	1913	IBU
George Chip	USA	1913 – 1914	USA
Eddie McGoorty	USA	1914	AUSTR
Jeff Smith	USA	1914	AUSTR
Al McCoy	USA	1914 – 1917	USA
Mick King	Australia	1914	AUSTR
Jeff Smith	USA	1914 – 1915	AUSTR
Les Darcy *	Australia	1915 – 1917	AUSTR
Mike O'Dowd	USA	1917 – 1920	
Johnny Wilson	USA	1920 – 1923	
Bryan Downey	USA	1922	OHIO
Dave Rosenberg	USA	1922	NY
Jock Malone	USA	1922 – 1923	OHIO
Mike O'Dowd *	USA	1922 – 1923	NY
Harry Greb	USA	1923 – 1926	
Tiger Flowers	USA	1926	
Mickey Walker *	USA	1926 – 1931	
Gorilla Jones	USA	1931 – 1932	NBA
Marcel Thil	France	1932	NBA/IBU
Marcel Thil	France	1932 – 1937	IBU
Ben Jeby	USA	1933	NY
Gorilla Jones	USA	1933	NBA
Lou Brouillard	Canada	1933	NY/NBA
Vince Dundee	USA	1933 – 1934	NY/NBA
Teddy Yarosz	USA	1934 – 1935	NY/NBA
Babe Risko	USA	1935 – 1936	NY/NBA
Freddie Steele	USA	1936 – 1937	NY/NBA
Freddie Steele	USA	1937 – 1938	NBA
Fred Apostoli	USA	1937 – 1938	IBU
Fred Apostoli	USA	1937 – 1939	NY
Edouard Tenet	France	1938	IBU
Al Hostak	USA	1938	NBA
Solly Krieger	USA	1938 – 1939	NBA
Al Hostak	USA	1939 – 1940	NBA
Ceferino Garcia	Philippines	1939 – 1940	NY
Ken Overlin	USA	1940 – 1941	NY
Tony Zale	USA	1940 – 1941	NBA
Billy Soose	USA	1941	NY
Tony Zale	USA	1941 – 1947	
Rocky Graziano	USA	1947 – 1948	
Tony Zale	USA	1948	
Marcel Cerdan	Algeria	1948 – 1949	
Jake la Motta	USA	1949 – 1950	
Jake la Motta	USA	1950 – 1951	NY/NBA
Sugar Ray Robinson	USA	1950 – 1951	PEN
Sugar Ray Robinson	USA	1951	
Randy Turpin	England	1951	
Sugar Ray Robinson *	USA	1951 – 1952	
Randy Turpin	GB	1953	EBU
Carl Bobo Olson	Hawaii	1953 – 1955	
Sugar Ray Robinson	USA	1955 – 1957	
Gene Fullmer	USA	1957	
Sugar Ray Robinson	USA	1957	
Carmen Basilio	USA	1957 – 1958	
Sugar Ray Robinson	USA	1958 – 1959	
Sugar Ray Robinson	USA	1959 – 1960	NY/EBU
Gene Fullmer	USA	1959 – 1962	NBA
Paul Pender	USA	1960 – 1961	NY/EBU
Terry Downes	England	1961 – 1962	NY/EBU
Paul Pender	USA	1962 – 1963	NY/EBU
Dick Tiger	Nigeria	1962 – 1963	NBA
Dick Tiger	Nigeria	1963	
Joey Giardello	USA	1963 – 1965	
Dick Tiger	Nigeria	1965 – 1966	
Emile Griffith	Virgin Islands	1966 – 1967	
Nino Benvenuti	Italy	1967	
Emile Griffith	Virgin Islands	1967 – 1968	
Nino Benvenuti	Italy	1968 – 1970	
Carlos Monzon	Argentine	1970 – 1974	
Carlos Monzon	Argentine	1974 – 1976	WBA
Rodrigo Valdez	Colombia	1974 – 1976	WBC
Carlos Monzon *	Argentine	1976 – 1977	
Rodrigo Valdez	Colombia	1977 – 1978	
Hugo Corro	Argentine	1978 – 1979	
Vito Antuofermo	Italy	1979 – 1980	
Alan Minter	England	1980	
Marvin Hagler	USA	1980 – 1987	
Marvin Hagler	USA	1987	WBC/IBF
Sugar Ray Leonard *	USA	1987	WBC
Frank Tate	USA	1987 –	IBF
Sumbu Kalambay	Zaire	1987 –	WBA
Thomas Hearns	USA	1987 –	WBC

Title Bouts

14.01.91 Bob Fitzsimmons W CO 13 Nonpareil Jack Dempsey, New Orleans, USA
26.09.94 Bob Fitzsimmons W CO 2 Dan Creedon, New Orleans, USA
Bob Fitzsimmons relinquished title (moved up to heavyweight)
17.12.97 Kid McCoy W PTS 15 Dan Creedon, New York C, USA
Kid McCoy lost general recognition (this came about when the Kid elected to campaign in the heavyweight division)
25.02.98 Tommy Ryan W CO 18 George Green, San Francisco, USA
13.06.98 Tommy Ryan W RSC 14 Tommy West, New York C, USA

24.10.98 Tommy Ryan W PTS 20 Jack Bonner, New York C, USA
18.09.99 Tommy Ryan W 10 Frank Craig, New York C, USA
04.03.01 Tommy Ryan W RTD 17 Tommy West, Louisville, USA
24.06.02 Tommy Ryan W CO 3 Johnny Gorman, London, England
15.09.02 Tommy Ryan W CO 6 Kid Carter, Fort Erie, Canada
Tommy Ryan relinquished title (retired)
04.07.07 Stanley Ketchell DREW 20 Joe Thomas, Marysville, USA
02.09.07 Stanley Ketchell W CO 32 Joe Thomas, San Francisco, USA
12.12.07 Stanley Ketchell W PTS 20 Joe Thomas, San Francisco, USA
22.02.08 Stanley Ketchell W CO 1 Mike Twin Sullivan, San Francisco, USA
09.05.08 Stanley Ketchell W CO 20 Jack Twin Sullivan, San Francisco, USA
04.06.08 Stanley Ketchell W PTS 10 Billy Papke, Milwaukee, USA
31.07.08 Stanley Ketchell W CO 3 Hugo Kelly, San Francisco, USA
18.08.08 Stanley Ketchell W CO 2 Joe Thomas, San Francisco, USA
07.09.08 Billy Papke W RSC 12 Stanley Ketchell, Los Angeles, USA
26.11.08 Stanley Ketchell W CO 11 Billy Papke, San Francisco, USA
02.06.09 Stanley Ketchell W CO 4 Tony Caponi, Schnectady, USA
09.06.09 Stanley Ketchell W RSC 3 Jack O'Brien, Philadelphia, USA
05.07.09 Stanley Ketchell W PTS 20 Billy Papke, San Francisco, USA
27.05.10 Stanley Ketchell W CO 2 Willie Lewis, New York C, USA
10.06.10 Stanley Ketchell W CO 5 Jim Smith, New York C, USA
Stanley Ketchell left title vacant (murdered in shooting incident)
08.06.11 Billy Papke W RTD 9 Jim Sullivan, London, England (GB)
22.02.12 Frank Mantell W PTS 20 Billy Papke, Sacramento, USA (USA)
30.03.12 Frank Mantell W PTS 20 Jack Henrick, Los Angeles, USA (USA)
Frank Mantell ceased to be recognised in the USA (this followed several bad defeats)
29.06.12 Billy Papke W RSC 16 Marcel Moreau, Paris, France (IBU)
23.10.12 Billy Papke W DIS 17 Georges Carpentier, Paris, France (IBU)
04.12.12 Billy Papke W CO 7 George Bernard, Paris, France (IBU)
05.03.13 Frank Klaus W DIS 15 Billy Papke, Paris France (IBU)
11.10.13 George Chip W CO 6 Frank Klaus, Pittsburgh, USA (USA)
23.12.13 George Chip W CO 5 Frank Klaus, Pittsburgh, USA (USA)
01.01.14 Eddie McGoorty W CO 1 Dave Smith, Sydney, Australia (AUSTR)
07.02.14 Eddie McGoorty W PTS 20 Pat Bradley, Sydney, Australia (AUSTR)
14.03.14 Jeff Smith W PTS 20 Eddie McGoorty, Sydney, Australia (AUSTR)
06.04.14 Al McCoy W CO 1 George Chip, New York C, USA (USA)
13.04.14 Jeff Smith W CO 16 Pat Bradley, Sydney, Australia (AUSTR)
06.06.14 Jeff Smith W PTS 20 Jimmy Clabby, Sydney, Australia (AUSTR)
28.11.14 Mick King W PTS 20 Jeff Smith, Sydney, Australia (AUSTR)
26.12.14 Jeff Smith W PTS 20 Mick King, Sydney, Australia (AUSTR)
23.01.15 Jeff Smith W DIS 5 Les Darcy, Sydney, Australia (AUSTR)
20.02.15 Jeff Smith W PTS 20 Mick King, Melbourne, Australia (AUSTR)
23.05.15 Les Darcy W DIS 2 Jeff Smith, Sydney, Australia (AUSTR)
12.06.15 Les Darcy W RTD 10 Mick King, Sydney, Australia (AUSTR)
31.07.15 Les Darcy W RSC 15 Eddie McGoorty, Sydney, Australia (AUSTR)
04.09.15 Les Darcy W PTS 20 Billy Murray, Sydney, Australia (AUSTR)
09.10.15 Les Darcy W RTD 6 Fred Dyer, Sydney, Australia (AUSTR)
23.10.15 Les Darcy W PTS 20 Jimmy Clabby, Sydney, Australia (AUSTR)
27.12.15 Les Darcy W RTD 8 Eddie McGoorty, Sydney, Australia (AUSTR)
15.01.16 Les Darcy W PTS 20 George Brown, Sydney, Australia (AUSTR)
25.03.16 Les Darcy W CO 7 Les O'Donnell, Sydney, Australia (AUSTR)
08.04.16 Les Darcy W PTS 20 George Brown, Sydney, Australia (AUSTR)
13.05.16 Les Darcy W RTD 4 Alex Costica, Sydney, Australia (AUSTR)
03.06.16 Les Darcy W CO 2 Buck Crouse, Sydney, Australia (AUSTR)
24.06.16 Les Darcy W CO 12 Dave Smith, Sydney, Australia (AUSTR)
26.06.16 Al McCoy W PTS 15 Hugh Ross, Bridgeport, USA (USA)
09.09.16 Les Darcy W PTS 20 Jimmy Clabby, Sydney, Australia (AUSTR)
30.09.16 Les Darcy W CO 9 George Chip, Sydney, Australia (AUSTR)
Les Darcy left Australian version of the title vacant (died from pneumonia)
14.11.17 Mike O'Dowd W CO 6 Al McCoy, New York C, USA
17.07.19 Mike O'Dowd W CO 3 Al McCoy, St. Paul, USA
06.11.19 Mike O'Dowd W CO 2 Billy Kramer, Paterson, USA
01.03.20 Mike O'Dowd W CO 2 Jack McCarron, Philadelphia, USA
30.03.20 Mike O'Dowd W CO 5 Joe Eagan, Boston, USA
06.05.20 Johnny Wilson W PTS 12 Mike O'Dowd, Boston, USA
17.03.21 Johnny Wilson W PTS 15 Mike O'Dowd, New York C, USA
27.07.21 Johnny Wilson W DIS 7 Bryan Downey, Cleveland, USA
22.02.22 Bryan Downey W PTS 12 Frank Carbone, Canton, USA (OHIO)
15.05.22 Bryan Downey W PTS 12 Mike O'Dowd, Columbus, USA (OHIO)
14.08.22 Dave Rosenberg W PTS 15 Phil Krug, New York C, USA (NY)
18.09.22 Jock Malone W PTS 12 Bryan Downey, Columbus, USA (OHIO)
30.11.22 Mike O'Dowd W DIS 8 Dave Rosenberg, New York C, USA (NY)
Mike O'Dowd relinquished NY version of title (retired)
24.07.23 Jock Malone W PTS 12 Bryan Downey, Columbus, USA (OHIO)
Jock Malone ceased to be recognised by Ohio (this followed a defeat by Lou Bogash in a non-title bout, October, 1923)
31.08.23 Harry Greb W PTS 15 Johnny Wilson, New York C, USA
03.12.23 Harry Greb W PTS 10 Bryan Downey, Pittsburgh, USA
18.01.24 Harry Greb W PTS 15 Johnny Wilson, New York C, USA
24.03.24 Harry Greb W RSC 12 Fay Keiser, Baltimore, USA
26.06.24 Harry Greb W PTS 15 Ted Moore, New York C, USA
02.07.25 Harry Greb W PTS 15 Mickey Walker, New York C, USA
13.11.25 Harry Greb W PTS 15 Tony Marullo, New Orleans, USA
26.02.26 Tiger Flowers W PTS 15 Harry Greb, New York C, USA
19.08.26 Tiger Flowers W PTS 15 Harry Greb, New York C, USA
03.12.26 Mickey Walker W PTS 10 Tiger Flowers, Chicago, USA
30.06.27 Mickey Walker W CO 10 Tommy Milligan, London, England
21.06.28 Mickey Walker W PTS 10 Ace Hudkins, Chicago, USA
29.10.29 Mickey Walker W PTS 10 Ace Hudkins, Los Angeles, USA
30.07.30 Mickey Walker W CO 3 Willie Oster, Newark, USA
Mickey Walker relinquished title (moved up to heavyweight)
25.08.31 Gorilla Jones W PTS 10 Tiger Thomas, Milwaukee, USA (NBA)
25.01.32 Gorilla Jones W RSC 6 Oddone Piazza, Milwaukee, USA (NBA)
26.04.32 Gorilla Jones W PTS 12 Young Terry, Trenton, USA (NBA)
11.06.32 Marcel Thil W DIS 11 Gorilla Jones, Paris, France (NBA/IBU)
04.07.32 Marcel Thil W PTS 15 Len Harvey, London, England (NBA/IBU)
Marcel Thil ceased to be recognised by the NBA (the authority once again supported the claims of Gorilla Jones)
11.11.32 Ben Jeby W PTS 15 Chuck Devlin, New York C, USA (NY)
13.01.33 Ben Jeby W RSC 12 Frank Battaglia, New York C, USA (NY)
30.01.33 Gorilla Jones W CO 7 Sammy Slaughter, Cleveland, USA (NBA)
Gorilla Jones ceased to be recognised by the NBA (failure to defend)
17.03.33 Ben Jeby DREW 15 Vince Dundee, New York C, USA (NY)
10.07.33 Ben Jeby W PTS 15 Young Terry, Newark, USA (NY)
09.08.33 Lou Brouillard W CO 7 Ben Jeby, New York C, USA (NY/NBA)
02.10.33 Marcel Thil W PTS 15 Kid Tunero, Paris, France (IBU)
30.10.33 Vince Dundee W PTS 15 Lou Brouillard, Boston, USA (NY/NBA)
08.12.33 Vince Dundee W PTS 15 Andy Callahan, Boston, USA (NY/NBA)
26.02.34 Marcel Thil W PTS 15 Ignacio Ara, Paris, France (IBU)
01.05.34 Vince Dundee W PTS 15 Al Diamond, Paterson, USA (NY/NBA)
03.05.34 Marcel Thil W PTS 15 Gustav Roth, Paris, USA (IBU)
11.09.34 Teddy Yarosz W PTS 15 Vince Dundee, Pittsburgh, USA (NY/NBA)
15.10.34 Marcel Thil DREW 15 Carmelo Candel, Paris, France (IBU)
04.05.35 Marcel Thil W RTD 14 Vilda Jaks, Paris, France (IBU)
03.06.35 Marcel Thil W PTS 15 Ignacio Ara, Madrid, Spain (IBU)
28.06.35 Marcel Thil W PTS 10 Carmelo Candel, Paris, France (IBU)
19.09.35 Babe Risko W PTS 15 Teddy Yarosz, Pittsburgh, USA (NY/NBA)
20.01.36 Marcel Thil W DIS 4 Lou Brouillard, Paris, France (IBU)
10.02.36 Babe Risko W PTS 15 Tony Fisher, Newark, USA (NY/NBA)
11.07.36 Freddie Steele W PTS 15 Babe Risko, Seattle, USA (NY/NBA)
01.01.37 Freddie Steele W PTS 10 Gorilla Jones, Milwaukee, USA (NY/NBA)
15.02.37 Marcel Thil W DIS 6 Lou Brouillard, Paris, France (IBU)
19.02.37 Freddie Steele W PTS 15 Babe Risko, New York C, USA (NY/NBA)
11.05.37 Freddie Steele W CO 3 Frank Battaglia, Seattle, USA (NY/NBA)
11.09.37 Freddie Steele W CO 4 Ken Overlin, Seattle, USA (NY/NBA)
Freddie Steele ceased to be recognised by NY (failure to defend against Fred Apostoli)
23.09.37 Fred Apostoli W RSC 10 Marcel Thil, New York C, USA (IBU)
Fred Apostoli forfeited IBU recognition (Thil was stripped of the European title and the IBU recognised the winner of the Tenet/Besselmann contest)
19.02.38 Freddie Steele W RTD 7 Carmen Barth, Cleveland, USA (NBA)
01.04.38 Fred Apostoli W PTS 15 Glen Lee, New York C, USA (NY)
07.04.38 Edouard Tenet W RTD 12 Josef Besselmann, Berlin, Germany (IBU)
Edouard Tenet ceased to be recognised by the IBU (this followed a defeat by Bep van Klaveren in a European title defence, July, 1938)
26.07.38 Al Hostak W CO 1 Freddie Steele, Seattle, USA (NBA)
01.11.38 Solly Krieger W PTS 15 Al Hostak, Seattle, USA (NBA)
18.11.38 Fred Apostoli W RSC 8 Young Corbett III, New York C, USA (NY)
27.06.39 Al Hostak W RSC 4 Solly Krieger, Seattle, USA (NBA)
02.10.39 Ceferino Garcia W RSC 7 Fred Apostoli, New York C, USA (NY)
11.12.39 Al Hostak W CO 1 Eric Seelig, Cleveland, USA (NBA)
23.12.39 Ceferino Garcia W CO 13 Glen Lee, Manila, Philippines (NY)
01.03.40 Ceferino Garcia DREW 10 Henry Armstrong, Los Angeles, USA (NY)
23.05.40 Ken Overlin W PTS 15 Ceferino Garcia, New York C, USA (NY)
19.07.40 Tony Zale W RTD 13 Al Hostak, Seattle, USA (NBA)
01.11.40 Ken Overlin W PTS 15 Steve Belloise, New York C, USA (NY)
13.12.40 Ken Overlin W PTS 15 Steve Belloise, New York C, USA (NY)
21.02.41 Tony Zale W CO 14 Steve Mamakos, Chicago, USA (NBA)
09.05.41 Billy Soose W PTS 15 Ken Overlin, New York C, USA (NY)
Billy Soose ceased to be recognised by NY (this followed a defeat by George Abrams in a non-title bout, July, 1941 and increasing weight problems)
28.05.41 Tony Zale W CO 2 Al Hostak, Chicago, USA (NBA)
28.11.41 Tony Zale W PTS 15 Georgie Abrams, New York C, USA
27.09.46 Tony Zale W CO 6 Rocky Graziano, New York C, USA
16.07.47 Rocky Graziano W RSC 6 Tony Zale, Chicago, USA
10.06.48 Tony Zale W CO 3 Rocky Graziano, Newark, USA
21.09.48 Marcel Cerdan W RSC 12 Tony Zale, Jersey C, USA
16.06.49 Jake la Motta W RTD 10 Marcel Cerdan, Detroit, USA
05.06.50 Sugar Ray Robinson W PTS 15 Robert Villemain, Philadelphia, USA (PEN)
12.07.50 Jake la Motta W PTS 15 Tiberio Mitri, New York C, USA (NY/NBA)
25.08.50 Sugar Ray Robinson W CO 1 Jose Basora, Scranton, USA (PEN)
13.09.50 Jake la Motta W CO 15 Laurent Dauthuille, Detroit, USA (NY/NBA)
26.10.50 Sugar Ray Robinson W CO 12 Carl Bobo Olson, Philadelphia, USA (PEN)
14.02.51 Sugar Ray Robinson W RSC 13 Jake la Motta, Chicago, USA
10.07.51 Randy Turpin W PTS 15 Sugar Ray Robinson, London, England
12.09.51 Sugar Ray Robinson W RSC 10 Randy Turpin, New York C, USA
13.03.52 Sugar Ray Robinson W PTS 15 Carl Bobo Olson, San Francisco, USA
16.04.52 Sugar Ray Robinson W CO 3 Rocky Graziano, Chicago, USA
Sugar Ray Robinson relinquished title (retired)
09.06.53 Randy Turpin W PTS 15 Charles Humez, London, England (EBU)
21.10.53 Carl Bobo Olson W PTS 15 Randy Turpin, New York C, USA
02.04.54 Carl Bobo Olson W PTS 15 Kid Gavilan, Chicago, USA
20.08.54 Carl Bobo Olson W PTS 15 Rocky Castellani, San Francisco, USA
15.12.54 Carl Bobo Olson W RSC 11 Pierre Langlois, San Francisco, USA
09.12.55 Sugar Ray Robinson W CO 2 Carl Bobo Olson, Chicago, USA
18.05.56 Sugar Ray Robinson W CO 4 Carl Bobo Olson, Los Angeles, USA
02.01.57 Gene Fullmer W PTS 15 Sugar Ray Robinson, New York C, USA
01.05.57 Sugar Ray Robinson W CO 5 Gene Fullmer, Chicago, USA
23.09.57 Carmen Basilio W PTS 15 Sugar Ray Robinson, New York C, USA

25.03.58	Sugar Ray Robinson W PTS 15 Carmen Basilio, Chicago, USA
	Sugar Ray Robinson forfeited NBA recognition (inactivity)
28.08.59	Gene Fullmer W RSC 14 Carmen Basilio, San Francisco, USA (NBA)
04.12.59	Gene Fullmer W PTS 15 Spider Webb, Logan, USA (NBA)
22.01.60	Paul Pender W PTS 15 Sugar Ray Robinson, Boston, USA (NY/EBU)
20.04.60	Gene Fullmer DREW 15 Joey Giardello, Bozeman, USA (NBA)
10.06.60	Paul Pender W PTS 15 Sugar Ray Robinson, Boston, USA (NY/EBU)
29.06.60	Gene Fullmer W RSC 12 Carmen Basilio, Salt Lake C, USA (NBA)
03.12.60	Gene Fullmer DREW 15 Sugar Ray Robinson, Los Angeles, USA (NBA)
14.01.61	Paul Pender W RSC 7 Terry Downes, Boston, USA (NY/EBU)
04.03.61	Gene Fullmer W PTS 15 Sugar Ray Robinson, Las Vegas, USA (NBA)
22.04.61	Paul Pender W PTS 15 Carmen Basilio, Boston, USA (NY/EBU)
11.07.61	Terry Downes W RTD 9 Paul Pender, Wembley, England (NY/EBU)
05.08.61	Gene Fullmer W PTS 15 Florentino Fernandez, Ogden, USA (NBA)
09.12.61	Gene Fullmer W CO 10 Benny Kid Paret, Las Vegas, USA (NBA)
07.04.62	Paul Pender W PTS 15 Terry Downes, Boston, USA (NY/EBU)
	Paul Pender forfeited NY/EBU recognition (failure to defend within stipulated period)
23.10.62	Dick Tiger W PTS 15 Gene Fullmer, San Francisco, USA (NBA)
23.02.63	Dick Tiger DREW 15 Gene Fullmer, Las Vegas, USA (NBA)
10.08.63	Dick Tiger W RTD 7 Gene Fullmer, Ibadan, Nigeria
07.12.63	Joey Giardello W PTS 15 Dick Tiger, Atlantic C, USA
14.12.64	Joey Giardello W PTS 15 Ruben Carter, Philadelphia, USA
21.10.65	Dick Tiger W PTS 15 Joey Giardello, New York C, USA
25.04.66	Emile Griffith W PTS 15 Dick Tiger, New York C, USA
13.07.66	Emile Griffith W PTS 15 Joey Archer, New York C, USA
23.01.67	Emile Griffith W PTS 15 Joey Archer, New York C, USA
17.04.67	Nino Benvenuti W PTS 15 Emile Griffith, New York C, USA
29.09.67	Emile Griffith W PTS 15 Nino Benvenuti, New York C, USA
04.03.68	Nino Benvenuti W PTS 15 Emile Griffith, New York C, USA
14.12.68	Nino Benvenuti W PTS 15 Don Fullmer, San Remo, Italy
04.10.69	Nino Benvenuti W DIS 7 Fraser Scott, Naples, Italy
22.11.69	Nino Benvenuti W CO 1 Luis Rodriguez, Rome, Italy
23.05.70	Nino Benvenuti W CO 8 Tom Bethea, Umag, Yugoslavia
07.11.70	Carlos Monzon W CO 12 Nino Benvenuti, Rome, Italy
08.05.71	Carlos Monzon W RSC 3 Nino Benvenuti, Monte Carlo
25.09.71	Carlos Monzon W RSC 14 Emile Griffith, Bs Aires, Argentine
04.03.72	Carlos Monzon W RSC 5 Denny Moyer, Rome, Italy
17.06.72	Carlos Monzon W RTD 12 Jean-Claude Bouttier, Colombes, France
19.08.72	Carlos Monzon W RSC 5 Tom Bogs, Copenhagen, Denmark
11.11.72	Carlos Monzon W PTS 15 Bennie Briscoe, Bs Aires, Argentine
02.06.73	Carlos Monzon W PTS 15 Emile Griffith, Monte Carlo
29.09.73	Carlos Monzon W PTS 15 Jean-Claude Bouttier, Paris, France
09.02.74	Carlos Monzon W RTD 6 Jose Napoles, Paris, France
	Carlos Monzon forfeited WBC recognition (failure to defend against Rodrigo Valdez)
25.05.74	Rodrigo Valdez W CO 7 Bennie Briscoe, Monte Carlo (WBC)
05.10.74	Carlos Monzon W CO 7 Tony Mundine, Bs Aires, Argentine (WBA)
30.11.74	Rodrigo Valdez W CO 11 Gratien Tonna, Paris, France (WBC)
31.05.75	Rodrigo Valdez W RSC 8 Ramon Mendez, Cali, Colombia (WBC)
30.06.75	Carlos Monzon W RSC 10 Tony Licata, New York C, USA (WBA)
16.08.75	Rodrigo Valdez W PTS 15 Rudy Robles, Cartagena, Colombia (WBC)
13.12.75	Carlos Monzon W CO 5 Gratien Tonna, Paris, France (WBA)
28.03.76	Rodrigo Valdez W RTD 4 Nessim Cohen, Paris, France (WBC)
26.06.76	Carlos Monzon W PTS 15 Rodrigo Valdez, Monte Carlo
30.07.77	Carlos Monzon W PTS 15 Rodrigo Valdez, Monte Carlo
	Carlos Monzon relinquished title (retired)
05.11.77	Rodrigo Valdez W PTS 15 Bennie Briscoe, Campione, Italy
22.04.78	Hugo Corro W PTS 15 Rodrigo Valdez, San Remo, Italy
05.08.78	Hugo Corro W PTS 15 Ronnie Harris, Bs Aires, Argentine
11.11.78	Hugo Corro W PTS 15 Rodrigo Valdez, Bs Aires, Argentine
30.06.79	Vito Antuofermo W PTS 15 Hugo Corro, Monte Carlo
30.11.79	Vito Antuofermo DREW 15 Marvin Hagler, Las Vegas, USA
16.03.80	Alan Minter W PTS 15 Vito Antuofermo, Las Vegas, USA
28.06.80	Alan Minter W RTD 8 Vito Antuofermo, Wembley, England
27.09.80	Marvin Hagler W RSC 3 Alan Minter, Wembley, England
17.01.81	Marvin Hagler W RSC 8 Fully Obelmejias, Boston, USA
13.06.81	Marvin Hagler W RTD 4 Vito Antuofermo, Boston, USA
03.10.81	Marvin Hagler W RSC 11 Mustafa Hamsho, Rosemont, USA
07.03.82	Marvin Hagler W RSC 1 Caveman Lee, Atlantic C, USA
30.10.82	Marvin Hagler W RSC 5 Fully Obelmejias, San Remo, Italy
11.02.83	Marvin Hagler W RSC 6 Tony Sibson, Worcester, USA
27.05.83	Marvin Hagler W CO 4 Wilford Scypion, Providence, USA
10.11.83	Marvin Hagler W PTS 15 Roberto Duran, Las Vegas, USA
30.03.84	Marvin Hagler W RSC 10 Juan Domingo Roldan, Las Vegas, USA
19.10.84	Marvin Hagler W RSC 3 Mustafa Hamsho, New York C, USA
16.04.85	Marvin Hagler W RSC 3 Thomas Hearns, Las Vegas, USA
10.03.86	Marvin Hagler W CO 11 John Mugabi, Las Vegas, USA
	Marvin Hagler forfeited WBA/IBF recognition (failure to meet Herol Graham inside the stipulated period and subsequently boxing Leonard)
06.04.87	Sugar Ray Leonard W PTS 12 Marvin Hagler, Las Vegas, USA (WBC)
	Sugar Ray Leonard relinquished WBC version of title (retired)
10.10.87	Frank Tate W PTS 15 Michael Olajide, Las Vegas, USA (IBF)
23.10.87	Sumbu Kalambay W PTS 15 Iran Barklay, Livorno, Italy (WBA)
29.10.87	Thomas Hearns W CO 4 Juan Domingo Roldan, Las Vegas, USA (WBC)
07.02.88	Frank Tate W CO 10 Tony Sibson, Stafford, England (IBF)
01.03.88	Sumbu Kalambay W PTS 12 Mike McCallum, Pesaro, Italy (WBA)

Super-Middleweight (168 lbs)

Title Holders

	Birthplace	Tenure	Status
Murray Sutherland	Scotland	1984	IBF
Chang-Pal Park *	S Korea	1984 – 1987	IBF
Chong-Pal Park	S Korea	1987 –	WBA
Graciano Rocchigiani	W Germany	1988 –	IBF

Title Bouts

28.03.84	Murray Sutherland W PTS 15 Ernie Singletary, Atlantic C, USA (IBF)
22.07.84	Chong-Pal Park W CO 11 Murray Sutherland, Seoul, S Korea (IBF)
02.01.85	Chong-Pal Park W CO 2 Roy Gumbs, Seoul, S Korea (IBF)
30.06.85	Chong-Pal Park W PTS 15 Vinnie Curto, Seoul, S Korea (IBF)
11.04.86	Chong-Pal Park W CO 15 Vinnie Curto, Los Angeles, USA (IBF)
06.07.86	Chong-Pal Park T DRAW 2 Lindell Holmes, Chungju, S Korea (IBF)
14.09.86	Chong-Pal Park W PTS 15 Marvin Mack, Pusan, S Korea (IBF)
25.01.87	Chong-Pal Park W RSC 15 Doug Sam, Seoul, S Korea (IBF)
03.05.87	Chong-Pal Park W PTS 15 Lindell Holmes, Inchon, S Korea (IBF)
26.07.87	Chong-Pal Park W RSC 4 Emmanuel Otti, Kwangju, S Korea (IBF)
	Chong-Pal Park relinquished title (contested the WBA version of the title)
06.12.87	Chong-Pal Park W RSC 2 Jesus Gallardo, Seoul, S Korea (WBA)
01.03.88	Chong-Pal Park W CO 5 Polly Pasieron, Chungju, S Korea (WBA)
12.03.88	Graciano Rocchigiani W RSC 8 Vince Boulware, Dusseldorf, W Germany (IBF)

Light-Heavyweight (175 lbs)

Title Holders

	Birthplace	Tenure	Status
Jack Root	Austria	1903	USA
George Gardner	Ireland	1903	USA
Bob Fitzsimmons	England	1903 – 1905	
Jack O'Brien *	USA	1905 – 1912	
Jack Dillon	USA	1912 – 1916	
Battling Levinsky	USA	1916 – 1920	
Georges Carpentier	France	1920 – 1922	
Battling Siki	Senegal	1922 – 1923	
Mike McTigue	Ireland	1923 – 1925	
Paul Berlenbach	USA	1925 – 1926	
Jack Delaney *	Canada	1926 – 1927	
Jimmy Slattery	USA	1927	NBA
Tommy Loughran	USA	1927	NY
Tommy Loughran *	USA	1927 – 1929	
Jimmy Slattery	USA	1930	NY
Maxie Rosenbloom	USA	1930 – 1933	NY
George Nichols	USA	1932	NBA
Bob Godwin	USA	1933	NBA
Maxie Rosenbloom	USA	1933 – 1934	
Bob Olin	USA	1934 – 1935	
John Henry Lewis *	USA	1935 – 1938	
Tiger Jack Fox	USA	1938 – 1939	NY
Melio Bettina	USA	1939	NY
Len Harvey	England	1939	GB
Billy Conn *	USA	1939 – 1940	
Anton Christoforidis	Greece	1941	NBA
Gus Lesnevich	USA	1941 – 1948	
Freddie Mills	England	1942 – 1946	GB
Freddie Mills	England	1948 – 1950	
Joey Maxim	USA	1950 – 1952	
Archie Moore	USA	1952 – 1961	
Archie Moore	USA	1961 – 1962	NY/EBU
Harold Johnson	USA	1961 – 1962	NBA
Harold Johnson	USA	1962 – 1963	
Willie Pastrano	USA	1963 – 1965	
Jose Torres	Puerto Rico	1965 – 1966	
Dick Tiger	Nigeria	1966 – 1968	
Bob Foster	USA	1968 – 1971	
Bob Foster	USA	1971 – 1972	WBC
Vicente Rondon	Venezuela	1971 – 1972	WBA
Bob Foster *	USA	1972 – 1974	
John Conteh	England	1974 – 1977	WBC
Victor Galindez	Argentine	1974 – 1978	WBA
Miguel Cuello	Argentine	1977 – 1978	WBC
Mate Parlov	Yugoslavia	1978	WBC
Mike Rossman	USA	1978 – 1979	WBA
Marvin Johnson	USA	1978 – 1979	WBC
Victor Galindez	Argentine	1979	WBA
Matt Saad Muhammad	USA	1979 – 1981	WBC
Marvin Johnson	USA	1979 – 1980	WBA
Mustafa Muhammad	USA	1980 – 1981	WBA
Michael Spinks	USA	1981 – 1983	WBA
Dwight Muhammad Qawi	USA	1981 – 1983	WBC
Michael Spinks *	USA	1983 – 1985	
J. B. Williamson	USA	1985 – 1986	WBC
Slobodan Kacar	Yugoslavia	1985 – 1986	IBF
Marvin Johnson	USA	1986 – 1987	WBA
Dennis Andries	Guyana	1986 – 1987	WBC
Bobby Czyz	USA	1986 – 1987	IBF

Thomas Hearns *	USA	1987	WBC
Leslie Stewart	Trinidad	1987	WBA
Virgil Hill	USA	1987 –	WBA
Charles Williams	USA	1987 –	IBF
Don Lalonde	Canada	1987 –	WBC

Title Bouts

22.04.03 Jack Root W PTS 10 Kid McCoy, Detroit, USA (USA)
04.07.03 George Gardner W CO 12 Jack Root, Fort Erie, Canada (USA)
25.11.03 Bob Fitzsimmons W PTS 20 George Gardner, San Francisco, USA
20.12.05 Jack O'Brien W RTD 13 Bob Fitzsimmons, San Francisco, USA
28.11.06 Jack O'Brien DREW 20 Tommy Burns, Los Angeles, USA
Jack O'Brien relinquished title (retired)
28.05.12 Jack Dillon W CO 3 Hugo Kelly, Indianapolis, USA
28.04.14 Jack Dillon W PTS 10 Al Norton, Kansas C, USA
25.04.16 Jack Dillon W PTS 15 Battling Levinsky, Kansas C, USA
24.10.16 Battling Levinsky W PTS 12 Jack Dillon, Boston, USA
03.05.20 Battling Levinsky W PTS 12 Clay Turner, Portland, USA
12.10.20 Georges Carpentier W CO 4 Battling Levinsky, Jersey C, USA
11.05.22 Georges Carpentier W CO 1 Ted Kid Lewis, London, England
24.09.22 Battling Siki W CO 6 Georges Carpentier, Paris, France
17.03.23 Mike McTigue W PTS 20 Battling Siki, Dublin, Ireland
04.10.23 Mike McTigue DREW 10 Young Stribling, Columbus, USA
30.05.25 Paul Berlenbach W PTS 15 Mike McTigue, New York C, USA
11.09.25 Paul Berlenbach W RSC 11 Jimmy Slattery, New York C, USA
11.12.25 Paul Berlenbach W PTS 15 Jack Delaney, New York C, USA
10.06.26 Paul Berlenbach W PTS 15 Young Stribling, New York C, USA
16.07.26 Jack Delaney W PTS 15 Paul Berlenbach, New York C, USA
Jack Delaney relinquished title (moved up to heavyweight)
30.08.27 Jimmy Slattery W PTS 10 Maxie Rosenbloom, Hartford, USA (NBA)
07.10.27 Tommy Loughran W PTS 15 Mike McTigue, New York C, USA (NY)
12.12.27 Tommy Loughran W PTS 15 Jimmy Slattery, New York C, USA
06.01.28 Tommy Loughran W PTS 15 Leo Lomski, New York C, USA
01.06.28 Tommy Loughran W PTS 15 Pete Latzo, New York C, USA
16.07.28 Tommy Loughran W PTS 10 Pete Latzo, Wilkes-Barre, USA
08.03.29 Tommy Loughran W PTS 10 Mickey Walker, Chicago, USA
18.07.29 Tommy Loughran W PTS 15 James J. Braddock, New York C, USA
Tommy Loughran relinquished title (moved up to heavyweight)
10.02.30 Jimmy Slattery W PTS 15 Lou Scozza, Buffalo, USA (NY)
25.06.30 Maxie Rosenbloom W PTS 15 Jimmy Slattery, Buffalo, USA (NY)
22.10.30 Maxie Rosenbloom W RSC 11 Abe Bain, New York C, USA (NY)
05.08.31 Maxie Rosenbloom W PTS 15 Jimmy Slattery, New York C, USA (NY)
18.03.32 George Nichols W PTS 10 Dave Maier, Chicago, USA (NBA)
George Nichols ceased to be recognised by the NBA (this followed a defeat by Lou Scozza in a non-title bout, May, 1932)
14.07.32 Maxie Rosenbloom W PTS 15 Lou Scozza, Buffalo, USA (NY)
22.02.33 Maxie Rosenbloom W PTS 10 Al Stillman, St Louis, USA (NY)
01.03.33 Bob Godwin W PTS 10 Joe Knight, Palm Beach, USA (NBA)
10.03.33 Maxie Rosenbloom W PTS 15 Adolf Heuser, New York C, USA (NY)
24.03.33 Maxie Rosenbloom W RSC 4 Bob Godwin, New York C, USA
03.11.33 Maxie Rosenbloom W PTS 15 Mickey Walker, New York C, USA
05.02.34 Maxie Rosenbloom DREW 15 Joe Knight, Miami, USA
16.11.34 Bob Olin W PTS 15 Maxie Rosenbloom, New York C, USA
31.10.35 John Henry Lewis W PTS 15 Bob Olin, St Louis, USA
13.03.36 John Henry Lewis W PTS 15 Jock McAvoy, New York C, USA
09.11.36 John Henry Lewis W PTS 15 Len Harvey, Wembley, England
03.06.37 John Henry Lewis W RSC 8 Bob Olin, St Louis, USA
25.04.38 John Henry Lewis W CO 4 Emilio Martinez, Minneapolis, USA
28.10.38 John Henry Lewis W PTS 15 Al Gainer, New Haven, USA
John Henry Lewis relinquished title (retired)
29.11.38 Tiger Jack Fox W PTS 15 Al Gainer, New York C, USA (NY)
03.02.39 Melio Bettina W RSC 9 Tiger Jack Fox, New York C, USA (NY)
10.07.39 Len Harvey W PTS 15 Jock McAvoy, London, England (GB)
Len Harvey failed to capitalise on GB recognition (wartime inactivity)
13.07.39 Billy Conn W PTS 15 Melio Bettina, New York C, USA
25.09.39 Billy Conn W PTS 15 Melio Bettina, Pittsburgh, USA
17.11.39 Billy Conn W PTS 15 Gus Lesnevich, New York C, USA
05.06.40 Billy Conn W PTS 15 Gus Lesnevich, Detroit, USA
Billy Conn relinquished title (moved up to heavyweight)
13.01.41 Anton Christoforidis W PTS 15 Melio Bettina, Cleveland, USA (NBA)
22.05.41 Gus Lesnevich W PTS 15 Anton Christoforidis, New York C, USA
26.08.41 Gus Lesnevich W PTS 15 Tami Mauriello, New York C, USA
14.11.41 Gus Lesnevich W PTS 15 Tami Mauriello, New York C, USA
20.06.42 Freddie Mills W CO 2 Len Harvey, London, England (GB)
14.05.46 Gus Lesnevich W RSC 10 Freddie Mills, London, England
28.02.47 Gus Lesnevich W RSC 10 Billy Fox, New York C, USA
05.03.48 Gus Lesnevich W CO 1 Billy Fox, New York C, USA
26.07.48 Freddie Mills W PTS 15 Gus Lesnevich, London, England
24.01.50 Joey Maxim W CO 10 Freddie Mills, London, England
22.08.51 Joey Maxim W PTS 15 Bob Murphy, New York C, USA
25.06.52 Joey Maxim W RTD 13 Sugar Ray Robinson, New York C, USA
17.12.52 Archie Moore W PTS 15 Joey Maxim, St Louis, USA
24.06.53 Archie Moore W PTS 15 Joey Maxim, Ogden, USA
27.01.54 Archie Moore W PTS 15 Joey Maxim, Miami, USA
11.08.54 Archie Moore W RSC 14 Harold Johnson, New York C, USA
22.06.55 Archie Moore W CO 3 Carl Bobo Olson, New York C, USA
05.06.56 Archie Moore W RSC 10 Yolande Pompey, London, England
20.09.57 Archie Moore W RSC 7 Tony Anthony, Los Angeles, USA
10.12.58 Archie Moore W CO 11 Yvon Durelle, Montreal, Canada
12.08.59 Archie Moore W CO 3 Yvon Durelle, Montreal, Canada
Archie Moore forfeited NBA recognition (inactivity)
07.02.61 Harold Johnson W RSC 9 Jesse Bowdry, Miami, USA (NBA)
24.04.61 Harold Johnson W RSC 2 Von Clay, Philadelphia, USA (NBA)
10.06.61 Archie Moore W PTS 15 Giulio Rinaldi, New York C, USA (NY/EBU)
Archie Moore forfeited NY/EBU recognition (failure to defend against either Harold Johnson or Doug Jones)
29.08.61 Harold Johnson W PTS 15 Eddie Cotton, Seattle, USA (NBA)
12.05.62 Harold Johnson W PTS 15 Doug Jones, Philadelphia, USA
23.06.62 Harold Johnson W PTS 15 Gustav Scholz, Berlin, W Germany
01.06.63 Willie Pastrano W PTS 15 Harold Johnson, Las Vegas, USA
10.04.64 Willie Pastrano W RSC 5 Greg Peralta, New Orleans, USA
30.11.64 Willie Pastrano W RSC 11 Terry Downes, Manchester, England
30.03.65 Jose Torres W RSC 9 Willie Pastrano, New York C, USA
21.05.66 Jose Torres W PTS 15 Wayne Thornton, New York C, USA
15.08.66 Jose Torres W PTS 15 Eddie Cotton, Las Vegas, USA
15.10.66 Jose Torres W CO 2 Chic Calderwood, San Juan, Puerto Rico
16.12.66 Dick Tiger W PTS 15 Jose Torres, New York C, USA
16.05.67 Dick Tiger W PTS 15 Jose Torres, New York C, USA
17.11.67 Dick Tiger W RSC 12 Roger Rouse, Las Vegas, USA
24.05.68 Bob Foster W CO 4 Dick Tiger, New York C, USA
23.01.69 Bob Foster W RSC 1 Frankie de Paula, New York C, USA
24.05.69 Bob Foster W RSC 4 Andy Kendall, Springfield, USA
04.04.70 Bob Foster W RSC 3 Roger Rouse, Missoula, USA
27.06.70 Bob Foster W CO 10 Mark Tessman, Baltimore, USA
Bob Foster forfeited WBA recognition (failure to defend against Jimmy Dupree)
27.02.71 Vicente Rondon W RSC 6 Jimmy Dupree, Caracas, Venezuela (WBA)
02.03.71 Bob Foster W CO 4 Hal Carroll, Scranton, USA (WBC)
24.04.71 Bob Foster W PTS 15 Ray Anderson, Tampa, USA (WBC)
05.06.71 Vicente Rondon W CO 1 Piero del Papa, Caracas, Venezuela (WBA)
21.08.71 Vicente Rondon W PTS 15 Eddie Jones, Caracas, Venezuela (WBA)
26.10.71 Vicente Rondon W RSC 12 Gomeo Brennan, Miami, USA (WBA)
29.10.71 Bob Foster W RSC 8 Tommy Hicks, Scranton, USA (WBC)
15.12.71 Vicente Rondon W CO 8 Doyle Baird, Cleveland, USA (WBA)
16.12.71 Bob Foster W RSC 3 Brian Kelly, Oklahoma C, USA (WBC)
07.04.72 Bob Foster W CO 2 Vicente Rondon, Miami, USA
27.06.72 Bob Foster W CO 4 Mike Quarry, Las Vegas, USA
26.09.72 Bob Foster W CO 14 Chris Finnegan, Wembley, England
21.08.73 Bob Foster W PTS 15 Pierre Fourie, Alburquerque, USA
01.12.73 Bob Foster W PTS 15 Pierre Fourie, Johannesburg, S Africa
17.06.74 Bob Foster DREW 15 Jorge Ahumada, Alburquerque, USA
Bob Foster relinquished title (retired)
01.10.74 John Conteh W PTS 15 Jorge Ahumada, Wembley, England (WBC)
07.12.74 Victor Galindez W RTD 12 Len Hutchins, Bs Aires, Argentine (WBA)
11.03.75 John Conteh W RSC 5 Lonnie Bennett, Wembley, England (WBC)
07.04.75 Victor Galindez W PTS 15 Pierre Fourie, Johannesburg, S Africa (WBA)
30.06.75 Victor Galindez W PTS 15 Jorge Ahumada, New York C, USA (WBA)
13.09.75 Victor Galindez W PTS 15 Pierre Fourie, Johannesburg, S Africa (WBA)
28.03.76 Victor Galindez W RTD 3 Harald Skog, Oslo, Norway (WBA)
22.05.76 Victor Galindez W CO 15 Richie Kates, Johannesburg, S Africa (WBA)
05.10.76 Victor Galindez W PTS 15 Kosie Smith, Johannesburg, S Africa (WBA)
09.10.76 John Conteh W PTS 15 Yaqui Lopez, Copenhagen, Denmark (WBC)
05.03.77 John Conteh W RSC 3 Len Hutchins, Liverpool, England (WBC)
John Conteh forfeited WBC version of title (withdrew from a scheduled defence against Miguel Cuello)
21.05.77 Miguel Cuello W CO 9 Jesse Burnett, Monte Carlo (WBC)
18.06.77 Victor Galindez W PTS 15 Richie Kates, Rome, Italy (WBA)
17.09.77 Victor Galindez W PTS 15 Yaqui Lopez, Rome, Italy (WBA)
20.11.77 Victor Galindez W PTS 15 Mustapha Muhammad, Turin, Italy (WBA)
07.01.78 Mate Parlov W CO 9 Miguel Cuello, Milan, Italy (WBC)
06.05.78 Victor Galindez W PTS 15 Yaqui Lopez, Reggio, Italy (WBA)
17.06.78 Mate Parlov W PTS 15 John Conteh, Belgrade, Yugoslavia (WBC)
15.09.78 Mike Rossman W RSC 13 Victor Galindez, New Orleans, USA (WBA)
02.12.78 Marvin Johnson W RSC 10 Mate Parlov, Marsala, Italy (WBC)
05.12.78 Mike Rossman W RSC 6 Aldo Traversaro, Philadelphia, USA (WBA)
14.04.79 Victor Galindez W RTD 9 Mike Rossman, New Orleans, USA (WBA)
22.04.79 Matt Saad Muhammad W RSC 8 Marvin Johnson, Indianapolis, USA (WBC)
18.08.79 Matt Saad Muhammad W PTS 15 John Conteh, Atlantic C, USA (WBC)
30.11.79 Marvin Johnson W RSC 11 Victor Galindez, New Orleans, USA (WBA)
29.03.80 Matt Saad Muhammad W RSC 4 John Conteh, Atlantic C, USA (WBC)
31.03.80 Mustapha Muhammad W RSC 11 Marvin Johnson, Knoxville, USA (WBA)
11.05.80 Matt Saad Muhammad W RSC 5 Louis Pergaud, Halifax, Canada (WBC)
13.07.80 Matt Saad Muhammad W RSC 14 Yaqui Lopez, McAfee, USA (WBC)
20.07.80 Mustapha Muhammad W RSC 10 Jerry Martin, McAfee, USA (WBA)
28.11.80 Matt Saad Muhammad W CO 4 Lotte Mwale, San Diego, USA (WBC)
29.11.80 Mustapha Muhammad W RSC 3 Rudi Koopmans, Los Angeles, USA (WBA)
28.02.81 Matt Saad Muhammad W RSC 11 Vonzell Johnson, Atlantic C, USA (WBC)
25.04.81 Matt Saad Muhammad W CO 9 Murray Sutherland, Atlantic C, USA (WBC)
18.07.81 Michael Spinks W PTS 15 Mustapha Muhammad, Las Vegas, USA (WBA)
26.09.81 Matt Saad Muhammad W RSC 11 Jerry Martin, Atlantic C, USA (WBC)
07.11.81 Michael Spinks W RSC 7 Vonzell Johnson, Atlantic C, USA (WBA)
19.12.81 Dwight Muhammad Qawi W RSC 10 Matt Saad Muhammad, Atlantic C, USA (WBC)
13.02.82 Michael Spinks W RSC 6 Mustapha Wasajja, Atlantic C, USA (WBA)
21.03.82 Dwight Muhummad Qawi W RSC 6 Jerry Martin, Las Vegas, USA (WBC)
11.04.82 Michael Spinks W RSC 8 Murray Sutherland, Atlantic C, USA (WBA)
12.06.82 Michael Spinks W RSC 8 Jerry Celestine, Atlantic C, USA (WBA)
07.08.82 Dwight Muhammad Qawi W RSC 6 Matt Saad Muhammad, Philadelphia, USA (WBC)

18.09.82 Michael Spinks W RSC 9 Johnny Davis, Atlantic C, USA (WBA)
20.11.82 Dwight Muhammad Qawi W RSC 11 Eddie Davis, Atlantic C, USA (WBC)
18.03.83 Michael Spinks W PTS 15 Dwight Muhammad Qawi, Atlantic C, USA
25.11.83 Michael Spinks W RSC 10 Oscar Rivadeneyra, Vancouver, Canada
25.02.84 Michael Spinks W PTS 12 Eddie Davis, Atlantic C, USA
23.02.85 Michael Spinks W RSC 3 David Sears, Atlantic C, USA
06.06.85 Michael Spinks W RSC 8 Jim MacDonald, Las Vegas, USA
Michael Spinks relinquished title (moved up to heavyweight)
10.12.85 J. B. Williamson W PTS 12 Prince Muhammed, Los Angeles, USA (WBC)
21.12.85 Slobodan Kacar W PTS 15 Mustafa Muhammad, Pesaro, Italy (IBF)
09.02.86 Marvin Johnson W RSC 7 Leslie Stewart, Indianapolis, USA (WBA)
30.04.86 Dennis Andries W PTS 12 J. B. Williamson, London, England (WBC)
06.09.86 Bobby Czyz W RSC 5 Slobodan Kacar, Las Vegas, USA (IBF)
10.09.86 Dennis Andries W RSC 9 Tony Sibson, London, England (WBC)
20.09.86 Marvin Johnson W RSC 13 Jean-Marie Emebe, Indianapolis, USA (WBA)
26.12.86 Bobby Czyz W RSC 1 David Sears, West Orange, USA (IBF)
21.02.87 Bobby Czyz W CO 2 Willie Edwards, Atlantic C, USA (IBF)
07.03.87 Thomas Hearns W RSC 10 Dennis Andries, Detroit, USA (WBC)
Thomas Hearns relinquished WBC version of title (moved down to the middleweight division)
03.05.87 Bobby Czyz W RSC 6 Jim MacDonald, Atlantic C, USA (IBF)
23.05.87 Leslie Stewart W RTD 8 Marvin Johnson, Port of Spain, Trinidad (WBA)
05.09.87 Virgil Hill W RSC 4 Leslie Stewart, Atlantic C, USA (WBA)
29.10.87 Charles Williams W RTD 9 Bobby Czyz, Las Vegas, USA (IBF)
21.11.87 Virgil Hill W PTS 12 Rufino Angulo, Paris, France (WBA)
27.11.87 Don Lalonde W RSC 2 Eddie Davis, Port of Spain, Trinidad (WBC)
03.04.88 Virgil Hill W RSC 11 Jean-Marie Emebe, Bismarck, USA (WBA)

Cruiserweight (190/195 lbs)

Title Holders

	Birthplace	Tenure	Status
Marvin Camel	USA	1979 – 1980	WBC
Carlos de Leon	Puerto Rico	1980 – 1982	WBC
Ossie Ocasio	Puerto Rico	1982 – 1984	WBA
S. T. Gordon	USA	1982 – 1983	WBC
Marvin Camel	USA	1983 – 1984	IBF
Carlos de Leon	Puerto Rico	1983 – 1985	WBC
Lee Roy Murphy	USA	1984 – 1986	IBF
Piet Crous	S Africa	1984 – 1985	WBA
Alfonso Ratliff	USA	1985	WBC
Dwight Muhammad Qawi	USA	1985 – 1986	WBA
Bernard Benton	USA	1985 – 1986	WBC
Carlos de Leon	Puerto Rico	1986 – 1988	WBC
Rickey Parkey	USA	1986 – 1987	IBF
Evander Holyfield	USA	1986 – 1987	WBA
Evander Holyfield	USA	1987 – 1988	WBA/IBF
Evander Holyfield	USA	1988 –	

Title Bouts

08.12.79 Marvin Camel DREW 15 Mate Parlov, Split, Yugoslavia (WBC)
31.03.80 Marvin Camel W PTS 15 Mate Parlov, Las Vegas, USA (WBC)
25.11.80 Carlos de Leon W PTS 15 Marvin Camel, New Orleans, USA (WBC)
13.02.82 Ossie Ocasio W PTS 15 Robbie Williams, Johannesburg, S Africa (WBA)
24.02.82 Carlos de Leon W RSC 8 Marvin Camel, Atlantic C, USA (WBC)
27.06.82 S. T. Gordon W RSC 2 Carlos de Leon, Cleveland, USA (WBC)
15.12.82 Ossie Ocasio W PTS 15 Young Joe Louis, Chicago, USA (WBA)
16.02.83 S. T. Gordon W RSC 8 Jesse Burnett, E Rutherford, USA (WBC)
20.05.83 Ossie Ocasio W PTS 15 Randy Stephens, Las Vegas, USA (WBA)
21.05.83 Marvin Camel W RSC 9 Rick Sekorski, Billings, USA (IBF)
17.07.83 Carlos de Leon W PTS 12 S. T. Gordon, Las Vegas, USA (WBC)
21.09.83 Carlos de Leon W RSC 4 Yaqui Lopez. San Jose, USA (WBC)
13.12.83 Marvin Camel W RSC 5 Rod MacDonald, Halifax, Canada (IBF)
09.03.84 Carlos de Leon W PTS 12 Anthony Davis, Las Vegas, USA (WBC)
05.05.84 Ossie Ocasio W RSC 15 John Odhiambo, San Juan, Puerto Rico (WBA)
02.06.84 Carlos de Leon W PTS 12 Bashiru Ali, Oakland, USA (WBC)
06.10.84 Lee Roy Murphy W RSC 14 Marvin Camel, Billings, USA (IBF)
01.12.84 Piet Crous W PTS 15 Ossie Ocasio, Sun C, S Africa (WBA)
20.12.84 Lee Roy Murphy W RSC 12 Young Joe Louis, Chicago, USA (IBF)
30.03.85 Piet Crous W RSC 3 Randy Stephens, Sun C, S Africa (WBA)
06.06.85 Alfonso Ratliff W PTS 12 Carlos de Leon, Las Vegas, USA (WBC)
27.07.85 Dwight Muhammad Qawi W CO 11 Piet Crous, Sun C, S Africa (WBA)
21.09.85 Bernard Benton W PTS 12 Alfonso Ratliff, Las Vegas, USA (WBC)
19.10.85 Lee Roy Murphy W CO 12 Chisanda Mutti, Monte Carlo (IBF)
22.03.86 Carlos de Leon W PTS 12 Bernard Benton, Las Vegas, USA (WBC)
23.03.86 Dwight Muhammed Qawi W RSC 6 Leon Spinks, Reno, USA (WBA)
19.04.86 Lee Roy Murphy W CO 9 Dorcey Gaymon, San Remo, Italy (IBF)
12.07.86 Evander Holyfield W PTS 15 Dwight Muhammad Qawi, Atlanta, USA (WBA)
10.08.86 Carlos de Leon W RSC 8 Michael Greer, Giardini Naxos, Italy (WBC)
25.10.86 Rickey Parkey W RSC 10 Lee Roy Murphy, Marsala, Italy (IBF)
14.02.87 Evander Holyfield W RSC 7 Henry Tillman, Reno, USA (WBA)
21.02.87 Carlos de Leon W RTD 4 Angelo Rottoli, Bergamo, Italy (WBC)
28.03.87 Rickey Parkey W RSC 12 Chisanda Mutti, Camaiore, Italy (IBF)
15.05.87 Evander Holyfield W RSC 3 Rickey Parkey, Las Vegas, USA (IBF)
15.08.87 Evander Holyfield W RSC 11 Ossie Ocasio, St Tropez, France (IBF/WBA)
05.12.87 Evander Holyfield W CO 4 Dwight Muhammad Qawi, Atlantic C, USA (IBF)
22.01.88 Carlos de Leon W PTS 12 Jose Mario Flores, Atlantic C, USA (WBC)
09.04.88 Evander Holyfield W RSC 8 Carlos de Leon, Las Vegas, USA

Heavyweight (190/195 lbs +)

Title Holders

	Birthplace	Tenure	Status
James J. Corbett	USA	1892 – 1897	
Bob Fitzsimmons	England	1897 – 1899	
James J. Jeffries *	USA	1899 – 1905	
Marvin Hart	USA	1905 – 1906	
Tommy Burns	Canada	1906 – 1908	
Jack Johnson	USA	1908 – 1915	
Jess Willard	USA	1915 – 1919	
Jack Dempsey	USA	1919 – 1926	
Gene Tunney *	USA	1926 – 1928	
Max Schmeling	Germany	1930 – 1932	
Jack Sharkey	USA	1932 – 1933	
Primo Carnera	Italy	1933 – 1934	
Max Baer	USA	1934 – 1935	
James J. Braddock	USA	1935 – 1937	
Joe Louis *	USA	1937 – 1949	
Ezzard Charles	USA	1949 – 1950	NBA
Lee Savold	USA	1950	GB/EBU
Ezzard Charles	USA	1950 – 1951	
Jersey Joe Walcott	USA	1951 – 1952	
Rocky Marciano *	USA	1952 – 1956	
Floyd Patterson	USA	1956 – 1959	
Ingemar Johannson	Sweden	1959 – 1960	
Floyd Patterson	USA	1960 – 1962	
Sonny Liston	USA	1962 – 1964	
Muhammad Ali	USA	1964 – 1965	
Muhammad Ali	USA	1965 – 1967	WBC
Ernie Terrell	USA	1965 – 1967	WBA
Muhammad Ali	USA	1967	
Joe Frazier	USA	1968 – 1970	WBC
Jimmy Ellis	USA	1968 – 1970	WBA
Joe Frazier	USA	1970 – 1973	
George Foreman	USA	1973 – 1974	
Muhammad Ali	USA	1974 – 1978	
Leon Spinks	USA	1978	
Leon Spinks	USA	1978	WBA
Larry Holmes *	USA	1978 – 1983	WBC
Muhammad Ali *	USA	1978 – 1979	WBA
John Tate	USA	1979 – 1980	WBA
Mike Weaver	USA	1980 – 1982	WBA
Michael Dokes	USA	1982 – 1983	WBA
Gerrie Coetzee	S Africa	1983 – 1984	WBA
Tim Witherspoon	USA	1984	WBC
Pinklon Thomas	USA	1984 – 1986	WBC
Larry Holmes	USA	1984 – 1985	IBF
Greg Page	USA	1984 – 1985	WBA
Tony Tubbs	USA	1985 – 1986	WBA
Michael Spinks	USA	1985 – 1987	IBF
Tim Witherspoon	USA	1986	WBA
Trevor Berbick	Jamaica	1986	WBC
Mike Tyson	USA	1986 – 1987	WBC
James Smith	USA	1986 – 1987	WBA
Mike Tyson	USA	1987	WBA/WBC
Tony Tucker	USA	1987	IBF
Mike Tyson	USA	1987 –	

Title Bouts

07.09.92 James J. Corbett W CO 21 John L. Sullivan, New Orleans, USA
25.01.94 James J. Corbett W CO 3 Charley Mitchell, Jacksonville, USA
17.03.97 Bob Fitzsimmons W CO 14 James J. Corbett, Carson C, USA
09.06.99 James J. Jeffries W CO 11 Bob Fitzsimmons, New York C, USA
03.11.99 James J. Jeffries W PTS 25 Tom Sharkey, New York C, USA
06.04.00 James J. Jeffries W CO 1 Jack Finnegan, Detroit, USA
11.05.00 James J. Jeffries W CO 23 James J. Corbett, New York C, USA
15.11.01 James J. Jeffries W RTD 5 Gus Ruhlin, San Francisco, USA
25.07.02 James J. Jeffries W CO 8 Bob Fitzsimmons, San Francisco, USA
14.08.03 James J. Jeffries W CO 10 James J. Corbett, San Francisco, USA
26.08.04 James J. Jeffries W CO 2 Jack Munroe, San Francisco, USA
James J. Jeffries relinquished title (retired)
03.07.05 Marvin Hart W RSC 12 Jack Root, Reno, USA
23.02.06 Tommy Burns W PTS 20 Marvin Hart, Los Angeles, USA
02.10.06 Tommy Burns W CO 15 Jim Flynn, Los Angeles, USA
28.11.06 Tommy Burns DREW 20 Jack O'Brien, Los Angeles, USA
08.05.07 Tommy Burns W PTS 20 Jack O'Brien, Los Angeles, USA
04.07.07 Tommy Burns W CO 1 Bill Squires, Los Angeles, USA
02.12.07 Tommy Burns W CO 10 Gunner Moir, London, England
10.02.08 Tommy Burns W CO 4 Jack Palmer, London, England
17.03.08 Tommy Burns W CO 1 Jem Roche, Dublin, Ireland
18.04.08 Tommy Burns W CO 5 Jewey Smith, Paris, France
13.06.08 Tommy Burns W CO 8 Bill Squires, Paris, France
24.08.08 Tommy Burns W CO 13 Bill Squires, Sydney, Australia
02.09.08 Tommy Burns W CO 6 Bill Lang, Melbourne, Australia
26.12.08 Jack Johnson W RSC 14 Tommy Burns, Sydney, Australia
16.10.09 Jack Johnson W CO 12 Stanley Ketchell, Los Angeles, USA
04.07.10 Jack Johnson W RSC 15 James J. Jeffries, Reno, USA
04.07.12 Jack Johnson W RSC 9 Jim Flynn, Las Vegas, USA
19.12.13 Jack Johnson DREW 10 Jim Johnson, Paris, France

27.06.14 Jack Johnson W PTS 20 Frank Moran, Paris, France
05.04.15 Jess Willard W CO 26 Jack Johnson, Havana, Cuba
04.07.19 Jack Dempsey W RTD 3 Jess Willard, Toledo, USA
06.09.20 Jack Dempsey W CO 3 Billy Miske, Benton Harbor, USA
14.12.20 Jack Dempsey W CO 12 Bill Brennan, New York C, USA
02.07.21 Jack Dempsey W CO 4 Georges Carpentier, Jersey C, USA
04.07.23 Jack Dempsey W PTS 15 Tommy Gibbons, Shelby, USA
14.09.23 Jack Dempsey W CO 2 Angel Firpo, New York C, USA
23.09.26 Gene Tunney W PTS 10 Jack Dempsey, Philadelphia, USA
22.09.27 Gene Tunney W PTS 10 Jack Dempsey, Chicago, USA
26.07.28 Gene Tunney W RSC 11 Tom Heeney, New York C, USA
Gene Tunney relinquished title (retired)
12.06.30 Max Schmeling W DIS 4 Jack Sharkey, New York C, USA
03.07.31 Max Schmeling W RSC 15 Young Stribling, Cleveland, USA
21.06.32 Jack Sharkey W PTS 15 Max Schmeling, New York C, USA
29.06.33 Primo Carnera W CO 6 Jack Sharkey, New York C, USA
22.10.33 Primo Carnera W PTS 15 Paolino Uzcudun, Rome, Italy
01.03.34 Primo Carnera W PTS 15 Tommy Loughran, Miami, USA
14.06.34 Max Baer W RSC 11 Primo Carnera, New York C, USA
13.06.35 James J. Braddock W PTS 15 Max Baer, New York C, USA
22.06.37 Joe Louis W CO 8 James J. Braddock, Chicago, USA
30.08.37 Joe Louis W PTS 15 Tommy Farr, New York C, USA
23.02.38 Joe Louis W CO 3 Nathan Mann, New York C, USA
01.04.38 Joe Louis W CO 5 Harry Thomas, Chicago, USA
22.06.38 Joe Louis W CO 1 Max Schmeling, New York C, USA
25.01.39 Joe Louis W RSC 1 John Henry Lewis, New York C, USA
17.04.39 Joe Louis W CO 1 Jack Roper, Los Angeles, USA
28.06.39 Joe Louis W RSC 4 Tony Galento, New York C, USA
20.09.39 Joe Louis W CO 11 Bob Pastor, Detroit, USA
09.02.40 Joe Louis W PTS 15 Arturo Godoy, New York C, USA
29.03.40 Joe Louis W CO 2 Johnny Paychek, New York C, USA
20.06.40 Joe Louis W RSC 8 Arturo Godoy, New York C, USA
16.12.40 Joe Louis W RTD 6 Al McCoy, Boston, USA
31.01.41 Joe Louis W CO 5 Red Burman, New York C, USA
17.02.41 Joe Louis W CO 2 Gus Dorazio, Philadelphia, USA
21.03.41 Joe Louis W RSC 13 Abe Simon, Detroit, USA
08.04.41 Joe Louis W RSC 9 Tony Musto, St Louis, USA
23.05.41 Joe Louis W DIS 7 Buddy Baer, Washington, USA
18.06.41 Joe Louis W CO 13 Billy Conn, New York C, USA
29.09.41 Joe Louis W RSC 6 Lou Nova, New York C, USA
09.01.42 Joe Louis W CO 1 Buddy Baer, New York C, USA
27.03.42 Joe Louis W CO 6 Abe Simon, New York C, USA
19.06.46 Joe Louis W CO 8 Billy Conn, New York C, USA
18.09.46 Joe Louis W CO 1 Tami Mauriello, New York C, USA
05.12.47 Joe Louis W PTS 15 Jersey Joe Walcott, New York C, USA
25.06.48 Joe Louis W CO 11 Jersey Joe Walcott, New York C, USA
Joe Louis relinquished title (retired)
22.06.49 Ezzard Charles W PTS 15 Jersey Joe Walcott, Chicago, USA (NBA)
10.08.49 Ezzard Charles W RSC 7 Gus Lesnevich, New York C, USA (NBA)
14.10.49 Ezzard Charles W CO 8 Pat Valentino, San Francisco, USA (NBA)
06.06.50 Lee Savold W RTD 4 Bruce Woodcock, London, England (GB/EBU)
Lee Savold ceased to be recognised by GB/EBU (this followed the announcement that Joe Louis was making a comeback)
15.08.50 Ezzard Charles W RSC 14 Freddie Beshore, Buffalo, USA (NBA)
27.09.50 Ezzard Charles W PTS 15 Joe Louis, New York C, USA
05.12.50 Ezzard Charles W CO 11 Nick Barone, Cincinnati, USA
12.01.51 Ezzard Charles W RSC 10 Lee Oma, New York C, USA
07.03.51 Ezzard Charles W PTS 15 Jersey Joe Walcott, Detroit, USA
30.05.51 Ezzard Charles W PTS 15 Joey Maxim, Chicago, USA
18.07.51 Jersey Joe Walcott W CO 7 Ezzard Charles, Pittsburgh, USA
05.06.52 Jersey Joe Walcott W PTS 15 Ezzard Charles, Philadelphia, USA
23.09.52 Rocky Marciano W CO 13 Jersey Joe Walcott, Philadelphia, USA
15.05.53 Rocky Marciano W CO 1 Jersey Joe Walcott, Chicago, USA
24.09.53 Rocky Marciano W RSC 11 Roland LaStarza, New York C, USA
17.06.54 Rocky Marciano W PTS 15 Ezzard Charles, New York C, USA
17.09.54 Rocky Marciano W CO 8 Ezzard Charles, New York C, USA
16.05.55 Rocky Marciano W RSC 9 Don Cockell, San Francisco, USA
21.09.55 Rocky Marciano W CO 9 Archie Moore, New York C, USA
Rocky Marciano relinquished title (retired)
30.11.56 Floyd Patterson W CO 5 Archie Moore, Chicago, USA
29.07.57 Floyd Patterson W RSC 10 Tommy Jackson, New York C, USA
22.08.57 Floyd Patterson W CO 6 Pete Rademacher, Seattle, USA
18.08.58 Floyd Patterson W RTD 12 Roy Harris, Los Angeles, USA
01.05.59 Floyd Patterson W CO 11 Brian London, Indianapolis, USA
26.06.59 Ingemar Johansson W RSC 3 Floyd Patterson, New York C, USA
20.06.60 Floyd Patterson W CO 5 Ingemar Johansson, New York C, USA
13.03.61 Floyd Patterson W CO 6 Ingemar Johansson, Miami, USA
04.12.61 Floyd Patterson W CO 4 Tom McNeeley, Toronto, Canada
25.09.62 Sonny Liston W CO 1 Floyd Patterson, Chicago, USA
22.07.63 Sonny Liston W CO 1 Floyd Patterson, Las Vegas, USA
25.02.64 Muhammad Ali W RTD 6 Sonny Liston, Miami, USA
Muhammad Ali forfeited WBA recognition (contractual dispute)
05.03.65 Ernie Terrell W PTS 15 Eddie Machen, Chicago, USA (WBA)
25.05.65 Muhammad Ali W CO 1 Sonny Liston, Lewiston, USA (WBC)
01.11.65 Ernie Terrell W PTS 15 George Chuvalo, Toronto, Canada (WBA)
22.11.65 Muhammad Ali W RSC 12 Floyd Patterson, Las Vegas, USA (WBC)
29.03.66 Muhammad Ali W PTS 15 George Chuvalo, Toronto, Canada (WBC)
21.05.66 Muhammad Ali W RSC 6 Henry Cooper, London, England (WBC)
28.06.66 Ernie Terrell W PTS 15 Doug Jones, Houston, USA (WBA)
06.08.66 Muhammad Ali W CO 3 Brian London, London, England (WBC)
10.09.66 Muhammad Ali W RSC 12 Karl Mildenberger, Frankfurt, W Germany (WBC)
14.11.66 Muhammad Ali W RSC 3 Cleveland Williams, Houston, USA (WBC)
06.02.67 Muhammad Ali W PTS 15 Ernie Terrell, Houston, USA
22.03.67 Muhammad Ali W CO 7 Zora Folley, New York C, USA
Muhammad Ali forfeited title (inactivity)
04.03.68 Joe Frazier W RSC 11 Buster Mathis, New York C, USA (WBC)
27.04.68 Jimmy Ellis W PTS 15 Jerry Quarry, Oakland, USA (WBA)
24.06.68 Joe Frazier W RTD 2 Manuel Ramos, New York C, USA (WBC)
14.09.68 Jimmy Ellis W PTS 15 Floyd Patterson, Stockholm, Sweden (WBA)
10.12.68 Joe Frazier W PTS 15 Oscar Bonavena, Philadelphia, USA (WBC)
22.04.69 Joe Frazier W CO 1 Dave Zyglewicz, Houston, USA (WBC)
23.06.69 Joe Frazier W RSC 7 Jerry Quarry, New York C, USA (WBC)
16.02.70 Joe Frazier W RTD 4 Jimmy Ellis, New York C, USA
18.11.70 Joe Frazier W CO 2 Bob Foster, Detroit, USA
08.03.71 Joe Frazier W PTS 15 Muhammad Ali, New York C, USA
15.01.72 Joe Frazier W RSC 4 Terry Daniels, New Orleans, USA
26.05.72 Joe Frazier W RSC 4 Ron Stander, Omaha, USA
22.01.73 George Foreman W RSC 2 Joe Frazier, Kingston, Jamaica
01.09.73 George Foreman W CO 1 Jose Roman, Tokyo, Japan
26.03.74 George Foreman W RSC 2 Ken Norton, Caracas, Venezuela
30.10.74 Muhammad Ali W CO 8 George Foreman, Kinshasha, Zaire
24.03.75 Muhammad Ali W RSC 15 Chuck Wepner, Cleveland, USA
16.05.75 Muhammad Ali W RSC 11 Ron Lyle, Las Vegas, USA
01.07.75 Muhammad Ali W PTS 15 Joe Bugner, Kuala Lumpar, Malaysia
01.10.75 Muhammad Ali W RTD 14 Joe Frazier, Manila, Philippines
20.02.76 Muhammad Ali W CO 5 Jean-Pierre Coopman, San Juan, Puerto Rico
30.04.76 Muhammad Ali W PTS 15 Jimmy Young, Landover, USA
25.05.76 Muhammad Ali W RSC 5 Richard Dunn, Munich, W Germany
28.09.76 Muhammad Ali W PTS 15 Ken Norton, New York C, USA
16.05.77 Muhammad Ali W PTS 15 Alfredo Evangelista, Landover, USA
29.09.77 Muhammad Ali W PTS 15 Ernie Shavers, New York C, USA
15.02.78 Leon Spinks W PTS 15 Muhammad Ali, Las Vegas, USA
Leon Spinks forfeited WBC recognition (failure to defend against Ken Norton)
09.06.78 Larry Holmes W PTS 15 Ken Norton, Las Vegas, USA (WBC)
15.09.78 Muhammad Ali W PTS 15 Leon Spinks, New Orleans, USA (WBA)
Muhammad Ali relinquished WBA version of title (retired)
10.11.78 Larry Holmes W CO 7 Alfredo Evangelista, Las Vegas, USA (WBC)
23.03.79 Larry Holmes W RSC 7 Ossie Ocasio, Las Vegas, USA (WBC)
22.06.79 Larry Holmes W RSC 12 Mike Weaver, New York C, USA (WBC)
28.09.79 Larry Holmes W RSC 11 Ernie Shavers, Las Vegas, USA (WBC)
20.10.79 John Tate W PTS 15 Gerrie Coetzee, Pretoria, S Africa (WBA)
03.02.80 Larry Holmes W CO 6 Lorenzo Zanon, Las Vegas, USA (WBC)
31.03.80 Mike Weaver W CO 15 John Tate, Knoxville, USA (WBA)
31.03.80 Larry Holmes W RSC 8 Leroy Jones, Las Vegas, USA (WBC)
07.07.80 Larry Holmes W RSC 7 Scott Ledoux, Minneapolis, USA (WBC)
02.10.80 Larry Holmes W RTD 10 Muhammad Ali, Las Vegas, USA (WBC)
25.10.80 Mike Weaver W CO 13 Gerrie Coetzee, Sun C, S Africa (WBA)
11.04.81 Larry Holmes W PTS 15 Trevor Berbick, Las Vegas, USA (WBC)
12.06.81 Larry Holmes W RSC 3 Leon Spinks, Detroit, USA (WBC)
03.10.81 Mike Weaver W PTS 15 James Tillis, Rosemont, USA (WBA)
06.11.81 Larry Holmes W RSC 11 Renaldo Snipes, Pittsburgh, USA (WBC)
11.06.82 Larry Holmes W RSC 13 Gerry Cooney, Las Vegas, USA (WBC)
26.11.82 Larry Holmes W PTS 15 Tex Cobb, Houston, USA (WBC)
10.12.82 Michael Dokes W RSC 1 Mike Weaver, Las Vegas, USA (WBA)
27.03.83 Larry Holmes W PTS 12 Lucien Rodriguez, Scranton, USA (WBC)
20.05.83 Michael Dokes DREW 15 Mike Weaver, Las Vegas, USA (WBA)
20.05.83 Larry Holmes W PTS 12 Tim Witherspoon, Las Vegas, USA (WBC)
10.09.83 Larry Holmes W RSC 5 Scott Frank, Atlantic C, USA (WBC)
23.09.83 Gerrie Coetzee W CO 10 Michael Dokes, Richfield, USA (WBA)
25.11.83 Larry Holmes W RSC 1 Marvis Frazier, Las Vegas, USA (WBC)
Larry Holmes relinquished WBC version of title (decided to box exclusively for the IBF)
09.03.84 Tim Witherspoon W PTS 12 Greg Page, Las Vegas, USA (WBC)
31.08.84 Pinklon Thomas W PTS 12 Tim Witherspoon, Las Vegas, USA (WBC)
09.11.84 Larry Holmes W RSC 12 James Smith, Las Vegas, USA (IBF)
01.12.84 Greg Page W CO 8 Gerrie Coetzee, Sun C, S Africa (WBA)
15.03.85 Larry Holmes W RSC 10 David Bey, Las Vegas, USA (IBF)
29.04.85 Tony Tubbs W PTS 15 Greg Page, Buffalo, USA (WBA)
20.05.85 Larry Holmes W PTS 15 Carl Williams, Reno, USA (IBF)
15.06.85 Pinklon Thomas W CO 8 Mike Weaver, Las Vegas, USA (WBC)
21.09.85 Michael Spinks W PTS 15 Larry Holmes, Las Vegas, USA (IBF)
17.01.86 Tim Witherspoon W PTS 15 Tony Tubbs, Atlanta, USA (WBA)
22.03.86 Trevor Berbick W PTS 12 Pinklon Thomas, Las Vegas, USA (WBC)
19.04.86 Michael Spinks W PTS 15 Larry Holmes, Las Vegas, USA (IBF)
19.07.86 Tim Witherspoon W RSC 11 Frank Bruno, Wembley, England (WBA)
06.09.86 Michael Spinks W RSC 4 Steffen Tangstad, Las Vegas, USA (IBF)
Michael Spinks forfeited title (refusal to defend against Tony Tucker)
22.11.86 Mike Tyson W RSC 2 Trevor Berbick, Las Vegas, USA (WBC)
12.12.86 James Smith W RSC 1 Tim Witherspoon, New York C, USA (WBA)
07.03.87 Mike Tyson W PTS 12 James Smith, Las Vegas, USA (WBA/WBC)
30.05.87 Mike Tyson W RSC 6 Pinklon Thomas, Las Vegas, USA (WBA/WBC)
30.05.87 Tony Tucker W RSC 10 James Douglas, Las Vegas, USA (IBF)
01.08.87 Mike Tyson W PTS 12 Tony Tucker, Las Vegas, USA
16.10.87 Mike Tyson W RSC 7 Tyrell Biggs, Atlantic C, USA
22.01.88 Mike Tyson W RSC 4 Larry Holmes, Atlantic C, USA (WBC/WBA)
21.03.88 Mike Tyson W RSC 2 Tony Tubbs, Tokyo, Japan (WBC/WBA)

Boxers' Record Index

Page numbers are shown *in italic* and where illustrations, **in bold**

General Index

Page numbers are shown *in italic* and where illustrations, **in bold**